TREASURY
of
DESSERTS

Publications International, Ltd.

ISBN: 0-7853-0198-4

Library of Congress Catalog Card Number: 93-84429

Cover photography by Sacco Productions Limited, Chicago

Pictured on the front cover *(clockwise from top right)*: Chocolate Raspberry Trifle *(page 152)*, Chocolate Marble Cheesecake *(page 63)*, Austrian Tea Cookies *(page 266)*, Peanut Butter Brownie Cups *(page 242)* and Fabulous Fruit Tart *(page 99)*.

Pictured on the back cover *(top to bottom)*: Apple Almond Pie *(page 87)*, Hot Fudge Sundae Cake *(page 124)* and Cut-Out Sugar Cookies *(page 174)*.

8 7 6 5 4 3 2 1

Manufactured in U.S.A.

Microwave Cooking: Microwave ovens vary in wattage. The cooking times given in this publication are approximate. Use the cooking times as guidelines and check for doneness before adding more time. Consult manufacturer's instructions for suitable microwave-safe cooking dishes.

CONTENTS

DESSERT BASICS

There is nothing quite like the tantalizing aromas and luscious flavors of homemade desserts. These delightful recipes will help you discover, or rediscover, the many pleasures of preparing sweet treats for family and friends.

From mile-high cakes to melt-in-your-mouth cookies, you can achieve success with every recipe. The following guidelines will help you master all types of basic skills, from angel food cake to pie crust. Each section focuses on a different type of dessert and takes you from preparing to storing. Even the most accomplished cooks will discover helpful tips to make their time in the kitchen easier and more enjoyable.

Combine all this information with over 650 kitchen-tested recipes developed by your favorite brand name food companies, and you have an impressive collection of dessert recipes to treasure for years to come.

A few recipes throughout this cookbook are noted as a sugar-free dessert. These recipes are sweetened with unsweetened fruit juice concentrates and fruit spreads and taste less sweet than a traditional dessert recipe.

GENERAL TECHNIQUES

These techniques lay the foundation of good cooking because they apply to a variety of recipes.

• Make sure you have all the necessary ingredients and utensils before preparing the recipe.

• Remove butter, margarine and cream cheese from the refrigerator to soften, if necessary.

• Toast and chop nuts, pare and slice fruit, and melt chocolate before preparing the recipe.

• Measure all the ingredients accurately and assemble them in the order they are called for in the recipe.

• Use the pan size specified in the recipe. Prepare the pan according to the recipe directions.

• Adjust oven racks and preheat oven. Check oven temperature for accuracy with an oven thermometer.

• Follow recipe directions and baking times exactly. Check for doneness using the test given in the recipe.

Measuring Ingredients

Dry Ingredients: Always use standardized measuring spoons and cups. Fill the correct measuring spoon or cup to overflowing and level off with a metal spatula or knife.

When measuring flour, lightly spoon it into a measuring cup and level off. Do not tap or bang the measuring cup as this will pack the flour. If a recipe calls for "sifted flour," sift the flour before measuring. If a recipe calls for "flour, sifted," measure the flour first and then sift it.

Liquid Ingredients: Use a standardized glass or plastic measuring cup with a pouring spout. Place the cup on a flat surface, fill to the desired mark and check the measurement at eye level.

When measuring sticky liquids such as honey or molasses, grease the measuring cup or spray with vegetable cooking spray before filling to make removal easier.

Beating Egg Whites

Separate eggs while cold because the yolk will be firm and less likely to break. Let egg whites stand at room temperature for 30 minutes before beating in order to achieve highest volume.

Make sure that the bowl and beaters you are using are clean and dry; any grease or yolk present will decrease the volume of the egg whites. For best results, use a copper, stainless steel or glass bowl (plastic bowls have an oily film on surface, even after repeated washings).

Add a pinch of cream of tartar and salt to the egg whites after they have been beaten slightly and are foamy; this will prevent them from collapsing.

When a recipe calls for sugar, as for a meringue, add the sugar slowly to the egg whites, beating well after each addition. If the mixture feels grainy to the touch, continue beating before adding more. If the egg whites are to be folded into other ingredients, this should be done immediately after they are beaten.

Whipping Cream

Chill the beaters, bowl and cream for the best results. Beat the cream slowly, increasing speed as it thickens to prevent spattering. To sweeten the cream, add granulated or powdered sugar in small amounts while beating until you reach the desired sweetness. If possible, whip cream shortly before using to prevent separation. If whipped ahead of time, use a wire whisk to briefly remix, if necessary.

Folding Ingredients

Folding is a technique that combines two mixtures while retaining the air in the lighter mixture. Place about one-third of the lighter mixture (egg whites or whipped cream) on top of the heavier mixture. Using a rubber spatula, cut down through the center of the mixture, then sweep across the bottom of the bowl and up the side using a circular motion. Turn the bowl slightly and repeat until blended. Add the remaining airy mixture and continue folding until combined.

Melting Chocolate

Make sure the utensils you use for melting are completely dry. Moisture makes the chocolate become stiff and grainy. If this happens, add ½ teaspoon shortening (not butter) for each ounce of chocolate and stir until smooth. Chocolate scorches easily, and once scorched cannot be used. Follow one of these three methods for successful melting.

Double Boiler: This is the safest method because it prevents scorching. Place the chocolate in the top of a double boiler or in a bowl over hot, not boiling, water; stir until smooth. (Make sure that the water remains just below a simmer and is one inch below the top pan.) Be careful that no steam or water gets into the chocolate.

Direct Heat: Place the chocolate in a heavy saucepan and melt over very low heat, stirring constantly. Remove the chocolate from the heat as soon as it is melted. Be sure to watch the chocolate carefully since it is easily scorched.

Microwave Oven: Place an unwrapped 1-ounce square or 1 cup of chips in a small microwavable bowl. Microwave on High (100% power) 1 to 1½ minutes, stirring after 1 minute. Stir the chocolate at 30-second intervals until smooth. Be sure to stir microwaved chocolate since it retains its original shape even when melted.

Toasting Nuts

Toasting nuts brings out their flavor and makes them crisp. Spread the nuts in a single layer on a rimmed baking sheet. Bake in a 325°F oven for 8 to 10 minutes or until golden. Shake the pan or stir the nuts occasionally to ensure even toasting. The nuts will darken and become crisper as they cool. To toast a small amount of nuts, place them in a dry skillet over low heat. Stir constantly for 2 to 4 minutes, until nuts darken slightly.

Toasting Coconut

Spread the flaked coconut in a thin layer on a rimmed baking sheet. Bake in a 325°F oven for 7 to 10 minutes. Shake the pan occasionally during baking to promote even browning and prevent burning.

Tinting Coconut

Dilute a few drops of food coloring with ½ teaspoon milk or water in a small bowl. Add 1 to 1⅓ cups flaked coconut and toss with a fork until evenly tinted.

PIES AND TARTS

Making flaky tender pie crusts can now be as easy as–pie! These few simple guidelines for combining ingredients and handling dough will ensure perfect pastry every time. Be sure to see pages 80–83 in the Pies & Tarts chapter for step-by-step photos of preparing pastry and fluting decorative edges. (Crumb crusts are used for many chilled and frozen pies.) Tarts are similar to single-crust pies and are baked in a fluted pan with shallow sides and a removable bottom.

Preparing Pastry

For tender, flaky pie crusts, follow these two basic rules: 1) keep the ingredients cold and 2) handle the dough as little as possible. Tough crusts are the result of overdeveloping gluten, a protein present in flour. Following these rules help prevent the development of gluten.

If you use butter in your pastry dough, it must be chilled. If the butter is soft, it cannot distribute evenly throughout the flour. Vegetable shortening and lard, although soft at room temperature, do not need to be chilled. Also make sure that the liquid you add is cold. The cold liquid keeps the fat solid.

Blend the flour and salt together, then cut the fat in quickly with a pastry blender, two knives or your fingertips until the fat particles are about the size of peas. Add cold water gradually, a tablespoon at a time, stirring lightly with a fork. Add just enough water so that the mixture holds together with slight pressure and can be gathered into a ball. Too little water produces a dry, crumbly pastry that will not hold together, and too much water makes the dough sticky and develops the gluten. Avoid overworking the dough or the pastry will be tough. Wrap the ball of dough in plastic wrap and refrigerate it for at least 1 hour. Chilling the dough makes it easier to handle and helps prevent shrinkage during baking.

Rolling

Place the chilled dough on a lightly floured surface and flatten it into a ½-inch-thick circle. Roll the dough with a floured rolling pin, pressing out from the center to the edge using quick, short strokes. Continue rolling until the dough is ⅛ inch thick and 2 inches larger than the inverted pie pan.

Loosely fold the dough into quarters and place the point of the folded dough into the center of the pie pan. Gently unfold the dough and ease it into the pan; do not stretch the dough or it will shrink during baking. For a single-crust pie, trim the dough and flute the edge.

Baking

Single-Crust Pies: Some single-crust pies, like custard pies, are baked in an unbaked pastry shell. Others require the shell to be prebaked so that it does not become soggy. If the pastry shell is to be baked "blind" (without the filling), prick the dough all over with a fork. Line the pastry with aluminum foil, waxed paper or parchment paper and spread dried beans or peas, or pie weights over the bottom. Weighing down the pastry prevents it from puffing and losing its shape during baking. (The dried beans are not edible after baking, but you can reuse them for blind baking.) The pastry can be fully or partially baked in this manner. Cool completely before adding the filling.

Double-Crust Pies: These pies are made by placing the filling (usually fruit) between two unbaked layers of pastry. Spoon the filling into the pastry shell and brush the rim of the shell with water. Roll out the top crust and place it over the filling. Press the pastry edges together to seal, then trim and flute. Cut a few slits or vents in the top crust to allow steam to escape. Before baking a double-crust pie, try glazing the top crust with milk or cream to promote browning. Brushing it with beaten egg will add color and shine; sprinkling it with granulated sugar will add a little sparkle.

If the top crust or edges of the pie shell are browning too quickly, cover the pie loosely with aluminum foil and continue baking.

Storing

Meringue-topped pies are best when served the day they are made; refrigerate any leftovers. Refrigerate custard or cream pies immediately after cooling. Fruit pies can be covered and stored at room temperature overnight; refrigerate them for longer storage.

To freeze unbaked pies, do not cut steam vents in the top crust. Cover the top with an inverted paper plate for extra protection and package in freezer bags or freezer wrap. To bake, do not thaw. Cut slits in the top crust and allow an additional 15 to 20 minutes of baking time. Baked pies can also be cooled and frozen. To serve, let the pie thaw at room temperature for 2 hours, then heat until warm. Pies with cream or custard fillings and meringue toppings are not recommended for freezing.

Unbaked pie dough can be frozen in bulk for later use. Simply flatten the dough into circles and stack them in a freezer bag with waxed paper separating each layer. Freeze prepared pastry shells in pie pans with waxed paper between the shells. Bulk pie dough must be thawed before using while pastry shells should be baked frozen.

COOKIES

The word cookie comes from the Dutch word, "koekje," meaning "little cake." The Dutch brought these little cakes to their first settlements in America, and they have been popular ever since. With so many flavors, shapes and sizes to choose from, cookies have definitely earned their place as America's favorite snack food.

Preparation Tips

Chill cookie dough before rolling or shaping it. This makes it much easier to handle. Remove only enough dough from the refrigerator that you will work with at one time. When making cut-out cookies, save any trimmings and re-roll them all at once to prevent the dough from becoming tough.

Cookies that are uniform in size and shape will finish baking at the same time. To easily shape drop cookies into a uniform size, use an ice cream scoop with a release bar. The bar usually has a number on it indicating the number of scoops that can be made from one quart of ice cream. The handiest size for cookies is a #80 or #90 scoop. This will yield about one rounded teaspoonful of dough for each cookie.

When baking brownies and bar cookies, always use the pan size called for in the recipe. Substituting a different pan will affect the cookies' texture. A smaller pan will give the bars a more cake-like texture and a larger pan will produce a flatter bar with a drier texture.

Baking

The best cookie sheets to use are those with little or no sides. They allow the heat to circulate easily during baking and achieve even browning. Another way to achieve even baking and browning is to place only one cookie sheet at a time in the center of the oven. If using more than one sheet at a time, or if your oven has uneven heat distribution, turn the cookie sheets halfway through the baking time.

When a recipe calls for greasing the cookie sheets, use shortening or a vegetable cooking spray for best results. Lining the cookie sheets with parchment paper is an alternative to greasing. It eliminates clean-up, bakes the cookies more evenly and allows them to cool right on the paper instead of on wire racks. Allow cookie sheets to cool between batches; the dough will spread if placed on a hot cookie sheet.

Most cookies bake quickly and should be watched carefully to avoid overbaking. Check them at the minimum baking time, then watch carefully to make sure they don't burn. It is generally better to slightly underbake, rather than to overbake cookies. Most cookies should be removed from cookie sheets immediately after baking and placed in a single layer on wire racks to cool. Fragile cookies may need to cool slightly on the cookie sheet before being moved to wire racks. Always cool cookies completely before stacking and storing. Bar cookies may be cooled and stored right in the baking pan.

Storing

Unbaked cookie dough can be refrigerated for up to two weeks or frozen for up to six weeks. Rolls of dough should be sealed tightly in plastic wrap; other doughs should be stored in airtight containers. Label dough with baking information for convenience.

Store soft and crisp cookies separately at room temperature to prevent changes in texture and flavor. Keep soft cookies in airtight containers. If they begin to dry out, add a piece of apple or bread to the container to help them retain moisture. Store crisp cookies in containers with loose-fitting lids to prevent moisture buildup. If they become soggy, heat undecorated cookies in a 300°F oven for 3 to 5 minutes to restore crispness. Store cookies with sticky glazes, fragile decorations and icings in single layers between sheets of waxed paper.

As a rule, crisp cookies freeze better than soft, moist cookies. Brownies are an exception to this rule since they freeze extremely well. Freeze baked cookies in airtight containers or freezer bags for up to 6 months. Thaw unwrapped cookies and brownies at room temperature. Meringue-based cookies do *not* freeze well and chocolate-dipped cookies will discolor if frozen.

CAKES

Cakes are divided into two basic categories according to what makes them rise. Butter cakes rely primarily on baking powder or baking soda for height while sponge cakes depend on the air trapped in the eggs during beating. Tortes are multi-layered cakes with rich fillings and are often made with little or no flour. Some cake recipes specifically call for cake flour. Cake flour contains less protein than all-purpose flour and produces a more tender cake.

Butter Cakes

Butter cakes include pound cakes and yellow, white, spice and chocolate layer cakes. These cakes use butter, shortening or oil for moistness and richness and are leavened with baking powder and/or baking soda. Before mixing the batter, soften the butter so that it mixes easily with the sugar.

Sponge Cakes

These cakes achieve their high volume from beaten eggs rather than a leavening agent like baking powder. Sponge cakes do not contain butter, oil or shortening. Angel food cakes are the most popular and are literally fat-free since they use only egg whites, not yolks. Yellow sponge cakes are prepared with whole eggs. Chiffon cakes are also lightened with beaten eggs, but they are not true sponge cakes because they contain vegetable oil.

When preparing sponge cakes, be sure to beat the eggs to the proper stage; do not over or underbeat them. Handle the beaten eggs gently when folding the other ingredients into them or they will lose air and volume. (See Folding Ingredients on page 6.)

Preparing Pans

Always use the exact pan size called for in the recipe. If the pan is too large, the cake will not rise properly or brown evenly. If the pan is too small, the cake will sink in the middle and the texture will be coarse; the batter may also run over the top of the pan during baking.

For butter cakes, grease and flour the pans before mixing the cake batter so that the cake can be baked immediately. To grease and flour cake pans, use a paper towel, waxed paper or your fingers to apply a thin, even layer of shortening. Sprinkle flour into the greased pan; shake or tilt the pan to coat evenly with flour, then tap lightly to remove any excess. To line pans with paper, trace the bottom of the cake pan onto a piece of waxed or parchment paper and cut to fit. Grease the pan, but do *not* flour it. Press the paper onto the bottom of the greased pan.

Sponge cakes are usually baked in tube pans. The center tube helps the heat circulate during baking and also supports the delicate structure of the cake. *Do not* grease the pans for sponge cakes. The ungreased pan lets the batter cling to the sides as it rises.

Baking

Place the cake pan(s) in the center of a preheated oven. Oven racks may need to be set lower for cakes baked in tube pans. If two racks are used, arrange them so they divide the oven into thirds and then stagger the pans so they are not directly over each other. Avoid opening the oven door during the first half of the baking time. The oven temperature must remain constant in order for the cake to rise properly.

A butter cake is done when it begins to pull away from the sides of the pan, the top springs back when lightly touched and a cake tester or wooden toothpick inserted into the center comes out clean and dry. A sponge cake is done when it is delicately browned and the top springs back when lightly touched.

Cooling

After removing butter cakes from the oven, let them stand in their pans on wire racks for ten minutes, or as the recipe directs. Run a knife around the edge of the cake to loosen it from the sides of the pan and invert it onto a wire rack. Remove the paper liner from the cake if one was used. Turn the cake top-side up onto a second rack to finish cooling.

Invert a sponge cake baked in a tube pan onto a heatproof funnel or bottle immediately after removing it from the oven. If it is cooled top-side up, it will fall. Do not remove a sponge cake from the pan until it is completely cool.

Frosting

Make sure the cake is completely cool before frosting it. Brush off any loose crumbs from the cake's surface. To keep the cake plate clean, place small pieces of waxed paper under the edges of the cake; remove them after frosting the cake. For best results, use a flat metal spatula for applying frosting. For a more professional look, first apply a thin layer of frosting on the cake as a base coat to help seal in any remaining crumbs.

Storing

Store one-layer cakes in their baking pan, tightly covered. Store two- or three-layer cakes in a cake-saver or under a large inverted bowl. If the cake has a fluffy or cooked frosting, insert a teaspoon handle under the edge of the cover to prevent an airtight seal and moisture buildup. Cakes with whipped cream frostings or cream fillings should be stored in the refrigerator.

Unfrosted cakes can be frozen for up to 4 months if well wrapped in plastic. Thaw in their wrapping at room temperature. Frosted cakes should be frozen unwrapped until the frosting hardens, and then wrapped and sealed; freeze for up to 2 months. To thaw, remove the wrapping and thaw at room temperature or in the refrigerator. Cakes with fruit or custard fillings do not freeze well as they become soggy when thawed.

Cheesecakes

Soften cream cheese before beginning the recipe. It will then combine easily with other ingredients and prevent lumps from forming in the batter. Beat cheesecake batter gently. Overbeating can cause the cheesecake to crack. Another common cause of cracks is overbaking. A simple doneness test is to gently shake the cheesecake—a 1-inch area in the center of the cheesecake should jiggle slightly. This area will firm during cooling. After baking, run a knife around the inside of the pan to loosen the edges of the crust. Let cool and then refrigerate for several hours before removing the rim of the pan. Cheesecakes can be stored in the refrigerator for up to one week, but for the best flavor, bring them to room temperature before serving. Cheesecakes are not recommended for freezing.

Baked Desserts

Bread puddings and custards, fruit cobblers and soufflés—baked desserts cover a wide range of sweets. Although many are long-time favorites, some of the techniques used may be new to you. These desserts can be better than you remember with only a quick review of some helpful tips.

Cobblers and Crisps

Always use the size dish called for in the recipe to allow room for the filling to bubble during baking. These desserts taste best when served warm. Ice cream or whipped cream are wonderful topping additions.

Bread Puddings

Always use the type of bread called for in the recipe. Substituting a different bread can affect the amount of liquid that is absorbed. The pudding is done when a knife inserted in the center comes out clean.

Store leftover cobblers, crisps and bread puddings in the refrigerator for up to two days. Reheat them, covered, in a 350°F oven until warm.

Baked Custards & Puddings

When preparing baked custards and puddings, beat the eggs just until blended. Do not beat until foamy to avoid bubbles on the baked surface.

Baking custards and puddings in a hot water bath is an important step. The hot water provides a constant, steady heat source, ensuring even, slow cooking. To test for doneness, insert a knife near the edge of the baking dish or cup. If the blade comes out clean, it is done and should be removed from the water bath immediately in order to stop the cooking process. If overcooked or cooked without a hot water bath, the custard or pudding will become rubbery. Once cooled, store covered in the refrigerator and serve within two to three days.

Soufflés

These light, airy desserts, which can be hot or cold, achieve their high volume from the air incorporated into stiffly beaten egg whites. The egg whites must be lightly folded into the base mixture just until blended. If the mixture is overmixed, the air is removed from the egg whites and the soufflé will not rise. Bake the soufflé on the middle rack of a preheated oven, allowing plenty of room for it to rise. Hot soufflés deflate quickly and should be served immediately after removing from the oven.

Frozen & Chilled Desserts

Many popular desserts fall into this category. Cold mousses, chilled soufflés and bavarian creams are molded desserts and hold their shape thanks to the addition of gelatin. Frozen desserts range from rich ice creams and refreshing sorbets to showstopping baked Alaskas.

Chilled Desserts

Mousses, cold soufflés and other pudding-like desserts are often prepared with gelatin. Gelatin is a natural protein that, when heated in liquid, becomes a sticky mixture that thickens or gels when chilled. Powdered gelatin is usually sold in ¼-ounce envelopes. One envelope gels about 2 cups of liquid. Gelatin is usually sprinkled over a small amount of liquid and allowed to stand for a few minutes; this gives the gelatin granules time to soften and swell. When this mixture is heated and stirred, the gelatin dissolves completely. Never use raw pineapple, papaya or figs in gelatin desserts. These uncooked fruits contain an enzyme that prevents the gelatin from setting.

Gelatin mixtures need to be refrigerated several hours or overnight until firm. Molded desserts must be loosened and inverted onto a plate for serving. To loosen the mold, simply lower it, just to the rim, in warm water for 5 to 10 seconds. Lift from the water and either shake the mold or gently pull the gelatin away from the edge of the mold with moist fingers to break the air lock. Place a moistened serving plate on top of the mold (moistening the plate allows you to move the mold, if necessary, after unmolding). Holding firmly, quickly turn both plate and mold over and shake to loosen; the dessert will fall smoothly onto the plate. Covered gelatin desserts can be stored in the refrigerator for two to three days.

Some cold soufflé recipes call for a collar of aluminum foil, waxed paper or parchment paper to be wrapped around the outside of the dish. This collar supports the mixture until it is set. When the collar is removed, the soufflé appears to rise out of the dish. Cold soufflés achieve their high volume from the air incorporated into stiffly beaten egg whites, just as hot soufflés.

Frozen Desserts

Two main types of desserts fall into this category—ices and ice creams. Ices are mixtures of pureed fruit, fruit juice, sugar and other flavorings. Ice creams are richer mixtures containing milk, cream and eggs. A few broad definitions will help clear up any confusion between the many variations.

Granité or Granita: The name of this sherbet-like dessert refers to its grainy texture. Serve this frozen mixture of water, sugar and fruit juice slightly thawed and slushy.

Sorbet: The French word for "sherbet", this frozen dessert can also be served as a palate refresher between courses. It is smoother in texture than a granité, with an intense fruit flavor.

Sherbet: Frozen sweetened fruit juice and water, sherbet also contains a small amount of milk or cream. It is lighter than ice cream but richer than granité or sorbet.

Ice Cream: Egg yolks, milk, cream and sugar all add to the richness of this favorite frozen treat. Ice cream recipes may call for the cream to be cooked with the eggs to form a custard, or the cream may be whipped first and then folded into the remaining ingredients. For food safety reasons, it is important to use clean, uncracked eggs in any uncooked ice cream recipe. Any number of flavorings, such as fruit, chocolate and nuts, can be added to the ice cream mixture—you're limited only by your imagination. Sauces, toppings and other additions turn a simple scoop of ice cream into a sundae or banana split.

Allow homemade ices and ice creams to ripen in the freezer for several hours before serving. Allow the ice cream to soften slightly before serving, either by transferring it to the refrigerator for 20 to 30 minutes or leaving it at room temperature for 10 to 15 minutes. Store leftover ice cream in the freezer for up to one week. Ice cream has a tendency to absorb other food odors and form ice crystals on the surface. Storing it in a covered, airtight container helps to extend its storage life.

Many types of ice cream freezers are available that take out some—or all—of the work involved in making homemade ice cream. The standard salt and ice-bucket freezer can either be hand cranked or run with an electric motor. As the blades inside the canister rotate through the ice cream, a mixture of salt and ice in the bucket outside freezes the ice cream.

A newer type of ice cream machine features a hollow metal canister that has a special coolant sealed inside. The canister is frozen, then filled with the ice cream mixture. A crank attached to the lid is periodically rotated by hand for 15 to 20 minutes until the mixture is frozen.

Some ice cream recipes give an option to freeze the mixture in a metal pan, bowl or ice cube tray. Freeze the mixture until half-frozen. Transfer to a chilled bowl and beat with an electric mixture until smooth. Return the mixture to the original container and freeze again. Repeat this procedure 1 to 2 more times to break up any ice crystals and incorporate air.

WEIGHTS AND MEASURES

Dash = less than ⅛ teaspoon

½ tablespoon = 1½ teaspoons

1 tablespoon = 3 teaspoons

2 tablespoons = ⅛ cup

¼ cup = 4 tablespoons

⅓ cup = 5 tablespoons plus 1 teaspoon

½ cup = 8 tablespoons

¾ cup = 12 tablespoons

1 cup = 16 tablespoons

½ pint = 1 cup or 8 fluid ounces

1 pint = 2 cups or 16 fluid ounces

1 quart = 4 cups or 2 pints or 32 fluid ounces

1 gallon = 16 cups or 4 quarts

1 pound = 16 ounces

EQUIVALENTS

Almonds, blanched, slivered	4 ounces = 1 cup
Apples	1 medium = 1 cup sliced
Bananas	1 medium, mashed = ⅓ cup
Blueberries	1 pint = about 3 cups
Butter or margarine	2 cups = 1 pound or 4 sticks 1 cup = ½ pound or 2 sticks ½ cup = 1 stick or 8 tablespoons ¼ cup = ½ stick or 4 tablespoons
Chocolate	1 (6-ounce) package chocolate chips = 1 cup chips or 6 (1-ounce) squares semisweet chocolate
Cocoa, unsweetened	1 (8-ounce) can = 2 cups
Coconut, flaked	3½ ounces = 1⅓ cups

Cookies, crushed
    Chocolate wafers
    Gingersnaps
    Graham crackers
    Vanilla wafers
	
	20 = 1 cup crumbs
	15 = 1 cup crumbs
	14 squares = 1 cup crumbs
	22 = 1 cup crumbs

Cranberries	12 ounces = 3 cups

Flour
    White or all-purpose
    Whole wheat
	
	1 pound = 3½ to 4 cups
	1 pound = 3¾ to 4 cups

Gelatin	¼ ounce envelope = about 1 tablespoon
Lemons	1 medium = 1 to 3 tablespoons juice and 2 to 3 teaspoons grated peel
Oranges	1 medium = 6 to 8 tablespoons juice and 2 to 3 tablespoons grated peel
Peaches	1 pound or 4 medium = 2 cups sliced
Pears	1 pound or 4 medium = 2 cups sliced
Pecans, shelled	1 pound = 4 cups halved, 3½ to 4 cups chopped
Raisins, seedless, whole	1 pound = 2¾ to 3 cups
Shortening	1 pound = 2½ cups
Sour cream	8 ounces = 1 cup
Strawberries, fresh	1 quart = 3½ to 4 cups sliced

Sugar
    Granulated
    Brown, packed
    Confectioners' or powdered
	
	1 pound = 2½ cups
	1 pound = 2¼ cups
	1 pound = 3¾ to 4 cups, unsifted

Walnuts, chopped	4½ ounces = 1 cup
Whipping cream	1 cup = 2 cups whipped

SUBSTITUTION LIST

If you don't have:	Use:
1 teaspoon baking powder	¼ teaspoon baking soda + ½ teaspoon cream of tartar
½ cup firmly packed brown sugar	½ cup granulated sugar mixed with 2 tablespoons molasses
1 cup buttermilk	1 tablespoon lemon juice or vinegar plus milk to equal 1 cup (Stir; let mixture stand 5 minutes.)
1 ounce (1 square) unsweetened baking chocolate	3 tablespoons unsweetened cocoa + 1 tablespoon shortening
3 ounces (3 squares) semisweet baking chocolate	3 ounces (½ cup) semi-sweet chocolate morsels
½ cup corn syrup	½ cup granulated sugar + 2 tablespoons liquid
1 tablespoon cornstarch	2 tablespoons all-purpose flour *or* 4 teaspoons quick-cooking tapioca
1 cup sweetened whipped cream	4½ ounces frozen whipped topping, thawed
1 cup heavy cream (for baking, not whipping)	¾ cup whole milk + ¼ cup butter
1 whole egg	2 egg yolks + 1 tablespoon water
1 cup cake flour	1 cup *minus* 2 tablespoons all-purpose flour
1 cup honey	1¼ cups granulated sugar + ¼ cup water
1 teaspoon freshly grated orange or lemon peel	½ teaspoon dried peel
1 teaspoon apple or pumpkin pie spice	Combine: ½ teaspoon ground cinnamon, ¼ teaspoon ground nutmeg, ⅛ teaspoon *each* ground allspice and cardamom

DESSERT DILEMMAS

Problems:

Solutions:

COOKIES

Uneven browning	Bake on only one oven rack at a time; use cookie sheets with little or no sides.
Cookies spread too much	Allow cookie sheets to cool between batches before reusing.
	If dough is too soft, chill slightly before baking.
	Avoid overgreasing cookie sheets.
Cut-out cookies are tough	Save dough scraps to reroll all at once; handle dough as little as possible.
	Use just enough flour on board to prevent sticking.

CAKES & CHEESECAKES

Cake falls in middle	Avoid overbeating - too much air is incorporated into batter.
	Avoid opening oven door before cake sets.
Cake peaks in center	Oven temperture may be too high and cake will rise too quickly; use oven thermometer to check for accuracy.
Cake is dry	Avoid overbeating egg whites. Avoid overbaking. Check cake for doneness at lower end of baking time range.
Cheesecake cracks	Avoid overbeating; too much air is incorporated into batter causing cheese cake to rise up, then fall and crack.
	Loosen rim of pan exactly as recipe directs to prevent cheesecake pulling away from sides and cracking.

PIE CRUSTS

Pastry is crumbly	Add additional water, 1 teaspoon at a time.
Pastry is tough	Add water gradually, stirring lightly after each addition.
	Avoid overworking dough; toss flour mixture and water together just until evenly moistened. Handle dough as little as possible.
Crust shrinks excessively	Roll pastry from the center outward; roll to an even thickness.
	Avoid stretching pastry when transferring from rolling surface to pie plate.

CUSTARDS

Texture is tough and rubbery	Bake custards in a hot water bath for slow, even cooking. Avoid overbaking.
	Remove custard from water bath as soon as it tests done to prevent any further cooking.

ICE CREAMS & SORBETS

Texture is lumpy	Ice cream mixture or fruit purée was not smooth before being frozen.
Texture is grainy	Mixture was not frozen quickly enough or was churned too slowly.
	Finished dessert was stored too long.

CAKES & TORTES

CHOCOLATE STRAWBERRY SHORTCAKE

Makes 12 servings

2 pints strawberries, hulled and cut in half
2 tablespoons sugar
1 teaspoon vanilla
2 (9-inch) layers ONE BOWL® Chocolate Cake
   (recipe follows)
   Semi-Sweet Chocolate Glaze (recipe follows)
3½ cups (8 ounces) COOL WHIP® Non-Dairy
   Whipped Topping, thawed, divided
   Chocolate-dipped strawberries (optional)

Mix strawberries, sugar and vanilla in medium bowl. Spoon half the strawberries on 1 cake layer. Drizzle with half the chocolate glaze; top with half the whipped topping. Repeat layers. Garnish with chocolate-dipped strawberries, if desired. Refrigerate.

Prep time: 15 minutes

ONE BOWL® CHOCOLATE CAKE

6 squares BAKER'S® Semi-Sweet Chocolate
¾ cup (1½ sticks) margarine or butter
1½ cups sugar
3 eggs
2 teaspoons vanilla
2½ cups all-purpose flour, divided
1 teaspoon baking soda
¼ teaspoon salt
1½ cups water

Preheat oven to 350°F.

Microwave chocolate and margarine in large microwavable bowl on HIGH (100% power) 2 minutes or until margarine is melted. Stir until chocolate is completely melted.

Stir sugar into melted chocolate mixture until well blended. Beat in eggs, one at a time, with electric mixer until completely mixed. Add vanilla. Add ½ cup flour, baking soda and salt; mix well. Beat in remaining 2 cups flour alternately with water until smooth. Pour into 2 greased and floured 9-inch layer pans.

Bake 35 minutes or until wooden toothpick inserted into centers comes out clean. Cool in pans 10 minutes. Remove from pans to cool on wire racks. Fill and frost as desired. *Makes 12 servings*

Prep time: 15 minutes
Bake time: 35 minutes

SEMI-SWEET CHOCOLATE GLAZE

3 squares BAKER'S® Semi-Sweet Chocolate
3 tablespoons water
1 tablespoon margarine or butter
1 cup powdered sugar
½ teaspoon vanilla

Microwave chocolate, water and margarine in large microwavable bowl on HIGH (100% power) 1 to 2 minutes or until chocolate is almost melted, stirring once. Stir until chocolate is completely melted.

Stir in sugar and vanilla until smooth. For thinner glaze, add ½ to 1 teaspoon additional water.

Makes about ¾ cup

Prep time: 10 minutes

Chocolate Strawberry Shortcake

DOUBLE BERRY LAYER CAKE

Makes 12 servings

1 package DUNCAN HINES® Moist Deluxe
    Strawberry Supreme Cake Mix
⅔ cup strawberry jam, divided
2½ cups fresh blueberries, rinsed, drained
    and divided
1 container (8 ounces) frozen whipped topping,
    thawed and divided
    Fresh strawberry slices, for garnish

1. Preheat oven to 350°F. Grease and flour two 9-inch round cake pans.

2. Prepare, bake and cool cake following package directions for basic recipe.

3. Place one cake layer on serving plate. Spread with ⅓ cup strawberry jam. Arrange 1 cup blueberries on jam. Spread half the whipped topping to within ½ inch of cake edge. Place second cake layer on top. Repeat with remaining ⅓ cup strawberry jam, 1 cup blueberries and remaining whipped topping. Garnish with strawberry slices and remaining ½ cup blueberries. Refrigerate until ready to serve.

Tip: For best results, cut cake with serrated knife; clean knife after each slice.

Berry Shortcake

BERRY SHORTCAKES

Makes 6 servings

1¾ cups all-purpose flour
1 tablespoon baking powder
⅛ teaspoon salt
½ cup cold butter or margarine
½ cup milk
1 teaspoon vanilla
1 egg
1 teaspoon water
1 cup sliced strawberries
1 cup raspberries
1 cup blueberries
3 tablespoons no-sugar-added strawberry
    pourable fruit*
4 tablespoons almond-flavored liqueur,** divided
1 cup heavy cream

Preheat oven to 425°F. Combine flour, baking powder and salt in medium bowl. Cut in butter with pastry blender or two knives until mixture resembles coarse crumbs. Add milk and vanilla; mix just until dry ingredients are moistened. Knead dough gently on lightly floured surface ten times. Roll or pat out to ½-inch thickness. Cut with 3-inch heart- or round-shaped biscuit cutter; place on ungreased cookie sheet. If necessary, reroll scraps of dough in order to make six shortcakes. Beat together egg and water; brush lightly over dough.

Bake 12 to 14 minutes or until golden brown. Cool slightly on wire rack. While shortcakes are baking, combine berries, pourable fruit and 3 tablespoons liqueur in medium bowl; let stand at room temperature 15 minutes. Beat cream with remaining 1 tablespoon liqueur in small bowl until soft peaks form. Split warm shortcakes; fill with about ⅔ of the berry and whipped cream mixtures. Replace tops of shortcakes; top with remaining berry and whipped cream mixtures.

*2 tablespoons no-sugar-added strawberry fruit spread combined with 1 tablespoon warm water may be substituted.

**3 tablespoons thawed frozen unsweetened apple juice concentrate *plus* ½ teaspoon almond extract may be substituted for the liqueur in the berry mixture, and 1 tablespoon thawed frozen unsweetened apple juice concentrate may be substituted for the liqueur in the whipped cream mixture.

Note: This is a sugar-free dessert.

CHERRY NUT CAKE

Makes 10 to 12 servings

1 (8-ounce) package PHILADELPHIA BRAND®
    Cream Cheese, softened
1 cup PARKAY® Margarine, softened
1½ cups granulated sugar
1½ teaspoons vanilla
4 eggs
2¼ cups sifted cake flour, divided
1½ teaspoons baking powder
¾ cup chopped maraschino cherries, well drained
½ cup chopped pecans
½ cup finely chopped pecans
1½ cups sifted powdered sugar
2 tablespoons milk

• Preheat oven to 325°F.

• Combine cream cheese, margarine, granulated sugar and vanilla in large bowl, mixing at medium speed on electric mixer until well blended. Add eggs, one at a time, mixing well after each addition.

• Sift together 2 cups flour and baking powder. Gradually add to cream cheese mixture; mix well. Toss remaining ¼ cup flour with cherries and chopped pecans; fold into batter.

• Grease 10-inch tube or fluted tube pan; sprinkle with finely chopped pecans. Pour batter into pan.

• Bake 1 hour and 10 minutes or until wooden toothpick inserted in center comes out clean. Cool 5 minutes; remove from pan. Cool on wire rack. Glaze with combined powdered sugar and milk. Garnish with additional pecan halves and maraschino cherry halves, if desired.

VARIATIONS

• Omit finely chopped nuts. Pour batter into three greased and floured 1-pound coffee cans. Bake at 325°F, 1 hour.

• Omit finely chopped nuts. Pour batter into four greased and floured 1-pound shortening cans. Bake at 325°F, 1 hour.

• Omit finely chopped nuts. Pour batter into five greased and floured 5¾ × 3¼-inch loaf pans. Bake at 325°F, 45 to 50 minutes.

• Substitute greased 9-inch springform pan with ring insert for 10-inch tube or fluted tube pan.

• Substitute ¾ cup chopped dried apricots for maraschino cherries and 2 tablespoons orange juice and 1 teaspoon grated orange peel for milk.

• Substitute 2 cups all-purpose flour for sifted cake flour.

Strawberry Chocolate Shortcake

STRAWBERRY CHOCOLATE SHORTCAKES

Makes 8 shortcakes

1 cup (6-ounce package) NESTLÉ® Toll House®
    Semi-Sweet Chocolate Morsels, divided
½ cup milk
2 cups all-purpose flour
¼ cup plus 2 tablespoons sugar, divided
1 tablespoon baking powder
1 teaspoon salt
½ cup butter
2 pints strawberries, washed, hulled and sliced
    Whipped cream

Preheat oven to 450°F. Combine over hot (not boiling) water, ½ cup Nestlé® Toll House® Semi-Sweet Chocolate Morsels and milk. Stir until morsels are melted and mixture is smooth. Set aside.

In large bowl, combine flour, 2 tablespoons sugar, baking powder and salt. With pastry blender or 2 knives, cut in butter until mixture resembles coarse crumbs. Add chocolate mixture; stir until blended. Knead in remaining ½ cup Nestlé® Toll House® Semi-Sweet Chocolate Morsels. On floured board, roll dough to ½-inch thickness. Cut dough into 8 pieces with 3-inch round cookie cutter. Place on ungreased cookie sheet.

Bake 8 to 10 minutes. Cool completely on wire rack. In medium bowl, toss strawberries with remaining ¼ cup sugar. Before serving, cut each shortcake in half crosswise. Top bottom half with strawberries and whipped cream. Cover with top half, more strawberries and whipped cream.

Toll House® Carrot Cake

TOLL HOUSE® CARROT CAKE

Makes 12 to 16 servings

2 cups all-purpose flour
1 teaspoon baking powder
1 teaspoon baking soda
1 teaspoon salt
1 teaspoon ground cinnamon
¼ teaspoon ground nutmeg
1¼ cups sugar
¾ cup vegetable oil
3 eggs
1 teaspoon vanilla extract
1¾ cups shredded carrots
1 (8-ounce) can crushed juice-packed pineapple, undrained
1 cup chopped nuts
1 cup (6-ounce package) NESTLÉ® Toll House® Semi-Sweet Chocolate Mini Morsels
Citrus Cream Cheese Frosting (recipe follows)

Preheat oven to 350°F. Grease and flour 13×9-inch baking pan.

In small bowl, combine flour, baking powder, baking soda, salt and spices. In large mixer bowl, beat sugar, oil, eggs and vanilla until well blended. Gradually beat in flour mixture. Stir in carrots, pineapple with juice, 1 cup nuts and Nestlé® Toll House® Semi-Sweet Chocolate Mini Morsels. Pour into pan.

Bake 45 to 50 minutes until wooden toothpick inserted into center comes out clean. Cool completely on wire rack. Spread with Citrus Cream Cheese Frosting. Garnish with additional chopped nuts, if desired.

Citrus Cream Cheese Frosting: In small mixer bowl, combine 4 ounces softened cream cheese and 2 tablespoons softened butter or margarine. Add 3 cups sifted powdered sugar; mix thoroughly. Stir in 1 tablespoon orange juice and 1 tablespoon lemon juice. Add additional orange juice if necessary until frosting is of spreading consistency.

CARROT CAKE WITH CREAM CHEESE GLAZE

Makes 1 cake

1½ cups butter, softened
1¾ cups firmly packed brown sugar
4 eggs
2 teaspoons vanilla
2¾ cups all-purpose flour
2½ teaspoons baking powder
¾ teaspoon salt
¾ teaspoon ground cinnamon
¾ teaspoon ground nutmeg
3 to 4 carrots, grated (about 2 cups)
1 can (8 ounces) crushed pineapple, well drained
½ cup raisins
½ cup chopped nuts
Cream Cheese Glaze (recipe follows)

Preheat oven to 350°F. In large bowl, beat butter until creamy. Gradually add sugar; beat until light and fluffy. Add eggs, 1 at a time, beating well after each addition. Stir in vanilla. In small bowl, combine flour, baking powder, salt and spices. Gradually add flour mixture to butter mixture; blend well. Stir in carrots, pineapple, raisins and nuts. Spoon batter into well-buttered and floured 12-cup Bundt® pan.

Bake 60 to 65 minutes or until wooden toothpick inserted into center of cake comes out clean. Let cool in pan on wire rack 15 minutes. Loosen edge; remove from pan. Cool completely on wire rack. Prepare Cream Cheese Glaze; drizzle over top of cake.

Cream Cheese Glaze: In small bowl, beat 1 package (3 ounces) softened cream cheese until fluffy. Beat in 2½ cups sifted powdered sugar. Stir in ½ teaspoon vanilla. Add 3 to 4 tablespoons milk to make a slightly thick glaze.

Favorite recipe from **American Dairy Association**

EASY CARROT CAKE

Makes 12 servings

1¼ cups MIRACLE WHIP® Salad Dressing
1 two-layer yellow cake mix
4 eggs
¼ cup cold water
2 teaspoons ground cinnamon
2 cups finely shredded carrots
½ cup chopped walnuts
1 (16-ounce) container ready-to-spread cream
   cheese frosting

• Preheat oven to 350°F.

• Beat salad dressing, cake mix, eggs, water and cinnamon in large bowl with electric mixer at medium speed until well blended. Stir in carrots and walnuts. Pour into greased 13×9-inch baking pan.

• Bake 30 to 35 minutes or until wooden toothpick inserted in center comes out clean. Cool completely. Spread cake with frosting. Garnish as desired.

Prep time: 15 minutes
Bake time: 35 minutes

CHOCOLATE APPLESAUCE CAKE

Makes about 12 servings

2½ cups all-purpose flour
⅓ cup unsweetened cocoa
2 teaspoons baking soda
¾ teaspoon salt
¾ cup shortening
1¾ cups sugar
2 eggs
1½ teaspoons vanilla
1½ cups sweetened applesauce
½ cup buttermilk

Preheat oven to 350°F. In small bowl, combine flour, cocoa, baking soda and salt. Using an electric mixer, beat shortening and sugar in large bowl until creamy. Beat in eggs and vanilla. In small bowl, combine applesauce and buttermilk; mix well. Add dry ingredients to sugar mixture alternately with applesauce mixture; mix until well blended. Pour batter into greased 13×9-inch pan.

Bake 35 to 40 minutes or until wooden toothpick inserted into center comes out clean. Cool completely in pan on wire rack. Serve plain or top with your favorite frosting.

Favorite recipe from **Western New York Apple Growers Association, Inc.**

COLONIAL APPLE CAKE

Makes about 16 servings

2¾ cups unsifted all-purpose flour
1 teaspoon baking powder
1 teaspoon ground cinnamon
¾ teaspoon salt
½ teaspoon baking soda
1¾ cups granulated sugar
1¼ cups CRISCO® Oil
2 eggs
¼ cup milk
1 teaspoon vanilla
2 cups chopped, peeled apples
½ cup chopped dates
1 teaspoon grated lemon peel
1 to 2 tablespoons confectioners sugar

1. Preheat oven to 350°F. Grease and flour 12-cup fluted tube pan. Set aside.

2. Mix flour, baking powder, cinnamon, salt and baking soda in medium mixing bowl. Set aside.

3. Combine granulated sugar, Crisco® Oil, eggs, milk and vanilla in large mixing bowl. Beat with electric mixer at medium speed until blended, scraping bowl constantly. Add flour mixture. Beat at medium speed 2 minutes longer, scraping bowl frequently. Stir in apples, dates and lemon peel. Pour batter into pan.

4. Bake at 350°F for 1 hour to 1 hour 15 minutes, or until wooden toothpick inserted in center comes out clean. Let stand 10 minutes. Invert onto serving plate. Cool slightly. Sift confectioners sugar onto cake. Serve warm. Top with whipped cream, if desired.

Easy Carrot Cake

PIÑA COLADA CAKE

Makes 16 servings

1 package DUNCAN HINES® Moist Deluxe
   Pineapple Supreme Cake Mix

FILLING

2 cups milk
1 package (8 ounces) cream cheese, softened
1 package (4-serving size) vanilla instant pudding
   and pie filling mix
¾ teaspoon rum flavoring or extract
1 can (8½ ounces) crushed pineapple,
   well drained

TOPPING

2 cups non-dairy whipped topping, thawed
½ cup flaked coconut, for garnish
½ cup pineapple tidbits, for garnish
½ cup maraschino cherries, for garnish

1. Preheat oven to 350°F. Grease and flour 10-inch tube pan.

2. Prepare, bake and cool cake following package directions for basic recipe.

3. Cut cooled cake into three equal layers (see Tip).

4. For Filling, combine milk, cream cheese, pudding mix and flavoring in medium bowl. Beat at medium speed with electric mixer for 2 minutes.

5. To assemble, place one cake layer on serving plate. Spread with half the Filling. Top with half the crushed pineapple. Repeat with second cake layer, remaining Filling and remaining crushed pineapple. Place third cake layer on top.

6. For Topping, spread whipped topping on sides and top of cake. Refrigerate until ready to serve. Garnish with coconut, pineapple tidbits and cherries, if desired.

Tip: To cut cake evenly, measure cake with ruler. Divide into 3 equal layers. Mark with toothpicks. Cut through layers using toothpicks as guide.

APRICOT CRUMBLE CAKE

Makes 16 servings

1 (8-ounce) package PHILADELPHIA BRAND®
   Cream Cheese, softened
1¼ cups granulated sugar
½ cup PARKAY® Margarine, softened
¼ cup milk
2 eggs
1 teaspoon vanilla
1¾ cups all-purpose flour
1 teaspoon baking powder
½ teaspoon baking soda
¼ teaspoon salt
1 (10-ounce) jar KRAFT® Apricot or Peach
   Preserves
2 cups flaked coconut
⅔ cup firmly packed brown sugar
1 teaspoon ground cinnamon
⅓ cup PARKAY® Margarine, melted

• Preheat oven to 350°F.

• Combine cream cheese, granulated sugar and ½ cup margarine in large bowl, mixing at medium speed on electric mixer until well blended. Gradually add milk, mixing well after each addition. Blend in eggs and vanilla.

• Add combined dry ingredients to cream cheese mixture; mix well. Pour half of batter into greased and floured 13×9-inch baking pan. Dot with preserves; cover with remaining batter.

• Bake 35 to 40 minutes or until wooden toothpick inserted in center comes out clean.

• Combine coconut, brown sugar, cinnamon and ⅓ cup margarine in medium bowl; mix well. Spread onto cake; broil 5 minutes, or until golden brown.

Piña Colada Cake

Seedy Lemon Cake

OLD-FASHIONED LEMON PUDDING CAKE

Makes 6 to 8 servings

1 cup sugar
¼ cup unsifted all-purpose flour
¼ teaspoon salt
3 eggs, separated
1 cup milk
¼ cup REALEMON® Lemon Juice from
   Concentrate

Preheat oven to 325°F. In medium bowl, combine sugar, flour and salt. In small bowl, beat egg yolks; stir in milk and ReaLemon® brand. Add to flour mixture; mix well. In small mixer bowl, beat egg whites until stiff but not dry; fold into egg yolk mixture. Pour into 1-quart baking dish. Place dish in larger pan; fill larger pan with 1 inch hot water.

Bake 50 to 55 minutes or until top is well browned. Cool about 30 minutes before serving. Refrigerate leftovers.

For Individual Servings: Pour mixture into 8 (6-ounce) custard cups; place in shallow pan. Fill shallow pan with 1 inch hot water. Bake 35 to 40 minutes or until tops are well browned. Cool about 30 minutes before serving. Refrigerate leftovers.

SEEDY LEMON CAKE

Makes two 9 × 5-inch loaves

1½ cups sugar
 1 cup sunflower oil
   Grated peel of 2 lemons
 6 eggs
1⅔ cups *plus* 1 tablespoon all-purpose flour, divided
 2 teaspoons baking powder
¼ teaspoon salt
½ cup sunflower kernels
   Whipped cream and lemon zest for garnish
   (optional)

Preheat oven to 300°F. Grease and flour two 9 × 5-inch loaf pans.

Beat together sugar, oil and lemon peel in large bowl. Add eggs, 1 at a time, beating well after each addition. Add 1⅔ cups flour, baking powder and salt; mix well. Combine remaining 1 tablespoon flour and sunflower kernels in small bowl; toss lightly. Stir into batter. Pour evenly into prepared pans.

Bake 1 hour or until wooden toothpick inserted in centers comes out clean. Cool loaves in pans on wire racks 10 minutes. Loosen edges and remove to wire racks to cool completely. Garnish as desired.

Favorite recipe from **National Sunflower Association**

LEMON RASPBERRY CHOCOLATE DELIGHT

Makes 12 to 16 servings

1 package DUNCAN HINES® Moist Deluxe
   Lemon Supreme Cake Mix
3 tablespoons margarine
¼ cup *plus* 2 tablespoons sugar
¼ cup water
2 tablespoons unsweetened cocoa
2 tablespoons light corn syrup
1 teaspoon vanilla extract
2 pints lemon sorbet
1 pint fresh raspberries, for garnish
   Mint leaves, for garnish

1. Preheat oven to 350°F. Grease and flour 13 × 9-inch pan.

2. Prepare, bake and cool cake following package directions for basic recipe.

3. Melt margarine over low heat in small saucepan. Remove from heat. Add sugar, water, cocoa and corn syrup. Cook over low heat, stirring constantly, until sauce is smooth and begins to boil. Remove from heat. Stir in vanilla extract. Cool slightly.

4. To serve, cut cake into squares. Top each square with scoop of lemon sorbet. Drizzle with 1 tablespoon cocoa sauce. Garnish with fresh raspberries and mint leaves.

Tip: To save time, purchase chocolate syrup to use in place of cocoa sauce.

GINGERBREAD WITH LEMON SAUCE

Makes 12 to 16 servings

CAKE
1 package DUNCAN HINES® Moist Deluxe Spice Cake Mix
3 eggs
1 cup water
⅓ cup CRISCO® Oil or CRISCO® PURITAN® Oil
2 tablespoons molasses
1 teaspoon ground ginger

LEMON SAUCE
1 cup sugar
¼ cup water
¼ cup fresh lemon juice
¼ cup butter or margarine
1 egg, well beaten
1¼ teaspoons finely grated lemon peel
Lemon peel strips, for garnish

1. Preheat oven to 350°F. Grease and flour 13×9-inch pan.

2. For Cake, combine cake mix, 3 eggs, 1 cup water, oil, molasses and ginger in large bowl. Beat at medium speed with electric mixer for 2 minutes. Pour into pan.

3. Bake at 350°F for 35 to 37 minutes or until wooden toothpick inserted in center comes out clean. Cool completely on wire rack.

4. For Lemon Sauce, combine sugar, ¼ cup water, lemon juice, butter, beaten egg and 1¼ teaspoons lemon peel in medium saucepan. Cook over medium heat, stirring constantly, until mixture comes to a boil. Remove from heat.

5. To serve, cut cake into squares. Spoon warm lemon sauce over cake squares. Garnish with additional lemon peel.

Tip: Lemon sauce can be stored in an airtight container in the refrigerator for up to 2 weeks.

DESSERT GINGERBREAD

Makes one 8-inch square cake

1½ cups sifted all-purpose flour
1 teaspoon ARM & HAMMER® Pure Baking Soda
1 teaspoon ground ginger
¼ teaspoon salt
⅓ cup vegetable shortening
½ cup sugar
1 egg
½ cup light molasses
¾ cup boiling water

Preheat oven to 350°F. Sift together flour, baking soda, ginger and salt in small bowl. Beat shortening in large bowl until light and fluffy. Add sugar gradually, beating well after each addition. Beat in egg thoroughly; blend in molasses.

Gradually stir flour mixture into shortening mixture. Beat thoroughly. Stir in water. Turn into greased and floured 8-inch square baking pan.

Bake 40 minutes or until wooden toothpick inserted in center of cake comes out clean. Cool in pan 10 minutes; remove from pan and cool on wire rack.

Gingerbread with Lemon Sauce

Ginger Pear Upside-Down Cake

GINGER PEAR UPSIDE-DOWN CAKE

Makes 8 servings

**8 tablespoons (½ cup) softened MAZOLA®
    Margarine, divided**
¾ cup KARO® Dark Corn Syrup, divided
**½ cup plus 2 tablespoons firmly packed brown
    sugar, divided**
1 can (16 ounces) pear halves, well drained
½ cup walnut halves
1⅓ cups all-purpose flour
1 teaspoon ground ginger
½ teaspoon baking soda
½ teaspoon ground cinnamon
¼ teaspoon salt
1 egg
½ cup buttermilk

Preheat oven to 350°F. In small saucepan, melt
2 tablespoons margarine. Stir in ¼ cup corn syrup
and 2 tablespoons brown sugar. Spread evenly in
ungreased 9-inch round cake pan. Arrange pear halves
and walnuts, rounded sides down, over corn syrup
mixture. In medium bowl, combine flour, ginger,
baking soda, cinnamon and salt. In large bowl, with
electric mixer at medium speed, beat remaining
6 tablespoons margarine, ½ cup corn syrup and ½ cup
brown sugar. Add egg and buttermilk; beat until well
blended. Add flour mixture; beat 1 minute or until
thoroughly combined. Carefully spoon batter over pears
and walnuts, smoothing top.

Bake 55 to 60 minutes or until wooden toothpick
inserted into center of cake comes out clean. Immediately
run spatula around edge of pan and invert cake onto
serving plate.

Prep time: 25 minutes
Bake time: 60 minutes

FRESH PEAR CAKE

Makes one 10-inch tube cake

4 cups chopped peeled pears
2 cups granulated sugar
1 cup chopped nuts
3 cups all-purpose flour
2 teaspoons baking soda
½ teaspoon salt
½ teaspoon ground cinnamon
½ teaspoon ground nutmeg
2 eggs
1 cup vegetable oil
1 teaspoon vanilla
    Powdered sugar for garnish (optional)

Preheat oven to 375°F. Grease and flour 10-inch fluted tube or tube pan.

Combine pears, granulated sugar and nuts in medium bowl; mix lightly. Let stand 1 hour, stirring frequently. Combine flour, baking soda, salt and spices in another medium bowl; set aside. Beat eggs in large bowl. Blend in oil and vanilla. Add flour mixture; mix well. Stir in pear mixture. Pour into prepared pan, spreading evenly to edges.

Bake 1 hour and 15 minutes or until wooden toothpick inserted in center comes out clean. Cool in pan on wire rack 10 minutes. Loosen edges and remove to rack to cool completely. Dust lightly with powdered sugar just before serving, if desired.

Favorite recipe from **New Mexico State Fair**

Tin Roof Sundae Cake

TIN ROOF SUNDAE CAKE

Makes one 3-layer cake

1 cup (2 sticks) butter, softened
2 cups granulated sugar
4 eggs
3 cups all-purpose flour
2 teaspoons baking powder
1 cup milk
1 teaspoon *each* vanilla and butter flavoring
3 tablespoons unsweetened cocoa powder
    Filling and Frosting (recipes follow)
    Melted white chocolate for garnish (optional)

Preheat oven to 350°F. Grease and flour three 8- to 9-inch round cake pans.

Beat together butter and sugar in large bowl until light and fluffy. Add eggs, 1 at a time, beating well after each addition. Combine flour and baking powder in small bowl. Add to butter mixture alternately with milk, beating well after each addition. Blend in vanilla and butter flavoring. Pour one third of batter into *each* of 2 prepared pans. Blend cocoa into remaining batter; pour into remaining pan.

Bake 30 minutes or until wooden toothpick inserted in centers comes out clean. Cool layers in pans on wire racks 10 minutes. Loosen edges and remove to racks to cool completely. To assemble, place 1 yellow layer on cake plate; spread with half of Filling. Cover with chocolate layer; spread with remaining Filling. Top with remaining layer. Frost with Frosting. Garnish as desired.

Filling: Beat together ½ cup (1 stick) softened butter and 4 ounces softened cream cheese in medium bowl until creamy. Gradually add 2 cups powdered sugar, beating until fluffy. Blend in ¾ cup crunchy peanut butter, 1 teaspoon vanilla and 1 teaspoon butter flavoring. Stir in ⅓ cup finely chopped peanuts. (Add 1 to 2 tablespoons milk if necessary for desired consistency.)

Frosting: Beat 4 ounces softened cream cheese and ¼ cup (½ stick) softened butter in medium bowl until creamy. Blend in 2 (1-ounce) squares melted unsweetened chocolate, 1 tablespoon lemon juice (optional) and 1 teaspoon vanilla. Gradually beat in 2 cups powdered sugar until fluffy.

Favorite recipe from **National Peanut Festival**

DELLA ROBBIA CAKE

Makes 12 to 16 servings

CAKE
1 package DUNCAN HINES® Angel Food
   Cake Mix
1½ teaspoons grated lemon peel

GLAZE
6 tablespoons sugar
1½ tablespoons cornstarch
1 cup water
1 tablespoon lemon juice
½ teaspoon vanilla extract
   Few drops red food coloring
6 cling peach slices
6 medium strawberries, sliced

1. Preheat oven to 375°F.

2. For Cake, prepare following package directions adding lemon peel with Cake Flour Mixture (red "B" packet). Bake and cool following package directions.

3. For Glaze, combine sugar, cornstarch and water in small saucepan. Cook over medium-high heat until mixture thickens and clears. Remove from heat. Stir in lemon juice, vanilla extract and red food coloring.

4. Alternate peach slices with strawberry slices around top of cooled cake. Pour glaze over fruit and top of cake. Refrigerate leftovers.

Tip: Use only metal or glass mixing bowls when preparing angel food cake mixes. Plastic or ceramic bowls can retain traces of grease which will prevent the egg whites from reaching full volume.

ZUCCHINI CHOCOLATE CAKE

Makes one 13×9-inch cake

½ cup (1 stick) margarine or butter, softened
½ cup vegetable oil
1⅔ cups granulated sugar
2 eggs
1 teaspoon vanilla
½ teaspoon chocolate flavoring
2½ cups all-purpose flour
¼ cup unsweetened cocoa powder
1 teaspoon baking soda
½ teaspoon salt
½ cup buttermilk
2 cups shredded zucchini
1 (6-ounce) package semisweet chocolate chips
½ cup chopped nuts

Preheat oven to 325°F. Grease and lightly flour 13×9-inch baking pan.

Beat together margarine, oil and sugar in large bowl until light and fluffy. Add eggs, 1 at a time, beating well after each addition. Blend in vanilla and chocolate flavoring. Combine dry ingredients in small bowl. Add to margarine mixture alternately with buttermilk, beating well after each addition. Stir in zucchini. Pour into prepared pan. Sprinkle with chocolate chips and nuts.

Bake 55 minutes or until wooden toothpick inserted in center comes out clean. Cool on wire rack. Cut into squares. Frost with your favorite chocolate frosting, if desired.

Favorite recipe from **Nebraska State Fair**

SWEET ZUCCHINI SPICE CAKE

Makes one 2-layer cake

3 cups grated peeled zucchini (approximately
   1 pound)
1 cup ground walnuts
1 cup flaked coconut
4 eggs
1 cup vegetable oil
2 tablespoons vanilla
2½ cups granulated sugar
3 cups all-purpose flour
2 teaspoons ground cinnamon
1½ teaspoons baking soda
1 teaspoon baking powder
1 teaspoon salt
   Pineapple Cream Cheese Icing (recipe follows)

Preheat oven to 350°F. Grease and flour two 10-inch round cake pans.

Combine zucchini, walnuts and coconut in medium bowl; set aside. Beat together eggs, oil and vanilla in large bowl until well blended. Beat in granulated sugar. Gradually add combined dry ingredients, beating well after each addition. Stir in zucchini mixture. Pour evenly into prepared pans.

Bake 35 to 40 minutes or until wooden toothpick inserted in centers comes out clean. Cool layers in pans on wire racks 10 minutes. Loosen edges and remove to wire racks to cool completely. Fill and frost with Pineapple Cream Cheese Icing.

Pineapple Cream Cheese Icing: Beat together 1 (8-ounce) package softened cream cheese and ½ cup (1 stick) softened margarine in large bowl until creamy. Add 1 (8-ounce) can drained crushed pineapple. Gradually add 1 pound (approximately 4½ cups) sifted powdered sugar, beating until smooth and of spreading consistency.

Favorite recipe from **New Mexico State Fair**

Sweet Zucchini Spice Cake

Peachy Upside-Down Cake

PEACHY UPSIDE-DOWN CAKE

Makes 12 to 16 servings

TOPPING
¼ cup margarine
½ cup firmly packed brown sugar
3 cups fresh chopped peaches (about 4 or
    5 medium)
3 maraschino cherries, cut into ⅛-inch strips

CAKE
1 package DUNCAN HINES® Moist Deluxe
    French Vanilla Cake Mix
Egg substitute equal to 3 eggs
1¼ cups water
⅓ cup CRISCO® Oil or CRISCO® PURITAN® Oil

1. Preheat oven to 350°F.

2. For Topping, place margarine in ungreased
13 × 9-inch pan in oven until melted. Remove from
oven. Stir in brown sugar. Spread to cover bottom of
pan. Arrange peaches and maraschino cherries in pan.
Set aside.

3. For Cake, combine cake mix, egg substitute, water
and oil in large bowl. Beat at medium speed with
electric mixer for 2 minutes. Pour batter evenly over
fruit mixture in pan.

4. Bake at 350°F for 45 minutes or until wooden
toothpick inserted in center of cake comes out clean.
Cool in pan 3 to 5 minutes. Invert onto large serving
tray; remove pan after 2 minutes. Serve warm or cool
completely.

Tip: Also delicious made with DUNCAN HINES®
Moist Deluxe Yellow Cake Mix.

PINEAPPLE
UPSIDE-DOWN CAKE

Makes 8 to 10 servings

1 can (20 ounces) DOLE® Pineapple Slices in Juice
⅔ cup margarine, softened, divided
⅔ cup brown sugar, packed
10 maraschino cherries
¾ cup granulated sugar, divided
2 eggs, separated
1 teaspoon grated lemon peel
1 teaspoon lemon juice
1 teaspoon vanilla extract
1½ cups all-purpose flour
1¾ teaspoons baking powder
¼ teaspoon salt
½ cup dairy sour cream

Preheat oven to 350°F. Drain pineapple; reserve
2 tablespoons juice.

In 9- or 10-inch cast iron skillet, melt ⅓ cup margarine.
Remove from heat. Add brown sugar and stir until
blended. Arrange pineapple slices in skillet. Place
1 cherry in center of each slice. In large bowl, beat
remaining ⅓ cup margarine with ½ cup granulated sugar
until fluffy. Beat in egg yolks, lemon peel, lemon juice
and vanilla. In medium bowl, combine flour, baking
powder and salt. Blend dry ingredients into margarine
mixture alternately with sour cream and reserved
pineapple juice. In large bowl, beat egg whites until
soft peaks form. Gradually beat in remaining ¼ cup
granulated sugar until stiff peaks form. Fold into batter.
Spread evenly over pineapple in skillet.

Bake 35 minutes or until cake springs back when
touched lightly in center. Let stand in skillet on wire
rack 10 minutes. Invert onto serving plate.

CHERRY-PINEAPPLE UPSIDE-DOWN CAKE

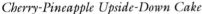

Makes one 9-inch cake

1¼ cups sifted cake flour
  2 teaspoons baking powder
¼ teaspoon salt
½ cup (1 stick) butter or margarine, softened,
    divided
¾ cup granulated sugar
  1 egg, beaten
½ cup milk
  1 teaspoon vanilla
¾ cup firmly packed brown sugar
  1 (20-ounce) can crushed pineapple, well drained
  1 (16-ounce) can sour pie cherries, drained
    Fresh mint leaves for garnish (optional)

Preheat oven to 350°F. Combine flour, baking powder and salt in small bowl; set aside. Beat together ¼ cup butter and granulated sugar in large bowl until light and fluffy. Blend in egg. Add flour mixture alternately with milk, beating well after each addition. Blend in vanilla. Melt remaining ¼ cup butter in 9-inch ovenproof skillet or 9-inch cake pan. Stir in brown sugar; spread to cover bottom of skillet. Cover with pineapple. Reserve a few cherries for garnish, if desired. Spoon remaining cherries over pineapple; top with batter.

Bake 50 minutes or until wooden toothpick inserted in center comes out clean. Cool in pan on wire rack 10 minutes. Loosen edges and turn upside down onto cake plate. Garnish with reserved cherries and mint leaves, if desired.

Favorite recipe from **Illinois State Fair**

Cherry-Pineapple Upside-Down Cake

Banana-Nut Cake

BANANA CHIP BUNDT CAKE

Makes 12 to 16 servings

1 package (18.5 ounces) banana cake mix (with pudding in the mix)
1 package (3½ ounces) instant banana cream pudding and pie filling
4 eggs
1 cup water
½ cup vegetable oil
1 cup HERSHEY'S MINI CHIPS® Semi-Sweet Chocolate
Chocolate Glaze (recipe follows)

Preheat oven to 350°F. Grease and flour 12-cup Bundt® pan.

In large mixer bowl, combine cake mix, pudding mix, eggs, water and oil; beat on low speed of electric mixer just until blended. Increase speed to medium; beat 2 minutes. Stir in small chocolate chips. Pour batter into prepared pan.

Bake 45 to 50 minutes or until wooden toothpick inserted in center comes out clean. Cool 10 minutes; remove from pan. Cool completely on wire rack. Drizzle with Chocolate Glaze.

Chocolate Glaze: In small saucepan, bring ⅓ cup sugar and ¼ cup water to a full boil, stirring until sugar dissolves. Remove from heat; add 1 cup HERSHEY'S Mini Chips® Semi-Sweet Chocolate. Stir with wire whisk until chips are melted and mixture is smooth. Cool to desired consistency; use immediately.

Makes about ⅔ cup glaze

BANANA-NUT CAKE

Makes 12 servings

2¼ cups all-purpose flour
¾ cup uncooked rolled oats
2 teaspoons baking powder
2 teaspoons ground cinnamon
1 teaspoon baking soda
¼ teaspoon salt
2 cups mashed ripe bananas (about 6 medium)
¾ cup thawed frozen unsweetened apple juice concentrate
4 eggs, beaten
½ cup butter or margarine, melted
2 teaspoons vanilla
¾ cup chopped walnuts
Easy Cream Cheese Glaze (recipe follows)

Preheat oven to 350°F. Combine dry ingredients in large bowl. Add bananas, juice concentrate, eggs, butter and vanilla; mix well. Stir in walnuts; spread into well-greased Bundt® or tube pan.

Bake 50 to 55 minutes or until wooden toothpick inserted in center comes out clean. Cool in pan on wire rack 15 minutes; turn cake out onto wire rack. Cool completely. Spoon Easy Cream Cheese Glaze over top of cake, letting excess glaze drip down sides. Serve at room temperature or chilled.

EASY CREAM CHEESE GLAZE

3 ounces regular *or* reduced calorie cream cheese, softened
2 tablespoons thawed frozen unsweetened apple juice concentrate
¼ teaspoon vanilla
⅛ teaspoon ground cinnamon

Combine all ingredients in small bowl; beat until smooth.

Note: This is a sugar-free dessert.

CHOCOLATE BANANA CAKE

Makes 9 servings

2 squares BAKER'S® Semi-Sweet Chocolate
⅓ cup margarine or butter
1¼ cups all-purpose flour
1 cup sugar
1 large ripe banana, mashed
¾ cup water
1 egg
1 teaspoon vanilla
½ teaspoon baking soda
¼ teaspoon salt
Semi-Sweet Chocolate Glaze (recipe follows)
Banana slices (optional)

To Microwave: Place chocolate and margarine in large microwavable bowl. Microwave on HIGH (100% power) 1 to 2 minutes or until margarine is melted. Stir until chocolate is completely melted.

Beat in flour, sugar, mashed banana, water, egg, vanilla, baking soda and salt until smooth. Pour into greased 8-inch square microwavable dish.

Microwave on HIGH 8 minutes or until wooden toothpick inserted into center comes out clean, rotating dish ¼ turn every 2 minutes. Cool in dish on countertop. Frost cake with Semi-Sweet Chocolate Glaze. Garnish with banana slices, if desired.

Prep time: 10 minutes
Microwave time: 8 minutes

SEMI-SWEET CHOCOLATE GLAZE

3 squares BAKER'S® Semi-Sweet Chocolate
3 tablespoons water
1 tablespoon margarine or butter
1 cup powdered sugar
½ teaspoon vanilla

Microwave chocolate, water and margarine in large microwavable bowl on HIGH (100% power) 1 to 2 minutes or until chocolate is almost melted, stirring once. Stir until chocolate is completely melted.

Stir in sugar and vanilla until smooth. For thinner glaze, add ½ to 1 teaspoon additional water.

Makes about ¾ cup

BOUNTIFUL BUTTERSCOTCH CAKE

Makes one 10-inch tube cake

2 cups (12-ounce package) NESTLÉ® Toll House® Butterscotch Flavored Morsels
¼ cup water
3 cups all-purpose flour
1 tablespoon baking powder
1 teaspoon salt
½ cup golden raisins
1 cup butter, softened
1 cup sugar
1 teaspoon vanilla extract
4 eggs
1 cup milk
½ cup finely chopped candied cherries
½ cup chopped toasted almonds
  Confectioners' sugar

Preheat oven to 350°F. Combine over hot (not boiling) water, Nestlé® Toll House® Butterscotch Flavored Morsels and water. Stir until morsels are melted and mixture is smooth. Set aside.

In medium bowl, combine flour, baking powder, salt and raisins; set aside. In large bowl, combine butter, sugar and vanilla extract; beat until creamy. Add eggs, 1 at a time, beating well after each addition. Gradually beat in flour mixture alternately with milk. Stir in butterscotch mixture, cherries and almonds. Pour into greased and floured 10-inch fluted tube pan.

Bake 1 hour or until wooden toothpick inserted in center comes out clean. Cool completely on wire rack; remove from pan. Sprinkle with confectioners' sugar. Garnish as desired.

Bountiful Butterscotch Cake

Date Torte

DATE TORTE

Makes one 2-layer cake

Chocolate Nut Filling (recipe follows)
½ pound pitted dates (about 1 cup)
9 egg whites
2 cups sifted powdered sugar
2 cups coarsely ground almonds
2 tablespoons dry bread crumbs
Additional powdered sugar for garnish (optional)

Prepare Chocolate Nut Filling; refrigerate until ready to use. Preheat oven to 350°F. Grease and flour two 9-inch round cake pans. Reserve a few dates for garnish, if desired; coarsely chop remaining dates.

Beat egg whites in large bowl at medium speed with electric mixer until foamy. Gradually add 2 cups sugar, beating at high speed until stiff peaks form. Stir together almonds and bread crumbs in small bowl; fold into egg white mixture. Fold in chopped dates. Pour evenly into prepared pans.

Bake 25 to 30 minutes or until lightly browned. Cool layers in pans on wire racks 10 minutes. Loosen edges and remove to racks to cool completely. To assemble, place 1 layer on cake plate; spread with filling. Cover with second layer. Dust lightly with additional powdered sugar just before serving and garnish with reserved dates, if desired.

Chocolate Nut Filling: Beat together ½ cup (1 stick) softened butter and 1 cup sifted powdered sugar in medium bowl until light and fluffy. Blend in 1 (1-ounce) square melted semisweet chocolate. Stir in ½ cup coarsely ground almonds.

Favorite recipe from **National Date Festival**

AMAZIN' RAISIN CAKE

Makes 1 (9-inch) layer cake

3 cups all-purpose flour
2 cups sugar
2 teaspoons baking soda
1½ teaspoons ground cinnamon
½ teaspoon salt
½ teaspoon ground nutmeg
¼ teaspoon ground cloves
1 cup HELLMANN'S® or BEST FOODS®
    Real, Light Reduced Calorie or Reduced Fat
    Cholesterol Free Mayonnaise Dressing
⅓ cup milk
2 eggs
3 cups coarsely chopped apples
1 cup raisins
1 cup coarsely chopped walnuts

Preheat oven to 350°F. Grease and flour two 9-inch round cake pans.

In large bowl, combine flour, sugar, baking soda, cinnamon, salt, nutmeg and cloves. Add mayonnaise, milk and eggs. Beat with electric mixer at low speed 2 minutes, scraping bowl frequently. (Batter will be thick.) With spoon, stir in apples, raisins and nuts. Spoon into prepared pans.

Bake 40 to 45 minutes or until cakes spring back when touched lightly in centers. Cool in pans on wire racks 10 minutes. Remove from pans; cool completely on racks. Fill and frost as desired.

SOLO® POPPY CAKE

Makes one 10-inch tube cake

1 cup butter or margarine, softened
1½ cups granulated sugar
1 can (12 ounces) SOLO® Poppy Filling
4 eggs, separated
1 cup sour cream
1 teaspoon vanilla
2½ cups all-purpose flour
1 teaspoon baking soda
¾ teaspoon salt
    Powdered sugar

Preheat oven to 350°F. In large bowl, beat butter and granulated sugar until light and fluffy. Blend in poppy filling. Add egg yolks, 1 at a time, beating well after each addition. Stir in sour cream and vanilla. In small bowl, combine flour, baking soda and salt. Gradually stir into poppy seed mixture, beating well after each addition. In large mixer bowl, beat egg whites at high speed until stiff but not dry peaks form; fold into batter. Pour batter into greased and lightly floured 10-inch tube pan.

Bake 1 hour and 10 minutes or until wooden toothpick inserted into center of cake comes out clean. Let cool in pan on wire rack 5 minutes. Loosen edges; remove from pan. Cool completely on wire rack. Sift powdered sugar over top of cake.

CHOCOLATE CHIP ORANGE POUND CAKE

Makes about 10 servings

½ cup butter, softened
4 ounces (½ of 8-ounce package) cream cheese, softened
¾ cup sugar
2 eggs
1 teaspoon vanilla extract
¼ teaspoon grated orange peel
1 cup all-purpose flour
1 teaspoon baking powder
1 cup HERSHEY'S MINI CHIPS® Semi-Sweet Chocolate
Powdered sugar

Preheat oven to 325°F. Grease and flour 9 × 5-inch loaf pan.

Cut butter and cream cheese into 1-inch slices; place in bowl of food processor. Add sugar; process until smooth, about 30 seconds. Add eggs, vanilla and orange peel; process until blended, about 10 seconds. Add flour and baking powder; process until blended, about 10 seconds. Stir in small chocolate chips. Pour batter into prepared pan.

Bake 45 to 50 minutes or until cake pulls away from sides of pan. Cool 10 minutes; remove from pan to wire rack. Cool completely on wire rack; sprinkle powdered sugar over cake.

Chocolate Almond Marble Pound Cake

CHOCOLATE ALMOND MARBLE POUND CAKE

Makes one 10-inch tube cake

1¼ cups (⅝ of 12-ounce package) NESTLÉ® Toll House® Semi-Sweet Chocolate Morsels, divided
3 cups all-purpose flour
2 teaspoons baking powder
½ teaspoon salt
1½ cups sugar
1 cup vegetable oil
¾ teaspoon almond extract
5 eggs
1 cup milk
Confectioners' sugar (optional)

Preheat oven to 350°F. Melt over hot (not boiling) water, ½ cup Nestlé® Toll House® Semi-Sweet Chocolate Morsels; stir until smooth. Set aside.

In medium bowl, combine flour, baking powder and salt; set aside. In large bowl, combine sugar, vegetable oil and almond extract; beat well. Add eggs, 1 at a time, beating well after each addition. Gradually beat in flour mixture alternately with milk. Divide batter in half. Stir melted morsels and remaining ¾ cup Nestlé® Toll House® Semi-Sweet Chocolate Morsels into half of batter; mix well. Pour half of plain batter into greased and floured 10-inch tube pan. Top with half of chocolate batter. Repeat layers with remaining batters.

Bake 65 to 70 minutes or until wooden toothpick inserted into center comes out clean. Cool 15 minutes; remove from pan. Cool completely on wire rack. Sprinkle with confectioners' sugar, if desired.

APPLE NUT POUND CAKE

Makes 16 servings

1 package DUNCAN HINES® Moist Deluxe Yellow Cake Mix
1 package (4-serving size) vanilla instant pudding and pie filling mix
2 teaspoons ground cinnamon
4 eggs
1 cup applesauce
1 cup raisins
1 cup chopped pecans
⅔ cup CRISCO® Oil or CRISCO® PURITAN® Oil
¼ cup chopped maraschino cherries
Confectioners sugar

1. Preheat oven to 350°F. Grease and flour 10-inch Bundt® pan.

2. Combine cake mix, pudding mix and cinnamon in large bowl. Add remaining ingredients except confectioners sugar; stir with wooden spoon until well blended. Pour into pan.

3. Bake at 350°F for 50 to 55 minutes or until wooden toothpick inserted in center comes out clean. Cool in pan 25 minutes. Invert onto serving plate. Cool completely. Dust with confectioners sugar.

Tip: For an enhanced flavor, toast the pecans before adding to cake batter. Spread pecans in a single layer on baking sheet. Bake at 325°F for about 5 minutes or until fragrant.

PINEAPPLE ORANGE POUND CAKE

Makes 12 to 16 servings

CAKE
1 package DUNCAN HINES® Moist Deluxe Pineapple Supreme Cake Mix
1 package (4-serving size) vanilla instant pudding and pie filling mix
4 eggs
1 cup orange juice
⅓ cup CRISCO® Oil or CRISCO® PURITAN® Oil
1 tablespoon grated orange peel

GLAZE
⅓ cup sugar
4 tablespoons orange juice

1. Preheat oven to 350°F. Grease and flour 10-inch Bundt® pan.

2. For Cake, combine cake mix, pudding mix, eggs, 1 cup orange juice, oil and peel in large bowl. Beat at medium speed with electric mixer for 2 minutes. Pour into pan.

3. Bake at 350°F for 50 to 60 minutes or until wooden toothpick inserted in center comes out clean. Cool 25 minutes in pan. Invert onto serving plate.

4. For Glaze, combine sugar and 4 tablespoons orange juice in small saucepan. Simmer 3 minutes. Brush warm glaze on cake.

Tip: Serve with peach ice cream.

Premier Pound Cake

PREMIER POUND CAKE

Makes two 9×5-inch loaves

3 cups sifted all-purpose flour
½ teaspoon baking powder
½ teaspoon baking soda
½ teaspoon salt
1 cup (2 sticks) butter or margarine, softened
2 cups superfine sugar
2 eggs
1 teaspoon vanilla
1 teaspoon lemon extract
1 cup buttermilk
Starfruit, strawberry slices and orange peel for garnish (optional)

Preheat oven to 350°F. Grease and flour two 9×5-inch loaf pans.

Combine flour, baking powder, baking soda and salt in medium bowl; set aside. Beat together butter and sugar in large bowl until light and fluffy. Add eggs, 1 at a time, beating well after each addition. Blend in vanilla and lemon extract. Add flour mixture alternately with buttermilk, beating well after each addition. Pour evenly into prepared pans.

Bake 35 to 40 minutes or until wooden toothpick inserted in centers comes out clean. Cool loaves in pans on wire racks 10 minutes. Loosen edges and remove to racks to cool completely. Garnish as desired.

Chocolate Angel Food Cake

CHOCOLATE ANGEL FOOD CAKE

Makes one 10-inch tube cake

1½ cups granulated sugar, divided
¾ cup sifted cake flour
¼ cup unsweetened cocoa powder
¼ teaspoon salt
12 egg whites
1½ teaspoons cream of tartar
1½ teaspoons vanilla
    Powdered sugar for garnish (optional)

Preheat oven to 375°F. Sift together ¾ cup granulated sugar, flour, cocoa and salt 2 times; set aside. Beat egg whites in large bowl at medium speed with electric mixer until foamy. Add cream of tartar; beat at high speed until soft peaks form. Gradually add remaining ¾ cup granulated sugar, 2 tablespoons at a time, beating until stiff peaks form. Blend in vanilla. Sift about one fourth of cocoa mixture over egg white mixture; fold in. Repeat with remaining cocoa mixture. Pour into ungreased 10-inch tube pan.

Bake 35 to 40 minutes or until cake springs back when lightly touched with finger. Invert pan over heatproof funnel or bottle; allow cake to cool completely before removing from pan. Turn cake onto cake plate. Dust lightly with powdered sugar just before serving, if desired. Garnish as desired.

Favorite recipe from **New Mexico State Fair**

LEMON ANGEL FOOD CAKE WITH BLUEBERRY SAUCE

Makes 12 to 16 servings

CAKE
1 cup *plus* 3 tablespoons water
2 tablespoons lemon juice
    Few drops yellow food coloring
1 package DUNCAN HINES® Angel Food
    Cake Mix
1 teaspoon grated lemon peel

SAUCE
⅔ cup sugar
2 tablespoons cornstarch
⅛ teaspoon salt
⅔ cup water
2 cups frozen dry pack blueberries
    Additional grated lemon peel, for garnish

1. Preheat oven to 375°F.

2. For Cake, combine 1 cup *plus* 3 tablespoons water, lemon juice and yellow food coloring in small bowl. Prepare Angel Food Cake following package directions *except* use water mixture for the 1⅓ cups water called for on the package. Add 1 teaspoon grated lemon peel and Cake Flour Mixture (red "B" packet). Bake and cool cake following package directions.

3. For Sauce, combine sugar, cornstarch and salt in small saucepan. Stir in ⅔ cup water. Cook over medium heat, stirring constantly, until thickened. Remove from heat. Stir in frozen blueberries. Refrigerate until chilled.

4. Spoon chilled blueberry sauce on top of cake. If desired, reserve a small amount of sauce to spoon over individual cake slices. Garnish with additional grated lemon peel. Refrigerate until ready to serve.

CINNAMON RIPPLE CAKE

Makes 12 to 16 servings

1 package DUNCAN HINES® Angel Food
    Cake Mix
1 tablespoon *plus* ¼ teaspoon ground cinnamon,
    divided
1½ cups frozen light whipped topping, thawed

1. Preheat oven to 375°F.

2. Prepare cake following package directions. Spoon one-fourth of batter into ungreased 10-inch tube pan. Spread evenly. Sprinkle 1 teaspoon cinnamon over batter with small fine sieve. Repeat layering 2 more times. Top with remaining cake batter.

3. Bake and cool following package directions.

4. Combine whipped topping and remaining ¼ teaspoon cinnamon in small bowl. Serve with cake slices.

Tip: For angel food cakes, always use a totally grease-free cake pan to get the best volume.

Cinnamon Ripple Cake

ANGEL FOOD CAKE

Makes one 10-inch tube cake

1¼ cups cake flour, sifted
1⅓ cups plus ½ cup sugar, divided
12 egg whites
1¾ teaspoons cream of tartar
    ¼ teaspoon salt
    1 teaspoon vanilla
    ¼ teaspoon almond extract
    Fresh strawberries for serving (optional)

Preheat oven to 350°F. Sift together flour with ½ cup sugar in small bowl 4 times. Beat egg whites with cream of tartar, salt, vanilla and almond extract in large bowl at high speed with electric mixer until stiff peaks form. Gradually add remaining 1⅓ cups sugar, mixing well after each addition. Fold in flour mixture. Pour into ungreased 10-inch tube pan.

Bake 35 to 40 minutes or until cake springs back when lightly touched with finger. Invert pan over heatproof funnel or bottle; allow cake to cool completely before removing from pan. Serve with strawberries, if desired.

Favorite recipe from **Michigan State Fair**

MARBLED ANGEL CAKE

Makes 12 to 16 servings

1 box (14.5 ounces) angel food cake mix
¼ cup HERSHEY'S Cocoa
    Chocolate Glaze (recipe follows)

Adjust oven rack to lowest position. Preheat oven to 375°F.

Prepare cake batter according to package directions. Measure 4 cups batter into separate bowl; gradually fold cocoa in until well blended, being careful not to deflate batter. Alternately pour vanilla and chocolate batters into ungreased 10-inch tube pan. Cut through batters with knife or spatula to marble.

Bake 30 to 35 minutes or until top crust is firm and looks very dry. Do not underbake. Invert pan on heatproof funnel or bottle; cool at least 1½ hours. Carefully run knife along side of pan to loosen cake. Place on serving plate; spread Chocolate Glaze over top of cake.

Chocolate Glaze: In small saucepan, bring ⅓ cup sugar and ¼ cup water to a full boil, stirring until sugar dissolves. Remove from heat; add 1 cup HERSHEY'S MINI CHIPS® Semi-Sweet Chocolate. Stir with wire whisk until chips are melted and mixture is smooth. Cool to desired consistency; use immediately.

Makes about ⅔ cup glaze

CHIFFON CAKE

Makes one 10-inch tube cake

5 eggs, separated
½ teaspoon cream of tartar
2¼ cups sifted all-purpose flour
1½ cups sugar
1 tablespoon baking powder
1 teaspoon salt
¾ cup water
½ cup vegetable oil
1 teaspoon vanilla
1 teaspoon almond extract
   Strawberries, kiwifruit and whipped cream for garnish (optional)

Preheat oven to 325°F. Beat egg whites and cream of tartar in large bowl with electric mixer at high speed until stiff peaks form. Set aside. Sift together dry ingredients into large bowl. Make a well in flour mixture. Add egg yolks, water, oil, vanilla and almond extract; mix well. Fold in egg white mixture. Pour immediately into ungreased 10-inch tube pan.

Bake 55 minutes. *Increase oven temperature to 350°F.* Continue baking an additional 10 minutes or until cake springs back when lightly touched with finger. Invert pan over heatproof funnel or bottle; allow cake to cool completely before removing from pan. Garnish as desired.

Favorite recipe from **Nebraska State Fair**

Chiffon Cake

MARBLE CHIFFON CAKE

Makes 12 to 16 servings

2 tablespoons plus 1½ cups sugar, divided
2 tablespoons plus ½ cup vegetable oil, divided
⅓ cup HERSHEY₂S Cocoa
1 cup cold water, divided
2 cups all-purpose flour
1 tablespoon baking powder
1 teaspoon salt
7 eggs, separated
2 teaspoons vanilla extract
½ teaspoon cream of tartar
   Vanilla Glaze or Quick Cocoa Glaze (recipes follow)

Preheat oven to 325°F. In small bowl, combine 2 tablespoons sugar, 2 tablespoons oil, cocoa and ¼ cup cold water; stir until smooth. Reserve. In small mixer bowl, stir together flour, remaining 1½ cups sugar, baking powder and salt. Add remaining ¾ cup cold water, ½ cup oil, egg yolks and vanilla. Beat on low speed until combined; continue beating on high speed 5 minutes. In large mixer bowl, with clean set of beaters, beat egg whites with cream of tartar until stiff peaks form. Pour batter in thin stream over beaten whites, gently folding with rubber spatula just until blended. Remove one-third of batter to separate bowl; gently fold in reserved chocolate mixture. Pour half of light batter into ungreased 10-inch tube pan; top with half of chocolate batter. Repeat layers. With spatula or knife, swirl gently through batters to marble.

Bake 65 to 70 minutes or until top springs back when touched lightly. Invert pan on heatproof funnel or bottle; cool cake completely. Loosen cake from pan; invert onto serving plate. Spread Vanilla Glaze or Quick Cocoa Glaze over top of cake, allowing glaze to drizzle down sides.

Vanilla Glaze: In small saucepan over low heat, melt ¼ cup butter or margarine; remove from heat. Gradually stir in 2 cups powdered sugar, 2 to 3 tablespoons hot water and 1 teaspoon vanilla extract; beat with wire whisk until smooth and slightly thickened.

QUICK COCOA GLAZE

2 tablespoons butter or margarine
¼ cup HERSHEY₂S Cocoa
3 tablespoons water
½ teaspoon vanilla extract
1¼ cups powdered sugar

In small saucepan over low heat, melt butter. Stir in cocoa and water. Cook, stirring constantly, until mixture thickens. Do not boil. Remove from heat. Stir in vanilla. Gradually add powdered sugar, beating with wire whisk until smooth. Add additional water, ½ teaspoon at a time, until desired consistency.

CHOCOLATE ANGEL FOOD ROLLS

Makes 16 to 20 servings

CAKE
1 package DUNCAN HINES® Angel Food
    Cake Mix
3 tablespoons unsweetened cocoa
    Confectioners sugar

FILLING
½ square grated semi-sweet chocolate
1 container (8 ounces) frozen whipped topping,
    thawed

DRIZZLE
2 squares (2 ounces) semi-sweet chocolate,
    chopped
2 teaspoons CRISCO® Shortening

1. Preheat oven to 350°F. Line two 15½×10½×1-inch jelly-roll pans with aluminum foil.

2. For Cake, combine Cake Flour Mixture (red "B" packet) and cocoa in small bowl. Prepare cake following package directions. Divide batter into pans. Spread evenly. Cut through batter with knife or spatula to remove large air bubbles.

3. Bake at 350°F for 15 minutes or until set. Invert cakes at once onto lint-free kitchen towels dusted with confectioners sugar. Remove foil carefully. Starting at short end, roll up each cake with towel jelly-roll fashion. Cool completely.

4. For Filling, fold grated chocolate into whipped topping. Unroll cakes. Spread half of filling to edges on each cake. Reroll cakes and place, seam-side down, on serving plate.

5. For Drizzle, combine chocolate and shortening in small resealable plastic bag. Place bag in bowl of hot water for several minutes. Dry with paper towel. Knead until blended and chocolate is smooth. Snip pinpoint corner in bag. Drizzle over rolls. Refrigerate until ready to serve.

Tip: For a quick finish, simply dust angel food rolls with confectioners sugar.

Chocolate Angel Food Roll

CHERRY ANGEL ROLLS

Makes 16 servings

1 package DUNCAN HINES® Angel Food
    Cake Mix
    Confectioners sugar
1 cup chopped maraschino cherries, drained
½ cup flaked coconut
1 teaspoon maraschino cherry juice
1 container (8 ounces) frozen whipped topping,
    thawed

1. Preheat oven to 350°F. Line two 15½×10½×1-inch jelly-roll pans with aluminum foil.

2. Prepare cake following package directions. Divide into pans. Spread evenly. Cut through batter with knife or spatula to remove large air bubbles.

3. Bake at 350°F for 15 minutes or until set. Invert cakes at once onto clean lint-free dishtowels dusted with confectioners sugar. Remove foil carefully. Starting at short end, roll up each cake with towel jelly-roll fashion. Cool completely.

4. Fold chopped cherries, coconut and cherry juice into whipped topping. Unroll cakes. Spread half of filling over each cake to edges. Reroll and place, seam-side down, on serving plate. Dust with confectioners sugar. Refrigerate until ready to serve.

Boston Cream Pie

BOSTON CREAM PIE

Makes one 9-inch cake

⅓ cup shortening
1 cup granulated sugar
1 egg
1 teaspoon vanilla
1¼ cups all-purpose flour
1½ teaspoons baking powder
½ teaspoon salt
¾ cup milk
    Filling (recipe follows)
    Glaze (recipe follows)

Preheat oven to 350°F. Grease and flour 9-inch round cake pan.

Beat together shortening and sugar in large bowl until light and fluffy. Blend in egg and vanilla. Add combined dry ingredients to sugar mixture alternately with milk, beating well after each addition. Pour into prepared pan.

Bake 35 minutes or until wooden toothpick inserted in center comes out clean. Cool in pan 10 minutes. Loosen edges and remove to wire rack to cool completely. When cool, split cake horizontally in half to make 2 thin layers. To assemble, place bottom half of cake on cake plate; spread with Filling. Cover with top half of cake layer. Spread top with Glaze; let cool. Serve when glaze is completely set. Refrigerate leftovers.

Filling: Combine ⅓ cup granulated sugar, 2 tablespoons cornstarch and ¼ teaspoon salt in 2-quart saucepan. Gradually stir in 1½ cups milk. Cook over medium heat, stirring constantly, until mixture thickens and comes to a boil. Boil 1 minute, stirring constantly. Gradually stir small amount of hot mixture into 2 slightly beaten egg yolks; mix thoroughly. Return to hot mixture in pan. Return to a boil; boil 1 minute, stirring constantly. (*Do not overcook.*) Remove from heat; stir in 2 teaspoons vanilla. Cool to room temperature. Cover; refrigerate until set.

Glaze: Combine 2 (1-ounce) squares unsweetened chocolate and 3 tablespoons butter in medium saucepan; stir over low heat until melted. Remove from heat; stir in 1 cup powdered sugar and ¾ teaspoon vanilla. Stir in 1 to 2 tablespoons water, a teaspoonful at a time, until glaze is of desired consistency. Cool slightly.

Favorite recipe from **The Essex Agricultural Society**

BOSTON CREAM TORTE

Makes 1 torte

1 package (4-serving size) JELL-O® Pudding and
    Pie Filling, Banana Cream or Vanilla Flavor
1¾ cups milk
2 baked 8-inch yellow cake layers, cooled
1 square BAKER'S® Unsweetened Chocolate
1 tablespoon butter or margarine
¾ cup confectioners sugar
1½ tablespoons hot milk
    Dash salt

Combine pudding mix and milk in medium saucepan; blend well. Cook and stir over medium heat until mixture comes to a full boil. Cover with plastic wrap; chill. Split cake layers horizontally to make 4 thin layers. Beat pudding until creamy. Spread about ⅔ cup pudding between each layer and stack.

Melt chocolate and butter in small saucepan over very low heat, stirring constantly. Combine sugar, hot milk and salt in small bowl; add chocolate mixture. Beat until smooth. Spread over top of cake. Chill. Store cake in refrigerator.

SOUTHERN PECAN CAKE

Makes 12 servings

2 cups pecan pieces
1 package DUNCAN HINES® Moist Deluxe
    French Vanilla Cake Mix
1 package (4-serving size) vanilla instant pudding
    and pie filling mix
4 eggs
1 cup water
⅓ cup CRISCO® Oil or CRISCO® PURITAN® Oil
1 container (16 ounces) DUNCAN HINES®
    Creamy Homestyle Cream Cheese Frosting

1. Preheat oven to 350°F. Grease and flour two 9-inch round cake pans.

2. Toast pecans on baking sheet at 350°F for 4 to 5 minutes or until fragrant. Cool. Chop finely. Measure 1½ cups. Reserve remaining pecans for garnish.

3. Combine cake mix, pudding mix, eggs, water and oil in large bowl. Beat at medium speed with electric mixer for 2 minutes. Fold in 1½ cups pecans. Pour into pans.

4. Bake at 350°F for 35 to 40 minutes or until wooden toothpick inserted in centers comes out clean. Cool in pans 15 minutes. Invert onto cooling racks. Cool completely.

5. Fill and frost cake with cream cheese frosting. Garnish with reserved pecans. Refrigerate until ready to serve.

Pudding Poke Cake

PUDDING POKE CAKE

Makes 18 servings

1 package (2-layer size) yellow or chocolate cake mix
2 packages (4-serving size each) JELL-O® Instant
    Pudding and Pie Filling, any flavor
1 cup confectioners sugar
4 cups cold milk

Prepare cake mix as directed on package, baking in
13 × 9-inch pan. Remove from oven. Immediately poke
holes down through cake to pan with round handle of
wooden spoon. (Or, poke holes with a plastic drinking
straw, using a turning motion to make large holes.)
Holes should be at 1-inch intervals.

Combine pudding mix with sugar in large bowl after
holes are made. Gradually stir in milk. Beat at low speed
of electric mixer for not more than 1 minute. (Do not
overbeat.) Quickly, before pudding mixture thickens,
pour about half of thin pudding mixture evenly over
warm cake and into holes to make stripes. Allow
remaining pudding mixture to thicken slightly; spoon
over top, swirling to "frost" cake. Chill at least 1 hour.
Store cake in refrigerator.

Prep time: 30 minutes
Chill time: 1 hour

GELATIN POKE LAYER CAKE

Makes one 8- or 9-inch cake

2 baked 8- or 9-inch white cake layers, cooled
2 packages (4-serving size) or 1 package (8-serving
    size) JELL-O® Brand Gelatin, any flavor
2 cups boiling water
3½ cups (8 ounces) COOL WHIP® Non-Dairy
    Whipped Topping, thawed, divided

Place cake layers, top-side up, in 2 clean 8- or 9-inch
cake pans. Prick each cake with fork at ½-inch intervals.
Completely dissolve gelatin in boiling water. Carefully
spoon over cake layers. Chill 3 to 4 hours. Dip 1 cake
pan in warm water for 10 seconds; then unmold onto
serving plate. Top with about 1 cup whipped topping.
Unmold second cake layer and carefully place on first
layer. Frost top and sides with remaining whipped
topping. Chill.

CHOCOLATE STRIPE CAKE

Makes 12 to 15 servings

1 package (18.25 ounces) white cake mix
1 envelope unflavored gelatin
¼ cup cold water
¼ cup boiling water
1 cup HERSHEY'S Syrup
    Whipped topping
    Additional HERSHEY'S Syrup for garnish

Preheat oven to 350°F. Grease and flour 13 × 9-inch
baking pan.

Prepare cake batter and bake according to package
directions. Cool 15 minutes. Do not remove cake from
pan. With fork, carefully pierce cake to bottom of pan,
making rows about 1 inch apart covering length and
width of cake.

In small bowl, sprinkle gelatin over cold water; let stand
1 minute to soften. Add boiling water; stir until gelatin
is completely dissolved and mixture is clear. Stir in 1 cup
syrup. Pour chocolate mixture evenly over cooled cake,
making sure entire top is covered and mixture has
flowed into holes.

Cover; refrigerate about 5 hours or until set. Serve
with whipped topping; garnish with additional syrup,
if desired. Refrigerate leftovers.

Left to right: Easy Peanut Butter-Chocolate Chip Cake, Double Marble Cake, Double Chocolate Snack Cake

DOUBLE CHOCOLATE SNACK CAKE

Makes 6 to 8 servings

1⅔ cups all-purpose flour
1 cup firmly packed light brown sugar
¼ cup HERSHEY'S® Cocoa
1 teaspoon baking soda
¼ teaspoon salt
1 cup water
⅓ cup vegetable oil
1 teaspoon white vinegar
¾ teaspoon vanilla extract
½ cup HERSHEY'S® Semi-Sweet Chocolate Chips

Preheat oven to 350°F. Grease and flour 8-inch square baking pan.

In large bowl, combine flour, sugar, cocoa, baking soda and salt. Add water, oil, vinegar and vanilla; beat with spoon or wire whisk until smooth. Pour batter into prepared pan. Sprinkle chocolate chips over top.

Bake 35 to 40 minutes or until wooden toothpick inserted in center comes out clean. Cool in pan on wire rack; cut into squares.

DOUBLE MARBLE CAKE

Makes 12 to 15 servings

1 package (18.25 or 19.75 ounces) fudge marble cake mix
3 eggs
⅓ cup vegetable oil
Water
1 cup HERSHEY'S® Semi-Sweet Chocolate Chips, divided
1 jar (7 ounces) marshmallow creme

Preheat oven to 350°F. Grease and flour 13×9-inch baking pan.

Prepare cake batters according to package directions, using eggs, oil and water. Stir ½ cup chocolate chips into chocolate batter. Spoon vanilla and chocolate batters into prepared pan; swirl as directed on package.

Bake 33 to 38 minutes or until wooden toothpick inserted in center comes out clean. Cool in pan on wire rack 5 minutes. Gently spread marshmallow creme over warm cake. In small saucepan over low heat, melt remaining ½ cup chips; swirl through marshmallow creme. Cool completely in pan on wire rack.

EASY PEANUT BUTTER-CHOCOLATE CHIP CAKE

Makes 12 to 15 servings

1 package (18.5 ounces) yellow cake mix (with pudding in the mix)
4 eggs
¾ cup water
⅓ cup vegetable oil
⅓ cup REESE'S™ Creamy Peanut Butter
1½ cups HERSHEY'S® Semi-Sweet Chocolate Chips, divided
¼ cup chopped, unsalted peanuts

Preheat oven to 350°F. Grease and lightly flour 13×9-inch baking pan.

Prepare cake batter according to package directions using eggs, water and oil. Blend in peanut butter. Spoon half of batter into prepared pan. Sprinkle ¾ cup chocolate chips over batter. Gently spread remaining batter over top. Sprinkle remaining ¾ cup chips and peanuts over top.

Bake 45 minutes or until wooden toothpick inserted in center comes out clean. Cool in pan on wire rack. Frost as desired.

Easy German Chocolate Cake

2 minutes or until mixture comes to a boil. Stir in coconut and ½ cup pecans. Spread evenly over cooled cake. Broil, 4 inches from heat, for 3 to 5 minutes or until golden brown. Cool completely.

Tip: Rotate cake under broiler for more even browning.

GERMAN SWEET CHOCOLATE CAKE

Makes 12 servings

1 package (4 ounces) BAKER'S® GERMAN'S®
    Sweet Chocolate
½ cup water
2¼ cups cake flour *or* 2 cups all-purpose flour
1 teaspoon baking soda
¼ teaspoon salt
1 cup (2 sticks) margarine or butter, softened
2 cups sugar
4 egg yolks
1 teaspoon vanilla
1 cup buttermilk
4 egg whites
    Classic Coconut-Pecan Filling and Frosting
    (recipe follows)

Preheat oven to 350°F. Line bottoms of three 9-inch layer pans with waxed paper.

Microwave chocolate and water in large microwavable bowl on HIGH (100% power) 1½ to 2 minutes or until chocolate is almost melted. Stir until chocolate is completely melted.

Mix flour, baking soda and salt in small bowl; set aside. Beat margarine and sugar in large bowl until light and fluffy. Add egg yolks, one at a time, beating well after each addition. Stir in melted chocolate mixture and vanilla. Add flour mixture alternately with buttermilk, beating after each addition until smooth.

Beat egg whites in large bowl with electric mixer on high speed until stiff peaks form. Fold into batter. Pour batter into prepared pans.

Bake 30 minutes or until cakes spring back when lightly touched. Remove from oven; immediately run spatula between cakes and sides of pans. Cool in pans 15 minutes. Remove from pans; peel off waxed paper. Cool on wire racks.

Spread Classic Coconut-Pecan Filling and Frosting between layers and over top of cake.

Note: This delicate cake will have a flat, slightly sugary top crust that tends to crack. This is normal and the frosting will cover it up.

EASY GERMAN CHOCOLATE CAKE

Makes 12 to 16 servings

CAKE
1 package DUNCAN HINES® Moist Deluxe
    Swiss Chocolate Cake Mix
3 eggs
1¼ cups water
½ cup CRISCO® Oil or CRISCO® PURITAN® Oil
½ cup chopped pecans

TOPPING
1 cup firmly packed brown sugar
⅓ cup butter or margarine, melted
¼ cup milk
1 can (3½ ounces) flaked coconut
½ cup chopped pecans

1. Preheat oven to 350°F. Grease and flour 13×9-inch pan.

2. For Cake, combine cake mix, eggs, water and oil in large bowl. Beat at medium speed with electric mixer for 2 minutes. Stir in ½ cup pecans. Pour batter into pan.

3. Bake at 350°F for 35 to 40 minutes or until wooden toothpick inserted in center comes out clean. Cool completely on wire rack.

4. For Topping, set oven to broil. Combine brown sugar, melted butter and milk in large microwave-safe bowl. Microwave on HIGH (100% power) for 1 to

CLASSIC COCONUT-PECAN FILLING AND FROSTING

1½ cups (12-ounce can) evaporated milk
1½ cups sugar
 4 egg yolks, slightly beaten
 ¾ cup (1½ sticks) margarine or butter
1½ teaspoons vanilla
 1 package (7 ounces) BAKER'S® ANGEL FLAKE®
    Coconut (about 2⅔ cups)
1½ cups chopped pecans

Combine milk, sugar, egg yolks, margarine and vanilla in large saucepan. Cook over medium heat until mixture thickens and is golden brown, about 12 minutes, stirring constantly. Remove from heat.

Stir in coconut and pecans. Cool to room temperature and of spreading consistency. *Makes about 4 ½ cups*

COOL AND MINTY PARTY CAKE

Makes one 9-inch cake

 1 (14-ounce) can EAGLE® Brand Sweetened
    Condensed Milk (NOT evaporated milk)
 2 teaspoons peppermint extract
 8 drops green food coloring
 2 cups (1 pint) whipping cream, whipped (*do not
    use non-dairy whipped topping*)
 1 (18¼- or 18½-ounce) package white cake mix
    Green creme de menthe liqueur
 1 (8-ounce) container frozen non-dairy whipped
    topping, thawed

Up to 3 to 10 days ahead
In large bowl, combine sweetened condensed milk, extract and food coloring. Fold in whipped cream. Pour into aluminum foil-lined 9-inch round layer cake pan; cover. Freeze at least 6 hours or until firm.

Up to 1 to 3 days ahead
Prepare and bake cake mix as package directs for two 9-inch round layers. Remove from pans; cool thoroughly.

Up to 1 to 3 days ahead
Prepare and bake cake mix as package directs for two 9-inch round layers. Remove from pans; cool thoroughly.

With fork, poke holes 1 inch apart and halfway through each cake layer. Spoon small amounts of creme de menthe in holes. Place 1 cake layer on serving plate; top with frozen whipped cream layer then second cake layer. Trim whipped cream layer even with edge of cake. Frost quickly with whipped topping. Return to freezer; freeze at least 6 hours before serving. Return leftovers to freezer.

FUDGE RIBBON CAKE

Makes one 10-inch tube cake

 1 (18¼- or 18½-ounce) package chocolate cake mix
 1 (8-ounce) package cream cheese, softened
 2 tablespoons margarine or butter, softened
 1 tablespoon cornstarch
 1 (14-ounce) can EAGLE® Brand Sweetened
    Condensed Milk (NOT evaporated milk)
 1 egg
 1 teaspoon vanilla extract
    Confectioners' sugar or Chocolate Drizzle
    (recipe follows)

Preheat oven to 350°F. Prepare cake mix as package directs. Pour batter into *well-greased* and floured 10-inch fluted tube pan. In small mixer bowl, beat cheese, margarine and cornstarch until fluffy. Gradually beat in sweetened condensed milk, then egg and vanilla until smooth. Pour evenly over cake batter.

Bake 50 to 55 minutes or until wooden toothpick inserted near center comes out clean. Cool 15 minutes; remove from pan. Cool. Sprinkle with confectioners' sugar or drizzle with Chocolate Drizzle.

Chocolate Drizzle: In small saucepan, over low heat, melt 1 (1-ounce) square unsweetened or semi-sweet chocolate, 1 tablespoon margarine or butter and 2 tablespoons water. Remove from heat. Stir in ¾ cup confectioners' sugar and ½ teaspoon vanilla extract. Stir until smooth and well blended. *Makes about ⅓ cup*

Fudge Ribbon Cake

OLD-FASHIONED CHOCOLATE CAKE

Makes 10 to 12 servings

1½ cups sugar
¾ cup (1½ sticks) butter, softened
2 eggs
1 teaspoon vanilla extract
2 cups all-purpose flour
1 cup water
⅓ cup NESTLÉ® Cocoa
1½ teaspoons baking soda
½ teaspoon salt

Preheat oven to 350°F. Grease and flour two 9-inch round baking pans.

In large mixer bowl, beat sugar, butter, eggs and vanilla extract until light and fluffy, about 5 minutes. Add flour, water, cocoa, baking soda and salt. Beat until blended and smooth. Pour into prepared pans.

Bake 28 to 33 minutes or until wooden toothpick inserted into centers comes out clean. Cool 5 minutes; remove from pans. Cool completely on wire racks. Fill and frost with favorite frosting.

Chocolate Mint Layer Cake

CHOCOLATE MINT LAYER CAKE

Makes one 2-layer cake

1 cup (⅔ of 10-ounce package) NESTLÉ®
    Toll House® Mint-Flavored Semi-Sweet
    Chocolate Morsels
1¼ cups water, divided
2¼ cups all-purpose flour
1 teaspoon salt
1 teaspoon baking soda
½ teaspoon baking powder
1½ cups firmly packed brown sugar
½ cup butter, softened
3 eggs
    Chocolate Mint Frosting (recipe follows)

Preheat oven to 375°F. In small saucepan, combine Nestlé® Toll House® Mint-Flavored Semi-Sweet Chocolate Morsels and ¼ cup water. Cook over medium heat, stirring constantly, until morsels are melted and mixture is smooth. Cool 10 minutes. In medium bowl, combine flour, salt, baking soda and baking powder; set aside. In large bowl, combine brown sugar and butter; beat until creamy. Add eggs, 1 at a time, beating well after each addition. Blend in chocolate mixture. Gradually beat in flour mixture alternately with remaining 1 cup water. Pour into 2 greased and floured 9-inch round baking pans.

Bake 25 to 30 minutes or until wooden toothpick inserted into centers comes out clean. Cool completely on wire racks. Fill and frost with Chocolate Mint Frosting. Garnish as desired.

CHOCOLATE MINT FROSTING

½ cup (⅓ of 10-ounce package) NESTLÉ®
    Toll House® Mint-Flavored Semi-Sweet
    Chocolate Morsels
¼ cup butter
1 teaspoon vanilla extract
¼ teaspoon salt
3 cups sifted confectioners' sugar
6 tablespoons milk

Combine over hot (not boiling) water, Nestlé® Toll House® Mint-Flavored Semi-Sweet Chocolate Morsels and butter. Stir until morsels are melted and mixture is smooth. Stir in vanilla extract and salt. Transfer to large bowl. Gradually beat in confectioners' sugar alternately with milk; beat until smooth.*

*If necessary, add more milk until frosting is of desired spreading consistency.

Top to bottom: German Sweet Chocolate Cake (page 46), Wellesley Fudge Cake

WELLESLEY FUDGE CAKE

Makes 12 servings

4 squares BAKER'S® Unsweetened Chocolate
1¾ cups sugar, divided
½ cup water
1⅔ cups all-purpose flour
1 teaspoon baking soda
¼ teaspoon salt
½ cup (1 stick) margarine or butter, softened
3 eggs
¾ cup milk
1 teaspoon vanilla
Easy Fudge Frosting (recipe follows)

Preheat oven to 350°F.

Microwave chocolate, ½ cup sugar and water in large microwavable bowl on HIGH (100% power) 1 to 2 minutes or until chocolate is almost melted, stirring once. Stir until chocolate is completely melted. Cool to lukewarm.

Mix flour, baking soda and salt in small bowl; set aside. Beat margarine and remaining 1¼ cups sugar in large bowl until light and fluffy. Add eggs, one at a time, beating well after each addition. Add flour mixture alternately with milk, beating after each addition until smooth. Stir in chocolate mixture and vanilla. Pour into 2 greased and floured 9-inch layer pans.

Bake 30 to 35 minutes or until cakes spring back when lightly pressed. Cool in pans 10 minutes. Remove from pans to cool on wire racks. Fill and frost with Easy Fudge Frosting.

Prep time: 30 minutes
Bake time: 30 to 35 minutes

EASY FUDGE FROSTING

4 squares BAKER'S® Unsweetened Chocolate
2 tablespoons margarine or butter
4 cups powdered sugar
½ cup milk
1 teaspoon vanilla

Microwave chocolate and margarine in large microwavable bowl on HIGH (100% power) 1 minute or until margarine is melted. Stir until chocolate is completely melted.

Stir in sugar, milk and vanilla until smooth. Let stand, if necessary, until of spreading consistency, stirring occasionally. Spread quickly. (Add 2 to 3 teaspoons additional milk if frosting becomes too thick.)

COCOA BUNDT CAKE

Makes 12 to 16 servings

1⅔ cups all-purpose flour
1½ cups sugar
½ cup HERSHEY'S Cocoa
1½ teaspoons baking soda
1 teaspoon salt
½ teaspoon baking powder
2 eggs
½ cup shortening
1½ cups buttermilk or sour milk*
1 teaspoon vanilla extract
Cocoa Glaze (recipe follows)

Preheat oven to 350°F. Generously grease and flour 12-cup Bundt® pan or 10-inch tight-fitting tube pan.

In large mixer bowl, blend flour, sugar, cocoa, baking soda, salt and baking powder; add eggs, shortening, buttermilk and vanilla. Beat on low speed with electric mixer 1 minute, scraping bowl constantly. Increase speed to high; beat 3 minutes, scraping bowl occasionally. Pour batter into prepared pan.

Bake 50 to 55 minutes or until wooden toothpick inserted in center of cake comes out clean. Cool 10 minutes; remove from pan to wire rack. Cool completely. Drizzle Cocoa Glaze over top of cake, allowing some to drizzle down sides.

*To sour milk: Combine 4½ teaspoons white vinegar plus enough milk to equal 1½ cups. Stir. Wait 5 minutes before using.

COCOA GLAZE

2 tablespoons butter or margarine
2 tablespoons HERSHEY'S Cocoa
2 tablespoons water
1 cup powdered sugar
½ teaspoon vanilla extract

In small saucepan, over low heat, melt butter; add cocoa and water, stirring constantly, until mixture thickens. *Do not boil.* Remove from heat; gradually add powdered sugar and vanilla, beating with wire whisk until smooth. Add additional water, ½ teaspoon at a time, until glaze is of desired consistency. *Makes about ¾ cup glaze*

Cocoa Sheet Cake: Prepare batter as directed; pour into greased and floured 13×9-inch baking pan. Bake at 350°F 35 to 40 minutes or until wooden toothpick inserted in center of cake comes out clean. Cool completely on wire rack; frost with desired frosting.

CHOCOLATE SYRUP SWIRL CAKE

Makes 12 to 16 servings

1 cup butter or margarine, softened
2 cups sugar
2 teaspoons vanilla extract
3 eggs
2¾ cups all-purpose flour
1¼ teaspoons baking soda, divided
½ teaspoon salt
1 cup buttermilk or sour milk*
1 cup HERSHEY'S Syrup
1 cup flaked coconut (optional)

Preheat oven to 350°F. Grease and flour 12-cup fluted tube pan or 10-inch tube pan.

In large mixer bowl, beat butter, sugar and vanilla until light and fluffy. Add eggs; beat well. Combine flour, 1 teaspoon baking soda and salt; add alternately with buttermilk to butter mixture. In small bowl, measure 2 cups batter; stir in syrup and remaining ¼ teaspoon baking soda. Add coconut, if desired, to remaining batter; pour into prepared pan. Pour chocolate batter over vanilla batter in pan; *do not mix.*

Bake 65 to 70 minutes or until wooden toothpick inserted in center comes out clean. Cool 15 minutes; remove from pan. Cool completely on wire rack; glaze or frost as desired.

*To sour milk: Combine 1 tablespoon white vinegar plus enough milk to equal 1 cup. Stir. Wait 5 minutes before using.

CHOCOLATE WALNUT CAKE

Makes 8 to 10 servings

1 (18¼- or 18½-ounce) package chocolate cake mix
1 cup coarsely chopped walnuts
1 (14-ounce) can EAGLE® Brand Sweetened Condensed Milk (NOT evaporated milk)
2 (1-ounce) squares unsweetened chocolate
Dash salt
1 tablespoon water
½ teaspoon vanilla extract

Prepare cake mix as package directs, adding ½ *cup* nuts. Bake according to package directions for 13×9-inch cake. Cool thoroughly. In heavy saucepan, over low heat, combine sweetened condensed milk, chocolate and salt. Cook and stir until chocolate melts and mixture thickens, about 10 minutes. Remove from heat. Stir in water and vanilla; cool. Spread on cake. Garnish with remaining nuts.

Chocolate Syrup Swirl Cake

Chocolate Confection Cake

CHOCOLATE CONFECTION CAKE

Makes 20 to 24 servings

1 package DUNCAN HINES® Moist Deluxe
  Devil's Food Cake Mix

FILLING
  1 cup evaporated milk
  1 cup granulated sugar
24 large marshmallows
  1 package (14 ounces) flaked coconut

TOPPING
  ½ cup butter or margarine
  ¼ cup *plus* 2 tablespoons milk
  ⅓ cup unsweetened cocoa
  1 pound confectioners sugar (3½ to 4 cups)
  1 teaspoon vanilla extract
  ¾ cup sliced almonds

1. Preheat oven to 350°F. Grease and flour
15½ × 10½ × 1-inch jelly-roll pan.

2. Prepare cake following package directions for basic
recipe. Pour into pan.

3. Bake at 350°F for 20 to 25 minutes or until wooden
toothpick inserted in center comes out clean.

4. For Filling, combine evaporated milk and granulated
sugar in large saucepan. Bring mixture to a boil. Add
marshmallows and stir until melted. Stir in coconut.
Spread on warm cake.

5. For Topping, combine butter, milk and cocoa in
medium saucepan. Stir over low heat until butter is
melted. Add confectioners sugar and vanilla extract,
stirring until smooth. Stir in almonds (see Tip). Pour
over filling. Spread evenly to edges. Cool completely.

Tip: For a pretty presentation, sprinkle the ¾ cup sliced
almonds over topping instead of stirring almonds into
topping.

CHOCOLATE-ORANGE PUDDING CAKE

Makes 6 to 8 servings

1 cup all-purpose flour
¾ cup granulated sugar
3 tablespoons plus ¼ cup HERSHEY'S Cocoa,
  divided
2 teaspoons baking powder
½ teaspoon salt
½ cup milk
2 tablespoons vegetable oil
1 teaspoon vanilla extract
½ cup chopped nuts, divided
¾ cup firmly packed light brown sugar
¼ to ½ teaspoon grated orange peel
1¼ cups boiling water
  Vanilla ice cream (optional)

To Microwave: In large bowl, stir together flour,
granulated sugar, 3 tablespoons cocoa, baking powder
and salt. Stir in milk, oil, vanilla and ¼ cup nuts. Spread
batter in 2- or 2½-quart microwave-safe casserole. In
small bowl, combine brown sugar, remaining ¼ cup
cocoa, remaining ¼ cup nuts, orange peel and water.
Carefully pour liquid mixture over batter in casserole;
do not mix.

Microwave at HIGH (100% power) 7 to 9 minutes,
rotating ¼ turn halfway through cooking time, or until
cake rises to the surface and sauce forms on bottom. Let
stand 10 minutes. Serve warm. Spoon into dessert
dishes, spooning sauce from bottom of casserole over
each serving. Top with scoop of ice cream, if desired.

CHOCOLATE SURPRISE CUPCAKES

Makes 18 cupcakes

FILLING:
  1 package (8 ounces) PHILADELPHIA BRAND®
    Cream Cheese, softened
  ⅓ cup granulated sugar
  1 egg
  ½ cup BAKER'S® Semi-Sweet Real Chocolate
    Chips

CUPCAKES:
  2 squares BAKER'S® Unsweetened Chocolate,
    melted
  ⅓ cup vegetable oil
  1¼ cups all-purpose flour
  1 cup granulated sugar
  ¾ cup water
  1 egg
  1 teaspoon vanilla
  ½ teaspoon baking soda
  ¼ teaspoon salt
    Powdered sugar (optional)

For Filling, beat cream cheese, ⅓ cup granulated sugar and 1 egg until smooth. Stir in chips; set aside.

For Cupcakes, preheat oven to 350°F. Microwave chocolate in large microwavable bowl on HIGH (100% power) 1 to 2 minutes or until almost melted, stirring after each minute. Stir until completely melted. Add oil, flour, 1 cup granulated sugar, water, 1 egg, vanilla, baking soda and salt; beat with wire whisk or fork until blended and smooth. Spoon half the batter evenly into 18 greased or paper-lined muffin cups. Top each with 1 tablespoon cream cheese mixture. Spoon the remaining batter evenly over cream cheese mixture.

Bake for 30 to 35 minutes or until wooden toothpick inserted in cake portion comes out clean. Remove from pans to cool on wire racks. Sprinkle with powdered sugar, if desired.

Prep time: 15 minutes
Bake time: 30 to 35 minutes

DEVIL'S FOOD CAKE

Makes 8 to 10 servings

  ¾ cup butter or margarine, softened
  1½ cups sugar
  1½ teaspoons vanilla extract
  2 eggs
  1¾ cups all-purpose flour
  ½ cup HERSHEY®'S Cocoa
  1 teaspoon baking soda
  ¼ teaspoon salt
  ½ cup buttermilk or sour milk*
  ½ cup boiling water

Preheat oven to 350°F. Grease and flour two 9-inch round baking pans.

Beat butter, sugar and vanilla in large mixer bowl until light and fluffy. Add eggs; beat well. Combine flour, cocoa, baking soda and salt; add alternately with buttermilk to sugar mixture. Add boiling water; beat just until smooth. Pour batter into prepared pans.

Bake 30 to 35 minutes or until cake tester inserted in centers comes out clean. Cool 10 minutes; remove cakes from pans. Cool completely on wire racks. Frost as desired.

*To sour milk: Combine 1½ teaspoons vinegar plus enough milk to equal ½ cup. Stir. Wait 5 minutes before using.

Chocolate Surprise Cupcakes

DEVIL'S DELIGHT CHOCOLATE GLAZED CAKE

Makes 12 to 16 servings

1 package (18.25 ounces) devil's food cake mix
　(with pudding in the mix)
4 eggs
1 cup water
½ cup vegetable oil
1 cup chopped nuts
1 cup miniature marshmallows
1 cup HERSHEY'S Semi-Sweet Chocolate Chips
½ cup raisins
　Powdered sugar or Chocolate Chip Glaze
　(recipe follows)

Preheat oven to 350°F. Grease and flour 12-cup Bundt® pan.

In large mixer bowl, combine cake mix, eggs, water and oil; beat on low speed just until blended. Increase speed to medium; beat 2 minutes. Stir in nuts, marshmallows, chocolate chips and raisins. Pour batter into prepared pan.

Bake 45 to 50 minutes or until wooden toothpick inserted in center comes out clean. Cool 10 minutes; remove from pan to wire rack. Cool completely on wire rack. Sprinkle powdered sugar over top or drizzle Chocolate Chip Glaze over top.

Chocolate Chip Glaze: In small saucepan, combine 2 tablespoons butter or margarine, 2 tablespoons light corn syrup and 2 tablespoons water. Cook over low heat, stirring constantly, until mixture begins to boil. Remove from heat; add 1 cup HERSHEY'S Semi-Sweet Chocolate Chips. Stir until chips are melted and mixture is smooth. Continue stirring until glaze is desired consistency. *Makes about 1 cup glaze*

CHOCOLATE ROYALE

Makes 12 to 16 servings

1 package DUNCAN HINES® Moist Deluxe
　Devil's Food Cake Mix

FROSTING

1 package (3 ounces) cream cheese, softened
½ cup confectioners sugar
1 teaspoon vanilla extract
1 cup whipping cream, whipped
2 large bananas, sliced
　Lemon juice
　Chocolate sprinkles

1. Preheat oven to 350°F. Grease and flour two 8-inch round pans.

2. Prepare, bake and cool cake following package directions for basic recipe.

3. For Frosting, combine cream cheese, confectioners sugar and vanilla extract in medium bowl. Beat at low speed with electric mixer until blended. Fold whipped cream into cheese mixture.

4. To assemble, place one cake layer on serving plate. Spread with thin layer of frosting. Reserve 12 banana slices for garnish; dip in lemon juice. Cover frosting with remaining banana slices. Spread another thin layer of frosting over bananas. Place second cake layer on top. Frost sides and top of cake with remaining frosting. Blot reserved banana slices dry on paper towel. Roll banana slices in chocolate sprinkles. Garnish top of cake with banana slices. Refrigerate until ready to serve.

Tip: To keep plate neat when frosting a layer cake, tuck four strips of waxed paper under edges of the bottom cake layer; carefully remove waxed paper after cake is frosted.

Chocolate Royale

CHOCOLATE SHEET CAKE

Makes one 15 × 10-inch cake

1¼ cups margarine or butter
½ cup unsweetened cocoa
1 cup water
2 cups unsifted all-purpose flour
1½ cups firmly packed brown sugar
1 teaspoon baking soda
1 teaspoon ground cinnamon
½ teaspoon salt
1 (14-ounce) can EAGLE® Brand Sweetened
   Condensed Milk (NOT evaporated milk)
2 eggs
1 teaspoon vanilla extract
1 cup confectioners' sugar
1 cup chopped nuts

Preheat oven to 350°F. In small saucepan, melt *1 cup* margarine; stir in *¼ cup* cocoa, then water. Bring to a boil; remove from heat. In large mixer bowl, combine flour, brown sugar, baking soda, cinnamon and salt. Add cocoa mixture; beat well. Stir in *⅓ cup* sweetened condensed milk, eggs and vanilla. Pour into greased 15 × 10-inch jellyroll pan.

Bake 15 minutes or until cake springs back when lightly touched. In small saucepan, melt remaining *¼ cup* margarine; add remaining *¼ cup* cocoa and remaining sweetened condensed milk. Stir in confectioners' sugar and nuts. Spread on warm cake.

CHOCOLATE STREUSEL CAKE

Makes 12 to 16 servings

STREUSEL
1 package DUNCAN HINES® Moist Deluxe
   Devil's Food Cake Mix, divided
1 cup finely chopped pecans
2 tablespoons firmly packed brown sugar
2 teaspoons ground cinnamon

CAKE
3 eggs
1⅓ cups water
½ cup CRISCO® Oil or CRISCO® PURITAN® Oil

TOPPING
1 container (8 ounces) frozen whipped topping,
   thawed
3 tablespoons sifted unsweetened cocoa
   Chopped pecans, for garnish
   Chocolate curls, for garnish (see Tip)

1. Preheat oven to 350°F. Grease and flour 10-inch Bundt® pan.

2. For Streusel, combine 2 tablespoons cake mix, 1 cup pecans, brown sugar and cinnamon in small bowl. Set aside.

3. For Cake, combine remaining cake mix, eggs, water and oil in large bowl. Beat at medium speed with electric mixer for 2 minutes. Pour two-thirds of batter into pan. Sprinkle with streusel mixture. Pour remaining batter evenly over streusel.

4. Bake at 350°F for 55 to 60 minutes or until wooden toothpick inserted in center comes out clean. Cool in pan 25 minutes. Invert onto serving plate. Cool completely.

5. For Topping, place whipped topping in medium bowl. Fold in cocoa until blended. Spread on cooled cake. Garnish with chopped pecans and chocolate curls, if desired. Refrigerate until ready to serve.

Tip: For chocolate curls, warm chocolate block in microwave oven at HIGH (100% power) for 5 to 10 seconds. Make chocolate curls by holding a sharp vegetable peeler against flat side of chocolate block and bringing blade toward you. Apply firm pressure for thicker, more open curls or light pressure for tighter curls.

Chocolate Streusel Cake

Chocolate Yogurt Cake

CHOCOLATE YOGURT CAKE

Makes one 2-layer cake

⅔ cup shortening
1¾ cups granulated sugar
2 eggs
1 teaspoon Cognac vanilla or vanilla
2½ cups sifted cake flour
1½ teaspoons baking soda
½ teaspoon salt
1 cup (8 ounces) plain yogurt
½ cup boiling water
½ cup unsweetened cocoa powder
   Filling (recipe follows)
   Fluffy Cocoa Frosting (recipe follows)
   Additional chopped hazelnuts for garnish
     (optional)
   Toasted flaked coconut for garnish (optional)

Preheat oven to 350°F. Grease and flour two 9-inch round cake pans.

Beat shortening and sugar in large bowl until light and fluffy. Add eggs, 1 at a time, beating well after each addition. Blend in vanilla. Combine flour, baking soda and salt in small bowl. Add to shortening mixture alternately with yogurt, beating well after each addition. Gradually add boiling water to cocoa, stirring until well blended; cool slightly. Add to batter; beat until well blended. Pour evenly into prepared pans.

Bake 35 minutes or until wooden toothpick inserted in centers comes out clean. Cool layers in pans on wire racks 10 minutes. Loosen edges and remove to racks to cool completely. To assemble, place 1 cake layer on cake plate; spread with Filling. Top with second cake layer. Frost with Fluffy Cocoa Frosting. Garnish as desired.

Filling: Combine ½ cup Fluffy Cocoa Frosting (recipe follows), 2 tablespoons chopped frozen cherries, thawed, ¼ cup flaked coconut and ¼ cup chopped toasted hazelnuts in small bowl, mixing until well blended.

Fluffy Cocoa Frosting: Combine 4 cups powdered sugar and ¾ cup cocoa in medium bowl; set aside. Beat ½ cup (1 stick) softened unsalted butter in large bowl until creamy. Beat in half of cocoa mixture until fluffy. Blend in ¼ cup evaporated milk and 1 teaspoon Cognac vanilla or vanilla. Gradually beat in remaining powdered sugar mixture. Beat in additional ¼ cup evaporated milk until spreadable. (Additional milk may be added, if desired, for a softer frosting.)

Favorite recipe from **Kentucky State Fair**

CHOCOLATE CHERRY TORTE

Makes 12 to 16 servings

1 package DUNCAN HINES® Moist Deluxe
   Devil's Food Cake Mix
1 can (21 ounces) cherry pie filling
¼ teaspoon almond extract
1 container (8 ounces) frozen whipped topping,
   thawed and divided
¼ cup toasted sliced almonds, for garnish (see Tip)

1. Preheat oven to 350°F. Grease and flour two 9-inch round cake pans.

2. Prepare, bake and cool cake following package directions for basic recipe. Combine cherry pie filling and almond extract in small bowl. Stir.

3. To assemble, place one cake layer on serving plate. Spread with 1 cup whipped topping, then half the pie filling mixture. Top with second cake layer. Spread remaining pie filling mixture to within 1½ inches of edge. Decorate cake edge with remaining whipped topping, as desired. Garnish with sliced almonds.

Tip: To toast almonds, spread in a single layer on baking sheet. Bake at 325°F for 4 to 6 minutes or until fragrant and golden.

HERSHEY® BAR CAKE

Makes 12 to 15 servings

1 HERSHEY®'S Milk Chocolate Bar (7 ounces),
   broken into pieces
¼ cup butter or margarine
1⅔ cups boiling water
2⅓ cups all-purpose flour
2 cups firmly packed light brown sugar
2 teaspoons baking soda
1 teaspoon salt
2 eggs
½ cup sour cream
1 teaspoon vanilla extract

Preheat oven to 350°F. Combine chocolate bar pieces, butter and boiling water in medium bowl; stir until chocolate is melted. Combine flour, brown sugar, baking soda and salt in large mixer bowl; gradually add chocolate mixture, beating until thoroughly blended. Blend in eggs, sour cream and vanilla; beat 1 minute on medium speed. Pour into greased and floured 13×9-inch pan.

Bake 35 to 40 minutes or until cake tester inserted in center comes out clean. Cool completely on wire rack. Frost as desired.

Chocolate Mayonnaise Cake

CHOCOLATE MAYONNAISE CAKE

Makes 1 (9-inch) layer cake

2 cups all-purpose flour
⅔ cup unsweetened cocoa
1¼ teaspoons baking soda
¼ teaspoon baking powder
3 eggs
1⅔ cups sugar
1 teaspoon vanilla
1 cup HELLMANN'S® or BEST FOODS®
    Real, Light Reduced Calorie or Reduced Fat
    Cholesterol Free Mayonnaise Dressing
1⅓ cups water

Preheat oven to 350°F. Grease and flour bottoms of two 9-inch round cake pans.

In medium bowl, combine flour, cocoa, baking soda and baking powder; set aside. In large bowl, with mixer at high speed, beat eggs, sugar and vanilla, scraping bowl occasionally, 3 minutes or until smooth and creamy. Reduce speed to low; beat in mayonnaise until blended. Add flour mixture in 4 additions alternately with water, beginning and ending with flour mixture. Pour into prepared pans.

Bake 30 to 35 minutes or until cakes spring back when touched lightly in centers. Cool in pans on wire racks 10 minutes. Remove from pans; cool completely on racks. Fill and frost as desired.

To Microwave: Prepare Chocolate Mayonnaise Cake batter as directed. Line bottoms of two 8-inch round microwavable cake pans with circles of waxed paper. Pour batter into prepared cake pans. Microwave 1 layer at a time. Place 1 cake pan on inverted microwavable pie plate in microwave oven.

Microwave on MEDIUM (50% power) 5 minutes. (If cake appears to be rising unevenly, rotate pan during cooking.) Microwave on HIGH (100% power) 3 to 5 minutes longer or just until cake begins to set on the outer edge. Center may appear to be slightly soft, but cake will firm as it cools. Repeat with remaining layer. Let stand in pans 10 minutes on flat heatproof surface. Remove from pans; remove waxed paper. Cool completely on wire racks. Fill and frost as desired.

BROWNIE CREAM CHIP TORTE

Makes 10 to 12 servings

TORTE:
2 cups (12-ounce package) NESTLÉ® Toll House® Semi-Sweet Chocolate Mini Morsels, divided
⅔ cup butter
1½ cups all-purpose flour
1 teaspoon baking powder
½ teaspoon salt
4 eggs
1½ cups sugar
1 teaspoon vanilla extract
½ cup chopped walnuts

CREAM CHIP FROSTING:
2 cups heavy cream
¼ cup sifted confectioners' sugar
1 teaspoon vanilla extract
¾ cup NESTLÉ® Toll House® Semi-Sweet Chocolate Mini Morsels, reserved from 12-ounce package

GARNISH:
¾ cup NESTLÉ® Toll House® Semi-Sweet Chocolate Mini Morsels, reserved from 12-ounce package

Torte: Preheat oven to 350°F. Line bottom and sides of 15½ × 10½ × 1-inch jelly-roll pan with heavy duty foil; grease foil and set aside. Combine over hot (not boiling) water, ½ cup Nestlé® Toll House® Semi-Sweet Chocolate Mini Morsels and butter. Stir until morsels are melted and mixture is smooth. Remove from heat; cool. In small bowl, combine flour, baking powder and salt; set aside. In large bowl, beat eggs and sugar until light and fluffy. Add cooled chocolate mixture; beat until well blended. Gradually blend in flour mixture. Stir in vanilla extract and walnuts. Spread batter into prepared pan.

Bake 18 to 20 minutes or until wooden toothpick inserted in center comes out clean. Loosen edges of cake; cool completely in pan. Invert onto cookie sheet; gently remove foil.

Cream Chip Frosting: In large bowl, combine heavy cream, confectioners' sugar and vanilla extract; beat until stiff. Fold in ¾ cup Nestlé® Toll House® Semi-Sweet Chocolate Mini Morsels.

Trim edges of cake; cut cake crosswise into four 10 × 3¾-inch sections. Spread about ¾ cup Cream Chip Frosting on 1 layer. Top with second layer. Repeat layers of Frosting and cake. Frost entire cake with remaining Frosting.

Garnish: Sprinkle cake with remaining ¾ cup Nestlé® Toll House® Semi-Sweet Chocolate Mini Morsels. Refrigerate until ready to serve.

PARTY SQUARES

Makes 16 servings

1 package DUNCAN HINES® Moist Deluxe Swiss Chocolate Cake Mix
1 container (12 ounces) DUNCAN HINES® Creamy Homestyle Vanilla Frosting, divided
Red food coloring
2 bars (1.55 ounces each) milk chocolate

1. Preheat oven to 350°F. Grease and flour 13 × 9-inch pan.

2. Prepare, bake and cool cake following package directions.

3. Reserve ⅓ cup Vanilla frosting. Tint remaining Vanilla frosting pink with red food coloring. Frost cake with pink frosting. Using a spatula, make diagonal lines in frosting across top of cake. Mark 16 servings with tip of knife.

4. Score milk chocolate bars into sections. Place chocolate pieces on top of each serving. Place star tip in pastry bag; fill with reserved Vanilla frosting. Pipe star partially on each chocolate piece to anchor. Cut cake into servings following lines in frosting.

Tip: This simple cake has many decorating options. Try reserving ⅓ cup Vanilla frosting and tinting with green food coloring. Leave remaining frosting white. Decorate as above except fit pastry bag with leaf tip.

Party Squares

CHEESECAKES

WHITE CHOCOLATE CHEESECAKE

Makes 12 servings

CRUST
½ cup (1 stick) butter, softened
¼ cup sugar
½ teaspoon vanilla
1 cup all-purpose flour

FILLING
4 (8-ounce) packages PHILADELPHIA BRAND®
    Cream Cheese, softened
½ cup sugar
1 teaspoon vanilla
4 eggs
12 ounces white chocolate, melted, slightly cooled

• Preheat oven to 325°F.

• For Crust, beat butter, sugar and vanilla in small bowl at medium speed with electric mixer until light and fluffy. Gradually add flour, mixing at low speed until blended. Press onto bottom of 9-inch springform pan; prick with fork.

• Bake 25 minutes or until edges are light golden brown.

• For Filling, beat cream cheese, sugar and vanilla at medium speed with electric mixer until well blended. Add eggs, 1 at a time, mixing at low speed after each addition, just until blended.

• Blend in melted chocolate; pour over crust.

• Bake 55 to 60 minutes or until center is almost set. Run knife or metal spatula around rim of pan to loosen cake; cool before removing rim of pan. Refrigerate 4 hours or overnight. Garnish as desired.

Macadamia Nut White Chocolate Cheesecake:
Add 1 (3½-ounce) jar macadamia nuts, chopped (about ¾ cup) to filling.

COCOA CHEESECAKE SUPREME

Makes 10 to 12 servings

    Chocolate Cookie Crust (recipe follows)
4 packages (3 ounces each) cream cheese, softened
3 tablespoons butter or margarine, softened
1 cup sugar
⅓ cup HERSHEY®S Cocoa
1½ teaspoons vanilla extract
2 eggs
1 cup (8 ounces) dairy sour cream
    Sweetened whipped cream (optional)

Prepare Chocolate Cookie Crust; set aside. Preheat oven to 325°F.

In large mixer bowl, beat cream cheese and butter until smooth; gradually beat in sugar. Beat in cocoa and vanilla until well blended. Add eggs, one at a time, beating well after each addition. Add sour cream; blend well. Pour batter into prepared crust.

Bake 30 minutes. Turn off oven; leave cheesecake in oven 15 minutes without opening oven door. Remove from oven. Loosen cheesecake from rim of pan; cool to room temperature. Cover; refrigerate several hours or overnight. Remove rim of pan. Garnish with sweetened whipped cream, if desired. Cover; refrigerate leftovers.

Chocolate Cookie Crust: Crush 22 chocolate wafers (one-half of 8½-ounce package) in food processor or blender to form fine crumbs (1 cup). Cut ¼ cup cold butter or margarine into ½-inch pieces. In medium bowl, place cookie crumbs and ⅛ teaspoon ground cinnamon; stir until combined. Cut in butter pieces until fine crumbs form. Press mixture onto bottom of 9-inch springform pan.

White Chocolate Cheesecake

Boston Cream Cheesecake

BOSTON CREAM CHEESECAKE

Makes 12 servings

CAKE BOTTOM
1 (9-ounce) package yellow cake mix (one-layer size)

FILLING
2 (8-ounce) packages PHILADELPHIA BRAND® Cream Cheese, softened
½ cup granulated sugar
1 teaspoon vanilla
2 eggs
⅓ cup sour cream

TOPPING
2 squares BAKER'S® Unsweetened Chocolate
3 tablespoons PARKAY® Margarine
2 tablespoons boiling water
1 cup powdered sugar
1 teaspoon vanilla

• Preheat oven to 350°F.

• For Cake Bottom, grease bottom of 9-inch springform pan. Prepare cake mix as directed on package; pour batter evenly into prepared pan. Bake 20 minutes.

• For Filling, beat cream cheese, granulated sugar and vanilla at medium speed with electric mixer until well blended. Add eggs, 1 at a time, mixing at low speed after each addition, just until blended. Blend in sour cream; pour over cake layer.

• Bake 35 minutes or until center is almost set. Run knife or metal spatula around rim of pan to loosen cake; cool before removing rim of pan.

• For Topping, melt chocolate and margarine in small saucepan over low heat, stirring until smooth. Remove from heat. Add remaining ingredients; mix well. Spread over cooled cheesecake. Refrigerate 4 hours or overnight.

NEAPOLITAN CHEESECAKE

Makes one 9-inch cheesecake

Chocolate Crumb Crust (recipe follows)
1 (10-ounce) package frozen strawberries, thawed and well drained
3 (8-ounce) packages cream cheese, softened
1½ cups sugar
3 eggs
⅓ cup sour cream
3 tablespoons plus 1 teaspoon flour, divided
½ teaspoon vanilla extract
¼ teaspoon salt
¼ teaspoon red food coloring (optional)
½ cup HERSHEY'S Semi-Sweet Chocolate Chips, melted

Prepare and bake Chocolate Crumb Crust. *Increase oven temperature to 400°F.*

In blender or food processor container, purée strawberries to yield ½ cup; set aside. In large mixer bowl, beat cream cheese with sugar until fluffy. Blend in eggs, sour cream, 3 tablespoons flour, vanilla and salt; beat until smooth. In separate bowl, stir together 1⅓ cups batter, remaining 1 teaspoon flour, puréed strawberries and food coloring if desired; mix well. Pour strawberry batter into prepared crust. Carefully spoon 2 cups vanilla batter over strawberry batter; smooth surface. Stir melted chocolate into remaining batter; carefully spoon over vanilla batter, smoothing surface.

Bake 10 minutes. *Reduce oven temperature to 350°F;* continue baking 55 to 60 minutes or until center is almost set. Remove from oven to wire rack. Cool 30 minutes. Loosen cheesecake from rim of pan; cool to room temperature. Refrigerate several hours or overnight. Just before serving, remove side of springform pan. Garnish as desired. Refrigerate leftovers.

Chocolate Crumb Crust: Preheat oven to 350°F. In medium bowl, combine 1½ cups vanilla wafer crumbs (about 45 wafers), ½ cup powdered sugar and ¼ cup HERSHEY'S Cocoa. Blend in ⅓ cup butter or margarine, melted. Press firmly on bottom of 9-inch springform pan. Bake 8 minutes; set aside.

COOKIES 'N' CREAM CHEESECAKE

Makes 10 to 12 servings

1 cup chocolate sandwich cookie crumbs
  (about 12 cookies)
1 tablespoon PARKAY® Margarine, melted
3 (8-ounce) packages PHILADELPHIA BRAND®
  Cream Cheese, softened
1 cup sugar
2 tablespoons all-purpose flour
1 teaspoon vanilla
3 eggs
1 cup coarsely chopped chocolate sandwich cookies
  (about 8 cookies)

• Preheat oven to 325°F.

• Mix together crumbs and margarine in small bowl. Press onto bottom of 9-inch springform pan. Bake 10 minutes.

• Beat cream cheese, sugar, flour and vanilla in large mixing bowl at medium speed with electric mixer until well blended.

• Add eggs, 1 at a time, mixing well after each addition. Fold in chopped cookies. Pour over crust.

• Bake 1 hour and 5 minutes or until center is almost set. Run knife or metal spatula around rim of pan to loosen cake; cool before removing rim of pan. Refrigerate 4 hours or overnight. Garnish with thawed COOL WHIP® Non-Dairy Whipped Topping, chocolate sandwich cookies, cut in half, and fresh mint leaves, if desired.

CHOCOLATE MARBLE CHEESECAKE

Makes 12 to 16 servings

CRUST
1 package DUNCAN HINES® Moist Deluxe
  Devil's Food Cake Mix
½ cup CRISCO® Oil or CRISCO® PURITAN® Oil

FILLING
3 packages (8 ounces each) cream cheese, softened
¾ cup sugar
½ teaspoon almond extract
3 eggs
1 square (1 ounce) unsweetened chocolate, melted

1. Preheat oven to 350°F. Grease 9-inch springform pan.

2. For Crust, combine cake mix and oil in large bowl. Stir until well blended. Press mixture into bottom of pan. Bake at 350°F for 22 minutes. Remove from oven. *Increase oven temperature to 450°F.*

3. For Filling, combine cream cheese, sugar and almond extract in large bowl. Beat at medium speed with electric mixer until blended. Add eggs, one at a time, beating well after each addition. Remove 1 cup batter to small bowl and add melted chocolate. Spoon plain filling into warm crust. Drop spoonfuls of chocolate batter over plain butter. Run knife through batters to marble.

4. Bake at 450°F for 7 minutes. *Reduce oven temperature to 250°F.* Bake 30 minutes longer or until cheesecake is set. Loosen cake from edge from pan with knife or spatula. Cool before removing from pan. Refrigerate until ready to serve.

Note: Oven temperature is reduced to prevent cheesecake from cracking.

Tip: To prevent chocolate from turning grainy, melt chocolate in saucepan over very low heat, stirring constantly, or melt in 1-cup glass measure in microwave oven at HIGH (100% power) for 1 to 1½ minutes (stir to make sure chocolate is melted).

Chocolate Marble Cheesecake

CHOCOLATE SWIRL CHEESECAKE

Makes 8 servings

4 packages (3 ounces each) cream cheese, softened
½ cup sugar
2 eggs
2 teaspoons vanilla extract
½ cup HERSHEY⸝S Semi-Sweet Chocolate Chips or HERSHEY⸝S MINI CHIPS₀ Semi-Sweet Chocolate
1 teaspoon shortening
1 packaged graham cracker crumb crust (6 ounces)

Preheat oven to 325°F. In large mixer bowl, beat cream cheese and sugar. Add eggs and vanilla; beat well. Reserve ½ cup cream cheese mixture in small bowl. Melt chocolate chips with shortening in top of double boiler over hot, not boiling, water; stir into reserved ½ cup cream cheese mixture. Pour vanilla mixture into crust. Spoon chocolate mixture by dollops onto vanilla mixture. Using tip of knife or spatula, gently swirl for marbled effect. Place filled crust on cookie sheet.

Bake 25 to 30 minutes or until center is almost set. Loosen cheesecake from rim of pan; cool to room temperature. Cover; refrigerate several hours or until firm. Remove rim of pan. Garnish as desired.

Chocolate Cherry Cheesecake

CHOCOLATE CHERRY CHEESECAKE

Makes 12 to 16 servings

CRUST
1 package DUNCAN HINES® Fudge Brownie Mix, Family Size, divided
2 tablespoons butter or margarine, softened
1 teaspoon water

FILLING
3 packages (8 ounces each) cream cheese, softened
¾ cup sugar
2 tablespoons all-purpose flour
3 eggs, lightly beaten
2 tablespoons lemon juice
1 teaspoon vanilla extract
1 can (21 ounces) cherry pie filling

1. Preheat oven to 350°F. Reserve 2½ cups dry brownie mix for Brownies, if desired (see recipe below).

2. For Crust, place remaining brownie mix in medium bowl. Cut in butter with pastry blender or 2 knives until mixture is crumbly. Stir in water. Pat mixture into bottom of ungreased 9-inch springform pan.

3. Bake at 350°F for 10 to 12 minutes or until set. Remove from oven. *Increase oven temperature to 450°F.*

4. For Filling, place cream cheese in large bowl. Beat at low speed with electric mixer, adding sugar and flour gradually. Add eggs, lemon juice and vanilla extract, mixing only until incorporated. Pour filling into crust.

5. Bake at 450°F for 10 minutes. *Reduce oven temperature to 250°F.* Bake for 28 to 33 minutes longer or until cheesecake is set. Loosen cake from sides of pan with knife or spatula. Cool completely. Remove sides of pan. Spoon cherry pie filling over top. Refrigerate at least 2 hours. Allow cheesecake to stand at room temperature 15 minutes before serving.

BROWNIES

2½ cups reserved brownie mix
1 egg
¼ cup CRISCO® Oil or CRISCO® PURITAN® Oil
3 tablespoons water

Preheat oven to 350°F. Grease bottom of 8-inch square pan. Combine reserved brownie mix, egg, Crisco® Oil and water in medium bowl. Stir with spoon until well blended, about 50 strokes. Spread in pan. Bake at 350°F for about 25 minutes or until set. Cool completely on wire rack. Cut into bars. *Makes 9 to 12 brownies*

CHOCOLATE HAZELNUT CHEESECAKE

Makes one 9-inch cheesecake

CRUST
1½ cups finely crushed chocolate wafer cookies
1 cup chopped toasted almonds
½ cup chopped toasted hazelnuts (skins removed)
⅓ cup sugar
6 tablespoons butter, melted

FILLING
1 cup sugar
3 (8-ounce) packages cream cheese, softened
4 eggs
⅓ cup whipping cream
¼ cup hazelnut-flavored liqueur
1 teaspoon vanilla
Topping (recipe follows)
Toasted sliced almonds for garnish (optional)

For Crust, preheat oven to 350°F. Grease bottom and side of 9-inch springform pan. Combine crumbs, almonds, hazelnuts, ⅓ cup sugar and butter in medium bowl; blend well. Press onto bottom and up side of prepared pan.

For Filling, beat together 1 cup sugar and cream cheese in large bowl until smooth and creamy. Add eggs, 1 at a time, beating well after each addition. Blend in whipping cream, liqueur and vanilla. Pour into crust.

Bake 40 to 45 minutes or until firm to the touch. Let stand on wire rack 5 minutes. Meanwhile, prepare Topping; carefully spread over cheesecake. Return cheesecake to oven; continue baking 5 minutes. Loosen cake from rim of pan; cool before removing rim of pan. Refrigerate. Garnish as desired.

Topping: Combine 2 cups light sour cream, 1 tablespoon sugar and 1 teaspoon vanilla in small bowl, mixing until well blended.

Chocolate Hazelnut Cheesecake

CHOCOLATE CHIP CHEESECAKE

Makes one 9-inch cheesecake

1½ cups finely crushed creme-filled chocolate sandwich cookies (about 18 cookies)
2 to 3 tablespoons margarine or butter, melted
3 (8-ounce) packages cream cheese, softened
1 (14-ounce) can EAGLE® Brand Sweetened Condensed Milk (NOT evaporated milk)
3 eggs
2 teaspoons vanilla extract
1 cup mini semi-sweet chocolate chips
1 teaspoon all-purpose flour

Preheat oven to 300°F. Combine crumbs and margarine; press firmly on bottom of 9-inch springform pan or 13×9-inch baking pan. In large mixer bowl, beat cheese until fluffy. Gradually beat in sweetened condensed milk until smooth. Add eggs and vanilla; mix well. In small bowl, toss together ½ *cup* chips with flour to coat; stir into cheese mixture. Pour into prepared pan. Sprinkle remaining chips evenly over top.

Bake 55 to 60 minutes or until set. Cool. Chill thoroughly. Just before serving, remove side of springform pan. Garnish as desired. Refrigerate leftovers.

APPLE CHEESECAKE

Makes one 9-inch cheesecake

1 cup graham cracker crumbs
  Sugar
1 teaspoon ground cinnamon, divided
3 tablespoons margarine, melted
2 (8-ounce) packages cream cheese, softened
2 eggs
½ teaspoon vanilla
4 cups peeled, thin apple slices (about 2½ pounds apples)
½ cup chopped pecans

Preheat oven to 350°F. Combine crumbs, 3 tablespoons sugar, ½ teaspoon cinnamon and margarine in small bowl; press onto bottom and up sides of 9-inch pie plate. Bake 10 minutes.

Beat together cream cheese and ½ cup sugar in large bowl until well blended. Add eggs, 1 at a time, beating well after each addition. Blend in vanilla; pour into crust. Toss apples with combined ⅓ cup sugar and remaining ½ teaspoon cinnamon. Spoon over cream cheese mixture; sprinkle with pecans.

Bake 1 hour and 10 minutes or until set. Cool to room temperature; refrigerate.

Favorite recipe from **Michigan Apple Committee**

AUTUMN CHEESECAKE

Makes 12 servings

CRUST
1 cup graham cracker crumbs
½ cup finely chopped pecans
3 tablespoons sugar
½ teaspoon ground cinnamon
¼ cup (½ stick) PARKAY® Margarine, melted

FILLING
2 (8-ounce) packages PHILADELPHIA BRAND® Cream Cheese, softened
½ cup sugar
½ teaspoon vanilla
2 eggs

TOPPING
4 cups thin peeled apple slices
⅓ cup sugar
½ teaspoon ground cinnamon
¼ cup chopped pecans

- Preheat oven to 325°F.

- For Crust, mix crumbs, pecans, sugar, cinnamon and margarine; press onto bottom of 9-inch springform pan. Bake 10 minutes.

- For Filling, beat cream cheese, sugar and vanilla at medium speed with electric mixer until well blended. Add eggs, 1 at a time, mixing at low speed after each addition, just until blended. Pour over crust.

- For Topping, toss apples with combined sugar and cinnamon. Spoon apple mixture over cream cheese layer; sprinkle with pecans.

- Bake 1 hour and 10 minutes to 1 hour and 15 minutes or until center is almost set. Run knife or metal spatula around rim of pan to loosen cake; cool before removing rim of pan. Refrigerate 4 hours or overnight.

TRADITIONAL CHEESECAKE

Makes one 9-inch cheesecake

¼ cup margarine or butter, melted
1½ cups graham cracker crumbs
1¾ cups sugar
3 (8-ounce) packages cream cheese, softened
4 eggs
¼ cup REALEMON® Lemon Juice from Concentrate
¼ teaspoon vanilla extract
  Peach Melba Topping (recipe follows)

Preheat oven to 300°F. Combine margarine, crumbs and ¼ cup sugar; press firmly on bottom of 9-inch springform pan. In large mixer bowl, beat cheese until fluffy. Beat in remaining 1½ cups sugar and eggs until smooth. On low speed, add ReaLemon® brand and vanilla; mix well. Pour into prepared pan.

Bake 65 to 70 minutes or until set. Carefully loosen cheesecake from edge of pan with knife tip. Cool to room temperature; chill. Just before serving, remove side of springform pan. Serve with Peach Melba Topping Refrigerate leftovers.

Peach Melba Topping: Thaw 1 (10-ounce) package frozen red raspberries; reserve ⅔ cup syrup. In small saucepan, combine reserved syrup, ¼ cup red currant jelly and 1 tablespoon cornstarch. Cook and stir until slightly thickened and clear. Cool. Stir in raspberries. Drain 1 (16-ounce) can peach slices; top cheesecake with peach slices and raspberry sauce.

Apple Cheesecake

Lemon Supreme Cheesecake

NORTHWEST CHEESECAKE SUPREME

Makes 10 to 12 servings

1 cup graham cracker crumbs
3 tablespoons sugar
3 tablespoons PARKAY® Margarine, melted
4 (8-ounce) packages PHILADELPHIA BRAND®
   Cream Cheese, softened
1 cup sugar
3 tablespoons all-purpose flour
4 eggs
1 cup sour cream
1 tablespoon vanilla
1 (21-ounce) can cherry pie filling

• Preheat oven to 325°F.

• Combine crumbs, 3 tablespoons sugar and margarine; press onto bottom of 9-inch springform pan. Bake 10 minutes. Remove from oven. *Increase oven temperature to 450°F.*

• Combine cream cheese, 1 cup sugar and flour, mixing at medium speed with electric mixer until well blended. Add eggs, 1 at a time, mixing well after each addition. Blend in sour cream and vanilla; pour over crust.

• Bake 10 minutes. *Reduce oven temperature to 250°F;* continue baking 1 hour or until center is almost set. Run knife or metal spatula around rim of pan to loosen cake; cool before removing rim of pan. Refrigerate 4 hours or overnight. Top with pie filling just before serving.

LEMON SUPREME CHEESECAKE

Makes one 9-inch cheesecake

CRUST
1 cup ground zwieback crackers
1 cup ground toasted almonds
6 tablespoons melted butter
2 tablespoons sugar

FILLING
4 (8-ounce) packages cream cheese, softened
¾ cup sugar
6 eggs
2 teaspoons grated lemon peel
¼ cup lemon juice
2 teaspoons vanilla
   Topping (recipe follows)
   Lemon Glaze (recipe follows)
   Kiwifruit and strawberry slices for garnish
   (optional)

For Crust, preheat oven to 350°F. Combine cracker crumbs, almonds, butter and 2 tablespoons sugar in medium bowl; press onto bottom and up side of 9-inch springform pan. Bake 5 minutes.

For Filling, beat cream cheese in large mixer bowl until creamy. Add ¾ cup sugar, mixing until well blended. Add eggs, 1 at a time, beating well after each addition. Blend in lemon peel, lemon juice and vanilla. Pour into crust.

Bake 45 to 50 minutes. Remove cheesecake from oven; carefully spoon Topping over cheesecake. Return cheesecake to oven; continue baking 12 minutes or until set. Cool 30 minutes. Meanwhile, prepare Lemon Glaze; let cool. Loosen cake from rim of pan; cool before removing rim of pan. Top cooled cheesecake with cooled Lemon Glaze. Refrigerate. Garnish as desired.

Topping: Combine 1 cup sour cream, 2 tablespoons sugar and ½ teaspoon vanilla in small bowl, mixing until well blended.

Lemon Glaze: Combine ½ cup sugar, 1½ tablespoons cornstarch and ¼ teaspoon salt in small saucepan. Add combined ¾ cup water, ⅓ cup lemon juice and 1 beaten egg yolk. Cook over low heat, stirring constantly, until mixture starts to boil and thickens. Stir in 1 tablespoon butter and 1 teaspoon grated lemon peel.

BUFFET LEMON CHEESECAKE

Makes 9 to 12 servings

1¼ cups graham cracker crumbs
3 tablespoons sugar
⅓ cup butter or margarine, melted
2 packages (8 ounces each) cream cheese, softened
4 cups cold milk, divided
2 packages (4-serving size) JELL-O® Lemon Flavor Instant Pudding and Pie Filling

Preheat oven to 350°F. Combine crumbs, sugar and butter in small bowl; mix well. Press firmly on bottom and up side of 9- or 10-inch springform pan. Bake 8 minutes, or until lightly browned. Cool on wire rack.

Place cream cheese in large bowl. With electric mixer at medium speed, beat until smooth. Gradually add 1 cup milk, blending until mixture is very smooth. Add remaining 3 cups milk and pudding mixes. Beat at low speed just until well blended, about 1 minute. Pour carefully into prepared crust. Chill until firm, about 3 hours. Just before serving, remove side of springform pan. Garnish with lemon slice and mint leaves, if desired.

BLUEBERRY CHEESECAKE

Makes 6 servings

1 (9-ounce) package ROYAL® No Bake Lite Cheesecake*
¼ cup BLUE BONNET® Spread, melted
1½ cups lowfat milk
Fresh blueberries or Blueberry Topping (recipe follows)

In small bowl, combine crumbs from cheesecake mix and Spread; press onto bottom and ½ inch up side of 8-inch springform pan. Refrigerate.

Prepare cheesecake filling according to package directions using milk; spread evenly into prepared crust. Refrigerate 1 hour.

To serve, cut cheesecake into wedges; top each wedge with blueberries or Blueberry Topping.

Blueberry Topping: In small saucepan, over medium-high heat, heat 2 cups fresh or frozen blueberries, ¼ cup water and 2 teaspoons lemon juice until mixture comes to a boil. In small bowl, blend 2 teaspoons cornstarch into 1 tablespoon water; slowly stir into blueberry mixture. Cook, stirring constantly, until mixture thickens and begins to boil. Reduce heat; simmer for 1 minute. Remove from heat; stir in 1 packet low-calorie sugar substitute. Cover; refrigerate.

*1 (11-ounce) package ROYAL® No Bake Cheesecake may be substituted.

HEAVENLY CHOCOLATE CHEESECAKE

Makes one 9-inch cheesecake

CRUST:
2 cups finely crushed vanilla wafers
1 cup ground toasted almonds
½ cup sugar
½ cup butter or margarine, melted

FILLING:
2 cups (11½-ounce package) NESTLÉ® Toll House® Milk Chocolate Morsels
½ cup milk
1 envelope unflavored gelatin
2 (8-ounce) packages cream cheese, softened
½ cup sour cream
½ teaspoon almond extract
½ cup whipping cream, whipped

Crust: In large bowl, combine vanilla wafer crumbs, almonds, sugar and butter; mix well. Press firmly onto bottom and 2 inches up sides of 9-inch springform pan; set aside.

Filling: Melt over hot (not boiling) water, Nestlé® Toll House® Milk Chocolate Morsels; stir until smooth. Set aside. Pour milk into small saucepan; sprinkle gelatin over top. Set aside for 1 minute to soften. Cook over low heat, stirring constantly, until gelatin dissolves. Set aside. In large bowl, combine cream cheese, sour cream and melted morsels; beat until fluffy. Beat in gelatin mixture and almond extract. Fold in whipped cream. Pour into prepared crust. Refrigerate until firm (about 3 hours). Run knife around edge of cake to separate from pan; remove sides. Garnish as desired.

Heavenly Chocolate Cheesecake

69

ORANGE NO-BAKE CHEESECAKE

Makes 12 to 16 servings

CRUST
1 package DUNCAN HINES® Moist Deluxe
    Pineapple Supreme Cake Mix
½ cup butter or margarine, melted

FILLING
1 package (4-serving size) orange gelatin
1 cup boiling water
2 teaspoons grated orange peel
2 packages (8 ounces each) cream cheese, softened
1 cup whipping cream
½ cup dairy sour cream
1 can (11 ounces) mandarin orange segments,
    drained

1. Preheat oven to 350°F.

2. For Crust, combine cake mix and melted butter in
large bowl. Mix at low speed with electric mixer until
crumbs form. Spread evenly in 9-inch springform pan.

Orange No-Bake Cheesecake

Lightly press crumbs 1 inch up sides. Smooth remaining
crumbs out in bottom of pan. Bake at 350°F for
20 minutes. Cool.

3. For Filling, dissolve gelatin in boiling water in small
saucepan. Add orange peel. Refrigerate until thickened.

4. Beat cream cheese in large bowl until smooth.
Gradually beat in gelatin mixture.

5. Beat whipping cream in large bowl until stiff. Fold
into cream cheese mixture. Pour into cooled crust.
Refrigerate until firm, about 3 hours.

6. Drop teaspoonfuls of sour cream around edge of
cheesecake. Garnish with drained orange segments.

Tip: You can use other fruit-flavored gelatin in place
of orange. Garnish with appropriate fruit.

APRICOT DELUXE CHEESECAKE

Makes 8 to 10 servings

  Shortbread Cookie Crust (recipe follows)
1 envelope unflavored gelatin
1 can (12 ounces) apricot nectar, divided
12 ounces cream cheese, softened
½ cup sugar
1 teaspoon grated lemon peel
1 tablespoon lemon juice
½ teaspoon vanilla
1 cup whipping cream
1 tablespoon sugar
2 teaspoons cornstarch
2 teaspoons rum (optional)

Prepare Shortbread Cookie Crust. In small saucepan,
sprinkle gelatin over ¾ cup apricot nectar; let stand
1 minute to soften. Cook and stir over low heat until
gelatin dissolves. Remove from heat; cool to room
temperature. Beat cream cheese, ½ cup sugar, lemon
peel, lemon juice and vanilla in large bowl with electric
mixer at medium speed until smooth. Add gelatin
mixture; beat until well blended. Beat whipping cream
in small bowl at high speed until soft peaks form; fold
into cream cheese mixture. Pour mixture into cooled
Shortbread Cookie Crust. Refrigerate, uncovered, until
set, at least 3 hours.

Mix 1 tablespoon sugar and cornstarch in small saucepan;
gradually blend in remaining ¾ cup apricot nectar. Cook
over medium heat, stirring constantly, until mixture
boils. Remove from heat. Stir in rum. Cool 10 minutes,
stirring frequently. Spread evenly over top of cheesecake;
refrigerate at least 30 minutes. Just before serving, remove
sides of pan.

No-Bake Chocolate Cheesecake

SHORTBREAD COOKIE CRUST

1⅓ cups ground shortbread cookies
½ teaspoon ground ginger (optional)
3 tablespoons butter, melted

Preheat oven to 350°F. In small bowl, thoroughly mix crumbs, ginger and butter. Press crumb mixture into bottom of greased 8-inch springform pan.

Bake about 5 minutes or until light brown. Cool on wire rack 30 minutes.

NO-BAKE CHOCOLATE CHEESECAKE

Makes about 8 servings

1½ cups HERSHEY'S Semi-Sweet Chocolate Chips
1 package (8 ounces) cream cheese, softened
1 package (3 ounces) cream cheese, softened
½ cup sugar
¼ cup (½ stick) butter or margarine, softened
2 cups frozen non-dairy whipped topping, thawed
1 packaged graham cracker crumb crust
   (6 ounces)

Place chocolate chips in small microwave-safe bowl. Microwave at HIGH (100% power) 1 to 1½ minutes or until chips are melted and mixture is smooth when stirred. Set aside to cool.

In large mixer bowl, beat cream cheese, sugar and butter until smooth. On low speed of electric mixer, blend in melted chocolate. Fold in whipped topping until blended. Spoon cheese mixture into crust. Cover; refrigerate until firm before serving. Garnish as desired. Refrigerate leftovers.

MOCHA CHOCOLATE CHIP CHEESECAKE

Makes one 9-inch cheesecake

CRUST:
2¼ cups graham cracker crumbs
2 cups (12-ounce package) NESTLÉ® Toll House®
   Semi-Sweet Chocolate Mini Morsels, divided
⅔ cup butter, melted and cooled to room
   temperature

FILLING:
½ cup milk
4 teaspoons TASTER'S CHOICE® Freeze Dried
   Coffee
1 envelope unflavored gelatin
2 (8-ounce) packages cream cheese, softened
1 (14-ounce) can sweetened condensed milk
2 cups whipping cream, whipped

Crust: In large bowl, combine graham cracker crumbs, 1 cup Nestlé® Toll House® Semi-Sweet Chocolate Mini Morsels and butter; mix well. Pat firmly into 9-inch springform pan, covering bottom and 2½ inches up sides. Set aside.

Filling: In small saucepan, combine milk and Taster's Choice® Freeze Dried Coffee; sprinkle gelatin over top. Let soften for 1 minute. Cook over low heat, stirring constantly, until gelatin and coffee dissolve. Set aside. In large bowl, beat cream cheese until creamy. Beat in sweetened condensed milk and gelatin mixture. Fold in whipped cream and remaining 1 cup Nestlé® Toll House® Semi-Sweet Chocolate Mini Morsels. Pour into prepared crust. Refrigerate until firm (about 2 hours). Run knife around edge of cheesecake to separate from pan; remove sides of pan.

Frozen Chocolate Cheesecake

FROZEN CHOCOLATE CHEESECAKE

Makes about 8 servings

1½ cups chocolate *or* vanilla wafer cookie crumbs
⅓ cup margarine, melted
1 package (8 ounces) cream cheese, softened
½ cup sugar, divided
2 eggs,* separated
1 cup semisweet chocolate chips, melted
1 teaspoon vanilla
1 cup whipping cream, lightly whipped
¾ cup chopped pecans
   Chocolate Curls (recipe follows)

Preheat oven to 325°F. Combine crumbs and margarine in small bowl; press onto bottom and up side of 9-inch pie plate. Bake 10 minutes. Cool completely on wire rack.

Combine cream cheese and ¼ cup sugar in large bowl. Beat egg yolks; gradually stir into cheese mixture with melted chocolate chips and vanilla. Beat egg whites in small bowl until foamy. Gradually add remaining ¼ cup sugar, beating until soft peaks form. Gently fold egg whites into chocolate mixture. Fold in whipped cream and pecans. Pour into prepared crust; freeze until firm. Garnish with chocolate curls.

*Use only grade A clean, uncracked eggs.

Chocolate Curls: Melt ¾ cup semisweet chocolate chips in small saucepan over low heat. Spread a thin layer on cold baking sheet. Refrigerate until firm, 15 minutes. Slip tip of straight-sided metal spatula under chocolate. Push spatula firmly along baking sheet, so chocolate curls as it is pushed up. Place completed curls on waxed paper.

FROZEN PEPPERMINT CHEESECAKE

Makes one 9-inch cheesecake

1¼ cups chocolate wafer cookie crumbs
   (about 24 wafers)
¼ cup sugar
¼ cup margarine or butter, melted
1 (8-ounce) package cream cheese, softened
1 (14-ounce) can EAGLE® Brand Sweetened
   Condensed Milk (NOT evaporated milk)
1 cup crushed hard peppermint candy
   Red food coloring (optional)
2 cups (1 pint) BORDEN® or MEADOW GOLD®
   Whipping Cream, whipped

Combine crumbs, sugar and margarine; press firmly on bottom and halfway up side of 9-inch springform pan. In large mixer bowl, beat cheese until fluffy. Gradually beat in sweetened condensed milk until smooth. Stir in crushed candy and food coloring if desired. Fold in whipped cream. Pour into prepared pan; cover.

Freeze 6 hours or until firm. Remove from freezer 5 minutes before serving. Remove side of springform pan. Garnish as desired. Freeze leftovers.

FROZEN PEACH AMARETTO CHEESECAKE

Makes 10 to 12 servings

1 cup graham cracker crumbs
¼ cup slivered almonds, toasted and finely chopped
2 tablespoons sugar
⅓ cup margarine or butter, melted
1 (8-ounce) package cream cheese, softened
1 (14-ounce) can EAGLE® Brand Sweetened
   Condensed Milk (NOT evaporated milk)
2 cups puréed fresh or thawed frozen peaches
⅓ cup amaretto liqueur
1 cup (½ pint) BORDEN® or MEADOW GOLD®
   Whipping Cream, whipped
   Fresh peach slices (optional)

Combine crumbs, almonds, sugar and margarine. Press firmly on bottom of 9-inch springform pan. In large mixer bowl, beat cheese until fluffy. Gradually beat in sweetened condensed milk until smooth. Stir in puréed peaches and liqueur. Fold in whipped cream. Pour into prepared pan; cover.

Freeze 6 hours or until firm. Remove from freezer 5 minutes before serving. Remove side of springform pan. Garnish with peach slices if desired. Freeze leftovers.

Frozen Mocha Cheesecake

FROZEN MOCHA CHEESECAKE

Makes one 8- or 9-inch cheesecake

1¼ cups chocolate wafer cookie crumbs
   (about 24 wafers)
¼ cup margarine or butter, melted
¼ cup sugar
1 (8-ounce) package cream cheese, softened
1 (14-ounce) can EAGLE® Brand Sweetened
   Condensed Milk (NOT evaporated milk)
⅔ cup chocolate-flavored syrup
1 to 2 tablespoons powdered instant coffee
1 teaspoon hot water
1 cup (½ pint) BORDEN® or MEADOW GOLD®
   whipping cream, whipped
   Additional chocolate wafer cookie crumbs
   (optional)

Combine 1¼ cups crumbs, margarine and sugar; press firmly on bottom and up side of 8- or 9-inch springform pan *or* 13×9-inch baking pan. In large mixer bowl, beat cheese until fluffy. Gradually beat in sweetened condensed milk and syrup until smooth. Dissolve coffee in water; add to cheese mixture. Mix well. Fold in whipped cream. Pour into prepared pan; cover.

Freeze 6 hours or until firm. Remove from freezer 5 minutes before serving. Remove side of springform pan. Garnish with additional chocolate crumbs if desired. Freeze leftovers.

LEMON CHEESECAKE CUPS

Makes 6 servings

1 package (4-serving size) JELL-O® Brand Lemon
   Flavor Sugar Free Gelatin
¾ cup boiling water
3 ounces Light PHILADELPHIA BRAND®
   Neufchatel Cheese, softened and cut into cubes
½ cup cold water
1 teaspoon grated lemon peel (optional)
½ cup thawed COOL WHIP® Non-Dairy Whipped
   Topping
   Graham cracker crumbs (optional)
   Lemon slices (optional)
   Mint leaves (optional)

Completely dissolve gelatin in boiling water in blender container. Cover; blend at medium speed 1 minute. Add cream cheese. Blend until smooth, about 1 minute. Add cold water and lemon peel. Cool slightly.

Blend whipped topping into gelatin mixture. Spoon into dessert dishes. Chill 1 hour. Sprinkle with graham cracker crumbs and garnish with lemon slices and mint leaves, if desired.

Prep time: 15 minutes
Chill time: 1 hour

SIMPLE CHOCOLATE CHEESECAKES

Makes 2 dozen cheesecakes

24 vanilla wafer cookies
2 packages (8 ounces each) cream cheese, softened
1¼ cups sugar
⅓ cup HERSHEY'S Cocoa
2 tablespoons all-purpose flour
3 eggs
1 cup dairy sour cream
1 teaspoon vanilla extract
    Sour Cream Topping (recipe follows)
    Canned cherry pie filling, chilled

Preheat oven to 325°F. Line 24 muffin cups with foil-laminated paper bake cups (2½ inches in diameter). Place one vanilla wafer in bottom of each cup.

In large mixer bowl, beat cream cheese and sugar. Blend in cocoa and flour. Add eggs; beat well. Blend in sour cream and vanilla. Fill each prepared cup almost full with cheese mixture.

Bake 15 to 20 minutes or just until set. Remove from oven; cool 5 to 10 minutes. Spread heaping teaspoonful Sour Cream Topping over top of each cup. Cool completely in pans; refrigerate. Garnish with cherry pie filling just before serving. Refrigerate leftovers.

Sour Cream Topping: In small bowl, combine 1 cup dairy sour cream, 2 tablespoons sugar and 1 teaspoon vanilla extract; stir until sugar dissolves.

INDIVIDUAL MICROWAVE CHEESECAKES

Makes 4 servings

    Graham Cracker Crust (recipe follows)
⅓ cup KARO® Light Corn Syrup
2 tablespoons sugar
1 egg
1 tablespoon ARGO® or KINGSFORD'S® Corn Starch
1 tablespoon lemon juice
1 package (8 ounces) cream cheese, cut into cubes
    Fruit, preserves, pie filling or chocolate curls

To Microwave: Prepare Graham Cracker Crust. In blender or food processor, process corn syrup, sugar, egg, corn starch and lemon juice until combined. Gradually add cream cheese; process 1 minute or until completely smooth. Pour into prepared cups. Arrange in circle in microwave oven.

Microwave on MEDIUM (50% power) 7 to 7½ minutes or just until set, rotating and rearranging three times. Cover and refrigerate 1 hour. Top with fruit, preserves, pie filling or chocolate curls.

Graham Cracker Crust: In small microwavable bowl, microwave 1 tablespoon MAZOLA® Margarine on HIGH (100% power) 30 seconds or until melted. Stir in ¼ cup graham cracker crumbs and 1 teaspoon sugar until evenly moistened. Press 1 tablespoon crust mixture into bottoms of 4 (6-ounce) microwavable custard cups or ramekins. Arrange in circle in microwave oven. Microwave on HIGH 1 minute, turning once; let stand while preparing filling.

Prep time: 20 minutes plus refrigerating

Individual Microwave Cheesecakes

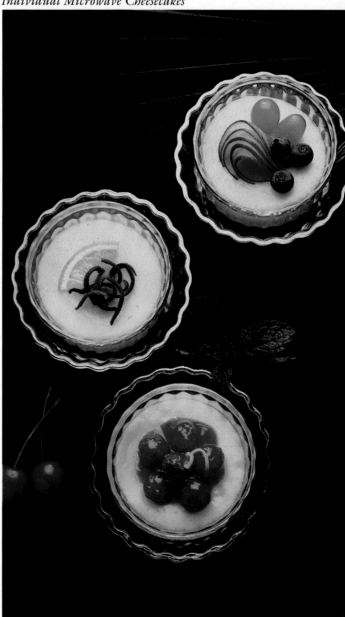

Strawberries and Cream Cheesecake Tarts

CHEESECAKES IN A CUP

Makes 8 servings

1 package (11 ounces) JELL-O® No Bake
    Cheesecake Mix
2 tablespoons sugar
⅓ cup PARKAY® Margarine, melted
1½ cups cold milk
    Raspberries or sliced strawberries
1 package (4-serving size) JELL-O® Brand Gelatin,
    Raspberry or Strawberry Flavor
¾ cup boiling water
½ cup cold water
    Ice cubes

Combine cheesecake crust crumbs and sugar in small
bowl. Mix in margarine. Press crumb mixture firmly
onto bottoms of 8 individual dessert glasses.

Mix milk with cheesecake filling mix in large bowl
at low speed of electric mixer until blended. Beat at
medium speed 3 minutes. Spoon filling over crusts.
Chill 30 minutes. Arrange fruit in single layer over
cheesecake filling.

Completely dissolve gelatin in boiling water in medium
bowl. Combine cold water and ice cubes to measure
1¼ cups. Add to gelatin, stirring until slightly thickened.
Remove any unmelted ice. Spoon gelatin over fruit.
Chill until firm, about 1½ hours.

Prep time: 20 minutes
Chill time: 2 hours

STRAWBERRIES AND CREAM CHEESECAKE TARTS

Makes 24 cheesecake tarts

CRUST
1 package DUNCAN HINES® Moist Deluxe
    Strawberry Supreme Cake Mix
¼ cup butter or margarine, melted

FILLING
2 packages (8 ounces each) cream cheese, softened
3 eggs
¾ cup sugar
1 teaspoon vanilla extract

TOPPING
1½ cups dairy sour cream
¼ cup sugar
12 fresh strawberries, halved

1. Preheat oven to 350°F. Place 2½-inch foil liners in
24 muffin cups.

2. For Crust, combine cake mix and melted butter in
large bowl. Beat at low speed with electric mixer for
1 minute. Divide mixture evenly into bottoms of muffin
cups. Level but do not press.

3. For Filling, combine cream cheese, eggs, ¾ cup sugar
and vanilla extract in medium bowl. Beat at medium
speed with electric mixer until smooth. Spoon evenly
into muffin cups.

4. Bake at 350°F for 20 minutes or until cheesecakes
are set.

5. For Topping, combine sour cream and ¼ cup sugar
in small bowl. Spoon evenly over cheesecakes. Return
to oven for an additional 5 minutes. Cool completely.

6. Garnish each cheesecake with strawberry half.
Refrigerate until ready to serve.

Tip: If you use dark-colored muffin pans, reduce the oven
temperature to 325°F to prevent overbaking the tarts.

INDIVIDUAL COCOA CHEESECAKES

Makes 6 cheesecakes

⅓ cup plus 1 tablespoon sugar, divided
⅓ cup graham cracker crumbs
1 tablespoon butter or margarine, melted
1 package (8 ounces) cream cheese, softened
3 tablespoons HERSHEY'S Cocoa
1 teaspoon vanilla extract
1 tablespoon milk
1 egg

To Microwave: In small bowl, combine 1 tablespoon sugar, graham cracker crumbs and butter. Press about 1 tablespoon crumb mixture onto bottoms of each of 6 microwave-safe ramekins (2½ to 3 inches in diameter). In small mixer bowl, beat cream cheese, remaining ⅓ cup sugar, cocoa and vanilla. Add milk and egg, beating just until smooth and well blended. Divide cheese mixture evenly among ramekins, filling each to ¼ inch from top.

Microwave at MEDIUM-HIGH (70% power) 2 minutes, rotating ramekins after 1 minute. Microwave at HIGH (100% power) 30 to 40 seconds or until puffed in center. Cool; refrigerate before serving. Garnish as desired.

Note: Substitute 6 paper-lined microwave-safe muffin cups (2½ inches in diameter) for ramekins, if desired.

BLACK-EYED SUSAN CHEESECAKES

Makes 2 dozen cheesecakes

24 vanilla wafer cookies
 2 packages (8 ounces each) cream cheese, softened
½ cup sugar
 2 eggs
½ teaspoon vanilla extract
 1 cup REESE'S® Peanut Butter Chips
½ cup HERSHEY®'S Semi-Sweet Chocolate Chips
 3 tablespoons butter or margarine
   Sliced almonds

Preheat oven to 350°F. Line 24 muffin cups with foil-laminated paper bake cups (2 inches in diameter). Place one vanilla wafer in bottom of each cup.

In large mixer bowl, beat cream cheese and sugar. Add eggs and vanilla; beat well. Stir in peanut butter chips. Spoon 1 heaping tablespoon cheese mixture into each cup.

Bake 15 minutes or just until set, but not browned. Cool. In small microwave-safe bowl, place chocolate chips and butter. Microwave at HIGH (100% power) 30 seconds to 1 minute or until chips are melted and mixture is smooth when stirred. Evenly spread teaspoonfuls of chocolate mixture onto center of each cheesecake, letting cheese filling show around edge. Place almond slices around chocolate mixture to resemble flower petals. Cover; refrigerate.

CHEESECAKE BARS

Makes about 40 bars

2 cups unsifted all-purpose flour
1½ cups firmly packed light brown sugar
 1 cup cold margarine or butter
1½ cups quick-cooking oats, uncooked
 2 (8-ounce) packages cream cheese, softened
½ cup granulated sugar
 3 eggs
¼ cup milk
 1 teaspoon vanilla extract
¼ cup REALEMON® Lemon Juice from
   Concentrate

Preheat oven to 350°F. In medium bowl, combine flour and brown sugar; cut in margarine until crumbly. Stir in oats. Reserving 1½ cups oat mixture, press remainder into 15 × 10 × 1-inch jelly-roll pan; bake 10 minutes. Meanwhile, in large mixer bowl, beat cheese and granulated sugar until fluffy. Add eggs; beat well. Add milk and vanilla, then ReaLemon® brand; beat well. Pour over baked crust; sprinkle with reserved oat mixture.

Bake 25 to 30 minutes or until lightly browned. Cool. Refrigerate.

SWIRL OF CHOCOLATE CHEESECAKE SQUARES

Makes 16 squares

1 cup graham cracker crumbs
½ cup plus 3 tablespoons sugar, divided
¼ cup butter or margarine, melted
1 package (8 ounces) cream cheese, softened
¾ cup undiluted CARNATION® Evaporated Milk
1 egg
2 tablespoons all-purpose flour
2 teaspoons vanilla
½ cup (3 ounces) semisweet chocolate chips

Preheat oven to 300°F. In small bowl, combine crumbs, 3 tablespoons sugar and butter. Press mixture firmly onto bottom of buttered 8-inch square pan. Place cream cheese, evaporated milk, remaining ½ cup sugar, egg, flour and vanilla in blender container; process until smooth. In small saucepan over low heat, melt chips. Gradually stir ½ cup cheese mixture into chocolate. Pour remaining cheese mixture over crumb crust. Pour chocolate mixture over cheese mixture. Swirl two mixtures to marble with spoon.

Bake 40 to 45 minutes or until set. Let cool in pan on wire rack. Cut into 2-inch squares to serve. Store, covered, in refrigerator.

PIES & TARTS

DELAWARE BLUEBERRY PIE

Makes one 9-inch pie

CRUST
Unbaked 9-inch Classic CRISCO® *Double* Crust
(page 80)

FILLING
4½ cups fresh blueberries, divided
½ cup granulated sugar
½ cup firmly packed brown sugar
2 tablespoons plus 1½ teaspoons cornstarch
½ teaspoon ground cinnamon
⅛ teaspoon salt
1 tablespoon butter or margarine
1 teaspoon peach schnapps
2 tablespoons quick-cooking tapioca
4 to 5 drops red food coloring (optional)

DECORATIONS
Reserved dough
2 tablespoons melted vanilla frozen yogurt

1. Preheat oven to 425°F. Reserve dough scraps for decorations, if desired.

2. For Filling, place ½ cup blueberries in resealable plastic sandwich bag. Crush berries. Pour juice and berries into strainer over liquid measuring cup. Press berries to extract all juice. Pour water over berries until juice measures ½ cup.

3. Combine sugars, cornstarch, cinnamon and salt in large saucepan. Add blueberry juice mixture. Cook and stir on medium heat until mixture boils. Remove from heat. Stir in butter and schnapps. Set pan in cold water about 5 minutes to cool. Stir in tapioca. Add food coloring, if desired. Carefully stir in remaining 4 cups blueberries. Spoon into unbaked pie crust. Moisten pastry edge with water.

4. Cover pie with top crust. Fold top edge under bottom crust; flute with fingers or fork.

5. For Decorations, cut stars and diamonds from reserved dough. Dip cutouts in melted yogurt. Place on top of pie and around edge. Cut slits in top crust to allow steam to escape.

6. Bake at 425°F for 15 minutes. Cover cutouts and edge of pie with foil, if necessary, to prevent overbrowning. *Reduce oven temperature to 375°F. Bake 20 to 25 minutes or until filling in center is bubbly and crust is golden brown. Cool to room temperature before serving.*

ROSY RASPBERRY PIE

Makes one 9-inch pie

CRUST
Unbaked 9-inch Classic CRISCO® *Double* Crust
(page 80)

FILLING
1¼ cups sugar
3 tablespoons cornstarch
⅛ teaspoon salt
5 cups fresh raspberries
2 tablespoons butter or margarine

1. Preheat oven to 375°F.

2. For Filling, combine sugar, cornstarch and salt in large bowl. Add raspberries. Toss gently to mix. Spoon into unbaked pie crust. Dot with butter. Moisten pastry edge with water.

3. Cover pie with top crust. Fold top edge under bottom crust; flute with fingers or fork. Cut slits or designs in top crust to allow steam to escape. Cover edge of pie with foil to prevent overbrowning.

4. Bake at 375°F for 35 minutes. Remove foil. Bake for 15 minutes or until filling in center is bubbly and crust is golden brown. Cool until barely warm or to room temperature before serving.

Delaware Blueberry Pie   79

CLASSIC CRISCO® CRUST

8-, 9- OR 10-INCH SINGLE CRUST
1⅓ cups all-purpose flour
½ teaspoon salt
½ cup CRISCO® Shortening
3 tablespoons cold water

8- OR 9-INCH DOUBLE CRUST
2 cups all-purpose flour
1 teaspoon salt
¾ cup CRISCO® Shortening
5 tablespoons cold water

10-INCH DOUBLE CRUST
2⅔ cups all-purpose flour
1 teaspoon salt
1 cup CRISCO® Shortening
7 to 8 tablespoons cold water

1. Spoon flour into measuring cup and level. Combine flour and salt in medium bowl.

2. Cut in Crisco® using pastry blender (or 2 knives) until all flour is blended to form pea-size chunks.

3. Sprinkle with water, 1 tablespoon at a time. Toss lightly with fork until dough will form a ball.

For Single-Crust Pies

4. Press dough between hands to form a 5- to 6-inch "pancake." Flour rolling surface and rolling pin lightly. Roll dough into circle. (Or, flour "pancake" lightly on both sides. Roll between sheets of waxed paper or plastic wrap on dampened countertop.)

5. Trim 1 inch larger than upside-down pie plate. Loosen dough carefully.

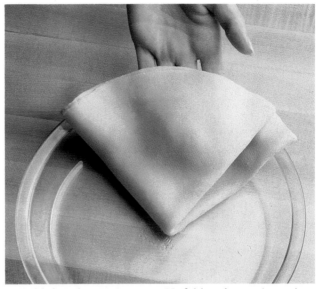

6. Fold dough into quarters. Unfold and press into pie plate. Fold edge under. Flute.

7. For recipes using a **baked** pie crust, heat oven to 425°F. Prick bottom and sides thoroughly with fork (50 times) to prevent shrinkage. Bake 10 to 15 minutes or until lightly browned. For recipes using an **unbaked** pie crust, follow baking directions given in that recipe.

For Double-Crust Pies

1. Divide dough in half. Roll each half separately. Transfer bottom crust to pie plate. Trim edge even with pie plate.

2. Add desired filling to unbaked pie crust. Moisten pastry edge with water. Lift top crust onto filled pie. Trim ½ inch beyond edge of pie plate. Fold top edge under bottom crust. Flute. Cut slits in top crust to allow steam to escape. Bake according to specific recipe directions.

DECORATIVE TIPS

Rope Edge

Fold overhang under and make stand-up edge. Press thumb into pastry at an angle. Pinch pastry between thumb and knuckle of index finger, rolling knuckle toward thumb. Place thumb in groove left by finger and continue around edge.

Cutouts

Trim edge even with pie plate. Cut desired shapes (about ¾ inch in size) from remaining pastry using tiny cookie cutter, thimble or bottlecap. Moisten pastry edge. Place cutouts on pastry edge, slightly overlapping. Press into place.

Fork Edge

Press pastry to rim of pie plate using 4-tined fork. Leave about 1¼ inches between marks. Go around crust edge again, filling in spaces with fork held at an angle.

Pinwheel

Fold edge under. Press flat. Cut slits around edge of pastry the width of the rim, leaving about 1 inch between slits. Fold under on a diagonal to form pinwheel points.

Woven Lattice Top

1. Leave overhang on bottom crust. Cut top crust into ten ½-inch strips. Place 5 strips evenly across filling. Fold every other strip back. Lay first strip across in opposite direction.

3. Trim ends of lattice strips even with crust overhang. Press together. Fold edge under. Flute.

2. Continue in this pattern, folding back every other strip each time you add a cross strip.

LEMON PASTRY

Makes one 9-inch pastry shell

1 cup unsifted all-purpose flour
½ teaspoon salt
⅓ cup shortening
1 egg
1 tablespoon REALEMON® Lemon Juice from
    Concentrate

Preheat oven to 400°F. In medium bowl, combine flour
and salt; cut in shortening until crumbly. In small bowl,
beat egg and ReaLemon® brand; sprinkle over flour
mixture. Stir until dough forms a ball. On floured
surface, roll out to about ⅛-inch thickness. Line 9-inch
pie plate; flute edges. Prick with fork.

Bake 12 to 15 minutes or until golden. Cool before
filling.

LOLA'S APPLE PIE

Makes one 10-inch pie

CRUST
    Unbaked 10-inch Classic CRISCO® *Double*
    Crust (page 80)

FILLING
    8 to 9 cups thinly sliced, peeled Granny Smith or
        other tart apples (about 3 pounds or 9 medium)
¾ to 1 cup sugar
2 tablespoons all-purpose flour
1 teaspoon ground cinnamon
⅛ teaspoon salt
⅛ teaspoon ground allspice
⅛ teaspoon ground cloves
2 tablespoons butter or margarine

TOPPING
    Sugar

1. Preheat oven to 400°F.

2. For Filling, place apples in large bowl. Combine
¾ to 1 cup sugar, flour, cinnamon, salt, allspice and
cloves. Sprinkle over apples; toss to coat. Spoon into
unbaked pie crust. Dot with butter. Moisten pastry edge
with water.

3. Cover pie with top crust. Fold top edge under
bottom crust; flute with fingers or fork. Cut slits or
shapes in top crust to allow steam to escape.

4. For Topping, sprinkle top crust with sugar.

5. Bake at 400°F for 50 to 55 minutes or until filling in
center is bubbly and crust is golden brown. Cover edge
of pie with foil, if necessary, to prevent overbrowning.
Serve barely warm or at room temperature.

Butterscotch Crumb Apple Pie

BUTTERSCOTCH CRUMB APPLE PIE

Makes one 9-inch pie

FILLING:
    4 cups pared, cored and thinly sliced tart cooking
        apples (about 1½ pounds)
2 cups (12-ounce package) NESTLÉ® Toll House®
    Butterscotch Flavored Morsels, divided
2 tablespoons all-purpose flour
1 teaspoon ground cinnamon
    One 9-inch unbaked pie shell

TOPPING:
1 cup (½ of 12-ounce package) NESTLÉ® Toll
    House® Butterscotch Flavored Morsels,
    reserved from above
¼ cup (½ stick) butter
¾ cup all-purpose flour
⅛ teaspoon salt
    Whipped cream or ice cream (optional)

Filling: Preheat oven to 350°F. In large bowl, stir
apples, 1 cup Nestlé® Toll House® Butterscotch
Flavored Morsels, flour and cinnamon until apples are
coated. Spoon into pie shell.* Bake 20 minutes.

Topping: Combine over hot (not boiling) water, 1 cup
Nestlé® Toll House® Butterscotch Flavored Morsels and
butter; stir until morsels are melted and mixture is

smooth. Remove from heat. Add flour and salt; blend until mixture forms large crumbs. Crumble topping over hot apple mixture.

Bake an additional 30 minutes or until apples are tender. Serve warm with whipped cream or ice cream, if desired.

*If using frozen pie shell, use deep-dish style, thawed. Bake pie on cookie sheet.

APPLE-CHEDDAR TART

Makes 8 servings

Cheddar Pastry (recipe follows)
1 egg white
6 cups peeled apple slices
2 teaspoons ground cinnamon
¼ teaspoon ground nutmeg
½ cup thawed frozen unsweetened apple juice concentrate
2 tablespoons cornstarch
2 tablespoons butter or margarine
Sharp Cheddar cheese (optional)

Prepare Cheddar Pastry. Preheat oven to 400°F. Roll out pastry dough to 12-inch circle. Place in 10-inch tart pan with removable bottom or 10-inch quiche dish; trim pastry and flute edges, sealing to side of pan. Prick bottom and sides of pastry with fork. Beat egg white until frothy; brush lightly over bottom of pastry.

Bake 15 minutes. Remove from oven. *Reduce oven temperature to 350°F.* Place apples in large bowl. Add cinnamon and nutmeg; toss lightly to coat. Combine apple juice concentrate and cornstarch in small bowl; mix well. Add to apple mixture; mix lightly. Spoon into partially baked crust; dot with butter. Return to oven.

Bake 35 to 40 minutes or until apples are tender and crust is golden brown. Cool on wire rack. Serve with sliced Cheddar cheese, if desired.

CHEDDAR PASTRY

1½ cups all-purpose flour
⅓ cup (1½ ounces) shredded sharp Cheddar cheese
¼ teaspoon salt
½ cup cold butter or margarine
3 to 4 tablespoons ice water

Combine flour, cheese and salt in medium bowl. Cut in butter with pastry blender or two knives until mixture forms coarse crumbs. Add water, 1 tablespoon at a time, mixing just until dough forms ball; wrap in plastic wrap. Refrigerate 1 hour.

Note: This is a sugar-free dessert.

APPLE CHESS PIE

Makes one 9-inch pie

1 (9-inch) unbaked pastry shell, pricked
4 eggs
1 (14-ounce) can EAGLE® Brand Sweetened Condensed Milk (NOT evaporated milk)
1 cup applesauce
½ cup margarine or butter, melted
½ cup shredded all-purpose apple
3 tablespoons REALEMON® Lemon Juice from Concentrate
2 tablespoons cornmeal

Preheat oven to 425°F. Bake pastry shell 8 minutes; remove from oven. *Reduce oven temperature to 350°F.*

Meanwhile, in large mixer bowl, beat eggs. Add remaining ingredients; mix well. Pour into prepared pastry shell.

Bake 40 minutes or until knife inserted near center comes out clean. Cool. Serve warm or chilled. Garnish as desired. Refrigerate leftovers.

Pineapple Chess Pie: Omit applesauce, shredded apple and ReaLemon® brand. Reduce margarine or butter to ⅓ cup. Add 1 (8-ounce) can juice-pack crushed pineapple, undrained, and ½ cup pineapple juice with remaining ingredients to eggs. Proceed as above.

Apple-Cheddar Tart

Apple Almond Pie

APPLE ALMOND PIE

Makes 8 servings

Easy-As-Pie Crust (page 102)
¾ cup sugar, divided
¼ cup ARGO® or KINGSFORD'S® Corn Starch
3 eggs
½ cup MAZOLA® Margarine, melted
½ cup KARO® Light or Dark Corn Syrup
¼ teaspoon almond extract
2 cups peeled, chopped apples (about 2 large)
1 cup sliced or slivered almonds, toasted
1 apple, peeled and thinly sliced (optional)
   Sliced almonds, toasted (optional)

Preheat oven to 375°F. Prepare Easy-As-Pie Crust.

Reserve 2 tablespoons sugar. In large bowl, combine remaining sugar and corn starch. Beat in eggs until well blended. Stir in margarine, corn syrup and almond extract. Mix in chopped apples and 1 cup almonds. Pour into unbaked pie crust. If desired, garnish with apple slices arranged in a circle around edge of pie; fill center with additional toasted almonds. Sprinkle reserved sugar over top.

Bake 50 minutes or until puffed and set. Cool on wire rack.

Prep time: 20 minutes
Bake time: 50 minutes plus cooling

NEW ENGLAND MAPLE APPLE PIE

Makes one 9-inch pie

1 (9-inch) unbaked pastry shell
2 pounds all-purpose apples, cored, pared and
   thinly sliced (about 6 cups)
½ cup plus 2 tablespoons unsifted all-purpose flour
½ cup CARY'S®, MAPLE ORCHARDS® or
   MACDONALD'S™ Pure Maple Syrup
2 tablespoons margarine or butter, melted
¼ cup firmly packed light brown sugar
1 teaspoon ground cinnamon
⅓ cup cold margarine or butter
½ cup chopped nuts

Place rack in lowest position in oven; preheat oven to 400°F. In large bowl, combine apples and *2 tablespoons flour*. Combine pure maple syrup and melted margarine. Pour over apples; mix well. Turn into pastry shell. In medium bowl, combine remaining *½ cup flour*, sugar and cinnamon; cut in cold margarine until crumbly. Add nuts; sprinkle over apples.

Bake 10 minutes. *Reduce oven temperature to 375°F;* bake 35 minutes longer or until golden brown. Serve warm. Garnish as desired.

FRESH PEAR CUSTARD PIE

Makes 6 to 8 servings

Pastry for single-crust 9-inch pie
4 eggs, beaten
3 ripe, medium pears, divided
2 cups milk
½ cup sugar
2 teaspoons grated lemon peel, divided
1 teaspoon lemon juice
1 teaspoon vanilla
¼ to ½ teaspoon ground ginger
¼ teaspoon salt
½ cup apricot preserves
1 tablespoon water
   Mint leaves (optional)

Preheat oven to 425°F. Roll out pastry on lightly floured surface into 10-inch circle. Carefully fit into 9-inch quiche dish or pie plate. Trim pastry even with rim of dish. Brush pie shell with small amount of beaten eggs. Prick bottom and sides with fork. Bake 5 to 10 minutes or until golden brown. Cool on wire rack.

Reduce oven temperature to 350°F. Pare and core 1 pear; cut into chunks. In food processor or blender, process pear chunks until smooth. In large bowl, combine remaining beaten eggs, milk, sugar, puréed pear, 1 teaspoon lemon peel, lemon juice, vanilla, ginger and salt; beat until combined. Pour into baked pie shell.

Bake 45 to 50 minutes or until knife inserted near center comes out clean. Cool on wire rack. In small bowl, mix preserves, water and remaining 1 teaspoon lemon peel. Core remaining 2 pears; cut lengthwise into thin slices. Arrange pear slices over top of pie. Pour apricot mixture evenly over pear slices. Serve warm or chilled. If desired, garnish with mint leaves.

Favorite recipe from **American Egg Board**

PEACH MELBA CHEESE PIE

Makes one 9-inch pie

1 (9-inch) unbaked pastry shell, pricked
1 (8-ounce) package cream cheese, softened
1 (14-ounce) can EAGLE® Brand Sweetened
    Condensed Milk (NOT evaporated milk)
1 egg
1 teaspoon vanilla extract
3 medium peaches, seeded, pared and sliced *or*
    1 (16 ounce) package frozen peach slices,
    thawed and well drained
    Raspberry Topping (recipe follows)

Preheat oven to 375°F. Bake pastry shell 15 minutes; remove from oven. *Reduce oven temperature to 300°F.*

In large mixer bowl, beat cheese until fluffy. Gradually beat in sweetened condensed milk until smooth. Add egg and vanilla; mix well. Pour into prepared pastry shell.

Bake 35 to 40 minutes or until set. Cool. Chill thoroughly. Just before serving, arrange peach slices on top of pie. Top with Raspberry Topping. Refrigerate leftovers.

Raspberry Topping: In small saucepan, combine ⅔ cup syrup reserved from 1 (10-ounce) package thawed frozen red raspberries in syrup, ¼ cup BAMA® Red Currant Jelly or Red Raspberry Jam and 1 tablespoon cornstarch. Over medium heat, cook and stir until thickened and clear. Cool. Stir in raspberries. Chill thoroughly. *Makes about 1⅓ cups*

Peach Melba Cheese Pie

PEACH DELIGHT PIE

Makes one 9-inch pie

FILLING
2½ cups sliced, peeled peaches (about 1¼ pounds
    or 2 to 3 large)
¾ cup granulated sugar
¼ cup quick-cooking tapioca
1 teaspoon lemon juice
1 teaspoon peach-flavored brandy

CRUMB MIXTURE
¼ cup all-purpose flour
¼ cup firmly packed brown sugar
¼ cup chopped almonds
3 tablespoons butter or margarine, melted

CRUST
    Unbaked 9-inch Classic CRISCO® *Double* Crust
    (page 80)

GLAZE
1 egg white, lightly beaten
    Additional granulated sugar

1. For Filling, combine peaches, ¾ cup granulated sugar, tapioca, lemon juice and brandy in medium bowl. Stir well. Let stand while preparing crumb mixture and crust.

2. For Crumb Mixture, combine flour, brown sugar, nuts and butter. Mix until crumbly.

3. Preheat oven to 425°F.

4. Sprinkle half of crumb mixture over unbaked pie crust. Add filling. Top with remaining crumb mixture. Moisten pastry edge with water.

5. Roll top crust same as bottom. Cut out heart shapes with cookie cutter. Place cutouts on filling around edge of pie.

6. For Glaze, brush cutouts with egg white. Sprinkle with additional granulated sugar. Cover edge of pie with foil to prevent overbrowning.

7. Bake at 425°F for 10 minutes. *Reduce oven temperature to 350°F.* Bake 25 minutes. Remove foil. Bake 5 minutes. Serve barely warm or at room temperature.

Georgia Peach Pie

GEORGIA PEACH PIE

Makes one 10-inch pie

CRUST
Unbaked 10-inch Classic CRISCO® *Double* Crust (page 80)

FILLING
1 can (29 ounces) yellow cling peaches in heavy syrup
3 tablespoons reserved peach syrup
3 tablespoons cornstarch
1 cup sugar, divided
3 eggs
⅓ cup buttermilk
½ cup butter or margarine, melted
1 teaspoon vanilla

GLAZE
2 tablespoons butter or margarine, melted
Additional sugar

1. Preheat oven to 400°F.

2. For Filling, drain peaches, reserving 3 tablespoons syrup. Set aside. Cut peaches into small pieces; place in large bowl. Combine cornstarch and 3 tablespoons sugar in medium bowl. Add 3 tablespoons reserved peach syrup; mix well. Add remaining sugar, eggs and buttermilk; mix well. Stir in ½ cup melted butter and vanilla. Pour over peaches; stir until peaches are coated. Pour filling into unbaked pie crust. Moisten pastry edge with water.

3. Cover pie with top crust. Fold top edge under bottom crust; flute with fingers or fork. Cut slits or designs in top crust to allow steam to escape.

4. For Glaze, brush top crust with 2 tablespoons melted butter. Sprinkle with additional sugar.

5. Bake at 400°F for 45 minutes or until filling in center is bubbly and crust is golden brown. Cool to room temperature before serving.

ALMOND CRUNCH PEACH PIE

Makes one 9-inch pie

FILLING
5 cups sliced, peeled fresh yellow cling peaches (4 large peaches)
½ cup sugar
2 tablespoons lemon juice
½ cup canned or packaged pure almond paste*
¼ cup all-purpose flour
¼ cup non-dairy powdered creamer

CRUST
Unbaked 9-inch Classic CRISCO® *Double* Crust (page 80)

TOPPING
1 egg white, lightly beaten
½ cup coarsely chopped or crushed almonds
3 tablespoons sugar

1. For Filling, combine peaches, ½ cup sugar and lemon juice in large bowl. Combine almond paste, flour and creamer in small bowl. Mix until crumbly. Add to peach mixture; stir well. Refrigerate while preparing crust.

2. Preheat oven to 375°F. Spoon filling into unbaked pie crust. Moisten pastry edge with water. Cover pie with top crust. Fold top edge under bottom crust; flute with fingers or fork. Cut slits in top crust to allow steam to escape.

3. For Topping, brush top crust with egg white. Sprinkle with almonds and 3 tablespoons sugar.

4. Bake at 375°F for 1 hour or until filling in center is bubbly and crust is golden brown. Cool until barely warm or to room temperature before serving.

*Use ½ cup very finely crushed or ground almonds mixed with ½ teaspoon almond extract, if almond paste is not available.

Classic Cherry Pie

CHERRY CHEESECAKE PIE

Makes one 9-inch pie

CRUST
  Unbaked 9-inch Classic CRISCO® *Single* Crust
  (page 80)

FILLING
  2 cans (16 ounces each) pitted red tart cherries,
    packed in water
  ¼ cup reserved cherry liquid
  ½ cup sugar
  1 tablespoon cornstarch
  1 teaspoon lemon juice
  ⅛ teaspoon almond extract

TOPPING
  1½ packages (8 ounces each) cream cheese, softened
  ½ cup sugar
  2 eggs
  ½ teaspoon vanilla
  Baked pastry cutouts (optional)

1. Preheat oven to 425°F. Reserve dough scraps from crust for decoration, if desired.

2. For Filling, drain cherries in large strainer over bowl, reserving ¼ cup liquid. Combine ½ cup sugar and cornstarch in large bowl. Stir in reserved ¼ cup cherry liquid, lemon juice and almond extract. Stir in cherries. Spoon into unbaked pie crust.

3. Bake at 425°F for 15 minutes. Remove from oven.

4. For Topping, combine cream cheese, ½ cup sugar, eggs and vanilla in medium bowl. Beat at medium speed of electric mixer until smooth. Spoon over hot cherry filling.

5. *Reduce oven temperature to 350°F.* Return pie to oven. Bake for 25 minutes or until topping is set. Cool to room temperature before serving. Garnish with baked pastry cutouts, if desired. Refrigerate leftovers.

CLASSIC CHERRY PIE

Makes one 9-inch pie

CRUST
  Unbaked 9-inch Classic CRISCO® *Double* Crust
  (page 80)

FILLING
  3 pounds pitted red tart cherries frozen with
    sugar, thawed*
  1½ cups reserved cherry juice*
  ⅓ cup firmly packed brown sugar
  ⅓ cup granulated sugar
  ¼ cup cornstarch
  ½ teaspoon ground cinnamon
  1½ tablespoons BUTTER FLAVOR CRISCO®
  1 tablespoon vanilla
  1 teaspoon almond extract

GLAZE
  Milk
  Additional granulated sugar

1. Preheat oven to 425°F.

2. For Filling, drain cherries in large strainer over bowl, reserving 1½ cups juice. Combine sugars, cornstarch and cinnamon in large saucepan. Stir in reserved 1½ cups cherry juice. Cook and stir on medium heat until mixture is thick and bubbly. Boil and stir 1 minute. Add cherries and cook 1 minute or until mixture comes to a boil. Remove from heat. Stir in Butter Flavor Crisco®, vanilla and almond extract. Spoon into unbaked pie crust. Moisten pastry edge with water.

3. Cover pie with top crust. Fold top edge under bottom crust; flute with fingers or fork. Cut slits in top crust to allow steam to escape.

4. For Glaze, brush top crust with milk. Sprinkle with additional granulated sugar. Bake at 425°F for 15 minutes. *Reduce oven temperature to 350°F.*

5. Bake 25 minutes or until filling in center is bubbly and crust is golden brown. Cool until barely warm or to room temperature before serving.

*Use 2 cans (1 pound each) red tart cherries packed in water in place of frozen. Reduce cherry liquid to 1 cup.

CLASSIC RHUBARB PIE

Makes one 9-inch pie

CRUST

Unbaked 9-inch Classic CRISCO® *Double* Crust (page 80)

FILLING

4 cups red rhubarb, cut into ½- to ¾-inch pieces
1⅓ to 1½ cups sugar, to taste
⅓ cup all-purpose flour
2 tablespoons butter or margarine

GLAZE

1 tablespoon milk
Additional sugar

1. Preheat oven to 400°F.

2. For Filling, combine rhubarb and sugar in large bowl; mix well. Stir in flour. Spoon into unbaked pie crust; dot with butter. Moisten pastry edge with water.

3. Cover pie with woven lattice top (see page 83).

4. For Glaze, brush top crust with milk. Sprinkle with additional sugar. Cover edge of pie with foil to prevent overbrowning.

5. Bake at 400°F for 20 minutes. *Reduce oven temperature to 325°F.* Remove foil. Bake 30 minutes or until filling in center is bubbly and crust is golden brown (if using frozen rhubarb, bake a total of 60 to 70 minutes). Cool until barely warm or to room temperature before serving.

STRAWBERRY RHUBARB PIE

Makes 8 servings

3 cups sliced fresh *or* frozen unsweetened rhubarb, divided
½ cup unsweetened white grape juice
2 tablespoons cornstarch
1 teaspoon ground cinnamon
¼ teaspoon salt
¼ teaspoon ground nutmeg
1 pint fresh strawberries, sliced (about 3½ cups)
¾ cup no-sugar-added strawberry fruit spread, divided
Pastry for double-crust 9-inch pie
1 egg yolk, lightly beaten
1 tablespoon sour cream *or* milk

Preheat oven to 450°F. Combine 2 cups rhubarb and grape juice in medium saucepan. Bring to a boil over medium heat. Reduce heat to low. Simmer, uncovered, until rhubarb is tender, 8 to 10 minutes for fresh or 5 minutes for frozen; drain.

Combine cornstarch, cinnamon, salt and nutmeg in medium bowl; mix well. Add strawberries; toss to coat. Stir in cooked rhubarb and ½ cup fruit spread. Stir in remaining 1 cup rhubarb.

Roll out half of pastry to 11-inch circle; place in 9-inch pie plate. Trim pastry and flute edges, sealing to edge of pie plate. Fill shell with fruit mixture; dot with remaining ¼ cup fruit spread. Roll out remaining pastry to 10-inch circle. Cut into ½-inch-wide strips. Form into lattice design over fruit. Combine egg yolk and sour cream; mix until well blended. Brush over pastry.

Bake 10 minutes. *Reduce oven temperature to 350°F.* Cover edge of pie with foil to prevent overbrowning. Continue baking 30 minutes or until pastry is golden brown and filling is hot and bubbly. Cool on wire rack. Serve warm or at room temperature.

Note: This is a sugar-free dessert.

Strawberry Rhubarb Pie

ReaLemon® Meringue Pie

REALEMON® MERINGUE PIE

Makes one 9-inch pie

1 (9-inch) baked pastry shell
1⅔ cups sugar
6 tablespoons cornstarch
½ cup REALEMON® Lemon Juice from
    Concentrate
4 eggs, separated*
1½ cups boiling water
2 tablespoons margarine or butter
¼ teaspoon cream of tartar

Preheat oven to 350°F. In heavy saucepan, combine
1⅓ *cups* sugar and cornstarch; add ReaLemon® brand.
In small bowl, beat egg *yolks*; add to lemon mixture.
Gradually add water, stirring constantly. Over medium
heat, cook and stir until mixture boils and thickens,
about 8 to 10 minutes. Remove from heat. Add margarine;
stir until melted. Pour into prepared pastry shell.

In small mixer bowl, beat egg *whites* with cream of
tartar to soft peaks; gradually add remaining ⅓ *cup*
sugar, beating until stiff but not dry. Spread on top
of pie, sealing carefully to edge of shell.

Bake 12 to 15 minutes or until golden. Cool. Chill
before serving. Garnish as desired. Refrigerate leftovers.

*Use only Grade A clean, uncracked eggs.

COOKIE CRUST LEMON PIE

Makes one 9-inch pie

1 (20-ounce) package refrigerated sugar cookie
    dough
1⅓ cups sugar
⅓ cup cornstarch
2 eggs
½ cup REALEMON® Lemon Juice from
    Concentrate
1½ cups boiling water
2 tablespoons margarine or butter
    Yellow food coloring (optional)
    Additional sugar

Preheat oven to 350°F. On floured surface, press
half the dough into 6-inch circle. Firmly press dough,
floured side down, on bottom and up side to rim
of 9-inch pie plate to form crust. In heavy saucepan,
combine 1⅓ cups sugar, cornstarch and eggs; mix well.
Over medium heat, gradually stir in ReaLemon® brand
then water, stirring constantly. Cook and stir until
thickened. Cook 1 minute longer. Remove from heat.
Add margarine; stir until melted. Add food coloring if
desired. Pour into prepared crust. Slice remaining
dough into 16 (¼-inch) rounds; arrange on top of
filling.

Bake 15 minutes or until golden. Sprinkle top of pie
with additional sugar. Cool. Chill. Refrigerate leftovers.

Lime Variation: Substitute REALIME® Lime Juice
from Concentrate for ReaLemon® brand and green
food coloring for yellow.

LEMONY BUTTERMILK PIE

Makes one 9-inch pie

Flaky Crust (recipe follows)
3 eggs
½ cup plus 2 teaspoons sugar, divided
1 cup buttermilk
1½ tablespoons all-purpose flour
2 teaspoons grated lemon peel
2 tablespoons fresh lemon juice
1 teaspoon vanilla
⅛ teaspoon ground cinnamon
⅛ teaspoon ground nutmeg
    Lemon slices (optional)
    Lemon leaves (optional)

Prepare Flaky Crust. *Reduce oven temperature to 375°F.*

In small mixer bowl, beat eggs and ½ cup sugar with
electric mixer on high speed until thick and lemon
colored, about 5 minutes. Stir in buttermilk, flour,
lemon peel, lemon juice and vanilla. Pour into baked
and cooled pie crust. In small bowl, combine remaining
2 teaspoons sugar, cinnamon and nutmeg. Sprinkle over
top of pie.

Bake 25 to 30 minutes or until knife inserted near
center comes out clean. Cool completely on wire rack.
If desired, garnish with lemon slices and lemon leaves.

FLAKY CRUST

1 cup all-purpose flour
⅛ teaspoon salt
3 tablespoons cold butter
3 tablespoons lard or shortening
3 to 4 tablespoons milk

Preheat oven to 425°F. In medium bowl, combine flour
and salt. Cut in butter and lard using pastry blender or
2 knives until mixture resembles coarse crumbs. Add
milk, 1 tablespoon at a time, mixing with fork until
dough just sticks together. Press into ball. Roll out on
lightly floured surface into 10-inch circle. Carefully fit
into 9-inch pie plate. Trim edge; flute as desired. Prick
bottom and side of pastry with fork.

Bake 10 minutes or until lightly browned. Cool
completely on wire rack.

Favorite recipe from **American Dairy Association**

LEMON SPONGE PIE

Makes one 9-inch pie

1 (9-inch) unbaked pastry shell, pricked
3 eggs, separated
1¼ cups granulated sugar
¼ cup unsifted all-purpose flour
¼ cup margarine or butter, melted
⅓ cup REALEMON® Lemon Juice from
    Concentrate
1 cup BORDEN® or MEADOW GOLD® Milk
    Confectioners' sugar

Preheat oven to 350°F. Bake pastry shell 8 minutes; remove from oven. Meanwhile, in small mixer bowl, beat egg *whites* until foamy; gradually add *¼ cup* granulated sugar, beating until soft peaks form. In large mixer bowl, combine remaining *1 cup* granulated sugar, flour, margarine and egg *yolks*; beat well. Stir in ReaLemon® brand. Gradually add milk; mix well. Fold egg white mixture into lemon mixture. Pour into prepared pastry shell.

Bake 40 minutes or until knife inserted near center comes out clean. Cool. Sprinkle with confectioners' sugar. Garnish as desired. Refrigerate leftovers.

KEY LIME PIE

Makes one 9- or 10-inch pie

1 (9- or 10-inch) baked pastry shell or graham
    cracker crumb crust*
6 egg yolks**
2 (14-ounce) cans EAGLE® Brand Sweetened
    Condensed Milk (NOT evaporated milk)
1 (8-ounce) bottle REALIME® Lime Juice from
    Concentrate
    Yellow or green food coloring (optional)
    Whipped cream or whipped topping

Preheat oven to 350°F. In large mixer bowl, beat egg yolks with sweetened condensed milk. Stir in ReaLime® brand and food coloring if desired. Pour into prepared pastry shell.

Bake 12 minutes or until set. Cool. Chill. Top with whipped cream. Garnish as desired. Refrigerate leftovers.

Key Lime Meringue Pie: Omit whipped cream. Prepare filling as above, reserving *4 egg whites*; do not bake. In small mixer bowl, beat egg whites with ¼ teaspoon cream of tartar until soft peaks form;

gradually add ½ cup sugar, beating until stiff but not dry. Spread on top of pie, sealing carefully to edge of pastry shell. Bake 12 to 15 minutes or until golden. Cool. Chill.

*If using frozen packaged pie shell or 6-ounce packaged graham cracker crumb pie crust, use 1 can Eagle® Brand Sweetened Condensed Milk, 3 egg yolks and ½ cup ReaLime® brand. Bake 8 minutes. Proceed as above.

**Use only Grade A clean, uncracked eggs.

ORANGE BLOSSOM PIE

Makes one 9-inch pie

1 (9-inch) unbaked pastry shell, pricked
1 (14-ounce) can EAGLE® Brand Sweetened
    Condensed Milk (NOT evaporated milk)
1 cup orange juice
2 egg yolks
1 tablespoon grated orange peel
1 (3-ounce) package cream cheese, softened
½ cup BORDEN® or MEADOW GOLD® Sour
    Cream, at room temperature
½ cup confectioners' sugar
½ teaspoon vanilla extract

Preheat oven to 375°F. Bake pastry shell 15 minutes; remove from oven. *Reduce oven temperature to 325°F.*

Meanwhile, in large bowl, combine sweetened condensed milk, orange juice, egg yolks and peel; mix well. Pour into prepared pastry shell (mixture will be thin).

Bake 35 minutes or until set. Meanwhile, in small mixer bowl, beat remaining ingredients until smooth; spread over pie. Bake 5 minutes longer. Cool. Chill. Garnish as desired. Refrigerate leftovers.

Lemon Sponge Pie

Double Blueberry Cheese Pie

DOUBLE BLUEBERRY CHEESE PIE

Makes one 9- or 9½-inch deep-dish pie

CRUST
Unbaked 9-inch Classic CRISCO® *Single* Crust (page 80)

FILLING
2 packages (8 ounces each) cream cheese, softened
1 cup granulated sugar
½ cup whipping cream
2 eggs
2 tablespoons all-purpose flour
2 teaspoons vanilla
2 cups fresh blueberries

TOPPING
2 cups whipping cream
2 tablespoons confectioners sugar
1 teaspoon vanilla
1 cup fresh blueberries

1. Preheat oven to 350°F. Press rolled crust into 9- or 9½-inch deep-dish pie plate.

2. For Filling, place cream cheese and granulated sugar in food processor bowl. Process, using steel blade, until smooth. Add ½ cup whipping cream, eggs, flour and 2 teaspoons vanilla through feed tube while processor is running. Process until blended. Add 2 cups blueberries. Pulse (quick on and off) twice. Pour into unbaked pie crust.

3. Bake at 350°F for 45 minutes. Turn oven off. Allow pie to remain in oven with door ajar for 1 hour. Cool to room temperature. Refrigerate 6 hours or overnight.

4. For Topping, beat 2 cups whipping cream in large bowl at high speed of electric mixer until stiff peaks form. Beat in confectioners sugar and 1 teaspoon vanilla. Spread over top of pie. Garnish with 1 cup blueberries. Serve immediately. Refrigerate leftover pie.

LUSCIOUS CRANBERRY AND BLUEBERRY PIE

Makes one 9-inch pie

CRUST
Unbaked 9-inch Classic CRISCO® *Double* Crust (page 80), prepared with ½ teaspoon ground mace added to flour mixture

FILLING
1 can (16 ounces) whole-berry cranberry sauce
⅓ cup firmly packed brown sugar
¼ cup granulated sugar
2 tablespoons all-purpose flour
2 tablespoons cornstarch
2 tablespoons orange juice
½ teaspoon dried grated orange peel
⅛ teaspoon salt
2 cups fresh or frozen blueberries
2 tablespoons butter or margarine

GLAZE
1 egg, beaten

1. Preheat oven to 425°F. Reserve dough scraps from crust for decorations, if desired.

2. For Filling, combine cranberry sauce, brown sugar, granulated sugar, flour, cornstarch, orange juice, orange peel and salt in large bowl. Stir in blueberries. Spoon into unbaked pie crust. Dot with butter. Moisten pastry edge with water.

3. Cover pie with top crust. Fold top edge under bottom crust; flute with fingers or fork. Cut dogwood blossoms in top crust to allow steam to escape.

4. Cut flowers or other shapes from reserved dough. Place on top of pie.

5. For Glaze, brush top crust with egg.

6. Bake at 425°F for 40 minutes or until filling in center is bubbly and crust is golden brown. Cover edge of pie with foil during last 10 minutes to prevent overbrowning. Cool to room temperature before serving.

Tropical Pineapple Pie

TROPICAL PINEAPPLE PIE

Makes one 9-inch pie

1 (9-inch) unbaked pastry shell, pricked
1 (14-ounce) can EAGLE® Brand Sweetened
   Condensed Milk (NOT evaporated milk)
½ cup frozen pineapple juice concentrate, thawed
3 egg *yolks*
1 (20-ounce) can juice-pack crushed pineapple,
   well drained, reserving ½ cup juice
1 (8-ounce) container BORDEN® or MEADOW
   GOLD® Sour Cream, at room temperature
2 tablespoons sugar
1½ teaspoons cornstarch

Preheat oven to 375°F. Bake pastry shell 15 minutes;
remove from oven. *Reduce oven temperature to 325°F.*

In large mixer bowl, beat sweetened condensed milk,
juice concentrate and egg yolks until well blended. Stir
in ¾ *cup* pineapple. Pour into prepared pastry shell.

Bake 25 minutes or until center is set. Top with sour
cream. Bake 5 minutes longer. Cool.

Meanwhile, in small saucepan, combine sugar and
cornstarch; gradually add reserved ½ cup pineapple juice
then remaining pineapple. Over low heat, cook and stir
until thickened. Cool. Spread over pie. Chill thoroughly.
Garnish as desired. Refrigerate leftovers.

PINEAPPLE MACADAMIA CHEESEPIE

Makes 8 servings

Macadamia Crust (recipe follows)
1 can (8 ounces) DOLE® Crushed Pineapple
   in Juice
12 ounces cream cheese, softened
¾ cup plain yogurt
½ cup sugar
1 egg
1 teaspoon vanilla extract

Preheat oven to 350°F. Prepare Macadamia Crust.
Drain pineapple well, pressing out excess juice with back
of spoon. Beat cream cheese in medium bowl until
smooth. Beat in yogurt, sugar, egg and vanilla until
blended. Spread pineapple over prepared crust,
reserving 2 tablespoons for garnish. Pour cream cheese
mixture over pineapple.

Bake 20 minutes or until set. Cool on wire rack;
refrigerate at least 2 hours. Just before serving, garnish
with reserved pineapple.

Macadamia Crust: In medium bowl, combine
1 cup chopped macadamia nuts, ¾ cup graham cracker
crumbs, 6 tablespoons melted margarine and
2 tablespoons sugar. Press onto bottom and sides of
8-inch pie plate. Refrigerate until ready to use.

COCONUT CUSTARD PIE

Makes one 9-inch pie

1 (9-inch) unbaked pastry shell, pricked
1 cup flaked coconut
3 eggs
1 (14-ounce) can EAGLE® Brand Sweetened
   Condensed Milk (NOT evaporated milk)
1¼ cups water
1 teaspoon vanilla extract
¼ teaspoon salt
⅛ teaspoon ground nutmeg

Preheat oven to 425°F. Reserving ½ *cup* coconut, toast
remainder. Bake pastry shell 8 minutes; cool slightly.

Meanwhile, in medium bowl, beat eggs. Add sweetened
condensed milk, water, vanilla, salt and nutmeg; mix
well. Stir in reserved ½ cup coconut. Pour into prepared
pastry shell. Sprinkle with toasted coconut.

Bake 10 minutes. *Reduce oven temperature to 350°F;*
bake 25 to 30 minutes longer or until knife inserted
near center comes out clean. Cool. Chill if desired.
Garnish as desired. Refrigerate leftovers.

Custard Pie: Omit coconut. Proceed as above.

SWEET POTATO PRALINE PIE

Makes one 9-inch pie

1 (9-inch) unbaked pastry shell
1 pound sweet potatoes or yams, cooked and peeled
¼ cup margarine or butter
1 (14-ounce) can EAGLE® Brand Sweetened
    Condensed Milk (NOT evaporated milk)
1 teaspoon vanilla extract
1 teaspoon ground cinnamon
1 teaspoon ground allspice
¼ teaspoon salt
2 eggs, beaten
    Praline Topping (recipe follows)

Preheat oven to 350°F. In large mixer bowl, beat *hot* sweet potatoes with margarine. Add sweetened condensed milk, vanilla, spices and salt; beat until smooth. Stir in eggs. Pour into pastry shell.

Bake 50 to 55 minutes or until center is set. Cool. Top with warm Praline Topping. Serve warm. Refrigerate leftovers.

Tip: 1 (16- to 18-ounce) can sweet potatoes or yams, drained, can be substituted for fresh. Melt margarine. Proceed as above.

Praline Topping: In small saucepan, combine ½ cup BORDEN® or MEADOW GOLD® Whipping Cream, *unwhipped*, ⅓ cup firmly packed brown sugar and ½ teaspoon vanilla extract. Cook and stir until sugar dissolves. Boil rapidly 5 to 8 minutes or until thickened, stirring occasionally. Remove from heat; stir in ½ cup chopped toasted pecans. Serve warm.

Makes about ⅔ cup

CALIFORNIA NUT PIE

Makes one 9-inch pie

1 (9-inch) unbaked pastry shell, pricked
1 (14-ounce) can EAGLE® Brand Sweetened
    Condensed Milk (NOT evaporated milk)
1 cup water
3 eggs
¼ cup amaretto liqueur or water
1 teaspoon vanilla extract
½ cup slivered almonds, toasted
½ cup chopped walnuts, toasted

Preheat oven to 425°F. Bake pastry shell 8 minutes; cool slightly.

Meanwhile, in small mixer bowl, beat sweetened condensed milk, water, eggs, liqueur and vanilla until well blended. Stir in nuts. Pour into prepared pastry shell.

Bake 10 minutes. *Reduce oven temperature to 350°F;* bake 25 minutes longer or until set. Cool. Serve warm or chilled. Garnish as desired. Refrigerate leftovers.

Top to bottom: Sweet Potato Praline Pie, California Nut Pie

Spring Fling Fruit Tart

SPRING FLING FRUIT TART

Makes 10 to 12 servings

1 cup all-purpose flour
¼ cup firmly packed brown sugar
½ cup PARKAY® Margarine
1 (8-ounce) package PHILADELPHIA BRAND®
  Cream Cheese, softened
¼ cup granulated sugar
1 tablespoon grated orange peel
¾ cup whipping cream, whipped
  Peeled kiwifruit slices
  Strawberry halves

• Preheat oven to 350°F.

• Stir together flour and brown sugar in medium bowl. Cut in margarine until mixture resembles coarse crumbs; knead mixture until well blended. Press onto bottom and ½ inch up sides of 10-inch tart pan with removable bottom.

• Bake 15 minutes or until golden brown. Cool.

• Beat cream cheese, granulated sugar and peel in large mixing bowl at medium speed with electric mixer until well blended. Fold in whipped cream; pour into crust. Chill until firm.

• Arrange fruit on top of tart just before serving. Carefully remove rim of pan. Garnish as desired.

Tip: When preparing crust, wet fingertips in cold water before pressing dough into pan.

STRAWBERRY TART GLACÉ

Makes 8 servings

Pastry for single-crust 9-inch pie
2 (8-ounce) packages Light PHILADELPHIA
  BRAND® Neufchatel Cheese, softened
½ cup sugar, divided
1 tablespoon milk
¼ teaspoon vanilla
1 quart strawberries, hulled, divided
1 tablespoon cornstarch
¼ cup water
  Few drops red food coloring (optional)

• Preheat oven to 450°F.

• On lightly floured surface, roll pastry into 12-inch circle. Place in 10-inch quiche dish. Trim edges of pastry, if necessary. Prick bottom and sides of pastry with fork. Bake 9 to 11 minutes or until golden brown. Cool.

• Combine neufchatel cheese, ¼ cup sugar, milk and vanilla in medium bowl at medium speed with electric mixer until well blended. Spread onto bottom of crust.

• Place 1 cup strawberries in food processor or blender container; process until smooth. Set aside.

• Press remaining 1 cup whole strawberries, hull side down, into neufchatel cheese mixture. Combine remaining ¼ cup sugar and cornstarch in saucepan; gradually add puréed strawberries and water. Cook, stirring constantly, over medium heat until mixture is clear and thickened. Stir in food coloring. Pour over whole strawberries; chill.

VARIATIONS

• Substitute 9-inch pie plate for 10-inch quiche dish.
• Substitute almond extract for vanilla.
• Substitute PHILADELPHIA BRAND® Cream Cheese for Neufchatel Cheese.

FABULOUS FRUIT TART

Makes 8 servings

Pastry for single-crust 9-inch pie
1 package (8 ounces) regular *or* reduced-calorie
  cream cheese, softened
⅓ cup no-sugar-added raspberry fruit spread
½ cup sliced peaches *or* nectarines
½ cup kiwifruit slices*
⅓ cup sliced strawberries*
⅓ cup raspberries*
3 tablespoons no-sugar-added apricot pourable
  fruit**
2 teaspoons raspberry-flavored liqueur (optional)

Preheat oven to 350°F. Roll out pastry to 12-inch circle; place in 10-inch tart pan with removable bottom or 10-inch quiche dish. Prick bottom and sides of pastry with fork. Bake 18 to 20 minutes or until golden brown. Cool completely on wire rack.

Combine cream cheese and fruit spread in small bowl; mix well. Spread onto bottom of cooled pastry shell. Refrigerate at least 1 hour. Just before serving, remove rim of pan. Arrange fruit over cream cheese layer. Combine pourable fruit and liqueur, if desired, in small bowl; brush evenly over fruit.

*Sliced bananas, plums or blueberries may be substituted.

**Two tablespoons no-sugar-added apricot fruit spread combined with 1 tablespoon warm water may be substituted.

Note: This is a sugar-free dessert.

Peanut Supreme Pie

Bake 50 to 55 minutes or until knife inserted halfway between center and edge comes out clean. Cool on wire rack.

California Pecan Pie: Stir ¼ cup sour cream into eggs until blended.

Kentucky Bourbon Pecan Pie: Add up to 2 tablespoons bourbon to filling.

Chocolate Pecan Pie: Reduce sugar to ⅓ cup. Melt 4 squares (1 ounce each) semisweet chocolate with margarine.

PEANUT SUPREME PIE

Makes one 9-inch pie

CRUST
Unbaked 9-inch Classic CRISCO® *Single* Crust (page 80)

PEANUT LAYER
½ cup chopped peanuts
½ cup JIF® Creamy Peanut Butter
½ cup confectioners sugar
½ cup half-and-half

FILLING
1 can (14 ounces) sweetened condensed milk
½ cup JIF® Creamy Peanut Butter
1 cup milk
1 package (6-serving size) vanilla flavor instant pudding and pie filling mix (not sugar-free)

TOPPING
¾ cup chopped peanuts

1. Preheat oven to 400°F.

2. For Peanut Layer, combine ½ cup nuts, ½ cup peanut butter, confectioners sugar and half-and-half in medium bowl. Stir until well blended. Pour into unbaked pie crust.

3. Bake at 400°F for 20 to 25 minutes or until crust is golden brown. Cool completely.

4. For Filling, combine sweetened condensed milk and ½ cup peanut butter in large bowl. Beat at low speed of electric mixer until well blended. Add milk slowly. Add pudding mix. Increase speed to medium. Beat 2 minutes. Pour over cooled peanut layer.

5. For Topping, sprinkle ¾ cup nuts over filling. Refrigerate at least 1 hour.

CLASSIC PECAN PIE

Makes 8 servings

Easy-As-Pie Crust (page 102)
3 eggs
1 cup sugar
1 cup KARO® Light or Dark Corn Syrup
2 tablespoons MAZOLA® Margarine, melted
1 teaspoon vanilla
1½ cups pecan halves

Preheat oven to 350°F. Prepare Easy-As-Pie Crust.

In medium bowl, beat eggs slightly. Add sugar, corn syrup, margarine and vanilla; stir until well blended. Stir in pecans. Pour into unbaked pie crust.

Chocolate Pie

CHOCOLATE SWEETHEART PIE

Makes 8 servings

1 package (8 ounces) BAKER'S® Semi-Sweet
    Chocolate, divided
⅔ cup corn syrup
1 cup (½ pint) heavy cream, divided
3 eggs
1 unbaked 9-inch pie shell
2 tablespoons sugar
½ teaspoon vanilla
1 pint strawberries, sliced

Preheat oven to 350°F.

Microwave 6 squares chocolate in large microwavable
bowl on HIGH (100% power) 1½ to 2½ minutes or
until almost melted, stirring after each minute. (Remove
from microwave). Stir until chocolate is completely
melted.

Stir in corn syrup and ½ cup cream. Add eggs, one at a
time, beating well after each addition. Pour into pie shell.

Bake for 45 minutes or until knife inserted 1 inch from
center comes out clean. Cool on wire rack. (Center of
pie will sink after cooling.)

Whip remaining ½ cup cream, sugar and vanilla until
soft peaks form; spoon into center of cooled pie. Top
with strawberries. Melt remaining 2 squares chocolate
and drizzle over strawberries. Garnish as desired.

Prep time: 30 minutes
Bake time: 45 minutes

CHOCOLATE PIE

Makes one 8-inch pie

CRUST
    Unbaked 8-inch Classic CRISCO® *Single* Crust
    (page 80)

FILLING
⅔ cup light corn syrup
⅔ cup dark corn syrup
¼ cup granulated sugar
¼ cup firmly packed brown sugar
¼ cup butter or margarine, softened
3 eggs
2 tablespoons all-purpose flour
1 square (1 ounce) unsweetened chocolate, melted
1½ teaspoons vanilla
¼ teaspoon salt
½ cup chopped walnuts
¼ cup shredded coconut
¼ cup semi-sweet miniature chocolate chips
6 walnut halves

1. Preheat oven to 450°F.

2. For Filling, combine light corn syrup, dark corn
syrup, granulated sugar, brown sugar, butter, eggs,
flour, unsweetened chocolate, vanilla and salt in large
bowl. Blend well. Fold in ½ cup walnuts, coconut and
chocolate chips. Pour into unbaked pie crust. Top
with nut halves.

3. Bake at 450°F for 10 minutes. *Reduce oven
temperature to 375°F.* Bake 40 to 45 minutes or until
filling is set in center. Cover edge of pie with foil, if
necessary, to prevent overbrowning. Cool to room
temperature before serving.

JACKPOT PIE

Makes 8 servings

Easy-As-Pie Crust (recipe follows)
1 cup flaked coconut
1 cup (6 ounces) semisweet chocolate chips
1 cup coarsely chopped pecans
⅔ cup KARO® Light or Dark Corn Syrup
½ cup granulated sugar
½ cup firmly packed brown sugar
4 eggs
2 tablespoons MAZOLA® Margarine, melted

Preheat oven to 350°F. Prepare Easy-As-Pie Crust.

In medium bowl, mix coconut, chocolate chips and pecans; sprinkle over bottom of unbaked pie crust. In same bowl, combine corn syrup, sugars, eggs and margarine until well blended. Pour over coconut mixture.

Bake 50 to 55 minutes or until puffed and set. Cool on wire rack.

EASY-AS-PIE CRUST

1¼ cups all-purpose flour
⅛ teaspoon salt
½ cup MAZOLA® Margarine
2 tablespoons cold water

In medium bowl, mix flour and salt. With pastry blender or 2 knives, cut in margarine until mixture resembles fine crumbs. Sprinkle water over flour mixture while tossing with fork to blend well. Press dough firmly into ball. On lightly floured surface, roll out to 12-inch circle. Fit loosely into 9-inch pie plate. Trim and flute edge. Fill and bake according to recipe.

CHOCOLATE CHIP PECAN PIE

Makes one 9-inch pie

CRUST
   Unbaked 9-inch Classic CRISCO® *Single* Crust
   (page 80)

FILLING
4 eggs
1 cup sugar
1 cup light corn syrup
3 tablespoons butter or margarine, melted
1 teaspoon vanilla
¼ teaspoon salt
2 cups pecan halves
½ cup semi-sweet chocolate chips
1 tablespoon plus 1½ teaspoons bourbon (optional)

1. Preheat oven to 375°F.

2. For Filling, beat eggs in large bowl at low speed of electric mixer until blended. Stir in sugar, corn syrup, butter, vanilla and salt with spoon until blended. Stir in nuts, chocolate chips and bourbon. Pour into unbaked pie crust.

3. Bake at 375°F for 55 to 60 minutes or until set. Cover edge of pie with foil, if necessary, to prevent overbrowning. Cool to room temperature before serving. Refrigerate leftover pie.

CHOCOLATE MACADAMIA NUT PIE

Makes 8 servings

Easy-As-Pie Crust (recipe opposite)
3 squares (1 ounce each) semisweet chocolate
¼ cup MAZOLA® Margarine
½ cup heavy cream
½ cup KARO® Light Corn Syrup
3 eggs
⅓ cup granulated sugar
⅓ cup firmly packed brown sugar
1 jar (3½ ounces) macadamia nuts, coarsely
   chopped and toasted (about ¾ cup)
   Whipped cream and macadamia nuts dipped in
   chocolate (optional)

Preheat oven to 350°F. Prepare Easy-As-Pie Crust.

In small heavy saucepan, combine chocolate and margarine; stir over low heat until melted and smooth. Remove from heat. Stir in cream and corn syrup until well blended. In medium bowl, beat eggs and sugars until well mixed. Stir in chocolate mixture until well blended. Stir in chopped and toasted macadamia nuts. Pour into unbaked pie crust.

Bake 40 minutes or until knife inserted halfway between center and edge comes out clean. Cool on wire rack. If desired, serve with whipped cream and macadamia nuts dipped in chocolate.

Prep time: 20 minutes
Bake time: 40 minutes plus cooling

Chocolate Chip Pecan Pie

Chocolate Oatmeal Cookie Pie

CHOCOLATE OATMEAL COOKIE PIE

Makes one 9-inch pie

½ cup firmly packed brown sugar
½ cup dark corn syrup
2 eggs
1 teaspoon vanilla extract
½ teaspoon ground cinnamon
2 cups (12-ounce package) NESTLÉ® Toll House® Semi-Sweet Chocolate Morsels, divided
1 cup chopped walnuts
½ cup quick oats, uncooked
½ cup raisins
1 tablespoon grated orange peel (optional)
1 (9-inch) unbaked pie shell
   Walnut halves
   Chocolate Leaves (directions follow)

Preheat oven to 350°F. In large bowl, combine brown sugar, corn syrup, eggs, vanilla extract and cinnamon; beat well. Stir in 1 cup Nestlé® Toll House® Semi-Sweet Chocolate Morsels, nuts, oats, raisins and orange peel. Pour into prepared pie shell.

Bake 35 to 40 minutes or until golden brown. Serve warm. Garnish with walnut halves and Chocolate Leaves.

Chocolate Leaves: Wash and thoroughly dry 12 nontoxic leaves, such as lemon leaves, grape leaves, rose leaves, violet leaves or nasturtium leaves. In small, heavy saucepan over low heat, melt remaining 1 cup Nestlé® Toll House® Semi-Sweet Chocolate Morsels, stirring until smooth; remove from heat. Spoon or brush chocolate about ⅟₁₆ inch thick onto back side of each leaf; do not spread over edge of leaf. Place on plate or cookie sheet; refrigerate about 30 minutes or until chocolate is set. Beginning at stem end, gently peel leaf away from chocolate. Refrigerate until ready to use.

GERMAN CHOCOLATE PIE

Makes one 9-inch pie

1 (9-inch) unbaked pastry shell, pricked
1 (4-ounce) package sweet cooking chocolate
¼ cup margarine or butter
1 (14-ounce) can EAGLE® Brand Sweetened Condensed Milk (NOT evaporated milk)
1 cup (½ pint) BORDEN® or MEADOW GOLD® Whipping Cream, *unwhipped*
½ cup biscuit baking mix
2 eggs plus 1 egg *yolk*
1½ teaspoons vanilla extract
½ cup flaked coconut
½ cup chopped pecans, toasted

Preheat oven to 375°F. Bake pastry shell 10 minutes; remove from oven. *Reduce oven temperature to 325°F.*

In small saucepan, melt chocolate with *2 tablespoons* margarine. In large mixer bowl, beat chocolate mixture, *⅔ cup* sweetened condensed milk, cream, biscuit mix, *2 eggs* and *1 teaspoon* vanilla until well blended. Pour into prepared pastry shell.

Bake 40 minutes or until center is set. In small saucepan, combine remaining sweetened condensed milk, egg *yolk*, *2 tablespoons* margarine and *½ teaspoon* vanilla. Over medium heat, cook and stir until thickened and bubbly, about 5 minutes. Add coconut and pecans; spread over top of pie. Serve warm or chilled. Refrigerate leftovers.

MOCHA-ALMOND PIE

Makes 8 to 10 servings

2 squares BAKER'S® Unsweetened Chocolate
2 squares BAKER'S® Semi-Sweet Chocolate
½ cup (1 stick) margarine or butter
1 tablespoon powdered instant coffee
1 cup sugar
¼ cup corn syrup
3 eggs
2 tablespoons sour cream or plain yogurt
1 teaspoon vanilla
1 unbaked 9-inch pie shell
½ cup sliced almonds

Preheat oven to 350°F.

Microwave chocolates, margarine and instant coffee in large microwavable bowl on HIGH (100% power) 2 minutes or until margarine is melted. Stir until chocolate is completely melted.

Stir in sugar and corn syrup. Beat in eggs, sour cream and vanilla. Pour into pie shell; sprinkle with almonds.

Bake for 45 minutes or until knife inserted 1 inch from center comes out clean. Cool on wire rack.

Prep time: 15 minutes
Bake time: 45 minutes

Saucepan preparation: Heat chocolates, margarine and instant coffee in 2-quart saucepan over very low heat until just melted, stirring constantly. Remove from heat. Continue as above.

CAPPUCCINO CHEESE PIE

Makes one 9-inch pie

1 (9-inch) unbaked pastry shell, pricked
2 to 3 tablespoons coffee-flavored liqueur
1 tablespoon instant coffee or espresso powder
1 (8-ounce) package cream cheese, softened
1 (14-ounce) can EAGLE® Brand Sweetened
    Condensed Milk (NOT evaporated milk)
2 eggs
2 tablespoons unsweetened cocoa
    BORDEN® or MEADOW GOLD® Whipping
    Cream, whipped

Preheat oven to 375°F. Bake pastry shell 15 minutes; remove from oven. *Reduce oven temperature to 325°F.*

Combine liqueur and coffee, stirring until coffee dissolves. In large mixer bowl, beat cheese until fluffy.

Gradually beat in sweetened condensed milk until smooth. Add eggs, liqueur mixture and cocoa; mix well. Pour into prepared pastry shell.

Bake 40 minutes or until set. Cool. Chill thoroughly. Serve with whipped cream. Garnish as desired. Refrigerate leftovers.

CHOCOLATE CHEESE PIE

Makes 6 to 8 servings

1 package (8 ounces) cream cheese, softened
1 package (3 ounces) cream cheese, softened
¾ cup sugar
1 teaspoon vanilla extract
¼ cup HERSHEY'S Cocoa
2 eggs
½ cup whipping cream
1 packaged crumb crust (6 ounces)
    Cherry or peach pie filling

Preheat oven to 350°F. In large mixer bowl, beat cream cheese, sugar and vanilla until well blended. Blend in cocoa, scraping sides of bowl and beaters frequently. Add eggs; blend well. Blend in whipping cream. Pour into crust.

Bake 35 to 40 minutes. (Center will be soft but will set upon cooling.) Cool to room temperature. Cover; refrigerate several hours or overnight. Serve topped with pie filling. Refrigerate leftovers.

Chocolate Cheese Pie

Top to bottom: Frozen Lemon Angel Pie (page 111), Margarita Parfait Pie

MARGARITA PARFAIT PIE

Makes one 9-inch pie

1¾ cups *finely* crushed SEYFERT'S® Pretzels
¼ cup sugar
½ cup plus 2 tablespoons margarine or butter, melted
1 (14-ounce) can EAGLE® Brand Sweetened Condensed Milk (NOT evaporated milk)
¼ cup REALIME® Lime Juice from Concentrate
¼ cup tequila
2 tablespoons triple sec or other orange-flavored liqueur
1 cup chopped fresh or frozen unsweetened strawberries, thawed and *well drained*
Red food coloring (optional)
1½ cups BORDEN® or MEADOW GOLD® Whipping Cream, whipped

Combine pretzel crumbs, sugar and margarine; press firmly on bottom and up side to rim of lightly buttered 9-inch pie plate to form crust. In large bowl, combine sweetened condensed milk, ReaLime® brand, tequila and triple sec; mix well. Divide mixture in half. Add strawberries and food coloring if desired to one half of mixture. Fold half the whipped cream into each mixture. Spoon mixtures alternately into prepared crust. With table knife or metal spatula, gently swirl through mixtures to marble. Freeze 4 hours or until firm. Remove from freezer 10 minutes before serving. Garnish as desired. Freeze ungarnished leftovers.

FRESH PINEAPPLE PIE

Makes 8 servings

Nut Crust (recipe follows)
1 large DOLE® Fresh Pineapple
½ cup sugar
2 tablespoons cornstarch
1 teaspoon grated lemon peel
⅛ teaspoon ground nutmeg
1½ cups water
3 drops yellow food coloring (optional)

Prepare Nut Crust. Twist crown from pineapple. Cut pineapple lengthwise into quarters. Cut fruit from shells with knife. Trim off core and cut fruit into bite-size chunks. In large saucepan, combine sugar, cornstarch, lemon peel and nutmeg. Stir in water and food coloring. Cook, stirring constantly, until sauce boils and is clear and thick. Remove from heat. Add pineapple. Cool. Spoon pineapple mixture into prepared crust. Refrigerate, covered, overnight.

Nut Crust: Preheat oven to 400°F. In large bowl, combine 1¾ cups vanilla wafer crumbs, ⅔ cup ground toasted walnuts, 5 tablespoons melted margarine and 1 tablespoon sugar. Press onto bottom and up sides of 9-inch pie plate. Bake 8 minutes. Cool.

CHERRY ALMOND MOUSSE PIE

Makes one 9-inch pie

1 (9-inch) baked pastry shell
1 (10-ounce) jar red maraschino cherries
1 (1-ounce) square unsweetened chocolate
1 (14-ounce) can EAGLE® Brand Sweetened Condensed Milk (NOT evaporated milk)
1 teaspoon almond extract
1 (8-ounce) package cream cheese, softened
1 cup cold water
1 package (4-serving size) *instant* vanilla flavor pudding mix
1 cup (½ pint) BORDEN® or MEADOW GOLD® Whipping Cream, whipped
½ cup chopped toasted almonds
Whole almonds and chocolate curls

Drain cherries. Reserve 5 or 6 whole cherries for garnish; chop remainder and set aside. In heavy saucepan, over low heat, melt chocolate with ½ *cup* sweetened condensed milk until thickened; stir in ¼ *teaspoon* almond extract. Spread on bottom of prepared pastry shell. In large mixer bowl, beat cheese until fluffy. Gradually beat in remaining sweetened condensed milk then water, pudding mix and remaining ¾ *teaspoon* almond extract. Fold in whipped cream, chopped cherries and chopped almonds. Pour into prepared pastry shell. Chill 4 hours or until set. Garnish with reserved cherries, whole almonds and chocolate curls. Refrigerate leftovers.

CHERRY CHEESE PIE

Makes one 9-inch pie

1 (9-inch) baked pastry shell or graham cracker crumb crust
1 (8-ounce) package cream cheese, softened
1 (14-ounce) can EAGLE® Brand Sweetened Condensed Milk (NOT evaporated milk)
⅓ cup REALEMON® Lemon Juice from Concentrate
1 teaspoon vanilla extract
1 (21-ounce) can cherry pie filling, chilled

In large mixer bowl, beat cheese until fluffy. Gradually beat in sweetened condensed milk until smooth. Stir in ReaLemon® brand and vanilla. Pour into prepared crust. Chill 3 hours or until set. Top with cherry pie filling before serving. Refrigerate leftovers.

BLACKBERRY ICE CREAM PIE

Makes one 9-inch pie

CRUST
Baked 9-inch Classic CRISCO® *Single* Crust
(page 80), cooled

FILLING
1 package (3 ounces) peach or berry flavor gelatin
(not sugar-free)
1 cup boiling water
1 pint vanilla ice cream, softened
1¾ cups fresh or frozen dry pack blackberries,
partially thawed

1. For Filling, combine gelatin and water in large bowl.
Stir until dissolved. Cut ice cream into small chunks.
Add to gelatin mixture, a spoonful at a time. Blend with
wire whisk after each addition.

2. Dry blackberries between paper towels. Fold into
gelatin mixture. Spoon into cooled baked pie crust.
Refrigerate or freeze several hours before serving.

Easy Raspberry Chiffon Pie

FROZEN FLUFFY
STRAWBERRY PIE

Makes one 9-inch pie

2½ cups flaked coconut, toasted
⅓ cup margarine or butter, melted
1 (3-ounce) package cream cheese, softened
1 (14-ounce) can EAGLE® Brand Sweetened
Condensed Milk (NOT evaporated milk)
2½ cups fresh or thawed frozen unsweetened
strawberries, puréed or mashed (about 1½ cups)
3 tablespoons REALEMON® Lemon Juice from
Concentrate
1 cup (½ pint) BORDEN® or MEADOW GOLD®
Whipping Cream, whipped

Combine coconut and margarine; press firmly on bottom
and up side to rim of 9-inch pie plate. In large mixer
bowl, beat cheese until fluffy; gradually beat in sweetened
condensed milk until smooth. Stir in puréed strawberries
and ReaLemon® brand. Fold in whipped cream. Pour
into prepared crust (mixture should mound slightly).
Freeze 4 hours or until firm. Before serving, garnish
with fresh strawberries if desired. Freeze leftovers.

Tip: One (9-inch) baked pastry shell can be substituted
for coconut crust.

EASY RASPBERRY
CHIFFON PIE

Makes 8 servings

Pastry for single-crust 9-inch pie
2 cups heavy cream
6 ounces cream cheese, softened
2 teaspoons vanilla
1 jar (10 ounces) no-sugar-added raspberry fruit
spread (about 1 cup)

Preheat oven to 375°F. Roll out pastry to 11-inch circle;
place in 9-inch pie plate. Trim and flute edges; prick
bottom and sides of pastry with fork. Bake 15 minutes
or until golden brown. Cool completely on wire rack.

Beat cream in small bowl at high speed with electric
mixer until stiff peaks form; set aside. Combine cream
cheese and vanilla in medium bowl; beat until light and
fluffy. Blend in fruit spread, scraping sides of bowl
frequently. Reserve ½ cup whipped cream for garnish;
fold remaining whipped cream into cream cheese
mixture until no white streaks remain. Spread evenly
into cooled pie shell. Refrigerate at least 2 hours or up
to 24 hours. Just before serving, pipe or spoon reserved
whipped cream around edge of pie. Garnish with
raspberries and mint leaves, if desired.

Note: This is a sugar-free dessert.

CLASSIC BANANA CREAM PIE

Makes 8 servings

2 eggs
½ cup plus 2 tablespoons sugar, divided
¼ cup all-purpose flour
2 cups milk, scalded
½ cup margarine
1 tablespoon vanilla extract
5 firm, medium DOLE® Bananas
1 baked 9-inch pastry shell
1 cup whipping cream

In heavy saucepan, beat eggs, ½ cup sugar and flour until pale lemon color. Gradually beat hot milk into egg mixture. Cook, stirring constantly, over medium heat until sauce thickens, about 5 minutes. Remove from heat. Stir in margarine and vanilla until blended. Press plastic wrap directly onto surface of filling. Cool.

To assemble pie, slice bananas; reserve a few slices for garnish, if desired. Fold remaining bananas into filling; spoon into baked pastry shell. Beat cream with remaining 2 tablespoons sugar until soft peaks form. Spread on top of pie. Garnish with reserved banana slices.

BANANA CREAM CHEESE PIE

Makes one 9-inch pie

1 (9-inch) graham cracker crumb crust or baked pastry shell
1 (8-ounce) package cream cheese, softened
1 (14-ounce) can EAGLE® Brand Sweetened Condensed Milk (NOT evaporated milk)
⅓ cup REALEMON® Lemon Juice from Concentrate
1 teaspoon vanilla extract
4 medium bananas
    Additional REALEMON® Brand
    Graham cracker crumbs (optional)

In large mixer bowl, beat cheese until fluffy. Gradually beat in sweetened condensed milk until smooth. Stir in ⅓ *cup* ReaLemon® brand and vanilla. Slice *2 bananas*; dip in additional ReaLemon® brand and drain. Cover bottom of crust with banana slices. Pour filling over banana slices; cover. Chill 3 hours or until set. Before serving, slice remaining *2 bananas*; dip in additional ReaLemon® brand. Drain. Coat with crumbs if desired. Arrange banana slices on top of pie. Refrigerate leftovers.

Frozen Peach Melba Pie

FROZEN PEACH MELBA PIE

Makes 1 (9-inch) pie

2 cups *crushed* granola or natural cereal
3 tablespoons all-purpose flour
3 tablespoons margarine or butter, melted
2 teaspoons ground cinnamon
1 (10-ounce) package frozen red raspberries in syrup, thawed and drained, reserving ⅔ cup syrup
¼ cup red currant jelly or red raspberry jam
1 tablespoon cornstarch
¼ teaspoon almond extract
½ (½-gallon) carton BORDEN® or MEADOW GOLD® Peach Premium Frozen Yogurt, softened

Preheat oven to 375°F. In medium bowl, combine granola, flour, margarine and cinnamon; press onto bottom and up side to rim of 9-inch pie plate to form crust. Bake 8 to 10 minutes. Cool.

In small saucepan, combine reserved raspberry syrup, jelly and cornstarch. Over medium heat, cook and stir until slightly thickened and glossy; stir in extract and raspberries. Cool. Scoop frozen yogurt into prepared crust; top with raspberry sauce. Freeze 6 hours or until firm. Remove from freezer 5 to 10 minutes before serving. Garnish as desired. Freeze ungarnished leftovers.

Top to bottom: Frozen Lemon Satin Pie, Cookie Crust Lemon Pie (page 93)

FROZEN LEMON SATIN PIE

Makes one 9-inch pie

1 (9-inch) graham cracker crumb crust or baked
    pastry shell
1 (8-ounce) package cream cheese, softened
1 (14-ounce) can EAGLE® Brand Sweetened
    Condensed Milk (NOT evaporated milk)
½ cup cold water
¼ cup REALEMON® Lemon Juice from
    Concentrate
1 (4-serving size) package instant lemon flavor
    pudding mix
    Yellow food coloring (optional)
1 cup (½ pint) BORDEN® or MEADOW GOLD®
    Whipping Cream, whipped
    Golden Lemon Sauce (recipe follows)

In large mixer bowl, beat cheese until fluffy. Gradually beat in sweetened condensed milk until smooth. Add water, ReaLemon® brand, pudding mix and food coloring if desired; mix well. Chill 15 minutes. Fold in whipped cream. Pour into prepared crust. Freeze 6 hours or until firm. Serve with Golden Lemon Sauce. Freeze leftover pie.

Golden Lemon Sauce: In heavy saucepan, combine ⅓ cup sugar, 1 tablespoon cornstarch and dash salt. Add ½ cup water, ¼ cup ReaLemon® brand and 1 egg *yolk*; mix well. Over medium heat, cook and stir until thickened and bubbly. Remove from heat; add 1 tablespoon margarine or butter and yellow food coloring if desired. Stir until well blended. Cool slightly. Serve warm. *Makes about 1 cup*

LEMON CHIFFON PIE

Makes 8 servings

3 egg yolks, slightly beaten
1½ cups water, divided
½ cup sugar, divided
1 package (4-serving size) JELL-O® Brand Lemon
    Flavor Gelatin
1½ teaspoons grated lemon peel
3 tablespoons lemon juice
3 egg whites
1 baked 9-inch pie shell or graham cracker crumb
    crust, cooled

Combine egg yolks and 1 cup water in small saucepan; add ¼ cup sugar. Cook and stir over low heat until slightly thickened. Remove from heat. Add gelatin; stir until dissolved. Add remaining ½ cup water, lemon peel and juice. Chill until slightly thickened.

Beat egg whites until foamy. Gradually beat in remaining ¼ cup sugar; continue beating until stiff peaks form. Fold in thickened gelatin mixture until well blended. Chill until mixture will mound from spoon. Spoon into pie shell. Chill until firm, about 4 hours. Garnish as desired.

Note: Use only Grade A clean, uncracked eggs.

Prep time: 30 minutes
Chill time: 4½ hours

FROZEN LEMON ANGEL PIE

Makes one 9-inch pie

3 egg whites*
½ teaspoon vanilla extract
¼ teaspoon cream of tartar
1½ cups sugar
2 cups (1 pint) BORDEN® or MEADOW GOLD®
    Whipping Cream, *unwhipped*
½ cup REALEMON® Lemon Juice from
    Concentrate
Yellow food coloring (optional)

Preheat oven to 275°F. In small mixer bowl, beat egg whites, vanilla and cream of tartar to soft peaks. Gradually add *½ cup* sugar, beating until stiff but not dry. Spread on bottom and up side of *well-buttered* 9-inch pie plate to form crust.

Bake 1 hour. Turn oven off; leave crust in oven 1 hour. Cool to room temperature. In large mixer bowl, combine cream, remaining *1 cup* sugar, ReaLemon® brand and food coloring if desired; beat until stiff. Spoon into prepared crust. Freeze 3 hours or until firm. Garnish as desired. Freeze ungarnished leftovers.

*Use only Grade A clean, uncracked eggs.

FLUFFY ORANGE PIE

Makes one 9-inch pie

2 cups vanilla wafer crumbs (about 50 wafers)
⅓ cup margarine or butter, melted
1 (8-ounce) package cream cheese, softened
1 (14-ounce) can EAGLE® Brand Sweetened
    Condensed Milk (NOT evaporated milk)
1 (6-ounce) can frozen orange juice concentrate,
    thawed
1 cup (½ pint) BORDEN® or MEADOW GOLD®
    Whipping Cream, whipped

Combine crumbs and margarine; press firmly on bottom and up side to rim of 9-inch pie plate. Chill. Meanwhile, in large mixer bowl, beat cheese until fluffy; gradually beat in sweetened condensed milk, then juice concentrate, until smooth. Fold in whipped cream. Pour into prepared crust. Chill 2 hours or until set. Garnish as desired. Refrigerate leftovers.

KEY LIME PIE

Makes 8 servings

2 packages (4-serving size each) or 1 package
    (8-serving size) JELL-O® Brand Lime
    Flavor Gelatin
2 cups boiling water
2 teaspoons grated lime peel
¼ cup lime juice
1 pint vanilla ice cream, softened
1 packaged graham cracker crumb crust
    COOL WHIP® Non-Dairy Whipped Topping,
    thawed (optional)

Completely dissolve gelatin in boiling water. Add lime peel and juice. Spoon in ice cream, stirring until melted and smooth. Chill until mixture will mound from spoon.

Spoon gelatin mixture into crust. Chill until firm, about 2 hours. Garnish with whipped topping, if desired.

Prep time: 15 minutes
Chill time: 2 hours

ICE CREAM SHOP PIE

Makes 8 servings

1½ cups cold half-and-half or milk
1 package (4-serving size) JELL-O® Instant
    Pudding and Pie Filling, any flavor
3½ cups (8 ounces) COOL WHIP® Non-Dairy
    Whipped Topping, thawed
    Ice Cream Shop Ingredients*
1 packaged chocolate, graham cracker or vanilla
    crumb crust

Pour half-and-half into large bowl. Add pudding mix. Beat with wire whisk until well blended, 1 to 2 minutes. Let stand 5 minutes or until slightly thickened.

Fold whipped topping and desired Ice Cream Shop Ingredients into pudding mixture. Spoon into crust.

Freeze pie until firm, about 6 hours or overnight. Remove from freezer. Let stand at room temperature about 10 minutes before serving to soften. Store any leftover pie in freezer.

Prep time: 15 minutes
Freezing time: 6 hours

*Rocky Road Pie: Use any chocolate flavor pudding mix and chocolate crumb crust. Fold in ½ cup *each* BAKER'S® Semi-Sweet Real Chocolate Chips, KRAFT® Miniature Marshmallows and chopped nuts with whipped topping. Serve with chocolate sauce, if desired.

*Toffee Bar Crunch Pie: Use French vanilla or vanilla flavor pudding mix and graham cracker crumb crust, spreading ⅓ cup butterscotch sauce onto bottom of crust before filling. Fold in 1 cup chopped chocolate-covered English toffee bars (about 6 bars) with whipped topping. Garnish with additional chopped toffee bars, if desired.

*Strawberry Banana Split Pie: Use French vanilla or vanilla flavor pudding mix, reducing half-and-half to ¾ cup and adding ¾ cup puréed BIRDS EYE® Quick Thaw Strawberries with the half-and-half. Use vanilla crumb crust and line bottom with banana slices. Garnish with whipped topping, maraschino cherries and chopped nuts. Serve with additional puréed strawberries if desired.

*Chocolate Cookie Pie: Use French vanilla or vanilla flavor pudding mix and chocolate crumb crust. Fold in 1 cup chopped chocolate sandwich cookies with whipped topping.

*Nutcracker Pie: Use butter pecan flavor pudding mix and graham cracker crumb crust. Fold in 1 cup chopped mixed nuts with whipped topping.

*Peppermint Stick Pie: Use French vanilla or vanilla flavor pudding mix and chocolate crumb crust. Fold in ½ cup crushed hard peppermint candies, ½ cup BAKER'S® Semi-Sweet Real Chocolate Chips and 2 teaspoons peppermint extract with whipped topping.

ANY SEASON LIGHT AND FRUITY PIE

Makes 8 servings

1 package (4-serving size) JELL-O® Brand Gelatin,
    any flavor
⅔ cup boiling water
½ cup cold water
    Ice cubes
3½ cups (8 ounces) COOL WHIP® Non-Dairy
    Whipped Topping, thawed
    Any Season Ingredients*
1 packaged graham cracker crumb crust

Completely dissolve gelatin in boiling water. Combine cold water and enough ice cubes to measure 1¼ cups. Add to gelatin; stir until slightly thickened. Remove any unmelted ice.

Blend whipped topping into gelatin using wire whisk. Fold in Any Season Ingredients. Chill until mixture is very thick.

Spoon gelatin mixture into crust. Chill 2 hours. Garnish with additional fruit and whipped topping, if desired.

Prep time: 20 minutes
Chill time: 2 hours

*Citrus Snowflake Pie (Winter): Use orange flavor gelatin. Fold in 1 cup drained mandarin orange sections, 1 small banana, sliced, and 2 tablespoons orange-flavored liqueur (optional). Garnish with additional whipped topping, mandarin orange sections and toasted coconut, if desired.

*Any Berry Pie (Spring): Use raspberry or strawberry flavor gelatin. Fold in ½ cup *each* blueberries, raspberries and sliced strawberries with 2 tablespoons raspberry-flavored liqueur (optional). Garnish with additional whipped topping and berries, if desired.

*Creamy Daiquiri Pie (Summer): Use lime flavor gelatin. Fold in ½ teaspoon grated lime peel, 2 tablespoons lime juice and 3 tablespoons rum (optional). Garnish with additional whipped topping and citrus curls, if desired.

*Autumn Harvest Pie (Fall): Use lemon flavor gelatin. Fold in 1 ripe pear, chopped, and 1 tablespoon lemon juice. Garnish with additional whipped topping and lemon slices, if desired.

Ice Cream Shop Pies: Rocky Road Pie (top), Toffee Bar Crunch Pie (center), Strawberry Banana Split Pie (bottom)

Quick Butterscotch Ice Cream Pie

QUICK BUTTERSCOTCH ICE CREAM PIE

Makes 8 to 10 servings

CRUST:
1½ cups chopped toasted pecans, divided
1 cup graham cracker crumbs
⅓ cup butter, melted

FILLING:
½ cup sugar
½ cup water
1 cup (½ of a 12-ounce package) NESTLÉ® Toll
    House® Butterscotch Flavored Morsels
2 eggs*
½ teaspoon salt
⅛ teaspoon nutmeg
1¾ cups heavy cream, whipped

Crust: In small bowl, combine ½ cup pecans, graham cracker crumbs and butter; mix well. Press crumb mixture into 9-inch pie plate; set aside.

Filling: In small saucepan, combine sugar and water. Bring to a boil over medium heat; boil 3 minutes. Remove from heat. In blender container, combine Nestlé® Toll House® Butterscotch Flavored Morsels and sugar mixture; cover and blend at high speed 30 seconds. Add eggs, salt and nutmeg; cover and blend at high speed 1 minute. Cool to room temperature. Fold into whipped cream. Spoon half of filling into prepared crust. Sprinkle ½ cup pecans over top; cover with remaining filling. Garnish with remaining ½ cup pecans. Freeze several hours or until firm.

*Use clean, uncracked eggs.

QUICK BUTTERSCOTCH CHEESE PIE

Makes one 9-inch pie

1 (9-inch) baked pastry shell or graham cracker
    crumb crust
1 (8-ounce) package cream cheese, softened
1 (14-ounce) can EAGLE® Brand Sweetened
    Condensed Milk (NOT evaporated milk)
¾ cup cold water
1 (4-serving size) package *instant* butterscotch
    flavor pudding mix
1 cup (½ pint) BORDEN® or MEADOW GOLD®
    Whipping Cream, whipped

In large mixer bowl, beat cheese until fluffy; gradually beat in sweetened condensed milk until smooth. On low speed, beat in water and pudding mix until smooth. Fold in whipped cream. Pour into prepared pastry shell. Chill 2 hours or until set. Garnish as desired. Refrigerate leftovers.

Chocolate Cheese Pie: Substitute *instant* chocolate flavor pudding mix for butterscotch. Add ¼ cup unsweetened cocoa with pudding mix. Proceed as above.

Coconut Cheese Pie: Substitute *instant* coconut cream flavor pudding mix for butterscotch. Fold in ½ cup flaked coconut with whipped cream. Proceed as above.

FLUFFY GRASSHOPPER PIE

Makes one 9-inch pie

2 cups finely crushed creme-filled chocolate
    sandwich cookies (about 20 cookies)
¼ cup margarine or butter, melted
1 (8-ounce) package cream cheese, softened
1 (14-ounce) can EAGLE® Brand Sweetened
    Condensed Milk (NOT evaporated milk)
3 tablespoons REALEMON® Lemon Juice from
    Concentrate
¼ cup green creme de menthe liqueur
¼ cup white creme de cacao liqueur
1 (4-ounce) container frozen non-dairy whipped
    topping, thawed *or* 1 cup (½ pint) BORDEN®
    or MEADOW GOLD® Whipping Cream,
    whipped

Combine crumbs and margarine; press firmly on bottom and up side to rim of buttered 9-inch pie plate. Chill. Meanwhile, in large mixer bowl, beat cheese until fluffy; gradually beat in sweetened condensed milk until smooth. Stir in ReaLemon® brand and liqueurs. Fold in whipped topping. Chill 20 minutes; pour into crust. Chill or freeze 4 hours or until set. Garnish as desired. Refrigerate or freeze leftovers.

ALMOND GINGER ICE CREAM PIE

Makes 8 to 10 servings

Almond Crust (recipe follows)
1 can (20 ounces) DOLE® Crushed Pineapple in Juice
1 quart vanilla ice cream, softened
½ cup DOLE® Blanched Slivered Almonds, toasted
¼ cup crystallized ginger, chopped
3 tablespoons almond-flavored liqueur
1 tablespoon grated orange peel

Prepare Almond Crust. Drain pineapple; reserve all but ½ cup juice. In large bowl, combine pineapple, reserved juice and remaining ingredients. Spoon into prepared crust; freeze overnight or until firm. Let soften slightly before slicing. Garnish as desired.

Almond Crust: In medium bowl, combine 1½ cups vanilla wafer crumbs, ⅔ cup toasted ground Dole® Almonds and ¼ cup melted margarine. Press onto bottom and up sides of 9-inch pie plate. Freeze until ready to use.

Fluffy Grasshopper Pie

PIÑA COLADA PIE

Makes 8 servings

1 can (20 ounces) DOLE® Crushed Pineapple in Juice, drained
3 tablespoons dark rum
3 tablespoons canned cream of coconut
1 quart vanilla ice cream, softened
Flaked coconut (optional)
DOLE® Pineapple (optional)

COCONUT CRUST
1½ cups vanilla wafer crumbs
1 cup flaked coconut, toasted (see Tip)
⅓ cup margarine, melted

Stir crushed pineapple, rum and cream of coconut into ice cream in large bowl. Freeze until ice cream holds shape.

Combine all crust ingredients in medium bowl. Press onto bottom and up side of 9-inch pie plate. Place in freezer until firm. Spoon filling into crust. Cover with plastic wrap and freeze overnight or until firm enough to cut. Garnish with additional coconut and pineapple, if desired.

Tip: To toast coconut, spread coconut on baking sheet. Bake at 350°F for 7 to 15 minutes or until golden, stirring frequently; cool.

HAWAIIAN CREAM PIE

Makes one 9-inch pie

2½ cups flaked coconut, toasted
⅓ cup margarine or butter, melted
1 (8-ounce) package cream cheese, softened
1 (14-ounce) can EAGLE® Brand Sweetened Condensed Milk (NOT evaporated milk)
1 (6-ounce) can frozen pineapple-orange juice concentrate, thawed
1 (8-ounce) can crushed pineapple, *well drained*
1 tablespoon grated orange peel
1 cup (½ pint) BORDEN® or MEADOW GOLD® Whipping Cream, whipped
Orange and pineapple slices

Combine coconut and margarine; press firmly on bottom and up side to rim of 9-inch pie plate. Chill. Meanwhile, in large mixer bowl, beat cheese until fluffy. Gradually beat in sweetened condensed milk, then juice concentrate, until smooth. Stir in crushed pineapple and orange peel. Fold in whipped cream. Pour into prepared crust. Chill or freeze 6 hours or until firm. Garnish with orange and pineapple slices. Refrigerate or freeze leftovers.

FLUFFY BLACK BOTTOM PIES

Makes 2 pies, 16 servings

1 package DUNCAN HINES® Fudge Brownie
    Mix, Family Size

FILLING
5½ cups (10½-ounce bag) miniature marshmallows
  1 cup milk
  ¼ teaspoon salt
  2 cups whipping cream, chilled
1½ teaspoons vanilla extract
  3 squares (1 ounce each) semi-sweet chocolate,
    coarsely chopped

TOPPING
1 tablespoon unsweetened cocoa, sifted
1 container (8 ounces) frozen whipped topping,
  thawed
  Semi-sweet chocolate shavings, for garnish
  Maraschino cherries, well drained, for garnish

1. Preheat oven to 350°F. Grease bottoms of two
9-inch pie pans.

2. Prepare brownies following package directions for
basic recipe. Spread half the batter evenly in each
pie pan.

3. Bake at 350°F for 17 minutes or until set. Cool
completely.

4. For Filling, combine marshmallows, milk and salt
in medium saucepan. Cook over low heat, stirring
constantly, until marshmallows are melted. Pour
mixture into large bowl. Refrigerate until set. Beat
whipping cream and vanilla extract in large bowl until
stiff peaks form. Fold whipped cream mixture and
chopped chocolate into marshmallow mixture. Pour half
the mixture evenly over each brownie crust. Refrigerate
at least 4 hours or until set.

5. For Topping, fold cocoa into whipped topping until
blended. Garnish pies with whipped topping mixture,
chocolate shavings and maraschino cherries. Refrigerate
until ready to serve.

Tip: For large chocolate shavings, use a vegetable
peeler; for fine chocolate shavings, use a hand grater.

Frozen Strawberry Fudge Pie

FROZEN STRAWBERRY
FUDGE PIE

Makes one 9-inch pie

2 (10-ounce packages) frozen quick thaw
  strawberries, thawed and drained
¼ cup corn syrup
1 (12-ounce container) frozen non-dairy whipped
  topping, thawed, divided
1 (9-inch) prepared chocolate crumb crust
1 cup (6-ounce package) NESTLÉ® Toll House®
  Semi-Sweet Chocolate Morsels

Place drained strawberries in blender or food processor
container. Cover; process until smooth. Transfer to
large bowl. Add corn syrup; mix well. Fold in 2 cups
whipped topping. Spoon into crust. Freeze until firm,
about 1½ hours. Combine over hot (not boiling) water,
1 cup whipped topping and Nestlé® Toll House® Semi-
Sweet Chocolate Morsels; stir until morsels are melted
and mixture is smooth. Spread evenly over strawberry
layer. Freeze until firm, about 1½ hours. Garnish with
remaining whipped topping and chocolate-dipped
strawberries, if desired.

ELEGANT RASPBERRY CHOCOLATE PIE

Makes 8 servings

1 package (4-serving size) JELL-O® Brand
    Raspberry Flavor Gelatin
1¼ cups boiling water
1 pint vanilla ice cream, softened
1 packaged chocolate crumb crust
3 tablespoons PARKAY® Margarine
2 squares BAKER'S® Semi-Sweet Chocolate
    COOL WHIP® Non-Dairy Whipped Topping,
    thawed (optional)
    Raspberries (optional)·

Completely dissolve gelatin in boiling water. Spoon in ice cream, stirring until melted and smooth. Chill until slightly thickened, about 10 minutes. Pour into crust. Chill until firm, about 2 hours.

Melt margarine with chocolate; cool. Spread over pie. Chill until chocolate mixture hardens. Garnish with whipped topping and raspberries, if desired.

Note: For ease in serving, let pie stand 5 minutes after spreading on chocolate. With knife, lightly score pie into serving-size pieces. Chill as directed above.

Prep time: 15 minutes
Chill time: 2½ hours

Elegant Raspberry Chocolate Pie

CHOCOLATE PEANUT BUTTER PIE

Makes 10 to 12 servings

¾ cup (1½ sticks) margarine or butter, softened
¾ cup peanut butter
½ cup firmly packed brown sugar
5¼ cups (12 ounces) COOL WHIP® Non-Dairy
    Whipped Topping, thawed, divided
    Chocolate Nut Crust (recipe follows)
    Peanuts (optional)
2 squares BAKER'S® Semi-Sweet Chocolate,
    melted (optional)

Beat margarine, peanut butter and sugar in large bowl until well blended. Reserve ¼ cup whipped topping for garnish. Gently stir in remaining 5 cups whipped topping until mixture is smooth and creamy. Spoon into Chocolate Nut Crust.

Refrigerate until firm, about 4 hours. Garnish with reserved whipped topping. Sprinkle with peanuts and drizzle melted chocolate over whipped topping, if desired.

Prep time: 20 minutes
Chill time: 4 hours

CHOCOLATE NUT CRUST

6 squares BAKER'S® Semi-Sweet Chocolate
1 tablespoon margarine or butter
1½ cups toasted finely chopped nuts

Line 9-inch pie plate with foil.

Microwave chocolate and margarine in large microwavable bowl on HIGH (100% power) 2 minutes or until margarine is melted. Stir until chocolate is completely melted.

Stir in nuts. Press mixture onto bottom and up sides of prepared pie plate. Refrigerate until firm, about 1 hour. Remove crust from pie plate; peel off foil. Return crust to pie plate or place on serving plate. Refrigerate.

Makes 1 (9-inch) crust

Prep time: 15 minutes
Chill time: 1 hour

Microwave Chocolate Mousse Pie

MICROWAVE CHOCOLATE MOUSSE PIE

Makes one 9-inch pie

1 (9-inch) baked pastry shell
4 (1-ounce) squares unsweetened chocolate
1 (14-ounce) can EAGLE® Brand Sweetened
   Condensed Milk (NOT evaporated milk)
2 teaspoons vanilla extract
2 cups (1 pint) BORDEN® or MEADOW GOLD®
   Whipping Cream, whipped

To Microwave: In 2-quart glass measure with handle, combine chocolate, sweetened condensed milk and vanilla; cook on 100% power (high) 2 to 4 minutes, stirring after each minute until chocolate is melted and mixture is smooth. Cool to room temperature, about 1½ hours. Beat until smooth. Fold in whipped cream. Pour into pastry shell. Chill 4 hours or until set. Garnish as desired. Refrigerate leftovers.

CHOCOLATE MOUSSE PIE

Makes 6 to 8 servings

1 envelope unflavored gelatin
2 tablespoons cold water
¼ cup boiling water
1 cup sugar
½ cup HERSHEY'S Cocoa
2 cups (1 pint) chilled whipping cream
2 teaspoons vanilla extract
1 packaged chocolate-flavored crumb crust
   (6 ounces)

In small bowl, sprinkle gelatin over cold water; let stand 5 minutes to soften. Add boiling water; stir until gelatin is completely dissolved and mixture is clear. Cool slightly. In large mixer bowl, stir together sugar and cocoa; add whipping cream and vanilla. Beat on medium speed of electric mixer, scraping bottom of bowl often, until stiff. Pour gelatin mixture into whipped cream mixture; beat until well blended. Spoon into crust. Cover; refrigerate at least 2 hours. Garnish as desired.

FROZEN CHOCOLATE MOUSSE PIE

Makes one 9-inch pie

2 cups finely crushed creme-filled chocolate
   sandwich cookies (about 20 cookies)
¼ cup margarine or butter, melted
1 (6-ounce) package semi-sweet chocolate chips
   (1 cup), *or* 4 (1-ounce) squares semi-sweet
   chocolate, melted
1 (14-ounce) can EAGLE® Brand Sweetened
   Condensed Milk (NOT evaporated milk)
1½ teaspoons vanilla extract
1 cup (½ pint) BORDEN® or MEADOW GOLD®
   Whipping Cream, stiffly whipped

Combine crumbs and margarine; press on bottom and up side to rim of lightly buttered 9-inch pie plate. Chill. In large mixer bowl, beat chocolate with sweetened condensed milk and vanilla until well blended. Chill 10 to 15 minutes. Fold in whipped cream. Pour into prepared crust. Freeze 6 hours or until firm. Garnish as desired. Freeze leftovers.

DOUBLE CHOCOLATE ALASKA PIE

Makes 6 to 8 servings

CRUST
⅓ cup margarine or butter, melted
¼ cup firmly packed brown sugar
1 tablespoon unsweetened cocoa
4 cups Rice CHEX® Brand Cereal, crushed to 1 cup

FILLING-MERINGUE
1 quart chocolate ice cream, softened
3 egg whites
½ teaspoon vanilla extract
¼ teaspoon cream of tartar
6 tablespoons granulated sugar

For Crust, preheat oven to 300°F. Grease 9-inch pie plate. Combine margarine, brown sugar and cocoa in large bowl. Add cereal; mix thoroughly. Press evenly onto bottom and up side of prepared pie plate. Bake 10 minutes. Cool completely.

For Filling, fill crust with ice cream. Freeze until firm, 6 hours or overnight.

For Meringue, beat egg whites with vanilla and cream of tartar in medium bowl until soft peaks form. Gradually add granulated sugar. Beat until stiff and glossy and sugar is dissolved. Spread meringue over ice cream. Seal to edges* and freeze.

At serving time, bake in preheated 475°F oven about 2½ minutes or until very lightly browned. Watch closely. Serve immediately.

*May be baked at this point according to above directions and frozen. Let stand a few minutes before serving.

Note: Best if stored in freezer no longer than 2 days.

GERMAN SWEET CHOCOLATE PIE

Makes 8 servings

1 package (4 ounces) BAKER'S® GERMAN'S® Sweet Chocolate
⅓ cup milk, divided
1 package (3 ounces) PHILADELPHIA BRAND® Cream Cheese, softened
2 tablespoons sugar (optional)
3½ cups (8 ounces) COOL WHIP® Non-Dairy Whipped Topping, thawed
1 (9-inch) prepared crumb crust

Microwave chocolate and 2 tablespoons milk in large microwavable bowl on HIGH (100% power) 1½ to 2 minutes or until chocolate is almost melted, stirring halfway through heating time. Stir until chocolate is completely melted.

Beat in cream cheese, sugar and remaining milk until well blended. Refrigerate until cool, about 10 minutes.

Gently stir in whipped topping until smooth. Spoon into crust. Freeze until firm, about 4 hours. Garnish as desired.

Prep time: 20 minutes
Freezing time: 4 hours

Saucepan preparation: Heat chocolate and 2 tablespoons milk in saucepan over very low heat until chocolate is melted, stirring constantly. Remove from heat. Continue as above.

German Sweet Chocolate Pie

Top to bottom: Cocoa Cloud Pie (page 122),
Peanut Butter Tart, Individual Chocolate Cream Pies

FROZEN PEANUT BUTTER PIE

Makes one 9- or 10-inch pie

Chocolate Crunch Crust (recipe follows)
1 (8-ounce) package cream cheese, softened
1 (14-ounce) can EAGLE® Brand Sweetened
　Condensed Milk (NOT evaporated milk)
¾ cup peanut butter
2 tablespoons REALEMON® Lemon Juice from
　Concentrate
1 teaspoon vanilla extract
1 cup (½ pint) BORDEN® or MEADOW GOLD®
　Whipping Cream, whipped, *or* 1 (4-ounce)
　container frozen non-dairy whipped topping,
　thawed
Chocolate fudge ice cream topping

Prepare Chocolate Crunch Crust. In large mixer bowl, beat cheese until fluffy. Gradually beat in sweetened condensed milk, then peanut butter until smooth. Stir in ReaLemon® brand and vanilla. Fold in whipped cream. Spoon into prepared crust. Drizzle fudge topping over pie. Freeze 4 hours or until firm. Return leftovers to freezer.

Chocolate Crunch Crust: In heavy saucepan, over low heat, melt ⅓ cup margarine or butter and 1 (6-ounce) package semi-sweet chocolate chips. Remove from heat; gently stir in 2½ cups oven-toasted rice cereal until completely coated. Press on bottom and up side to rim of buttered 9- or 10-inch pie plate. Chill 30 minutes.

PEANUT BUTTER TARTS

Makes 6 servings

1 package (3½ ounces) instant vanilla pudding and
　pie filling
1½ cups milk, divided
1 cup REESE'S® Peanut Butter Chips
6 single-serve graham cracker crumb crusts
　(4-ounce package)
Whipped topping
Fresh fruit

In small mixer bowl, blend pudding mix and 1 cup milk; set aside. In top of double boiler over hot, not boiling, water, melt peanut butter chips with remaining ½ cup milk, stirring constantly to blend. (Or, in small microwave-safe bowl, place chips and ½ cup milk. Microwave at HIGH [100% power] 45 seconds; stir. If necessary, microwave at HIGH additional 15 seconds or until melted and smooth when stirred.) Gradually add to pudding, blending well. Spoon into crusts. Cover; refrigerate until set. Garnish with whipped topping and fruit.

INDIVIDUAL CHOCOLATE CREAM PIES

Makes 6 servings

1½ ounces (½ of 3-ounce package) cream cheese,
　softened
6 tablespoons sugar
½ teaspoon vanilla extract
2½ tablespoons HERSHEY'S Cocoa
2½ tablespoons milk
1 cup (½ pint) chilled whipping cream
6 single-serve graham cracker crumb crusts
　(4-ounce package)
Whipped topping
HERSHEY'S MINI CHIPS® Semi-Sweet
　Chocolate

In small mixer bowl, beat cream cheese, sugar and vanilla until well blended. Add cocoa alternately with milk, beating until smooth. In small mixer bowl, beat whipping cream until stiff; fold into chocolate mixture. Spoon into crusts. Cover; refrigerate until set. Garnish with whipped topping and small chocolate chips.

PISTACHIO CHOCOLATE CRUNCH PIE

Makes one 9-inch pie

½ cup blanched almonds
2 cups (1 pint) sour cream, divided
2 cups cold milk, divided
1 package (4-serving size) JELL-O® Pistachio
　Flavor Instant Pudding and Pie Filling
1 baked 9-inch pie shell, cooled
1 cup thawed COOL WHIP® Non-Dairy Whipped
　Topping
1 cup graham cracker or vanilla or chocolate wafer
　crumbs
1 package (4-serving size) JELL-O® Chocolate
　Flavor Instant Pudding and Pie Filling

Preheat oven to 350°F. Toast almonds in shallow pan 3 to 5 minutes, stirring once. Chop nuts; set aside. Place 1 cup sour cream and 1 cup milk in medium bowl. Add pistachio flavor pudding mix. With electric mixer at low speed, beat for 1 minute. Pour into pie shell. Spread whipped topping over filling; sprinkle with nuts and crumbs.

Place remaining 1 cup sour cream and remaining 1 cup milk in another medium bowl. Add chocolate flavor pudding mix. With electric mixer at low speed, beat for 1 minute. Spoon over nuts and crumbs. Chill about 4 hours. Garnish with additional whipped topping and multi-colored sprinkles, if desired.

COCOA CLOUD PIE

Makes 6 to 8 servings

2 packages (3 ounces each) cream cheese, softened
1 cup powdered sugar
2 teaspoons vanilla extract
½ cup HERSHEY'S Cocoa
¼ cup milk
2 cups (1 pint) chilled whipping cream
1 packaged graham cracker crumb crust (6 ounces)

In large mixer bowl, beat cream cheese, powdered sugar and vanilla until well blended. Add cocoa alternately with milk, beating until smooth. Gradually add whipping cream, beating until stiff. Spoon into crust. Cover; refrigerate several hours or overnight. Garnish as desired.

CHOCOLATE COFFEE PIE

Makes one 9-inch pie

CRUST

1¼ cups chocolate wafer crumbs
¼ cup (½ stick) butter, melted

FILLING

2 pints coffee ice cream, softened, divided
½ cup chocolate fudge topping, divided
⅓ cup chopped salted nuts, divided
1 pint chocolate ice cream, softened
1 cup whipping cream
2 tablespoons confectioners' sugar
2 tablespoons unsweetened cocoa powder

For Crust, combine crumbs and butter. Press mixture firmly on bottom and up sides of a 9-inch pie plate. Freeze until firm.

For Filling, spread 1 pint coffee ice cream over crust. Spread half the chocolate topping over coffee ice cream; sprinkle with half the nuts. Freeze until firm, about 1 hour. Spread chocolate ice cream over nuts and topping. Top with remaining ¼ cup chocolate topping and nuts. Freeze until firm, about 1 hour. Spread remaining coffee ice cream over nuts and topping. Freeze several hours or overnight.

Combine whipping cream, sugar and cocoa in small bowl. Cover; refrigerate 30 minutes. Whip cream mixture until stiff. Swirl over top of pie. Freeze until whipped cream mixture is firm, at least 1 hour. To serve, let stand at room temperature about 15 minutes; cut into small wedges.

Favorite recipe from **American Dairy Association**

Black Forest Pie

BLACK FOREST PIE

Makes one 9- or 10-inch pie

1 (9- or 10-inch) baked pastry shell
4 (1-ounce) squares unsweetened chocolate
1 (14-ounce) can EAGLE® Brand Sweetened
  Condensed Milk (NOT evaporated milk)
1 teaspoon almond extract
1½ cups BORDEN® or MEADOW GOLD®
  Whipping Cream, whipped
1 (21-ounce) can cherry pie filling, chilled
  Toasted sliced almonds (optional)

In heavy saucepan, over medium-low heat, melt chocolate with sweetened condensed milk. Remove from heat; stir in extract. Pour into large bowl; cool or chill thoroughly. Beat until smooth. Gradually fold in whipped cream. Pour into prepared pastry shell. Chill 4 hours or until set. Top with pie filling. Garnish with almonds if desired. Refrigerate leftovers.

Microwave Tip: In 1-quart glass measure with handle, combine chocolate and sweetened condensed milk. Cook on 100% power (high) 2 to 4 minutes, stirring after each minute until smooth. Proceed as above.

CLASSIC MUD PIE

Makes one 9-inch pie

CHOCOLATE COOKIE CRUST:
2 cups (12-ounce package) NESTLÉ® Toll House®
    Semi-Sweet Chocolate Morsels, divided
3 tablespoons butter
1¼ cups chocolate wafer crumbs

FUDGE SAUCE:
1½ cups NESTLÉ® Toll House® Semi-Sweet
    Chocolate Morsels, reserved from
    12-ounce package
½ cup heavy cream
3 tablespoons butter
1 tablespoon coffee-flavored liqueur

FILLING:
1 quart coffee ice cream, softened
2 tablespoons coffee-flavored liqueur

Chocolate Cookie Crust: Combine over hot (not boiling) water, ½ cup Nestlé® Toll House® Semi-Sweet Chocolate Morsels and butter; stir until morsels are melted and mixture is smooth. Add chocolate wafer crumbs; stir until well blended. Press on bottom and up side of 9-inch pie pan. Refrigerate until firm, 35 to 45 minutes.

Fudge Sauce: Combine over hot (not boiling) water, remaining 1½ cups Nestlé® Toll House® Semi-Sweet Chocolate Morsels, heavy cream and butter. Stir until morsels are melted and mixture is smooth. Remove from heat; stir in coffee-flavored liqueur. Refrigerate 10 minutes. Spread ½ cup sauce over bottom of prepared Chocolate Cookie Crust. Refrigerate 15 minutes.

Filling: In large bowl, combine ice cream and coffee-flavored liqueur. Spoon over Fudge Sauce layer. Freeze several hours or until firm. Reheat remaining Fudge Sauce over hot (not boiling) water. Serve pie with warm Fudge Sauce. Top with whipped cream, if desired.

CHOCOLATE MINT DREAM PIE

Makes 8 servings

2 envelopes DREAM WHIP® Whipped
    Topping Mix
2½ cups cold milk, divided
2 packages (4-serving size) JELL-O® Chocolate
    Flavor Instant Pudding and Pie Filling
3 tablespoons white creme de menthe liqueur*
1 packaged chocolate crumb crust
    Mint leaves (optional)

Combine whipped topping mix with 1 cup milk in large bowl. Beat at high speed with electric mixer until topping thickens and forms stiff peaks, about 6 minutes. Add remaining 1½ cups milk, pudding mix and liqueur; blend at low speed. Beat at high speed for 2 minutes, scraping sides of bowl occasionally.

Spoon filling mixture into crust. Chill at least 4 hours or overnight. Garnish with additional whipped topping and mint leaves, if desired.

* ¼ teaspoon peppermint extract may be substituted for creme de menthe liqueur.

Prep time: 10 minutes
Chill time: 4 hours

Classic Mud Pie

FROZEN & CHILLED DESSERTS

HOT FUDGE SUNDAE CAKE

Makes 12 to 16 servings

1 package DUNCAN HINES® Moist Deluxe
    Dark Dutch Fudge Cake Mix
½ gallon brick vanilla ice cream

FUDGE SAUCE
 1 can (12 ounces) evaporated milk
1¾ cups sugar
 4 squares (1 ounce each) unsweetened chocolate
 ¼ cup butter or margarine
1½ teaspoons vanilla extract
 ¼ teaspoon salt
    Whipped cream, maraschino cherries and mint
    leaves for garnish

1. Preheat oven to 350°F. Grease and flour 13×9-inch pan.

2. Prepare, bake and cool cake following package directions for basic recipe.

3. Remove cake from pan. Split cake in half horizontally. Place bottom layer back in pan. Cut ice cream into even slices and place evenly over bottom cake layer (use all the ice cream). Place remaining cake layer over ice cream. Cover and freeze until firm.

4. For Fudge Sauce, combine evaporated milk and sugar in medium saucepan. Stir constantly over medium heat until mixture comes to a rolling boil. Boil and stir for 1 minute. Add unsweetened chocolate and stir until melted. Beat over medium heat until smooth. Remove from heat. Stir in butter, vanilla and salt.

5. To serve, cut cake into serving squares. Spoon hot fudge sauce on top of each cake square. Garnish with whipped cream, maraschino cherries and mint leaves, if desired.

PEACH ICE CREAM CHARLOTTE

Makes 1 cake

1 package (3 ounces) ladyfingers, thawed if frozen
    and split in half horizontally
1 quart peach ice cream, softened
¼ cup chopped almonds, toasted
3 tablespoons almond-flavored liqueur *or*
    2 teaspoons almond extract
1 cup whipping cream
1 tablespoon confectioners' sugar
¼ teaspoon almond extract
    Sliced almonds
    Sliced peaches

Butter bottom and side of charlotte mold or 2½-quart bowl. Line side and bottom with ladyfingers, cut side facing in; set aside. Combine peach ice cream, chopped almonds and liqueur in medium bowl. Spoon into mold. Cover; freeze several hours or overnight. Remove mold from freezer; dip in warm water. Unmold onto serving plate. Return to freezer up to 3 hours. Just before serving, combine whipping cream, sugar and extract in large bowl. Beat until stiff peaks form. Pipe through pastry tube fitted with fluted tip onto top of mold. Garnish with sliced almonds and peaches. Serve immediately.

Favorite recipe from **American Dairy Association**

Hot Fudge Sundae Cake

Chocolate Frozen Dessert

CHOCOLATE FROZEN DESSERT

Makes 16 to 18 servings

1 package (16 ounces) chocolate sandwich cookies, crushed (about 1¾ cups)
½ cup (1 stick) butter or margarine, melted
½ gallon vanilla ice cream (in rectangular block)
Chocolate Sauce (recipe follows)
⅔ cup pecan pieces (optional)

In medium bowl, stir together crushed cookies and butter. Press mixture onto bottom of 13×9-inch pan or two 8-inch square pans. Cut ice cream into 1-inch slices; place over crust. Cover; freeze 1 to 2 hours or until firm. Uncover pan; pour Chocolate Sauce over ice cream. Sprinkle pecan pieces over top, if desired. Cover; freeze until firm.

CHOCOLATE SAUCE

2 cups powdered sugar
1½ cups (12-ounce can) evaporated milk
1 cup HERSHEY'S Semi-Sweet Chocolate Chips
½ cup butter or margarine

In medium saucepan, combine powdered sugar, evaporated milk, chocolate chips and butter. Cook over medium heat, stirring constantly, until mixture boils; boil and stir 8 minutes. Remove from heat; cool slightly.

Makes about 2½ cups

LEMON CREAM DESSERT

Makes 9 to 12 servings

2 cups vanilla wafer crumbs
1 cup MIRACLE WHIP® Salad Dressing, divided
1 (12-ounce) container (4½ cups) frozen whipped topping, thawed
1 (6-ounce) can frozen lemonade or limeade concentrate, softened

Preheat oven to 350°F. Combine crumbs and ½ cup salad dressing in medium bowl; mix well. Press mixture onto bottom of 8-inch square baking pan. Bake 10 minutes. Cool.

Combine remaining ½ cup salad dressing, whipped topping and lemonade concentrate in another medium bowl, mixing until well blended. Spoon over crust; cover tightly. Freeze until firm. Place in refrigerator 10 minutes before cutting into squares to serve. Garnish as desired.

Prep time: 20 minutes plus freezing

Variation: Substitute strawberry or peach daiquiri frozen concentrate mix for lemonade concentrate.

BROWNIE MINT SUNDAE SQUARES

Makes 10 to 12 servings

1 (21.5-ounce) package fudge brownie mix
¾ cup coarsely chopped walnuts
1 (14-ounce) can EAGLE® Brand Sweetened Condensed Milk (NOT evaporated milk)
2 teaspoons peppermint extract
4 to 6 drops green food coloring (optional)
2 cups (1 pint) BORDEN® or MEADOW GOLD® Whipping Cream, whipped
½ cup mini chocolate chips
Hot fudge sauce or chocolate-flavored syrup

Prepare brownie mix as package directs; stir in walnuts. Turn into aluminum foil-lined and greased 13×9-inch baking pan. Bake as directed. Cool completely. In large bowl, combine sweetened condensed milk, peppermint extract and food coloring if desired. Fold in whipped cream and chips. Pour over cooled brownie layer. Cover; freeze 6 hours or until firm. To serve, lift from pan with foil; cut into squares. Serve with hot fudge sauce. Garnish as desired. Freeze leftovers.

PINEAPPLE PARFAIT SQUARES

Makes 9 to 12 servings

1 (20-ounce) can crushed pineapple, well drained
1 (16-ounce) container BORDEN® Sour Cream
1 (14-ounce) can EAGLE® Brand Sweetened
    Condensed Milk (NOT evaporated milk)
¼ cup REALEMON® Lemon Juice from
    Concentrate
¾ cup chopped pecans
12 maraschino cherries

In large bowl, combine pineapple, sour cream, sweetened condensed milk and ReaLemon® brand; mix well. Spread into 8-inch square pan; garnish with nuts and cherries. Cover; freeze 3 hours or until firm. Remove from freezer 10 minutes before serving. Cut into squares. Freeze leftovers.

BANANA SPLIT SQUARES

Makes 12 to 16 servings

1 (21.5- or 23.6-ounce) package fudge brownie mix
2 bananas, thinly sliced, dipped in REALEMON®
    Lemon Juice from Concentrate and drained
½ cup chopped nuts (optional)
2 quarts plus 1 pint BORDEN® or MEADOW
    GOLD® Ice Cream, any 3 flavors, softened
Chocolate ice cream topping, whipped cream,
    banana slices, nuts, cherries

Preheat oven to 350°F. Prepare brownie mix as package directs; spread in 13×9-inch baking pan. Bake 20 to 25 minutes; cool. Layer bananas, nuts, 1 quart ice cream, 1 pint ice cream and 1 quart ice cream on brownie in pan. Cover; freeze 6 hours or until firm. Remove from freezer 10 minutes before serving. Cut into squares; garnish with ice cream topping, whipped cream, banana slices, nuts and cherries. Freeze leftovers.

FUDGY ICE CREAM SQUARES

Makes 10 to 12 servings

1½ cups finely crushed creme-filled chocolate
    sandwich cookies (about 18 cookies)
2 to 3 tablespoons margarine or butter, melted
3 (1-ounce) squares unsweetened chocolate, melted
1 (14-ounce) can EAGLE® Brand Sweetened
    Condensed Milk (NOT evaporated milk)
2 teaspoons vanilla extract
1 cup chopped nuts (optional)
2 cups (1 pint) BORDEN® or MEADOW GOLD®
    Whipping Cream, whipped
Whipped topping

Combine crumbs and margarine; press firmly on bottom of 13×9-inch baking pan. In large mixer bowl, beat melted chocolate with sweetened condensed milk and vanilla until well blended. Stir in nuts if desired. Fold in whipped cream. Pour into prepared pan. Top with whipped topping. Cover; freeze 6 hours or until firm. Cut into squares. Garnish as desired. Freeze leftovers.

Banana Split Square

BERRY GOOD SUNDAES

Makes 4 servings

4 (6-inch) flour tortillas
1½ cups diced peeled nectarines
1½ cups diced strawberries or raspberries
2 tablespoons sugar
½ teaspoon grated lemon peel
4 scoops (3 ounces each) vanilla ice milk
   Sprigs of fresh mint, for garnish

Preheat oven to 350°F. Soften tortillas according to package directions. Press each tortilla down into ungreased 10-ounce custard cup. Bake 10 to 15 minutes or until crisp. Set aside to cool.

Combine nectarines, strawberries, sugar and lemon peel in large bowl; mix gently until well blended. To assemble, remove tortillas from custard cups. Place each tortilla shell on dessert plate and fill with 1 scoop of ice milk. Spoon equal portions of fruit mixture over tops. Garnish with mint sprigs.

Berry Good Sundae

HOT PEANUT FUDGE SUNDAES

Makes 6 sundaes (about 2 cups sauce)

1 package (6 ounces) semi-sweet chocolate chips
¾ cup evaporated milk
½ cup peanut butter
½ cup marshmallow creme
1 quart vanilla ice cream
½ cup chopped roasted peanuts

Melt chocolate in double boiler or in small saucepan over very low heat. Add evaporated milk, peanut butter and marshmallow creme. Beat until thoroughly combined. Scoop ice cream into 6 sundae dishes. Ladle on warm sauce; garnish with peanuts.

Favorite recipe from **Oklahoma Peanut Commission**

BUTTER RUM SUNDAES

Makes 6 to 8 sundaes (1½ cups sauce)

1 cup firmly packed light brown sugar
⅓ cup BUTTER FLAVOR CRISCO®
½ cup dark corn syrup
¼ cup milk
1 to 2 teaspoons imitation rum flavoring
   Vanilla ice cream

1. Blend brown sugar, Butter Flavor Crisco® and corn syrup in 1-quart saucepan. Cook and stir over medium heat until mixture comes to a boil. Boil 1 minute. Remove from heat. Gradually blend in milk until smooth. Stir in rum flavoring.

2. Cool until warm. Stir well. Serve over vanilla ice cream. Cover and refrigerate any leftover sauce. Reheat over low heat, stirring constantly, before serving.

PINEAPPLE PISTACHIO DESSERT

Makes 6 servings

1 can (8 ounces) DOLE® Crushed Pineapple in Juice, drained
2 ounces chopped DOLE® Pistachios
2 tablespoons orange-flavored liqueur
   Grated peel from 1 DOLE® Orange
1 quart vanilla ice cream, softened

Gently fold pineapple, pistachios, liqueur and orange peel into ice cream. Turn into 1½-quart mold. Cover; freeze 4 hours or until firm. Dip bottom of mold in hot water for 20 seconds to unmold. Invert onto serving plate. Garnish as desired.

Frozen Piña Colada Torte

BANANA SPLIT BOMBE

Makes 10 to 12 servings

2 pints strawberry ice cream, slightly softened
1½ pints chocolate ice cream, slightly softened
1 pint vanilla ice cream,* slightly softened
1 cup puréed bananas* (about 2 medium)
¼ teaspoon lemon juice*
  Whipped cream
  Strawberries
  Banana slices

Chill 7-cup mold in freezer. Using an ice cream spade or large spoon, pack ¾-inch layer of strawberry ice cream over bottom and up side of chilled mold. Freeze until firm. Spoon layer of chocolate ice cream over strawberry shell; pack firmly. Freeze until firm. Combine vanilla ice cream, puréed bananas and lemon juice. Pack into center of chocolate shell. Cover and freeze at least 6 hours or overnight.

To unmold, dip mold in lukewarm water just to rim for a few seconds. Loosen ice cream from mold with thin metal spatula. Invert onto chilled serving plate. Return to freezer until firm. To serve, pipe whipped cream in strips up side of bombe. Arrange strawberries and banana slices around base.

*One pint banana ice cream may be substituted for vanilla ice cream, puréed bananas and lemon juice.

Favorite recipe from **American Dairy Association**

FROZEN PIÑA COLADA TORTE

Makes 12 to 15 servings

1 (7-ounce) package flaked coconut, toasted (2⅓ cups)
3 tablespoons margarine or butter, melted
1 (14-ounce) can EAGLE® Brand Sweetened Condensed Milk (NOT evaporated milk)
½ cup COCO LOPEZ® Cream of Coconut
1 (20-ounce) can crushed pineapple, well drained
2 cups (1 pint) BORDEN® or MEADOW GOLD® Whipping Cream, whipped (*do not use non-dairy whipped topping*)
  Maraschino cherries

Reserving ¾ *cup* coconut, combine remaining coconut and margarine; press firmly on bottom of 9-inch springform pan, 13×9-inch baking pan *or* 9-inch square pan. In large bowl, combine sweetened condensed milk and cream of coconut; stir in *1 cup* pineapple. Fold in whipped cream. Pour half the mixture into prepared pan. Sprinkle with ½ *cup* reserved coconut; top with remaining whipped cream mixture. Cover; freeze 6 hours or until firm. Just before serving, garnish with remaining coconut, remaining pineapple and cherries. Freeze leftovers.

Strawberry-Banana Granité

STRAWBERRY-BANANA GRANITÉ

Makes 5 servings

2 ripe medium bananas, peeled and sliced
   (about 2 cups)
2 cups unsweetened frozen strawberries
   (do not thaw)
¼ cup no-sugar-added strawberry pourable fruit*
   Whole fresh strawberries (optional)
   Fresh mint leaves (optional)

Place banana slices in plastic freezer bag; freeze until firm. Place frozen banana slices and frozen strawberries in food processor container. Let stand 10 minutes for fruit to soften slightly. Add pourable fruit. Remove plunger from top of food processor to allow air to be incorporated. Process until smooth, scraping down sides of container frequently. Serve immediately. Garnish with fresh strawberries and mint leaves, if desired. Freeze leftovers.

*3 tablespoons no-sugar-added strawberry fruit spread combined with 1 tablespoon warm water may be substituted.

Notes: Granité may be transferred to airtight container and frozen up to 1 month. Let stand at room temperature 10 minutes to soften slightly before serving.

This is a sugar-free dessert.

RASPBERRY SORBET

Makes 10 servings

1 package (10 ounces) BIRDS EYE® Quick Thaw
   Red Raspberries, thawed
1 cup cold water
1 package (4-serving size) JELL-O® Brand Gelatin,
   Raspberry Flavor
1 cup sugar
2 cups boiling water

Place raspberries and cold water in blender; cover. Blend at high speed until smooth. Strain to remove seeds.

Completely dissolve gelatin and sugar in boiling water. Add raspberry purée. Pour into 9-inch square pan. Freeze until ice crystals form 1 inch around edge, about 1 hour.

Spoon gelatin mixture into chilled blender container; cover. Blend at high speed until smooth, about 30 seconds. Return mixture to pan. Freeze until firm, about 6 hours or overnight.

FRUIT FLAVOR FREEZE

Makes 10 servings

1 package (4-serving size) JELL-O® Brand Gelatin,
   any flavor
¾ cup sugar
1 cup boiling water
2 cups milk
¾ cup (4 ounces) COOL WHIP® Non-Dairy
   Whipped Topping, thawed
   Assorted cookies (optional)

Completely dissolve gelatin and sugar in boiling water. Stir in milk. (Mixture will appear curdled but will be smooth when frozen.) Pour into 13×9-inch pan. Freeze until ice crystals form 1 inch around edge, about 1 hour.

Spoon gelatin mixture into chilled bowl. Beat until smooth. Blend in whipped topping. Return to pan. Freeze until firm, about 4 hours. Serve with assorted cookies, if desired.

Prep time: 15 minutes
Freezing time: 5 hours

TANGERINE SORBET

Makes about 1 quart

½ cup sugar
1 envelope unflavored gelatin
3 cups fresh Florida tangerine juice, divided
1 teaspoon grated tangerine peel

In medium bowl, combine sugar and gelatin. Heat 1 cup tangerine juice to boiling. Add to gelatin mixture; stir until gelatin and sugar are completely dissolved. Stir in remaining 2 cups juice and grated peel. Cool. Pour into 9×9-inch pan; cover and freeze. When almost frozen, scrape into large bowl. Beat until smooth. Return to pan; cover and freeze until almost frozen. Scrape into bowl and beat again. Spoon into pan; cover and freeze until firm.

Favorite recipe from **Florida Department of Citrus**

Clockwise from top: Honeydew Ice, Cantaloupe Ice, Watermelon Ice

WATERMELON ICE

Makes 6 servings

4 cups seeded 1-inch watermelon chunks
¼ cup thawed frozen unsweetened pineapple juice
 concentrate
2 tablespoons fresh lime juice
 Fresh melon balls (optional)
 Fresh mint leaves (optional)

Place melon chunks in single layer in plastic freezer bag; freeze until firm, about 8 hours. Place frozen melon in food processor container. Let stand 15 minutes for fruit to soften slightly. Add pineapple juice and lime juice. Remover plunger from top of food processor to allow air to be incorporated. Process until smooth, scraping down sides of container frequently. Serve immediately. Garnish with melon balls and mint leaves, if desired. Freeze leftovers.

Honeydew Ice: Substitute honeydew for the watermelon and unsweetened pineapple-guava-orange juice concentrate for the pineapple juice concentrate.

Cantaloupe Ice: Substitute cantaloupe for the watermelon and unsweetened pineapple-guava-orange juice concentrate for the pineapple juice concentrate.

Notes: Ices may be transferred to airtight container and frozen up to 1 month. Let stand at room temperature 10 minutes to soften slightly before serving.

This is a sugar-free dessert.

BLACKBERRY-LEMON ICE CREAM

Makes about 2 quarts

3 cups (1½ pints) BORDEN® or MEADOW
 GOLD® Half-and-Half
2 cups frozen unsweetened blackberries, mashed
1 (14-ounce) can EAGLE® Brand Sweetened
 Condensed Milk (NOT evaporated milk)
¼ cup plus 2 tablespoons REALEMON® Lemon
 Juice from Concentrate
1 teaspoon grated lemon peel (optional)

In ice cream freezer container, combine ingredients; mix well. Freeze according to manufacturer's instructions. Freeze leftovers.

BANANA MOCHA ICE CREAM

Makes about 1½ quarts, 6 servings

3 extra-ripe, medium DOLE® Bananas, peeled
4 eggs*
2 cups whipping cream, unwhipped
1 cup half-and-half
1 cup sugar
½ cup chocolate syrup
2 tablespoons instant coffee crystals
2 teaspoons vanilla extract
¼ teaspoon ground cinnamon
⅛ teaspoon salt

Slice bananas into blender; process until smooth (1½ cups). Add eggs; process to blend.

Pour mixture and remaining ingredients into ice cream freezer container. Stir until sugar and coffee dissolve and mixture is blended. Freeze according to manufacturer's instructions.

*Use only grade A clean, uncracked eggs.

EASY HOMEMADE VANILLA ICE CREAM

Makes about 1½ quarts

1 (14-ounce) can EAGLE® Brand Sweetened Condensed Milk (NOT evaporated milk)
4 teaspoons vanilla extract
2 cups (1 pint) BORDEN® or MEADOW GOLD® Whipping Cream, whipped (*do not use non-dairy whipped topping*)

In large bowl, combine sweetened condensed milk and vanilla. Fold in whipped cream. Pour into 9 × 5-inch loaf pan or other 2-quart container; cover. Freeze 6 hours or until firm. Garnish as desired. Freeze leftovers.

Vanilla Nut Ice Cream: Add ¾ cup chopped nuts to sweetened condensed milk mixture. Proceed as above.

Coffee Ice Cream: Dissolve 1 tablespoon instant coffee granules in 1 teaspoon hot water; add to sweetened condensed milk mixture. Proceed as above.

Chocolate Chip Ice Cream: Add ½ cup mini chocolate chips to sweetened condensed milk mixture. Proceed as above.

COFFEE BRICKLE ICE CREAM

Makes about 2 quarts

2 tablespoons instant coffee granules
2 teaspoons hot water
4 cups (1 quart) BORDEN® or MEADOW GOLD® Half-and-Half
1 (14-ounce) can EAGLE® Brand Sweetened Condensed Milk (NOT evaporated milk)
¾ cup chopped almonds, toasted
⅓ cup almond brickle chips
2 teaspoons vanilla extract
1 teaspoon almond extract

In small bowl, dissolve coffee in water. In ice cream freezer container, combine coffee mixture and remaining ingredients; mix well. Freeze according to manufacturer's instructions. Freeze leftovers.

PEACH ICE CREAM

Makes about 1½ quarts

3 cups (1½ pints) BORDEN® or MEADOW GOLD® Half-and-Half
1 (14-ounce) can EAGLE® Brand Sweetened Condensed Milk (NOT evaporated milk)
1 cup puréed or mashed peaches
1 tablespoon vanilla extract
Yellow food coloring (optional)

In ice cream freezer container, combine all ingredients; mix well. Freeze according to manufacturer's instructions. Freeze leftovers.

Refrigerator-Freezer Method: Omit half-and-half. In large bowl, combine sweetened condensed milk, puréed peaches and vanilla; add food coloring if desired. Fold in 2 cups (1 pint) BORDEN® or MEADOW GOLD® Whipping Cream, whipped (*do not use non-dairy whipped topping*). Pour into 9 × 5-inch loaf pan or other 2-quart container; cover. Freeze 6 hours or until firm. Freeze leftovers.

Peach Ice Cream

133

OLD-FASHIONED ORANGE ICE CREAM

Makes about 2 quarts

2 cups milk
1 cup sugar
4 eggs, lightly beaten
2 cups (1 pint) whipping cream, unwhipped
1 can (12 ounces) Florida frozen orange juice
   concentrate, thawed, undiluted

In top of double boiler, over simmering water, combine milk, sugar and eggs. Cook, stirring constantly, until mixture thickens and coats the back of a spoon. Cool. Stir in whipping cream and orange juice concentrate.

Transfer mixture to ice cream freezer container. Freeze according to manufacturer's directions. Or, turn into 9 × 5-inch loaf pan; cover and freeze 2 to 3 hours or until almost firm. Turn mixture into bowl; beat until light and fluffy. Return to loaf pan; cover. Freeze 3 to 4 hours or until completely firm.

Favorite recipe from **Florida Department of Citrus**

CHOCO-CHERRY ICE CREAM LOAF

Makes 8 to 10 servings

2 cups finely crushed creme-filled chocolate
   sandwich cookies (about 20 cookies)
3 tablespoons margarine or butter, melted
1 (14-ounce) can EAGLE® Brand Sweetened
   Condensed Milk (NOT evaporated milk)
⅓ cup chocolate-flavored syrup
1 (16-ounce) can dark sweet pitted cherries,
   well drained and coarsely chopped
¾ cup chopped nuts
½ to 1 teaspoon almond extract
2 cups (1 pint) BORDEN® or MEADOW GOLD®
   Whipping Cream, whipped (*do not use
   non-dairy whipped topping*)

Line 9 × 5-inch loaf pan with aluminum foil, extending foil above sides of pan. Combine crumbs and margarine; press firmly on bottom and halfway up sides of prepared pan. In large bowl, combine sweetened condensed milk and syrup. Stir in cherries, nuts and extract. Fold in whipped cream. Pour into prepared pan. Cover; freeze 6 hours or overnight. To serve, remove from pan; peel off foil and slice. Garnish as desired. Freeze leftovers.

MINT CHOCOLATE CHIP ICE CREAM

Makes about 1½ quarts

1 (14-ounce) can EAGLE® Brand Sweetened
   Condensed Milk (NOT evaporated milk)
2 teaspoons peppermint extract
   Green food coloring (optional)
2 cups (1 pint) BORDEN® or MEADOW GOLD®
   Half-and-Half
2 cups (1 pint) BORDEN® or MEADOW GOLD®
   Whipping Cream, *unwhipped*
¾ cup mini chocolate chips

In large bowl, combine sweetened condensed milk, extract and food coloring if desired; mix well. Stir in remaining ingredients. Pour into ice cream freezer container. Freeze according to manufacturer's instructions. Freeze leftovers.

Refrigerator-Freezer Method: Omit half-and-half; reduce mini chocolate chips to ½ cup. Whip whipping cream. In large bowl, combine sweetened condensed milk, extract and food coloring if desired; mix well. Fold in whipped cream and chocolate chips. Pour into 9 × 5-inch loaf pan or other 2-quart container; cover. Freeze 6 hours or until firm. Freeze leftovers.

Left to right: Butter Pecan Ice Cream, Mint Chocolate Chip Ice Cream

EASY HOMEMADE CHOCOLATE ICE CREAM

Makes about 1½ quarts

1 (14-ounce) can EAGLE® Brand Sweetened Condensed Milk (NOT evaporated milk)
⅔ cup chocolate-flavored syrup
2 cups (1 pint) BORDEN® or MEADOW GOLD® Whipping Cream, whipped (*do not use non-dairy whipped topping*)

In large bowl, combine sweetened condensed milk and syrup. Fold in whipped cream. Pour into 9 × 5-inch loaf pan or other 2-quart container; cover. Freeze 6 hours or until firm. Garnish as desired. Freeze leftovers.

Chocolate Mocha Ice Cream: Add 1 tablespoon instant coffee granules to sweetened condensed milk and syrup. Let stand 10 minutes. Proceed as above.

Chocolate Peanut Butter Ice Cream: Add ½ cup peanut butter to sweetened condensed milk and syrup. Proceed as above.

Chocolate Nut Ice Cream: Add ¾ cup chopped nuts to sweetened condensed milk and syrup. Proceed as above.

Chocolate Rocky Road Ice Cream: Add ½ cup chopped peanuts and 1 cup CAMPFIRE® Miniature Marshmallows to sweetened condensed milk and syrup. Proceed as above.

Chocolate Mint Ice Cream: Add 1 teaspoon peppermint extract to sweetened condensed milk and syrup. Proceed as above.

Chocolate Chocolate Chip Ice Cream: Add ¾ cup mini chocolate chips to sweetened condensed milk and syrup. Proceed as above.

BUTTER PECAN ICE CREAM

Makes about 2 quarts

1 (14-ounce) can EAGLE® Brand Sweetened Condensed Milk (NOT evaporated milk)
1 to 1½ cups chopped pecans, toasted
3 tablespoons butter or margarine, melted
1 teaspoon maple flavoring
2 cups (1 pint) BORDEN® or MEADOW GOLD® Half-and-Half
2 cups (1 pint) BORDEN® or MEADOW GOLD® Whipping Cream, *unwhipped*

In large bowl, combine sweetened condensed milk, pecans, butter and maple flavoring; mix well. Stir in remaining ingredients. Pour into ice cream freezer container. Freeze according to manufacturer's instructions. Freeze leftovers.

Fresh Berry Ice Cream

Refrigerator-Freezer Method: Omit half-and-half. Whip whipping cream. In large bowl, combine sweetened condensed milk, pecans, butter and maple flavoring; mix well. Fold in whipped cream. Pour into 9 × 5-inch loaf pan or other 2-quart container; cover. Freeze 6 hours or until firm. Freeze leftovers.

FRESH BERRY ICE CREAM

Makes about 1½ quarts

3 cups (1½ pints) BORDEN® or MEADOW GOLD® Half-and-Half
1 (14-ounce) can EAGLE® Brand Sweetened Condensed Milk (NOT evaporated milk)
2 cups fresh or frozen unsweetened raspberries, strawberries or other berries, mashed or puréed (about 1 cup)
1 tablespoon vanilla extract
Few drops red food coloring (optional)

In large bowl, combine ingredients; mix well. Pour into ice cream freezer container. Freeze according to manufacturer's instructions. Garnish as desired. Freeze leftovers.

Refrigerator-Freezer Method: Omit half-and-half. In large bowl, combine sweetened condensed milk, mashed or puréed fruit and vanilla. Stir in food coloring if desired. Fold in 2 cups (1 pint) BORDEN® or MEADOW GOLD® Whipping Cream, whipped (*do not use non-dairy whipped topping.*) Pour into 9 × 5-inch loaf pan or other 2-quart container; cover. Freeze 6 hours or until firm. Freeze leftovers.

PINEAPPLE BAKED ALASKA

Makes 6 servings

1 large DOLE® Fresh Pineapple
1 pint ice cream or sorbet, any flavor, softened
4 egg whites, at room temperature
¼ teaspoon cream of tartar
½ cup sugar

Cut pineapple in half lengthwise through crown. Cut fruit from shells with a knife, leaving shells intact. Turn shells upside down to drain. Trim off core and dice fruit. Reserve 2 cups for Pineapple Baked Alaska; refrigerate remainder for another use.

Spread ice cream in shells. Top with diced pineapple. Cover with plastic wrap; freeze 4 hours or until frozen.

Preheat oven to 450°F. Beat egg whites and cream of tartar in large bowl until soft peaks form. Gradually add sugar, beating until glossy and stiff peaks form. Spread meringue over ice cream and diced pineapple, sealing edges well. Make peaks in meringue with back of spoon. Cover crowns with foil. Bake 4 to 5 minutes until meringue is lightly browned. Remove foil. Serve immediately.

Brownie Alaska

BROWNIE ALASKA

Makes 2 Brownie Alaskas, 8 to 10 servings each

1 package DUNCAN HINES® Chocolate Lovers' Double Fudge Brownie Mix
½ gallon brick strawberry ice cream
6 egg whites
2 cups marshmallow creme

1. Preheat oven to 350°F. Line 13×9-inch pan with aluminum foil.

2. Prepare, bake and cool brownie mix following package directions.

3. Invert brownie onto cookie sheet. Remove foil and cut in half crosswise so each half measures about 9×6½ inches. Cut brick ice cream in half lengthwise. Place each half on brownie halves. Chill in freezer.

4. For meringue, preheat oven to 475°F. Beat egg whites until soft peaks form. Add marshmallow creme, ¼ cup at a time. Beat well after each addition. Beat until stiff peaks form. Divide between two brownie halves. Spread over top and sides, sealing edges completely.

5. Bake at 475°F for 2 to 3 minutes or until meringue is lightly browned. Serve immediately.

Note: Recipe makes two Brownie Alaskas; one to serve and one to freeze for a quick dessert at a later time. To freeze, loosely wrap with aluminum foil.

Tip: For delicious variations, try different ice creams such as mint chocolate chip, peppermint or chocolate.

MUD PIE

Makes one 9-inch pie

1 (14-ounce) can EAGLE® Brand Sweetened Condensed Milk (NOT evaporated milk)
4 teaspoons vanilla extract
1 cup coarsely crushed creme-filled chocolate sandwich cookies (12 cookies)
2 cups (1 pint) BORDEN® or MEADOW GOLD® Whipping Cream, whipped (*do not use non-dairy whipped topping*)
1 (9-inch) prepared chocolate crumb crust
   Chocolate fudge ice cream topping or chocolate-flavored syrup
   Chopped nuts

In large bowl, combine sweetened condensed milk and vanilla. Fold in cookies and whipped cream. Pour into 9×5-inch loaf pan or other 2-quart container; cover. Freeze 6 hours or until firm. Scoop ice cream into prepared crust. Drizzle with topping. Garnish with nuts. Freeze leftovers.

Left to right: Cherry-Crowned Cocoa Pudding (page 364), Choco-Berry Frozen Dessert

CHOCO-BERRY FROZEN DESSERT

Makes about 10 servings

3 packages (3 ounces each) cream cheese, softened and divided
1 cup HERSHEY'S Syrup
½ cup water
4½ cups (about 12 ounces) frozen non-dairy whipped topping, thawed and divided
¾ cup puréed strawberries (fresh, sweetened *or* frozen, thawed and drained berries)

Line 9×5-inch loaf pan with aluminum foil. In large mixer bowl, beat 2 packages cream cheese. Blend in syrup and water; beat until smooth. Fold in 3 cups whipped topping. Spoon half of chocolate mixture into prepared pan; freeze 15 minutes. Refrigerate remaining chocolate mixture. In small mixer bowl, beat remaining package cream cheese. Blend in strawberries until smooth. Fold in remaining 1½ cups whipped topping. Spoon strawberry mixture over chocolate layer in pan. Top with refrigerated chocolate mixture. Cover; freeze several hours or overnight until firm. Unmold about 10 minutes before serving. Peel off foil before slicing. Garnish as desired.

PEPPERMINT ICE CREAM LOAF

Makes 8 to 10 servings

2 cups finely crushed creme-filled chocolate sandwich cookies (about 20 cookies)
3 tablespoons margarine or butter, melted
1 cup crushed hard peppermint candy
¼ cup boiling water
1 (14-ounce) can EAGLE® Brand Sweetened Condensed Milk (NOT evaporated milk)
1 to 2 drops red food coloring (optional)
2 cups (1 pint) BORDEN® or MEADOW GOLD® Whipping Cream, whipped (*do not use non-dairy whipped topping*)

Line 9×5-inch loaf pan with aluminum foil, extending foil above sides of pan. Combine crumbs and margarine; press firmly on bottom and halfway up sides of prepared pan. In blender container, blend ¼ *cup* peppermint candy and boiling water until candy dissolves; cool. In large mixer bowl, beat sweetened condensed milk, food coloring if desired, ½ *cup* crushed candy and peppermint liquid until well blended. Fold in whipped cream and remaining ¼ *cup* crushed candy. Pour into prepared pan. Cover; freeze 6 hours or overnight. To serve, remove from pan; peel off foil and slice. Garnish as desired. Freeze leftovers.

TROPICAL FROZEN MOUSSE

Makes 6 servings

2½ cups mango chunks (2 to 4 mangos, peeled and
    cut into bite-size pieces)
⅓ cup sugar
1 tablespoon kirsch
1 teaspoon grated lime peel
¼ teaspoon fresh lime juice
2 cups whipped cream
    Mango slices and fresh mint leaves for garnish

Place mango chunks in food processor or blender
container. Cover; process until smooth. Transfer to
large bowl. Blend in sugar, kirsch, lime peel and lime
juice. Fold whipped cream into mango mixture. Pour
into sherbet glasses or 8-inch square pan. Cover and
freeze 4 hours or until firm. Let stand at room
temperature 30 minutes before serving. Garnish with
mango slices and mint leaves just before serving.

FROZEN CHOCOLATE MOUSSE

Makes 6 to 8 servings

1 cup (6 ounces) semi-sweet chocolate chips
1 (14-ounce) can EAGLE® Brand Sweetened
    Condensed Milk (NOT evaporated milk)
1½ teaspoons vanilla extract
2 cups (1 pint) BORDEN® or MEADOW GOLD®
    Whipping Cream, whipped (*do not use
    non-dairy whipped topping*)

In medium saucepan over low heat, melt chips; remove
from heat. Add sweetened condensed milk and vanilla;
mix well. Cool to room temperature or chill 20 to 30
minutes. Fold in whipped cream. Spoon equal portions
into individual serving dishes. Freeze 2 hours or until
firm. Garnish as desired. Freeze leftovers.

QUICK CHOCOLATE MOUSSE

Makes 8 to 10 servings

1 (14-ounce) can EAGLE® Brand Sweetened
    Condensed Milk (NOT evaporated milk)
1 cup cold water
1 (4-serving size) package *instant* chocolate flavor
    pudding mix
1 cup (½ pint) BORDEN® or MEADOW GOLD®
    Whipping Cream, whipped

In large bowl, combine sweetened condensed milk and
water. Add pudding mix; beat well. Chill 5 minutes.
Fold in whipped cream. Spoon into serving dishes; chill.
Garnish as desired. Refrigerate leftovers.

FROZEN MINT CHOCOLATE MOUSSE

Makes 6 to 8 servings

1 (14-ounce) can EAGLE® Brand Sweetened
    Condensed Milk (NOT evaporated milk)
⅔ cup chocolate-flavored syrup
¾ teaspoon peppermint extract
1 cup (½ pint) BORDEN® or MEADOW GOLD®
    Whipping Cream, whipped (*do not use
    non-dairy whipped topping*)

In large bowl, combine sweetened condensed milk,
syrup and extract; mix well. Fold in whipped cream.
Spoon equal portions into individual serving dishes.
Freeze 3 to 4 hours or until firm. Garnish as desired.
Freeze leftovers.

FROZEN CHOCOLATE BANANA LOAF

Makes 8 to 10 servings

1½ cups chocolate wafer cookie crumbs
    (about 30 wafers)
¼ cup sugar
3 tablespoons margarine or butter, melted
1 (14-ounce) can EAGLE® Brand Sweetened
    Condensed Milk (NOT evaporated milk)
⅔ cup chocolate-flavored syrup
2 small ripe bananas, mashed (¾ cup)
2 cups (1 pint) BORDEN® or MEADOW GOLD®
    Whipping Cream, whipped (*do not use
    non-dairy whipped topping*)

Line 9 × 5-inch loaf pan with aluminum foil, extending
foil above sides of pan; butter foil. Combine crumbs,
sugar and margarine; press firmly on bottom and halfway
up sides of prepared pan. In large bowl, combine
sweetened condensed milk, syrup and bananas; mix
well. Fold in whipped cream. Pour into prepared pan;
cover. Freeze 6 hours or until firm. To serve, remove
from pan; peel off foil. Garnish as desired. Slice to serve.
Freeze leftovers.

Tropical Frozen Mousse

FRUIT SPARKLES

Makes 6 (½ cup) servings

1 package (4-serving size) JELL-O® Brand
    Sugar Free Gelatin, any flavor
1 cup boiling water
1 cup cold fruit-flavor seltzer, sparkling water,
    club soda or other sugar-free carbonated
    beverage
1 cup sliced bananas and strawberries*

Completely dissolve gelatin in boiling water. Add
seltzer. Chill until slightly thickened. Add fruit.
Pour into individual dessert dishes. Chill until firm,
about 1 hour. Garnish with additional fruit and mint
leaves, if desired.

*1 cup drained mandarin orange sections or crushed
pineapple may be substituted for bananas and
strawberries.

Prep time: 15 minutes
Chill time: 2 hours

Fruit Sparkles

PEACH MELBA DESSERT

Makes 10 servings

1 package (4-serving size) JELL-O® Brand Peach
    Flavor Gelatin
2 cups boiling water, divided
¾ cup cold water
1 package (4-serving size) JELL-O® Brand
    Raspberry Flavor Gelatin
1 pint vanilla ice cream, softened
1 can (8¾ ounces) sliced peaches, drained*
2 cups fresh raspberries
  Mint leaves (optional)

Completely dissolve peach flavor gelatin in 1 cup boiling
water. Add cold water. Chill until slightly thickened.

Completely dissolve raspberry flavor gelatin in remaining
1 cup boiling water. Spoon in ice cream, stirring until
melted and smooth. Pour into serving bowl. Chill until
set but not firm.

Arrange peach slices and raspberries on ice cream
mixture in bowl. Add mint leaves, if desired. Spoon
peach gelatin over fruit. Chill until firm, about 3 hours.

*One fresh peach, peeled and sliced, may be substituted
for canned peaches.

Prep time: 20 minutes
Chill time: 4 hours

VANILLA RICE PUDDING

Makes 10 servings

1 package (4-serving size) JELL-O® Pudding
    and Pie Filling, French Vanilla, Vanilla or
    Coconut Cream Flavor
4 cups milk
1 egg, well beaten
1 cup MINUTE® Rice, uncooked
¼ cup raisins (optional)
¼ teaspoon ground cinnamon
⅛ teaspoon ground nutmeg

Place pudding mix in medium saucepan. Gradually stir
in milk and egg. Add rice and raisins. Cook and stir over
medium heat until mixture just comes to a boil. Cool
5 minutes, stirring twice. Pour into dessert dishes or
serving bowl. Sprinkle with cinnamon and nutmeg.
Serve warm.

Note: For chilled pudding, place plastic wrap on surface
of hot pudding; cool slightly. Chill about 1 hour. Stir
before serving. Sprinkle with cinnamon and nutmeg.

Prep time: 20 minutes

CREAMY RICE PUDDING

Makes 4 to 6 servings

2½ cups water
½ cup uncooked long grain rice
1 cinnamon stick *or* ¼ teaspoon ground cinnamon
2 (½-inch) pieces lemon peel
   Dash salt
1 (14-ounce) can EAGLE® Brand Sweetened
   Condensed Milk (NOT evaporated milk)
   Additional ground cinnamon

In medium saucepan, combine water, rice, cinnamon, lemon peel and salt; let stand 30 minutes. Bring to a boil, stirring occasionally. Add sweetened condensed milk; mix well. Return to a boil; stir. Reduce heat to medium. Cook, uncovered, stirring frequently, until liquid is absorbed to top of rice, about 15 minutes. Cool (pudding thickens as it cools). Remove cinnamon stick and lemon peel. Sprinkle with additional cinnamon. Serve warm or chilled. Refrigerate leftovers.

FROSTY ORANGE DESSERT

Makes 6 to 8 servings

1 (3-ounce) package orange flavored gelatin
1 cup boiling water
½ cup cold water
⅓ cup orange juice
1 teaspoon grated orange peel
1 (8-ounce) package Light PHILADELPHIA
   BRAND® Neufchatel Cheese, softened
¼ cup sugar

• Dissolve gelatin in boiling water in medium bowl; add cold water, juice and peel.

• Combine neufchatel cheese and sugar in small bowl, mixing until well blended. Gradually add gelatin mixture to neufchatel cheese mixture, mixing until blended.

• Chill, stirring occasionally, until thickened but not set. Beat with electric mixer until fluffy. Spoon into individual parfait glasses; chill several hours or overnight.

VARIATIONS

• Substitute PHILADELPHIA BRAND® Cream Cheese for Neufchatel Cheese.

• Substitute lime flavored gelatin for orange flavored gelatin. Reduce orange juice to ¼ cup. Add 2 tablespoons lime juice with orange juice. Substitute lime peel for orange peel.

Creamy Banana Pudding

CREAMY BANANA PUDDING

Makes 8 to 10 servings

1 (14-ounce) can EAGLE® Brand Sweetened
   Condensed Milk (NOT evaporated milk)
1½ cups cold water
1 (4-serving size) package *instant* vanilla flavor
   pudding mix
2 cups (1 pint) BORDEN® or MEADOW GOLD®
   Whipping Cream, whipped
36 vanilla wafers
3 medium bananas, sliced and dipped in
   REALEMON® Lemon Juice from Concentrate

In large bowl, combine sweetened condensed milk and water. Add pudding mix; beat well. Chill 5 minutes. Fold in whipped cream. Spoon *1 cup* pudding mixture into 2½-quart glass serving bowl. Top with one-third *each* of the wafers, bananas and pudding. Repeat layers twice, ending with pudding. Cover; chill. Garnish as desired. Refrigerate leftovers.

Tip: Mixture can be layered in individual serving dishes.

Three-in-One Chocolate Pudding & Pie Filling

THREE-IN-ONE CHOCOLATE PUDDING & PIE FILLING

Makes 4 servings

¾ cup sugar
⅓ cup HERSHEY₂'S Cocoa
2 tablespoons cornstarch
2 tablespoons all-purpose flour
¼ teaspoon salt
2 cups milk
2 egg yolks, slightly beaten
2 tablespoons butter or margarine
1 teaspoon vanilla extract

In medium saucepan, combine sugar, cocoa, cornstarch, flour and salt; blend in milk and egg yolks. Cook over medium heat, stirring constantly, until mixture boils; boil and stir 1 minute. Remove from heat; blend in butter and vanilla. Pour into medium bowl or individual serving dishes; press plastic wrap directly onto surface. Cool; refrigerate.

To Microwave: In 2-quart microwave-safe bowl, combine sugar, cocoa, cornstarch, flour and salt; blend in milk and egg yolks. Microwave at HIGH (100% power) 5 minutes, stirring several times, or until mixture boils. Microwave at HIGH 1 to 2 additional minutes or until mixture is smooth and thickened. Stir in butter and vanilla. Pour into medium bowl or individual serving dishes; press plastic wrap directly onto surface. Cool; refrigerate.

Pie: Reduce milk to 1¾ cups; cook as directed above. Pour hot pudding into 1 packaged (6-ounce) graham cracker crumb crust; press plastic wrap onto surface. Refrigerate; top with sweetened whipped cream or whipped topping before serving.

Parfaits: Alternate layers of cold pudding and sweetened whipped cream in parfait glasses.

CHOCO-BERRY BAVARIAN CREAM

Makes 8 to 10 servings

1 package (10-ounce) frozen strawberries in syrup, thawed *or* 1 cup sweetened sliced fresh strawberries
2 envelopes unflavored gelatin
½ cup sugar
1 cup HERSHEY₂'S Mini Chips₍₎ Semi-Sweet Chocolate
2¼ cups milk, divided
1 teaspoon vanilla extract
1 cup (½ pint) cold whipping cream
    Strawberry Cream (recipe follows)
    Fresh strawberries (optional)

Drain strawberries; reserve syrup. Add enough water to reserved strawberry liquid to equal ¾ cup. Sprinkle gelatin over liquid; set aside. In medium saucepan, stir together sugar, chips and ½ cup milk. Cook over low heat, stirring constantly until mixture is smooth and very hot. Add gelatin mixture, stirring until gelatin is completely dissolved. Remove from heat; add remaining 1¾ cups milk and vanilla. Pour into bowl; refrigerate, stirring occasionally, until mixture mounds when dropped from spoon. In small bowl, beat whipping cream until stiff; fold in chocolate mixture. Pour into oiled 5- or 6-cup mold; refrigerate until firm. Unmold; garnish with Strawberry Cream and fresh strawberries, if desired.

Strawberry Cream: Mash or purée reserved strawberries from Bavarian Cream recipe to equal ½ cup. In medium mixer bowl, beat 1 cup (½ pint) cold whipping cream and 1 teaspoon vanilla extract until stiff. Fold in strawberry purée and 2 to 3 drops red food color. Store, covered, in refrigerator.

TRIPLE LAYER DESSERTS

Makes 8 servings

3 cups cold half-and-half, divided
3 cups cold milk, divided
¼ cup chocolate liqueur, divided (optional)
1 package (4-serving size) JELL-O® Instant Pudding and Pie Filling, French Vanilla or Vanilla Flavor
2 packages (4-serving size each) JELL-O® Instant Pudding and Pie Filling, Chocolate Flavor
½ cup thawed COOL WHIP® Non-Dairy Whipped Topping
2 squares BAKER'S® Semi-Sweet Chocolate, melted

Pour 1 cup half-and-half, 1 cup milk and 2 tablespoons liqueur into small bowl. Add vanilla pudding mix. Beat with wire whisk until well blended, 1 to 2 minutes. Let stand until slightly thickened, about 5 minutes. Spoon into individual dessert glasses.

Pour remaining 2 cups half-and-half and 2 cups milk into medium bowl. Add chocolate pudding mixes. Beat with wire whisk until well blended, 1 to 2 minutes. Fold whipped topping into half the chocolate pudding; let stand until slightly thickened. Spoon over vanilla pudding in glasses. Stir melted chocolate and remaining 2 tablespoons liqueur into remaining chocolate pudding; let stand until slightly thickened. Spoon into glasses. Chill until ready to serve. Garnish as desired.

Prep time: 20 minutes

ORANGE NUT CREAM DESSERTS

Makes 6 to 8 servings

1 (14-ounce) can EAGLE® Brand Sweetened Condensed Milk (NOT evaporated milk)
1 (6-ounce) can frozen orange juice concentrate, thawed
1 (8-ounce) container BORDEN® Sour Cream
1 cup flaked coconut
½ cup chopped pecans
1 tablespoon grated orange peel
Fresh orange sections

In medium bowl, combine sweetened condensed milk and juice concentrate. Stir in sour cream. In small bowl, combine coconut, nuts and peel. Layer half *each* of sweetened condensed milk mixture, coconut mixture then orange sections in dessert dishes. Repeat, ending with orange sections. Chill. Refrigerate leftovers.

Triple Layer Desserts

Orange Terrine with Strawberry Sauce

ORANGE TERRINE WITH STRAWBERRY SAUCE

Makes 12 servings

1 package (3 ounces) ladyfingers, split, divided
2 packages (4-serving size each) or 1 package
    (8-serving size) JELL-O® Brand Orange Flavor
    Sugar Free Gelatin
1½ cups boiling water
1 cup cold orange juice
    Ice cubes
1 tablespoon orange liqueur (optional)
2 teaspoons grated orange peel
3¼ cups (8 ounces) COOL WHIP® LITE®
    Non-Dairy Whipped Topping, thawed, divided
1 package (10 ounces) BIRDS EYE® Strawberries
    in Syrup, thawed
1 cup fresh strawberries

• Line bottom and sides of 9×5-inch loaf pan with plastic wrap. Stand enough ladyfingers to fit evenly along 2 long sides of pan (cut sides should be facing in).

• Completely dissolve gelatin in boiling water. Combine orange juice and enough ice cubes to measure 1¾ cups. Add to gelatin; stir until slightly thickened. Remove any unmelted ice. Stir in liqueur and orange peel. Gently stir in 2½ cups whipped topping.

• Spoon gelatin mixture into prepared pan. If necessary, trim ladyfingers to make even with top of gelatin mixture. Arrange remaining ladyfingers evenly on top of gelatin mixture. Chill until firm, at least 3 hours.

• When ready to serve, place thawed frozen strawberries in blender container; cover. Blend until puréed; strain. Unmold terrine onto serving plate; remove plastic wrap. Decorate with remaining ¾ cup whipped topping and fresh strawberries. Cut into slices. Serve on strawberry purée.

ALPINE STRAWBERRY BAVARIAN

Makes 10 servings

3 cups cold water, divided
2 (3-ounce) packages JELL-O® Brand Lemon
    Flavor Sugar Free Gelatin
1 (8-ounce) container Light PHILADELPHIA
    BRAND® Pasteurized Process Cream Cheese
    Product
1 pint strawberry ice milk or ice cream, softened
1 tablespoon lemon juice
2 cups strawberry slices

• Bring 1½ cups cold water to a boil. Gradually add to gelatin in medium bowl; stir until dissolved. Stir in remaining 1½ cups cold water.

• Gradually add gelatin to cream cheese product in large mixing bowl, mixing at medium speed with electric mixer until well blended.

• Stir in ice milk and lemon juice; fold in strawberries. Spoon into ten parfait glasses or a 1½-quart bowl. Chill.

• Garnish each serving with whipped topping, chocolate curls and additional strawberries, if desired.

Prep time: 20 minutes plus chilling

LEMON CRUNCH PARFAITS

Makes 4 to 6 servings

½ cup unsifted all-purpose flour
¼ cup chopped nuts
2 tablespoons firmly packed light brown sugar
¼ cup margarine or butter, melted
1 (14-ounce) can EAGLE® Brand Sweetened
    Condensed Milk (NOT evaporated milk)
¼ cup REALEMON® Lemon Juice from
    Concentrate
1 (8-ounce) container BORDEN® Lite-line®
    Lemon Yogurt
    Few drops yellow food coloring (optional)

Preheat oven to 350°F. Combine flour, nuts, sugar and margarine. Spread in 8-inch square baking pan. Bake 10 minutes, stirring after 5 minutes. Cool. In medium bowl, combine sweetened condensed milk, ReaLemon® brand, yogurt and food coloring if desired. In parfait or dessert glasses, layer crumbs and yogurt mixture. Chill. Refrigerate leftovers.

Combine crumbs and ¼ cup sugar in small bowl. Mix in margarine. Press mixture evenly onto bottom of 13×9-inch pan. (If desired, bake at 375°F for 8 minutes. Cool on wire rack.)

Beat cream cheese with remaining ¼ cup sugar and 2 tablespoons milk in medium bowl until smooth. Fold in half the whipped topping. Spread over crust. Arrange strawberries in even layer on cream cheese mixture.

Pour remaining milk into medium bowl. Add pudding mix. Beat with wire whisk until well blended, 1 to 2 minutes. Pour over strawberries. Chill 4 hours or overnight.

Spread remaining whipped topping over pudding just before serving. Garnish with additional strawberries, if desired.

Prep time: 35 minutes
Chill time: 4 hours

STRIPED DELIGHT

Makes 18 servings

1 cup all-purpose flour
1 cup finely chopped pecans
¾ cup sugar, divided
½ cup PARKAY® Margarine, melted
1 package (8 ounces) PHILADELPHIA BRAND®
    Cream Cheese, softened
2⅔ cups cold milk, divided
3½ cups (8 ounces) COOL WHIP® Non-Dairy
    Whipped Topping, thawed, divided
1 package (6-serving size) JELL-O® Instant
    Pudding and Pie Filling, any flavor

Preheat oven to 350°F. Combine flour, pecans, ½ cup sugar and margarine in medium bowl; mix until flour is moistened. Press mixture evenly onto bottom of 13×9-inch pan. Bake 20 minutes or until lightly browned. Cool on wire rack.

Beat cream cheese, remaining ¼ cup sugar and 2 tablespoons milk in medium bowl until smooth. Fold in half the whipped topping. Spread over cooled crust.

Pour remaining milk into medium bowl. Add pudding mix. Beat with wire whisk until well blended, 1 to 2 minutes. Pour over cream cheese layer. Chill 4 hours or overnight.

Spread remaining whipped topping over pudding just before serving. Garnish, if desired.

Prep time: 30 minutes
Bake time: 20 minutes
Chill time: 4 hours

Top to bottom: Striped Delight, Berried Delight

BERRIED DELIGHT

Makes 18 servings

1 cup graham cracker crumbs
½ cup sugar, divided
⅓ cup PARKAY® Margarine, melted
1 package (8 ounces) PHILADELPHIA BRAND®
    Cream Cheese, softened
2⅔ cups cold milk, divided
3½ cups (8 ounces) COOL WHIP® Non-Dairy
    Whipped Topping, thawed, divided
2 pints strawberries, hulled and halved
1 package (6-serving size) JELL-O® Instant
    Pudding and Pie Filling, French Vanilla or
    Vanilla Flavor

PINWHEEL CAKE AND CREAM

Makes 10 servings

1 package (4-serving size) JELL-O® Instant
    Pudding and Pie Filling, French Vanilla or
    Vanilla Flavor
2 cups cold milk
1 cup thawed COOL WHIP® Non-Dairy Whipped
    Topping
1 small peach or nectarine, cut into bite-size pieces
1 teaspoon grated orange peel
1 pound cake loaf (10 ounces), cut into slices
2 cups summer fruit*

Prepare pudding mix with milk as directed on package.
Let stand 5 minutes or until slightly thickened. Fold in
whipped topping, peach and orange peel.

Arrange pound cake slices on round serving plate. Spoon
pudding mixture evenly over center of cake slices. Arrange
fruit over pudding mixture. Chill until ready to serve.

*We suggest any variety of berries, seedless grapes or
sliced peaches, nectarines or plums.

Prep time: 15 minutes

Pinwheel Cake and Cream

BERRIES 'N' BITS PUDDING

Makes 8 to 10 servings

1 (14-ounce) can EAGLE® Brand Sweetened
    Condensed Milk (NOT evaporated milk)
1½ cups cold water
1 (4-serving size) package *instant* vanilla flavor
    pudding mix
2 cups (1 pint) BORDEN® or MEADOW GOLD®
    Whipping Cream, whipped
36 vanilla wafers
1 quart fresh strawberries, hulled and sliced
¾ cup mini chocolate chips

In large bowl, combine sweetened condensed milk and
water. Add pudding mix; beat well. Chill 5 minutes. Fold
in whipped cream. Spoon *2 cups* pudding mixture into
3-quart glass serving bowl; top with half *each* of the
vanilla wafers, strawberries, mini chocolate chips and half
of remaining pudding mixture. Repeat layering. Cover;
chill. Garnish with additional mini chocolate chips, vanilla
wafers and strawberries if desired. Refrigerate leftovers.

STRAWBERRIES & CREAM DESSERT

Makes 10 to 12 servings

1 (14-ounce) can EAGLE® Brand Sweetened
    Condensed Milk (NOT evaporated milk)
½ cup cold water
1 (4-serving size) package *instant* vanilla flavor
    pudding mix
2 cups (1 pint) BORDEN® or MEADOW GOLD®
    Whipping Cream, whipped
1 (10¾- or 12-ounce) prepared loaf pound cake,
    cut into cubes (about 6 cups)
1 quart fresh strawberries, hulled and sliced
½ cup strawberry preserves
    Additional fresh strawberries, sliced
    Toasted slivered almonds

In large bowl, combine sweetened condensed milk and
water. Add pudding mix; beat well. Chill 5 minutes.
Fold in whipped cream. Spoon *2 cups* pudding mixture
into 4-quart glass serving bowl; top with half the cake
cubes, 2 cups strawberries, half the preserves and half
the remaining pudding. Repeat layering, ending with
pudding. Garnish with additional strawberries and
almonds. Cover; chill. Refrigerate leftovers.

HAWAIIAN TRIFLE

Makes 8 servings

2 packages (3⅛ ounces each) vanilla flavor pudding
    and pie filling mix (not instant)
2 cups milk
1½ cups DOLE® Pineapple Juice
2 cups whipping cream, divided
1 package (16 ounces) frozen pound cake, thawed
½ cup cream sherry
1 cup raspberry jam, melted
1 can (20 ounces) DOLE® Crushed Pineapple in
    Juice, drained
    Maraschino cherries (optional)

Prepare pudding mix according to package directions, using milk and pineapple juice as liquid. Place saucepan in bowl of ice water to cool pudding; stir often. In medium bowl, beat 1 cup cream until soft peaks form; fold into cooled pudding. Cut pound cake in half lengthwise. Drizzle sherry over cake halves; cut cake into chunks.

Spoon 1 cup pudding mixture into 2½- to 3-quart glass serving bowl. Top with half the cake and half the jam. Reserve ½ cup pineapple for garnish. Spoon half the remaining pineapple on top of jam in serving bowl. Spoon half the remaining pudding on top. Repeat layering with remaining cake, jam and pineapple. Top with remaining pudding. Refrigerate, covered, overnight.

In medium bowl, beat remaining 1 cup cream until soft peaks form; spread over top of trifle. Garnish trifle with reserved pineapple and maraschino cherries, if desired.

TRIFLE CUPS

Makes 6 servings

1 package (4-serving size) JELL-O® Brand
    Raspberry Flavor Gelatin
¾ cup boiling water
1 package BIRDS EYE® Quick Thaw Red
    Raspberries, thawed
    Ice cubes
12 shortbread or sugar cookies
1½ cups cold half-and-half or milk
1 package (4-serving size) JELL-O® Instant
    Pudding and Pie Filling, French Vanilla or
    Vanilla Flavor
½ cup thawed COOL WHIP® Non-Dairy Whipped
    Topping

Completely dissolve gelatin in boiling water. Drain raspberries, reserving syrup. Combine syrup and enough ice cubes to measure 1 cup. Add to gelatin, stirring until ice is melted. Place bowl in larger bowl of ice and water. Let stand, stirring occasionally, until gelatin is slightly thickened, about 5 minutes. Reserve 6 raspberries for garnish, if desired. Stir remaining raspberries into gelatin.

Crumble cookies into individual dessert dishes. Spoon gelatin mixture over cookies; chill until set but not firm.

Pour half-and-half into small bowl. Add pudding mix. Beat with wire whisk until well blended, about 1 to 2 minutes. Let stand 5 minutes or until slightly thickened. Fold in whipped topping. Spoon over gelatin mixture. Chill until set, about 1 hour. Garnish with reserved raspberries and additional whipped topping, if desired.

Prep time: 20 minutes
Chill time: 1 hour

CHOCOLATE RASPBERRY TRIFLE

Makes 8 to 10 servings

CUSTARD:
3 tablespoons cornstarch
1 tablespoon sugar
⅛ teaspoon salt
2 cups milk
3 egg yolks
2 cups (11½-ounce package) NESTLÉ® Toll House®
    Milk Chocolate Morsels, divided

TRIFLE:
1 cup heavy cream
1 tablespoon sugar
1 (10¾-ounce) frozen pound cake, thawed
2 tablespoons creme de cacao, divided
¼ cup seedless raspberry jam, divided
    Raspberries and NESTLÉ® Cocoa, for garnish

Custard: In 2-quart heavy-gauge saucepan, combine cornstarch, sugar and salt. Gradually add milk. Whisk in egg yolks until smooth. Cook over medium heat, stirring constantly, until mixture comes to a boil; boil 1 minute. Remove from heat. Stir in 1½ cups Nestlé® Toll House® Milk Chocolate Morsels until smooth. Press plastic wrap on surface; refrigerate until chilled.

Trifle: In small mixer bowl, beat heavy cream and sugar until stiff peaks form. Cut cake into ½-inch-thick slices. Cut 1 cake slice into thin strips; reserve for top. Arrange about half of remaining slices in bottom of 2-quart dessert bowl; sprinkle with 1 tablespoon creme de cacao. Spread 2 tablespoons raspberry jam over cake. Spoon half of custard over jam and cake; gently top with half of whipped cream. Repeat cake slices, liqueur, jam and custard layers once. Arrange cake strips on top of custard. Pipe or spoon remaining whipped cream between strips. Garnish with raspberries and sprinkle with cocoa. Top with remaining ½ cup Nestlé® Toll House® Milk Chocolate Morsels, if desired.

Chocolate Raspberry Trifle

Trifle Spectacular

TRIFLE SPECTACULAR

Makes 10 to 12 servings

1 package DUNCAN HINES® Moist Deluxe
   Devil's Food Cake Mix
1 can (14 ounces) sweetened condensed milk
1 cup water
1 package (4-serving size) vanilla instant pudding
   and pie filling mix
2 cups whipping cream, whipped
2 tablespoons orange juice, divided
2½ cups sliced fresh strawberries, divided
1 pint fresh raspberries, divided
2 kiwifruit, peeled and sliced, divided
1½ cups frozen whipped topping, thawed, for garnish
   Mint leaves, for garnish (optional)

1. Preheat oven to 350°F. Grease and flour two 9-inch
round cake pans.

2. Prepare, bake and cool cake following package
directions for basic recipe. Cut one cake layer into
1-inch cubes. Freeze other cake layer for later use.

3. Combine sweetened condensed milk and water in
large bowl. Stir until blended. Add pudding mix. Beat
until thoroughly blended. Refrigerate 5 minutes. Fold
whipped cream into pudding mixture.

4. To assemble, spread 2 cups pudding mixture into
3-quart trifle dish (or 3-quart clear glass bowl with
straight sides). Arrange half the cake cubes over pudding
mixture. Sprinkle with 1 tablespoon orange juice. Layer
with 1 cup strawberry slices, half the raspberries and
one-third of kiwifruit slices. Repeat layers. Top with
remaining pudding mixture. Garnish with whipped
topping, remaining ½ cup strawberry slices, kiwifruit
slices and mint leaves, if desired.

Tip: Since the different layers contribute to the beauty
of this recipe, arrange the fruit pieces to show attractively
along the sides of the trifle dish.

CHILLY STRAWBERRY SOUFFLÉS

Makes 8 to 10 servings

1 (10-ounce) package frozen strawberries, thawed
2 envelopes unflavored gelatin
2¼ cups cold water, divided
1 (8-ounce) package Light PHILADELPHIA
   BRAND® Neufchatel Cheese, softened
¼ cup sugar
1 tablespoon lemon juice
   Few drops red food coloring (optional)
2 cups thawed frozen whipped topping

• Drain strawberries, reserving liquid. Chop
strawberries; set aside.

• Soften gelatin in ½ cup water in saucepan for
1 minute; stir over low heat until dissolved. Add
remaining 1¾ cups water.

• Combine neufchatel cheese and sugar in large bowl,
mixing until well blended. Gradually add gelatin mixture
to neufchatel cheese mixture, mixing until well blended.
Stir in reserved strawberry liquid, lemon juice and food
coloring.

• Chill, stirring occasionally, until thickened but not
set. Beat with electric mixer or wire whisk until smooth.
Fold in strawberries and whipped topping.

• Wrap 3-inch collars of foil around individual dessert
dishes or cups; secure with tape. Pour mixture into
dishes; chill until firm. Remove collars before serving.

VARIATIONS

• Substitute 1-quart soufflé dish for individual dessert
dishes.

• Substitute PHILADELPHIA BRAND® Cream
Cheese for Neufchatel Cheese. Increase sugar to ⅔ cup.
Substitute 1 cup whipping cream, whipped, for whipped
topping.

CHILLED RASPBERRY SOUFFLÉ

Makes 6 cups

2 cups (two 10-ounce packages) frozen sweetened
     raspberries in syrup, thawed
3 ounces cream cheese
⅓ cup sugar
½ teaspoon vanilla
2 envelopes unflavored gelatin
¾ cup water
½ cup dry CARNATION® Nonfat Dry Milk
½ cup ice water
2 tablespoons lemon juice

Place raspberries and syrup, cream cheese, sugar and
vanilla in blender container. Cover; process until well
blended. Sprinkle gelatin over ¾ cup water in small
saucepan; let stand 1 minute to soften. Stir over low
heat until dissolved. Add to raspberry mixture in blender.
Cover; process until well blended. Strain into medium
bowl to remove seeds; discard seeds. Chill until mixture
mounds from spoon.

Fold piece of aluminum foil or waxed paper into a
24 × 3-inch strip. Wrap around a 4- to 5-cup soufflé
dish, allowing foil to extend 2 inches above top of dish;
secure with tape. Spray inside of foil strip with nonstick
cooking spray.

Combine dry nonfat milk, ice water and lemon juice in
small mixer bowl. Beat on high speed until stiff peaks
form, 4 to 6 minutes. Fold into raspberry mixture.
Spoon into soufflé dish. Chill until firm. Remove collar
from dish before serving.

FROZEN LEMON SOUFFLÉ

Makes 6 to 8 servings

1½ cups sugar
3 tablespoons cornstarch
1 envelope unflavored gelatin
1 cup water
⅔ cup REALEMON® Lemon Juice from
     Concentrate *or* REALIME® Lime Juice
     from Concentrate
Few drops yellow or green food coloring
     (optional)
3 egg whites*
1 cup (½ pint) whipping cream

In large saucepan, combine sugar, cornstarch and
gelatin; add water and ReaLemon® brand. Over medium
heat, cook and stir until slightly thickened; stir in food
coloring if desired. Cool. Chill until partially set, about
1 hour, stirring occasionally. In small mixer bowl, beat
egg whites until stiff but not dry; fold into sugar mixture.

In small mixer bowl, beat whipping cream until stiff
peaks form; fold into sugar mixture. Tape or tie a 3-inch
waxed paper or aluminum foil "collar" securely around
rim of 1-quart soufflé dish. Pour mixture into dish.
Freeze 6 hours or overnight. Remove "collar." Garnish
as desired. Return leftovers to freezer.

*Use only Grade A clean, uncracked eggs.

Tip: Soufflé can be chilled in refrigerator 6 hours
instead of frozen.

COLD APRICOT SOUFFLÉ

Makes 5 to 6 servings

9 fresh California apricots (13 ounces)
2 envelopes unflavored gelatin
½ cup water
¾ cup sugar
⅓ cup apricot brandy
6 eggs, separated*
1 cup whipping cream, whipped
     Additional apricot halves and mint sprigs
     (optional)

Tape a 3-inch waxed paper collar around a 5- to 6-cup
soufflé dish; oil dish and inside of waxed paper. Halve
9 apricots and discard pits. Place apricot halves in covered
blender container; process until smooth. Sprinkle gelatin
over water in medium saucepan; let stand 1 minute to
soften. Stir over low heat until gelatin is dissolved. Stir
in blended apricots, sugar and brandy.

Lightly beat yolks in small bowl; whisk into apricot
mixture. Cook over low heat until mixture thickens
slightly; pour into large bowl. Refrigerate until mixture
mounds slightly from spoon. Beat egg whites in large
bowl with electric mixer at high speed until stiff peaks
form. Stir about ½ cup egg whites into apricot mixture.
Gently fold in whipped cream and remaining egg whites.
Pour into soufflé dish; refrigerate at least 4 hours.
Remove paper collar before serving. Garnish with
additional apricot halves and mint sprigs, if desired.

*Use only clean, uncracked eggs

Favorite recipe from **California Apricot Advisory Board**

BAKED DESSERTS

BERRY COBBLER

Makes 6 servings

1 pint fresh raspberries (2½ cups)*
1 pint fresh blueberries *or* strawberries, sliced
   (2½ cups)*
2 tablespoons cornstarch
½ to ¾ cup sugar
1 cup all-purpose flour
1½ teaspoons baking powder
¼ teaspoon salt
⅓ cup milk
⅓ cup butter or margarine, melted
2 tablespoons thawed frozen unsweetened apple
   juice concentrate
¼ teaspoon ground nutmeg

Preheat oven to 375°F. Combine berries and cornstarch in medium bowl; toss lightly to coat. Add sugar; mix well. Spoon into 1½-quart or 8-inch square baking dish. Combine flour, baking powder and salt in medium bowl. Add milk, butter and concentrate; mix just until dry ingredients are moistened. Drop six heaping tablespoonfuls of batter evenly over berries; sprinkle with nutmeg.

Bake 25 minutes or until topping is golden brown and fruit is bubbly. Cool on wire rack. Serve warm or at room temperature.

*One (16-ounce) bag frozen raspberries and one (16-ounce) bag frozen blueberries or strawberries may be substituted for fresh berries. Thaw berries, reserving juices. Increase cornstarch to 3 tablespoons.

BLUEBERRY STREUSEL COBBLER

Makes 8 to 12 servings

1 pint fresh or frozen blueberries, rinsed
   and sorted
1 (14-ounce) can EAGLE® Brand Sweetened
   Condensed Milk (NOT evaporated milk)
2 teaspoons grated lemon peel
¾ cup plus 2 tablespoons cold margarine or butter
2 cups biscuit baking mix
½ cup firmly packed brown sugar
½ cup chopped nuts
   Blueberry Sauce (recipe follows)

Preheat oven to 325°F. In medium bowl, combine blueberries, sweetened condensed milk and peel. In large bowl, cut *¾ cup* margarine into *1½ cups* biscuit mix until crumbly; add blueberry mixture. Spread in greased 9-inch square baking pan. In small bowl, combine remaining *½ cup* biscuit mix and sugar; cut in remaining *2 tablespoons* margarine until crumbly. Add nuts. Sprinkle over blueberry mixture.

Bake 1 hour and 10 minutes or until golden. Serve warm with vanilla ice cream and Blueberry Sauce. Refrigerate leftovers.

Blueberry Sauce: In small saucepan, combine ½ cup granulated sugar, 1 tablespoon cornstarch, ½ teaspoon ground cinnamon and ¼ teaspoon ground nutmeg. Gradually add ½ cup water. Cook and stir until thickened. Stir in 1 pint fresh or frozen blueberries; cook and stir until hot. *Makes about 1⅔ cups*

Berry Cobbler

MINCE RASPBERRY COBBLER

Makes one 8-inch pie

Pastry for 1-crust pie
1 jar NONE SUCH® Ready-to-Use Mincemeat
    (Regular *or* Brandy & Rum)
1 (10-ounce) package frozen red raspberries in
    syrup, thawed
1 tablespoon cornstarch
1 egg yolk
2 tablespoons water

Preheat oven to 425°F. In medium bowl, combine
mincemeat, raspberries and cornstarch. Turn into 8-inch
square baking dish. Roll pastry to 9-inch square; cut slits
near center. Place pastry over filling; turn under edges,
seal and flute. Mix egg yolk and water; brush over entire
surface of pie.

Bake 30 minutes or until golden brown. Serve warm
with ice cream if desired.

BUTTERY CRANBERRY COBBLER

Makes 10 to 12 servings

1 package DUNCAN HINES® Moist Deluxe
    Butter Recipe Golden Cake Mix, divided
1 cup quick-cooking oats (not instant or
    old-fashioned), uncooked
¾ cup butter or margarine, softened and divided
2 eggs
⅓ cup water
1 can (16 ounces) whole-berry cranberry sauce

1. Preheat oven to 375°F. Grease and flour 13×9-
inch pan.

2. For topping, combine ½ cup dry cake mix, oats and
¼ cup butter in medium bowl with fork until crumbly.
Set aside.

3. For base, place remaining dry cake mix in large bowl.
Cut in remaining ½ cup butter with fork until crumbly.
Stir in eggs and water until mixture is moistened.
Spread in bottom of pan.

4. Stir cranberry sauce until smooth. Spread over batter
in pan. Sprinkle with topping.

5. Bake at 375°F for 35 to 40 minutes or until wooden
toothpick inserted in center comes out clean. Cool
10 minutes before serving.

Tip: To quickly soften cold butter, place 1 unwrapped
stick of butter in microwave oven and microwave at
HIGH (100% power) for 10 seconds.

DEEP DISH APPLE COBBLER

Makes 12 to 16 servings

CRUST AND TOPPING
1 package DUNCAN HINES® Moist Deluxe
    Yellow Cake Mix
1 cup quick-cooking oats (not instant or
    old-fashioned), uncooked
1 cup chopped walnuts
¾ cup butter or margarine, melted

FILLING
7½ cups peeled and sliced apples (about 6 large)
½ cup raisins
½ cup water
3 tablespoons sugar
2 teaspoons ground cinnamon
½ teaspoon ground nutmeg

1. Preheat oven to 350°F. Grease and flour 13×9-
inch pan.

2. For Crust and Topping, stir together cake mix, oats,
walnuts and melted butter in large bowl. Sprinkle half
of mixture into pan.

3. For Filling, combine apples, raisins, water, sugar,
cinnamon and nutmeg in large saucepan. Stir occasionally
over low heat for 10 minutes. Spread filling over crust
in pan. Sprinkle remaining topping mixture over filling.

4. Bake at 350°F for 35 minutes or until lightly browned.
Serve warm or at room temperature.

Tip: For a quick and easy preparation, apple filling can
be heated in the microwave oven. Combine filling
ingredients in microwave-safe bowl and microwave at
HIGH (100% power) for 6 minutes, stirring once.

BUTTERSCOTCH APPLE PECAN COBBLER

Makes 10 to 12 servings

FILLING:
2 cups (12-ounce package) NESTLÉ® Toll
    House® Butterscotch Flavored Morsels
¼ cup all-purpose flour
½ teaspoon ground cinnamon
2½ pounds tart apples, peeled, sliced

TOPPING:
½ cup all-purpose flour
¼ cup firmly packed brown sugar
¼ cup (½ stick) butter
1 cup chopped pecans
¾ cup quick or old-fashioned oats, uncooked
    Whipped cream or ice cream (optional)

Filling: Preheat oven to 350°F. In small bowl, combine Nestlé® Toll House® Butterscotch Flavored Morsels, flour and cinnamon; set aside. Place apples in ungreased 13×9-inch baking pan; sprinkle morsel mixture over apples. Bake 20 minutes.

Topping: In small bowl, combine flour and brown sugar. With pastry blender or 2 knives, cut in butter until crumbly. Stir in pecans and oats. Sprinkle over filling.

Bake 30 to 40 minutes longer until apples are tender. Cool slightly. Serve warm with whipped cream or ice cream.

BLUEBERRY PEAR CREAM CHEESE CRISP

Makes 16 servings

2 cups old-fashioned or quick oats, uncooked
1 cup all-purpose flour
⅓ cup granulated sugar
⅓ cup firmly packed brown sugar
½ cup PARKAY® Margarine, melted
2 (8-ounce) containers Light PHILADELPHIA
    BRAND® Pasteurized Process Cream
    Cheese Product
½ cup granulated sugar
2 eggs
1 tablespoon grated lemon peel
2 tablespoons lemon juice
2 pears, peeled, cored, sliced, halved
1 pint blueberries

• Preheat oven to 325°F.

• Mix together oats, flour, ⅓ cup granulated sugar and brown sugar in medium bowl until well blended. Stir in margarine.

• Reserve 1 cup oat mixture for topping. Press remaining oat mixture onto bottom of 13×9-inch baking pan. Bake 10 minutes.

• Beat cream cheese product and ½ cup granulated sugar in large mixing bowl at medium speed with electric mixer until well blended. Add eggs, one at a time, mixing well after each addition. Stir in lemon peel and juice; pour over crust.

• Layer pears evenly over cream cheese mixture; top with blueberries. Sprinkle reserved oat mixture over fruit.

• Bake 45 minutes. Serve warm with vanilla ice cream, if desired.

Prep time: 20 minutes
Cook time: 55 minutes

Pineapple Cherry-Berry Crunch

PINEAPPLE CHERRY-BERRY CRUNCH

Makes 9 to 12 servings

1 package DUNCAN HINES® Blueberry
    Muffin Mix
1 can (20 ounces) crushed pineapple with juice,
    undrained
1 can (21 ounces) cherry pie filling
1 cup quick-cooking oats (not instant or
    old-fashioned), uncooked
¼ cup chopped pecans
½ cup butter or margarine, melted

1. Preheat oven to 350°F.

2. Rinse blueberries from Mix with cold water and drain.

3. Spoon pineapple with juice evenly into ungreased 9-inch square pan. Spread pie filling over pineapple. Spoon blueberries over pie filling. Combine muffin mix and oats; sprinkle evenly over fruit. Sprinkle with pecans. Drizzle melted butter over top.

4. Bake at 350°F for 55 to 60 minutes or until golden brown and bubbly. Serve warm.

OLD-FASHIONED APPLE CRISP

Makes 8 servings

FRUIT
**4 cups sliced, peeled cooking apples (about
    1⅓ pounds or 3 to 4 medium)**
3 tablespoons apple juice

CRUMB MIXTURE
⅔ cup firmly packed brown sugar
½ cup all-purpose flour
**½ cup quick-cooking oats (not instant or
    old-fashioned), uncooked**
½ teaspoon ground cinnamon
¼ teaspoon salt
⅓ cup BUTTER FLAVOR CRISCO®
1 tablespoon milk
1 teaspoon vanilla

1. Preheat oven to 375°F.

2. For Fruit, toss apples with apple juice. Spoon into
8-inch square glass baking dish.

3. For Crumb Mixture, combine brown sugar, flour,
oats, cinnamon and salt in large bowl. Cut in Butter
Flavor Crisco® until coarse crumbs form. Combine milk
and vanilla. Drizzle over crumbs while tossing with fork.
Sprinkle over apple mixture.

4. Bake at 375°F for 35 to 40 minutes or until fruit is
tender, center is bubbly and crumbs are browned. Serve
warm with cream, whipped cream or ice cream, if desired.

Old-Fashioned Peach or Pear Crisp: Follow
above recipe using peaches or pears and substituting
1 tablespoon lemon juice for the apple juice.

Old-Fashioned Blueberry Crisp: Follow above
recipe using 3 cups blueberries and substituting
1 tablespoon lemon juice for the apple juice.

Apple-Raisin Crisp

APPLE-RAISIN CRISP

Makes 6 servings

**1 cup *plus* 3 tablespoons thawed frozen
    unsweetened apple juice concentrate, divided**
¼ cup uncooked rolled oats
**4 large cooking apples,* peeled, cored and sliced
    (about 6 cups sliced)**
¾ cup raisins
2 tablespoons cornstarch
2 teaspoons ground cinnamon, divided
½ teaspoon ground nutmeg
¼ teaspoon salt
½ cup all-purpose flour
¼ cup cold butter or margarine
**½ cup chopped walnuts or pecans (optional)
    Unsweetened whipped cream (optional)**

Preheat oven to 375°F. Combine 3 tablespoons apple
juice concentrate and oats in small bowl; mix lightly. Set
aside. Combine apples and raisins in large bowl; set aside.

*Use Jonathan, McIntosh or Rome Beauty apples.

Combine cornstarch, 1½ teaspoons cinnamon, nutmeg and salt in medium bowl; mix well. Blend in remaining 1 cup apple juice concentrate. Add to apple mixture; mix lightly to coat. Spoon into shallow 1½-quart or 8-inch square baking dish. Combine flour and remaining ½ teaspoon cinnamon; cut in butter with pastry blender or two knives until mixture resembles coarse crumbs. Add oat mixture; mix lightly. Stir in walnuts, if desired; sprinkle evenly over apple mixture.

Bake 35 minutes or until apples are tender. Serve warm, at room temperature or chilled with whipped cream, if desired.

Note: This is a sugar-free dessert.

PEACHY BLUEBERRY CRUNCH

Makes 9 servings

1 package DUNCAN HINES® Bakery Style
    Blueberry Muffin Mix
4 cups peeled, sliced peaches (about 4 large)
½ cup water
3 tablespoons firmly packed brown sugar
½ cup chopped pecans
⅓ cup butter or margarine, melted
    Whipped topping or ice cream (optional)

1. Preheat oven to 350°F.

2. Rinse blueberries from Mix with cold water and drain.

3. Arrange peach slices in ungreased 9-inch square pan. Sprinkle blueberries over peaches. Combine water and brown sugar in liquid measuring cup. Pour over fruit.

4. Combine muffin mix, pecans and melted butter in large bowl. Stir until thoroughly blended. (Mixture will be crumbly.) Sprinkle crumb mixture over fruit mixture. Sprinkle contents of topping packet from Mix over crumb mixture.

5. Bake at 350°F for 50 to 55 minutes or until lightly browned and bubbly. Serve warm with whipped topping or ice cream, if desired.

Tip: If peaches are not fully ripened when purchased, place several peaches in a paper bag at room temperature; loosely close and check daily. Peaches are ripe when they give to slight pressure.

TROPICAL CRISP

Makes 8 servings

1 DOLE® Fresh Pineapple
4 ripe, medium DOLE® Bananas, peeled
1 cup brown sugar, packed, divided
1 cup all-purpose flour
¾ cup rolled oats, uncooked
½ cup flaked coconut
½ teaspoon ground nutmeg
½ cup margarine

Preheat oven to 350°F. Twist crown from pineapple. Cut pineapple lengthwise into quarters. Cut fruit from shells with a knife. Trim off core and cut fruit into chunks. Cut bananas into chunks. In 9-inch baking dish, toss pineapple and bananas with ¼ cup brown sugar. In medium bowl, combine remaining ¾ cup brown sugar, flour, oats, coconut and nutmeg. Cut in margarine until crumbly. Sprinkle over fruit mixture.

Bake 45 to 50 minutes or until topping is crisp and juices have begun to bubble around edges. Serve warm.

Tropical Crisp

Blueberry Crisp

BLUEBERRY CRISP

Makes 8 servings

3 cups cooked brown rice
3 cups fresh blueberries*
¼ cup plus 3 tablespoons firmly packed brown
    sugar, divided
    Nonstick cooking spray
⅓ cup rice bran
¼ cup whole wheat flour
¼ cup chopped walnuts
1 teaspoon ground cinnamon
3 tablespoons margarine

Preheat oven to 375°F. Combine rice, blueberries, and 3 tablespoons sugar in large bowl. Coat 8 individual custard cups or 2-quart baking dish with cooking spray. Place rice mixture in cups or baking dish; set aside. Combine bran, flour, walnuts, remaining ¼ cup sugar, and cinnamon in small bowl. Cut in margarine with pastry blender until mixture resembles coarse meal. Sprinkle over rice mixture.

Bake 15 to 20 minutes or until thoroughly heated. Serve warm.

To Microwave: Prepare as directed using 2-quart microproof baking dish. Cook, uncovered, on HIGH (100% power) 4 to 5 minutes, rotating dish once during cooking time. Let stand 5 minutes. Serve warm.

*Substitute frozen unsweetened blueberries for the fresh blueberries, if desired. Thaw and drain before using. Or, substitute your choice of fresh fruit or combinations of fruit for the blueberries, if desired.

Favorite recipe from **USA Rice Council**

CHOCOLATE-APRICOT STEAMED PUDDING

Makes 8 servings

½ cup dried apricots, finely chopped
¼ cup apricot brandy *or* fruit juice, divided
2 packages (4-serving size each) JELL-O®
    Chocolate Flavor Pudding and Pie Filling
¼ cup all-purpose flour
¼ teaspoon CALUMET® Baking Powder
¼ teaspoon salt
4 eggs, separated
¼ cup sugar
¼ cup (½ stick) PARKAY® Margarine, melted
½ teaspoon vanilla
1 package (4-serving size) JELL-O® Vanilla Flavor
    Pudding and Pie Filling
3 cups milk

Soak apricots in 2 tablespoons brandy; set aside.

Combine chocolate pudding mixes, flour, baking powder and salt; set aside. Beat egg whites in medium bowl at high speed of electric mixer until foamy. Gradually add sugar; continue beating until stiff peaks form. Beat egg yolks in large bowl until thick and light in color. Fold in egg white mixture. Gently stir in flour mixture. Fold in apricot mixture, margarine and vanilla.

Pour into well-greased 1-quart mold; cover tightly with foil. Set mold on rack in large saucepan. Add enough hot water to saucepan to come halfway up side of mold. Heat water to boiling. Reduce heat; cover and steam 1½ hours.

Combine vanilla pudding mix with milk in medium saucepan. Cook and stir over medium heat until mixture comes to a full boil. Stir in remaining 2 tablespoons brandy. Unmold steamed pudding. Serve with warm sauce mixture.

Prep time: 30 minutes
Cook time: 1½ hours

BANANA BREAD PUDDING

Makes about 8 servings

2 extra-ripe, medium DOLE® Bananas, peeled
    and cut into chunks
4 slices bread, cubed
¼ cup DOLE® Raisins
1¼ cups milk
2 firm, medium DOLE® Bananas, peeled
2 eggs, lightly beaten
½ cup sugar
1 tablespoon margarine, melted
1 teaspoon vanilla extract
½ teaspoon ground nutmeg, divided
¼ teaspoon salt

Preheat oven to 350°F. Grease 1½-quart casserole dish. Place 2 extra-ripe bananas in blender. Process until puréed; use 1 cup for recipe.

In large bowl, combine bread cubes and raisins. Stir in puréed bananas and milk. Let stand 5 minutes. Slice 2 firm bananas; stir into bread mixture. Stir in eggs, sugar, margarine, vanilla, ¼ teaspoon nutmeg and salt. Pour into prepared dish. Sprinkle with remaining ¼ teaspoon nutmeg.

Place casserole in large pan. Pour boiling water into large pan to depth of 2 inches. Bake 1 hour or until knife inserted in center comes out clean. Remove casserole from water; serve warm.

Chocolate Cinnamon Bread Pudding

CHOCOLATE CINNAMON BREAD PUDDING

Makes 6 to 8 servings

4 cups soft white bread cubes (5 slices)
½ cup chopped nuts
3 eggs
¼ cup unsweetened cocoa
2 teaspoons vanilla extract
1 teaspoon ground cinnamon
½ teaspoon salt
1 (14 ounce) can EAGLE® Brand Sweetened
    Condensed Milk (NOT evaporated milk)
2¾ cups water
2 tablespoons margarine or butter, melted
    Cinnamon Cream Sauce (recipe follows)

Preheat oven to 350°F. Butter 9-inch square baking pan. Place bread cubes and nuts in prepared pan. In large bowl, beat eggs, cocoa, vanilla, cinnamon and salt; add sweetened condensed milk, water and margarine. Pour evenly over bread, moistening completely.

Bake 40 to 45 minutes or until knife inserted in center comes out clean. Cool slightly. Serve warm with Cinnamon Cream Sauce. Refrigerate leftovers.

Cinnamon Cream Sauce: In medium saucepan, combine 1 cup (½ pint) BORDEN® or MEADOW GOLD® Whipping Cream, ⅔ cup firmly packed brown sugar, 1 teaspoon vanilla extract and ½ teaspoon ground cinnamon. Bring to a boil; reduce heat and boil rapidly 6 to 8 minutes or until thickened, stirring occasionally. Cool slightly. Serve warm.   *Makes about 1 cup sauce*

GOLDEN BREAD PUDDING

Makes 6 to 8 servings

4 cups soft white bread cubes (5 slices)
3 eggs
1 teaspoon ground cinnamon
3 cups water
1 (14-ounce) can EAGLE® Brand Sweetened
    Condensed Milk (NOT evaporated milk)
2 tablespoons margarine or butter, melted
2 teaspoons vanilla extract
½ teaspoon salt

Preheat oven to 350°F. Place bread cubes in buttered 9-inch square baking pan. In large bowl, beat eggs and cinnamon; stir in remaining ingredients. Pour evenly over bread, moistening completely.

Bake 45 to 50 minutes or until knife inserted in center comes out clean. Cool. Serve warm or chilled. Refrigerate leftovers.

Tip: For a softer, more custard-like bread pudding, decrease bread cubes to 3 cups (4 slices).

Apple Bread Pudding: Arrange 2 cups pared, cored, chopped all-purpose apples (3 medium) and ½ cup raisins in baking pan. Add bread cubes. Increase margarine to ¼ cup. Reduce water to 1¾ cups. Proceed as above.

Pineapple Bread Pudding: Add 1 (8- or 8¼-ounce) can crushed pineapple, undrained, to bread cubes. Reduce water to 2¾ cups. Proceed as above.

FRENCH APPLE BREAD PUDDING

Makes 6 to 8 servings

3 eggs
1 (14-ounce) can EAGLE® Brand Sweetened
    Condensed Milk (NOT evaporated milk)
3 medium all-purpose apples, pared, cored and
    finely chopped (about 2 cups)
1¾ cups hot water
¼ cup margarine or butter, melted
1 teaspoon ground cinnamon
1 teaspoon vanilla extract
4 cups French bread cubes (about 6 ounces)
½ cup raisins (optional)
    BORDEN® or MEADOW GOLD® Whipping
    Cream, whipped

Preheat oven to 350°F. In large bowl, beat eggs; add sweetened condensed milk, apples, water, margarine, cinnamon and vanilla. Stir in bread and raisins, completely moistening bread. Turn into buttered 9-inch square baking pan.

Bake 1 hour or until knife inserted near center comes out clean. Cool. Serve warm with whipped cream. Garnish as desired. Refrigerate leftovers.

BAKED LEMON SPONGE PUDDING

Makes 6 servings

2 eggs, separated
1 cup *undiluted* CARNATION® Evaporated Milk
⅓ cup sugar
⅓ cup all-purpose flour
3 tablespoons lemon juice
2 tablespoons butter or margarine, melted
2 teaspoons grated lemon peel
¼ cup sugar
    Additional grated lemon peel
    Raspberry Sauce (recipe follows)

Baked Lemon Sponge Pudding

Preheat oven to 350°F. In medium bowl, beat egg yolks with wire whisk. Blend in evaporated milk, *⅓ cup* sugar, flour, lemon juice, butter, and *2 teaspoons* grated lemon peel. In small mixer bowl, beat egg whites just until soft peaks form. Gradually add ¼ *cup* sugar, beating just until stiff peaks form and sugar is dissolved. Do not overbeat. Carefully fold egg white mixture into lemon mixture. Spoon into six 6-ounce ungreased custard cups. Place cups in 13×9-inch baking pan. Fill outer pan with hot water to depth of 1 inch.

Bake 35 to 45 minutes or until light golden brown. Carefully remove custard cups from hot water. Sprinkle tops with additional grated lemon peel. Serve immediately with Raspberry Sauce.

Raspberry Sauce: In small saucepan, combine 1½ cups (12-ounce package) whole, unsweetened frozen raspberries, thawed, and ¼ cup sugar. Cook and stir until sugar is dissolved. Place mixture in blender or food processor; process until smooth. Strain mixture through sieve into bowl to remove seeds. Serve warm.

Peaches and Cinnamon Rice Pudding

PEACHES AND CINNAMON RICE PUDDING

Makes 4 servings

1 cup water
⅓ cup uncooked rice (*not* converted)
1 tablespoon butter or margarine
⅛ teaspoon salt
1 can (16 ounces) sliced peaches in unsweetened juice, undrained
½ cup milk, divided
2 teaspoons cornstarch
½ teaspoon ground cinnamon
¼ cup no-sugar-added peach fruit spread
½ cup heavy cream (optional)
1 tablespoon no-sugar-added peach fruit spread (optional)
   Fresh peach slices (optional)
   Cinnamon sticks (optional)

Combine water, rice, butter and salt in medium saucepan. Bring to a boil over high heat. Reduce heat to low. Cover; simmer until rice is tender, about 25 minutes. Remove from heat.

Drain canned peaches, reserving ½ cup juice; set peaches aside. Add reserved juice and ¼ cup milk to rice mixture; set aside. Combine cornstarch and cinnamon in small bowl; mix well. Gradually add remaining ¼ cup milk, stirring until smooth. Add to rice mixture; return to heat. Bring to a boil over medium-high heat, stirring constantly. Reduce heat to low. Simmer, stirring frequently, until thickened, about 2 minutes. Remove from heat; stir in ¼ cup fruit spread. Cool to room temperature, stirring occasionally. Chop drained peaches; stir into pudding. Serve at room temperature or chilled.

If desired, beat cream and 1 tablespoon fruit spread until soft peaks form. Serve with pudding. Garnish with fresh peach slices and cinnamon sticks, if desired.

Note: This is a sugar-free dessert.

BAKED ALMOND PUDDING

Makes 8 to 10 servings

¼ cup firmly packed brown sugar
¾ cup slivered almonds, toasted
1 (14-ounce) can EAGLE® Brand Sweetened Condensed Milk (NOT evaporated milk)
5 eggs
1 cup (½ pint) BORDEN® or MEADOW GOLD® Whipping Cream
¼ cup water
½ teaspoon almond extract
   Additional toasted almonds (optional)

Preheat oven to 325°F. In 8-inch round layer cake pan, sprinkle brown sugar; set aside.

In blender or food processor container, grind ¾ *cup* nuts; add sweetened condensed milk, eggs, ½ *cup* cream, water and extract. Blend thoroughly. Pour into prepared pan; set in larger pan. Fill larger pan with 1 inch hot water.

Bake 40 to 45 minutes or until knife inserted near center comes out clean. Cool. Chill. Invert onto serving plate. Beat remaining ½ *cup* cream for garnish; top with additional nuts if desired. Refrigerate leftovers.

FRUIT GLAZED BAKED CUSTARDS

Makes 6 servings

3 eggs
1 (14-ounce) can EAGLE® Brand Sweetened
    Condensed Milk (NOT evaporated milk)
1 cup water
1 teaspoon vanilla extract
½ cup red currant jelly
2 tablespoons orange-flavored liqueur or
    orange juice
1 tablespoon cornstarch
    Few drops red food coloring (optional)
    Fresh strawberries or other fruit

Preheat oven to 350°F. In medium mixing bowl, beat eggs; stir in sweetened condensed milk, water and vanilla. Pour equal portions of mixture into six 6-ounce custard cups. Set cups in shallow pan; fill pan with 1 inch hot water.

Bake 45 to 50 minutes or until knife inserted in centers comes out clean. Cool.

In small saucepan, combine jelly, liqueur and cornstarch. Cook and stir until jelly melts and mixture comes to a boil. Stir in food coloring if desired. Cool to room temperature.

Invert custards onto serving plates. Top with sauce and strawberries. Refrigerate leftovers.

CARAMEL FLAN

Makes 10 to 12 servings

¾ cup sugar
4 eggs
1¾ cups water
1 (14-ounce) can EAGLE® Brand Sweetened
    Condensed Milk (NOT evaporated milk)
½ teaspoon vanilla extract
⅛ teaspoon salt

Preheat oven to 350°F. In heavy skillet, over medium heat, cook sugar, stirring constantly until melted and caramel colored. Pour into ungreased 9-inch round layer cake pan, tilting to coat bottom completely. In medium bowl, beat eggs; stir in water, sweetened condensed milk, vanilla and salt. Pour over caramelized sugar; set cake pan in larger pan. Fill larger pan with 1 inch hot water.

Bake 55 to 60 minutes or until knife inserted near center comes out clean. Cool. Chill thoroughly. Loosen side of flan with knife; invert onto serving plate with rim. Garnish as desired. Refrigerate leftovers.

CARAMEL PUMPKIN FLAN

Makes about 6 servings

¾ cup sugar, divided
4 eggs
1 cup canned pumpkin
1 teaspoon ground cinnamon
¼ teaspoon salt
¼ teaspoon ground ginger
¼ teaspoon ground allspice
¼ teaspoon ground nutmeg
1 cup half-and-half
½ teaspoon vanilla
    Boiling water

Preheat oven to 350°F. Melt ½ cup sugar in 8-inch skillet over medium heat, stirring constantly, until sugar is caramelized. Immediately pour caramel syrup into 1-quart soufflé dish or other baking dish 7 to 8 inches in diameter. Tilt dish so caramel syrup flows over bottom and slightly up side. Let cool 10 minutes.

Beat eggs slightly on medium speed in large bowl with electric mixer. Add remaining ¼ cup sugar, pumpkin, cinnamon, salt, ginger, allspice and nutmeg. Beat until well blended. Add half-and-half and vanilla; beat until smooth. Pour over caramel syrup. Set dish in larger pan. Pour boiling water into larger pan to depth of 1½ inches.

Bake 45 to 50 minutes or until knife inserted in center comes out clean. Remove from water; place on wire rack to cool. Refrigerate, loosely covered, 6 hours or overnight.

To unmold, run knife around edge of dish; cover with rimmed serving plate. Holding plate in place, invert dish. Flan and caramel syrup will slide onto plate. Cut into wedges to serve; spoon caramel syrup over top.

BUTTERSCOTCH APPLE SQUARES

Makes about 12 servings

¼ cup margarine or butter
½ cup graham cracker crumbs
2 small all-purpose apples, pared, cored and chopped (about 1¼ cups)
1 (6-ounce) package butterscotch-flavored chips
1 (14-ounce) can EAGLE® Brand Sweetened Condensed Milk (NOT evaporated milk)
1 (3½-ounce) can flaked coconut (1⅓ cups)
1 cup chopped nuts

Preheat oven to 350°F (325°F for glass dish). In 13×9-inch baking pan, melt margarine in oven. Sprinkle crumbs evenly over margarine; top with apples. In heavy saucepan, over medium heat, melt chips with sweetened condensed milk. Pour butterscotch mixture evenly over apples. Top with coconut and nuts; press down firmly.

Bake 25 to 30 minutes or until lightly browned. Cool. Cut into squares. Garnish as desired. Refrigerate leftovers.

To Microwave: In 12×7-inch microwave-safe baking dish, melt margarine on 100% power (high) 1 minute. Sprinkle crumbs evenly over margarine; top with apples. In 1-quart glass measure with handle, melt chips with sweetened condensed milk on 70% power (medium-high) 2 to 3 minutes. Stir until smooth. Pour butterscotch mixture evenly over apples. Top with coconut and nuts. Press down firmly. Cook on 100% power (high) 8 to 9 minutes. Proceed as above.

Butterscotch Apple Square

"KEY" LIME DESSERT SQUARES

Makes about 16 servings

CRUST
½ cup chopped pecans
1 package DUNCAN HINES® Moist Deluxe White Cake Mix
½ cup butter or margarine, melted

FILLING
3 egg yolks
1 can (14 ounces) sweetened condensed milk
⅔ cup lime juice
1 drop green food coloring

TOPPING
1 container (8 ounces) frozen non-dairy whipped topping, thawed
Lime slices (optional)

1. Preheat oven to 350°F.

2. For Crust, spread pecans in shallow baking pan. Bake 5 minutes, stirring occasionally, or until lightly browned.

3. Combine pecans, cake mix and butter in large bowl. Stir until crumbs form. Spread in bottom of ungreased 13×9-inch pan. Press lightly.

4. For Filling, combine egg yolks, sweetened condensed milk, lime juice and food coloring in medium bowl. Stir until well blended. Spread over crust.

5. Bake at 350°F for 15 minutes or until set. Cool 15 minutes. Refrigerate until chilled, about 2 hours. Cut into squares. Top with dollops of whipped topping and lime slices, if desired.

Tip: Leftover egg whites will keep refrigerated in airtight container for a few days.

CRUNCHY LEMON SQUARES

Makes 9 servings

1 cup unsifted all-purpose flour
1 cup quick-cooking oats, uncooked
½ cup coarsely chopped pecans
½ cup firmly packed light brown sugar
½ cup flaked coconut
1 teaspoon baking powder
½ cup margarine or butter, melted
1 (14-ounce) can EAGLE® Brand Sweetened Condensed Milk (NOT evaporated milk)
½ cup REALEMON® Lemon Juice from Concentrate
1 tablespoon grated lemon peel

Preheat oven to 350°F (325°F for glass dish). In medium bowl, combine flour, oats, nuts, sugar, coconut, baking powder and margarine; stir until crumbly. Reserving half the crumb mixture, press remainder evenly on bottom of 9-inch square baking pan. In medium bowl, combine sweetened condensed milk, ReaLemon® brand and peel; spread into prepared pan. Sprinkle with reserved crumb mixture.

Bake 25 to 30 minutes or until lightly browned. Cool. Chill. Cut into squares. Garnish as desired. Refrigerate leftovers.

Pumpkin Squares

PUMPKIN SQUARES

Makes 12 to 16 servings

CRUST
1 package DUNCAN HINES® Moist Deluxe
   Spice Cake Mix
½ cup CRISCO® Oil or CRISCO® PURITAN® Oil
½ teaspoon salt
¼ teaspoon baking soda

TOPPING
1 can (16 ounces) solid-pack pumpkin
1 can (12 ounces) evaporated milk
2 eggs, lightly beaten
¾ cup sugar
1 teaspoon ground cinnamon
½ teaspoon salt
½ teaspoon ground ginger
¼ teaspoon ground cloves
   Whipped topping, for garnish
   Pecan halves, for garnish

1. Preheat oven to 350°F.

2. For Crust, combine cake mix, Crisco® Oil, ½ teaspoon salt and baking soda in large bowl. Stir until thoroughly blended. Spread evenly in ungreased 13×9-inch pan.

3. Bake at 350°F for 20 to 25 minutes or until set.

4. For Topping, combine pumpkin, evaporated milk, eggs, sugar, cinnamon, ½ teaspoon salt, ginger and cloves in large bowl. Stir until well blended. Pour pumpkin mixture over hot crust.

5. Bake at 350°F for 25 to 30 minutes or until center is firm. Cool completely. Refrigerate until ready to serve. Cut into squares. Garnish with dollops of whipped topping. Decorate with pecan halves.

Tip: For a different presentation, serve with ice cream and garnish with shaved chocolate.

OATMEAL APPLESAUCE SQUARES

Makes about 12 squares

1 package DUNCAN HINES® Moist Deluxe Spice
   Cake Mix
2 eggs
½ cup butter or margarine, softened
2 cups applesauce
1 cup quick-cooking oats (not instant or
   old-fashioned), uncooked
½ cup firmly packed brown sugar

1. Preheat oven to 350°F. Grease 13×9-inch pan.

2. Combine cake mix, eggs and butter in large bowl. Beat at low speed with electric mixer until blended. Spread in pan.

3. Bake at 350°F for 15 minutes. Remove from oven.

4. Pour applesauce over baked layer. Combine oats and brown sugar in small bowl. Mix until crumbly. Sprinkle over applesauce. Return to oven.

5. Bake at 350°F for 10 minutes or until lightly browned. Cool. Cut into squares.

Tip: You can use flavored applesauce in place of regular applesauce.

CHERRY TURNOVERS

Makes 6 turnovers

8 frozen phyllo dough sheets, thawed
¼ cup butter or margarine, melted
6 tablespoons no-sugar-added black cherry fruit
    spread
1½ tablespoons cherry-flavored liqueur (optional)
1 egg
1 teaspoon cold water

Preheat oven to 400°F. Lightly brush each phyllo sheet with butter; stack. Cut through all sheets to form six (5-inch) squares. Combine fruit spread and cherry liqueur, if desired. Place 1 tablespoon fruit spread mixture in center of each stack of eight phyllo squares; brush edges of phyllo with butter. Fold edges over to form triangle; gently press edges together to seal. Place on ungreased cookie sheet. Beat together egg and water; brush over phyllo triangles.

Bake 10 minutes or until golden brown. Cool on wire rack. Serve warm or at room temperature.

Note: This is a sugar-free dessert.

POLYNESIAN CHOCOLATE CRÊPES

Makes 16 to 18 servings

Pineapple Cream Filling (recipe follows)
3 eggs
¾ cup water
½ cup BORDEN® or MEADOW GOLD® Coffee
    Cream *or* Half-and-Half
¾ cup plus 2 tablespoons unsifted all-purpose flour
3 tablespoons unsweetened cocoa
2 tablespoons sugar
⅛ teaspoon salt
3 tablespoons margarine or butter, melted
    and cooled
Orange Fudge Topping (recipe follows)

Prepare Pineapple Cream Filling. In blender or food processor container, combine eggs, water and cream; blend 10 seconds. Add flour, cocoa, sugar, salt and margarine; blend until smooth. Let stand at room temperature 10 minutes.

Lightly oil 6-inch crêpe pan. Over medium heat, pour 2 to 3 tablespoons batter into pan. Lift and tilt pan to spread batter. Return to heat; cook until surface begins to dry. Loosen crêpe around edges; turn and lightly cook other side. Invert pan over waxed paper; remove crêpe. Repeat with remaining batter.

Spoon about ¼ cup Pineapple Cream Filling onto each crêpe; roll up. Place seam-side-down on serving plate. Serve with Orange Fudge Topping. Refrigerate leftovers.

PINEAPPLE CREAM FILLING

1 (14-ounce) can EAGLE® Brand Sweetened
    Condensed Milk (NOT evaporated milk)
1 (15¼-ounce) can crushed juice-pack pineapple,
    well drained
1 teaspoon grated orange peel
¼ cup orange juice
3 tablespoons REALEMON® Lemon Juice from
    Concentrate
1 cup (½ pint) BORDEN® or MEADOW GOLD®
    Whipping Cream, whipped

In medium bowl, combine all ingredients except whipped cream; mix well. Cover; chill at least 2 hours. Just before using, fold in whipped cream.

Makes about 4 cups

Orange Fudge Topping: In heavy saucepan, over low heat, melt 2 tablespoons margarine or butter; stir in ⅓ cup unsweetened cocoa. Add ¼ cup orange juice and 3 tablespoons water; mix well. Stir in 1 (14-ounce) can Eagle® Brand Sweetened Condensed Milk (NOT evaporated milk). Over medium heat, cook and stir until thickened and bubbly, about 5 minutes. Remove from heat; stir in 1 teaspoon vanilla extract. Serve warm.

Makes about 1½ cups

KIWIFRUIT AND PEAR PASTRY

Makes 12 to 16 servings

1 package (17¼ ounces) frozen puff pastry sheets,
    thawed according to package directions
4 ounces almond paste, sliced very thin
½ pound California kiwifruit, pared, sliced
1 pear, pared, cored and sliced
Powdered sugar

Preheat oven to 425°F. Place 1 puff pastry sheet on ungreased cookie sheet. Layer almond paste, kiwifruit and pear slices on pastry to within ½ inch of edges. Top with remaining puff pastry sheet; press edges together to seal. Use knife to pierce steam vents in decorative design on top pastry.

Bake 20 minutes or until golden brown. Let pastry cool slightly before carefully sliding it onto serving plate. Cool completely. Sprinkle with powdered sugar. Cut into squares.

Favorite recipe from **California Kiwifruit Commission**

Cherry Turnovers

Quick "Baked" Apple

QUICK "BAKED" APPLES

Makes 4 servings

4 cooking apples*
2 tablespoons chopped raisins
2 tablespoons chopped dates
2 tablespoons chopped walnuts or pecans
1 tablespoon butter or margarine, melted
1 teaspoon cornstarch
¾ teaspoon ground cinnamon
¾ cup thawed frozen unsweetened apple juice
    concentrate
Sour cream or crème frâiche (optional)

To Microwave: Remove peel from top and halfway down sides of each apple, starting at stem end. With apple corer or sharp knife, remove core to within ¼ inch of bottom of apple, leaving bottom stem end intact. Place apples in 9-inch microwavable pie plate or shallow baking dish. Combine raisins, dates, walnuts and butter; spoon into centers of apples. Combine cornstarch and cinnamon. Blend in apple juice concentrate; drizzle over apples.

Microwave, uncovered, on HIGH (100% power) 10 to 12 minutes or until apples are tender when pierced with sharp knife, rotating dish every 6 minutes. Let stand 5 to 10 minutes before serving. Spoon juices from dish over apples. Serve warm or at room temperature with sour cream, if desired.

*Use Jonathon, McIntosh or Rome Beauty apples.

Notes: For 2 servings, cut all ingredients in half. Peel, core and fill apples as directed. Place in 9-inch microwavable pie plate or shallow baking dish. Microwave on HIGH 5 to 8 minutes or until tender when pierced with sharp knife, rotating dish after 4 minutes. Continue as directed.

This is a sugar-free dessert.

APPLE DUMPLINGS

Makes 6 dumplings

PASTRY
Unbaked 9-inch Classic CRISCO® *Double* Crust (page 80)

FILLING
6 baking apples (about 3 inches in diameter), peeled and cored
⅓ cup chopped pecans
⅓ cup raisins
½ teaspoon ground cinnamon

SYRUP
2 cups firmly packed brown sugar
1 cup water

TOPPING
Whipped cream (optional)

1. Heat oven to 425°F. Grease 11½ × 8-inch baking dish.

2. For Pastry, roll out two-thirds of pastry into 14-inch square on lightly floured surface. Cut into 4 squares. Roll remaining pastry into 14 × 7-inch rectangle. Cut into 2 squares.

3. For Filling, place 1 apple in center of each pastry square. Combine nuts, raisins and cinnamon. Spoon into centers of apples.

4. Moisten corners of each pastry square. Bring 2 opposite corners of pastry up over apple and press together. Repeat with other corners. Press pastry seams together along sides of dumpling. Place dumplings in prepared baking dish.

5. For Syrup, combine brown sugar and water in medium saucepan on low heat. Stir until mixture comes to a boil. Pour carefully around dumplings.

6. Bake at 425°F for 40 minutes or until apples are tender and pastry is golden brown. Spoon syrup over dumplings several times during baking. Serve warm with whipped cream, if desired.

CHOCOLATE PUFF

Makes 6 servings

1 package (8 ounces) BAKER'S® Semi-Sweet
   Chocolate
⅔ cup corn syrup
4 eggs
¼ cup milk
1 package (3 ounces) PHILADELPHIA BRAND®
   Cream Cheese, cubed and softened
   Powdered sugar (optional)

Preheat oven to 375°F.

Microwave chocolate and corn syrup in large microwavable bowl on HIGH (100% power) 2 minutes. Stir until chocolate is completely melted. Cool slightly.

Blend eggs and milk in blender or food processor until smooth. With blender running, gradually add cream cheese, blending until smooth. Add chocolate mixture; blend until well mixed. Pour into ungreased 1½-quart soufflé or baking dish.

Bake for 50 to 55 minutes or until knife inserted into center comes out clean. Sprinkle with powdered sugar, if desired.

Prep time: 15 minutes
Bake time: 50 to 55 minutes

Saucepan Preparation: Heat chocolate and corn syrup in heavy 2-quart saucepan over very low heat until chocolate is melted, stirring constantly. Continue as above.

INDIVIDUAL FUDGE SOUFFLÉS

Makes 8 servings

½ cup (1 stick) butter or margarine, softened
1¼ cups granulated sugar
1 teaspoon vanilla extract
4 eggs
⅔ cup milk
½ teaspoon powdered instant coffee
⅔ cup all-purpose flour
⅔ cup HERSHEY'S Cocoa
1½ teaspoons baking powder
1 cup (½ pint) whipping cream
2 tablespoons powdered sugar

Preheat oven to 325°F. Grease and sugar eight 6-ounce ramekins or custard cups; set aside. In large mixer bowl, beat butter, granulated sugar and vanilla until light and fluffy. Add eggs, one at a time, beating well after each addition. Scald milk; remove from heat and add powdered coffee, stirring until dissolved. Combine flour, cocoa and baking powder; add alternately with milk mixture to butter mixture. Beat 1 minute on medium speed.

Divide batter evenly among prepared ramekins. Place ramekins in two 8-inch square pans; place pans in oven. Pour hot water into pans to a depth of ⅛ inch.

Bake 45 to 50 minutes, adding more water if necessary, until wooden toothpick inserted in centers comes out clean. Remove pans from oven; allow ramekins to stand in water 5 minutes. Remove ramekins from water; cool slightly. Serve in ramekins or invert onto dessert dishes. Beat cream with powdered sugar until stiff; spoon onto warm soufflés.

PUMPKIN SOUFFLÉ

Makes 1½-quart soufflé

¼ cup butter
¼ cup all-purpose flour
1 cup milk
½ cup LIBBY'S® Solid Pack Pumpkin
½ teaspoon ground cloves
¼ teaspoon ground cinnamon
¼ teaspoon ground nutmeg
4 eggs, separated
½ teaspoon cream of tartar
⅓ cup granulated sugar
   Powdered sugar (optional)

Preheat oven to 350°F. In 2-quart saucepan, melt butter; whisk in flour. Cook, stirring constantly, for 2 minutes. Remove from heat; stir in milk. Cook over medium heat, stirring constantly, 3 to 5 minutes or until thickened. Remove from heat; stir in pumpkin, cloves, cinnamon and nutmeg.

In small mixer bowl, beat egg yolks about 5 minutes or until thick and lemon colored. Add small amount of pumpkin mixture to yolks; mix well. Add yolk mixture to pumpkin mixture; stir well. In large mixer bowl, beat egg whites and cream of tartar until frothy. Gradually beat in granulated sugar until stiff peaks form. Fold *one-fourth* of beaten egg whites into pumpkin mixture to lighten mixture. Fold in *remaining* egg whites. Butter 1½ quart soufflé dish; dust with powdered sugar, if desired. Spoon mixture into soufflé dish.

Bake for 40 to 45 minutes, or until long wooden skewer or knife inserted near center comes out clean. Sprinkle with powdered sugar, if desired. Serve immediately.

COOKIES

CUT-OUT SUGAR COOKIES

Makes about 3 dozen cookies

⅔ cup **BUTTER FLAVOR CRISCO®**
¾ **cup sugar**
1 **tablespoon plus 1 teaspoon milk**
1 **teaspoon vanilla**
1 **egg**
2 **cups all-purpose flour**
1½ **teaspoons baking powder**
¼ **teaspoon salt**
   Colored sugars and decors (optional)

1. Combine Butter Flavor Crisco®, sugar, milk and vanilla in large bowl. Beat at medium speed of electric mixer until well blended and creamy. Beat in egg.

2. Combine flour, baking powder and salt. Mix into creamed mixture at low speed until well blended. Cover and refrigerate several hours or overnight.

3. Preheat oven to 375°F. Roll out dough, half at a time, to about ⅛-inch thickness on floured surface. Cut dough out with cookie cutters. Place 2 inches apart on ungreased cookie sheet. Sprinkle with colored sugars and decors or leave plain and frost when cooled.

4. Bake 7 to 9 minutes, or until set. Remove immediately to wire rack.

Lemon or Orange Cut-Out Sugar Cookies: Add 1 teaspoon grated lemon or orange peel and 1 teaspoon lemon or orange extract to dough in Step 1.

Creamy Vanilla Frosting: Combine ½ cup Butter Flavor Crisco®, 1 pound (4 cups) powdered sugar, ⅓ cup milk and 1 teaspoon vanilla in medium bowl. Beat at low speed of electric mixer until well blended. Scrape bowl. Beat at high speed for 2 minutes, or until smooth and creamy. One or two drops food color can be used to tint each cup of frosting, if desired. Frost cooled cookies. (This frosting works well in decorating tube.)

Lemon or Orange Creamy Frosting: Prepare Creamy Vanilla Frosting, adding ⅓ cup lemon or orange juice in place of milk. Add 1 teaspoon orange peel with orange juice.

Easy Chocolate Frosting: Place ⅓ cup Butter Flavor Crisco® in medium microwave-safe bowl. Cover with waxed paper. Microwave at HIGH (100% power) until melted (or melt on rangetop in small saucepan on low heat). Add ¾ cup unsweetened cocoa and ¼ teaspoon salt. Beat at low speed of electric mixer until blended. Add ½ cup milk and 2 teaspoons vanilla. Beat at low speed. Add 1 pound (4 cups) powdered sugar, 1 cup at a time. Beat at low speed after each addition until smooth and creamy. Add more sugar to thicken or milk to thin until of good spreading consistency.

Chocolate Dipped Cut-Out Sugar Cookies: Combine 1 cup semi-sweet chocolate chips and 1 teaspoon Butter Flavor Crisco® in microwave-safe measuring cup. Microwave at MEDIUM (50% power). Stir after 1 minute. Repeat until smooth (or melt on rangetop in small saucepan on very low heat). Dip one end of cooled cookie halfway up in chocolate. Place on waxed paper until chocolate is firm.

Chocolate Nut Cut-Out Sugar Cookies: Dip cookie in melted chocolate as directed. Sprinkle with finely chopped nuts before chocolate hardens.

DROP SUGAR COOKIES

Makes about 5½ dozen cookies

2½ cups sifted all-purpose flour
¾ teaspoon salt
½ teaspoon ARM & HAMMER® Pure Baking Soda
½ cup butter or margarine, softened
½ cup vegetable shortening
1 cup sugar
1 egg
1 teaspoon vanilla extract
2 tablespoons milk

Preheat oven to 400°F. Sift together flour, salt and baking soda. Set aside. Beat butter and shortening in large bowl with electric mixer on medium speed until blended; add sugar gradually and continue beating until light and fluffy. Beat in egg and vanilla. Add flour mixture and beat until smooth; blend in milk. Drop dough by teaspoonfuls about 3 inches apart onto greased cookie sheets. Flatten with bottom of greased glass that has been dipped in sugar.

Bake 12 minutes or until edges are lightly browned. Cool on wire racks.

Lemon Cookies

"PHILLY" APRICOT COOKIES

Makes about 7 dozen cookies

1½ cups PARKAY® Margarine, softened
1½ cups granulated sugar
1 (8-ounce) package PHILADELPHIA BRAND® Cream Cheese, softened
2 eggs
1½ teaspoons grated lemon peel
2 tablespoons lemon juice
4½ cups all-purpose flour
1½ teaspoons baking powder
    KRAFT® Apricot Preserves
    Powdered sugar

• Combine margarine, granulated sugar and cream cheese in large bowl, mixing until well blended. Blend in eggs, peel and juice. Add combined flour and baking powder; mix well. Cover; refrigerate several hours.

• Preheat oven to 350°F.

• Shape level measuring tablespoonfuls of dough into balls. Place on ungreased cookie sheet; flatten slightly. Indent centers; fill with preserves.

• Bake 15 minutes or until lightly browned. Cool on wire rack; sprinkle with powdered sugar.

LEMON COOKIES

Makes about 4 dozen cookies

⅔ cup MIRACLE WHIP® Salad Dressing
1 two-layer yellow cake mix
2 eggs
2 teaspoons grated lemon peel
⅔ cup ready-to-spread vanilla frosting
4 teaspoons lemon juice

• Preheat oven to 375°F.

• Blend salad dressing, cake mix and eggs at low speed with electric mixer until moistened. Add peel. Beat on medium speed 2 minutes. (Dough will be stiff.)

• Drop rounded teaspoonfuls of dough, 2 inches apart, onto greased cookie sheet.

• Bake 9 to 11 minutes or until lightly browned. (Cookies will still appear soft.) Cool 1 minute; remove from cookie sheet. Cool completely on wire rack.

• Stir together frosting and juice until well blended. Spread on cookies.

RASPBERRY FRECKLES

Makes about 3 dozen cookies

COOKIES
1 cup sugar
½ cup BUTTER FLAVOR CRISCO®
1 egg
1 tablespoon raspberry-flavored liqueur
2⅔ cups all-purpose flour
1 teaspoon baking powder
½ teaspoon baking soda
½ teaspoon salt
½ cup dairy sour cream
1 cup cubed (⅛- to ¼-inch) white confectionery
     coating
¾ cup mini chocolate chips
½ cup (2¼-ounce bag) sliced almonds, crushed

TOPPING
¼ cup seedless red raspberry jam
1 teaspoon raspberry-flavored liqueur
⅓ cup chopped white confectionery coating
2 teaspoons BUTTER FLAVOR CRISCO®

1. Preheat oven to 375°F. Grease cookie sheet with
Butter Flavor Crisco®.

2. For Cookies, combine sugar and ½ cup Butter Flavor
Crisco® in large bowl. Stir with spoon until well blended
and creamy. Stir in egg and 1 tablespoon liqueur.

3. Combine flour, baking powder, baking soda and salt.
Add alternately with sour cream to creamed mixture.
Stir in cubed confectionery coating, chocolate chips
and nuts.

4. Roll dough to ¼-inch thickness on floured surface.
Cut with 3-inch scalloped round cutter. Place 2 inches
apart on greased cookie sheet.

5. Bake at 375°F for 7 minutes or just until beginning to
brown. Cool 2 minutes on cookie sheet before removing
to paper towels. Cool completely.

6. For Topping, combine raspberry jam and 1 teaspoon
liqueur in microwave-safe measuring cup or bowl.
Microwave at MEDIUM (50% power) until jam melts
(or melt on rangetop in small saucepan on very low
heat). Drop mixture in 10 to 12 dots to resemble
freckles on top of each cookie.

7. Combine chopped confectionery coating and 2
teaspoons Butter Flavor Crisco® in heavy resealable
sandwich bag. Seal. Microwave at MEDIUM. Knead
bag after 1 minute. Repeat until smooth (or melt by
placing in bowl of hot water). Cut tiny tip off corner
of bag. Squeeze out and drizzle over cookies.

Raspberry Freckles

ALMOND-RASPBERRY THUMBPRINT COOKIES

Makes about 5 dozen cookies

1 cup butter or margarine, softened
1 cup sugar
1 can SOLO® *or* 1 jar BAKER® Almond Filling
2 egg yolks
1 teaspoon almond extract
2½ cups all-purpose flour
½ teaspoon baking powder
½ teaspoon salt
1 can SOLO® *or* 1 jar BAKER® Raspberry or
     Strawberry Filling

Beat butter and sugar in medium bowl with electric
mixer until light and fluffy. Add almond filling, egg
yolks and almond extract; beat until blended. Stir in
flour, baking powder and salt with wooden spoon to
make soft dough. Cover; refrigerate at least 3 hours
or overnight.

Preheat oven to 350°F. Shape dough into 1-inch balls.
Place on ungreased cookie sheets, about 1½ inches
apart. Press thumb into center of each ball to make
indentation. Spoon ½ teaspoon raspberry filling into
each indentation.

Bake 11 to 13 minutes or until edges of cookies are
golden brown. Cool on cookie sheets 1 minute. Remove
from cookie sheets; cool completely on wire racks.

Butter-Flavored Brickle Drizzles

BUTTER-FLAVORED BRICKLE DRIZZLES

Makes about 6 dozen cookies

COOKIES

1 cup BUTTER FLAVOR CRISCO®
1 cup granulated sugar
1 cup firmly packed brown sugar
1 can (14 ounces) sweetened condensed milk
    (not evaporated milk)
1 teaspoon vanilla
1¾ cups all-purpose flour
1 teaspoon salt
½ teaspoon baking soda
3 cups quick-cooking oats (not instant or
    old-fashioned), uncooked
1 cup almond brickle chips

DRIZZLE

1 cup milk chocolate chips

1. Preheat oven to 350°F. Grease cookie sheet with Butter Flavor Crisco®.

2. For Cookies, combine Butter Flavor Crisco®, granulated sugar and brown sugar in large bowl. Stir with spoon until well blended and creamy. Stir in condensed milk and vanilla. Mix well.

3. Combine flour, salt and baking soda. Stir into creamed mixture. Stir in oats.

4. Shape dough into 1-inch balls. Press tops into brickle chips. Place, brickle side up, 2 inches apart on greased cookie sheet.

5. Bake at 350°F for 9 to 10 minutes or until set but not browned. Remove to wire rack. Cool completely.

6. For Drizzle, place chocolate chips in heavy resealable sandwich bag. Seal. Microwave at MEDIUM (50% power). Knead bag after 1 minute. Repeat until smooth (or melt by placing in bowl of hot water). Cut tiny tip off corner of bag. Squeeze out and drizzle over cookies.

BUTTER PECAN CRISPS

Makes about 5 dozen cookies

1 cup unsalted butter, softened
¾ cup granulated sugar
¾ cup firmly packed brown sugar
½ teaspoon salt
2 eggs
1 teaspoon vanilla
1½ cups finely ground pecans
2½ cups sifted all-purpose flour
1 teaspoon baking soda
30 pecan halves
4 squares (1 ounce each) semisweet chocolate
1 tablespoon shortening

Preheat oven to 375°F. In large bowl, beat butter, sugars and salt until light and fluffy. Add eggs, 1 at a time, beating well after each addition. Beat in vanilla and ground pecans. In small bowl, combine flour and baking soda. Gradually stir flour mixture into butter mixture. Spoon dough into large pastry bag fitted with ⅜-inch round tip; fill bag halfway. Shake down dough to remove air bubbles. Hold bag perpendicular to and about ½ inch above parchment paper-lined cookie sheets. Pipe dough into 1¼-inch balls, spacing 3 inches apart. Cut each pecan half lengthwise into 2 slivers. Press 1 sliver in center of each dough ball.

Bake 9 to 12 minutes or until lightly browned. Cool 5 minutes on cookie sheets. Remove to wire racks; cool completely. In small, heavy saucepan over low heat, melt chocolate and shortening; stir to blend. Drizzle chocolate mixture over cookies. Let stand until chocolate is set.

GINGERSNAPS

Makes about 4 dozen cookies

1 cup firmly packed brown sugar
¾ cup unsalted butter, softened
¼ teaspoon salt
1 egg
¼ cup light molasses
1 tablespoon ground ginger
2 teaspoons baking soda
1 teaspoon ground cinnamon
½ teaspoon ground cloves
2¼ cups all-purpose flour
⅓ to ½ cup granulated sugar
½ cup powdered sugar, sifted
1 to 1½ teaspoons strong brewed coffee, cooled
¼ teaspoon lemon juice

In large bowl, beat brown sugar, butter and salt until light and fluffy. Beat in egg. Gradually add molasses; mix well. Add ginger, baking soda, cinnamon and cloves. Beat until blended. Using rubber spatula, gradually fold in flour. (Dough will be soft and sticky.) Divide dough into quarters. Wrap each portion; refrigerate until firm, about 1½ hours.

Preheat oven to 350°F. Shape slightly rounded tablespoonfuls of dough into balls. Roll balls in granulated sugar to coat generously. Place 4 inches apart on greased cookie sheets.

Bake about 10 minutes or until centers of cookies feel slightly firm. Cool 5 minutes on cookie sheets. Remove to wire racks; cool completely.

In small bowl, mix powdered sugar, 1 teaspoon coffee and lemon juice. Stir until smooth. Stir in as much of remaining coffee as needed to make stiff icing for piping. Fit pastry bag with small round tip. Pipe icing on cookies, forming spiral design. Let stand until icing is firm.

ORANGE DROP COOKIES

Makes about 3 dozen cookies

COOKIES
1 package DUNCAN HINES® Golden Sugar
   Cookie Mix
1 egg
½ teaspoon grated orange peel
1 tablespoon orange juice
¾ cup flaked coconut
½ cup chopped pecans

GLAZE
1 cup confectioners sugar
2 teaspoons lemon juice
1 teaspoon grated orange peel
2 teaspoons orange juice

1. Preheat oven to 375°F.

2. For Cookies, combine cookie mix, contents of buttery flavor packet from Mix, egg, ½ teaspoon orange peel and 1 tablespoon orange juice in large bowl. Stir with spoon until well blended. Stir in coconut and pecans. Drop by rounded teaspoonfuls 2 inches apart onto ungreased cookie sheet.

3. Bake at 375°F for 7 to 8 minutes or until set. Cool 1 minute on cookie sheet. Remove to wire rack. Cool completely.

4. For Glaze, combine confectioners sugar, lemon juice, 1 teaspoon orange peel and 2 teaspoons orange juice in small bowl. Stir until blended. Drizzle over tops of cooled cookies. Allow glaze to set before storing between layers of waxed paper in airtight container.

Tip: When grating orange peel, avoid the bitter white portion known as the pith.

Orange Drop Cookies

Marvelous Macaroons

MARVELOUS MACAROONS

Makes about 3½ dozen cookies

1 can (8 ounces) DOLE® Crushed Pineapple
    in Juice
1 can (14 ounces) sweetened condensed milk
1 package (7 ounces) flaked coconut
½ cup margarine, melted
½ cup DOLE® Chopped Almonds, toasted
1 teaspoon grated lemon peel
¼ teaspoon almond extract
1 cup all-purpose flour
1 teaspoon baking powder

Preheat oven to 350°F. Drain pineapple well, pressing out excess juice with back of spoon. In large bowl, combine drained pineapple, milk, coconut, margarine, almonds, lemon peel and almond extract. In small bowl, combine flour and baking powder. Beat into pineapple mixture until blended. Drop heaping tablespoonfuls of dough 1 inch apart onto greased cookie sheets.

Bake 13 to 15 minutes or until lightly browned. Garnish with whole almonds, if desired. Cool on wire racks. Store in covered container in refrigerator.

ALMOND MACAROONS

Makes about 3 dozen cookies

4 egg whites
⅔ cup sugar
2 cups (12-ounce package) NESTLÉ® Toll House®
    Semi-Sweet Chocolate Mini Morsels
1½ cups ground blanched almonds
½ teaspoon almond extract

Preheat oven to 350°F. Grease cookie sheets. In large mixer bowl, beat egg whites until foamy. Gradually add sugar, beating until stiff peaks form. Fold in Nestlé® Toll House® Semi-Sweet Mini Morsels, almonds and almond extract. Drop by heaping teaspoonfuls onto prepared cookie sheets.

Bake 20 minutes or until lightly browned and set. Let stand on cookie sheets 2 minutes. Remove from cookie sheets; cool on wire racks.

SPICY SOUR CREAM COOKIES

Makes about 4½ dozen cookies

1 package DUNCAN HINES® Moist Deluxe
    Spice Cake Mix
1 cup dairy sour cream
1 cup chopped pecans or walnuts
¼ cup butter or margarine, softened
1 egg

1. Preheat oven to 350°F. Grease cookie sheet.

2. Combine cake mix, sour cream, pecans, butter and egg in large bowl. Mix at low speed with electric mixer until blended.

3. Drop by rounded teaspoonfuls onto cookie sheet.

4. Bake at 350°F for 9 to 11 minutes or until lightly browned. Cool 2 minutes on cookie sheet. Remove to wire rack.

Tip: Sprinkle cooled cookies with confectioners sugar.

QUICK PUDDING COOKIES

Makes about 2 dozen cookies

1 package (4-serving size) JELL-O® Instant
    Pudding and Pie Filling, any flavor
1 cup all-purpose biscuit mix
¼ cup vegetable oil
1 egg, slightly beaten
3 tablespoons water

Preheat oven to 375°F. Combine pudding mix and biscuit mix in medium bowl. Stir in oil, egg and water, blending well. Drop by teaspoonfuls 2 inches apart onto ungreased cookie sheets.

Bake about 12 minutes, or until lightly browned. Remove from cookie sheets and cool on wire racks. Store in tightly covered container.

Quick Pudding Chip Cookies: Prepare Quick Pudding Cookies as directed, stirring in ½ cup BAKER'S® Semi-Sweet Real Chocolate Chips just before baking.

Makes about 2½ dozen cookies

Note: Cookie dough may be pressed through cookie press, or rolled into 1-inch balls and flattened on cookie sheets with fork or greased glass dipped in flour; reduce water to 2 tablespoons.

ALMOND CREAM CHEESE COOKIES

Makes about 4 dozen cookies

3 ounces cream cheese, softened
1 cup butter, softened
1 cup sugar
1 egg yolk
1 tablespoon milk
⅛ teaspoon almond extract
2½ cups sifted cake flour
1 cup BLUE DIAMOND® Sliced Natural
    Almonds, toasted

Beat cream cheese with butter and sugar in large bowl until fluffy. Blend in egg yolk, milk and almond extract. Gradually mix in cake flour. Gently stir in almonds. (Dough will be sticky.) Divide dough in half; place each half on large sheet of waxed paper. Working through waxed paper, shape each half into 12 × 1½-inch roll. Refrigerate until very firm.

Preheat oven to 325°F. Cut rolls into ¼-inch-thick slices.

Bake on ungreased cookie sheets 10 to 15 minutes or until edges are golden. *Cookies should not brown.* Cool on wire racks.

Triple Treat Cookies

TRIPLE TREAT COOKIES

Makes about 3 dozen cookies

2 packages DUNCAN HINES® Golden Sugar
    Cookie Mix
2 eggs
2 tablespoons water
¾ cup semi-sweet miniature chocolate chips
½ cup chopped pecans
½ cup flaked coconut

1. Preheat oven to 375°F.

2. Combine cookie mixes, contents of buttery flavor packets from Mixes, eggs and water in large bowl. Stir until thoroughly blended.

3. Place chocolate chips, pecans and coconut on 3 individual plates. Shape 3 measuring teaspoonfuls of dough into 3 balls. Roll 1 ball in chocolate chips, 1 ball in pecans and 1 ball in coconut. Place balls together with sides touching on ungreased cookie sheet. Repeat with remaining dough, placing balls 2 inches apart.

4. Bake at 375°F for 8 to 10 minutes or until light golden brown. Cool 1 minute on cookie sheet. Carefully remove to wire rack. Cool completely. Store in airtight container.

Tip: To save time when forming dough into balls, use a 1-inch spring-operated cookie scoop. Spring-operated cookie scoops are available at kitchen specialty shops.

BISCOCHITOS

Makes 4 to 5 dozen cookies

3 cups all-purpose flour
2 teaspoons anise seed
1½ teaspoons baking powder
½ teaspoon salt
1 cup lard or butter
¾ cup sugar, divided
1 egg
¼ cup orange juice
2 teaspoons ground cinnamon

Preheat oven to 350°F. Combine flour, anise seed, baking powder and salt in medium bowl; set aside. Beat lard in large bowl of electric mixer on medium speed until creamy. Add ½ cup sugar; beat until fluffy. Blend in egg. Gradually add flour mixture alternately with orange juice, mixing well after each addition. Divide dough in half; shape each portion into a ball. Wrap in plastic wrap; refrigerate 1 hour.

Roll out balls, 1 at a time, on lightly floured surface to ¼-inch thickness; cover remaining dough to prevent drying. Cut out cookies with fancy cookie cutters 2 to 2½ inches in diameter. As you cut cookies, add scraps to remaining dough. If dough becomes too soft to handle, refrigerate briefly. Place cookies, slightly apart, on ungreased cookie sheet.

To prepare cinnamon topping, combine remaining ¼ cup sugar and cinnamon; lightly sprinkle over cookies.

Bake 8 to 10 minutes or until edges are lightly browned. Cool on wire racks. Store in airtight container.

Butterscotch Granola Cookies

BUTTERSCOTCH GRANOLA COOKIES

Makes about 5 dozen cookies

1½ cups all-purpose flour
 1 teaspoon ground cinnamon
 ½ teaspoon salt
 ½ teaspoon baking powder
 ½ teaspoon baking soda
 ½ cup butter, softened
 ½ cup honey
 ½ cup firmly packed brown sugar
 1 egg
 1 teaspoon vanilla extract
 ¼ cup milk
 2 cups (12-ounce package) NESTLÉ® Toll House® Butterscotch Flavored Morsels
 1 cup quick-cooking oats, uncooked
 1 cup chopped walnuts
 ¾ cup raisins
 ¼ cup wheat germ

Preheat oven to 350°F. In small bowl, combine flour, cinnamon, salt, baking powder and baking soda; set aside. In large bowl, combine butter, honey and brown sugar; beat until creamy. Beat in egg and vanilla extract. Blend in flour mixture alternately with milk. Stir in Nestlé® Toll House® Butterscotch Flavored Morsels, oats, walnuts, raisins and wheat germ. Drop by rounded teaspoonfuls onto greased cookie sheets.

Bake 8 to 10 minutes or until lightly browned. Allow to stand 2 minutes; remove from cookie sheets. Cool completely on wire racks.

BUTTERSCOTCH LEMON COOKIES

Makes about 1½ dozen cookies

1½ cups all-purpose flour
 2 teaspoons baking powder
 ½ teaspoon salt
 ¾ cup sugar
 ½ cup butter, softened
 1 egg
 2 tablespoons milk
 1 teaspoon grated lemon peel
 1 tablespoon lemon juice
1½ cups (¾ of 12-ounce package) NESTLÉ® Toll House® Butterscotch Flavored Morsels

Preheat oven to 375°F. In small bowl, combine flour, baking powder and salt; set aside. In large bowl, combine sugar and butter; beat until creamy. Add egg, milk, lemon peel and lemon juice; beat well. (Mixture will appear curdled.) Gradually blend in flour mixture. Stir in Nestlé® Toll House® Butterscotch Flavored Morsels. Drop by rounded tablespoonfuls onto greased cookie sheets.

Bake 8 to 10 minutes or until lightly browned. Allow to stand 2 minutes before removing from cookie sheets. Cool completely on wire racks.

CHOCOLATE-DIPPED CINNAMON THINS

Makes about 2 dozen

1¼ cups all-purpose flour
1½ teaspoons ground cinnamon
1 cup unsalted butter, softened
1 cup powdered sugar
1 large egg
1 teaspoon vanilla
¼ teaspoon salt
4 ounces broken bittersweet chocolate

Place flour and cinnamon in small bowl; stir to combine.

Beat butter in large bowl with electric mixer at medium speed until light and fluffy, scraping down side of bowl once. Add sugar; beat well. Add egg, vanilla and salt; beat well, scraping down side of bowl once. Gradually add flour mixture. Beat at low speed, scraping down side of bowl occasionally, until well blended.

Place dough on sheet of waxed paper. Using waxed paper to hold dough, roll it back and forth to form a log about 12 inches long and 2½ inches wide. Securely wrap log in plastic wrap. Refrigerate at least 2 hours or until firm. (Log may be frozen up to 3 months; thaw in refrigerator before baking).

Preheat oven to 350°F. Cut dough with long, sharp knife into ¼-inch-thick slices. Place 2 inches apart on ungreased cookie sheets.

Bake 10 minutes or until set. Let cookies stand on cookie sheets 2 minutes. Remove cookies with spatula to wire racks; cool completely.

Melt chocolate in 1-cup glass measure set in bowl of very hot water, stirring twice. Dip each cookie into chocolate, coating 1 inch up sides. Let excess chocolate drip back into cup.

Transfer to wire racks or waxed paper; let stand at cool room temperature about 40 minutes until chocolate is set. Store between sheets of waxed paper at cool room temperature or in refrigerator.

Note: These cookies do not freeze well.

Chocolate-Dipped Cinnamon Thins

WHOLE WHEAT OATMEAL COOKIES

Makes about 3 dozen cookies

¾ cup BUTTER FLAVOR CRISCO®
¾ cup firmly packed brown sugar
⅓ cup apple juice
¼ cup molasses
¼ cup honey
1 egg
1 teaspoon vanilla
1 cup whole wheat flour
1 teaspoon ground cinnamon
½ teaspoon baking soda
¼ teaspoon salt
⅛ teaspoon ground nutmeg
3 cups quick-cooking oats (not instant or
   old-fashioned), uncooked
¾ cup raisins
¾ cup chopped walnuts

1. Preheat oven to 350°F. Grease cookie sheet with Butter Flavor Crisco®.

2. Combine Butter Flavor Crisco®, sugar, juice, molasses, honey, egg and vanilla in large bowl. Beat at medium speed of electric mixer until blended and creamy.

3. Combine flour, cinnamon, baking soda, salt and nutmeg. Mix into creamed mixture at low speed until just blended. Stir in oats, raisins and nuts with spoon. Drop rounded tablespoonfuls of dough 2 inches apart onto greased cookie sheet.

4. Bake at 350°F for 13 to 14 minutes or until set. Cool 5 minutes on cookie sheet. Remove to wire rack.

COWBOY MACAROONS

Makes about 4 dozen cookies

1 cup BUTTER FLAVOR CRISCO®
1 cup firmly packed brown sugar
1 cup granulated sugar
2 eggs
1 teaspoon vanilla
2 cups all-purpose flour
1 teaspoon baking powder
1 teaspoon salt
½ teaspoon baking soda
2 cups quick-cooking oats (not instant or old-fashioned), uncooked
2 cups corn flakes
1 cup finely chopped pecans
1 cup flake coconut
½ cup maraschino cherries, cut into quarters (optional)

1. Preheat oven to 350°F. Grease cookie sheet with Butter Flavor Crisco®.

2. Combine Butter Flavor Crisco®, brown sugar and granulated sugar in large bowl. Beat at medium speed of electric mixer until well blended and creamy. Beat in eggs and vanilla.

3. Combine flour, baking powder, salt and baking soda. Mix into creamed mixture at low speed until just blended. Stir in oats, corn flakes and nuts with spoon. Stir in coconut and cherries.

4. Form dough into 1-inch balls. Place 2 inches apart on greased cookie sheet.

5. Bake at 350°F for 12 to 14 minutes or until set. Cool 1 minute on cookie sheet. Remove to wire rack.

OLD-FASHIONED HARVEST COOKIES

Makes about 4 dozen cookies

¾ cup BUTTER FLAVOR CRISCO®
1 cup firmly packed dark brown sugar
¾ cup canned solid-pack pumpkin
1 egg
2 tablespoons molasses
1½ cups all-purpose flour
1 teaspoon ground nutmeg
½ teaspoon baking powder
½ teaspoon baking soda
¼ teaspoon salt
¼ teaspoon ground cinnamon
2½ cups quick-cooking oats (not instant or old-fashioned), uncooked
1½ cups finely chopped dates
½ cup chopped walnuts

1. Preheat oven to 350°F. Grease cookie sheet with Butter Flavor Crisco®.

2. Combine Butter Flavor Crisco® and sugar in large bowl. Beat at medium speed of electric mixer until well blended. Beat in pumpkin, egg and molasses.

3. Combine flour, nutmeg, baking powder, baking soda, salt and cinnamon. Mix into creamed mixture at low speed until just blended. Stir in, one a time, oats, dates and nuts with spoon.

4. Drop rounded tablespoonfuls of dough 2 inches apart onto cookie sheet.

5. Bake at 350°F for 10 to 12 minutes or until bottoms are lightly browned. Cool 2 minutes on cookie sheet. Remove to wire rack.

Old-Fashioned Harvest Cookies

185

OATMEAL SCOTCHIES

Makes about 4 dozen cookies

1¼ cups all-purpose flour
1 teaspoon baking soda
½ teaspoon salt
½ teaspoon ground cinnamon
1 cup (2 sticks) butter, softened
¾ cup granulated sugar
¾ cup firmly packed brown sugar
2 eggs
1 teaspoon vanilla extract *or* grated peel of 1 orange
3 cups quick or old-fashioned oats, uncooked
2 cups (12-ounce package) NESTLÉ® Toll House® Butterscotch Flavored Morsels

Preheat oven to 375°F. In small bowl, combine flour, baking soda, salt and cinnamon; set aside.

In large mixer bowl, beat butter, granulated sugar, brown sugar, eggs and vanilla extract until creamy. Gradually beat in flour mixture. Stir in oats and Nestlé® Toll House® Butterscotch Flavored Morsels. Drop by rounded tablespoonfuls onto ungreased cookie sheets.

Bake 7 to 8 minutes for chewy cookies or 9 to 10 minutes for crisp cookies. Let stand on cookie sheets 2 minutes. Remove from cookie sheets; cool on wire racks.

Oatmeal Scotchie Pan Cookies: Preheat oven to 375°F. Spread dough in greased 15½×10½×1-inch jelly-roll pan. Bake 18 to 22 minutes or until very lightly browned. Cool completely in pan on wire rack. Cut into bars. *Makes about 4 dozen bars*

KENTUCKY OATMEAL-JAM COOKIES

Makes about 2 dozen cookies

½ cup BUTTER FLAVOR CRISCO®
¾ cup sugar
½ cup strawberry jam
¼ cup buttermilk*
1 egg
1 teaspoon vanilla
1 cup all-purpose flour
½ cup unsweetened cocoa powder
1 teaspoon ground cinnamon
½ teaspoon baking soda
¼ teaspoon ground nutmeg
¼ teaspoon ground cloves
1½ cups quick-cooking oats (not instant or old-fashioned), uncooked
½ cup raisins
½ cup chopped pecans (optional)
  About 24 pecan halves (optional)

1. Preheat oven to 350°F. Grease cookie sheet with Butter Flavor Crisco®.

2. Combine Butter Flavor Crisco®, sugar, jam, buttermilk, egg and vanilla in large bowl. Beat at medium speed of electric mixer until well blended and creamy.

3. Combine flour, cocoa, cinnamon, baking soda, nutmeg and cloves. Mix into creamed mixture at low speed until blended. Stir in oats, raisins and chopped nuts with spoon.

4. Drop 2 tablespoonfuls of dough in a mound onto greased cookie sheet. Repeat for each cookie, keeping mounds 3 inches apart. Top each with pecan half.

5. Bake at 350°F for 10 to 12 minutes or until set. Cool 2 minutes on cookie sheet. Remove to wire rack.

*You may substitute ¾ teaspoon lemon juice or vinegar plus enough milk to equal ¼ cup for the buttermilk. Stir. Wait 5 minutes before using.

OATMEAL LEMON-CHEESE COOKIES

Makes about 6 dozen cookies

1 cup BUTTER FLAVOR CRISCO®
1 package (3 ounces) cream cheese, softened
1¼ cups sugar
1 egg, separated
2 teaspoons grated lemon peel
1 teaspoon lemon extract
1¼ cups all-purpose flour
1¼ cups quick-cooking oats (not instant or old-fashioned), uncooked
½ teaspoon salt
1 egg
  Additional sugar for sprinkling
½ cup sliced almonds

1. Preheat oven to 350°F.

2. Combine Butter Flavor Crisco®, cream cheese and 1¼ cups sugar in large bowl. Beat at medium speed of electric mixer until well blended and creamy. Beat in egg yolk, lemon peel and lemon extract.

3. Combine flour, oats and salt. Stir into creamed mixture with spoon until blended.

4. Drop rounded teaspoonfuls of dough 2 inches apart onto ungreased cookie sheet. Beat whole egg with egg white. Brush over tops of cookies. Lightly sprinkle with additional sugar. Lightly press almond slices on top.

5. Bake at 350°F for 10 to 12 minutes or until edges are lightly browned. Cool 2 minutes on cookie sheet. Remove to wire rack.

Oatmeal Scotchies

Oatmeal Apple Cookies

OATMEAL APPLE COOKIES

Makes about 2½ dozen cookies

1¼ cups firmly packed brown sugar
¾ cup BUTTER FLAVOR CRISCO®
¼ cup milk
1 egg
1½ teaspoons vanilla
1 cup all-purpose flour
1¼ teaspoons ground cinnamon
½ teaspoon salt
¼ teaspoon baking soda
¼ teaspoon ground nutmeg
3 cups quick-cooking oats (not instant or old-fashioned), uncooked
1 cup diced, peeled apples
¾ cup raisins (optional)
¾ cup coarsely chopped walnuts (optional)

1. Preheat oven to 375°F. Grease cookie sheet with Butter Flavor Crisco®.

2. Combine brown sugar, Butter Flavor Crisco®, milk, egg and vanilla in large bowl. Beat at medium speed of electric mixer until well blended and creamy.

3. Combine flour, cinnamon, salt, baking soda and nutmeg. Add gradually to creamed mixture at low speed. Mix just until blended. Stir in, one at a time,

oats, apples, raisins and nuts with spoon. Drop by rounded tablespoonfuls 2 inches apart onto greased cookie sheet.

4. Bake at 375°F for 13 minutes or until set. Cool 2 minutes on cookie sheet before removing to wire rack.

CHUNKY OATMEAL COOKIES

Makes about 3 dozen cookies

1 package DUNCAN HINES® Moist Deluxe French Vanilla Cake Mix
¾ cup butter or margarine, softened
2 eggs
1 teaspoon vanilla extract
1 cup quick-cooking oats (not instant or old-fashioned), uncooked
1 cup macadamia nuts, coarsely chopped
1 cup vanilla milk chips

1. Preheat oven to 375°F.

2. Combine cake mix, butter, eggs and vanilla extract in large bowl. Beat at low speed with electric mixer until moistened. Beat at medium speed until mixture is

blended. Stir in oats, macadamia nuts and vanilla milk chips. Drop by rounded tablespoonfuls 2 inches apart onto ungreased cookie sheets.

3. Bake at 375°F for 12 to 13 minutes or until edges are light golden brown. Cool 1 minute on cookie sheets. Remove to wire racks. Cool completely. Store in airtight container.

Tip: For a delicious flavor variation, use DUNCAN HINES® Moist Deluxe Swiss Chocolate Cake Mix in place of French Vanilla Cake Mix.

OATMEAL SHAGGIES

Makes 2½ to 3 dozen cookies

COOKIES
2 cups quick-cooking oats (not instant or old-fashioned), uncooked
1 cup finely shredded carrots
1 cup firmly packed brown sugar
1 cup raisins
1 cup all-purpose flour
1 teaspoon baking powder
1 teaspoon baking soda
1 teaspoon salt
½ teaspoon ground cinnamon
½ teaspoon ground cloves
½ cup BUTTER FLAVOR CRISCO®
⅓ cup milk
2 eggs, beaten
1 cup shredded coconut
½ cup finely chopped walnuts

FROSTING
1 cup confectioners sugar
2 tablespoons butter or margarine, softened
2 teaspoons grated orange peel
1 tablespoon plus 1 teaspoon orange juice

1. Preheat oven to 350°F. Grease cookie sheet with Butter Flavor Crisco®.

2. For Cookies, combine oats, carrots, brown sugar and raisins in large bowl.

3. Combine flour, baking powder, baking soda, salt, cinnamon and cloves. Stir into oat mixture with spoon.

4. Combine Butter Flavor Crisco®, milk and eggs. Stir into oat mixture. Stir in coconut and nuts. Drop by rounded tablespoonfuls 2½ inches apart onto greased cookie sheet.

5. Bake at 350°F for 10 to 12 minutes or until lightly browned. Remove to wire rack. Cool completely.

6. For Frosting, combine confectioners sugar, butter, orange peel and orange juice in small bowl. Stir until smooth and of spreading consistency. Frost cookies.

OATMEAL COOKIES

Makes about 5 dozen cookies

1¼ cups BUTTER FLAVOR CRISCO®
¾ cup firmly packed brown sugar
3 tablespoons milk
1 teaspoon water
½ teaspoon vanilla
½ teaspoon coconut flavor
1 egg
1¼ cups all-purpose flour
1 teaspoon baking soda
¾ teaspoon salt
3 cups uncooked rolled oats
½ cup pecan pieces
½ cup raisins

1. Preheat oven to 325°F.

2. Combine Butter Flavor Crisco®, brown sugar, milk, water, vanilla and coconut flavor in large bowl. Beat at medium speed of electric mixer until well blended and creamy. Beat in egg.

3. Combine flour, baking soda and salt. Add gradually to creamed mixture at speed. Mix until well blended. Stir in oats, nuts and raisins with spoon. Drop by rounded teaspoonfuls 2 inches apart onto ungreased cookie sheet.

4. Bake at 325°F for 10 to 12 minutes or until slightly browned and slightly moist in center. Cool 2 minutes on cookie sheet before removing to wire rack.

Oatmeal Shaggies

CHOCOLATE-PEANUT COOKIES

Makes about 5 dozen cookies

1 cup butter or margarine, softened
¾ cup granulated sugar
¾ cup firmly packed light brown sugar
2 eggs
1 teaspoon vanilla
1 teaspoon baking soda
¼ teaspoon salt
2¼ cups all-purpose flour
2 cups chocolate-covered peanuts

Preheat oven to 375°F. Line cookie sheets with parchment paper or leave ungreased.

Beat butter with sugars, eggs and vanilla in large bowl until light. Beat in baking soda and salt. Stir in flour to make stiff dough. Blend in chocolate-covered peanuts. Drop by rounded teaspoonfuls 2 inches apart onto cookie sheets.

Bake 9 to 11 minutes or until just barely golden. Do not overbake. Remove to wire racks to cool.

COCOA SNICKERDOODLES

Makes about 4½ dozen cookies

1 cup butter or margarine, softened
¾ cup firmly packed brown sugar
¾ cup plus 2 tablespoons granulated sugar, divided
2 eggs
2 cups uncooked rolled oats
1½ cups all-purpose flour
¼ cup plus 2 tablespoons unsweetened cocoa, divided
1 teaspoon baking soda
2 tablespoons ground cinnamon

Preheat oven to 375°F. Lightly grease cookie sheets or line with parchment paper.

Beat butter, brown sugar and ¾ cup granulated sugar in large bowl until light and fluffy. Add eggs; mix well. Combine oats, flour, ¼ cup cocoa and baking soda in medium bowl. Stir into butter mixture until blended. Mix remaining 2 tablespoons granulated sugar, cinnamon and remaining 2 tablespoons cocoa in small bowl. Drop dough by rounded teaspoonfuls into cinnamon mixture; toss to coat. Place 2 inches apart on prepared cookie sheets.

Bake 8 to 10 minutes or until firm in center. Do not overbake. Remove to wire racks to cool.

Cocoa Snickerdoodles, Chocolate-Peanut Cookies

CHOCOLATE CHIP WAFER COOKIES

Makes about 2 dozen cookies

½ cup butter or margarine, softened
½ cup sugar
1 egg
1 teaspoon vanilla
½ cup all-purpose flour
   Dash salt
1 cup (6 ounces) semisweet chocolate chips
⅓ cup chopped pecans or walnuts

Preheat oven to 350°F. Line cookie sheets with foil; lightly grease foil.

Beat butter and sugar in large bowl until light. Add egg; beat until creamy. Stir in vanilla, flour and salt. Add chocolate chips and nuts; mix until well blended. Drop dough by teaspoonfuls 3 inches apart onto prepared cookie sheets.

Bake 7 to 10 minutes or until edges are golden and centers are set. (Cookies are soft when hot, but become crispy as they cool.) Cool completely on foil, then peel foil from cookies.

MRS. J'S CHIP COOKIES

Makes about 8 dozen cookies

4 cups crispy rice cereal
1 milk chocolate crunch bar (5 ounces), broken into squares
2 cups all-purpose flour
1 teaspoon baking powder
1 teaspoon baking soda
¼ teaspoon salt
1 cup butter or margarine, softened
1 cup granulated sugar
1 cup firmly packed light brown sugar
2 eggs
1 teaspoon vanilla
1 package (12 ounces) semisweet chocolate chips
1½ cups chopped walnuts

Preheat oven to 375°F. Line cookie sheets with parchment paper or leave ungreased.

Process cereal in blender or food processor until pulverized. Add chocolate bar; continue processing until both chocolate and cereal are completely ground. Add flour, baking powder, baking soda and salt; process until blended. Beat butter and sugars in large bowl until well blended. Add eggs; beat until light. Blend in vanilla. Add flour mixture; blend until smooth. Stir in chocolate chips and walnuts until blended. Shape dough into walnut-sized balls. Place 2 inches apart on cookie sheets.

Bake 10 to 12 minutes or until firm in center. Do not overbake. Remove to wire racks to cool.

CHOCOLATE CHIP CINNAMON CRINKLES

Makes about 3½ dozen cookies

½ cup butter or margarine, softened
½ cup firmly packed brown sugar
¼ cup plus 2 tablespoons granulated sugar, divided
1 egg
1 teaspoon vanilla
1 teaspoon cream of tartar
½ teaspoon baking soda
⅛ teaspoon salt
1⅓ cups all-purpose flour
1 cup (6 ounces) semisweet chocolate chips
2 teaspoons unsweetened cocoa
1 teaspoon ground cinnamon

Preheat oven to 400°F. Line cookie sheets with parchment paper or leave ungreased.

Beat butter, brown sugar, ¼ cup granulated sugar, egg and vanilla in large bowl until light and fluffy. Beat in cream of tartar, baking soda and salt. Add flour; mix until dough is blended and stiff. Stir in chocolate chips. Combine remaining 2 tablespoons granulated sugar, cocoa and cinnamon in small bowl. Shape rounded teaspoonfuls of dough into balls about 1¼ inches in diameter. Roll balls in cinnamon mixture until coated on all sides. Place 2 inches apart on cookie sheets.

Bake 8 to 10 minutes or until firm. Do not overbake. Remove to wire racks to cool.

Top to bottom: Mrs. J's Chip Cookies, Chocolate Chip Wafer Cookies, Chocolate Chip Cinnamon Crinkles

BANANA CHOCOLATE CHIP SOFTIES

Makes about 3 dozen cookies

1 ripe, medium banana
1¼ cups all-purpose flour
1 teaspoon baking powder
½ teaspoon salt
⅓ cup butter or margarine, softened
⅓ cup granulated sugar
⅓ cup firmly packed light brown sugar
1 large egg
1 teaspoon vanilla
1 cup milk chocolate chips
½ cup coarsely chopped walnuts (optional)

Preheat oven to 375°F. Lightly grease cookie sheets.

Peel banana and place in small bowl. Mash enough banana with fork to measure ½ cup. Set aside. Place flour, baking powder and salt in small bowl; stir to combine.

Beat butter, granulated sugar and brown sugar in large bowl with electric mixer at medium speed until light and fluffy, scraping down side of bowl once. Beat in banana, egg and vanilla, scraping down side of bowl once. Add flour mixture. Beat at low speed until well blended, scraping down side of bowl once. Stir in chips and walnuts with mixing spoon. (Dough will be soft.)

Drop rounded teaspoonfuls of dough 2 inches apart onto prepared cookie sheets.

Bake 9 to 11 minutes or until edges are golden brown. Let cookies stand on cookie sheets 2 minutes. Remove cookies with spatula to wire racks; cool completely. Store tightly covered at room temperature.

Note: These cookies do not freeze well.

ORANGE-WALNUT CHIPPERS

Makes about 3 dozen cookies

½ cup all-purpose flour
¼ teaspoon baking soda
¼ teaspoon salt
½ cup butter or margarine, softened
1 cup firmly packed light brown sugar
1 large egg
1 tablespoon orange peel
1½ cups uncooked quick-cooking or
      old-fashioned oats
1 cup semisweet chocolate chips
½ cup coarsely chopped walnuts

Preheat oven to 375°F. Lightly grease cookie sheets; set aside.

Place flour, baking soda and salt in small bowl; stir to combine.

Beat butter and sugar in large bowl with electric mixer at medium speed until light and fluffy, scraping down side of bowl once. Beat in egg and orange peel, scraping down side of bowl once. Add flour mixture. Beat at low speed, scraping down side of bowl once. Stir in oats with wooden spoon. Stir in chips and nuts.

Drop teaspoonfuls of dough 2 inches apart onto prepared cookie sheets.

Bake 10 to 12 minutes or until golden brown. Let cookies stand on cookie sheets 2 minutes. Remove cookies with spatula to wire racks; cool completely. Store tightly covered at room temperature or freeze up to 3 months.

CHERRY CORDIAL COOKIES

Makes about 4 dozen cookies

1 package (18.25 ounces) cherry cake mix
¾ cup butter or margarine, softened
2 eggs
1 cup HERSHEY'S MINI CHIPS® Semi-Sweet
      Chocolate
MINI CHIPS® Glaze (recipe follows)

Preheat oven to 350°F. In large mixer bowl, combine cake mix, butter and eggs; mix well. Stir in small chocolate chips. Drop by rounded teaspoonfuls onto ungreased cookie sheet.

Bake 10 to 12 minutes or until almost set. Cool slightly; remove from cookie sheet to wire rack. Cool completely. Drizzle Mini Chips® Glaze onto cooled cookies; let stand until set.

Mini Chips® Glaze: In small microwave-safe bowl, place 1 cup HERSHEY'S MINI CHIPS® Semi-Sweet Chocolate and 3 tablespoons vegetable shortening (not butter, margarine or oil). Microwave at HIGH (100% power) 45 seconds; stir. If necessary, microwave at HIGH additional 15 seconds or until melted and smooth when stirred. Use immediately.

Banana Chocolate Chip Softies

Black Forest Oatmeal Fancies

BLACK FOREST OATMEAL FANCIES

Makes about 3 dozen cookies

1 cup BUTTER FLAVOR CRISCO®
1 cup granulated sugar
1 cup firmly packed brown sugar
2 eggs
2 teaspoons vanilla
1⅔ cups all-purpose flour
1 teaspoon baking soda
1 teaspoon salt
½ teaspoon baking powder
3 cups quick-cooking oats (not instant or
    old-fashioned), uncooked
1 cup vanilla milk chips
6 squares (1 ounce each) semi-sweet baking
    chocolate, coarsely chopped
½ cup coarsely chopped red candied cherries
½ cup sliced almonds

1. Preheat oven to 375°F.

2. Combine Butter Flavor Crisco®, granulated sugar, brown sugar, eggs and vanilla in large bowl. Beat at medium speed of electric mixer until well blended and creamy.

3. Combine flour, baking soda, salt and baking powder. Add gradually to creamed mixture at low speed. Mix until well blended. Stir in, one at a time, oats, vanilla milk chips, chocolate, cherries and nuts with spoon. Drop by rounded tablespoonfuls 2 inches apart onto ungreased cookie sheet.

4. Bake at 375°F for 9 to 11 minutes or until set. Cool 2 minutes on cookie sheet before removing to wire rack.

CHUNK FULL OF CHOCOLATE SURPRISE COOKIES

Makes about 3 dozen cookies

1¼ cups firmly packed brown sugar
 1 cup BUTTER FLAVOR CRISCO®
 ½ cup granulated sugar
 2 eggs
 2 teaspoons vanilla
 ½ teaspoon water
 3 cups all-purpose flour
 1 teaspoon baking soda
 ½ teaspoon salt
 1 package (10 ounces) semi-sweet chocolate chunks
 1 package (4 ounces) German's sweet chocolate,
    cut into small, chunk-size pieces
 2 white baking bars (2 ounces each), cut into
    small, chunk-size pieces
 1 cup flake coconut
 ½ cup almond brickle chips

1. Preheat oven to 350°F.

2. Combine brown sugar, Butter Flavor Crisco® and granulated sugar in large bowl. Beat at medium speed of electric mixer until well blended. Add eggs, vanilla and water. Beat until well blended.

3. Combine flour, baking soda and salt. Add, 1 cup at a time, to creamed mixture. Beat at low speed until blended. Stir in semi-sweet chocolate chunks, sweet chocolate pieces, white baking bar pieces, coconut and brickle chips with spoon until blended. Drop by heaping tablespoonfuls 3 inches apart onto ungreased cookie sheet.

4. Bake at 350°F for 10 to 12 minutes or until set but not browned. Cool 1 minute on cookie sheet before removing to wire rack.

CHOCOLATE CHIP CORDIALS

Makes 28 cordials

COOKIES

1 package DUNCAN HINES® Chocolate Chip
   Cookie Mix
1 egg
2 teaspoons water
1 cup chopped pecans
¼ cup chopped red candied cherries
¼ cup flaked coconut
   Pecan halves, for garnish
   Red or green candied cherry halves, for garnish

CHOCOLATE GLAZE

1 square (1 ounce) semi-sweet chocolate
1½ tablespoons butter or margarine

1. Preheat oven to 375°F. Place 1¾-inch paper liners in 28 mini muffin cups.

2. For Cookies, combine cookie mix, buttery flavor packet from Mix, egg and water in large bowl. Stir until thoroughly blended. Stir in chopped pecans, chopped cherries and coconut. Fill cups with cookie dough. Top with pecan or cherry halves.

Chocolate Chip Cordials

3. Bake at 375°F for 13 to 15 minutes or until light golden brown. Remove from muffin tins; cool completely on wire racks.

4. For Chocolate Glaze, melt chocolate and butter in small bowl over hot water. Stir until smooth. Drizzle over cordials. Refrigerate until chocolate is firm. Store in airtight container.

Tip: You can also prepare glaze in microwave oven. Place chocolate and butter in microwave-safe bowl. Microwave at MEDIUM (50% power) for 45 to 60 seconds; stir until smooth.

CHOCOLATE CHIP CARAMEL NUT COOKIES

Makes 2 to 2½ dozen cookies

18 caramels, unwrapped
1 cup BUTTER FLAVOR CRISCO®
1 cup granulated sugar
½ cup firmly packed brown sugar
2 eggs, beaten
2¾ cups all-purpose flour
1 teaspoon baking soda
1 teaspoon salt
1 teaspoon vanilla
½ teaspoon hot water
1 cup semi-sweet miniature chocolate chips
½ cup coarsely chopped unsalted peanuts

1. Preheat oven to 400°F.

2. Cut each caramel into 4 pieces. Cut each fourth into 6 pieces.

3. Combine Butter Flavor Crisco®, granulated sugar and brown sugar in large bowl. Beat at medium speed of electric mixer until well blended and creamy. Beat in eggs.

4. Combine flour, baking soda and salt. Add gradually to creamed mixture at low speed. Mix until well blended. Beat in vanilla and hot water. Stir in caramels, chocolate chips and nuts with spoon. Mound two slightly rounded tablespoonfuls of dough on ungreased cookie sheet. Repeat for each cookie, keeping mounds 3 inches apart. Shape dough into circles, 2 inches in diameter and 1 inch high.

5. Bake at 400°F for 7 to 9 minutes or until light golden brown. Cool 5 minutes on cookie sheet before removing to wire rack.

EASY PEANUTTY SNICKERDOODLES

Makes about 2 dozen cookies

2 tablespoons sugar
2 teaspoons ground cinnamon
1 package (15 ounces) golden sugar cookie mix
1 egg
1 tablespoon water
1 cup REESE'S® Peanut Butter Chips

Preheat oven to 375°F. In small bowl, combine sugar and cinnamon. In medium bowl, combine cookie mix (and enclosed flavor packet), egg and water; mix with spoon or fork until thoroughly blended. Stir in peanut butter chips. Shape dough into 1-inch balls. (If dough is too soft, cover and refrigerate about 1 hour.) Roll balls in cinnamon-sugar. Place on ungreased cookie sheet.

Bake 8 to 10 minutes or until very lightly browned. Cool slightly; remove from cookie sheet to wire rack. Cool completely.

Top to bottom: Chocolate Chip 'n' Oatmeal Cookies, Easy Peanutty Snickerdoodles, Chocolate Kiss Cookies (page 215)

CHOCOLATE CHIP 'N' OATMEAL COOKIES

Makes about 4 dozen cookies

1 package (about 18.25 ounces) yellow cake mix
1 cup quick-cooking rolled oats, uncooked
¾ cup butter or margarine, softened
2 eggs
1 cup HERSHEY'S Semi-Sweet Chocolate Chips

Preheat oven to 350°F. In large mixer bowl, combine cake mix, oats, butter and eggs; mix well. Stir in chocolate chips. Drop by rounded teaspoonfuls onto ungreased cookie sheet.

Bake 10 to 12 minutes or until very lightly browned. Cool slightly; remove from cookie sheet to wire rack. Cool completely.

EVERYBODY'S FAVORITE CHOCOLATE CHIP COOKIE

Makes about 3 dozen cookies

1 cup BUTTER FLAVOR CRISCO®
¾ cup firmly packed brown sugar
¾ cup granulated sugar
2 eggs
1 teaspoon vanilla
1½ cups all-purpose flour
1 teaspoon baking soda
1 teaspoon salt
1 teaspoon hot water
3 cups quick-cooking oats (not instant or old-fashioned), uncooked
½ cup semi-sweet chocolate chips
½ cup butterscotch flavored chips
½ cups coarsely chopped walnuts or pecans

1. Preheat oven to 350°F.

2. Combine Butter Flavor Crisco®, brown sugar, granulated sugar, eggs and vanilla in large bowl. Beat at medium speed of electric mixer until well blended.

3. Combine flour, baking soda and salt. Mix into creamed mixture at low speed until just blended. Beat in hot water. Stir in, one at a time, oats, chocolate chips, butterscotch chips and nuts.

4. Drop rounded tablespoonfuls of dough 2 inches apart onto ungreased cookie sheet. Make crisscross marks on top of dough with floured fork tines.

5. Bake at 350°F for 10 to 11 minutes or until set. (Cookies will look moist.) Cool 2 minutes on cookie sheet. Remove to wire rack.

BAKER'S CHOCOLATE CHIP COOKIES

Makes about 6 dozen cookies

1 cup (2 sticks) margarine or butter, softened
¾ cup firmly packed brown sugar
¾ cup granulated sugar
2 eggs
1 teaspoon vanilla
2¼ cups all-purpose flour
1 teaspoon baking soda
¼ teaspoon salt
1 package (12 ounces) BAKER'S® Semi-Sweet
    Real Chocolate Chips
1 cup chopped nuts (optional)

Preheat oven to 375°F.

Beat margarine, sugars, eggs and vanilla in large bowl until light and fluffy. Mix in flour, baking soda and salt. Stir in chips and nuts. Drop by rounded teaspoonfuls, 2 inches apart, onto ungreased cookie sheets.

Bake for 8 to 10 minutes or until golden brown. Remove from cookie sheets to cool on wire racks.

Prep time: 15 minutes
Bake time: 8 to 10 minutes

Whole Grain Chippers

CHOCOLATE CHUNK COOKIES

Makes about 4½ dozen cookies

3 eggs
1 cup vegetable oil
¾ cup firmly packed brown sugar
1 teaspoon baking powder
1 teaspoon vanilla
¼ teaspoon baking soda
¼ teaspoon salt
2 cups all-purpose flour
1 package (12 ounces) semisweet chocolate chunks

Preheat oven to 350°F. Lightly grease cookie sheets or line with parchment paper.

Beat eggs in large bowl until foamy. Add oil and sugar; beat until light and frothy. Blend in baking powder, vanilla, baking soda and salt. Mix in flour until dough is smooth. Stir in chocolate chunks. Shape dough into walnut-sized balls. Place 2 inches apart on prepared cookie sheets.

Bake 10 to 12 minutes or until lightly browned. Remove to wire racks to cool.

WHOLE GRAIN CHIPPERS

Makes about 6 dozen cookies

1 cup butter or margarine, softened
1 cup firmly packed light brown sugar
⅔ cup granulated sugar
2 eggs
1 teaspoon baking soda
1 teaspoon vanilla
    Pinch salt
1 cup whole wheat flour
1 cup all-purpose flour
2 cups uncooked rolled oats
1 package (12 ounces) semisweet chocolate chips
1 cup sunflower seeds

Preheat oven to 375°F. Lightly grease cookie sheets or line with parchment paper.

Beat butter with sugars and eggs in large bowl until light and fluffy. Beat in baking soda, vanilla and salt. Blend in flours and oats to make a stiff dough. Stir in chocolate chips. Shape rounded teaspoonfuls of dough into balls; roll in sunflower seeds. Place 2 inches apart on prepared cookie sheets.

Bake 8 to 10 minutes or until firm. Do not overbake. Cool a few minutes on cookie sheet; remove to wire racks to cool completely.

Almond Milk Chocolate Chippers

Drop rounded teaspoonfuls of dough 2 inches apart onto ungreased cookie sheets.

Bake 9 to 10 minutes or until edges are golden brown. Let cookies stand on cookie sheets 2 minutes. Remove cookies with spatula to wire racks; cool completely. Store tightly covered at room temperature or freeze up to 3 months.

ULTIMATE CHIPPERS

Makes about 6 dozen cookies

2½ cups all-purpose flour
 1 teaspoon baking soda
 ½ teaspoon salt
 1 cup butter or margarine, softened
 1 cup firmly packed light brown sugar
 ½ cup granulated sugar
 2 large eggs
 1 tablespoon vanilla
 1 cup semisweet chocolate chips
 1 cup milk chocolate chips
 1 cup vanilla chips
 ½ cup coarsely chopped pecans (optional)

Preheat oven to 375°F.

Place flour, baking soda and salt in medium bowl; stir to combine.

Beat butter, brown sugar and granulated sugar in large bowl with electric mixer at medium speed until light and fluffy, scraping down side of bowl once. Beat in eggs and vanilla, scraping down side of bowl once. Add flour mixture. Beat at low speed scraping down side of bowl once. Stir in chips and pecans with wooden spoon.

Drop heaping teaspoonfuls of dough 2 inches apart onto ungreased cookie sheets.

Bake 10 to 12 minutes or until edges are golden brown. Let cookies stand on cookie sheets 2 minutes. Remove cookies with spatula to wire racks; cool completely. Store tightly covered at room temperature or freeze up to 3 months.

ALMOND MILK CHOCOLATE CHIPPERS

Makes about 3 dozen cookies

1¼ cups all-purpose flour
 ½ teaspoon baking soda
 ½ teaspoon salt
 ½ cup butter or margarine, softened
 ½ cup firmly packed light brown sugar
 ⅓ cup granulated sugar
 1 large egg
 2 tablespoons almond-flavored liqueur
 1 cup milk chocolate chips
 ½ cup toasted slivered almonds

Preheat oven to 375°F.

Place flour, baking soda and salt in small bowl; stir to combine.

Beat butter, brown sugar and granulated sugar in large bowl with electric mixer at medium speed until light and fluffy, scraping down side of bowl once. Beat in egg until well blended. Beat in liqueur. Gradually add flour mixture. Beat at low speed until well blended, scraping down side of bowl once. Stir in chips and almonds with wooden spoon.

WHITE CHOCOLATE BIGGIES

Makes about 2 dozen cookies

2 cups butter or margarine, softened
1 cup granulated sugar
¾ cup firmly packed light brown sugar
2 eggs
2 teaspoons vanilla
2½ cups all-purpose flour
⅔ cup unsweetened cocoa
1 teaspoon baking soda
½ teaspoon salt
1 package (10 ounces) large white chocolate chips
¾ cup pecan halves, coarsely chopped
½ cup golden raisins

Preheat oven to 350°F. Lightly grease cookie sheets or line with parchment paper.

Beat butter, sugars, eggs and vanilla in large bowl until light and creamy. Combine flour, cocoa, baking soda and salt in medium bowl; blend into creamed mixture until smooth. Stir in white chocolate chips, pecans and raisins. Scoop out about ⅓ cupful of dough for each cookie. Place on prepared cookie sheets, spacing about 4 inches apart. Press each cookie to flatten slightly.

Bake 12 to 14 minutes or until firm in center. Cool 5 minutes on cookie sheet, then remove to wire racks to cool completely.

COWBOY COOKIES

Makes about 4 dozen cookies

½ cup butter or margarine, softened
½ cup firmly packed light brown sugar
¼ cup granulated sugar
1 egg
1 teaspoon vanilla
1 cup all-purpose flour
2 tablespoons unsweetened cocoa
½ teaspoon baking powder
¼ teaspoon baking soda
1 cup uncooked rolled oats
1 cup (6 ounces) semisweet chocolate chips
½ cup raisins
½ cup chopped nuts

Preheat oven to 375°F. Lightly grease cookie sheets or line with parchment paper.

Beat butter with sugars in large bowl until blended. Add egg and vanilla; beat until fluffy. Combine flour, cocoa, baking powder and baking soda in small bowl; stir into butter mixture with oats, chocolate chips, raisins and nuts. Drop teaspoonfuls of dough 2 inches apart onto prepared cookie sheets.

Bake 10 to 12 minutes or until lightly browned around edges. Remove to wire racks to cool.

PEANUT BUTTER JUMBOS

Makes about 1½ dozen cookies

½ cup butter or margarine, softened
1 cup firmly packed brown sugar
1 cup granulated sugar
1½ cups peanut butter
3 eggs
2 teaspoons baking soda
1 teaspoon vanilla
4½ cups uncooked rolled oats
1 cup (6 ounces) semisweet chocolate chips
1 cup candy-coated chocolate pieces

Preheat oven to 350°F. Lightly grease cookie sheets or line with parchment paper.

Beat butter, sugars, peanut butter and eggs in large bowl until light. Blend in baking soda, vanilla and oats until well mixed. Stir in chocolate chips and candy pieces. Scoop out about ⅓ cupful of dough for each cookie. Place on prepared cookie sheets, spacing about 4 inches apart. Press each cookie to flatten slightly.

Bake 15 to 20 minutes or until firm in center. Remove to wire racks to cool.

Left to right: Peanut Butter Jumbos, White Chocolate Biggies

Top to bottom: Choco-Dipped Peanut Butter Cookies, Easy Peanut Butter Cookies, Peanut Blossoms

EASY PEANUT BUTTER COOKIES

Makes about 5 dozen cookies

1 (14-ounce) can EAGLE® Brand Sweetened
   Condensed Milk (NOT evaporated milk)
¾ to 1 cup peanut butter
1 egg
1 teaspoon vanilla extract
2 cups biscuit baking mix
   Granulated sugar

In large mixer bowl, beat sweetened condensed milk, peanut butter, egg and vanilla until smooth. Add biscuit mix; mix well. Cover; refrigerate at least 1 hour.

Preheat oven to 350°F. Shape dough into 1-inch balls. Roll in sugar. Place 2 inches apart on ungreased cookie sheets. Flatten with fork.

Bake 6 to 8 minutes or until *lightly* browned. *Do not overbake.* Cool. Store tightly covered at room temperature.

Choco-Dipped Peanut Butter Cookies: Shape as above; omit sugar. *Do not flatten.* Bake as directed. Cool. Melt 1 pound chocolate-flavored candy coating.* Partially dip each cookie into candy coating. Place on waxed paper-lined cookie sheets. Let stand or refrigerate until chocolate is set.

Peanut Blossoms: Shape as above; roll in sugar. *Do not flatten.* Bake as directed. Press solid milk chocolate candy drop in center of each cookie immediately after baking.

*Candy coating (also called confectioners' or summer coating) is usually purchased in grocery store baking sections or in candy specialty stores.

PEANUT BUTTER SENSATIONS

Makes about 2 dozen cookies

1 cup JIF® Creamy Peanut Butter
¾ cup granulated sugar
½ cup firmly packed brown sugar
½ cup BUTTER FLAVOR CRISCO®
1 tablespoon milk
1 teaspoon vanilla
1 egg
1¼ cups all-purpose flour
¾ teaspoon baking soda
½ teaspoon baking powder
¼ teaspoon salt

1. Preheat oven to 375°F.

2. Combine Jif® Creamy Peanut Butter, granulated sugar, brown sugar, Butter Flavor Crisco®, milk and vanilla in large bowl. Beat at medium speed of electric mixer until well blended and creamy. Beat in egg.

3. Combine flour, baking soda, baking powder and salt. Add gradually to creamed mixture at low speed. Mix just until blended. Drop by rounded tablespoonfuls 2 inches apart onto ungreased cookie sheet. Make crisscross marks on top with floured fork tines.

4. Bake at 375°F for 8 to 10 minutes. Cool 2 minutes on cookie sheet before removing to wire rack.

NUTTY TOPPERS

Makes about 4 dozen cookies

PEANUT BUTTER LAYER
¾ cup BUTTER FLAVOR CRISCO®
1 cup JIF® Creamy Peanut Butter
1 cup sugar
2 eggs
1 teaspoon vanilla
1 teaspoon water
2 cups all-purpose flour
1 teaspoon baking soda
¼ teaspoon salt

CHOCOLATE LAYER
½ cup dough from Peanut Butter Layer
1 egg
1 tablespoon unsweetened cocoa
48 pecans or walnut halves

1. Preheat oven to 375°F.

2. For Peanut Butter Layer, combine Butter Flavor Crisco®, Jif® Creamy Peanut Butter, sugar, 2 eggs, vanilla and water in large bowl. Beat at medium speed of electric mixer until well blended and creamy.

3. Combine flour, baking soda and salt. Mix into creamed mixture at low speed until blended.

4. For Chocolate Layer, combine ½ cup of dough from Peanut Butter Layer, 1 egg and cocoa. Beat at low speed until blended.

5. Form Peanut Butter Layer dough into 1-inch balls. Place 2 inches apart on ungreased cookie sheets. Flatten slightly with bottom of greased and sugared glass. Place leveled ½ teaspoonful of Chocolate Layer on flattened dough. Press nut into each center. Repeat with remaining dough.

6. Bake at 375°F for 10 minutes or until edges are lightly browned. Cool 2 minutes on cookie sheets. Remove to wire rack.

PEANUT BUTTER SPRITZ SANDWICHES

Makes 2½ to 3 dozen sandwich cookies

1 package DUNCAN HINES® Peanut Butter
  Cookie Mix
1 egg
3 bars (1.55 ounces each) milk chocolate

1. Preheat oven to 375°F.

2. Combine cookie mix, contents of peanut butter packet from Mix and egg in large bowl. Stir until thoroughly blended. Fill cookie press with dough. Press desired shapes 2 inches apart onto ungreased cookie sheet.

3. Bake at 375°F for 7 to 9 minutes or until set but not browned. Cool 1 minute on cookie sheet.

4. Cut each milk chocolate bar into 12 sections by following division marks on bars.

Peanut Butter Spritz Sandwiches

5. To assemble, carefully remove one cookie from cookie sheet. Place one milk chocolate section on bottom of warm cookie; top with second cookie. Press together to make sandwich. Repeat with remaining cookies. Place sandwich cookies on wire rack until chocolate is set. Store in airtight container.

Tip: For best appearance, use cookie press plates that give solid shapes.

PEANUT BUTTER COCOA COOKIES

Makes about 6 dozen cookies

1 cup BUTTER FLAVOR CRISCO®
1 cup JIF® Extra Crunchy Peanut Butter
1 cup firmly packed brown sugar
1 cup granulated sugar
2 eggs
1 teaspoon vanilla
2 cups all-purpose flour
½ cup unsweetened cocoa
1 teaspoon baking powder
1 teaspoon baking soda
1 cup milk chocolate chips

1. Preheat oven to 350°F.

2. Combine Butter Flavor Crisco®, Jif® Extra Crunchy Peanut Butter, brown sugar and granulated sugar in large bowl. Beat at medium speed of electric mixer until well blended. Beat in eggs and vanilla. Beat until blended and creamy.

3. Combine flour, cocoa, baking powder and baking soda. Mix into creamed mixture at low speed until just blended. Stir in milk chocolate chips.

4. Drop rounded tablespoonfuls of dough 2 inches apart onto ungreased cookie sheet.

5. Bake at 350°F for 10 to 12 minutes or until edges are lightly browned. Cool 2 minutes on cookie sheet. Remove to wire rack.

Left to right: Double Peanut Butter Supremes, Nutty Toppers (page 201), Oatmeal Lemon-Cheese Cookies (page 186)

DOUBLE PEANUT BUTTER SUPREMES

Makes about 4 dozen cookies

COOKIES
½ cup BUTTER FLAVOR CRISCO®
1 cup JIF® Creamy Peanut Butter
½ cup firmly packed brown sugar
½ cup granulated sugar
⅓ cup dairy sour cream
1 egg
1 teaspoon vanilla
2 cups all-purpose flour
¾ teaspoon baking soda
½ teaspoon baking powder
½ teaspoon salt
   Additional granulated sugar for rolling

FILLING
1 package (8 ounces) cream cheese, softened
½ cup JIF® Creamy Peanut Butter
1 egg, slightly beaten
⅓ cup granulated sugar
   Dash salt
1 cup semi-sweet miniature chocolate chips

1. For Cookies, combine Butter Flavor Crisco®, 1 cup Jif® Creamy Peanut Butter, brown sugar, ½ cup granulated sugar, sour cream, 1 egg and vanilla in large bowl. Beat at medium speed of electric mixer until well blended and creamy.

2. Combine flour, baking soda, baking powder and ½ teaspoon salt. Mix into creamed mixture at low speed until blended. Cover and refrigerate 1 hour.

3. For Filling, combine cream cheese, ½ cup Jif® Creamy Peanut Butter, 1 egg, ⅓ cup sugar and dash salt. Beat at medium speed of electric mixer until blended. Stir in miniature chocolate chips.

4. Preheat oven to 350°F.

5. Form dough into 1-inch balls. Roll in additional granulated sugar. Place 2 inches apart on ungreased cookie sheet. Press thumb gently in center of each cookie. Fill center with rounded teaspoonful of filling.

6. Bake at 350°F for 12 to 13 minutes or until lightly browned. Cool 2 minutes on cookie sheet. Remove to wire rack.

PEANUT BUTTER CHOCOLATE CHIPPERS

Makes about 2 dozen cookies

1 cup creamy or chunky peanut butter
1 cup firmly packed light brown sugar
1 large egg
¾ cup milk chocolate chips
   Granulated sugar

Preheat oven to 350°F.

Combine peanut butter, brown sugar and egg in medium bowl; mix with mixing spoon until well blended. Add chips; mix well.

Roll heaping tablespoonfuls of dough into 1½-inch balls.* Place balls 2 inches apart on ungreased cookie sheets.

Dip table fork into granulated sugar; press criss-cross fashion onto each ball, flattening to ½-inch thickness.

Bake 12 minutes or until set. Let cookies stand on cookie sheets 2 minutes. Remove cookies with spatula to wire racks; cool completely. Store tightly covered at room temperature or freeze up to 3 months.

*Or, use small ice cream scoop (1½ inches in diameter) filled with dough and pressed against side of bowl to level.

DOUBLE PEANUT BUTTER JOY

Makes about 3 dozen cookies

1 cup granulated sugar
1 cup firmly packed brown sugar
1 cup JIF® Creamy Peanut Butter
½ cup BUTTER FLAVOR CRISCO®
2 eggs
1½ cups all-purpose flour
½ teaspoon baking soda
¼ teaspoon salt
2 cups peanut butter chips

1. Preheat oven to 350°F.

2. Combine granulated sugar, brown sugar, Jif® Creamy Peanut Butter and Butter Flavor Crisco® in large bowl. Beat at medium speed of electric mixer until well blended and creamy. Add eggs, one at a time, beating after each addition.

3. Combine flour, baking soda and salt. Add gradually to creamed mixture at low speed. Mix just until well blended. Stir in peanut butter chips with spoon. (Dough will be stiff.) Shape into 1½-inch balls. Place 2 inches apart on ungreased cookie sheet. Make crisscross marks on top with floured forked tines, smoothing edges of cookies, if necessary.

4. Bake at 350°F for 8 to 10 minutes or until edges are set and tops are moist. Cool about 8 minutes on cookie sheet before removing to wire rack.

CHOCOLATE & PEANUT BUTTER TWEED COOKIES

Makes about 6 dozen cookies

1 cup butter or margarine, softened
½ cup firmly packed light brown sugar
¼ cup granulated sugar
1 egg
¼ teaspoon baking soda
2½ cups all-purpose flour
½ cup *each* semisweet chocolate chips and peanut butter chips, chopped*

Beat butter and sugars in large bowl until smooth. Add egg and baking soda; beat until light. Stir in flour until dough is smooth. Blend in chopped chips. Divide dough into 4 parts. Shape each part into a roll, about 1½ inches in diameter. Wrap in plastic wrap; refrigerate until firm, at least 1 hour or up to 2 weeks. (For longer storage, freeze up to 6 weeks.)

Preheat oven to 375°F. Lightly grease cookie sheets or line with parchment paper. Cut rolls into ⅛-inch-thick slices; place 2 inches apart on prepared cookie sheets.

Bake 10 to 12 minutes or until lightly browned. Remove to wire racks to cool.

*Chips can be chopped in a food processor.

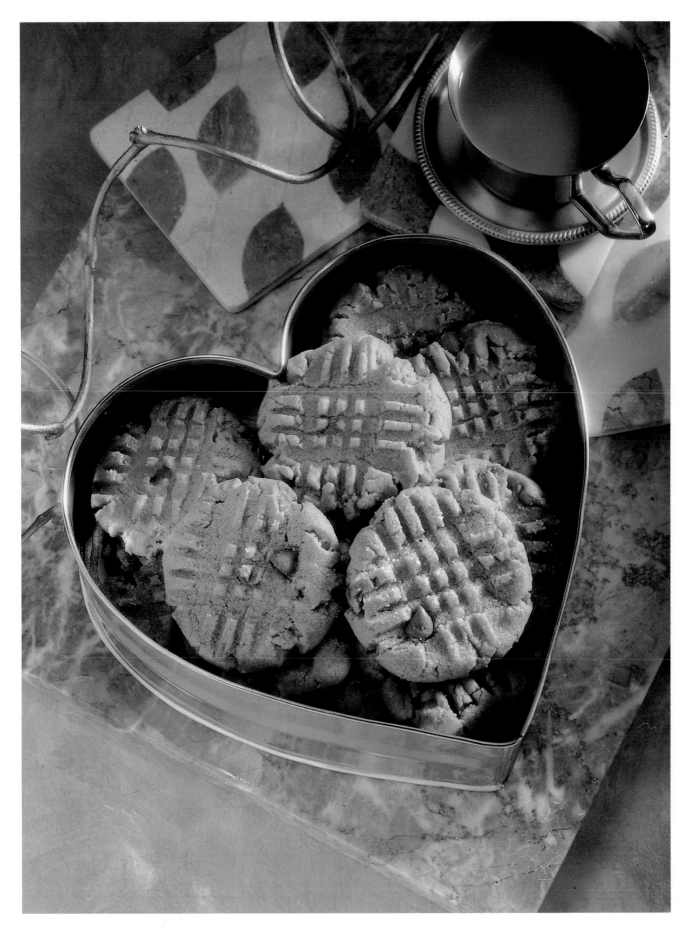

Peanut Butter Chocolate Chippers

CHOCOLATE SUGAR DROPS

Makes about 5 dozen cookies

½ cup butter or margarine, softened
½ cup vegetable oil
½ cup powdered sugar
½ cup granulated sugar
1 egg
2 cups all-purpose flour
¼ cup unsweetened cocoa
½ teaspoon baking soda
½ teaspoon cream of tartar
¼ teaspoon salt
1 teaspoon vanilla
   Additional granulated sugar

Beat butter, oil, powdered sugar, ½ cup granulated sugar and egg in large bowl until light and fluffy. Combine flour, cocoa, baking soda, cream of tartar and salt in small bowl. Add to butter mixture with vanilla, stirring until dough is smooth. Cover; refrigerate 30 minutes or overnight, if desired.

Preheat oven to 350°F. Lightly grease cookie sheets or line with parchment paper. Shape dough into marble-sized balls. Place 2 inches apart on prepared cookie

Chocolate Sugar Drops, Chocolate-Coconut Cookies, Chocolate & Peanut Butter Tweed Cookies (page 204)

sheets. Flatten each cookie to about ⅓-inch thickness with bottom of greased glass dipped in additional granulated sugar.

Bake 10 minutes or until firm. Do not overbake. Remove to wire racks to cool.

CHOCOLATE-COCONUT COOKIES

Makes about 4 dozen cookies

2 squares (1 ounce each) unsweetened chocolate
½ cup butter or margarine, softened
1 cup firmly packed light brown sugar
1 egg
1¼ cups all-purpose flour
¼ teaspoon baking powder
⅛ teaspoon baking soda
   Dash salt
2 cups chopped walnuts or pecans
½ cup flaked coconut
   Pecan halves or red candied cherry halves

Preheat oven to 350°F. Lightly grease cookie sheets or line with parchment paper.

Melt chocolate in top of double boiler over hot, not boiling, water. Remove from heat; cool. Beat butter and sugar in large bowl until blended. Add egg and melted chocolate; beat until light. Combine flour, baking powder, baking soda and salt in small bowl. Stir into butter mixture until blended. Mix in nuts and coconut. Drop dough by teaspoonfuls 2 inches apart onto prepared cookie sheets. Press a pecan or cherry half into center of each cookie.

Bake 10 to 12 minutes or until firm. Remove to wire racks to cool.

DOUBLE CHOCOLATE TREASURES

Makes about 5 dozen cookies

1 package (12 ounces) semi-sweet chocolate pieces
   (2 cups), divided
½ cup (1 stick) margarine, softened
¾ cup granulated sugar
2 eggs
1 teaspoon vanilla
2 cups QUAKER® Oats (quick or old-fashioned,
   uncooked)
1½ cups all-purpose flour
2 teaspoons baking powder
¼ teaspoon salt (optional)
½ cup powdered sugar

Preheat oven to 350°F. In small saucepan over low heat, melt 1 cup chocolate pieces, stirring constantly until smooth; cool slightly.* Beat margarine and sugar in large bowl until light and fluffy. Blend in eggs, vanilla and melted chocolate. Combine oats, flour, baking powder and salt. Stir into chocolate mixture; mix well. Stir in remaining 1 cup chocolate pieces. Shape into 1-inch balls. Roll in powdered sugar, coating heavily. Place on ungreased cookie sheet.

Bake 10 to 12 minutes. Cool 1 minute on cookie sheet; remove to wire rack. Cool completely. Store tightly covered.

To Microwave: Place chocolate pieces in microwaveable bowl. Microwave at HIGH (100% power) 1 to 2 minutes, stirring every 30 seconds until smooth.

DOUBLE CHOCOLATE CHUNK COOKIES

Makes about 2 dozen cookies

8 squares BAKER'S® Semi-Sweet Chocolate, divided
½ cup (1 stick) margarine or butter, slightly softened
2 cups firmly packed brown sugar
½ cup granulated sugar
1 egg
1 teaspoon vanilla
1 cup all-purpose flour
½ teaspoon CALUMET® Baking Powder
¼ teaspoon salt
¾ cup chopped walnuts (optional)

Microwave 1 square chocolate in small microwavable bowl on HIGH (100% power) 1 to 2 minutes or until melted, stirring after each minute. Stir until completely melted. Set aside. Cut 3 squares chocolate into large (½-inch) chunks; set aside.

Beat margarine, sugars, egg and vanilla in large bowl until light and fluffy. Stir in 1 square melted chocolate. Mix in flour, baking powder and salt. Stir in chocolate chunks and walnuts. Refrigerate 30 minutes.

Preheat oven to 350°F. Drop dough by heaping tablespoonfuls, about 2 inches apart, onto greased cookie sheets. Bake for 8 minutes or until lightly browned. Cool 5 minutes on cookie sheets. Remove and finish cooling on wire racks.

Microwave remaining 4 squares chocolate in small microwavable bowl on HIGH 1½ to 2½ minutes or until melted, stirring after each minute. Stir until completely melted. Dip half of each cookie into melted chocolate. Let stand on waxed paper until chocolate is firm.

Double Chocolate Chunk Cookies

QUICK CHOCOLATE SOFTIES

Makes about 2 dozen large or 4 dozen small cookies

1 package (18.25 ounces) devil's food chocolate cake mix
⅓ cup water
⅓ cup butter or margarine, softened
1 large egg
1 cup large vanilla baking chips
½ cup coarsely chopped walnuts

Preheat oven to 350°F. Lightly grease cookie sheets.

Combine cake mix, water, butter and egg in large bowl. Beat with electric mixer at low speed until moistened, scraping down side of bowl once. Increase speed to medium; beat 1 minute, scraping down side of bowl once. (Dough will be thick.) Stir in chips and nuts with wooden spoon until well blended.

Drop heaping *teaspoonfuls* of dough 2 inches apart (for smaller cookies) or heaping *tablespoonfuls* 3 inches apart (for larger cookies) onto prepared cookie sheets.

Bake 10 to 12 minutes or until set. Let cookies stand on cookie sheets 1 minute. Remove cookies with spatula to wire racks; cool completely. Store tightly covered at room temperature or freeze up to 3 months.

*Left to right: Chocolate Mint Meltaways,
Chocolate Mint Cookies*

Bake 8 to 10 minutes or until set. Let stand on cookie sheet 3 minutes. Cool completely on wire racks.

Glaze: Combine over hot (not boiling) water, remaining ½ cup Nestlé® Toll House® Mint-Flavored Semi-Sweet Chocolate Morsels and vegetable shortening. Stir until morsels are melted and mixture is smooth.

Drizzle each cookie with ½ teaspoon Glaze; sprinkle with almonds. Refrigerate until Glaze sets (about 10 minutes). Store in airtight container in refrigerator.

CHOCOLATE MINT COOKIES

Makes about 3½ dozen cookies

COOKIES:
1½ cups (10-ounce package) NESTLÉ® Toll House®
   Mint-Flavored Semi-Sweet Chocolate Morsels,
   divided
 1 cup all-purpose flour
 ¾ teaspoon baking powder
 ¼ teaspoon baking soda
 ¼ teaspoon salt
 ¼ cup butter, softened
 ⅓ cup sugar
 ½ teaspoon vanilla extract
 1 egg

GLAZE:
 1 cup NESTLÉ® Toll House® Mint-Flavored
   Semi-Sweet Chocolate Morsels, reserved
   from 10-ounce package
 ¼ cup vegetable shortening
 3 tablespoons corn syrup
 2¼ teaspoons water

Cookies: Melt over hot (not boiling) water, ½ cup Nestlé® Toll House® Mint-Flavored Semi-Sweet Chocolate Morsels; stir until smooth. Set aside. In small bowl, combine flour, baking powder, baking soda and salt; set aside. In large bowl, combine butter, sugar and vanilla extract; beat until creamy. Beat in egg; blend in melted morsels. Gradually beat in flour mixture. Shape dough into ball and wrap in plastic wrap. Refrigerate about 1 hour or until firm.

Preheat oven to 350°F. On lightly floured board, roll dough to ³⁄₁₆-inch thickness. Cut with 2-inch heart-shaped or round cookie cutter. Reroll remaining dough and cut out cookies. Place on ungreased cookie sheets.

Bake 8 to 10 minutes or until set. Let stand 2 minutes. Remove from cookie sheets; cool completely on wire racks.

CHOCOLATE MINT MELTAWAYS

Makes about 4 dozen cookies

COOKIES:
1½ cups (10-ounce package) NESTLÉ® Toll House®
   Mint-Flavored Semi-Sweet Chocolate Morsels,
   divided
 ¾ cup butter, softened
 ½ cup sifted confectioners' sugar
 1 egg yolk
 1¼ cups all-purpose flour

GLAZE:
 ½ cup NESTLÉ® Toll House® Mint-Flavored
   Semi-Sweet Chocolate Morsels, reserved from
   10-ounce package
 1 tablespoon vegetable shortening
 2 tablespoons chopped toasted almonds

Cookies: Preheat oven to 350°F. Melt over hot (not boiling) water, 1 cup Nestlé® Toll House® Mint-Flavored Semi-Sweet Chocolate Morsels; stir until smooth. Set aside. In large bowl, beat butter, confectioners' sugar and egg yolk until creamy. Add melted morsels and flour; beat until well blended. Drop by heaping teaspoonfuls onto ungreased cookie sheets.

Glaze: Combine over hot (not boiling) water, remaining 1 cup Nestlé® Toll House® Mint-Flavored Semi-Sweet Chocolate Morsels, vegetable shortening, corn syrup and water; stir until morsels are melted and mixture is smooth. Remove from heat, but keep mixture over hot water.

Dip half of each cookie into Glaze; shake off any excess Glaze. Place cookies on waxed paper-lined cookie sheets. Refrigerate until Glaze sets (about 10 minutes). Store in airtight container in refrigerator.

MOCHA MINT CRISPS

Makes about 4 dozen cookies

1 cup (2 sticks) butter or margarine, softened
1 cup sugar
¼ cup light corn syrup
1 egg
¼ teaspoon peppermint extract
1 teaspoon powdered instant coffee
1 teaspoon hot water
2 cups all-purpose flour
6 tablespoons HERSHEY'S Cocoa
2 teaspoons baking soda
¼ teaspoon salt
  Mocha Mint Sugar (recipe follows)

Preheat oven to 350°F. In large mixer bowl, beat butter and sugar until light and fluffy. Add corn syrup, egg and peppermint extract; mix thoroughly. Dissolve instant coffee in water; stir into butter mixture. Stir together flour, cocoa, baking soda and salt; gradually add to butter mixture, blending thoroughly. Shape dough into 1-inch balls. (Dough may be refrigerated for a short time for easier handling.) Prepare Mocha Mint Sugar. Roll dough balls in Mocha Mint Sugar. Place balls on ungreased cookie sheet about 2 inches apart.

Bake 8 to 10 minutes or until no imprint remains when touched lightly. Cool slightly; remove from cookie sheet to wire rack. Cool completely.

Mocha Mint Sugar: In small bowl, stir together ¼ cup powdered sugar, 2 tablespoons crushed hard peppermint candies (about 6 candies) and 1½ teaspoons powdered instant coffee.

Quick Chocolate Macaroons

QUICK CHOCOLATE MACAROONS

Makes about 2 dozen cookies

1 square BAKER'S® Unsweetened Chocolate
1⅓ cups BAKER'S® ANGEL FLAKE® Coconut
⅓ cup sweetened condensed milk
½ teaspoon vanilla

Preheat oven to 350°F.

Microwave chocolate in large microwavable bowl on HIGH (100% power) 1 to 2 minutes or until almost melted, stirring after each minute. Stir until chocolate is completely melted. Stir in coconut, condensed milk and vanilla. Drop by teaspoonfuls, 1 inch apart, onto well-greased cookie sheets.

Bake for 10 to 12 minutes or until set. Immediately remove from cookie sheets to cool on wire racks.

Prep time: 10 minutes
Bake time: 10 to 12 minutes

*Top to bottom: Chocolate Sugar Cookies, Jam-Filled
Chocolate Sugar Cookies, Chocolate-Caramel Sugar Cookies*

CHOCOLATE SUGAR COOKIES

Makes about 3½ dozen cookies

3 squares BAKER'S® Unsweetened Chocolate
1 cup (2 sticks) margarine or butter
1 cup sugar
1 egg
1 teaspoon vanilla
2 cups all-purpose flour
1 teaspoon baking soda
1 teaspoon salt
  Additional sugar

Microwave chocolate and margarine in large microwavable bowl on HIGH (100% power) 2 minutes or until margarine is melted. Stir until chocolate is completely melted.

Stir 1 cup sugar into melted chocolate mixture until well blended. Stir in egg and vanilla until completely mixed. Mix in flour, baking soda and salt. Refrigerate 30 minutes.

Preheat oven to 375°F. Shape dough into 1-inch balls; roll in additional sugar. Place on ungreased cookie sheets. (If a flatter, crisper cookie is desired, flatten ball with bottom of drinking glass.)

Bake for 8 to 10 minutes or until set. Remove from cookie sheets to cool on wire racks.

Prep time: 15 minutes
Chill time: 30 minutes
Bake time: 8 to 10 minutes

Jam-Filled Chocolate Sugar Cookies: Prepare Chocolate Sugar Cookie dough as directed; roll in finely chopped nuts in place of sugar. Make indentation in center of each ball; fill center with your favorite jam. Bake as directed.

Chocolate-Caramel Sugar Cookies: Prepare Chocolate Sugar Cookie dough as directed. Roll in finely chopped nuts in place of sugar. Make indentation in each ball; bake as directed. Microwave 1 package (14 ounces) KRAFT® Caramels with 2 tablespoons milk in medium microwavable bowl on HIGH (100% power) 3 minutes or until melted, stirring after 2 minutes. Fill centers of cookies with caramel mixture. Drizzle with melted BAKER'S® Semi-Sweet Chocolate, if desired.

CHOCOLATE CRACKLES

Makes 4 to 5 dozen cookies

1½ cups granulated sugar
½ cup CRISCO® Oil
1½ teaspoons vanilla
3 eggs
1⅔ cups unsifted all-purpose flour
½ cup unsweetened cocoa
1½ teaspoons baking powder
½ teaspoon salt
⅓ to ½ cup confectioners sugar

1. Combine granulated sugar, Crisco® Oil and vanilla in medium mixing bowl; mix until well blended. Add eggs, one at a time, mixing well after each addition. Stir in flour, cocoa, baking powder and salt. Cover and refrigerate about 3 hours.

2. Preheat oven to 350°F. Lightly grease cookie sheet. Place confectioners sugar in shallow dish or large plastic food bag. Shape dough into 1-inch balls. Roll in confectioners sugar or add to bag and shake to coat. Place about 2 inches apart on greased cookie sheet.

3. Bake at 350°F about 10 minutes,* or until almost no indentation remains when touched lightly. Cool on wire rack.

*For softer cookies, bake about 8 minutes.

CHOCOLATE OATMEAL WALNUT COOKIES

Makes about 4½ dozen cookies

1 package DUNCAN HINES® Chocolate Lovers' Walnut Brownie Mix
½ teaspoon ground cinnamon
1 egg
⅓ cup water
⅓ cup CRISCO® Oil or CRISCO® PURITAN® Oil
1¼ cups quick-cooking oats (not instant or old-fashioned), uncooked
  Confectioners sugar (optional)

1. Preheat oven to 350°F. Grease cookie sheet.

2. Combine brownie mix and cinnamon in large bowl. Add egg, water and oil. Stir with spoon until well blended, about 50 strokes. Stir in oats and nut packet from Mix. Drop by measuring tablespoonfuls 2 inches apart onto greased cookie sheet.

3. Bake at 350°F for 8 to 10 minutes or until set. Cool 2 minutes on cookie sheet. Remove to wire rack. Cool completely Dust with confectioners sugar, if desired. Store in airtight container.

CHOCOLATE BISCOTTI

Makes 4 dozen cookies

1½ cups all-purpose flour
½ cup NESTLÉ® Cocoa
1½ teaspoons baking powder
½ teaspoon baking soda
⅔ cup sugar
3 tablespoons butter, softened
2 eggs
½ teaspoon almond extract
½ cup coarsely chopped almonds

Preheat oven to 350°F. In small bowl, combine flour, cocoa, baking powder and baking soda; set aside.

In large mixer bowl, beat sugar, butter, eggs and almond extract until creamy. Gradually beat in flour mixture. Stir in almonds. Divide dough in half. On greased cookie sheet, shape into two 12-inch long logs. Flatten slightly.

Bake 25 minutes. Cool on wire rack 5 minutes. Cut into ½-inch thick slices; return slices to cookie sheet, cut-sides down. Bake 20 minutes longer. Remove from cookie sheet; cool completely on wire rack.

Chocolate Biscotti

COCOA SHORTBREAD

Makes about 2 dozen cookies

2 cups all-purpose flour
½ cup NESTLÉ® Cocoa
1 cup (2 sticks) butter, softened
1 cup sifted confectioners' sugar
1½ teaspoons vanilla extract

Preheat oven to 300°F. In small bowl, combine flour and Nestlé® Cocoa; set aside.

In large mixer bowl, beat butter, confectioners' sugar and vanilla extract until creamy. Gradually blend in flour mixture. On lightly floured board, roll dough ½ inch thick; cut into 2 × 1-inch strips. With fork, pierce surface. Place on ungreased cookie sheets.

Bake 20 minutes or just until firm. Let stand on cookie sheets 2 minutes. Remove from cookies sheets; cool completely on wire racks.

MOCHA SHORTBREAD COOKIES

Makes about 1½ dozen cookies

1 teaspoon NESCAFÉ® Classic Instant Coffee
1 teaspoon boiling water
2 cups (12-ounce package) NESTLÉ® Toll House®
    Semi-Sweet Chocolate Morsels, divided
¾ cup butter, softened
1¼ cups sifted confectioners' sugar
1 cup all-purpose flour
⅛ teaspoon salt

Preheat oven to 250°F. In cup, dissolve Nescafé® Classic Instant Coffee in boiling water; set aside. Melt over hot (not boiling) water, 1 cup Nestlé® Toll House® Semi-Sweet Chocolate Morsels; stir until smooth. Remove from heat; set aside. In large bowl, combine butter, confectioners' sugar and coffee mixture; beat until smooth. Gradually blend in flour and salt. Stir in melted morsels. Roll dough between two pieces of waxed paper to ³⁄₁₆-inch thickness. Remove top sheet; cut out cookies using 2½-inch cookie cutter. Remove from waxed paper and place on ungreased cookie sheets.

Bake 25 minutes. Cool completely on wire racks. Melt over hot (not boiling) water, remaining 1 cup Nestlé® Toll House® Semi-Sweet Chocolate Morsels; stir until smooth. Spread slightly rounded teaspoonfuls of melted chocolate on flat side of cookie; top with second cookie. Repeat with remaining cookies. Refrigerate until set. Let stand at room temperature 15 minutes before serving.

CHOCOLATE PECAN TASSIES

Makes 3 dozen tassies

CRUST
½ cup (1 stick) margarine or butter, softened
1 package (3 ounces) PHILADELPHIA BRAND®
    Cream Cheese, softened
1 cup all-purpose flour

FILLING
1 square BAKER'S® Unsweetened Chocolate
1 tablespoon margarine or butter
¾ cup firmly packed brown sugar
1 egg
1 teaspoon vanilla
1 cup chopped pecans
    Powdered sugar (optional)

Beat ½ cup margarine and cream cheese in medium bowl until well blended. Beat in flour until just blended. Wrap dough in plastic wrap; refrigerate 1 hour.

Preheat oven to 350°F. Microwave chocolate and 1 tablespoon margarine in large microwavable bowl on HIGH (100% power) 1 minute or until margarine is melted. Stir until chocolate is completely melted.

Beat in sugar, egg and vanilla until thickened. Stir in pecans.

Shape chilled crust mixture into 36 (1-inch) balls. Flatten each ball and press onto bottom and up sides of ungreased miniature muffin cups. Spoon about 1 teaspoon filling into each cup.

Bake for 20 minutes. Cool in pans on wire racks 15 minutes. Remove from pans. Cool completely. Sprinkle with powdered sugar, if desired.

Prep time: 45 minutes
Chill time: 1 hour
Bake time: 20 minutes

Chocolate Clouds

CHOCOLATE CLOUDS

Makes about 2½ dozen cookies

3 egg whites
⅛ teaspoon cream of tartar
¾ cup sugar
1 teaspoon vanilla extract
2 tablespoons HERSHEY'S Cocoa
1¾ cups (10-ounce package) HERSHEY'S
    Semi-Sweet Chocolate Chunks *or* 2 cups
    (12-ounce package) HERSHEY'S
    Semi-Sweet Chocolate Chips

Preheat oven to 300°F. Place parchment paper or foil on cookie sheets. In large mixer bowl, beat egg whites and cream of tartar until soft peaks form. Gradually add sugar and vanilla, beating until stiff peaks form, sugar is dissolved and mixture is glossy. Sift cocoa onto egg white mixture; gently fold in just until combined. Fold in chocolate chunks. Drop by heaping tablespoonfuls onto prepared cookie sheets.

Bake 35 to 40 minutes or just until dry. Cool slightly; carefully peel cookies off paper. Cool completely on wire racks. Store, covered, at room temperature.

Marshmallow Sandwich Cookies

MARSHMALLOW SANDWICH COOKIES

Makes about 2 dozen sandwich cookies

2 cups all-purpose flour
½ cup unsweetened cocoa
2 teaspoons baking soda
¼ teaspoon salt
⅔ cup butter or margarine, softened
1¼ cups sugar
¼ cup light corn syrup
1 large egg
1 teaspoon vanilla
  Additional sugar
24 large marshmallows

Preheat oven to 350°F.

Place flour, cocoa, baking soda and salt in medium bowl; stir to combine.

Beat butter and 1¼ cups sugar in large bowl with electric mixer at medium speed until light and fluffy, scraping down side of bowl once. Beat in corn syrup, egg and vanilla, scraping down side of bowl once. Gradually add flour mixture. Beat at low speed, scraping down side of bowl occasionally. Cover and refrigerate dough 15 minutes or until firm enough to roll into balls.

Place additional sugar in shallow dish. Roll tablespoonfuls of dough into 1-inch balls; roll in sugar to coat. Place 3 inches apart on ungreased cookie sheets.

Bake 10 to 11 minutes or until set. Remove cookies with spatula to wire rack; cool completely.

To assemble sandwiches,* place one marshmallow on flat side of one cookie on paper plate. Microwave at HIGH (100% power) 12 seconds or until marshmallow is hot. Immediately place another cookie, flat side down, over marshmallow; press together slightly. Store tightly covered at room temperature.

*Cookies also taste great just as they are!

Note: These cookies do not freeze well.

CHOCOLATE CHIP SANDWICH COOKIES

Makes about 1½ dozen sandwich cookies

COOKIES
  1 package DUNCAN HINES® Chocolate Chip
    Cookie Mix
  1 egg
  2 teaspoons water

CREAM FILLING
  1 cup marshmallow creme
  ½ cup butter or margarine, softened
1⅔ cups confectioners sugar
  1 teaspoon vanilla extract

1. Preheat oven to 375°F.

2. For Cookies, combine cookie mix, buttery flavor packet from Mix, egg and water in large bowl. Stir until thoroughly blended. Drop by rounded teaspoonfuls 2 inches apart onto ungreased cookie sheet.

3. Bake at 375°F for 8 to 10 minutes or until light golden brown. Cool 1 minute on cookie sheet. Remove to wire rack.

4. For Cream Filling, combine marshmallow creme and butter in small bowl. Add confectioners sugar and vanilla extract, beating until smooth.

5. To assemble, spread bottoms of half the cookies with 1 tablespoon each cream filling; top with remaining cookies. Press together to make sandwich cookies. Refrigerate to quickly firm the filling, if desired.

Tip: After chilling the assembled cookies, wrap individually in plastic wrap. Store in the refrigerator until ready to serve.

CHOCOLATE KISS COOKIES

Makes about 3½ dozen cookies

1 package (15 ounces) golden sugar cookie mix
½ cup HERSHEY'S Cocoa
1 egg
2 tablespoons water
⅔ cup finely chopped nuts
1 bag (9 ounces) HERSHEY'S KISSES®
    Chocolates, unwrapped (about 42)

Preheat oven to 350°F. In medium bowl, combine cookie mix (and enclosed flavor packet), cocoa, egg and water; mix with spoon or fork until thoroughly blended. Shape dough into 1-inch balls. Roll balls in nuts; place on ungreased cookie sheet.

Bake 8 minutes or until lightly browned. Remove from oven; cool 5 minutes. Place chocolate piece on top of each cookie, pressing down so cookie cracks around edges. Remove from cookie sheet to wire rack. Cool completely.

Chocolate Chip Sandwich Cookies

YUMMY CHOCOLATE COOKIES WITH ORANGE FROSTING

Makes about 3 dozen cookies

COOKIES
1 cup granulated sugar
¾ cup BUTTER FLAVOR CRISCO®
1 egg
½ teaspoon vanilla
1¾ cups all-purpose flour
½ cup unsweetened cocoa
1 teaspoon baking soda
½ teaspoon salt
1 cup mashed ripe bananas
    (2 to 3 medium bananas)
1 cup raisins
½ teaspoon grated orange peel
2 teaspoons orange juice

FROSTING
1 package (3 ounces) cream cheese, softened
¼ cup BUTTER FLAVOR CRISCO®
3 cups confectioners sugar
2 tablespoons orange juice
⅛ teaspoon grated orange peel (optional)
    Yellow and red food color (optional)

1. Preheat oven to 350°F. Grease cookie sheet with Butter Flavor Crisco®.

2. For Cookies, combine granulated sugar, ¾ cup Butter Flavor Crisco®, egg and vanilla in large bowl. Beat at medium speed of electric mixer until well blended and creamy.

3. Combine flour, cocoa, baking soda and salt in medium bowl. Stir well. Add alternately with bananas to creamed mixture, beating at low speed until well blended. Stir in raisins, ½ teaspoon orange peel and 2 teaspoons orange juice with spoon. Drop by heaping teaspoonfuls 2 inches apart onto greased cookie sheet.

4. Bake at 350°F for 12 minutes or until set. Cool 2 minutes on cookie sheet before removing to wire rack. Cool completely.

5. For Frosting, combine cream cheese and ¼ cup Butter Flavor Crisco® in medium bowl. Beat at medium speed until well blended. Gradually add confectioners sugar and 2 tablespoons orange juice; beat until creamy. Add ⅛ teaspoon orange peel and food color, if desired. Beat until blended. Frost cookies.

BROWNIES & BARS

BANANA SPLIT BARS

Makes about 2 dozen bars

⅓ cup margarine or butter, softened
1 cup sugar
1 egg
1 banana, mashed
½ teaspoon vanilla
1¼ cups all-purpose flour
1 teaspoon CALUMET® Baking Powder
¼ teaspoon salt
⅓ cup chopped nuts
2 cups KRAFT® Miniature Marshmallows
1 cup BAKER'S® Semi-Sweet Real Chocolate Chips
⅓ cup drained maraschino cherries, quartered

Preheat oven to 350°F.

Beat margarine and sugar until light and fluffy. Add egg, banana and vanilla; mix well. Mix in flour, baking powder and salt. Stir in nuts. Pour into greased 13×9-inch pan.

Bake for 20 minutes. Remove from oven. Sprinkle with marshmallows, chips and cherries. Bake 10 to 15 minutes longer or until wooden toothpick inserted in center comes out clean. Cool in pan on wire rack. Cut into bars.

Prep time: 20 minutes
Bake time: 30 to 35 minutes

LAYERED CHOCOLATE CHEESE BARS

Makes about 2 dozen bars

¼ cup (½ stick) margarine or butter
1½ cups graham cracker crumbs
¾ cup sugar, divided
1 package (4 ounces) BAKER'S® GERMAN'S® Sweet Chocolate
1 package (8 ounces) PHILADELPHIA BRAND® Cream Cheese, softened
1 egg
1 cup BAKER'S® ANGEL FLAKE® Coconut
1 cup chopped nuts

Preheat oven to 350°F.

Melt margarine in oven in 13×9-inch pan. Carefully add graham cracker crumbs and ¼ cup sugar; mix well. Press into pan. Bake for 10 minutes.

Microwave chocolate in large microwavable bowl on HIGH (100% power) 1½ to 2½ minutes or until almost melted, stirring after each minute. Stir until completely melted. Stir in remaining ½ cup sugar, cream cheese and egg. Spread over crust. Sprinkle with coconut and nuts; press lightly.

Bake for 30 minutes. Cool completely in pan on wire rack. Cut into bars.

Top plate (clockwise from top): Layered Chocolate Cheese Bar, Banana Split Bar,
Chocolate Peanut Butter Bar (page 218)

CHOCOLATE PEANUT BUTTER BARS

Makes about 2 dozen bars

2 cups peanut butter
1 cup sugar
2 eggs
1 package (8 ounces) BAKER'S® Semi-Sweet
   Chocolate, divided
1 cup chopped peanuts

Preheat oven to 350°F.

Beat peanut butter, sugar and eggs in large bowl until light and fluffy. Reserve 1 cup peanut butter mixture; set aside.

Microwave 4 squares chocolate in small microwavable bowl on HIGH (100% power) 1½ to 2½ minutes or until almost melted, stirring after each minute. Stir until completely melted. Add to peanut butter mixture in bowl; mix well. Press into ungreased 13×9-inch pan. Top with reserved peanut butter mixture.

Bake for 30 minutes or until edges are lightly browned. Melt remaining 4 squares chocolate as above; spread evenly over entire surface. Sprinkle with peanuts. Cool in pan on wire rack until chocolate is set. Cut into bars.

Prep time: 15 minutes
Bake time: 30 minutes

Chocolate Peanut Goodies

CHEWY CHOCOLATE PEANUT BUTTER BARS

Makes about 4½ dozen bars

1 cup firmly packed brown sugar
⅔ cup (10⅔ tablespoons) butter, softened
⅓ cup light corn syrup
1 teaspoon vanilla extract
4 cups quick oats, uncooked
1 cup (6-ounce package) NESTLÉ® Toll House®
   Semi-Sweet Chocolate Morsels
⅔ cup peanut butter
½ cup chopped peanuts

Preheat oven to 350°F. Grease 13×9-inch baking pan.

In large mixer bowl, beat brown sugar and butter until creamy. Beat in corn syrup and vanilla extract. Stir in oats. Press into bottom of prepared pan. Bake 15 minutes. Cool slightly.

In small heavy saucepan, combine Nestlé® Toll House® Semi-Sweet Chocolate Morsels and peanut butter. Cook over low heat, stirring constantly, until morsels melt and mixture is smooth. Spread over crust. Sprinkle with peanuts; cool completely in pan on wire rack. Refrigerate 10 minutes to set chocolate mixture. Cut into bars.

CHOCOLATE PEANUT GOODIES

Makes 3 dozen pieces

1 container (16 ounces) DUNCAN HINES®
   Creamy Homestyle Milk Chocolate Frosting
½ cup JIF® Creamy Peanut Butter
3 cups quick-cooking oats (not instant or
   old-fashioned), uncooked
1 cup chopped peanuts
36 peanut halves, for garnish

1. Combine Milk Chocolate frosting and peanut butter in large bowl. Stir with wooden spoon until blended. Add oats and peanuts. Stir until thoroughly blended.

2. Press mixture into ungreased 8-inch square pan. Cut into 36 pieces. Garnish tops with peanut halves. Store in airtight container in refrigerator.

Left to right: Chocolate Peanut Bars, Pecan Caramel Brownies (page 244)

CHOCOLATE PEANUT BARS

Makes about 5 dozen bars

½ cup butter or margarine, softened
1 cup firmly packed brown sugar, divided
¼ cup granulated sugar
2 eggs, separated
1 teaspoon vanilla
2 cups all-purpose flour
2 teaspoons baking powder
½ teaspoon baking soda
¼ teaspoon salt
2 to 4 tablespoons milk
1 cup (6 ounces) semisweet chocolate chips
¾ cup salted peanuts, coarsely chopped

Preheat oven to 350°F. Lightly grease 13×9-inch pan.

Beat butter, ¼ cup brown sugar and granulated sugar in large bowl until creamy. Beat in egg yolks and vanilla. Combine flour, baking powder, baking soda and salt in small bowl. Blend into creamed mixture. Stir in enough milk to make a smooth, light dough. Press on bottom of prepared pan. Sprinkle chocolate chips over top; press down lightly into dough.

In clean, dry bowl, beat egg whites until stiff, but not dry peaks form. Gradually beat in remaining ¾ cup brown sugar. Spread mixture evenly over dough in pan; top with peanuts.

Bake 25 to 30 minutes or until top is puffed, lightly browned and feels dry. Cut into bars while still warm.

MICROWAVE CHEWY GRANOLA SQUARES

Makes about 16 squares

½ cup (1 stick) margarine or butter
½ cup firmly packed brown sugar
1 egg
½ teaspoon vanilla
1 cup quick oats, uncooked
½ cup all-purpose flour
½ teaspoon baking soda
½ teaspoon ground cinnamon
¼ teaspoon salt
1 cup BAKER'S® Semi-Sweet Real Chocolate Chips, divided
½ cup raisins

To Microwave: Beat margarine, sugar, egg and vanilla until light and fluffy in large bowl.

Stir in oats, flour, baking soda, cinnamon and salt. Stir in ½ cup chips and raisins. Spread into greased 8-inch square microwavable dish.

Microwave on HIGH (100% power) 2 minutes; rotate dish. Microwave 2 minutes longer or until wooden toothpick inserted into center comes out clean. Sprinkle with remaining ½ cup chips; microwave 1 minute longer. Cool in pan on counter top 15 minutes; cut into squares.

Prep time: 15 minutes
Microwave time: 5 minutes

219

HEAVENLY OAT BARS

Makes about 2 dozen bars

½ cup MAZOLA® Margarine, softened
½ cup firmly packed brown sugar
½ cup KARO® Light or Dark Corn Syrup
1 teaspoon vanilla
3 cups uncooked quick or old-fashioned oats
1 cup (6 ounces) semi-sweet chocolate chips
½ cup SKIPPY® Creamy Peanut Butter

Preheat oven to 350°F. Lightly grease 9-inch square baking pan. In large bowl with mixer at medium speed, beat margarine, brown sugar, corn syrup and vanilla until blended and smooth. Stir in oats. Spread in prepared pan.

Bake 25 minutes or until center is just firm. Cool slightly on wire rack. In small heavy saucepan over low heat, stir chocolate chips until melted and smooth. Remove from heat; stir in peanut butter until smooth. Spread over warm bars. Cool completely in pan on wire rack before cutting.

Tip: To melt chocolate chips in microwave, place in dry microwavable bowl or glass measuring cup. Microwave on HIGH (100% power) 1 minute; stir. Microwave on HIGH 1 minute longer. Stir until chocolate is smooth.

CHOCOLATE 'N' OAT BARS

Makes about 3 dozen bars

1 cup unsifted all-purpose flour
1 cup quick-cooking oats, uncooked
¾ cup firmly packed light brown sugar
½ cup margarine or butter, softened
1 (14-ounce) can EAGLE® Brand Sweetened Condensed Milk (NOT evaporated milk)
1 cup chopped nuts
1 (6-ounce) package semi-sweet chocolate chips

Preheat oven to 350°F (325°F for glass dish). In large bowl, combine flour, oats, sugar and margarine; mix well. Reserving ½ cup oat mixture, press remainder on bottom of 13×9-inch baking pan.

Bake 10 minutes. Pour sweetened condensed milk evenly over crust. Sprinkle with nuts and chocolate chips. Top with remaining oat mixture; press down firmly.

Bake 25 to 30 minutes or until lightly browned. Cool. Cut into bars. Store covered at room temperature.

Top to bottom: Double Chocolate Raspberry Bars, Easy Apricot Oatmeal Bars (page 238)

DOUBLE CHOCOLATE RASPBERRY BARS

Makes about 3 dozen bars

BARS
1¾ cups all-purpose flour
1 cup granulated sugar
¼ cup unsweetened cocoa
1 cup cold butter or margarine
1 egg, lightly beaten
1 teaspoon vanilla
1 can SOLO® *or* 1 jar BAKER® Raspberry Filling
1 cup chopped almonds *or* pecans
6 squares (1 ounce each) semi-sweet chocolate, finely chopped, *or* 1 package (6 ounces) semi-sweet chocolate morsels

GLAZE
1 cup powdered sugar
1 to 2 tablespoons milk

Preheat oven to 350°F. Grease 13×9-inch baking pan; set aside.

For Bars, combine flour, granulated sugar and cocoa in medium bowl. Cut in butter until mixture resembles coarse crumbs. Add egg and vanilla; stir well. Set aside 1 cup cocoa mixture. Press remaining mixture into bottom of prepared pan. Top with raspberry filling. Combine reserved cocoa mixture, almonds and chocolate. Sprinkle over filling.

Bake 40 minutes. Cool completely in pan on wire rack.

For Glaze, combine powdered sugar and milk in small bowl; stir until smooth. Drizzle glaze in zig-zag pattern over cooled top. Let stand until glaze is set. Cut into bars.

CHOCOLATE RASPBERRY COCONUT BARS

Makes about 3 dozen bars

COOKIE BASE:
1 cup all-purpose flour
¼ cup firmly packed brown sugar
½ cup (1 stick) butter

TOPPING:
1 (14-ounce) can sweetened condensed milk
½ cup all-purpose flour
½ teaspoon baking powder
¼ teaspoon salt
2 eggs
1 cup (6-ounce package) NESTLÉ® Toll House® Semi-Sweet Chocolate Morsels
1 (3½-ounce) can flaked coconut (1⅓ cups), divided
½ cup chopped pecans
½ cup raspberry preserves

Cookie Base: Preheat oven to 350°F. In medium bowl, combine flour and brown sugar. With pastry blender or 2 knives, cut in butter until mixture resembles coarse crumbs. Press into greased 9-inch square baking pan. Bake 20 minutes.

Topping: In large bowl, combine sweetened condensed milk, flour, baking powder, salt and eggs; mix well. Stir in Nestlé® Toll House® Semi-Sweet Chocolate Morsels, 1 cup coconut and pecans. Pour over baked cookie base.

Bake 25 minutes or until topping is set. Remove from oven. Spread preserves over top of bars. Sprinkle with remaining ⅓ cup coconut. Cool completely in pan on wire rack. Cut into bars.

CHOCOLATE CREAM CHEESE SUGAR COOKIE BARS

Makes about 16 bars

1 box (15 ounces) golden sugar cookie mix
1 package (8 ounces) cream cheese, softened
¼ cup butter or margarine, softened
½ cup granulated sugar
¼ cup HERSHEY'S® Cocoa
1 egg
1 teaspoon vanilla extract
Powdered sugar (optional)

Preheat oven to 350°F. Prepare cookie dough as directed on package; spread into ungreased 9-inch square baking pan. In small mixer bowl, beat cream cheese and butter until light and fluffy. Stir together granulated sugar and cocoa; add to butter mixture. Add egg and vanilla; beat until smooth. Spread cream cheese mixture evenly over cookie dough.

Bake 40 minutes or until no imprint remains when touched lightly in center. Cool completely in pan on wire rack. Sprinkle powdered sugar over top, if desired. Cut into bars. Cover; store in refrigerator.

Chocolate Raspberry Coconut Bars

Chocolate Macaroon Squares

MACAROON ALMOND CRUMB BARS

Makes about 3 dozen bars

1 (18¼- or 18½-ounce) package chocolate cake mix
¼ cup vegetable oil
2 eggs
1 (14-ounce) can EAGLE® Brand Sweetened
    Condensed Milk (NOT evaporated milk)
½ to 1 teaspoon almond extract
1½ cups coconut macaroon crumbs
    (about 8 macaroons)
1 cup chopped slivered almonds

Preheat oven to 350°F (325°F for glass dish). In large mixer bowl, combine cake mix, oil and *1 egg*; beat on medium speed until crumbly. Press firmly on bottom of greased 13×9-inch baking pan. In medium bowl, combine sweetened condensed milk, remaining egg and extract; mix well. Add *1 cup* macaroon crumbs and almonds. Spread evenly over crust. Sprinkle with remaining *½ cup* crumbs.

Bake 30 to 35 minutes or until lightly browned. Cool. Cut into bars. Store loosely covered at room temperature.

CHOCOLATE MACAROON SQUARES

Makes about 2 dozen squares

BASE:
1 (18½-ounce) package chocolate cake mix
⅓ cup butter, softened
1 egg

TOPPING:
1 (14-ounce) can sweetened condensed milk
1 egg
1 teaspoon vanilla extract
1 (3½-ounce) can flaked coconut (1⅓ cups), divided
1 cup chopped pecans
1 cup (6-ounce package) NESTLÉ® Toll House®
    Semi-Sweet Chocolate Morsels

Base: Preheat oven to 350°F. In large bowl, combine cake mix, butter and egg; mix until crumbly. Press into greased 13×9-inch baking pan.

Topping: In large bowl, combine sweetened condensed milk, egg and vanilla extract; beat until well blended. Stir in 1 cup coconut, pecans and Nestlé® Toll House® Semi-Sweet Chocolate Morsels.

Spread topping over base. Sprinkle remaining ⅓ cup coconut over top.

Bake 30 to 40 minutes. Cool completely in pan on wire rack. Cut into squares.

Note: Center may appear loose but will set upon cooling.

DELUXE TOLL HOUSE® MUD BARS

Makes about 2 dozen bars

1 cup plus 2 tablespoons all-purpose flour
½ teaspoon baking soda
½ teaspoon salt
¾ cup firmly packed brown sugar
½ cup (1 stick) butter, softened
1 teaspoon vanilla extract
1 egg
2 cups (12-ounce package) NESTLÉ® Toll House®
    Semi-Sweet Chocolate Morsels, divided
½ cup chopped walnuts

Preheat oven to 375°F. In small bowl, combine flour, baking soda and salt; set aside. In large mixer bowl, beat brown sugar, butter and vanilla extract until creamy. Beat in egg. Gradually add flour mixture. Stir in 1⅓ cups Nestlé® Toll House® Semi-Sweet Chocolate Morsels and walnuts. Spread into greased 9-inch square baking pan.

Bake 23 to 25 minutes or just until top begins to brown. Immediately sprinkle remaining ⅔ cup Nestlé® Toll House® Semi-Sweet Chocolate Morsels over top. Let stand until morsels become shiny and soft. Spread chocolate over top with spatula. Refrigerate 5 to 10 minutes to set chocolate. Cut into bars.

MISSISSIPPI MUD BARS

Makes about 3 dozen bars

½ cup butter or margarine, softened
¾ cup firmly packed brown sugar
1 egg
1 teaspoon vanilla
½ teaspoon baking soda
¼ teaspoon salt
1 cup plus 2 tablespoons all-purpose flour
1 cup (6 ounces) semisweet chocolate chips, divided
1 cup (6 ounces) white chocolate chips, divided
½ cup chopped walnuts or pecans

Preheat oven to 375°F. Line 9-inch square baking pan with foil; grease foil.

Beat butter and sugar in large bowl until blended and smooth. Beat in egg and vanilla until light. Blend in baking soda and salt. Add flour, mixing until well blended. Stir in ¾ cup semisweet chocolate chips, ¾ cup white chocolate chips and nuts. Spread dough in prepared pan.

Bake 23 to 25 minutes or until center feels firm. Do not overbake. Remove from oven; sprinkle remaining ¼ cup each semisweet and white chocolate chips over the top. Let stand a few minutes until chips melt, then spread evenly over bars. Cool in pan on wire rack until chocolate is set. Cut into bars.

COCONUT-ALMOND MOUND BARS

Makes about 3 dozen bars

2 cups graham cracker crumbs
½ cup butter or margarine, softened
¼ cup powdered sugar
2 cups flaked coconut
1 can (14 ounces) sweetened condensed milk
½ cup whole blanched almonds
1 cup (6 ounces) milk chocolate chips

Preheat oven to 350°F. Lightly grease 13×9-inch pan.

Combine crumbs, butter and sugar in large bowl until blended and smooth. Press on bottom of prepared pan.

Bake 10 to 12 minutes or just until golden. Combine coconut and sweetened condensed milk in small bowl; spread evenly over baked crust. Arrange almonds evenly over coconut mixture.

Bake 15 to 18 minutes or until almonds are toasted. Remove from oven; sprinkle chocolate chips over top. Let stand a few minutes until chips melt; spread evenly over top. Cool completely in pan on wire rack. Cut into bars.

CHOCOLATE ALMOND COCONUT BARS

Makes about 2 dozen bars

1 package (6 ounces) slivered almonds, chopped
1 package DUNCAN HINES® Moist Deluxe Devil's Food Cake Mix
½ cup butter or margarine, melted
1½ cups flaked coconut, packed
3 eggs
1 cup semi-sweet miniature chocolate chips

1. Preheat oven to 350°F. Toast almonds on baking sheet at 350°F about 5 minutes, stirring occasionally, or until fragrant and light golden brown. Cool completely.

2. Combine cake mix, toasted almonds and melted butter in medium bowl. Press mixture into bottom of ungreased 13×9-inch pan.

3. Combine coconut and eggs in medium bowl. Stir with spoon until well blended. Spread over crust. Sprinkle with miniature chocolate chips.

4. Bake at 350°F for 20 to 25 minutes. Cool completely in pan on wire rack. Refrigerate until well chilled. Cut into bars.

CHOCOLATE CHIP SHORTBREAD

Makes 16 cookies

½ cup butter, softened
½ cup sugar
1 teaspoon vanilla
1 cup all-purpose flour
¼ teaspoon salt
½ cup miniature semisweet chocolate chips

1. Preheat oven to 375°F.

2. Beat butter and sugar in large bowl with electric mixer at medium speed until light and fluffy, scraping down side of bowl occasionally. Beat in vanilla. Add flour and salt. Beat at low speed, scraping down side of bowl once. Stir in chocolate chips with wooden spoon.

3. Divide dough in half. Press each half into ungreased 8-inch round cake pan.

4. Bake 12 minutes or until edges are golden brown. Score hot shortbread with sharp knife, taking care not to cut completely through shortbread. Make 8 wedges per pan.

5. Let pans stand on wire racks 10 minutes. Invert shortbread onto wire racks; cool completely. Break into triangles.

6. Store tightly covered at room temperature or freeze up to 3 months.

MILK CHOCOLATE PECAN BARS

Makes about 4½ dozen bars

COOKIE BASE:
1 cup all-purpose flour
½ cup firmly packed brown sugar
½ teaspoon baking soda
¼ cup butter

TOPPING:
2 cups (11½-ounce package) NESTLÉ® Toll House® Milk Chocolate Morsels
2 eggs
¼ cup firmly packed brown sugar
1 teaspoon vanilla extract
¼ teaspoon salt
1 cup chopped pecans, divided

Cookie Base: Preheat oven to 350°F. In large bowl, combine flour, brown sugar and baking soda; mix well. With pastry blender or 2 knives, cut in butter until mixture resembles fine crumbs. Press evenly into greased 13×9-inch baking pan. Bake for 10 minutes.

Topping: Melt over hot (not boiling) water, Nestlé® Toll House® Milk Chocolate Morsels; stir until smooth. Remove from heat. In medium bowl, combine eggs, brown sugar, vanilla extract and salt; beat 2 minutes with electric mixer at high speed. Add melted morsels; mix well. Stir in ½ cup pecans.

Pour topping over cookie base; sprinkle with remaining ½ cup pecans.

Bake 20 minutes. Cool completely in pan on wire rack. Cut into bars.

CHOCOLATE CHIP PECAN SQUARES

Makes 16 squares

½ cup BUTTER FLAVOR CRISCO®
½ cup firmly packed brown sugar
1 egg
1 tablespoon milk
1 teaspoon vanilla
¾ cup all-purpose flour
2 cups milk chocolate chips,* divided
¾ cup chopped pecans, divided

1. Preheat oven to 350°F. Grease 8×8-inch pan with Butter Flavor Crisco®.

2. Combine Butter Flavor Crisco®, sugar, egg, milk and vanilla in large bowl. Beat at medium speed of electric mixer until well blended.

3. Mix in flour at low speed. Stir in 1 cup chocolate chips and ½ cup nuts. Spread in pan.

4. Bake at 350°F for 25 to 30 minutes or until lightly browned. Remove from oven. Sprinkle with remaining 1 cup chocolate chips. Wait 5 minutes, or until chips soften. Spread evenly. Sprinkle remaining ¼ cup nuts over top, if desired. Cool in pan on wire rack. Cut into 2-inch squares.

*You may substitute semi-sweet chocolate chips for the milk chocolate chips.

Chocolate Chip Shortbread

Top to bottom: Double Chocolate Fantasy Bars, Macaroon Almond Crumb Bars (page 222) and Toffee Bars (page 228)

DOUBLE CHOCOLATE FANTASY BARS

Makes about 3 dozen bars

1 (18¼- or 18½-ounce) package chocolate cake mix
¼ cup vegetable oil
1 egg
1 cup chopped nuts
1 (14-ounce) can EAGLE® Brand Sweetened
    Condensed Milk (NOT evaporated milk)
1 (6-ounce) package semi-sweet chocolate chips
1 teaspoon vanilla extract
    Dash salt

Preheat oven to 350°F. In large mixer bowl, combine cake mix, oil and egg; beat on medium speed until crumbly. Stir in nuts. Reserving 1½ cups crumb mixture, press remainder on bottom of greased 13×9-inch baking pan. In small saucepan, combine remaining ingredients. Over medium heat, cook and stir until chips melt. Pour evenly over prepared crust. Sprinkle reserved crumb mixture evenly over top.

Bake 25 to 30 minutes or until set. Cool. Cut into bars. Store loosely covered at room temperature.

MARBLE SQUARES

Makes about 2 dozen squares

¾ cup water
½ cup PARKAY® Margarine
1½ (1-ounce) squares unsweetened chocolate
2 cups all-purpose flour
2 cups sugar
1 teaspoon baking soda
½ teaspoon salt
2 eggs, beaten
½ cup sour cream
1 (8-ounce) package PHILADELPHIA BRAND®
    Cream Cheese, softened
⅓ cup sugar
1 egg
1 (6-ounce) package semi-sweet chocolate pieces

- Preheat oven to 375°F.

- Combine water, margarine and chocolate in saucepan; bring to a boil. Remove from heat. Stir in combined flour, 2 cups sugar, baking soda and salt. Add 2 beaten eggs and sour cream; mix well. Pour into greased and floured 15 × 10 × 1-inch jelly roll pan.

- Combine cream cheese and ⅓ cup sugar, mixing until well blended. Blend in 1 egg. Spoon over chocolate batter. Cut through batter with knife several times for marble effect. Sprinkle with chocolate pieces.

- Bake 25 to 30 minutes or until wooden toothpick inserted in center comes out clean. Cool in pan on wire rack. Cut into squares.

COCOA BANANA BARS

Makes about 9 bars

BARS
⅔ cup QUAKER® Oat Bran hot cereal, uncooked
⅔ cup all-purpose flour
½ cup granulated sugar
⅓ cup unsweetened cocoa
½ cup mashed ripe banana (about 1 large)
¼ cup liquid vegetable oil margarine
3 tablespoons light corn syrup
2 egg whites, slightly beaten
1 teaspoon vanilla

GLAZE
2 teaspoons unsweetened cocoa
2 teaspoons liquid vegetable oil margarine
¼ cup powdered sugar
2 to 2½ teaspoons warm water
Strawberry halves (optional)

For Bars, preheat oven to 350°F. Lightly spray 8-inch square baking pan with nonstick cooking spray or oil lightly.

Combine oat bran cereal, flour, granulated sugar and ⅓ cup cocoa in large bowl. Add combined banana, ¼ cup margarine, corn syrup, egg whites and vanilla; mix well. Pour into prepared pan, spreading evenly.

Bake 23 to 25 minutes or until center is set. Cool in pan on wire rack.

For Glaze, combine 2 teaspoons cocoa and 2 teaspoons margarine in small bowl. Stir in powdered sugar and 1 teaspoon water. Gradually add remaining 1 to 1½ teaspoons water to make a medium-thick glaze, mixing well. Drizzle glaze over brownies. Top with strawberry halves, if desired. Cut into bars. Store tightly covered.

APPLESAUCE FUDGE BARS

Makes about 3 dozen bars

3 squares (1 ounce each) semisweet chocolate
½ cup butter or margarine
1 cup firmly packed light brown sugar
⅔ cup unsweetened applesauce
2 eggs, beaten
1 teaspoon vanilla
1 cup all-purpose flour
½ teaspoon baking powder
¼ teaspoon baking soda
½ cup walnuts, chopped
1 cup (6 ounces) milk chocolate chips

Preheat oven to 350°F. Grease 9-inch square pan.

Melt semisweet chocolate and butter in small heavy saucepan over low heat, stirring frequently. Remove from heat; cool. Combine sugar, applesauce, eggs and vanilla in large bowl. Combine flour, baking powder and baking soda in small bowl. Mix flour mixture into applesauce mixture; blend in chocolate mixture. Spread batter evenly in prepared pan. Sprinkle nuts over top.

Bake 25 to 30 minutes or just until set. Remove from oven; sprinkle chocolate chips over top. Let stand a few minutes until chips melt; spread evenly over top. Cool in pan on wire rack. Cut into bars.

Cocoa Banana Bars

FAVORITE LAYER BARS

Makes about 3 dozen bars

1½ cups graham cracker crumbs
¼ cup sugar
¼ cup PARKAY® Margarine, melted
1 (8-ounce) package PHILADELPHIA BRAND®
    Cream Cheese, softened
½ cup sugar
1 egg
¾ cup flaked coconut
¾ cup chopped nuts
1 (6-ounce) package semi-sweet chocolate pieces

• Preheat oven to 325°F.

• Combine crumbs, ¼ cup sugar and margarine; press onto bottom of 13×9-inch baking pan. Bake 10 minutes.

• Combine cream cheese, ½ cup sugar and egg, mixing until well blended. Spread over crust. Sprinkle with combined coconut, nuts and chocolate; press lightly into surface.

• Bake 25 to 30 minutes or until lightly browned. Cool completely in pan on wire rack. Cut into bars.

ALMOND TOFFEE SQUARES

Makes about 2 dozen squares

1 cup (2 sticks) margarine or butter, softened
1 cup firmly packed brown sugar
1 egg
1 teaspoon vanilla
2 cups all-purpose flour
¼ teaspoon salt
2 packages (4 ounces each) BAKER'S® GERMAN'S®
    Sweet Chocolate, broken into squares
½ cup toasted slivered almonds
½ cup lightly toasted BAKER'S® ANGEL FLAKE®
    Coconut

Preheat oven to 350°F.

Beat margarine, sugar, egg and vanilla. Mix in flour and salt. Press into greased 13×9-inch pan.

Bake for 30 minutes or until edges are golden brown. Remove from oven. Immediately top with chocolate squares. Cover with foil; let stand 5 minutes or until chocolate is softened.

Spread chocolate evenly over entire surface; sprinkle with almonds and coconut. Cut into squares while still warm. Cool in pan on wire rack.

Prep time: 20 minutes
Bake time: 30 minutes

ENGLISH TOFFEE BARS

Makes about 3 dozen bars

2 cups all-purpose flour
1 cup firmly packed light brown sugar
½ cup butter
1 cup pecan halves
    Toffee Topping (recipe follows)
1 cup HERSHEY'S Milk Chocolate Chips

Preheat oven to 350°F. In large mixer bowl, combine flour and brown sugar. With pastry blender or 2 knives, cut in butter until fine crumbs form. (A few large crumbs may remain.) Press into ungreased 13×9-inch baking pan. Sprinkle pecans over crust. Prepare Toffee Topping; drizzle evenly over pecans and crust.

Bake 20 to 22 minutes or until Toffee Topping is bubbly and golden. Remove from oven. Immediately sprinkle chocolate chips over top; press gently into surface with back of spoon. Cool completely in pan on wire rack. Cut into bars.

Toffee Topping: In small saucepan, combine ⅔ cup butter and ⅓ cup firmly packed light brown sugar. Cook over medium heat, stirring constantly, until mixture comes to a boil. Continue boiling, stirring constantly, 30 seconds; use immediately.

TOFFEE BARS

Makes about 3 dozen bars

½ cup margarine or butter, melted
1 cup rolled oats, uncooked
½ cup firmly packed brown sugar
½ cup unsifted all-purpose flour
½ cup finely chopped walnuts
¼ teaspoon baking soda
1 (14-ounce) can EAGLE® Brand Sweetened
    Condensed Milk (NOT evaporated milk)
2 teaspoons vanilla extract
1 (6-ounce) package semi-sweet chocolate chips

Preheat oven to 350°F. Combine *6 tablespoons* margarine, oats, sugar, flour, nuts and baking soda. Press firmly on bottom of greased 13×9-inch baking pan; bake 10 to 15 minutes or until lightly browned.

Meanwhile, in medium saucepan, combine remaining *2 tablespoons* margarine and sweetened condensed milk. Over medium heat, cook and stir until mixture thickens slightly, about 15 minutes. Remove from heat; stir in vanilla. Pour over crust. Return to oven.

Bake 10 to 15 minutes longer or until golden brown. Remove from oven; immediately sprinkle chips over top. Let stand 1 minute; spread while still warm. Cool. Cut into bars. Store tightly covered at room temperature.

SCRUMPTIOUS CHOCOLATE LAYER BARS

Makes about 3 dozen bars

2 cups (12-ounce package) HERSHEY'S
    Semi-Sweet Chocolate Chips
1 package (8 ounces) cream cheese
⅔ cup (5-ounce can) evaporated milk
1 cup chopped walnuts
¼ cup sesame seeds (optional)
1 teaspoon almond extract, divided
3 cups all-purpose flour
1½ cups sugar
1 cup (2 sticks) butter or margarine, softened
2 eggs
1 teaspoon baking powder
½ teaspoon salt

Preheat oven to 375°F. Grease 13 × 9-inch baking pan.

In medium saucepan, combine chocolate chips, cream cheese and evaporated milk. Cook over low heat, stirring constantly, until chips are melted and mixture is smooth. Remove from heat; stir in walnuts, sesame seeds, if desired, and ½ teaspoon almond extract. Blend well; set aside.

Stir together flour, sugar, butter, eggs, baking powder, salt and remaining ½ teaspoon almond extract in large mixer bowl; blend with electric mixer on low speed until mixture resembles coarse crumbs. Press half of crumb mixture into prepared pan; spread with chocolate mixture. Sprinkle remaining crumb mixture over filling.

Bake 35 to 40 minutes or until golden brown. Cool completely in pan on wire rack. Cut into bars.

Clockwise from top right: Scrumptious Chocolate Layer Bars, Best Brownies (page 249), Peanut Butter Paisley Brownies (page 243)

Special Treat No-Bake Squares

SPECIAL TREAT NO-BAKE SQUARES

Makes 3 dozen squares

CRUST
½ cup butter or margarine
¼ cup granulated sugar
¼ cup unsweetened cocoa
1 large egg
¼ teaspoon salt
1½ cups graham cracker crumbs (about 18 graham crackers)
¾ cup flaked coconut
½ cup chopped pecans

FILLING
⅓ cup butter or margarine, softened
1 package (3 ounces) cream cheese, softened
1 teaspoon vanilla
1 cup powdered sugar

GLAZE
2 ounces dark sweet or bittersweet chocolate candy bar, broken into ½-inch pieces
1 teaspoon butter or margarine

Line 9-inch square pan with foil, shiny side up, allowing a 2-inch overhang on sides. Or, lightly grease pan.

For Crust, combine ½ cup butter, granulated sugar, cocoa, egg and salt in medium saucepan. Cook over medium heat, stirring constantly, until mixture thickens, about 2 minutes. Remove from heat; stir in graham cracker crumbs, coconut and pecans. Press evenly into prepared pan.

For Filling, beat ⅓ cup butter, cream cheese and vanilla in small bowl with electric mixer at medium speed until smooth, scraping down side of bowl once. Gradually beat in powdered sugar. Spread over crust; refrigerate 30 minutes.

For Glaze, combine chocolate and 1 teaspoon butter in small resealable plastic freezer bag; seal bag. Microwave at HIGH (100% power) 50 seconds. Turn bag over; microwave at HIGH 40 to 50 seconds or until melted. Knead bag until chocolate is smooth and completely melted. Cut off tiny corner of bag; drizzle chocolate over filling. Refrigerate until firm, about 20 minutes. Remove bars with foil from pan. Cut into 1½-inch squares. Store tightly covered in refrigerator.

CHOCOLATE CARAMEL BARS

Makes 20 to 24 bars

1 package DUNCAN HINES® Moist Deluxe Swiss Chocolate Cake Mix
1 package (14 ounces) caramels
¾ cup butter or margarine
1 can (5 ounces) evaporated milk
1 cup chopped pecans
1 package (6 ounces) semi-sweet chocolate chips

1. Preheat oven to 350°F. Grease and flour 13×9-inch pan.

2. Prepare cake mix following package directions for basic recipe. Pour half of batter into pan. Bake at 350°F for 15 minutes.

3. Combine caramels, butter and evaporated milk in small saucepan. Cook over low heat until caramels are melted, stirring occasionally. Stir in pecans. Pour over hot baked layer. Sprinkle with chocolate chips. Spread remaining cake batter over top.

4. Bake at 350°F for 35 to 45 minutes. Cool completely in pan on wire rack. Cut into bars.

Tip: Cake will not test done with toothpick. Bake until top looks dry or press cake gently with your fingertip. Cake is done if it springs back.

CHEWY CHOCOLATE CHIP COOKIE SQUARES

Makes about 4 dozen squares

2¼ cups firmly packed brown sugar
½ cup BUTTER FLAVOR CRISCO®, melted
2 cups self-rising flour*
2 eggs
1 teaspoon vanilla
1 cup semi-sweet chocolate chips
¾ cup chopped pecans

1. Preheat oven to 325°F. Grease 13×9-inch pan with Butter Flavor Crisco®.

2. Combine brown sugar and Butter Flavor Crisco® in large bowl. Beat at low speed of electric mixer until well blended. Add, one at a time, flour, eggs and vanilla. Beat until blended. Add chocolate chips and nuts. Beat just until blended. Spread in greased pan.

3. Bake at 325°F for 30 to 35 minutes or until wooden toothpick inserted in center comes out clean. *Do not overbake.* Cool in pan on wire rack. Cut into squares.

*Substitute 2 cups all-purpose flour plus 1 tablespoon baking powder and ¼ teaspoon salt in place of self-rising flour, if desired.

Blueberry Cheesecake Bars

BLUEBERRY CHEESECAKE BARS

Makes about 16 bars

1 package DUNCAN HINES® Bakery Style
   Blueberry Muffin Mix
¼ cup butter or margarine
⅓ cup finely chopped pecans
1 package (8 ounces) cream cheese, softened
½ cup sugar
1 egg
1 teaspoon grated lemon peel
3 tablespoons lemon juice

1. Preheat oven to 350°F. Grease 9-inch square pan.

2. Rinse blueberries from Mix with cold water and drain.

3. Place muffin mix in medium bowl. Cut in butter with pastry blender or two knives until mixture resembles coarse crumbs. Stir in pecans. Press into bottom of pan. Bake at 350°F for 15 minutes or until set.

4. Combine cream cheese and sugar in medium bowl. Beat until smooth. Add egg, lemon peel and lemon juice. Beat well. Spread over baked crust. Sprinkle with blueberries. Sprinkle topping packet from Mix over blueberries. Return to oven.

5. Bake at 350°F for 35 to 40 minutes or until filling is set. Cool completely in pan on wire rack. Refrigerate until ready to serve. Cut into bars.

Tip: Lower oven temperature by 25°F when using glass baking dish. Glass heats more quickly and retains heat longer.

BLUEBERRY BRAN BARS

Makes about 15 bars

1¾ cups QUAKER® Oats (quick or old-fashioned, uncooked)
1 cup QUAKER® Oat Bran hot cereal, uncooked
½ cup all-purpose flour
½ cup firmly packed brown sugar
½ teaspoon baking powder
¼ teaspoon salt (optional)
⅓ cup liquid vegetable oil margarine
⅓ cup light corn syrup
2 cups fresh or frozen blueberries (about 1 pint)
½ cup granulated sugar
3 tablespoons water, divided
2 tablespoons cornstarch
2 teaspoons lemon juice

Preheat oven to 350°F. Lightly spray 11 × 7-inch baking dish with nonstick cooking spray or oil lightly.

Combine oats, oat bran cereal, flour, brown sugar, baking powder and salt. Add margarine and corn syrup, mixing until mixture resembles coarse crumbs; reserve 1 cup. Press remaining mixture onto bottom of prepared dish.

Bake 10 minutes. Meanwhile, combine blueberries, granulated sugar and 2 tablespoons water in small saucepan. Bring to a boil; simmer 2 minutes, uncovered, stirring occasionally. Combine remaining 1 tablespoon water, cornstarch and lemon juice; mix well. Gradually stir into blueberry mixture; cook and stir about 30 seconds or until thickened and clear. Spread over partially baked base to within ¼ inch of edge; sprinkle with reserved oat mixture.

Bake 18 to 20 minutes or until topping is lightly browned. Cool in pan on wire rack. Cut into bars. Store loosely covered.

STRAWBERRY BARS

Makes about 16 bars

1 package DUNCAN HINES® Golden Sugar
   Cookie Mix
1 teaspoon grated lemon peel
¼ teaspoon ground cinnamon
1 egg white
¾ cup strawberry preserves
   Confectioners sugar

1. Preheat oven to 350°F. Grease sides of 9-inch square pan (see Tip).

2. Combine cookie mix, lemon peel and cinnamon in large bowl. Add contents of buttery flavor packet from Mix and egg white. Stir until thoroughly blended. Press half the dough into bottom of pan. Spread with preserves. Make ropes with remaining dough to form lattice top; place over preserves as shown in photograph.

4. Bake at 350°F for 30 to 32 minutes or until lattice top is golden. Cool completely in pan on wire rack. Dust with confectioners sugar. Cut into bars.

Tip: Strawberry Bars will be easier to remove from the pan if the sides have been greased.

Strawberry Bar

MAGIC APPLE COOKIE BARS

Makes about 3 dozen bars

1 cup uncooked rolled oats
¾ cup graham cracker crumbs
¼ cup BUTTER FLAVOR CRISCO®
1½ cups very finely chopped, peeled Granny Smith
   or other firm, tart cooking apples
½ cup butterscotch chips (optional)
½ cup flake coconut
½ cup finely chopped nuts
1 can (14 ounces) sweetened condensed milk
   (not evaporated milk)

1. Preheat oven to 350°F. Grease 11×7-inch glass baking dish with Butter Flavor Crisco®.

2. Combine oats, graham cracker crumbs and Butter Flavor Crisco®. Stir well. Press firmly in bottom of greased baking dish. Top with apples, butterscotch chips, coconut and nuts. Pour condensed milk over top.

3. Bake at 350°F for 30 to 35 minutes or until lightly browned. Loosen from sides of dish while still warm with knife. Cool completely in pan on wire rack. Cut into bars. Serve immediately or refrigerate.

APPLE CINNAMON BARS

Makes about 3 dozen bars

1 cup applesauce
¾ cup ROMAN MEAL® Apple Cinnamon
   Multi-Bran Cereal
⅔ cup raisins, plumped*
½ teaspoon freshly grated orange peel
½ cup margarine, softened
¾ cup firmly packed brown sugar
2 eggs *or* 4 egg whites
1½ cups all-purpose flour
1 teaspoon baking powder
½ teaspoon baking soda
½ teaspoon salt
½ teaspoon ground cinnamon
½ teaspoon ground nutmeg
½ cup chopped walnuts

Preheat oven to 375°F. In medium bowl, combine applesauce, cereal, raisins and orange peel. Set aside. In large bowl, beat margarine and sugar until creamy. Add eggs; beat well. Stir in combined dry ingredients. Blend in applesauce mixture and nuts. Spread evenly in well-greased 13×9-inch baking pan.

Bake 18 to 22 minutes or until lightly browned. Cool in pan on wire rack. Cut into bars.

*To plump raisins, place raisins in small bowl. Cover with warm water. Let stand 10 minutes; drain.

BANANA GINGERBREAD BARS

Makes about 2½ dozen bars

1 extra-ripe medium DOLE® Banana, peeled
1 package (14.5 ounces) gingerbread cake mix
½ cup lukewarm water
1 egg
1 small DOLE® Banana, peeled and chopped
   (½ cup)
½ cup DOLE® Raisins
½ cup DOLE® Slivered Almonds
1½ cups powdered sugar
   Juice from 1 DOLE® Lemon (3 tablespoons)

• Preheat oven to 350°F. Place medium banana in blender. Process until puréed; use ½ cup for recipe.

• Combine gingerbread mix, water, ½ cup puréed banana and egg in large bowl. Beat well. Stir in chopped banana, raisins and almonds. Spread batter in greased 13×9-inch baking pan.

• Bake 20 to 25 minutes until wooden toothpick inserted in center comes out clean.

• Mix powdered sugar and lemon juice in medium bowl to make thin glaze. Spread over warm gingerbread. Cool in pan on wire rack. Cut into bars. Sprinkle with additional powdered sugar if desired.

Banana Gingerbread Bars

NO-CHOLESTEROL PECAN DATE BARS

Makes about 2½ dozen bars

CRUST
   1 package DUNCAN HINES® Moist Deluxe
      White Cake Mix
   ⅓ cup margarine
   1 egg white

TOPPING
   1 package (8 ounces) pitted dates, chopped
1¼ cups chopped pecans
   1 cup water
   ½ teaspoon vanilla extract
      Confectioners sugar

1. Preheat oven to 350°F. Grease and flour 13×9-inch pan.

2. For Crust, place cake mix in large bowl. Cut in margarine with pastry blender or 2 knives until mixture is crumbly. Add egg white; stir well (mixture will be crumbly). Press into bottom of pan.

3. For Topping, combine dates, pecans and water in medium saucepan. Bring to a boil. Reduce heat and simmer until mixture thickens, stirring constantly. Remove from heat. Stir in vanilla extract. Spread date mixture evenly over crust.

4. Bake at 350°F for 25 to 30 minutes or until set. Cool completely in pan on wire rack. Dust with confectioners sugar. Cut into bars.

Tip: To save time, use 1 package (8 ounces) chopped, sugared dates in place of pitted dates.

PECAN PIE BARS

Makes about 4 dozen bars

CRUST
   1 package DUNCAN HINES® Golden Sugar
      Cookie Mix
   1 tablespoon water

TOPPING
   3 eggs, lightly beaten
   ¾ cup dark corn syrup
   ¾ cup firmly packed brown sugar
   3 tablespoons butter or margarine, melted
1½ teaspoons vanilla extract
   ¼ teaspoon salt
   1 cup chopped pecans

1. Preheat oven to 375°F.

2. For Crust, empty cookie mix into ungreased 13×9-inch baking pan. Drizzle with buttery flavor packet from Mix and water. Toss with fork until crumbs form. Press crumbs lightly into bottom of pan with floured fork.

3. Bake at 375°F for 10 to 12 minutes or until light brown. Lightly press surface with fork to level. *Reduce oven temperature to 350°F.*

4. For Topping, combine eggs, corn syrup, brown sugar, melted butter, vanilla extract and salt in large bowl. Stir until well blended. Stir in pecans. Pour over partially baked crust. Return to oven.

5. Bake at 350°F for about 30 minutes or until center is set. Loosen from edge of pan with knife. Cool completely in pan on wire rack. Cut into bars.

PINEAPPLE DREAM BARS

Makes about 1½ dozen bars

½ cup margarine, softened
1 cup dark brown sugar, packed, divided
1⅓ cups all-purpose flour, divided
2 eggs
1 teaspoon rum extract
1 teaspoon baking powder
1 teaspoon ground cinnamon
¼ teaspoon salt
¼ teaspoon ground nutmeg
1 can (8¼ ounces) DOLE® Crushed Pineapple in Syrup,* drained
1½ cups flaked coconut
1 cup chopped walnuts
½ cup chopped maraschino cherries

Preheat oven to 350°F. In medium mixer bowl, beat margarine and ⅓ cup brown sugar. Blend in 1 cup flour until mixture is crumbly. Pat into bottom of 13×9-inch baking pan. Bake 10 to 15 minutes or until golden. Cool slightly.

In large bowl, beat eggs with remaining ⅔ cup brown sugar and extract until thick. In small bowl, combine remaining ⅓ cup flour, baking powder, cinnamon, salt and nutmeg. Stir flour mixture into egg mixture. Fold in pineapple, coconut, nuts and cherries. Spread over baked crust.

Bake 30 minutes or until set. Cool slightly in pan on wire rack before cutting into bars.

*Use pineapple packed in juice, if desired.

Pineapple Pecan Bars

PINEAPPLE PECAN BARS

Makes 1½ to 2 dozen bars

2⅓ cups all-purpose flour, divided
⅔ cup powdered sugar
1 cup margarine, cut into chunks
1 can (20 ounces) DOLE® Crushed Pineapple in Juice, drained
4 eggs, lightly beaten
¾ cup brown sugar, packed
2 cups coarsely chopped pecans

Preheat oven to 350°F. In large bowl, combine 2 cups flour and powdered sugar. Cut in margarine with pastry blender or 2 knives until mixture is crumbly. Using bottom of metal measuring cup, pat dough into 13×9-inch baking pan. Bake 15 minutes. Cool slightly.

In medium bowl, combine pineapple, eggs, brown sugar and remaining ⅓ cup flour. Stir in pecans. Pour over partially baked crust.

Bake 30 to 35 minutes or until set. Cool completely in pan on wire rack. Cut into bars.

LEMON RASPBERRY CHEESECAKE BARS

Makes about 3 dozen bars

CRUST
¾ cup BUTTER FLAVOR CRISCO®
⅓ cup firmly packed brown sugar
1¼ cups all-purpose flour
1 cup uncooked rolled oats
¼ teaspoon salt

FILLING
½ cup seedless red raspberry jam
2 packages (8 ounces each) cream cheese, softened
¾ cup granulated sugar
2 tablespoons all-purpose flour
2 eggs
2 teaspoons grated lemon peel
3 tablespoons lemon juice

1. Preheat oven to 350°F. Grease 13×9-inch pan with Butter Flavor Crisco®.

2. For Crust, combine Butter Flavor Crisco® and brown sugar. Beat at medium speed of electric mixer until well blended. Gradually add 1¼ cups flour, oats and salt at low speed. Mix until well blended. Press into bottom of greased pan.

3. Bake at 350°F for 20 minutes or until lightly browned.

4. For Filling, spoon jam immediately on hot crust. Spread carefully to cover.

5. Combine cream cheese, granulated sugar and 2 tablespoons flour in large bowl. Beat at low speed until well blended. Add eggs. Mix well. Add lemon peel and lemon juice. Beat until smooth. Pour over raspberry layer.

6. Bake at 350°F for 25 minutes or until set. Cool to room temperature on wire rack. Cut into bars. Cover; refrigerate.

RICH LEMON BARS

Makes about 2½ dozen bars

1½ cups plus 3 tablespoons unsifted all-purpose flour
½ cup confectioners' sugar
¾ cup cold margarine or butter
4 eggs, slightly beaten
1½ cups granulated sugar
1 teaspoon baking powder
½ cup REALEMON® Lemon Juice from Concentrate
Additional confectioners' sugar

Preheat oven to 350°F. In medium bowl, com[...]
1½ cups flour and ½ cup confectioners' sugar; [...]
margarine until crumbly. Press onto bottom [...]
greased 13×9-inch baking pan; bake 15 mi[...]

Meanwhile, in large bowl, combine eggs, [...]
sugar, remaining 3 tablespoons flour, bakin[...]
ReaLemon® brand; mix well. Pour over [...]

Bake 20 to 25 minutes or until golden[...]
Cut into bars. Sprinkle with additiona[...]
sugar. Store covered in refrigerator; [...]
temperature.

Lemon Pecan Bars: Omit 3 tab[...]
lemon mixture. Sprinkle ¾ cup finely chopp[...]
over top of lemon mixture. Bake as above.

Coconut Lemon Bars: Omit 3 tablespoons flour in lemon mixture. Sprinkle ¾ cup flaked coconut over top of lemon mixture. Bake as above.

LEMON NUT BARS

Makes about 3 dozen bars

1⅓ cups all-purpose flour
½ cup firmly packed brown sugar
¼ cup granulated sugar
¾ cup PARKAY® Margarine
1 cup old-fashioned or quick oats, uncooked
½ cup chopped nuts
1 (8-ounce) package PHILADELPHIA BRAND® Cream Cheese, softened
1 egg
1 tablespoon grated lemon peel
3 tablespoons lemon juice

• Preheat oven to 350°F.

• Stir together flour and sugars in medium bowl. Cut in margarine until mixture resembles coarse crumbs. Stir in oats and nuts. Reserve 1 cup crumb mixture; press remaining crumb mixture onto bottom of greased 13×9-inch baking pan. Bake 15 minutes.

• Beat cream cheese, egg, peel and juice in small mixing bowl at medium speed with electric mixer until well blended. Pour over crust; sprinkle with reserved crumb mixture.

• Bake 25 minutes. Cool in pan on wire rack. Cut into bars.

Prep time: 30 minutes
Cook time: 25 minutes

Lemon Nut Bars

BUTTERSCOTCH CHEESE CRUNCHERS

Makes about 6 dozen bars

2 cups (12-ounce package) NESTLÉ® Toll House®
   Butterscotch Flavored Morsels
6 tablespoons butter
2 cups graham cracker crumbs
2 cups chopped walnuts
2 (8-ounce) packages cream cheese, softened
½ cup sugar
4 eggs
¼ cup all-purpose flour
2 tablespoons lemon juice

Preheat oven to 350°F. Combine over hot (not boiling) water, Nestlé® Toll House® Butterscotch Flavored Morsels and butter; stir until morsels are melted and mixture is smooth. Transfer to large bowl; stir in graham cracker crumbs and walnuts with a fork until mixture resembles fine crumbs. Reserve 2 cups crumb mixture for topping. Press remaining mixture into ungreased 15½ × 10½ × 1-inch jelly-roll pan.

Bake 12 minutes. Meanwhile, in large bowl, combine cream cheese and sugar; beat until creamy. Add eggs, 1 at a time, beating well after each addition. Blend in flour and lemon juice. Pour evenly over hot baked crust. Sprinkle reserved crumb mixture on top.

Bake 25 minutes. Cool completely in pan on wire rack; cut into bars. Refrigerate before serving.

Butterscotch Cheese Crunchers

SPICE ISLANDS BUTTERSCOTCH BARS

Makes about 4½ dozen bars

1¾ cups all-purpose flour
1 teaspoon ground ginger
½ teaspoon baking soda
¼ teaspoon ground cloves
¾ cup plus 2 tablespoons vegetable oil
½ cup molasses
¼ cup firmly packed brown sugar
1 egg
1 cup chopped nuts
1 cup (½ of 12-ounce package) NESTLÉ® Toll
   House® Butterscotch Flavored Morsels
Confectioners' sugar

Preheat oven to 350°F. In small bowl, combine flour, ginger, baking soda and cloves; set aside. In large bowl, combine vegetable oil, molasses, brown sugar and egg; beat well. Gradually beat in flour mixture. Stir in nuts and Nestlé® Toll House® Butterscotch Flavored Morsels. Pour into greased 13 × 9-inch baking pan.

Bake at 350°F for 20 to 25 minutes. Cool completely in pan on wire rack. Sprinkle with confectioners' sugar. Cut into bars.

EASY APRICOT OATMEAL BARS

Makes about 3 dozen bars

1½ cups all-purpose flour
¾ cup firmly packed brown sugar
1 teaspoon baking powder
1 cup cold butter or margarine
1½ cups quick-cooking oats, uncooked
½ cup flaked coconut
½ cup coarsely chopped walnuts
1 can SOLO® *or* 1 jar BAKER® Apricot,
   Raspberry or Strawberry Filling

Preheat oven to 350°F. Grease 13 × 9-inch baking pan; set aside.

Combine flour, brown sugar and baking powder in medium bowl. Cut in butter until mixture resembles coarse crumbs. Add oats, coconut and walnuts; mix until crumbly. Press half of mixture into bottom of prepared pan. Spoon apricot filling over crumb mixture. Sprinkle remaining crumb mixture over apricot layer.

Bake 25 to 30 minutes or until lightly browned. (Center may seem soft but will set when cool.) Cool completely in pan on wire rack. Cut into bars.

Top to bottom: Chocolate Chip Pecan Squares (page 224), Streusel Peanut Butter Bars

STREUSEL PEANUT BUTTER BARS

Makes about 2½ dozen bars

BASE
½ cup BUTTER FLAVOR CRISCO®
1½ cups firmly packed brown sugar
⅔ cup JIF® Creamy or Extra Crunchy Peanut Butter
2 eggs
1 teaspoon vanilla
1½ cups all-purpose flour
½ teaspoon salt
¼ cup milk

STREUSEL TOPPING
3 tablespoons BUTTER FLAVOR CRISCO®
⅓ cup all-purpose flour
⅓ cup firmly packed brown sugar
1 tablespoon JIF® Creamy or Extra Crunchy Peanut Butter
¼ cup finely chopped peanuts

1. Preheat oven to 350°F. Grease 13×9-inch pan with Butter Flavor Crisco®.

2. For Base, combine ½ cup Butter Flavor Crisco®, 1½ cups sugar and ⅔ cup Jif® Peanut Butter in large bowl. Beat at medium speed of electric mixer until well blended and creamy. Beat in eggs and vanilla.

3. Combine 1½ cups flour and salt. Add alternately with milk to creamed mixture at low speed. Beat until well blended. Spread in pan.

4. For Topping, combine 3 tablespoons Butter Flavor Crisco®, ⅓ cup flour, ⅓ cup sugar and 1 tablespoon Jif® Peanut Butter. Mix with spoon until well blended and coarse crumbs form. Sprinkle over base. Sprinkle nuts over topping.

5. Bake at 350°F for 30 to 33 minutes or until golden brown and center is set. Cool in pan on wire rack. Cut into bars.

YUMMY PEANUT BUTTER BARS

Makes about 1½ dozen bars

BARS
1 package DUNCAN HINES® Peanut Butter Cookie Mix
1 egg
1 tablespoon water
⅓ cup chopped peanuts

WHITE GLAZE
¼ cup confectioners sugar
1 to 2 teaspoons water

CHOCOLATE GLAZE
¼ cup semi-sweet chocolate chips
2 teaspoons CRISCO® Shortening

1. Preheat oven to 350°F.

2. For Bars, combine cookie mix, peanut butter packet from Mix, egg and water in large bowl. Stir until thoroughly blended. Stir in peanuts. Spread in ungreased 8-inch square pan.

3. Bake at 350°F for 23 to 25 minutes or until edges are light golden brown. Cool completely in pan on wire rack.

4. For White Glaze, combine confectioners sugar and water in small bowl. Stir until smooth. Drizzle over cooled bars.

5. For Chocolate Glaze, place chocolate chips and shortening in small resealable plastic bag; seal. Place bag in hot water for several minutes. Dry with paper towel. Knead until blended and chocolate is smooth. Snip a tiny piece off one corner of bag. Drizzle chocolate over white glaze. Allow glazes to set before cutting into bars.

Freezing Instructions: Store cooled bars between layers of waxed paper in airtight container. Freeze for up to 6 months.

Decadent Blonde Brownies

DECADENT BLONDE BROWNIES

Makes 2 dozen brownies

1 jar (3½ ounces) macadamia nuts
1½ cups all-purpose flour
1 teaspoon baking powder
½ teaspoon salt
½ cup butter or margarine, softened
¾ cup granulated sugar
¾ cup firmly packed light brown sugar
2 large eggs
2 teaspoons vanilla
1 package (10 ounces) semisweet chocolate chunks*

Preheat oven to 350°F. Grease 13×9-inch baking pan.

Coarsely chop macadamia nuts to measure ¾ cup; set aside. Combine flour, baking powder and salt in small bowl.

Beat butter, granulated sugar and brown sugar in large bowl with electric mixer at medium speed until light and fluffy, scraping down side of bowl once. Beat in eggs and vanilla, scraping down side of bowl once. Add flour mixture. Beat at low speed until well blended, scraping down side of bowl once. Stir in chocolate chunks and macadamia nuts with wooden spoon. Spread batter evenly into prepared pan.

Bake 25 to 30 minutes or until golden brown. Remove pan to wire rack; cool completely. Cut into 3¼×1½-inch bars. Store tightly covered at room temperature or freeze up to 3 months.

*If chocolate chunks are not available, cut one 10-ounce thick chocolate candy bar into ½-inch pieces to equal 1½ cups.

HERSHEY'S CHOCOLATE CHIP BLONDIES

Makes about 16 bars

6 tablespoons butter or margarine, softened
¾ cup firmly packed light brown sugar
1 egg
1 tablespoon milk
1 teaspoon vanilla extract
1 cup all-purpose flour
½ teaspoon baking soda
⅛ teaspoon salt
2 cups (12-ounce package) HERSHEY'S Semi-Sweet Chocolate Chips
½ cup coarsely chopped nuts (optional)

Preheat oven to 350°F. Grease 9-inch square baking pan.

In large mixer bowl, beat butter and brown sugar until light and fluffy. Add egg, milk and vanilla; beat well. Stir together flour, baking soda and salt; add to butter mixture, stirring well. Stir in chocolate chips and nuts, if desired. Spread in prepared pan.

Bake 20 to 25 minutes or until lightly browned. Cool completely in pan on wire rack. Cut into bars.

DOUBLE CHOCOLATE CHIP BROWNIES

Makes about 2 dozen brownies

2 cups (12-ounce package) NESTLÉ® Toll House® Semi-Sweet Chocolate Morsels, divided
½ cup butter
3 eggs
1¼ cups all-purpose flour
1 cup sugar
1 teaspoon vanilla extract
¼ teaspoon baking soda
½ cup chopped nuts

Preheat oven to 350°F. In large heavy saucepan over low heat, melt 1 cup Nestlé® Toll House® Semi-Sweet Chocolate Morsels and butter; stir until smooth. Remove from heat. Add eggs; stir well. Add flour, sugar, vanilla and baking soda; stir well. Stir in remaining 1 cup Nestlé® Toll House® Semi-Sweet Morsels and nuts. Spread into greased 13×9-inch baking pan.

Bake 18 to 22 minutes or just until set. Cool completely in pan on wire rack. Cut into squares.

White Chocolate Chunk Brownies

WHITE CHOCOLATE CHUNK BROWNIES

Makes 16 brownies

**4 squares (1 ounce each) unsweetened chocolate,
    coarsely chopped**
½ cup butter or margarine
2 large eggs
1¼ cups granulated sugar
1 teaspoon vanilla
½ cup all-purpose flour
½ teaspoon salt
6 ounces white baking bar, cut into ¼-inch pieces
½ cup coarsely chopped walnuts
    Powdered sugar for garnish (optional)

Preheat oven to 350°F. Grease 8-inch square
baking pan.

Melt unsweetened chocolate and butter in small, heavy
saucepan over low heat, stirring constantly; set aside.

Beat eggs in large bowl with electric mixer at medium
speed 30 seconds. Gradually add granulated sugar,
beating at medium speed about 4 minutes until very
thick and lemon colored.

Beat in chocolate mixture and vanilla. Beat in flour and
salt at low speed just until blended. Stir in baking bar
pieces and walnuts with wooden spoon. Spread batter
evenly into prepared pan.

Bake 30 minutes or until edges just begin to pull away
from sides of pan and center is set. Remove pan to wire
rack; cool completely. Cut into 2-inch squares. Sprinkle
powdered sugar over brownies, if desired. Store tightly
covered at room temperature or freeze up to 3 months.

PEANUT BUTTER BROWNIE CUPS

Makes 2 dozen cups

BROWNIE CUPS
**1 package DUNCAN HINES® Chocolate Lovers'
    Double Fudge Brownie Mix**
2 eggs
⅓ cup water
¼ cup CRISCO® Oil or CRISCO® PURITAN® Oil

TOPPING
⅓ cup sugar
⅓ cup light corn syrup
½ cup peanut butter

CHOCOLATE GLAZE
¾ cup semi-sweet chocolate chips
3 tablespoons butter or margarine
1 tablespoon light corn syrup
3 tablespoons chopped peanuts, for garnish

1. Preheat oven to 350°F. Place 24 (2-inch) foil liners
on cookie sheets.

2. For Brownie Cups, combine brownie mix, fudge
packet from Mix, eggs, water and Crisco® Oil in large
bowl. Stir with spoon until well blended, about
50 strokes. Place 2 level measuring tablespoons batter
in each foil liner.

3. Bake at 350°F for 20 to 22 minutes or until set. Cool
completely on wire rack.

4. For Topping, combine sugar and ⅓ cup corn syrup in
small heavy saucepan. Bring to a boil over medium heat.
Stir in peanut butter. Drop by rounded teaspoonfuls
onto each brownie cup.

5. For Chocolate Glaze, combine chocolate chips, butter
and 1 tablespoon corn syrup in small heavy saucepan.
Cook, stirring constantly, over low heat until melted.
Spoon 1 rounded teaspoonful chocolate glaze onto peanut
butter topping. Sprinkle with chopped peanuts. Refrigerate
15 minutes or until chocolate is firm.

Tip: For a different presentation, spread the chocolate
glaze evenly to brownie edges.

PEANUT BUTTER PAISLEY BROWNIES

Makes about 3 dozen brownies

½ cup butter or margarine, softened
¼ cup REESE'S™ Peanut Butter
1 cup granulated sugar
1 cup firmly packed light brown sugar
3 eggs
1 teaspoon vanilla extract
2 cups all-purpose flour
2 teaspoons baking powder
¼ teaspoon salt
½ cup (5½-ounce can) HERSHEY'S® Syrup

Preheat oven to 350°F. Grease 13×9-inch baking pan.

In large mixer bowl, blend butter and peanut butter. Add granulated sugar and brown sugar; beat well. Add eggs, one at a time, beating well after each addition. Blend in vanilla. Stir together flour, baking powder and salt; mix into peanut butter mixture, blending well.

Spread half the batter into prepared pan. Spoon syrup over top. Carefully spread with remaining batter. Swirl with spatula or knife for marbled effect.

Bake 35 to 40 minutes or until lightly browned. Cool completely in pan on wire rack. Cut into squares.

ONE BOWL® BROWNIES

Makes about 2 dozen brownies

4 squares BAKER'S® Unsweetened Chocolate
¾ cup (1½ sticks) margarine or butter
2 cups sugar
3 eggs
1 teaspoon vanilla
1 cup all-purpose flour
1 cup chopped nuts (optional)

Preheat oven to 350°F.

Microwave chocolate and margarine in large microwavable bowl on HIGH (100% power) 2 minutes or until margarine is melted. Stir until chocolate is completely melted.

Stir sugar into melted chocolate mixture. Mix in eggs and vanilla until well blended. Stir in flour and nuts. Spread in greased 13×9-inch pan.

Bake for 30 to 35 minutes or until wooden toothpick inserted into center comes out with fudgy crumbs. Do not overbake. Cool in pan on wire rack. Cut into squares.

Tip: For cake-like brownies, stir in ½ cup milk with eggs and vanilla. Increase flour to 1½ cups.

ROCKY ROAD BROWNIES

Prepare One Bowl® Brownies as directed; spread in greased 13×9-inch pan. Bake at 350°F for 30 minutes.

Immediately sprinkle 2 cups KRAFT® Miniature Marshmallows, 1 cup BAKER'S® Semi-Sweet Real Chocolate Chips and 1 cup chopped nuts over brownies. Continue baking 3 to 5 minutes or until toppings begin to melt together. Cool in pan on wire rack. Cut into squares.   *Makes about 2 dozen brownies*

PEANUT BUTTER SWIRL BROWNIES

Prepare One Bowl® Brownie batter as directed, reserving 1 tablespoon margarine and 2 tablespoons sugar. Spread in greased 13×9-inch pan.

Add reserved ingredients to ⅔ cup peanut butter; mix well. Place spoonfuls of peanut butter mixture over brownie batter. Swirl with knife to marbleize.

Bake at 350°F for 30 to 35 minutes or until wooden toothpick inserted into center comes out with fudgy crumbs. Cool in pan on wire rack. Cut into squares.
Makes about 2 dozen brownies

Tip: For more peanut butter flavor, use 1 cup peanut butter.

One Bowl® Brownies: Peanut Butter Swirl Brownies (top), Rocky Road Brownies (bottom)

SEMI-SWEET CHOCOLATE BROWNIES

Makes about 16 brownies

6 squares BAKER'S® Semi-Sweet Chocolate
½ cup (1 stick) margarine or butter
⅔ cup sugar
2 eggs
1 teaspoon vanilla
1 cup all-purpose flour
⅓ cup chopped nuts (optional)

Preheat oven to 350°F.

Microwave chocolate and margarine in large microwavable bowl on HIGH (100% power) 2 minutes or until margarine is melted. Stir until chocolate is completely melted.

Stir sugar into melted chocolate mixture. Mix in eggs and vanilla until well blended. Stir in flour and nuts. Spread in greased 8-inch square pan.

Bake for 30 minutes or until wooden toothpick inserted into center comes out with fudgy crumbs. Do not overbake. Cool in pan on wire rack. Cut into squares.

Prep time: 10 minutes
Bake time: 30 minutes

Caramel-Layered Brownie

CARAMEL-LAYERED BROWNIES

Makes about 2 dozen brownies

4 squares BAKER'S® Unsweetened Chocolate
¾ cup (1½ sticks) margarine or butter
2 cups sugar
3 eggs
1 teaspoon vanilla
1 cup all-purpose flour
1 cup BAKER'S® Semi-Sweet Real Chocolate Chips
1½ cups chopped nuts, divided
1 package (14 ounces) KRAFT® Caramels
⅓ cup evaporated milk

Preheat oven to 350°F.

Microwave chocolate and margarine in large microwavable bowl on HIGH (100% power) 2 minutes or until margarine is melted. Stir until chocolate is completely melted.

Stir sugar into melted chocolate mixture. Mix in eggs and vanilla until well blended. Stir in flour. Remove 1 cup of batter; set aside. Spread remaining batter in greased 13×9-inch pan. Sprinkle with chips and 1 cup nuts.

Microwave caramels and evaporated milk in medium microwavable bowl on HIGH (100% power) 4 minutes, stirring after 2 minutes. Stir until caramels are completely melted and smooth. Spoon over chips and nuts, spreading to edges of pan. Gently spread reserved batter over caramel mixture. Sprinkle with remaining ½ cup nuts.

Bake for 40 minutes or until wooden toothpick inserted into center comes out with fudgy crumbs. Do not overbake. Cool in pan on wire rack. Cut into squares.

Prep time: 20 minutes
Bake time: 40 minutes

PECAN CARAMEL BROWNIES

Makes about 2 dozen brownies

50 caramel candy cubes
2 tablespoons milk
1½ cups granulated sugar
1 cup butter or margarine, melted
4 eggs
2 teaspoons vanilla
1 cup all-purpose flour
⅔ cup unsweetened cocoa
½ teaspoon baking powder
¼ teaspoon salt
1 cup (6 ounces) semisweet chocolate chips
   Easy Cocoa Glaze (recipe follows)
⅓ cup pecan halves, toasted

Preheat oven to 350°F. Butter 13×9-inch pan.

Unwrap caramels; melt with milk in small heavy saucepan over medium to low heat, stirring until caramels melt completely. Keep warm. Combine granulated sugar, butter, eggs, vanilla, flour, cocoa, baking powder and salt in large bowl. Beat with electric mixer at medium speed until smooth. Spread half the batter in prepared pan.

Bake 15 minutes. Carefully remove from oven; sprinkle with chocolate chips. Drizzle melted caramel mixture over top, covering evenly. Cover with remaining batter. Return to oven.

Bake 20 minutes. Do not overbake. Cool slightly in pan on wire rack. Prepare Easy Cocoa Glaze. Pour over warm brownies; arrange toasted pecans on top. Cool completely in pan on wire rack. Cut into squares.

EASY COCOA GLAZE

2 tablespoons butter or margarine
2 tablespoons unsweetened cocoa
2 tablespoons milk
    Dash salt
1 cup powdered sugar
1 teaspoon vanilla

Combine butter, cocoa, milk and salt in small heavy saucepan. Bring to a boil over medium heat, stirring constantly. Remove from heat; add powdered sugar and beat until smooth. Stir in vanilla.

BROWNIE PIZZA

Makes 12 servings

BROWNIE LAYER:
4 squares BAKER'S® Unsweetened Chocolate
¾ cup (1½ sticks) margarine or butter
2 cups sugar
4 eggs
1 teaspoon vanilla
1 cup all-purpose flour

TOPPING:
1 package (8 ounces) PHILADELPHIA BRAND®
    Cream Cheese, softened
¼ cup sugar
1 egg
½ teaspoon vanilla
    Assorted sliced fruit
2 squares BAKER'S® Semi-Sweet Chocolate,
    melted

Brownie Pizza

Preheat oven to 350°F. Line 12×½-inch pizza pan with foil (to lift brownie from pan after baking); grease foil.

Microwave unsweetened chocolate and margarine in large microwavable bowl on HIGH (100% power) 2 minutes or until margarine is melted. Stir until chocolate is completely melted.

Stir 2 cups sugar into melted chocolate mixture. Mix in 4 eggs and 1 teaspoon vanilla until well blended. Stir in flour until well blended. Spread in prepared pan.

Bake for 30 minutes. Mix cream cheese, ¼ cup sugar, 1 egg and ½ teaspoon vanilla in small bowl until well blended. Pour over baked brownie crust.

Bake 10 minutes longer or until toothpick inserted into center comes out with fudgy crumbs. Do not overbake. Cool in pan on wire rack. Lift brownie pizza out of pan; peel off foil. Place brownie pizza on serving plate. Arrange fruit over cream cheese layer. Drizzle with melted semi-sweet chocolate. Let stand until chocolate is set. Cut into wedges to serve.

MINTED CHOCOLATE CHIP BROWNIES

Makes 16 brownies

¾ cup granulated sugar
½ cup butter or margarine
2 tablespoons water
1 cup semisweet chocolate chips or miniature
    chocolate chips
1½ teaspoons vanilla
2 large eggs
1¼ cups all-purpose flour
½ teaspoon baking soda
½ teaspoon salt
1 cup mint chocolate chips
    Powdered sugar for garnish

Preheat oven to 350°F. Grease 9-inch square baking pan.

Combine granulated sugar, butter and water in medium microwavable bowl. Microwave at HIGH (100% power) 2½ to 3 minutes or until butter is melted. Stir in semisweet chips; stir gently until chips are melted and mixture is well blended. Stir in vanilla; let stand 5 minutes to cool.

Beat eggs into chocolate mixture, 1 at a time, with wooden spoon. Combine flour, baking soda and salt in small bowl. Add to chocolate mixture; mix well. Stir in mint chips. Spread batter evenly into prepared pan.

Bake 25 minutes for fudgy brownies or 30 to 35 minutes for cake-like brownies. Remove pan to wire rack; cool completely. Cut into 2¼-inch squares. Sprinkle powdered sugar over brownies, if desired. Store tightly covered at room temperature or freeze up to 3 months.

MOCHA BROWNIES

Makes about 32 brownies

1¼ cups all-purpose flour
1 teaspoon baking powder
½ teaspoon salt
4 (1-ounce) squares semi-sweet chocolate
¾ cup BLUE BONNET® Spread
1 tablespoon instant coffee granules
1 cup granulated sugar
4 eggs
1 teaspoon vanilla extract
1¼ cups PLANTERS® Chopped Walnuts, divided
    Creamy Coffee Frosting (recipe follows)

Preheat oven to 350°F. In small bowl, combine flour, baking powder and salt; set aside.

In large saucepan over low heat, melt chocolate, Spread and 1 tablespoon coffee granules until melted and well blended. Remove from heat; stir in granulated sugar. Add eggs, 1 at a time, beating well after each addition. Stir in vanilla. Stir in 1 cup walnuts. Spread in greased 13×9-inch baking pan.

Bake 25 to 30 minutes. Cool in pan on wire rack. Spread with Creamy Coffee Frosting; sprinkle with remaining ¼ cup walnuts. Cut into bars.

Creamy Coffee Frosting: Dissolve 1 teaspoon instant coffee granules in ¼ cup milk. In small bowl with electric mixer at high speed, beat 4 ounces cream cheese and coffee mixture until creamy. Gradually beat in 1 (16-ounce) package confectioner's sugar until well blended and of good spreading consistency.

MADISON AVENUE MOCHA BROWNIES

Makes about 4 dozen brownies

1 (20- to 23-ounce) package brownie mix
1 (8-ounce) package PHILADELPHIA BRAND® Cream Cheese, softened
⅓ cup sugar
1 egg
1½ teaspoons MAXWELL HOUSE® Instant Coffee
1 teaspoon vanilla

• Preheat oven to 350°F.

• Prepare brownie mix according to package directions. Pour into greased 13×9-inch baking pan.

• Beat cream cheese, sugar and egg in small mixing bowl at medium speed with electric mixer until well blended.

• Dissolve coffee in vanilla; add to cream cheese mixture, mixing until well blended.

• Spoon cream cheese mixture over brownie batter; cut through batter with knife several times for marble effect.

• Bake 35 to 40 minutes or until set. Cool in pan on wire rack. Cut into bars.

Prep time: 20 minutes
Cook time: 40 minutes

Minted Chocolate Chip Brownies

RICH 'N' CREAMY BROWNIE BARS

Makes about 4 dozen brownies

BROWNIES
1 package DUNCAN HINES® Chocolate Lovers' Double Fudge Brownie Mix

2 eggs

⅓ cup water

¼ cup CRISCO® Oil or CRISCO® PURITAN® Oil

½ cup chopped pecans

TOPPING
1 package (8 ounces) cream cheese, softened

2 eggs

1 pound (3½ cups) confectioners sugar

1 teaspoon vanilla extract

1. Preheat oven to 350°F. Grease bottom of 13×9-inch pan.

2. For Brownies, combine brownie mix, fudge packet from Mix, 2 eggs, water and Crisco® Oil in large bowl. Stir with spoon until well blended, about 50 strokes. Stir in pecans. Spread evenly in pan.

3. For Topping, beat cream cheese in large bowl at medium speed with electric mixer until smooth. Beat in 2 eggs, confectioners sugar and vanilla extract until smooth. Spread evenly over brownie mixture.

4. Bake at 350°F for 45 to 50 minutes or until edges and top are golden brown and shiny. Cool completely in pan on wire rack. Refrigerate until well chilled. Cut into bars.

BITTERSWEET BROWNIES

Makes 16 brownies

MAZOLA® No Stick™ Corn Oil Cooking Spray

4 squares (1 ounce each) unsweetened chocolate, melted

1 cup sugar

½ cup HELLMANN'S® or BEST FOODS® Real, Light Reduced Calorie or Reduced Fat Cholesterol Free Mayonnaise Dressing

2 eggs

1 teaspoon vanilla

¾ cup all-purpose flour

½ teaspoon baking powder

¼ teaspoon salt

½ cup chopped walnuts

Preheat oven to 350°F. Spray 8×8-inch baking pan with cooking spray. In large bowl, stir chocolate, sugar, mayonnaise, eggs and vanilla until smooth. Mix in flour, baking powder and salt until well blended. Stir in walnuts. Spread evenly in prepared pan.

Bake 25 to 30 minutes or until wooden toothpick inserted into center comes out clean. Cool in pan on wire rack. Cut into 2-inch squares.

OUTRAGEOUS BROWNIES

Makes about 2 dozen brownies

½ cup MIRACLE WHIP® Salad Dressing

2 eggs, beaten

¼ cup cold water

1 (21.5-ounce) package fudge brownie mix

3 (7-ounce) milk chocolate bars, divided

• Preheat oven to 350°F.

• Mix together salad dressing, eggs and water until well blended. Stir in brownie mix, mixing just until moistened.

• Coarsely chop two chocolate bars; stir into brownie mixture. Pour into greased 13×9-inch baking pan. Chop remaining chocolate bar; reserve.

• Bake 30 to 35 minutes or until edges begin to pull away from sides of pan. Immediately top with reserved chocolate bar. Let stand about 5 minutes or until melted; spread evenly over brownies. Garnish with walnut halves, if desired. Cool in pan on wire rack. Cut into squares.

Rich 'n' Creamy Brownie Bars

BEST BROWNIES

Makes about 16 brownies

½ cup (1 stick) butter or margarine, melted
1 cup sugar
1 teaspoon vanilla extract
2 eggs
½ cup all-purpose flour
⅓ cup HERSHEY®'S Cocoa
¼ teaspoon baking powder
¼ teaspoon salt
½ cup chopped nuts (optional)
Creamy Brownie Frosting (recipe follows)

Preheat oven to 350°F. Grease 9-inch square baking pan.

In medium bowl, stir together butter, sugar and vanilla with wooden spoon. Add eggs; beat well. Stir together flour, cocoa, baking powder and salt; gradually add to egg mixture, beating until combined. Stir in nuts, if desired. Spread batter evenly into prepared pan.

Bake 20 to 25 minutes or until brownies begin to pull away from sides of pan. Cool completely in pan on wire rack. Frost with Creamy Brownie Frosting. Cut into squares.

CREAMY BROWNIE FROSTING

3 tablespoons butter or margarine, softened
3 tablespoons HERSHEY®'S Cocoa
1 tablespoon light corn syrup *or* honey
½ teaspoon vanilla extract
1 cup powdered sugar
1 to 2 tablespoons milk

In small mixer bowl, beat butter, cocoa, corn syrup and vanilla until well blended. Add powdered sugar and milk; beat to spreading consistency.

Makes about 1 cup frosting

SOUR CREAM WALNUT BROWNIES

Makes about 2 dozen brownies

BROWNIES
1 package DUNCAN HINES® Chocolate Lovers'
    Walnut Brownie Mix
¾ cup dairy sour cream
1 egg
1 teaspoon water

CHOCOLATE DRIZZLE
½ cup semi-sweet chocolate chips
2 teaspoons CRISCO® Shortening

Sour Cream Walnut Brownies

1. Preheat oven to 350°F. Grease 13×9-inch pan.

2. For Brownies, combine brownie mix, sour cream, egg and water in large bowl. Stir with spoon until well blended, about 50 strokes. Spread in pan. Sprinkle with contents of walnut packet from Mix.

3. Bake at 350°F for 25 to 28 minutes or until set.

4. For Chocolate Drizzle, place chocolate chips and shortening in small resealable plastic bag; seal. Place bag in bowl of hot water for several minutes. Dry with paper towel. Knead until blended and chocolate is smooth. Snip a tiny piece off one corner of bag. Drizzle chocolate over brownies. Cool completely in pan on wire rack. Cut into bars.

Tip: Overbaking brownies will cause them to become dry. Follow the recommended baking times given in recipes closely.

SPECIAL OCCASIONS

CHOCOLATE AND PEAR TART

Makes 12 servings

Chocolate Tart Crust (recipe follows)
1 cup milk
2 egg yolks, beaten
2 tablespoons sugar
⅛ teaspoon salt
1 cup HERSHEY₂S Semi-Sweet Chocolate Chips
3 large fresh pears
Apricot Glaze (recipe follows)

Prepare Chocolate Tart Crust; set aside. In top of double boiler over hot, not boiling, water, scald milk; gradually stir in egg yolks, sugar and salt. Cook over hot water, stirring constantly, until slightly thickened; do not boil. Remove from heat; immediately add chocolate chips, stirring until chips are melted and mixture is smooth. Pour into baked Chocolate Tart Crust; refrigerate several hours or until firm. Core and peel pears; cut into thin slices. Place in circular pattern on top of filling. Immediately prepare Apricot Glaze. Spoon over top of fruit, covering completely. Refrigerate several hours or until firm. Remove rim of pan. Serve cold. Cover; refrigerate leftovers.

Chocolate Tart Crust: Preheat oven to 325°F. Grease and flour 9-inch round tart pan with removable bottom. In small mixer bowl, stir together ¾ cup all-purpose flour, ¼ cup powdered sugar and 1 tablespoon HERSHEY₂S Cocoa. At low speed of electric mixer, beat in 6 tablespoons chilled margarine until blended and smooth. Press evenly onto bottom and up side of prepared pan. Bake 10 to 15 minutes; cool.

APRICOT GLAZE

¾ teaspoon unflavored gelatin
2 teaspoons cold water
½ cup apricot nectar
¼ cup sugar
1 tablespoon arrowroot
1 teaspoon lemon juice

In small bowl or cup, sprinkle gelatin over cold water; let stand several minutes to soften. In small saucepan, combine apricot nectar, sugar, arrowroot and lemon juice; cook over medium heat, stirring constantly, until mixture is thickened. Remove from heat; immediately add gelatin mixture. Stir until smooth.

Chocolate and Pear Tart

PASTRY CHEF TARTS

Makes 10 servings

1 package (10 ounces) pie crust mix
1 egg, beaten
1 to 2 tablespoons cold water
1½ cups cold half-and-half or milk
1 package (4-serving size) JELL-O® Instant
    Pudding and Pie Filling, French Vanilla or
    Vanilla Flavor
    Assorted berries or fruit*
    Mint leaves (optional)

Preheat oven to 425°F. Combine pie crust mix with egg. Add just enough water to form dough. Form 2 to 3 tablespoons dough into a round. Repeat to make 10 rounds. Press each round onto bottom and up sides of

*We suggest any variety of berries, mandarin orange sections, melon balls, halved seedless grapes, sliced peaches, kiwifruit or plums.

Pastry Chef Tarts

ten 3- to 4-inch tart pans. (Use tart pans with removable bottoms, if possible.) Pierce pastry several times with fork. Place on baking pans. Bake for 10 minutes or until golden. Cool slightly. Remove tart shells from pans; cool completely on wire racks.

Pour half-and-half into small bowl. Add pudding mix. Beat with wire whisk until well blended, 1 to 2 minutes. Spoon into tart shells. Chill until ready to serve.

Arrange fruit on pudding. Garnish with mint leaves, if desired.

Note: Individual graham cracker crumb tart shells may be substituted for baked tart shells.

CHOCOLATE CREAM STRAWBERRY TART

Makes one 9-inch tart

TART SHELL:
    Pastry for single crust 9-inch pie

PASTRY CREAM:
  ¼ cup sugar
  3 tablespoons all-purpose flour
  ¼ teaspoon salt
  1 cup milk
  4 egg yolks
  1 cup (6-ounce package) NESTLÉ® Toll House®
    Semi-Sweet Chocolate Morsels
  2 tablespoons butter
  2 teaspoons vanilla extract
  2 pints strawberries, washed and hulled
  2 tablespoons strawberry jelly

Tart Shell: Preheat oven to 425°F. Fit pastry dough into 9-inch tart pan with removable bottom. Press dough firmly into bottom and sides of pan; trim edges. Line pastry dough with foil; weight with dried beans.

Bake 10 minutes or until lightly browned. Remove foil and beans; bake additional 2 to 3 minutes. Cool completely. Remove from pan; place on serving plate.

Pastry Cream: In medium saucepan, combine sugar, flour and salt. Gradually add milk. Cook over low heat, stirring constantly, until mixture boils. Boil 2 minutes, stirring constantly; remove from heat. Beat in egg yolks. Return to heat; cook 1 minute longer. Remove from heat. Add Nestlé® Toll House® Semi-Sweet Chocolate Morsels, butter and vanilla extract. Stir until morsels are melted and mixture is smooth. Place plastic wrap on surface of pastry cream. Refrigerate 30 minutes. Stir; spread evenly into baked tart shell. Arrange strawberries, hull-side down, on top. In small saucepan over low heat, melt strawberry jelly. Brush over strawberries. Refrigerate several hours. Let stand at room temperature 15 minutes before serving.

CHOCOLATE RASPBERRY TART

Makes 8 to 10 servings

1 package (4-serving size) JELL-O® Vanilla Flavor
    Pudding and Pie Filling
1¾ cups half-and-half or milk
    Chocolate Crumb Crust (recipe follows)
1 pint raspberries
2 squares BAKER'S® Semi-Sweet Chocolate, melted

Microwave pudding mix and half-and-half in large microwavable bowl on HIGH (100% power) 3 minutes; stir well. Microwave on HIGH 3 minutes longer; stir again. Microwave on HIGH 1 minute longer or until mixture comes to a boil. Cool slightly; cover surface with plastic wrap. Refrigerate at least 4 hours.

Just before serving, spoon filling into Chocolate Crumb Crust. Arrange raspberries on top of filling. Drizzle with melted chocolate.

Prep time: 30 minutes
Chill time: 4 hours

Saucepan preparation: Combine pudding mix and half-and-half in 2-quart saucepan. Cook over medium heat until mixture comes to a full boil, stirring constantly. Continue as above.

CHOCOLATE CRUMB CRUST

3 squares BAKER'S® Semi-Sweet Chocolate
3 tablespoons margarine or butter
1 cup graham cracker crumbs

Preheat oven to 375°F.

Microwave chocolate and margarine in small microwavable bowl on HIGH (100% power) 2 minutes or until margarine is melted. Stir until chocolate is completely melted.

Stir in crumbs. Press mixture onto bottom and up sides of 9-inch tart pan or pie plate. Freeze 10 minutes. Bake 8 minutes. Cool on wire rack.

Makes 1 (9-inch) crust

Prep time: 5 minutes
Freezing time: 10 minutes
Bake time: 8 minutes

Jubilee Pie

JUBILEE PIE

Makes 8 servings

1 cup milk
3 eggs
½ cup all-purpose baking mix with buttermilk
½ cup KARO® Light or Dark Corn Syrup
¼ cup MAZOLA® Margarine, softened
1 cup (6 ounces) semisweet chocolate chips, melted
1 can (21 ounces) cherry pie filling
¼ teaspoon almond extract
1 cup whipping cream, whipped
    Chocolate curls (optional)

Preheat oven to 350°F. Grease 9-inch pie plate.

In blender or food processor, blend milk, eggs, baking mix, corn syrup, margarine and melted chocolate 1 minute. Pour into prepared pie plate; let stand 5 minutes.

Bake 35 to 40 minutes or until filling is puffed and set. Cool on wire rack 1 hour. (Center of pie will fall, forming a well). While pie is baking, mix cherry pie filling and almond extract; refrigerate. Fill center of cooled pie with cherry mixture. Refrigerate at least 1 hour. Before serving, pipe or swirl whipped cream around edge. If desired, garnish with chocolate curls.

Prep time: 20 minutes
Bake time: 40 minutes, plus cooling and chilling

French Apple Pie

FRENCH APPLE PIE

Makes one 9-inch pie

CRUST
Unbaked 9-inch Classic CRISCO® *Double* Crust
(page 80)

NUT FILLING
¾ cup ground walnuts
2 tablespoons firmly packed brown sugar
2 tablespoons beaten egg
1 tablespoon milk
1 tablespoon butter or margarine, softened
¼ teaspoon vanilla
¼ teaspoon lemon juice

APPLE FILLING
5 cups sliced, peeled Granny Smith apples
(about 1¾ pounds or 5 medium)
1 teaspoon lemon juice
¾ cup granulated sugar
2 tablespoons all-purpose flour
1 teaspoon ground cinnamon
¼ teaspoon salt
¼ teaspoon ground nutmeg
2 tablespoons butter or margarine

1. Preheat oven to 425°F.

2. For Nut Filling, combine nuts, brown sugar, egg, milk,
1 tablespoon butter, vanilla and ¼ teaspoon lemon juice
in small bowl. Spread over bottom of unbaked pie crust.

3. For Apple Filling, place apples in large bowl. Sprinkle
with 1 teaspoon lemon juice. Combine granulated sugar,
flour, cinnamon, salt and nutmeg. Sprinkle over apples.
Toss to coat. Spoon over nut filling. Dot with 2 tablespoons
butter. Moisten pastry edge with water.

4. Cover pie with top crust. Fold top edge under bottom
crust; flute with fingers or fork. Cut slits in top crust to
allow steam to escape.

5. Bake at 425°F for 50 minutes or until filling in center
is bubbly and crust is golden brown. Cover edge of pie
with foil, if necessary, to prevent overbrowning. Cool
until barely warm or room temperature before serving.

APPLE CREAM CRUMBLE PIE

Makes 12 servings

½ package (15-ounce) refrigerated pie crusts
(1 crust)
1 (8-ounce) package PHILADELPHIA BRAND®
Cream Cheese, softened
⅓ cup sugar
1 teaspoon vanilla
1 egg
⅔ cup BREAKSTONE'S® Sour Cream
3 apples, sliced
½ cup all-purpose flour
¼ cup sugar
1 teaspoon ground cinnamon
⅓ cup PARKAY® Margarine
½ cup chopped pecans

Preheat oven to 350°F.

On lightly floured surface, roll pastry into 12-inch circle.
Place in 10-inch quiche dish or tart pan with removable
bottom. Trim edges of pastry even with top of dish.
Prick bottom and sides of pastry with fork. Bake
15 minutes.

Beat cream cheese, ⅓ cup sugar and vanilla in large
mixing bowl at medium speed with electric mixer until
well blended. Add egg; mix well. Blend in sour cream.
Pour into crust. Top evenly with apples.

Mix together flour, ¼ cup sugar and cinnamon in
medium bowl; cut in margarine until mixture resembles
coarse crumbs. Stir in pecans; sprinkle over apples.

Bake 50 minutes. Cool. Garnish with cinnamon sticks
tied with orange peel, if desired.

Prep time: 30 minutes
Cook time: 65 minutes

COUNTRY CRUNCH RHUBARB PIE

Makes one 10-inch pie

CRUST
Baked 10-inch Classic CRISCO® *Single* Crust
(page 80), cooled

CRUNCH LAYER
1 cup chopped pecans
¼ cup all-purpose flour
¼ cup quick-cooking oats (not instant or
    old-fashioned), uncooked
¼ cup firmly packed brown sugar
¼ cup butter or margarine, softened
½ teaspoon ground cinnamon
¼ teaspoon ground nutmeg

FILLING
3½ cups fresh or frozen cut rhubarb (¼-to ½-inch
    pieces)
1½ cups granulated sugar
¼ cup all-purpose flour
2 tablespoons quick-cooking tapioca
1 tablespoon butter or margarine
½ teaspoon ground cinnamon
½ teaspoon ground nutmeg
2 eggs, lightly beaten
1 can (16 ounces) pitted red tart cherries packed
    in water, well drained

MERINGUE
3 egg whites
1 teaspoon cream of tartar
⅔ cup granulated sugar

1. Preheat oven to 350°F.

2. For Crunch Layer, combine nuts, ¼ cup flour, oats, brown sugar, ¼ cup butter, ½ teaspoon cinnamon and ¼ teaspoon nutmeg in medium bowl. Spread on baking sheet.

3. Bake at 350°F for 10 minutes, stirring several times. Cool. Break into small pieces. Place half of crunch mixture in bottom of baked pie crust. Set aside remaining crunch mixture.

4. For Filling, combine rhubarb, 1½ cups granulated sugar, ¼ cup flour, tapioca, 1 tablespoon butter, ½ teaspoon cinnamon and ½ teaspoon nutmeg in large saucepan. Cook and stir over medium heat until rhubarb begins to soften. Remove from heat. Stir small amount of hot mixture slowly into eggs, mixing thoroughly. Return mixture to saucepan. Cook and stir until mixture starts to thicken. Add cherries. Cook and stir until thickened. Cool slightly. Pour over crunch layer. Top with remaining crunch mixture.

5. For Meringue, beat egg whites and cream of tartar in medium bowl at high speed of electric mixer until foamy. Beat in ⅔ cup granulated sugar, 1 tablespoon at a time, until sugar is dissolved and stiff peaks form. Spoon over crunch layer, spreading to edge.

6. Bake at 350°F for 10 minutes or until meringue is lightly browned. Cool to room temperature before serving. Refrigerate leftover pie.

BLUEBERRY PIE

Makes 8 servings

Cream Cheese Pastry (recipe follows)
2 pints (4 cups) fresh or thawed unsweetened
    frozen blueberries
2 tablespoons cornstarch
⅔ cup no-sugar-added blueberry preserves, melted
¼ teaspoon ground nutmeg
1 egg yolk
1 tablespoon sour cream

Preheat oven to 425°F. Prepare Cream Cheese Pastry. On lightly floured surface or pastry cloth, roll out half of dough to 11-inch circle. Place in 9-inch pie plate; set aside.

Combine blueberries and cornstarch in medium bowl; toss lightly to coat. Add preserves and nutmeg; mix lightly. Spoon into crust. Roll out remaining dough to 11-inch circle; place over fruit mixture. Turn edges under; flute. Cut several slits or circle in top crust to allow steam to escape. If desired, cut leaves from pastry scraps to decorate top of pie.

Bake 10 minutes. Remove pie from oven. *Reduce oven temperature to 350°F.* Combine egg yolk and sour cream; brush lightly over crust. Return pie to oven; continue baking 40 minutes or until crust is golden brown. Cool on wire rack. Serve warm, at room temperature or chilled.

CREAM CHEESE PASTRY

1½ cups all-purpose flour
½ cup cold butter or margarine
3 ounces cream cheese, cubed
1 teaspoon vanilla

Place flour in large bowl. Cut in butter with pastry blender or two knives until mixture resembles coarse crumbs. Cut in cream cheese until mixture forms dough. Blend in vanilla.

Notes: Pastry can be prepared in food processor with steel blade attached.

This is a sugar-free dessert.

PATRIOTIC PIE

Makes 8 servings

CRUST
1 package DUNCAN HINES® Blueberry Muffin
Mix
¼ cup butter or margarine

FILLING
1 quart vanilla ice cream, softened (see Tip)
½ cup crumb mixture, reserved from Crust

TOPPING
Can of blueberries from Mix
1 pint fresh strawberries, rinsed, drained and sliced
2 tablespoons sugar (optional)

1. Preheat oven to 400°F. Grease 9-inch pie plate.

2. For Crust, place muffin mix in medium bowl. Stir
with fork to break into small crumbs. Cut in butter
with pastry blender or 2 knives until mixture is crumbly.
Sprinkle evenly in ungreased 9-inch square baking pan.
Do not press.

3. Bake at 400°F for 10 to 12 minutes. Stir. Cool slightly.
Reserve ½ cup crumbs for filling. Press remaining crumbs
onto bottom and up side of 9-inch pie plate to form
crust. Cool completely.

3. For Filling, spread ice cream over crust. Sprinkle
with reserved crumbs. Freeze several hours or until firm.

4. For Topping, rinse blueberries from Mix with cold
water and drain. Combine strawberries and sugar, if
desired.

5. To serve, let pie stand 5 minutes at room temperature.
Top with blueberries and strawberries. Cut into 8 wedges
using sharp knife.

Tip: Ice cream can be softened by allowing to stand
at room temperature for 15 minutes or placing in
refrigerator for 30 minutes.

BLUEBERRY CELEBRATION PIE

Makes one 9-inch pie

CRUST
Baked and cooled 9-inch Classic CRISCO®
Single Crust (page 80), prepared with
2 tablespoons finely chopped, blanched
almonds added to flour mixture

BLUEBERRY FILLING
2 cups fresh or thawed frozen blueberries, divided
2 tablespoons cornstarch
2 tablespoons granulated sugar
1 tablespoon grated lemon peel
1 tablespoon lemon juice
2 tablespoons butter or margarine
2 teaspoons creme de cassis liqueur (optional)

ALMOND FILLING
6 bars (1¼ ounces each) white chocolate candy bars
with almonds
1 egg yolk*
2 tablespoons water
¼ teaspoon vanilla
⅛ teaspoon almond extract
2 tablespoons confectioners sugar
1 cup whipping cream, whipped

WHIPPED CREAM LAYER
1 cup whipping cream
¼ cup confectioners sugar
¼ teaspoon vanilla

1. For Blueberry Filling, place 1 cup blueberries in
medium saucepan. Combine cornstarch, granulated
sugar, lemon peel and lemon juice. Add to saucepan.
Cook over low heat, mashing blueberries and stirring
until thickened and clear. Add remaining 1 cup
blueberries, butter and cassis, if desired. Cool slightly.
Spoon into baked pie crust.

2. For Almond Filling, break up candy bars and place
in small saucepan. Melt candy bars over low heat, stirring
constantly. Combine egg yolk and water; add to melted
candy bars. Blend well. Cool. Stir in ¼ teaspoon vanilla
and the almond extract.

3. Beat 2 tablespoons confectioners sugar into whipped
cream. Stir a few spoonfuls into candy bar mixture. Fold
in remaining sweetened whipped cream. Spread evenly
over blueberry layer.

4. For Whipped Cream Layer, combine whipping
cream, ¼ cup confectioners sugar and ¼ teaspoon vanilla
in small bowl. Beat at high speed of electric mixer until
stiff. Spread over almond filling. Garnish as desired.

*Use clean, uncracked egg.

Patriotic Pie

PEACHES AND CREAM PIE

Makes one 9-inch pie

CRUST
Unbaked 9-inch Classic CRISCO® *Double* Crust
(page 80)
1 egg white, lightly beaten
Granulated sugar

NUT LAYER
½ cup sliced natural almonds
2 teaspoons butter or margarine

FILLING
1 package (8 ounces) cream cheese, softened
1 cup confectioners sugar
1 teaspoon vanilla
1 cup whipping cream, whipped

TOPPING AND GLAZE
3½ cups sliced, peeled fresh peaches* (about
     2 pounds or 5 to 6 medium), divided
1 tablespoon lemon juice
½ cup granulated sugar
2 tablespoons cornstarch

1. For Crust, preheat oven to 425°F. Press bottom crust into 9-inch pie plate; set aside. Roll out second half and cut out small leaf shapes using cookie cutter. Place around edge of pie crust. Brush with egg white; sprinkle with granulated sugar. Thoroughly prick bottom and sides with fork (50 times) to prevent shrinkage. Cover with plastic wrap and freeze 10 minutes.

2. Remove plastic wrap and bake pie crust 10 to 15 minutes or until lightly browned. Cool. *Increase oven temperature to 450°F.*

3. For Nut Layer, place nuts and butter in baking pan. Bake at 450°F until golden brown, stirring often. Cool. Sprinkle nut mixture over bottom of baked and cooled pie crust.

4. For Filling, combine cream cheese, confectioners sugar and vanilla in medium bowl. Beat at medium speed of electric mixer until well blended. Fold in whipped cream. Spoon over nuts in pie crust. Refrigerate 1 hour.

5. For Topping and Glaze, combine 1¾ cups peaches and lemon juice in blender. Blend well. Combine ½ cup granulated sugar and cornstarch. Add to blender. Blend well. Pour mixture into small saucepan. Cook and stir on medium heat until mixture boils and thickens. Boil 1 minute. Remove from heat. Cool. Arrange remaining 1¾ cups peach slices on top of filling. Spoon glaze over peaches. Refrigerate until firm.

*Use 1 bag (20 ounces) frozen unsweetened freestone peach slices if fresh peaches are not available. Use half of package for glaze and half for topping.

Peaches and Cream Pie

ARIZONA'S SUPREME CITRUS PIE

Makes one 9- or 9½-inch deep-dish pie

CRUST
Baked 9-inch Classic CRISCO® *Single* Crust
(page 80), cooled

FLUFFY FILLING
1 package (8 ounces) cream cheese, softened
1 can (14 ounces) sweetened condensed milk
1 can (6 ounces) frozen lemonade concentrate,
     thawed
1 package (4-serving size) lemon flavor instant
     pudding and pie filling mix (not sugar-free)
1 cup whipping cream, whipped

CLEAR FILLING
½ cup cornstarch
⅓ cup water
4 egg yolks
½ cup fresh lemon juice
1½ cups granulated sugar
1½ cups water
1 tablespoon butter or margarine

TOPPING
1 cup whipping cream
2 tablespoons confectioners sugar
¾ teaspoon vanilla

1. For Fluffy Filling, combine cream cheese and sweetened condensed milk in large bowl. Beat at low speed of electric mixer until smooth. Add lemonade concentrate. Blend well. Beat in pudding mix until smooth. Fold in whipped cream. Spoon into baked pie crust. Make shallow depression in filling 1 inch from edge. Refrigerate.

3. For Clear Filling, combine cornstarch and ⅓ cup water in small bowl. Stir to blend. Combine egg yolks and lemon juice in medium bowl. Beat until smooth. Combine granulated sugar and 1½ cups water in medium saucepan. Cook over medium heat until mixture comes to a boil. Slowly stir in cornstarch mixture. Cook and stir until thickened and clear. Remove from heat. Slowly stir in egg yolk mixture until blended. Return to heat. Cook and stir 1 to 2 minutes or until mixture comes to a boil. Remove from heat. Stir in butter until blended. Cool completely. Spread gently in depression over fluffy filling.

4. For Topping, beat whipping cream in small bowl at high speed of electric mixer until stiff peaks form. Beat in confectioners sugar and vanilla. Spread over clear filling. Refrigerate until firm.

HEAVENLY CHOCOLATE CREAM PIES

Makes 2 pies, 16 servings

CRUST
  1 package DUNCAN HINES® Moist Deluxe Swiss Chocolate Cake Mix
  ¾ cup butter or margarine

1st LAYER
  1 package (8 ounces) cream cheese, softened
  1 cup confectioners sugar
  1 cup frozen non-dairy whipped topping, thawed

2nd LAYER
  2 packages (4-serving size each) chocolate instant pudding and pie filling mix
  3 cups cold milk

3rd LAYER
  2 cups frozen non-dairy whipped topping, thawed, divided
  Chocolate leaves, for garnish (optional)
  Mint leaves, for garnish (optional)

1. Preheat oven to 350°F. Grease two 9-inch pie plates.

2. For Crust, place cake mix in large bowl. Cut in butter using pastry blender or 2 knives until coarse crumbs form. Place half the crumbs in each plate. Press on bottom and up sides of each plate. Bake at 350°F for 15 minutes. Cool.

3. For 1st layer, combine cream cheese and confectioners sugar in small bowl. Beat at medium speed with electric mixer until smooth. Stir in 1 cup whipped topping. Spread half the mixture evenly over each crust. Refrigerate until set.

4. For 2nd layer, prepare pudding mixes following package directions, using 3 cups milk. Spoon half the pudding over cream cheese mixture in each plate. Refrigerate until set.

5. For 3rd layer, spread 1 cup whipped topping over pudding mixture in each plate. Refrigerate until ready to serve. Garnish with chocolate leaves and mint leaves, if desired.

Note: One container (8 ounces) frozen non-dairy whipped topping will be enough for recipe.

Tip: For Heavenly Lemon Cream Pies use DUNCAN HINES® Moist Deluxe Lemon Supreme Cake Mix in place of Swiss Chocolate Cake Mix and lemon instant pudding and pie filling mix in place of chocolate instant pudding and pie filling mix.

Heavenly Chocolate Cream Pies

Top to bottom: Pear Fans, Fruit in Cream

FRUIT IN CREAM

Vanilla Sauce (recipe page 261)
Assorted fruit*
Quick Chocolate Sauce (recipe follows)
Mint leaves (optional)

Spoon Vanilla Sauce onto each serving plate to cover bottom. Arrange fruit in sauce in center of plate. Swirl Quick Chocolate Sauce around outside edge of Vanilla Sauce to form design. Garnish with mint leaves, if desired.

*We suggest any variety of berries, mandarin orange sections, melon balls, halved seedless grapes, sliced peaches, kiwifruit or plums.

QUICK CHOCOLATE SAUCE

¾ cup light corn syrup
1 package (4-serving size) JELL-O® Instant Pudding and Pie Filling, Chocolate or Chocolate Fudge Flavor
¾ cup evaporated milk or half-and-half

Pour corn syrup into small bowl. Blend in pudding mix. Gradually add evaporated milk, stirring constantly. Let stand 10 minutes or until slightly thickened.

Makes about 2 cups

Note: Store leftover sauces in covered containers in refrigerator.

PEAR FANS

Canned pear halves, drained
Vanilla Sauce (recipe follows)
Berry Cream Sauce (recipe follows)
Cinnamon stick, cut into ¾-inch pieces (optional)
Mint leaves (optional)

Cut pear halves into thin slices with sharp knife, up to but not cutting through stem ends. Holding stem end in place, gently fan out slices from stem. Place pear fan in center of each plate. Spoon Vanilla Sauce around pears. Swirl Berry Cream Sauce around outside edge of Vanilla Sauce to form design. Place cinnamon stick piece and mint leaf at stem end of each pear, if desired.

VANILLA SAUCE

3½ cups cold half-and-half or milk
1 package (4-serving size) JELL-O® Instant Pudding and Pie Filling, French Vanilla or Vanilla Flavor

Pour half-and-half into medium bowl. Add pudding mix. Beat with wire whisk until well blended, 1 to 2 minutes. Let stand 10 minutes or until slightly thickened.

Makes 3½ cups

BERRY CREAM SAUCE

2 packages (10 ounces each) BIRDS EYE® Quick Thaw Red Raspberries or Strawberries, thawed
1½ cups cold half-and-half or milk
1 package (4-serving size) JELL-O® Instant Pudding and Pie Filling, French Vanilla or Vanilla Flavor

Process raspberries in food processor or blender until smooth; strain to remove seeds. Pour half-and-half into medium bowl. Add pudding mix. Beat with wire whisk until well blended, 1 to 2 minutes. Stir in raspberry purée. Let stand 10 minutes or until slightly thickened.

Makes 3½ cups

Note: Store leftover sauces in covered containers in refrigerator.

CHOCOLATE TRUFFLE LOAF WITH EASY RASPBERRY SAUCE

Makes 12 servings

2 cups whipping cream, divided
3 egg yolks
16 squares (1 ounce each) semisweet chocolate
½ cup KARO® Light or Dark Corn Syrup
½ cup MAZOLA® Margarine
¼ cup confectioners sugar
1 teaspoon vanilla
Easy Raspberry Sauce (recipe follows)

Line 9¼ × 5¼-inch loaf pan with plastic wrap. In small bowl, mix ½ cup cream with egg yolks. In large saucepan, combine chocolate, corn syrup and margarine; cook and stir over medium heat until melted. Add egg mixture. Cook 3 minutes over medium heat, stirring constantly. Cool to room temperature. In small bowl with mixer at medium speed, beat remaining 1½ cups cream, sugar and vanilla until soft peaks form. Gently fold into chocolate mixture just until combined. Pour into prepared pan; cover with plastic wrap. Refrigerate overnight or chill in freezer 3 hours. Invert onto serving dish; slice and serve with Easy Raspberry Sauce.

Easy Raspberry Sauce: In blender or food processor, blend 1 package (10 ounces) thawed frozen raspberries until smooth; strain to remove seeds. Stir in ⅓ cup KARO® Light Corn Syrup.

Prep time: 30 minutes, plus chilling.

Microwave Directions: Prepare loaf pan and egg mixture as above. In 3-quart microwavable bowl, mix chocolate, corn syrup and margarine. Microwave on HIGH (100% power) 2 to 2½ minutes or until chocolate is melted and mixture is smooth, stirring twice. Stir in egg mixture. Microwave 3 minutes on HIGH, stirring twice. Continue as above.

Chocolate Truffle Loaf with Easy Raspberry Sauce

ST. PATRICK'S DAY PARFAITS

Makes 6 servings

3 cups miniature marshmallows *or* 30 large
   marshmallows
½ cup milk
2 tablespoons green creme de menthe liqueur
1 cup HERSHEY₀S Semi-Sweet Chocolate Chips
¼ cup powdered sugar
1½ cups whipping cream

In medium saucepan over low heat, combine marshmallows and milk. Cook, stirring constantly, until marshmallows are melted and mixture is smooth. Measure 1 cup marshmallow mixture into small bowl. Blend in creme de menthe; set aside. Add chocolate chips and powdered sugar to remaining marshmallow mixture in saucepan. Return to low heat; stir until chips are melted. Remove from heat; cool to room temperature.

In small bowl, beat whipping cream until stiff; fold 1½ cups into mint mixture. Fold remaining whipped cream into chocolate mixture. Alternately spoon chocolate and mint mixtures into parfait glasses. Refrigerate or freeze. Garnish as desired.

St. Patrick's Day Parfaits

CHOCOLATE PASSION TRIFLE

Makes 16 servings

Semi-Sweet Chocolate Brownies (recipe page 244)
1 cup chopped toasted pecans, divided
2 tablespoons coffee-flavored liqueur, divided
2 cups cold half-and-half or milk
1 package (4-serving size) JELL-O® Chocolate
   Flavor Instant Pudding and Pie Filling
3½ cups (8 ounces) COOL WHIP® Non-Dairy
   Whipped Topping, thawed, divided
½ pint raspberries
4 (1.4-ounce) chocolate-covered English toffee
   bars, chopped

Prepare Semi-Sweet Chocolate Brownies as directed, substituting ½ cup pecans for the ⅓ cup nuts. Sprinkle warm baked brownies with 1 tablespoon liqueur. Cool in pan; cut into ½-inch squares.

Pour half-and-half into large bowl. Add pudding mix. Beat with wire whisk until well blended, about 2 minutes. Let stand 5 minutes. Gently stir in remaining 1 tablespoon liqueur and 2 cups whipped topping until well blended. Refrigerate 1 hour.

Reserve a few raspberries and pecans for garnish. Layer half *each* of the brownies, remaining raspberries, chopped toffee, remaining pecans and pudding mixture in 2-quart glass serving bowl; repeat layers. Garnish with remaining 1½ cups whipped topping, reserved raspberries and pecans. Cover; refrigerate at least 1 hour.

Prep time: 1 hour
Chill time: 2 hours

ORANGE CREAM TIMBALES

Makes 4 servings

1 package (4-serving size) JELL-O® Brand Orange
   Flavor Gelatin
1 cup boiling water
½ cup cold water
   Ice cubes
1¾ cups (4 ounces) COOL WHIP® Non-Dairy
   Whipped Topping, thawed, divided
1 can (11 ounces) mandarin orange sections, well
   drained
   Mint leaves (optional)

Completely dissolve gelatin in boiling water. Combine cold water and enough ice cubes to measure 1 cup. Add to gelatin, stirring until ice is melted. If necessary, place bowl in larger bowl of ice and water; let stand, stirring occasionally, until slightly thickened, about 5 minutes.

Fold 1⅓ cups whipped topping into gelatin mixture. Pour half the gelatin mixture evenly into 6 (6-ounce) custard cups, filling each cup about half full. Place dollop of remaining whipped topping in center of each dessert; press orange section into whipped topping. Fill cups with remaining gelatin mixture. Chill until firm, about 3 hours.

Place remaining orange sections in food processor or blender; cover. Process until smooth. Unmold gelatin cups onto individual dessert plates. Spoon orange purée around desserts. Garnish with mint leaves, if desired. (Or, omit orange purée. Garnish desserts with whole orange sections and mint leaves.)

Prep time: 20 minutes
Chill time: 3 hours

STRAWBERRY-CHOCOLATE BAVARIAN CREAM

Makes 8 to 10 servings

1 package (10 ounces) frozen sliced strawberries, thawed*
2 envelopes unflavored gelatin
1 cup HERSHEY'S Semi-Sweet Chocolate Chips
½ cup sugar
2¼ cups milk, divided
1 teaspoon vanilla extract
1 cup (½ pint) cold whipping cream
Strawberry Cream (recipe follows)

Lightly oil 5- or 6-cup mold. Drain strawberries; reserve syrup. Add water to syrup to equal ¾ cup. Stir gelatin into syrup mixture; set aside. Refrigerate drained berries for Strawberry Cream.

In medium saucepan, combine chocolate chips, sugar and ½ cup milk; cook over low heat, stirring constantly, until chips are melted and mixture is smooth and very hot. Add gelatin mixture, stirring until gelatin is completely dissolved. Remove from heat; add remaining 1¾ cups milk and vanilla. Pour into large bowl; refrigerate, stirring occasionally, until mixture mounds when dropped from a spoon.

Beat whipping cream until stiff; fold into chocolate mixture. Pour into prepared mold; refrigerate until firm. Unmold; garnish with Strawberry Cream.

*One cup sweetened sliced fresh strawberries may be substituted for frozen.

Strawberry Cream: Mash or purée reserved strawberries to equal ½ cup. In small mixer bowl, beat 1 cup (½ pint) cold whipping cream and 1 teaspoon vanilla extract until stiff. Fold in strawberry purée and 2 to 3 drops red food color.

Charlotte Russe

CHARLOTTE RUSSE

Makes 10 servings

2 packages (4-serving size each) or 1 package (8-serving size) JELL-O® Brand Gelatin, any red flavor
2 cups boiling water
1 quart vanilla ice cream, softened
12 ladyfingers, split
COOL WHIP® Non-Dairy Whipped Topping, thawed (optional)
Fresh raspberries (optional)
Mint leaves (optional)

Completely dissolve gelatin in boiling water. Spoon in ice cream, stirring until melted and smooth. Chill until thickened but not set.

Trim about 1 inch off one end of each ladyfinger; reserve trimmed ends for snacking or other use. Vertically place ladyfingers, cut-ends-down, around sides of 8-inch springform pan. Spoon gelatin mixture into pan. Chill until firm, about 3 hours. Remove sides of pan. Garnish with whipped topping, raspberries and mint leaves, if desired.

Prep time: 20 minutes
Chill time: 3 hours

Chocolate Mint Baked Alaska

CHOCOLATE MINT BAKED ALASKA

Makes one baked Alaska

CRUST:
1½ cups (10-ounce package) NESTLÉ® Toll House® Mint-Flavored Semi-Sweet Chocolate Morsels, divided
3 tablespoons butter
1¼ cups chocolate wafer crumbs

FILLING:
2 tablespoons corn syrup
2 tablespoons whipping cream
3 pints vanilla ice cream, softened

MERINGUE:
4 egg whites
½ teaspoon cream of tartar
¾ cup sugar

Crust: Combine over hot (not boiling) water, ½ cup Nestlé® Toll House® Mint-Flavored Semi-Sweet Chocolate Morsels and butter. Stir until morsels are melted and mixture is smooth. Add chocolate wafer crumbs; stir until well blended. Press into bottom of 9-inch springform pan; freeze until firm.

Filling: Combine over hot (not boiling) water, remaining 1 cup Nestlé® Toll House® Mint-Flavored Semi-Sweet Chocolate Morsels, corn syrup and cream. Stir until morsels are melted and mixture is smooth. Cool to room temperature. In large bowl, beat ice cream until smooth but not melted. Gradually stir in chocolate mixture (flecks will appear in ice cream). Spoon into center of crust, spreading to within ¾ inch of edge and mounding high in center. Using spatula, smooth to form dome. Freeze until firm.

Meringue: In large bowl, combine egg whites and cream of tartar; beat until soft peaks form. Gradually add sugar; beat until stiff peaks form.

Preheat oven to 450°F. Remove sides of pan. Spread meringue over filling and crust to cover completely; swirl to decorate.

Bake for 4 to 6 minutes or until lightly browned. Serve immediately.

MINTED GRAPEFRUIT ICE

Makes 10 to 12 servings

½ cup *plus* 1 tablespoon sugar, divided
1½ teaspoons unflavored gelatin
½ cup water
1 teaspoon dried mint leaves, crushed
3 cups Florida grapefruit juice
1 egg white*

In small saucepan, mix ½ cup sugar and gelatin. Add water and mint; stir. Let stand 1 minute. Bring to a boil over medium heat, stirring constantly, until gelatin dissolves. Remove from heat. Cover; let stand 10 minutes.

Pour grapefruit juice into large metal bowl. Strain gelatin mixture into grapefruit juice through a very fine sieve or several layers of cheesecloth to remove mint leaves. Stir.

Freeze 3 hours or until ice crystals form, 2 inches deep, around edge of bowl. Mix well with wire whisk to break up crystals. Freeze 1½ to 2 hours longer or until firm.

With electric mixer, beat egg white until soft peaks form. Add remaining 1 tablespoon sugar; beat until stiff peaks form. Beat grapefruit ice until smooth; fold in beaten egg white mixture. Freeze 1 hour. Stir and freeze until firm.

*Use only Grade A clean, uncracked egg.

Favorite recipe from **Florida Department of Citrus**

FROZEN PASSION

Makes 2 to 3 quarts

2 (14-ounce) cans EAGLE® Brand Sweetened
  Condensed Milk (NOT evaporated milk)
1 (2-liter) bottle *or* 5 (12-ounce) cans carbonated
  beverage, any flavor
Chocolate Ice Cream Cups (recipe follows)

In ice cream freezer container, combine all ingredients
except Chocolate Ice Cream Cups; mix well. Freeze
according to manufacturer's instructions. Just before
serving, scoop into Chocolate Ice Cream Cups. Freeze
leftovers.

CHOCOLATE ICE CREAM CUPS

2 cups (12 ounces) semi-sweet chocolate chips
1 (14-ounce) can EAGLE® Brand Sweetened
  ` Condensed Milk (NOT evaporated milk)
1 cup finely ground nuts
1 teaspoon vanilla extract

In small saucepan, over low heat, melt chips with
sweetened condensed milk, stirring frequently, until
chips are melted and mixture is smooth. Remove from
heat. Stir in nuts and vanilla. In 2½-inch foil-lined muffin
cups, spread about 2 tablespoons chocolate mixture on
bottom and up side to rim of each cup with spoon. Freeze
2 hours or until firm. Before filling, remove foil liners.
Store unfilled cups tightly covered in freezer.

Makes about 1½ dozen

HOT CHOCOLATE SOUFFLÉ

Makes 8 to 10 servings

¾ cup HERSHEY'S Cocoa
1 cup sugar, divided
½ cup all-purpose flour
¼ teaspoon salt
2 cups milk
6 egg yolks, well beaten
2 tablespoons butter or margarine
1 teaspoon vanilla extract
8 egg whites
¼ teaspoon cream of tartar
  Sweetened whipped cream

Adjust oven rack to lowest position. Preheat oven to
350°F. Lightly butter 2½-quart soufflé dish; sprinkle
with sugar. For collar, cut a length of heavy-duty
aluminum foil to fit around soufflé dish; fold in thirds
lengthwise. Lightly butter one side. Attach foil, buttered
side in, around outside of dish allowing foil to extend at
least 2 inches above dish. Secure foil with tape or string.

In large saucepan, stir together cocoa, ¾ cup sugar, flour
and salt; gradually stir in milk. Cook over medium heat,
stirring constantly with wire whisk, until mixture boils;
remove from heat. Gradually stir small amount of
chocolate mixture into beaten egg yolks; blend well.
Add egg mixture to chocolate mixture in pan, blending
well. Cook and stir 1 minute. Add butter and vanilla,
stirring until blended. Set aside; cool 20 minutes. In
large mixer bowl, beat egg whites with cream of tartar
until soft peaks form; gradually add remaining ¼ cup
sugar, beating until stiff peaks form. Gently fold about one-
third of beaten egg white mixture into chocolate mixture.
Lightly fold chocolate mixture, half at a time, into
remaining beaten egg white mixture just until blended;
do not overfold.

Gently pour mixture into prepared dish; smooth top
with spatula. Gently place dish in larger baking pan;
pour hot water into larger pan to depth of 1 inch.

Bake 65 to 70 minutes or until puffed and set. Remove
soufflé dish from water. Carefully remove foil. Serve
immediately with sweetened whipped cream.

Hot Chocolate Soufflé

ALMOND RICE MADELEINES

Makes about 3 dozen madeleines

Nonstick cooking spray
1 cup whole blanched almonds, lightly toasted
1½ cups sugar
¾ cup flaked coconut
3 cups cooked rice, chilled
3 egg whites
Fresh raspberries (optional)
Frozen nondairy whipped topping, thawed (optional)
Powdered sugar (optional)

Preheat oven to 350°F. Coat madeleine pans* with nonstick cooking spray. Place almonds in food processor; process until finely ground. Add sugar and coconut to processor; process until coconut is finely minced. Add rice; pulse to blend. Add egg whites; pulse to blend. Spoon mixture evenly into madeleine pans, filling to tops.

Bake 25 to 30 minutes or until lightly browned. Cool completely in pans on wire racks. Cover and refrigerate 2 hours before serving. Run a sharp knife around each madeleine and gently invert onto serving plates. Serve with raspberries and whipped topping, if desired. Sprinkle with powdered sugar, if desired.

*You may substitute miniature muffin pans for the madeleine pans, if desired.

Favorite recipe from **USA Rice Council**

AUSTRIAN TEA COOKIES

Makes about 3½ dozen cookies

1½ cups sugar, divided
½ cup butter, softened
½ cup vegetable shortening
1 egg, beaten
½ teaspoon vanilla extract
2 cups all-purpose flour
2 cups HONEY ALMOND DELIGHT® Brand Cereal, crushed to 1 cup
½ teaspoon baking powder
¼ teaspoon ground cinnamon
14 ounces almond paste
2 egg whites
5 tablespoons raspberry or apricot jam, warmed

In large bowl, beat 1 cup sugar, butter and shortening until well blended. Add egg and vanilla; mix well. Stir in flour, cereal, baking powder and cinnamon until well blended. Cover; refrigerate 1 to 2 hours or until firm.

Preheat oven to 350°F. Roll out dough on lightly floured surface to ¼-inch thickness; cut into 2-inch circles with floured cookie cutter. Place 2 inches apart on ungreased cookie sheet; set aside. In small bowl, beat almond paste, egg whites and remaining ½ cup sugar until smooth. With pastry tube fitted with medium-sized star tip, pipe almond paste mixture ½ inch thick on top of each cookie along outside edge. Place ¼ teaspoon jam in center of each cookie, spreading out to almond paste border.

Bake 8 to 10 minutes or until lightly browned. Let stand 1 minute on cookie sheet. Remove to wire rack; cool completely.

RASPBERRY ALMOND SANDWICH COOKIES

Makes 4½ to 5 dozen sandwich cookies

1 package DUNCAN HINES® Golden Sugar Cookie Mix
1 egg
1 tablespoon water
½ teaspoon almond extract
¾ cup sliced natural almonds, broken
Seedless red raspberry jam

1. Preheat oven to 375°F.

2. Combine cookie mix, buttery flavor packet from Mix, egg, water and almond extract in large bowl. Stir until thoroughly blended. Drop half the dough by level measuring teaspoons 2 inches apart onto ungreased cookie sheets. (It is a small amount of dough but will spread during baking to 1½ to 1¾ inches.)

3. Place nuts on waxed paper. Drop remaining half of dough by level measuring teaspoons onto nuts. Place, almond-side-up, 2 inches apart on cookie sheets.

4. Bake both plain and almond cookies at 375°F for 6 minutes or until set but not browned. Cool 1 minute on cookie sheets. Remove to wire racks. Cool completely.

5. Spread bottoms of plain cookies with jam; top with almond cookies. Press together to make sandwiches. Store in airtight container.

Tip: For evenly baked cookies, place the cookie sheets in center of oven, not touching sides.

Almond Rice Madeleines

Heavenly Oatmeal Heart

3. Combine flour, baking soda and salt. Add gradually to creamed mixture at low speed. Mix until well blended. Stir in oats, 1 cup chocolate chips, 1 cup vanilla chips and nuts with spoon.

4. Place 3-inch heart-shaped cookie cutter on ungreased cookie sheet. Place ⅓ cup dough inside cutter. Press to edges and level. Remove cutter. Repeat to form remaining cookies, spacing 2½ inches apart.

5. Bake at 375°F for 9 minutes or until light golden brown. Cool on cookie sheet until slightly warm before removing to wire rack. Cool completely.

6. For Drizzle, place ½ cup chocolate chips and ½ cup vanilla chips in separate heavy resealable sandwich bags. Add ½ teaspoon Butter Flavor Crisco® to each bag. Seal. Microwave 1 bag at MEDIUM (50% power). Knead bag after 1 minute. Repeat until mixture is smooth (or melt by placing each in bowl of hot water). Repeat with remaining bag. Cut tiny piece off corner of each bag. Squeeze out and drizzle both mixtures over cookies. To serve, cut cookies in half, if desired.

HEAVENLY OATMEAL HEARTS

Makes about 2 dozen heart cookies

COOKIES
 1 cup plus 2 tablespoons BUTTER FLAVOR CRISCO®
 1 cup firmly packed brown sugar
 ½ cup granulated sugar
 2 eggs
 1 teaspoon vanilla
 1½ cups plus ⅓ cup all-purpose flour
 1½ teaspoons baking soda
 ¾ teaspoon salt
 3 cups rolled oats, uncooked
 1 cup milk chocolate chips
 1 cup vanilla chips
 1 cup plus 2 tablespoons cinnamon-roasted peanuts,* chopped

DRIZZLE
 ½ cup milk chocolate chips
 ½ cup vanilla chips
 1 teaspoon BUTTER FLAVOR CRISCO®, divided

1. Preheat oven to 375°F.

2. For Cookies, combine 1 cup plus 2 tablespoons Butter Flavor Crisco®, brown sugar and granulated sugar in large bowl. Beat at medium speed of electric mixer until light and fluffy. Beat in eggs and vanilla until creamy.

*Substitute honey-roasted peanuts combined with 1½ teaspoons ground cinnamon if cinnamon-roasted peanuts are unavailable.

GREETING CARD COOKIES

Makes about 1 dozen cookies

 ½ cup (1 stick) butter or margarine, softened
 ¾ cup sugar
 1 egg
 1 teaspoon vanilla extract
 1½ cups all-purpose flour
 ⅓ cup HERSHEY®S Cocoa
 ½ teaspoon baking powder
 ½ teaspoon baking soda
 ¼ teaspoon salt
 Decorative Frosting (recipe follows)

In large mixer bowl, beat butter, sugar, egg and vanilla until light and fluffy. Stir together flour, cocoa, baking powder, baking soda and salt; add to butter mixture, blending well. Refrigerate about 1 hour or until firm enough to roll.

Preheat oven to 350°F. Cut cardboard rectangle for pattern, 4 × 2¼ inches; wrap in plastic wrap. On lightly floured board or between two pieces of waxed paper, roll out half of dough to ¼-inch thickness. For each cookie, place pattern on dough; cut through dough around pattern with sharp paring knife. (Save dough trimmings and reroll for remaining cookies.) Carefully place 2 inches apart on lightly greased cookie sheet.

Bake 8 to 10 minutes or until set. Cool 1 minute on cookie sheet. (If cookies have lost their shape, trim irregular edges while cookies are still hot.) Carefully transfer to wire rack. Cool completely. Repeat procedure with remaining dough. Prepare Decorative Frosting; spoon into pastry bag fitted with decorating tip. Pipe names or greetings onto cookies; decorate as desired.

Decorative Frosting: In small mixer bowl, beat 3 cups powdered sugar and ⅓ cup shortening; gradually add 2 to 3 tablespoons milk, beating until smooth and slightly thickened. Divide frosting and tint with red or green food color as desired. Cover until ready to use.

CHOCOLATE CHIP RUGALACH

Makes 4 dozen pieces

1 cup (2 sticks) butter or margarine, slightly
    softened
2 cups all-purpose flour
1 cup vanilla ice cream, softened
½ cup strawberry jam, divided
1 cup BAKER'S® Semi-Sweet Real Chocolate
    Chips, divided
1 cup finely chopped nuts, divided
    Powdered sugar (optional)

Beat butter and flour in large bowl until well blended. Beat in ice cream until well blended. Divide dough into 4 balls; wrap each in waxed paper. Refrigerate until firm, about 1 hour.

Preheat oven to 350°F. Roll dough, one ball at a time, on floured surface into 11 × 6-inch rectangle, about ⅛ inch thick. Spread with 2 tablespoons jam; sprinkle with ¼ cup chips and ¼ cup nuts. Starting at short end, roll up jelly-roll fashion. Place on ungreased cookie sheet. Cut 12 diagonal slits in roll, being careful not to cut all the way through. Repeat with remaining dough, jam, chips and nuts.

Bake for 35 minutes or until golden brown. Cool 5 minutes on cookie sheet. Cut through each roll; separate pieces. Cool completely on wire racks. Sprinkle with powdered sugar, if desired.

Prep time: 30 minutes
Chill time: 1 hour
Bake time: 35 minutes

ICE CREAM COOKIES

Makes about 8 dozen cookies

2 squares (1 ounce each) unsweetened chocolate
1 cup butter, softened
1 cup powdered sugar
4 egg yolks
1 teaspoon vanilla
3 cups all-purpose flour
    Additional powdered sugar

Melt chocolate in top of double boiler over hot, not boiling, water. Remove from heat; cool. Beat butter and 1 cup sugar in large bowl until blended. Add egg yolks, vanilla and melted chocolate; beat until light. Blend in flour to make stiff dough. Divide dough into 4 parts. Shape each part into a roll, about 1½ inches in diameter. Wrap in plastic wrap; refrigerate until firm, at least 30 minutes or up to 2 weeks. (For longer storage, freeze up to 6 weeks.)

Preheat oven to 350°F. Line cookie sheets with parchment paper or leave ungreased. Cut rolls into ⅛-inch-thick slices; place 2 inches apart on prepared cookie sheets. Bake 8 to 10 minutes or just until set, but not browned. Cool on wire racks. Dust with powdered sugar.

Ice Cream Cookie Sandwiches: Prepare and bake cookies as directed; cool completely. Spread desired amount of softened ice cream on bottoms of half the cookies. Top with remaining cookies, bottom sides down, forming sandwiches. Dust tops with powdered sugar; serve immediately.

Makes about 4 dozen sandwich cookies

Ice Cream Cookie Sandwiches

CHOCOLATE CHIPS THUMBPRINT COOKIES

Makes about 2½ dozen cookies

1 cup HERSHEY'S Semi-Sweet Chocolate Chips, divided
¼ cup shortening
¼ cup (1 stick) butter or margarine, softened
½ cup sugar
1 egg, separated
½ teaspoon vanilla extract
1 cup all-purpose flour
¼ teaspoon salt
1 cup finely chopped nuts

Preheat oven to 350°F. In small microwave-safe bowl, place ¼ cup chocolate chips. Microwave at HIGH (100% power) 20 to 30 seconds or just until chocolate is melted and smooth when stirred; set aside to cool slightly. In large mixer bowl, blend shortening, butter, sugar, melted chocolate, egg yolk and vanilla; stir in flour and salt. Shape dough into 1-inch balls. With fork, slightly beat egg white. Dip each ball into egg white; roll in chopped nuts. Place balls about 1 inch apart on ungreased cookie sheet. Press thumb in center of each ball to make indentation.

Bake 10 to 12 minutes or until set. Remove from oven; immediately place several chocolate chips in center of each cookie. Carefully remove from cookie sheet to wire rack. After several minutes, swirl melted chocolate in each thumbprint. Cool completely.

Chocolate Chips Thumbprint Cookies

CHOCOLATE NUT SLICES

Makes about 2½ dozen cookies

COOKIES
¾ cup BUTTER FLAVOR CRISCO®
½ cup granulated sugar
⅓ cup firmly packed brown sugar
2 tablespoons milk
1½ teaspoons vanilla
1 egg
1¼ cups all-purpose flour
⅓ cup unsweetened cocoa powder
½ teaspoon baking soda
½ teaspoon salt
¾ cup coarsely chopped pecans
½ cup semisweet chocolate chips

DRIZZLE
½ teaspoon BUTTER FLAVOR CRISCO®
½ cup chopped white confectionery coating
Chopped pecans (optional)

1. Preheat oven to 350°F.

2. For Cookies, combine ¾ cup Butter Flavor Crisco®, granulated sugar, brown sugar, milk and vanilla in large bowl. Beat at medium speed of electric mixer until well blended and creamy. Beat in egg.

3. Combine flour, cocoa, baking soda and salt. Mix into creamed mixture at low speed until blended. Stir in nuts and chocolate chips.

4. Divide dough into 4 equal portions. Form each into 8 × 1-inch roll on waxed paper. Pick up ends of waxed paper and roll dough back and forth to get a nicely shaped roll. Place rolls 3 inches apart on ungreased cookie sheet.

5. Bake 10 minutes or until set. Cool on cookie sheet.

6. For Drizzle, combine ½ teaspoon Butter Flavor Crisco® and white confectionery coating in microwave-safe cup. Microwave at MEDIUM (50% power). Stir after 1 minute. Repeat until smooth (or melt on range top in small saucepan on very low heat). Drizzle back and forth over cooled cookie rolls. Sprinkle with nuts before drizzle hardens, if desired.

7. Cut diagonally into 1-inch slices.

Chocolate-Raspberry Kolachy

off

SPECIAL OCCASIONS

Preheat oven to 375°F. Lightly grease cookie sheets; set aside.

Roll each dough disc on well-floured surface with stockinette-covered rolling pin to ¼- to ⅛-inch thickness. Cut out with 3-inch round cookie cutter. Place 2 inches apart on prepared cookie sheets. Place rounded ½ teaspoon jam in center of each circle. Bring three edges of dough circles up over jam; pinch edges together to seal, leaving center of triangle slightly open.

Bake 10 minutes or until set. Let cookies stand on cookie sheets 2 minutes. Remove cookies with spatula to wire racks; cool completely. Just before serving, sprinkle with powdered sugar. Store tightly covered in refrigerator; let stand for 30 minutes at room temperature before serving.

Note: These cookies do not freeze well.

Chocolate-Raspberry Kolachy Cups: Fit dough circles into greased mini-muffin cups; fill with a heaping teaspoon of jam. Bake 10 minutes or until set. Cool completely in muffin pans on wire rack. Remove cups and dust with powdered sugar before serving.

CHOCOLATE-RASPBERRY KOLACHY

Makes about 1½ dozen cookies

2 squares (1 ounce each) semisweet chocolate, coarsely chopped
1½ cups all-purpose flour
¼ teaspoon baking soda
¼ teaspoon salt
½ cup butter or margarine, softened
3 ounces cream cheese or light cream cheese, softened
⅓ cup granulated sugar
1 teaspoon vanilla
Seedless raspberry jam
Powdered sugar

Place chocolate in 1-cup glass measure. Microwave at HIGH (100% power) 1 to 2 minutes or until chocolate is melted, stirring after 1 minute; set aside.

Combine flour, baking soda and salt in small bowl; stir well. Beat butter and cream cheese in large bowl with electric mixer at medium speed until well blended, scraping down side of bowl occasionally. Beat in granulated sugar until light and fluffy, scraping down side of bowl once. Beat in vanilla and chocolate. Gradually add flour mixture. Beat at low speed, scraping down side of bowl once. Divide dough in half; flatten each half into a disc. Wrap separately in plastic wrap. Refrigerate until firm, 1 to 2 hours.

CHOCOLATE-DIPPED ALMOND HORNS

Makes about 16 cookies

1 can SOLO® Almond Paste
3 egg whites
½ cup superfine sugar
½ teaspoon almond extract
¼ cup plus 2 tablespoons all-purpose flour
½ cup sliced almonds
5 squares (1 ounce each) semisweet chocolate, melted and cooled

Preheat oven to 350°F. Grease 2 cookie sheets; set aside. Break almond paste into small pieces and place in medium bowl or food processor container. Add egg whites, sugar and almond extract. Beat with electric mixer or process until mixture is very smooth. Add flour and beat or process until blended.

Spoon almond mixture into pastry bag fitted with ½-inch (#8) plain tip. Pipe mixture into 5- or 6-inch crescent shapes on prepared cookie sheets, about 1½ inches apart. Sprinkle with sliced almonds.

Bake 13 to 15 minutes or until edges are golden brown. Cool on cookie sheets on wire racks 2 minutes. Remove from cookie sheets and cool completely on wire racks. Dip ends of cookies in melted chocolate and place on aluminum foil. Let stand until chocolate is set.

off

271

PINWHEELS AND CHECKERBOARDS

Makes about 2½ dozen cookies

2 cups all-purpose flour
1 teaspoon CALUMET® Baking Powder
½ teaspoon salt
⅔ cup butter or margarine, softened
1 cup sugar
1 egg
1 teaspoon vanilla
2 squares BAKER'S® Unsweetened Chocolate, melted

Mix flour, baking powder and salt in small bowl; set aside. Beat butter in large bowl until light and fluffy. Gradually add sugar and continue beating until well blended. Add egg and vanilla; beat well. Gradually add flour mixture, mixing well after each addition. Divide dough in half; blend chocolate into one half. Use prepared doughs to make Pinwheels or Checkerboards.

Pinwheels: Roll chocolate and vanilla doughs separately between sheets of waxed paper into 12 × 8-inch rectangles. Remove top sheets of paper and invert vanilla dough onto chocolate dough. Remove remaining paper. Starting at short end, roll up jelly-roll fashion; wrap in waxed paper. Refrigerate until firm, at least 3 hours (or freeze 1 hour).

Preheat oven to 375°F. Cut roll into ¼-inch slices, using very sharp knife. Place 2 inches apart on cookie sheets. Bake 10 minutes or until cookies just begin to brown around edges. Cool on wire racks.

Checkerboards: Put small amount of milk in bowl. Roll chocolate and vanilla doughs separately on lightly floured surface into 9 × 4½-inch rectangles. Brush chocolate dough lightly with milk and top with vanilla dough. Using long sharp knife, cut lengthwise into 3 strips, 1½ inches wide. Stack strips, alternating colors and brushing each layer with milk. Cut lengthwise again into 3 strips, ½ inch wide. Invert middle section so that colors alternate; brush sides with milk. Press strips together lightly to form a rectangle. Wrap in waxed paper. Refrigerate overnight.

Preheat oven to 375°F. Cut roll into ¼-inch slices, using very sharp knife. Place on cookie sheets. Bake 8 minutes or just until white portions begin to brown. Cool on wire racks.

Mint Chocolate Pinwheels

MINT CHOCOLATE PINWHEELS

Makes about 3 dozen cookies

1¼ cups all-purpose flour
1 teaspoon baking powder
½ teaspoon salt
⅔ cup butter or margarine, softened
1 cup sugar
1 large egg
1 teaspoon vanilla
1 cup quick-cooking oats, uncooked
1 cup mint chocolate chips

Combine flour, baking powder and salt in small bowl; stir well. Beat butter and sugar in large bowl with electric mixer at medium speed until light and fluffy, scraping down side of bowl once. Add egg and vanilla; beat well, scraping down side of bowl once. Gradually add flour mixture. Beat at low speed, scraping down side of bowl once. Stir in oats with wooden spoon.

Place mint chocolate chips in 1-cup glass measure. Microwave at HIGH (100% power) about 2 minutes or until melted, stirring after 1½ minutes.

Divide cookie dough in half. Add melted chocolate to one half; mix well.

Roll out each half of dough between two sheets of waxed paper into 15 × 10-inch rectangles. Remove waxed paper from top of each rectangle. Place chocolate dough over plain dough; remove bottom sheet of waxed paper from chocolate dough. Using bottom sheet of waxed paper as a guide, starting at long side, tightly roll up dough jelly-roll fashion, removing waxed paper while rolling.

Wrap dough roll in plastic wrap; refrigerate at least 2 hours or up to 24 hours.

Preheat oven to 350°F. Lightly grease cookie sheets. Unwrap roll. With long, sharp knife, cut dough into ¼-inch slices. Place 3 inches apart on prepared cookie sheets.

Bake 10 to 12 minutes or until set. Remove cookies with spatula to wire racks; cool completely. Store tightly covered at room temperature or freeze up to 3 months.

DOUBLE-DIPPED CHOCOLATE PEANUT BUTTER COOKIES

Makes about 2 dozen cookies

1¼ cups all-purpose flour
½ teaspoon baking powder
½ teaspoon baking soda
½ teaspoon salt
½ cup butter or margarine, softened
½ cup granulated sugar
½ cup firmly packed light brown sugar
½ cup creamy or chunky peanut butter
1 large egg
1 teaspoon vanilla
   Additional granulated sugar
1½ cups semisweet chocolate chips
3 teaspoons shortening, divided
1½ cups milk chocolate chips

Preheat oven to 350°F.

Combine flour, baking powder, baking soda and salt in small bowl; stir well. Beat butter, ½ cup granulated sugar and brown sugar in large bowl with electric mixer at medium speed until light and fluffy, scraping down side of bowl once. Beat in peanut butter, egg and vanilla, scraping down side of bowl once. Gradually stir in flour mixture with wooden spoon, blending well.

Roll heaping tablespoonfuls of dough into 1½-inch balls. Place balls 2 inches apart on ungreased cookie sheets. (If dough is too soft to roll into balls, refrigerate 30 minutes.) Dip fork into additional granulated sugar; press criss-cross fashion into each ball, flattening to ½-inch thickness.

Bake 12 minutes or until set. Let cookies stand on cookie sheets 2 minutes. Remove cookies with spatula to wire racks; cool completely.

Melt semisweet chocolate chips and 1½ teaspoons shortening in top of double boiler over hot, not boiling, water. Dip one end of each cookie one third the way up; place on waxed paper. Let stand until chocolate is set, about 30 minutes.

Melt milk chocolate chips with remaining 1½ teaspoons shortening in top of double boiler over hot, not boiling, water. Dip undipped end of each cookie one third the way up; place on waxed paper. Let stand until chocolate is set, about 30 minutes. Store cookies between sheets of waxed paper at cool room temperature or freeze up to 3 months.

Double-Dipped Chocolate Peanut Butter Cookies

CHOCOLATE-EDGED LACE COOKIES

Makes about 2½ dozen cookies

⅔ **cup ground almonds**
½ **cup butter**
½ **cup sugar**
⅓ **cup all-purpose flour**
2 **tablespoons whipping cream**
¼ **teaspoon salt**
4 **ounces dark sweet or bittersweet chocolate candy bar, broken into pieces**

Preheat oven to 375°F. Spread ground almonds onto baking sheet. Bake 5 minutes or until light golden brown and fragrant.

Combine butter, sugar, flour, cream and salt in medium, heavy saucepan. Add almonds; cook over medium heat, stirring constantly, about 5 minutes or until butter melts and small bubbles form around side of saucepan. Remove from heat; stir well. Drop rounded teaspoonfuls of batter 6 inches apart on greased cookie sheets. (Bake only 4 cookies per sheet.)

Bake 6 to 8 minutes or until cookies are deep golden brown around edges. Let cookies stand on cookie sheets 2 minutes. Remove cookies with spatula to wire rack;* cool completely.

Melt chocolate in small, heavy saucepan over low heat, stirring constantly. Tilt saucepan to pool chocolate at one end; dip edge of each cookie in chocolate, turning cookie slowly so entire edge is tinged with chocolate. Let cookies stand on waxed paper until chocolate is set. Store tightly covered at room temperature. Do not freeze.

*For tuile-shaped cookies, balance a wooden spoon over two cans of the same height. Working quickly when cookies are still hot, drape the cookies over the handle of the spoon so that both sides hang down and form a taco shape; cool completely. Dip both edges of cookies into chocolate.

CHOCOLATE-GILDED DANISH SUGAR CONES

Makes 16 cookies

½ **cup butter or margarine, softened**
½ **cup sugar**
½ **cup all-purpose flour**
2 **egg whites**
1 **teaspoon vanilla**
3 **ounces bittersweet chocolate** *or* ½ **cup semisweet chocolate chips**

Preheat oven to 400°F. Generously grease 4 cookie sheets.

Beat butter and sugar in large bowl until light and fluffy. Blend in flour. In clean, dry bowl, beat egg whites until frothy. Blend into butter mixture with vanilla. Place 4 mounds of dough 4 inches apart on each prepared cookie sheet. Spread mounds with small spatula dipped in water to 3-inch diameter.

Bake 1 sheet at a time 5 to 6 minutes or until edges are just barely golden. (Do not overbake or cookies become crisp too quickly and are difficult to shape.) Remove from oven and quickly loosen each cookie from cookie sheet with a thin spatula. Shape each cookie into a cone; cones will firm as they cool. (If cookies become too firm to shape, return to oven for a few seconds to soften.)

Melt chocolate in small bowl over hot water. Stir until smooth. When all cookies are baked and cooled, dip flared ends into melted chocolate; let stand on waxed paper until chocolate is set. If desired, serve cones by standing them in a bowl. (Adding about 1 inch of sugar to bottom of bowl may be necessary to hold them upright.)

CHOCOLATE-DIPPED BRANDY SNAPS

Makes about 3 dozen cookies

½ **cup butter**
½ **cup sugar**
⅓ **cup dark corn syrup**
½ **teaspoon ground cinnamon**
¼ **teaspoon ground ginger**
1 **cup all-purpose flour**
2 **teaspoons brandy**
1 **cup (6-ounce package) NESTLÉ® Toll House® Semi-Sweet Chocolate Morsels**
1 **tablespoon vegetable shortening**
⅓ **cup finely chopped nuts**

Preheat oven to 300°F. In medium, heavy saucepan, combine butter, sugar, dark corn syrup, cinnamon and ginger; cook over medium heat, stirring constantly, until melted and smooth. Remove from heat; stir in flour and brandy. Drop by rounded teaspoonfuls onto ungreased cookie sheets about 3 inches apart. (*Do not* bake more than 6 cookies at one time.)

Bake 10 to 14 minutes or until deep caramel color. Let stand on cookie sheets a few seconds. Remove from cookie sheets and immediately roll around wooden spoon handle; cool completely. Combine over hot (not boiling) water, Nestlé® Toll House® Semi-Sweet Chocolate Morsels and vegetable shortening; stir until morsels are melted and mixture is smooth. Dip cookies halfway into melted chocolate; shake off excess. Sprinkle with nuts; set on waxed paper-lined cookie sheets. Refrigerate 10 minutes or until chocolate is set. Store in airtight container in refrigerator.

Chocolate-Gilded Danish Sugar Cones

CHOCOLATE MACAROONS

Makes about 3 dozen cookies

12 ounces semisweet baking chocolate or
    chocolate chips
 1 can (8 ounces) almond paste
 2 large egg whites
½ cup powdered sugar
 2 tablespoons all-purpose flour
    Additional powdered sugar (optional)

Preheat oven to 300°F. Line cookie sheets with
parchment paper; set aside.

Melt chocolate in small, heavy saucepan over low heat,
stirring constantly; set aside. Beat almond paste, egg
whites and ½ cup sugar in large bowl with electric mixer
at medium speed for 1 minute, scraping down side of
bowl once. Beat in chocolate until well combined. Beat
in flour at low speed, scraping down side of bowl once.

Spoon dough into pastry tube fitted with rosette tip.
Pipe 1½-inch spirals 1 inch apart onto prepared cookie
sheets. (Pipe all dough at once; dough will get stiff
upon standing.)

Bake 20 minutes or until set. Carefully remove parchment
paper to countertop; cool completely. Peel cookies off
parchment paper. Place additional powdered sugar in
fine-mesh strainer; sprinkle over cookies, if desired.
Store tightly covered at room temperature or freeze up
to 3 months.

Chocolate Macaroons

CHOCOLATE-DIPPED
OAT COOKIES

Makes about 6 dozen cookies

 2 cups uncooked rolled oats
¾ cup firmly packed brown sugar
½ cup vegetable oil
½ cup finely chopped walnuts
 1 egg
 2 teaspoons grated orange peel
¼ teaspoon salt
 1 package (12 ounces) milk chocolate chips

Combine oats, sugar, oil, walnuts, egg, orange peel and
salt in large bowl until blended. Cover; refrigerate
overnight.

Preheat oven to 350°F. Lightly grease cookie sheets or
line with parchment paper. Melt chocolate chips in top
of double boiler over hot, not boiling, water; keep
warm. Shape oat mixture into large marble-sized balls.
Place 2 inches apart on prepared cookie sheets.

Bake 10 to 12 minutes or until golden and crisp. Cool
10 minutes on wire racks. Dip tops of cookies, one at a
time, into melted chocolate. Place on waxed paper; cool
until chocolate is set.

SPUMONI BARS

Makes 4 dozen cookies

¾ cup butter or margarine, softened
⅔ cup sugar
 3 egg yolks
 1 teaspoon vanilla
¼ teaspoon baking powder
⅛ teaspoon salt
 2 cups all-purpose flour
12 maraschino cherries, well drained and chopped
¼ cup chopped walnuts
¼ cup mint-flavored or plain semisweet chocolate
    chips
 2 teaspoons water, divided

Preheat oven to 350°F. Beat butter and sugar in large
bowl until blended. Beat in egg yolks, vanilla, baking
powder and salt until light. Stir in flour to make a stiff
dough. Divide dough into 3 equal parts; place each part
in small bowl. Add cherries and walnuts to one part,

Spumoni Bars, Chocolate Pistachio Fingers, Chocolate-Dipped Oat Cookies

blending well. Melt chocolate chips in small bowl over hot water. Stir until smooth. Add melted chocolate and 1 teaspoon water to second part, blending well. Stir remaining 1 teaspoon water into third part. (If doughs are soft, refrigerate 10 minutes.)

Divide each color of dough into 4 equal parts. Shape each part into a 6-inch rope by rolling on lightly floured surface. Place one rope of each color side by side on ungreased cookie sheet. Flatten ropes so they attach together making 1 strip of 3 colors. With rolling pin, roll strip directly on cookie sheet until it measures 12 × 3 inches. With straight edge of knife, score strip crosswise at 1 inch intervals. Repeat with remaining ropes to make a total of 4 tri-colored strips of dough.

Bake 12 to 13 minutes or until set but not completely browned. While cookies are still warm, trim lengthwise edges to make even. Cut into individual cookies along score marks. (Cookies will bake together but are easy to cut apart while still warm.) Cool on cookie sheets.

CHOCOLATE PISTACHIO FINGERS

Makes 8 dozen cookies

¾ cup butter or margarine, softened
⅓ cup sugar
3 ounces (about ⅓ cup) almond paste
1 egg yolk
1⅔ cups all-purpose flour
1 cup (6 ounces) semisweet chocolate chips
½ cup finely chopped natural pistachios

Preheat oven to 350°F. Line cookie sheets with parchment paper or lightly grease and dust with flour.

Beat butter and sugar in large bowl until blended. Add almond paste and egg yolk; beat until light. Blend in flour to make a smooth dough. (If dough is too soft to handle, cover and refrigerate until firm.) Turn out onto lightly floured surface. Divide into 8 equal pieces; divide each piece in half. Roll each half into a 12-inch rope; cut each rope into 2-inch lengths. Place 2 inches apart on prepared cookie sheets.

Bake 10 to 12 minutes or until edges just begin to brown. Remove to wire racks to cool. Melt chocolate chips in small bowl over hot water. Stir until smooth. Dip both ends of cookies about ½ inch into melted chocolate; dip chocolate ends into pistachios. Place on waxed paper; let stand until chocolate is set.

Clockwise from top right: Chocolate Macadamia Bars, Naomi's Revel Bars, Double Chocolate Crispy Bars

CHOCOLATE MACADAMIA BARS

Makes about 3 dozen bars

12 squares (1 ounce each) bittersweet chocolate *or* 1 package (12 ounces) semisweet chocolate chips
1 package (8 ounces) cream cheese
⅔ cup whipping cream *or* undiluted evaporated milk
1 cup chopped macadamia nuts or almonds
1 teaspoon vanilla, divided
1 cup butter or margarine, softened
1½ cups sugar
1 egg
3 cups all-purpose flour
1 teaspoon baking powder
¼ teaspoon salt

Preheat oven to 375°F. Lightly grease 13×9-inch pan.

Combine chocolate, cream cheese and cream in large heavy saucepan. Stir over low heat until chocolate is melted and mixture is smooth. Remove from heat; stir in nuts and ½ teaspoon vanilla.

Beat butter and sugar in large bowl. Beat in egg and remaining ½ teaspoon vanilla. Add flour, baking powder and salt, blending well. Press half of dough on bottom of prepared pan. Spread chocolate mixture evenly over top. Sprinkle remaining dough over chocolate mixture.

Bake 35 to 40 minutes or until golden brown. Cool in pan on wire rack. Cut into bars.

DOUBLE CHOCOLATE CRISPY BARS

Makes about 3 dozen bars

6 cups crispy rice cereal
½ cup peanut butter
⅓ cup butter or margarine
2 squares (1 ounce each) unsweetened chocolate
1 package (8 ounces) marshmallows
1 cup (6 ounces) semisweet chocolate chips *or* 6 ounces bittersweet chocolate, chopped
6 ounces white chocolate, chopped
2 teaspoons shortening, divided

Preheat oven to 350°F. Spread cereal on cookie sheet; toast in oven 10 minutes or until light brown. Place in large bowl. Line 13×9-inch pan with waxed paper.

Meanwhile, combine peanut butter, butter and unsweetened chocolate in large heavy saucepan. Stir over low heat until chocolate is melted. Add marshmallows; stir until melted and smooth. Pour chocolate mixture over cereal; mix until evenly coated. Press firmly into prepared pan.

Place semisweet chocolate and white chocolate into separate bowls. Add 1 teaspoon shortening to each bowl. Place bowls over very warm water; stir until chocolates are melted and mixtures are smooth. Spread top of cereal mixture with melted semisweet chocolate; cool until chocolate is set. Turn cereal mixture out of pan onto sheet of waxed paper, chocolate-side-down. Remove waxed paper from cereal mixture; spread white chocolate over surface. Cool until white chocolate is set. Cut into bars using sharp, thin knife.

NAOMI'S REVEL BARS

Makes about 3 dozen bars

1 cup plus 2 tablespoons butter or margarine, softened, divided
2 cups firmly packed brown sugar
2 eggs
2 teaspoons vanilla
2½ cups all-purpose flour
1 teaspoon baking soda
3 cups uncooked rolled oats
1 package (12 ounces) semisweet chocolate chips
1 can (14 ounces) sweetened condensed milk

Preheat oven to 325°F. Lightly grease 13×9-inch pan.

Beat 1 cup butter and sugar in large bowl. Add eggs; beat until light and creamy. Blend in vanilla. Combine flour and baking soda; stir into creamed mixture. Blend in oats. Spread ¾ of oat mixture evenly in prepared pan. Combine chocolate chips, milk and remaining 2 tablespoons butter in small heavy saucepan. Stir over low heat until chocolate is melted and mixture is smooth. Pour chocolate mixture evenly over mixture in pan. Dot with remaining oat mixture.

Bake 20 to 25 minutes or until oat mixture is browned. Cool in pan on wire rack. Cut into bars.

WALNUT CRUNCH BROWNIES

Makes about 2 dozen brownies

BROWNIE LAYER
4 squares BAKER'S® Unsweetened Chocolate
¾ cup (1½ sticks) margarine or butter
2 cups granulated sugar
4 eggs
1 teaspoon vanilla
1 cup all-purpose flour

WALNUT TOPPING
¼ cup (½ stick) margarine or butter
¾ cup firmly packed brown sugar
2 eggs
2 tablespoons all-purpose flour
1 teaspoon vanilla
4 cups chopped walnuts

Preheat oven to 350°F.

Microwave chocolate and ¾ cup margarine in large microwavable bowl on HIGH (100% power) 2 minutes or until margarine is melted. Stir until chocolate is completely melted.

Stir granulated sugar into melted chocolate mixture. Mix in 4 eggs and 1 teaspoon vanilla until well blended. Stir in 1 cup flour. Spread in greased 13×9-inch pan.

Microwave ¼ cup margarine and brown sugar in medium microwaveable bowl on HIGH 1 minute or until margarine is melted. Stir in 2 eggs, 2 tablespoons flour and 1 teaspoon vanilla until completely mixed. Stir in walnuts. Spread evenly over brownie batter.

Bake for 45 minutes or until wooden toothpick inserted into center comes out with fudgy crumbs. Do not overbake. Cool in pan on wire rack. Cut into squares.

Prep time: 20 minutes
Bake time: 45 minutes

Clockwise from top right: Peanut-Layered Brownies (page 281), Almond Macaroon Brownies (page 280), Walnut Crunch Brownies

COCONUT-CROWNED CAPPUCCINO BROWNIES

Makes 16 brownies

6 squares (1 ounce each) semisweet chocolate,
    coarsely chopped
1 tablespoon freeze-dried coffee granules
1 tablespoon boiling water
¾ cup all-purpose flour
¾ teaspoon ground cinnamon
½ teaspoon baking powder
¼ teaspoon salt
½ cup sugar
¼ cup butter or margarine, softened
3 large eggs, divided
¼ cup whipping cream
1 teaspoon vanilla
¾ cup flaked coconut, divided
½ cup semisweet chocolate chips, divided

Preheat oven to 350°F. Grease 8-inch square baking
pan. Melt chocolate squares in small, heavy saucepan
over low heat, stirring constantly; set aside. Dissolve
coffee in boiling water in small cup; set aside.

Combine flour, cinnamon, baking powder and salt in
small bowl; stir well. Beat sugar and butter in large bowl
with electric mixer at medium speed until light and
fluffy, scraping down side of bowl once. Beat in 2 eggs,
1 at a time, scraping down side of bowl after each
addition. Beat in chocolate mixture and coffee mixture
until well combined. Add flour mixture. Beat at low
speed until well blended, scraping down side of bowl
once. Spread batter evenly into prepared pan.

Coconut-Crowned Cappuccino Brownies

For topping, combine cream, remaining 1 egg and
vanilla in small bowl; mix well. Stir in ½ cup coconut
and ¼ cup chips. Spread evenly over brownie base;
sprinkle with remaining ¼ cup coconut and ¼ cup chips.

Bake 30 to 35 minutes or until coconut is browned and
center is set. Remove pan to wire rack; cool completely.
Cut into 2-inch squares. Store tightly covered at room
temperature or freeze up to 3 months.

ALMOND MACAROON BROWNIES

Makes about 16 brownies

BROWNIE LAYER

6 squares BAKER'S® Semi-Sweet Chocolate
½ cup (1 stick) margarine or butter
⅔ cup sugar
2 eggs
1 teaspoon vanilla
1 cup all-purpose flour
⅓ cup chopped toasted almonds

CREAM CHEESE TOPPING

4 ounces PHILADELPHIA BRAND® Cream
    Cheese, softened
⅓ cup sugar
1 egg
1 tablespoon all-purpose flour
⅓ cup chopped toasted almonds
1 cup BAKER'S® ANGEL FLAKE® Coconut
    Whole almonds (optional)
1 square BAKER'S® Semi-Sweet Chocolate,
    melted (optional)

Preheat oven to 350°F.

Microwave 6 squares chocolate and margarine in large
microwavable bowl on HIGH (100% power) 2 minutes
or until margarine is melted. Stir until chocolate is
completely melted.

Stir ⅔ cup sugar into melted chocolate mixture. Mix in
2 eggs and vanilla until well blended. Stir in 1 cup flour
and ⅓ cup chopped almonds. Spread in greased 8-inch
square pan.

Mix cream cheese, ⅓ cup sugar, 1 egg and 1 tablespoon
flour in small bowl until smooth. Stir in ⅓ cup chopped
almonds and coconut. Spread over brownie batter. Garnish
with whole almonds, if desired.

Bake for 35 minutes or until wooden toothpick inserted
into center comes out with fudgy crumbs. Do not
overbake. Cool in pan on wire rack. Drizzle with 1 square
melted chocolate, if desired. Cool until chocolate is set.
Cut into squares.

5. For Chocolate Drizzle, place chocolate chips and shortening in resealable plastic bag; seal. Place bag in bowl of hot water for several minutes. Dry with paper towel. Knead until blended and chocolate is smooth. Snip a tiny piece off one corner of bag. Drizzle chocolate mixture over brownies. Store in single layer in airtight containers.

Tip: Place waxed paper under wire rack to catch excess glaze.

PEANUT-LAYERED BROWNIES

Makes about 2 dozen brownies

BROWNIE LAYER
4 squares BAKER'S® Unsweetened Chocolate
¾ cup (1½ sticks) margarine or butter
2 cups granulated sugar
3 eggs
1 teaspoon vanilla
1 cup all-purpose flour
1 cup chopped peanuts

PEANUT BUTTER LAYER
1 cup peanut butter
½ cup powdered sugar
1 teaspoon vanilla

GLAZE
4 squares BAKER'S® Semi-Sweet Chocolate
¼ cup (½ stick) margarine or butter

Preheat oven to 350°F.

Microwave unsweetened chocolate and ¾ cup margarine in large microwavable bowl on HIGH (100% power) 2 minutes or until margarine is melted. Stir until chocolate is completely melted.

Stir granulated sugar into melted chocolate mixture. Mix in eggs and 1 teaspoon vanilla until well blended. Stir in flour and peanuts. Spread in greased 13×9-inch pan.

Bake for 30 to 35 minutes or until wooden toothpick inserted into center comes out with fudgy crumbs. Do not overbake. Cool in pan on wire rack.

Mix peanut butter, powdered sugar and 1 teaspoon vanilla in small bowl until well blended and smooth. Spread over brownies.

Microwave semi-sweet chocolate and ¼ cup margarine in small microwavable bowl on HIGH 2 minutes or until margarine is melted. Stir until chocolate is completely melted. Spread over peanut butter layer. Cool until chocolate is set. Cut into squares.

Prep time: 20 minutes
Bake time: 30 to 35 minutes

Fancy Walnut Brownies

FANCY WALNUT BROWNIES

Makes 2 dozen brownies

BROWNIES
1 package DUNCAN HINES® Chocolate Lovers' Walnut Brownie Mix
1 egg
⅓ cup water
⅓ cup CRISCO® Oil or CRISCO® PURITAN® Oil

GLAZE
4½ cups confectioners sugar
½ cup milk or water
24 walnut halves, for garnish

CHOCOLATE DRIZZLE
⅓ cup semi-sweet chocolate chips
1 tablespoon CRISCO® Shortening

1. Preheat oven to 350°F. Place 24 (2-inch) foil liners on cookie sheets.

2. For Brownies, combine brownie mix, egg, water and Crisco® Oil in large bowl. Stir with spoon until well blended, about 50 strokes. Stir in contents of walnut packet from Mix. Fill each foil liner with 2 generous tablespoons batter.

3. Bake at 350°F for 20 to 25 minutes or until set. Remove from cookie sheet; cool completely on wire rack. Remove liners. Turn brownies upside down on wire rack.

4. For Glaze, combine confectioners sugar and milk in medium bowl. Blend until smooth. Spoon glaze over 1 brownie to completely cover. Top immediately with walnut half. Repeat with remaining brownies. Allow glaze to set.

Jelly Roll Diploma

JELLY ROLL DIPLOMA

Makes 8 to 10 servings

1 package DUNCAN HINES® Angel Food
   Cake Mix
1 cup water
¾ cup CRISCO® Oil or CRISCO® PURITAN® Oil
¼ cup all-purpose flour
3 eggs
2 tablespoons grated lemon peel
½ teaspoon vanilla extract
   Confectioners sugar
⅔ cup any red jam or preserves
   Ribbon for bow

1. Preheat oven to 350°F. Line 15½×10½×1-inch jelly-roll pan with waxed paper; grease waxed paper. Place 2½-inch paper or foil liners in 24 muffin cups.*

2. Combine water and egg white mixture (blue packet) in large bowl. Beat at low speed with electric mixer for 1 minute. Beat at high speed until stiff peaks form. Combine flour mixture (red packet), Crisco® Oil, flour, eggs, lemon peel and vanilla extract in medium bowl. Beat at low speed until blended. Beat at medium speed 3 minutes. Fold beaten egg white mixture into yellow batter. Pour enough batter into jelly-roll pan to fill to within ¼ inch of top. Spread evenly.

3. Bake at 350°F for 30 minutes or until wooden toothpick inserted in center comes out clean. Immediately invert cake onto dish towel covered with confectioners sugar. Peel off paper and trim edges of cake. Starting at short end, roll up cake with towel jelly-roll fashion. Cool completely. Unroll cake and spread with jam. Reroll and place, seam-side-down, on serving plate. Sprinkle top with confectioners sugar. Tie a ribbon around diploma.

*For Cupcakes: While jelly-roll cake is baking, spoon remaining batter into muffin cups, filling each about two-thirds full. Bake at 350°F for 15 to 20 minutes. Cool. Frost as desired.   *Makes 24 cupcakes*

Tip: For Graduation prediction cupcakes write predictions such as "Your job interview will be a winner" on small piece of white paper. Roll up. Tuck paper in small cut in bottom of each cake. Frost as desired.

LEMON CREAM ALMOND TORTE

Makes 8 to 10 servings

½ cup sifted cake flour
½ teaspoon baking powder
⅛ teaspoon salt
½ cup butter or margarine, softened
¾ cup granulated sugar
1 cup BLUE DIAMOND® Blanched Almond Paste
3 eggs
1 tablespoon brandy
1 teaspoon vanilla
⅛ teaspoon almond extract
   Lemon Cream (recipe follows)
   Powdered sugar (optional)
   Lemon slices (optional)

Preheat oven to 325°F. In small bowl, combine flour, baking powder and salt. In large bowl, beat butter and granulated sugar until creamy. Add almond paste; beat until smooth. Add eggs, 1 at a time, beating well after each addition. Mix in brandy, vanilla and almond extract. Stir in flour mixture until well blended. Pour into greased and floured 8-inch round pan.

Bake 45 minutes or until wooden toothpick inserted into center comes out clean. Let cool in pan on wire rack 15 minutes. Loosen edge; remove from pan. Cool completely on wire rack.

Meanwhile, prepare Lemon Cream. Slice cake horizontally in half. Spread Lemon Cream over cut side of bottom layer; top with second layer, cut-side-down. Refrigerate until serving time. To serve, if desired, place lace doily over top of torte. Sift powdered sugar evenly over top; carefully remove doily. Garnish with lemon slices, if desired.

LEMON CREAM

3 egg yolks
⅓ cup granulated sugar
2 tablespoons all-purpose flour
1 cup milk, scalded
2 teaspoons grated lemon peel
2 tablespoons lemon juice
½ teaspoon vanilla

In medium saucepan, beat egg yolks and sugar until thick and pale yellow. Stir in flour. Gradually pour in hot milk, stirring constantly. Stir in lemon peel. Bring mixture to a boil over medium heat, stirring constantly. Boil and stir 1 minute. Remove from heat; add lemon juice and vanilla. Cool completely, stirring occasionally.

EASTER BASKET CAKE

Makes 12 to 16 servings

1 package DUNCAN HINES® Moist Deluxe
   Cake Mix (any flavor)
1 container (16 ounces) DUNCAN HINES®
   Creamy Homestyle Chocolate Frosting
   Green food coloring
½ teaspoon water
1 cup flaked coconut
   Assorted Easter candies
2 (12-inch) chenille stems
   Pastel ribbon

1. Preheat oven to 350°F. Grease and flour two 9-inch round cake pans.

2. Prepare, bake and cool cakes following package directions for basic recipe.

3. Place one cake layer on serving plate. Spread with Chocolate frosting. Top with second cake layer. Frost top with thin layer of frosting. Frost sides and outer 1 inch of cake top with remaining frosting. Make basketweave pattern in frosting with fork tines as shown in photograph.

Easter Basket Cake

4. Combine several drops green food coloring and water in small bowl. Add coconut. Toss with fork until evenly tinted. Place tinted coconut on top of center of cake for grass. Arrange candies on top.

5. Make handle with chenille stem ends twisted together. Wrap handle with ribbon. Insert in cake. Tie bow on one side of handle.

Tip: To stiffen ribbon for a pretty bow; place ribbon between sheets of waxed paper on ironing board. With iron set on low heat, press for several seconds.

JACK-O-LANTERN CAKE

Makes 12 to 16 servings

1 package DUNCAN HINES® Moist Deluxe Cake
   Mix (any flavor)
2 containers (16 ounces each) DUNCAN HINES®
   Creamy Homestyle Vanilla Frosting, divided
1 flat-bottom ice cream cone
   Green, red and yellow food coloring

1. Preheat oven to 375°F. Grease and flour 10-inch Bundt® pan.

2. Prepare, bake and cool cake following package directions for basic recipe. Place on serving plate.

3. Measure ¼ cup Vanilla frosting into small bowl. Tint with green food coloring; stir well. Place ice cream cone upside down on waxed paper. Frost with green frosting. Refrigerate.

4. Tint remaining Vanilla frosting with red and yellow food coloring until frosting is desired orange color. Measure 3 tablespoons orange frosting in small bowl; add green food coloring to make brown frosting.

5. Frost cake with orange frosting. Make eyes, mouth and nose with brown frosting as desired on pumpkin. Place green-frosted ice cream cone in center hole of cake for stem.

Tip: Decorate serving plate with green-tinted coconut, if desired.

Flag Cake

FLAG CAKE

Makes 12 servings

1 cup MIRACLE WHIP® Salad Dressing
3 eggs
1¾ cups sugar
2 teaspoons vanilla
2 cups flour
¾ cup unsweetened cocoa
1¼ teaspoons baking soda
¼ teaspoon *each*: baking powder, salt
1⅓ cups cold water
1 (16-ounce) container COOL WHIP® Non-Dairy
   Whipped Topping, thawed, divided
2 pints strawberries, halved
½ cup blueberries

• Preheat oven to 350°F.

• Beat salad dressing, eggs, sugar and vanilla at medium speed with electric mixer until well blended.

• Add combined dry ingredients alternately with water, mixing well after each addition. Pour into greased and floured 13×9-inch baking pan.

• Bake 40 to 45 minutes or until wooden toothpick inserted in center comes out clean. Cool 10 minutes on wire rack; remove from pan. Cool completely on wire rack.

• Reserve 1 cup whipped topping for decorating cake. Frost top and sides of cake with remaining whipped topping. Decorate with fruit and reserved whipped topping to resemble American flag.

Prep time: 25 minutes
Bake time: 45 minutes

ELEGANT CHOCOLATE LOG

Makes one log

3¼ cups sifted powdered sugar, divided
5 tablespoons sifted all-purpose flour
5 tablespoons unsweetened cocoa
½ teaspoon salt
6 eggs, separated
¼ teaspoon cream of tartar
1 tablespoon water
1¼ teaspoons vanilla
   Additional powdered sugar
1 cup whipping cream
2 tablespoons granulated sugar
12 large marshmallows, cut up, *or* ¾ cup
   miniature marshmallows
1 (1-ounce) square unsweetened chocolate,
   melted, cooled
3 to 4 tablespoons light cream, half-and-half,
   or milk
¼ cup chopped pecans

Preheat oven to 375°F. Grease 15×10×1-inch jelly-roll pan; line with waxed paper.

Sift together 1¾ cups powdered sugar, flour, cocoa and salt 3 times; set aside. Beat egg whites in large bowl at high speed with electric mixer until foamy. Add cream of tartar; beat until stiff peaks form. Set aside. Beat egg yolks in separate large bowl at high speed with electric mixer until thick and lemon-colored. Blend in water and vanilla. Add cocoa mixture; beat on medium speed until well blended. Fold in egg white mixture. Spread into prepared pan.

Bake 15 to 20 minutes or until wooden toothpick inserted in center comes out clean. Meanwhile, lightly dust clean dish towel with additional powdered sugar. Loosen warm cake from edges of pan with spatula; invert onto towel. Remove pan; carefully peel off paper. Cut off crisp edges with sharp knife. Roll up cake gently, starting at narrow end, by folding cake over and then tucking it in towel. Continue rolling cake, using towel as an aid. Cool completely in towel on wire rack.

Beat whipping cream in medium bowl at high speed with electric mixer until thickened. Gradually add granulated sugar, beating until soft peaks form. Fold in marshmallows. Unroll cake; remove towel. Spread with whipped cream mixture; reroll cake. Combine melted chocolate and remaining 1½ cups powdered sugar in separate medium bowl. Stir in light cream, 1 tablespoonful at a time, until frosting is of spreading consistency. Spread over cake roll; sprinkle with pecans. Refrigerate until ready to serve.

Favorite recipe from **Illinois State Fair**

ELEGANT CHOCOLATE TORTE

Makes 10 to 12 servings

6 eggs
1 cup sugar
1 teaspoon vanilla extract
½ cup all-purpose flour
½ cup HERSHEY'S Cocoa
½ cup (1 stick) butter or margarine, melted and
    cooled slightly
    Peanut Butter Cream Filling (recipe follows)
6 tablespoons strained apricot preserves, divided
    Fresh fruit slices (optional)

Preheat oven to 350°F. Grease and flour three 8-inch round baking pans.

In large mixer bowl, beat eggs until foamy. Gradually add sugar; continue beating until thick and lemon colored, about 5 minutes. Blend in vanilla. Stir together flour and cocoa; with rubber spatula gradually fold into egg mixture. Fold in melted butter until well blended. Divide batter evenly among prepared pans.

Bake 15 minutes or until cakes spring back when touched lightly in centers. Cool 5 minutes; remove from pans. Cool completely on wire racks. Meanwhile, prepare Peanut Butter Cream Filling. Spread top of each cake layer with 2 tablespoons apricot preserves. Place one cake layer, apricot-side up, on serving plate. Spread one-

Elegant Chocolate Torte

third of filling over preserves. Set second layer, apricot-side up, on top of first layer; spread one-third of filling over preserves. Top with third cake layer, apricot-side up; spread remaining filling over preserves. Cover; refrigerate until just before serving. Garnish with fresh fruit, if desired.

PEANUT BUTTER CREAM FILLING

1½ cups miniature marshmallows
 1 cup REESE'S® Peanut Butter Chips
 ⅓ cup milk
 1 cup (½ pint) chilled whipping cream
 ½ teaspoon vanilla extract

In top of double boiler over hot, not boiling, water place marshmallows, peanut butter chips and milk. Stir until mixture is melted and smooth; cool to lukewarm. In large cold mixer bowl, beat whipping cream until stiff; fold in vanilla and peanut butter mixture. Refrigerate until chilled.

Note: If filling is too soft to spread, refrigerate for a short time. Torte will stack best if each layer is spread with filling and refrigerated until set.

ORANGE COCOA CAKE

Makes 10 to 12 servings

½ cup HERSHEY'S Cocoa
½ cup boiling water
¼ cup (½ stick) butter or margarine, softened
¼ cup shortening
2 cups granulated sugar
1 teaspoon vanilla extract
⅛ teaspoon salt
2 eggs
1½ teaspoons plus ⅛ teaspoon baking soda, divided
 1 cup plus 3 tablespoons buttermilk or sour milk,*
    divided
1¾ cups all-purpose flour
¾ teaspoon grated orange peel
¼ teaspoon orange extract
    Orange Buttercream Frosting (recipe follows)

Preheat oven to 350°F. Grease three 8- or 9-inch baking pans; line with waxed paper.

In small bowl, stir together cocoa and water until smooth; set aside. In large mixer bowl, beat butter, shortening, granulated sugar, vanilla and salt until fluffy. Add eggs; beat well. Stir 1½ teaspoons baking soda into 1 cup buttermilk; add to butter mixture alternately with flour.

In small bowl, measure 1⅔ cups batter. Stir in remaining ⅛ teaspoon baking soda, remaining 3 tablespoons buttermilk, orange peel and orange extract; pour into one prepared pan. Stir cocoa mixture into remaining batter; divide evenly among remaining two prepared pans.

Bake 25 to 30 minutes or until wooden toothpick inserted into centers comes out clean. Cool 10 minutes; remove from pans to wire racks. Cool completely. Place one chocolate layer on serving plate; spread with a portion of Orange Buttercream Frosting. Top with orange layer; spread with a portion of frosting. Top with remaining chocolate layer; frost top and side of cake with remaining frosting.

*To sour milk: Use 1 tablespoon white vinegar plus enough milk to equal 1 cup; stir. Wait 5 minutes before using. Use ½ teaspoon white vinegar plus enough milk to equal 3 tablespoons; stir. Wait 5 minutes before using.

ORANGE BUTTERCREAM FROSTING

⅔ cup butter or margarine, softened
6 cups powdered sugar, divided
2 teaspoons grated orange peel
1½ teaspoons vanilla extract
4 to 6 tablespoons milk

In large mixer bowl, beat butter, 1 cup powdered sugar, orange peel and vanilla until creamy. Add remaining powdered sugar alternately with milk, beating to spreading consistency.

RICH CHOCOLATE MINI-CAKES

Makes 2 dozen mini-cakes

⅔ cup all-purpose flour
½ cup sugar
3 tablespoons HERSHEY'S Cocoa or
    HERSHEY'S European Style Cocoa
½ teaspoon baking powder
¼ teaspoon baking soda
¼ teaspoon salt
½ cup water
3 tablespoons vegetable oil
1 teaspoon vanilla extract
    Chocolate Glaze (recipe follows)
    Vanilla Drizzle (recipe follows)

Preheat oven to 350°F. Lightly grease 24 small muffin cups (1¾ inches in diameter).

In medium bowl, stir together flour, sugar, cocoa, baking powder, baking soda and salt. Add water, oil and vanilla; stir or whisk until batter is smooth and blended. (Batter will be thin.) Spoon batter into prepared cups, filling ⅔ full.

Rich Chocolate Mini-Cakes

Bake 12 to 14 minutes or until tops spring back when touched lightly in centers. Cool in pans on wire rack 3 minutes; invert onto rack. Cool completely on wire rack. Prepare Chocolate Glaze; dip rounded top of each mini-cake into glaze or spread glaze on tops. Place on waxed paper-covered tray or cookie sheet; refrigerate 10 minutes to set glaze. Prepare Vanilla Drizzle; drizzle onto mini-cakes. Decorate as desired.

Chocolate Glaze: In small saucepan over low heat, melt 2 tablespoons butter or margarine; add 2 tablespoons Hershey's Cocoa and 2 tablespoons water. Cook, stirring constantly, until smooth and slightly thickened; do not boil. Remove from heat; cool slightly. Gradually blend in 1 cup powdered sugar and ½ teaspoon vanilla extract; beat with wire whisk until smooth.

Vanilla Drizzle: In small microwave-safe bowl, microwave ½ cup HERSHEY'S Vanilla Milk Chips and 1 tablespoon shortening at HIGH (100% power) 30 seconds; stir until smooth. If necessary, microwave at HIGH additional 15 seconds or just until chips are melted and mixture is smooth when stirred.

TURTLE PECAN CHEESECAKE

Makes one 9-inch cheesecake

2 cups crushed chocolate cookies or vanilla wafers
　　(approximately 8 ounces cookies)
¼ cup (½ stick) butter, melted
2½ (8-ounce) packages cream cheese, softened
1 cup sugar
1½ tablespoons all-purpose flour
1 teaspoon vanilla
¼ teaspoon salt
3 eggs
2 tablespoons whipping cream
　　Caramel and Chocolate Toppings (recipes follow)
1 cup chopped toasted pecans

Preheat oven to 450°F. Combine cookie crumbs and butter; press onto bottom of 9-inch springform pan. Beat cream cheese in large bowl until creamy. Add sugar, flour, vanilla and salt; mix well. Add eggs, 1 at a time, beating well after each addition. Blend in cream. Pour over crust.

Bake 10 minutes. *Reduce oven temperature to 200°F;* continue baking 35 to 40 minutes or until set. Loosen cake from rim of pan; cool before removing rim of pan. Drizzle with Caramel Topping and Chocolate Topping. Refrigerate. Sprinkle with pecans just before serving.

Caramel Topping: Combine ½ (14-ounce) bag caramels and ⅓ cup whipping cream in small saucepan; stir over low heat until melted and smooth.

Chocolate Topping: Combine 1 (4-ounce) package chopped German sweet chocolate, 2 tablespoons whipping cream and 1 teaspoon butter in small saucepan; stir over low heat until melted and smooth.

Favorite recipe from **Illinois State Fair**

Turtle Pecan Cheesecake

CHOCOLATE MARBLE PRALINE CHEESECAKE

Makes 12 to 16 servings

CRUST

1 package DUNCAN HINES® Golden Sugar
    Cookie Mix
1 egg
½ cup finely chopped pecans (see Tip)

FILLING

1¼ cups firmly packed brown sugar
2 tablespoons all-purpose flour
3 packages (8 ounces each) cream cheese, softened
3 eggs, lightly beaten
1½ teaspoons vanilla extract
1 square (1 ounce) unsweetened chocolate, melted
20 to 25 pecan halves (about ½ cup)
    Caramel flavor topping

1. Preheat oven to 350°F.

2. For Crust, combine cookie mix, contents of buttery flavor packet from Mix, 1 egg and chopped pecans in large bowl. Stir until thoroughly blended. Press mixture into bottom of ungreased 9-inch springform pan.

3. Bake at 350°F for 20 to 22 minutes or until edge is light brown and center is set. Cool slightly.

4. For Filling, combine brown sugar and flour in small bowl; set aside. Place cream cheese in large bowl. Beat at low speed with electric mixer, adding brown sugar mixture gradually. Add beaten eggs and vanilla extract, mixing only until combined. Remove 1 cup batter to small bowl; add melted chocolate. Pour remaining plain batter over warm crust. Drop spoonfuls of chocolate batter onto plain batter. Run knife through batters to marble. Arrange pecan halves around edge.

5. Bake at 350°F for 45 to 55 minutes or until set. Loosen cake from sides of pan with knife or spatula. Cool completely on wire rack. Refrigerate 2 hours before serving.

6. To serve, remove sides of pan. Spread a thin layer of caramel flavor topping over top of cheesecake and nuts. Cut into slices and serve with additional caramel flavor topping, if desired.

Tip: For added flavor, toast pecans before chopping. Spread pecans in single layer on baking sheet. Toast in 350°F oven for 3 to 5 minutes, stirring occasionally, or until fragrant. Cool completely.

BROWNIE BOTTOM CHEESECAKE

Makes 12 servings

BROWNIE BOTTOM

½ cup (1 stick) butter
4 squares BAKER'S® Unsweetened Chocolate
1½ cups sugar
2 eggs
¼ cup milk
1 teaspoon vanilla
1 cup all-purpose flour
½ teaspoon salt

CHEESECAKE

3 (8-ounce) packages PHILADELPHIA BRAND®
    Cream Cheese, softened
¾ cup sugar
1 teaspoon vanilla
3 eggs
½ cup sour cream

• Preheat oven to 325°F.

• For Brownie Bottom, melt butter and chocolate in heavy 3-quart saucepan over low heat, stirring constantly; cool.

• Stir in sugar. Add eggs, 1 at a time, mixing after each addition just until blended. Blend in milk and vanilla.

• Stir in combined flour and salt, mixing just until blended.

• Spoon into greased and floured 9 × 3-inch springform pan, spreading evenly. Bake 25 minutes.

• For Cheesecake, beat cream cheese, sugar and vanilla at medium speed with electric mixer until well blended. Add eggs, 1 at a time, mixing at low speed after each addition, just until blended.

• Blend in sour cream; pour over brownie bottom (filling will almost come to top of pan).

• Bake 55 to 60 minutes or until center is almost set. Run knife or metal spatula around rim of pan to loosen cake; cool before removing rim of pan. Refrigerate 4 hours or overnight. Let stand 30 minutes at room temperature before serving. Drizzle with assorted ice cream toppings, if desired.

KIDS' CORNER

CLOWN PARTY CAKE

Makes 12 to 16 servings

1 package DUNCAN HINES® Moist Deluxe
   Cake Mix (any flavor)

DECORATOR FROSTING
   5 cups confectioners sugar
   ¾ cup CRISCO® Shortening
   ½ cup water
   ⅓ cup non-dairy powdered creamer
   2 teaspoons vanilla extract
   ½ teaspoon salt
      Red and yellow food coloring
      Assorted candies

1. Preheat oven to 350°F. Grease and flour one 8-inch round cake pan and one 8-inch square baking pan.

2. Prepare cake mix following package directions for basic recipe. Pour 2 cups batter into round pan and 3 cups batter into square pan. Bake and cool cakes following package directions.

3. For Decorator Frosting, combine confectioners sugar, Crisco® shortening, water, non-dairy powdered creamer, vanilla extract and salt in large bowl. Beat at medium speed with electric mixer for 3 minutes. Beat at high speed for 5 minutes. Add more confectioners sugar to thicken or more water to thin as needed. Tint 1½ cups frosting with red food coloring; set aside. Tint 1 cup frosting with yellow food coloring; set aside. Reserve remaining white frosting.

4. To assemble, cut cooled cakes and arrange on large baking sheet or piece of sturdy cardboard as shown (see Tip). Spread sides and top of round cake with some of the white frosting. Spread sides and top of remaining cake with red frosting. Place star tip in decorating bag. Fill with remaining white frosting. Pipe border around edges of hat and collar. Decorate with assorted candies. Use candies to make eyes, nose and mouth on face. Place large star tip in clean decorating bag. Fill with yellow frosting. Pipe hair around face.

Tip: Cover baking sheet or sturdy cardboard rectangle with colored foil to coordinate with the cake.

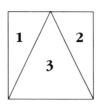

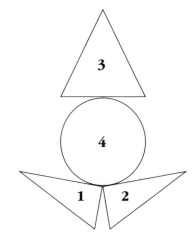

Clown Party Cake

Butterfly Cake

CHOCOLATE BANANA CAKE

Makes 12 to 16 servings

1 package DUNCAN HINES® Moist Deluxe
   Swiss Chocolate Cake Mix
1½ cups light vanilla nonfat yogurt, divided
2 medium bananas, sliced and divided
1 tablespoon chopped pecans

1. Preheat oven to 350°F. Grease and flour 10-inch
tube pan.

2. Prepare, bake and cool cake following package
directions for No Cholesterol recipe.

3. Split cake into thirds horizontally. Place bottom cake
layer on serving plate. Spread ½ cup yogurt on cake.
Arrange half the banana slices on yogurt. Place middle
cake layer on top of bananas. Repeat with ½ cup yogurt
and remaining banana slices. Place top cake layer on top
of bananas. Spread top with remaining ½ cup yogurt.
Sprinkle with pecans. Refrigerate until ready to serve.

Tip: To save time, simply cut cake into serving slices,
top with yogurt and garnish with banana slices and
chopped pecans.

BUTTERFLY CAKES

Makes 2 cakes, 16 servings

1 package DUNCAN HINES® Moist Deluxe Cake
   Mix (any flavor)
1 container (16 ounces) DUNCAN HINES®
   Creamy Homestyle Vanilla Frosting, divided
   Assorted candies such as chocolate chips, peanut
    butter chips, vanilla milk chips, halved
    gumdrops, halved jelly beans and candy-coated
    chocolate pieces
4 bars (2 to 2½ ounces each) chocolate-covered
   crunchy peanut butter candy
4 chocolate-covered peanut butter cups
   Spaghetti (uncooked)

1. Preheat oven to 350°F. Grease and flour two 9-inch
round cake pans.

2. Prepare, bake and cool cake following package
directions for basic recipe.

3. To assemble, cut each cake in half to form 2 semicircles
(see Tip). Arrange on serving platters as shown in
photograph. Reserve 1 tablespoon Vanilla frosting for
candies. Frost sides and tops of cakes with remaining
frosting. Use tip of knife to mark sections of wings.
Decorate each section with candy pieces. Spread a portion
of reserved frosting on flat side of one candy bar. Top
with second candy bar; press together. Repeat with
remaining candy bars. Place between cake semicircles
for bodies. Spread a portion of reserved frosting on flat
side of one peanut butter cup. Top with second peanut
butter cup; press together. Repeat with remaining peanut
butter cups. Place at top end of candy bars for head.
Use vanilla milk chips for eyes and spaghetti for antennas.

Tip: Cakes are easier to frost when completely frozen.
After cutting into semicircles, place in freezer while
organizing candies for decorations.

KANSAS KIDS' CAKE

Makes one 13 × 9-inch cake

¾ cup honey
½ cup (1 stick) butter, softened
¼ cup peanut butter
2 eggs
1 teaspoon vanilla
1 cup all-purpose flour
1 cup whole wheat flour
1½ teaspoons baking powder
¾ teaspoon baking soda
½ teaspoon salt
¾ cup buttermilk
   Peanut Butter Topping (recipe follows)

Preheat oven to 350°F. Grease and lightly flour 13×9-inch baking pan.

Beat together honey, butter and peanut butter in large bowl until well blended. Blend in eggs and vanilla. Sift together dry ingredients; add to peanut butter mixture alternately with buttermilk, beating well after each addition. Pour into prepared pan. Prepare Peanut Butter Topping; sprinkle over batter.

Bake 25 to 30 minutes or until wooden toothpick inserted in center comes out clean. Cool on wire rack. Serve warm or at room temperature.

Peanut Butter Topping: Combine ¾ cup sugar, ½ cup peanut butter, and 2 tablespoons all-purpose flour in small bowl, mixing until well blended. Stir in 1 cup semisweet chocolate chips.

Favorite recipe from **Celebrate! Kansas Food Recipe Contest**

ICE CREAM CONE CAKES

Makes 2 dozen cones

1 package (2-layer size) yellow cake mix
24 flat-bottom ice cream cones
    Fluffy Pudding Frosting (recipe follows)
    Candy sprinkles (optional)

Preheat oven to 350°F. Prepare cake mix as directed on package. Spoon about ¼ cup batter into each cone. Set cones on baking sheet.

Bake for 25 minutes. Cool on rack. Spoon Fluffy Pudding Frosting over cakes; garnish with sprinkles, if desired.

Prep time: 15 minutes
Bake time: 25 minutes

Note: Store frosted cakes in refrigerator.

FLUFFY PUDDING FROSTING

1 cup cold milk
1 package (4-serving size) JELL-O® Instant
    Pudding and Pie Filling, any flavor
¼ cup confectioners sugar
3½ cups (8 ounces) COOL WHIP® Non-Dairy
    Whipped Topping, thawed

Pour milk into large bowl. Add pudding mix and sugar. Beat with wire whisk until well blended, 1 to 2 minutes. Fold in whipped topping. Use immediately.

Makes about 4 cups

DRUM LAYER CAKE

Makes 12 to 16 servings

1 package DUNCAN HINES® Moist Deluxe
    Cake Mix (any flavor)
2 containers (16 ounces each) DUNCAN HINES®
    Creamy Homestyle Vanilla Frosting, divided
    Green food coloring
    Thin pretzel sticks
    Candy-coated chocolate pieces
2 Lollipops

1. Preheat oven to 350°F. Grease and flour two 8-inch round cake pans.

2. Prepare, bake and cool cake following package directions for basic recipe.

3. To assemble, place one cake layer on serving plate. Spread with half of Vanilla frosting from one frosting container. Top with second cake layer. Tint frosting in second container with green food coloring. Spread green frosting on sides of cake. Spread remaining Vanilla frosting on top of cake. Arrange pretzel sticks and candy-coated chocolates on sides of cake as shown in photograph. Place lollipops on top of cake for drumsticks.

Tip: For a brighter green frosting, as shown in photograph, use paste food colors available from cake decorating and specialty shops.

Drum Layer Cake

HOPSCOTCH CAKE

Makes 12 to 16 servings

1 package DUNCAN HINES® Moist Deluxe
    Yellow Cake Mix
1 container (16 ounces) DUNCAN HINES®
    Creamy Homestyle Vanilla Frosting, divided
    Green food coloring
1 cup flaked coconut, tinted green (see Tip)
    Thin pretzel sticks
    Candy-coated chocolate pieces

1. Preheat oven to 350°F. Grease and flour 13×9-inch pan.

2. Prepare, bake and cool cake following package directions for basic recipe. Remove from pan; place on large baking sheet or piece of sturdy cardboard (see Tip on page 292).

3. Tint 1 cup Vanilla frosting with 3 to 4 drops green food coloring; frost sides and 1-inch border along top edge of cake. Frost remaining cake top with remaining Vanilla frosting. Sprinkle tinted coconut on green frosting to form grass. Outline sidewalk and chalk marks with pretzel sticks as shown in photograph. Form numbers with candy-coated chocolate pieces.

Tip: To tint coconut, place 3 drops green food coloring, 1 teaspoon water and 1 cup coconut in large resealable plastic bag. Seal bag and shake until evenly tinted.

Hopscotch Cake

SURPRISE-FILLED CUPCAKES

Makes 24 cupcakes

1 package DUNCAN HINES® Moist Deluxe
    Dark Dutch Fudge Cake Mix
1 jar (7 ounces) marshmallow creme, divided
1 container (16 ounces) DUNCAN HINES®
    Creamy Homestyle Dark Chocolate Frosting
½ cup confectioners sugar
2½ teaspoons milk

1. Preheat oven to 350°F. Place 24 (2½-inch) paper liners in muffin cups.

2. Prepare, bake and cool cupcakes following package directions for basic recipe.

3. Reserve 2 tablespoons marshmallow creme; set aside. Place remaining marshmallow creme in decorating bag fitted with large star tip. Push tip into top center of each cupcake about 1 inch deep. Tightly squeeze bag for 5 to 7 seconds to fill cupcake.

4. Frost tops of cupcakes with Dark Chocolate frosting. Combine reserved marshmallow creme and confectioners sugar in small bowl. Add milk, 1 teaspoon at a time, stirring until smooth. Place in small resealable plastic bag. Snip a tiny piece off corner of bag. Squeeze design over each cupcake.

Tip: For an extra surprise, tint marshmallow creme filling with a few drops of your favorite food coloring.

HALLOWEEN PARTY CUPCAKES

Makes 24 cupcakes

1 package DUNCAN HINES® Moist Deluxe
    Orange Supreme Cake Mix
1 container (16 ounces) DUNCAN HINES®
    Creamy Homestyle Chocolate Frosting
    Assorted Halloween candies, for garnish

1. Preheat oven to 350°F. Place 2½-inch paper liners in 24 muffin cups.

2. Prepare, bake and cool cupcakes following package directions for basic recipe.

3. Frost cupcakes with Chocolate frosting. Decorate with assorted Halloween candies.

Tip: Cupcakes can be made special for many occasions by decorating with holiday candies. Choose your favorite flavors of cake mix and frosting to complement the candies.

Back-to-School Pencil Cake

speed for 5 minutes. Add more confectioners sugar to thicken or water to thin as needed. Tint 1 cup frosting pink with red food coloring. Tint remaining frosting with yellow food coloring.

4. To assemble, cut cooled cake and arrange on large baking sheet or piece of sturdy cardboard (see Tip on page 292). Spread pink frosting on cake for eraser at one end and for wood at other end. Spread yellow frosting over remaining cake. Decorate with chocolate sprinkles for pencil tip and eraser band as shown in photograph.

Tip: To make this cake even more special, reserve ¼ cup frosting before tinting yellow. Place writing tip in decorator bag. Fill with frosting. Pipe name of child, teacher or school on pencil.

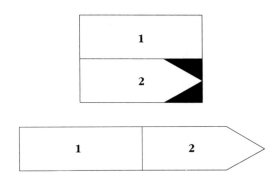

BACK-TO-SCHOOL PENCIL CAKE

Makes 12 to 16 servings

1 package DUNCAN HINES® Moist Deluxe
   Cake Mix (any flavor)

DECORATOR FROSTING
5 cups confectioners sugar
¾ cup CRISCO® Shortening
½ cup water
⅓ cup non-dairy powdered creamer
2 teaspoons vanilla extract
½ teaspoon salt
   Red and yellow food coloring
   Chocolate sprinkles

1. Preheat oven to 350°F. Grease and flour 13×9-inch pan.

2. Prepare, bake and cool cake following package directions for basic recipe.

3. For Decorator Frosting, combine confectioners sugar, shortening, water, non-dairy powdered creamer, vanilla extract and salt in large bowl. Beat at medium speed with electric mixer for 3 minutes. Beat at high

ICE CREAM PARTY CAKE

Makes 1 (9-inch) cake

8 finger-shaped creme-filled chocolate snack cakes
½ gallon BORDEN® or MEADOW GOLD®
   Ice Cream, any flavor, slightly softened
1 tablespoon chocolate-flavored syrup
   Maraschino cherries and whipped topping
   (optional)
   Additional chocolate-flavored syrup (optional)

Cut 5 cakes in half crosswise, then lengthwise. In 9-inch springform pan, place cake pieces vertically around side. Cut each remaining cake crosswise into 8 pieces; line bottom of pan. Spoon ice cream into prepared pan, covering cake pieces. Drizzle with 1 tablespoon chocolate syrup. Cover. Freeze overnight or until firm. Garnish with cherries and whipped topping if desired. Remove side of pan; let stand 10 minutes before serving. Serve with additional chocolate syrup if desired. Freeze leftovers.

Tip: Snack cakes slice easier when frozen or chilled.

MICROWAVE BANANA CARAMEL PIE

Makes 1 pie

¼ cup margarine or butter
1 (14-ounce) can EAGLE® Brand Sweetened
  Condensed Milk (NOT evaporated milk)
1 teaspoon vanilla extract
1 cup (½ pint) BORDEN® or MEADOW GOLD®
  Whipping Cream
3 medium bananas
  REALEMON® Lemon Juice from Concentrate
1 (6-ounce) packaged graham cracker crumb
  pie crust

To Microwave: In 2-quart glass measure with handle, melt margarine on 100% power (high) 1 minute. Stir in sweetened condensed milk and vanilla. Cook on 100% power (high) 6 to 10 minutes, stirring briskly after each minute until smooth. Stir in ¼ cup *unwhipped* cream. Freeze 5 minutes. Meanwhile, slice *2 bananas;* dip in ReaLemon® brand and drain. Arrange on bottom of crust. Pour filling over bananas; cover. Chill at least 2 hours. In small mixer bowl, whip remaining ¾ *cup* cream. Spread on top of pie. Slice remaining banana; dip in ReaLemon® brand, drain and garnish pie. Refrigerate leftovers.

PINK LEMONADE PIE

Makes one 8- or 9-inch pie

1 (8- or 9-inch) baked pastry shell
1 (8-ounce) package cream cheese, softened
1 (14-ounce) can EAGLE® Brand Sweetened
  Condensed Milk (NOT evaporated milk)
1 (6-ounce) can frozen pink lemonade concentrate,
  thawed
  Few drops red food coloring (optional)
1 (4-ounce) container frozen non-dairy whipped
  topping, thawed
½ cup pink-tinted coconut*

In large mixer bowl, beat cheese until fluffy; gradually beat in sweetened condensed milk, then lemonade concentrate and food coloring if desired. Fold in whipped topping. Pour into prepared pastry shell. Chill 4 hours or until set. Garnish with tinted coconut. Refrigerate leftovers.

*****To tint coconut:** Combine ½ cup flaked coconut, ½ teaspoon water and 2 drops red food coloring in small plastic bag or bowl. Shake or mix well.

BANANA CHOCOLATE CREAM PIE

Makes 1 pie

Chocolate Crumb Crust (recipe follows)
2 packages (3½ ounces each) chocolate flavor
  pudding and pie filling mix (not instant)
1 quart (4 cups) milk
2 squares (2 ounces) unsweetened chocolate,
  melted
2 firm, large DOLE® Bananas

Prepare Chocolate Crumb Crust. In medium saucepan, combine pudding mix and milk. Prepare pudding mix according to package directions for pie filling. Stir in melted chocolate. Remove from heat. Cool.

Slice bananas. Alternately layer pudding and bananas in prepared crust. Refrigerate until ready to serve. Garnish with whipped cream and additional banana slices, if desired.

Chocolate Crumb Crust: In medium bowl, combine 2 cups chocolate wafer crumbs and ½ cup melted margarine. Press mixture evenly onto bottom and sides of 8- or 9-inch pie plate. Refrigerate until ready to use.

BANANA CREAM PIE

Makes 8 servings

  Vanilla wafers
  Teddy bear cookies
1 large banana
2½ cups cold milk
1 package (6-serving size) JELL-O® Instant
  Pudding and Pie Filling, Banana Cream,
  Chocolate or Vanilla Flavor
1 cup thawed COOL WHIP® Non-Dairy Whipped
  Topping (optional)
  Additional banana slices (optional)
  Gumdrop slices (optional)

Cover bottom of 9-inch pie plate with vanilla wafers. Arrange additional vanilla wafers and teddy bear cookies alternately around sides. Slice banana; place slices over wafers on bottom of plate.

Pour milk into small bowl. Add pudding mix. Beat with wire whisk until well blended, 1 to 2 minutes. Pour over bananas in pie plate. Chill 2 hours. Garnish with whipped topping, additional banana slices and gumdrop slices to resemble tic-tac-toe game, if desired.

Prep time: 15 minutes
Chill time: 2 hours

Top to bottom: Banana Split Brownie Pie (page 301), Microwave Banana Caramel Pie

Cookies and Cream Pie

COOKIES AND CREAM PIE

Makes 8 servings

Chocolate sandwich cookies
1½ cups cold milk
1 cup ice cream, any flavor, softened
1 package (6-serving size) JELL-O® Instant
    Pudding and Pie Filling, any flavor
COOL WHIP® Non-Dairy Whipped Topping,
    thawed (optional)

Line bottom and sides of 9-inch pie plate with cookies.

Blend milk and ice cream in medium bowl. Add pudding mix. Beat with wire whisk or at low speed of electric mixer until blended, 1 to 2 minutes. Pour immediately into pie plate. Chill until set, about 3 hours. Garnish with whipped topping, if desired.

Prep time: 15 minutes
Chill time: 3 hours

PEANUT CANDY BAR PIE

Makes one 9-inch pie

1 (9-inch) baked pastry shell, cooled
1 (8-ounce) package cream cheese, softened
1 (14-ounce) can EAGLE® Brand Sweetened
    Condensed Milk (NOT evaporated milk)
¾ cup creamy peanut butter
1 teaspoon vanilla extract
2 (2-ounce) chocolate-coated peanut candy bars,
    chopped into small pieces
1 cup (½ pint) BORDEN® or MEADOW GOLD®
    Whipping Cream, whipped
Hot Fudge Sauce (recipe page 301) or chocolate
    fudge ice cream topping, warmed

In large mixer bowl, beat cheese until fluffy. Gradually beat in sweetened condensed milk then peanut butter and vanilla until smooth. Stir in candy pieces. Fold in whipped cream. Pour into prepared pastry shell. Freeze 4 hours or until firm. Remove from freezer 10 minutes before serving. Serve with Hot Fudge Sauce. Garnish with additional candy pieces if desired. Freeze leftovers.

BANANA SPLIT BROWNIE PIE

Makes one 9-inch pie

1 (12.9- or 15-ounce) package fudge brownie mix
2 medium bananas, sliced, dipped in REALEMON®
    Lemon Juice from Concentrate and well drained
BORDEN® or MEADOW GOLD® Vanilla,
    Chocolate and Strawberry Ice Creams
Hot Fudge Sauce (recipe follows)
Chopped toasted pecans
BORDEN® or MEADOW GOLD® Whipping
    Cream, whipped
Maraschino cherries (optional)

Preheat oven to 350°F. Prepare brownie mix as package directs. Spoon batter into greased 9-inch round layer cake pan; bake 25 minutes. Cool 10 minutes; remove from pan.

On serving plate, place brownie; top with bananas, scoops of ice cream and Hot Fudge Sauce. Garnish with nuts, whipped cream and cherries if desired. Serve immediately. Freeze leftovers.

Hot Fudge Sauce: In heavy saucepan, over medium heat, melt 1 cup (6 ounces) semi-sweet chocolate chips and 2 tablespoons margarine or butter with 1 (14-ounce) can EAGLE® Brand Sweetened Condensed Milk and 2 tablespoons water. Cook and stir constantly until thickened, about 5 minutes. Add 1 teaspoon vanilla extract. Serve warm. Refrigerate leftovers.

Makes about 2 cups

Fudge Brownie Pie

FUDGE BROWNIE PIE

Makes 6 to 8 servings

2 eggs
1 cup sugar
½ cup (½ stick) butter or margarine, melted
½ cup all-purpose flour
⅓ cup HERSHEY'S Cocoa
¼ teaspoon salt
1 teaspoon vanilla extract
½ cup chopped nuts (optional)
    Ice cream
    Quick Hot Fudge Sauce (recipe follows)

Preheat oven to 350°F. Lightly grease 8-inch pie plate.

In small mixer bowl, beat eggs; blend in sugar and melted butter. In separate bowl, stir together flour, cocoa and salt; add to butter mixture. Stir in vanilla and nuts, if desired. Pour into prepared pie plate.

Bake 25 to 30 minutes or until almost set. (Pie will not test done in center.) Cool; cut into wedges. Serve topped with scoop of ice cream; drizzle with Quick Hot Fudge Sauce.

QUICK HOT FUDGE SAUCE

¾ cup sugar
½ cup HERSHEY'S Cocoa
½ cup plus 2 tablespoons (5-ounce can)
    evaporated milk
⅓ cup light corn syrup
⅓ cup butter or margarine
1 teaspoon vanilla extract

In small saucepan, stir together sugar and cocoa; blend in evaporated milk and corn syrup. Cook over medium heat, stirring constantly, until mixture boils; boil and stir 1 minute. Remove from heat; stir in butter and vanilla. Serve warm. *Makes about 1¾ cups sauce*

CHERRY FUDGE TARTS

Makes 14 tarts

3 (1-ounce) squares unsweetened or semisweet
    chocolate
1 (14-ounce) can EAGLE® Brand Sweetened
    Condensed Milk (NOT evaporated milk)
¼ teaspoon salt
¼ cup water
2 egg yolks, beaten
1 teaspoon almond extract
1 cup (½ pint) BORDEN® or MEADOW GOLD®
    Whipping Cream, whipped
14 (3-inch) prepared tart-size graham cracker crumb
    or baked pastry crusts
1 (21-ounce) can cherry pie filling, chilled

In heavy saucepan, over medium heat, melt chocolate
with sweetened condensed milk and salt. Cook and stir
rapidly until *very thick* and bubbly, 5 to 8 minutes. Add
water and egg yolks; cook and stir rapidly until mixture
thickens and bubbles again. Remove from heat; stir in
extract. Cool 15 minutes. *Chill thoroughly*, about
30 minutes; stir. Fold in whipped cream. Spoon into
crusts. Chill 1 hour or until set. Top with cherry pie
filling. Refrigerate leftovers.

Cherry Fudge Tarts

MINI FRUIT CHEESE TARTS

Makes 24 tarts

24 (2- or 3-inch) prepared tart-size graham cracker
    crumb or baked pastry crusts
1 (8-ounce) package cream cheese, softened
1 (14-ounce) can EAGLE® Brand Sweetened
    Condensed Milk (NOT evaporated milk)
⅓ cup REALEMON® Lemon Juice from
    Concentrate
1 teaspoon vanilla extract
    Assorted fruit (strawberries, blueberries,
    banana slices, raspberries, orange segments,
    cherries, kiwifruit slices, grapes, pineapple
    chunks, etc.)
¼ cup apple jelly, melted

In large mixer bowl, beat cheese until fluffy. Gradually
beat in sweetened condensed milk until smooth. Stir in
ReaLemon® brand and vanilla. Spoon equal portions
into crusts. Top with fruit; brush with jelly. Chill 2 hours
or until set. Refrigerate leftovers.

GREEN MOUNTAIN PIE
IN CHEWY CRUST

Makes one 9-inch pie or 8 servings

CRUST
1¾ cups soft macaroon crumbs (about seven 2-inch
    macaroons crumbled with fingers)
¼ cup BUTTER FLAVOR CRISCO®, melted

FILLING
2 pints lime sherbet, softened, divided
1 quart vanilla ice cream, softened
1½ cups soft macaroon crumbs (about six 2-inch
    macaroons crumbled with fingers)

1. For Crust, preheat oven to 350°F. Lightly grease
9-inch pie plate with Butter Flavor Crisco®.

2. Combine 1¾ cups crumbs and melted Butter Flavor
Crisco® in small bowl. Press into greased pie plate.

3. Bake at 350°F for 10 minutes. Cool completely
before filling.

4. For Filling, spread 1 pint sherbet in cooled crust.
Freeze about 1 hour or until firm.

5. Combine ice cream and 1½ cups crumbs. Spread
evenly over sherbet. Freeze about 1 hour or until firm.

6. Spread remaining sherbet over ice cream. Freeze
several hours. Remove from freezer 10 to 15 minutes
before serving.

Note: Lemon sherbet may be used in place of lime.

FROZEN STRAWBERRY YOGURT PIE

Makes 8 servings

CRUST
1 package DUNCAN HINES® Golden Sugar
    Cookie Mix
1 egg white

FILLING
1 quart frozen strawberry nonfat yogurt, softened
    (see Tip)
Fresh strawberries, for garnish

1. Preheat oven to 400°F.

2. For Crust, place cookie mix in large bowl. Stir in
contents of buttery flavor packet from Mix and egg
white until mixture is crumbly. Spread evenly in
ungreased 9-inch square pan. Do not press.

3. Bake at 400°F for 12 to 14 minutes. Stir. Reserve ½
cup crumbs for topping. Press remaining crumbs into
bottom and up sides of ungreased 9-inch pie pan to
form crust. Cool completely.

4. For Filling, spread softened yogurt over cooled crust.
Sprinkle with reserved crumbs. Cover and freeze for
3 to 4 hours or overnight until firm.

5. To serve, let pie stand at room temperature for 5
minutes. Cut into wedges with sharp knife. Garnish
with fresh strawberries.

Tip: Frozen yogurt can be softened by allowing to
stand at room temperature for 15 minutes.

Frozen Strawberry Yogurt Pie

TEDDY PEANUT BUTTER SWIRL PIE

Makes 6 servings

2 cups TEDDY GRAHAMS® Graham Snacks,
    any flavor, divided
1 (9-inch) HONEY MAID® Honey Graham
    Pie Crust
½ cup creamy peanut butter
1 quart vanilla ice milk, softened
¼ cup PLANTERS® Dry Roasted Peanuts, chopped

Place ½ cup Teddy Grahams® in bottom of pie crust.
Heat peanut butter over low heat until smooth and
pourable; drizzle ¼ cup over cookies in crust. Fold
1 cup Teddy Grahams® into ice milk; spread into pie
crust. Drizzle remaining ¼ cup peanut butter over pie;
quickly swirl with knife to create a marbled effect. Top
with remaining ½ cup Teddy Grahams® and chopped
peanuts. Cover and freeze until firm, about 4 hours.

BANANA SPLIT PIE

Makes 8 servings

20 chocolate sandwich cookies
¼ cup margarine, melted
2 medium DOLE® Bananas, peeled, sliced
1 quart strawberry ice cream, softened
1 can (20 ounces) DOLE® Crushed Pineapple
    in Juice, drained
1 cup whipping cream, whipped
¼ cup chopped nuts
Maraschino cherry (optional)

Preheat oven to 350°F. For crust, process cookies in
food processor or blender until finely ground. Add melted
margarine. Process until blended. Press into bottom and
up side of 9-inch pie plate. Bake 5 minutes. Cool.

Arrange sliced bananas over crust. Spread ice cream over
bananas. Top with pineapple. Cover pie with whipped
cream. Sprinkle with nuts. Freeze 4 hours or until firm.
Remove from freezer 30 minutes before serving.
Garnish with maraschino cherry, if desired.

Prep time: 20 minutes
Bake time: 5 minutes
Freezing time: 4 hours

Banana Cookie Ice Cream

BANANA COOKIE ICE CREAM

Makes about 8 servings

2 ripe DOLE® Bananas, peeled, mashed
10 chocolate sandwich cookies, finely chopped
1 quart vanilla ice cream, softened
¼ cup chocolate syrup
 Additional chocolate syrup
 DOLE® Banana slices
 Maraschino cherries

Fold 2 mashed bananas and cookies into ice cream in large bowl. Spoon into 8 × 8-inch pan. Drizzle with ¼ cup chocolate syrup. Run knife through mixture to make swirls. Cover; freeze until firm.

To serve, scoop into sundae glasses. Top with additional chocolate sauce, banana slices and maraschino cherries, if desired.

FROZEN PEANUT BANANA YOGURT

Makes about 1½ quarts

1½ cups mashed ripe bananas (1½ pounds or about 3 bananas)
2 tablespoons lemon juice
1 cup peanut butter
⅓ cup honey
3 (8-ounce) cartons lemon-flavored yogurt
½ cup chopped peanuts

Combine mashed bananas and lemon juice in small bowl. Combine peanut butter and honey in large bowl; stir in banana mixture. Add yogurt and chopped peanuts; mix well. Place in ice cream freezer container. Freeze according to manufacturer's instructions.

Refrigerator-Freezer Method: Pour mixture into 3 ice cube trays or two 9 × 5-inch loaf pans. Freeze until solid. Break into chunks and beat in large bowl with electric mixer until smooth. Cover; freeze until firm. If mixture becomes too hard, let stand in refrigerator 30 minutes before serving.

Favorite recipe from **Oklahoma Peanut Commission**

CREAMY SODA FREEZE

Makes 2 to 3 quarts

2 (14-ounce) cans EAGLE® Brand Sweetened Condensed Milk (NOT evaporated milk)
1 (2-liter) bottle *or* 5 (12-ounce) cans carbonated beverage, any flavor

In ice cream freezer container, combine ingredients; mix well. Freeze according to manufacturer's instructions. Freeze leftovers.

Creamy Soda Shakes: In blender container, combine one-half (14-ounce) can Eagle® Brand Sweetened Condensed Milk, 1 (12-ounce) can carbonated beverage and 3 cups ice. Blend until smooth. Repeat for additional shakes. Store leftovers in freezer. *Makes 1 to 2 quarts*

Frozen Pops: Combine 1 (14-ounce) can Eagle® Brand Sweetened Condensed Milk with 2 (12-ounce) cans carbonated beverage; mix well. Pour equal portions into 8 (5-ounce) paper cold-drink cups. Cover each cup with aluminum foil; make small hole in center of foil. Insert a wooden stick into each cup through hole. Freeze 6 hours or until firm. *Makes 8 servings*

EASY HOMEMADE VANILLA ICE CREAM 'N' COOKIES

Makes about 1½ quarts

1 (14-ounce) can EAGLE® Brand Sweetened Condensed Milk (NOT evaporated milk)
4 teaspoons vanilla extract
2 cups (1 pint) BORDEN® or MEADOW GOLD® Whipping Cream, whipped (*do not use non-dairy whipped topping*)
1 cup coarsely crushed creme-filled chocolate sandwich cookies (about 12 cookies)

In large bowl, combine sweetened condensed milk and vanilla. Fold in whipped cream and cookies. Pour into 9 × 5-inch loaf pan or other 2-quart container; cover. Freeze 6 hours or until firm. Let stand 5 minutes before serving. Freeze leftovers.

Dish of Dirt

FUDGY ROCKY ROAD ICE CREAM

Makes about 2 quarts

5 (1-ounce) squares unsweetened chocolate, melted
1 (14-ounce) can EAGLE® Brand Sweetened Condensed Milk (NOT evaporated milk)
2 teaspoons vanilla extract
2 cups (1 pint) BORDEN® or MEADOW GOLD® Half-and-Half
2 cups (1 pint) BORDEN® or MEADOW GOLD® Whipping Cream, unwhipped
1½ cups CAMPFIRE® Miniature Marshmallows
¾ cup chopped peanuts

In large mixer bowl, beat chocolate, sweetened condensed milk and vanilla. Stir in remaining ingredients. Pour into ice cream freezer container. Freeze according to manufacturer's instructions. Freeze leftovers.

Fudgy Chocolate Chip Ice Cream: Omit marshmallows and reduce peanuts to ½ cup. Add ¾ cup mini chocolate chips. Proceed as above.

DISH OF DIRT

Makes 4 servings

14 OREO® Chocolate Sandwich Cookies, finely crushed (about 1 cup crumbs)
1 pint chocolate ice cream
¼ cup chocolate-flavored syrup
Gummy worms and prepared whipped topping, for garnish

In each of 4 dessert dishes, place 2 tablespoons cookie crumbs. Top each with ½ cup ice cream, remaining 2 tablespoons cookie crumbs and 1 tablespoon syrup. Garnish with gummy worms and whipped topping.

CHERRY CHEESECAKE ICE CREAM

Makes about 1½ quarts

1 (3-ounce) package cream cheese, softened
1 (14-ounce) can EAGLE® Brand Sweetened Condensed Milk (NOT evaporated milk)
2 cups (1 pint) BORDEN® or MEADOW GOLD® Half-and-Half
2 cups (1 pint) BORDEN® or MEADOW GOLD® Whipping Cream, unwhipped
1 (10-ounce) jar maraschino cherries, well drained and chopped (about 1 cup)
1 tablespoon vanilla extract
½ teaspoon almond extract

In large mixer bowl, beat cream cheese until fluffy. Gradually beat in sweetened condensed milk until smooth. Add remaining ingredients; mix well. Pour into ice cream freezer container. Freeze according to manufacturer's instructions. Freeze leftovers.

Tip: 1 (17-ounce) can pitted dark sweet cherries, well drained and chopped, can be substituted for maraschino cherries.

CHOCOLATE CHIP ICE CREAM SANDWICHES

Makes 12 to 15 servings

1 (14-ounce) can EAGLE® Brand Sweetened
  Condensed Milk (NOT evaporated milk)
2 tablespoons vanilla extract
2 cups (1 pint) BORDEN® or MEADOW GOLD®
  Whipping Cream, whipped (*do not use
  non-dairy whipped topping*)
¾ cup mini chocolate chips
24 to 30 chocolate chip or chocolate wafer cookies

In large bowl, combine sweetened condensed milk and
vanilla; mix well. Fold in whipped cream and chips. Pour
into 9 × 5-inch loaf pan or other 2-quart container; cover.
Freeze 6 hours or until firm.

Scoop about ¼ cup ice cream onto bottom of 1 cookie;
top with another cookie, top side up. Press gently. Wrap
tightly with plastic wrap. Repeat for remaining
sandwiches. Store in freezer.

FROZEN FRUITY BARS

Makes 8 servings

1 package (4-serving size) JELL-O® Brand Gelatin,
  any flavor
½ cup sugar
2 cups boiling water
2 cups cold water

Completely dissolve gelatin and sugar in boiling water.
Add cold water. Pour into pop molds or paper or plastic
cups. Freeze until almost firm, about 2 hours. Insert
wooden stick or spoon into each mold or cup. Freeze
until firm, about 8 hours or overnight.

Prep time: 15 minutes
Freezing time: 10 hours

FROZEN PUDDING BARS

Makes 6 servings

1 package (4-serving size) JELL-O® Instant
  Pudding and Pie filling, any flavor
2 cups cold milk

Prepare pudding mix with milk as directed on package.
Pour into pop molds or paper or plastic cups. Insert
wooden stick or spoon into each mold or cup. Freeze
until firm, about 5 hours.

Prep time: 10 minutes
Freezing time: 5 hours

CHOCOLATE-CHERRY SUNDAES

Makes 6 servings

1 package (4-serving size) JELL-O® Brand
  Cherry Flavor Gelatin
1 cup boiling water
½ cup cold water
1 cup chocolate ice cream, softened
  COOL WHIP® Non-Dairy Whipped Topping,
  thawed
  Chocolate syrup
  Maraschino cherries (optional)

Completely dissolve gelatin in boiling water. Measure
½ cup of gelatin into small bowl. Add cold water; set
aside. Spoon ice cream into remaining gelatin, stirring
until melted and smooth. Spoon into individual dessert
dishes. Chill until set but not firm, about 10 minutes.

Spoon reserved gelatin over creamy layer in dishes. Chill
until set, about 1 hour. Top each dessert with dollop of
whipped topping; drizzle with chocolate syrup. Garnish
with cherries, if desired.

Prep time: 15 minutes
Chill time: 70 minutes

Frozen Fruity Bars, Frozen Pudding Bars

CHOCOLATE-COVERED BANANA POPS

Makes 9 pops

3 ripe, large bananas
9 wooden ice cream sticks or skewers
2 cups (12-ounce package) HERSHEY'S
    Semi-Sweet Chocolate Chips
2 tablespoons shortening
1½ cups coarsely chopped unsalted, roasted peanuts

Peel bananas; cut each into thirds. Insert a wooden stick into each banana piece; place on waxed paper-covered tray or cookie sheet. Cover tray; freeze until firm. In top of double boiler over hot, not boiling, water, melt chocolate chips and shortening. Remove bananas from freezer just before dipping. Dip each piece into warm chocolate, covering completely; allow excess to drip off. Immediately roll in peanuts. Return to waxed paper-covered tray or cookie sheet. Cover tray; return to freezer. Serve frozen.

FRUIT PARFAITS

Makes 6 servings

1 package DUNCAN HINES® Moist Deluxe
    Yellow Cake Mix
2 cups fresh peaches, peeled, pitted and diced
1 cup miniature marshmallows
¼ cup flaked coconut
1½ cups whipping cream
2 tablespoons confectioners sugar
½ teaspoon almond extract
6 peach slices

1. Preheat oven to 350°F. Grease and flour two 9-inch round cake pans.

2. Prepare, bake and cool cake following package directions for basic recipe.

3. Cut one cake layer into 1-inch cubes. (Freeze other layer of cake in large airtight plastic bag to use later.) Place in large bowl. Add diced peaches, marshmallows and coconut. Toss to mix.

4. Combine whipping cream, confectioners sugar and almond extract in large bowl. Beat at high speed with electric mixer until stiff. Set aside enough whipped cream mixture for garnish. Fold remaining whipped cream mixture into cake mixture. Spoon into 6 parfait dishes. Top each with reserved whipped cream mixture and peach slice. Refrigerate until ready to serve.

GELATIN SUNDAES

Makes 4 servings

1 package (4-serving size) JELL-O® Brand Gelatin,
    any flavor
¾ cup boiling water
½ cup cold water
    Ice cubes
1 pint ice cream, any flavor
1 cup thawed COOL WHIP® Non-Dairy Whipped
    Topping
¼ cup chopped nuts

Completely dissolve gelatin in boiling water. Combine cold water and enough ice cubes to measure 1¼ cups. Add to gelatin, stirring until thickened. Remove any unmelted ice. Refrigerate until firm.

Spoon ice cream and gelatin alternately into tall sundae dishes, ending with gelatin and filling to within ½ inch of top of dish. Top with whipped topping and nuts. Serve immediately.

Prep time: 15 minutes

GELATIN BANANA SPLITS

Makes 3 to 4 servings

1 package (4-serving size) JELL-O® Brand Gelatin,
    any flavor
1 cup boiling water
1 cup cold water
3 or 4 medium bananas
    Lemon juice
½ cup thawed COOL WHIP® Non-Dairy Whipped
    Topping
3 or 4 maraschino cherries
    Chopped nuts

Completely dissolve gelatin in boiling water. Add cold water and pour into deep narrow bowl. Chill until firm. Just before serving, peel bananas and cut in half lengthwise; brush with lemon juice and arrange in banana split dishes. Scoop gelatin onto bananas. Garnish with whipped topping, cherries and nuts.

Bavarian Forest Cheesecake

BAVARIAN FOREST CHEESECAKE

Makes 10 to 12 servings

WHOPPERS® CRUST
1 package (8 ounces) WHOPPERS® Malted Milk
    Candy, crushed
½ cup graham cracker crumbs
¼ cup butter or margarine, melted

FILLING
3 packages (8 ounces each) cream cheese, softened
½ cup sugar
1 teaspoon vanilla
6 eggs
1 package (8 ounces) WHOPPERS® Malted Milk
    Candy, crushed
Whipped cream, additional WHOPPERS®
    Malted Milk Candy and maraschino cherries
    for garnish

For Whoppers® Crust, in small bowl, combine all crust ingredients; mix well. Grease bottom of 9-inch springform pan. Press crust mixture onto bottom of pan.

For Filling, preheat oven to 350°F. In large bowl, beat cream cheese until fluffy. Gradually add sugar, beating constantly; beat in vanilla. Add eggs, 1 at a time, beating thoroughly after each addition. Pour batter over prepared crust.

Bake 30 minutes. Remove from oven; sprinkle 1 package crushed Whoppers® over top. Continue baking 10 minutes or until set. Loosen cake from rim of pan; cool completely in pan on wire rack. Cover; refrigerate at least 2 hours. Before serving, remove side of springform pan. Garnish cake with whipped cream, additional Whoppers® and cherries. Store, covered, in refrigerator.

"RADICAL" PEANUT BUTTER PIZZA COOKIES

Makes 22 cookies

COOKIES
1 cup BUTTER FLAVOR CRISCO®
1¼ cups granulated sugar, divided
1 cup firmly packed dark brown sugar
1 cup JIF® Creamy Peanut Butter
2 eggs
1 teaspoon baking soda
1 teaspoon vanilla
½ teaspoon salt
2 cups all-purpose flour
2 cups quick-cooking oats (not instant or old-fashioned), uncooked

PIZZA SAUCE
1 package (11½ ounces) milk chocolate chips (2 cups)
¼ cup BUTTER FLAVOR CRISCO®

PIZZA TOPPING
Any of the following:
Mmmmm – candy-coated chocolate pieces
Beary good – gummy bears
Jumbo jewels – small pieces of gumdrops
Bubble-gum like – round sprinkles and balls
German chocolate – chopped pecans and flake coconut
Cherries jubilee – candied cherries and slivered almonds
Rocky road – miniature marshmallows and miniature semi-sweet chocolate chips
Harvest mix – candy corn and chopped peanuts
Ants and logs – cashews and raisins

DRIZZLE
1 cup chopped white confectionery coating

1. Preheat oven to 350°F.

2. For Cookies, combine 1 cup Butter Flavor Crisco®, 1 cup granulated sugar and brown sugar in large bowl. Beat at low speed of electric mixer until well blended. Add Jif® Creamy Peanut Butter, eggs, baking soda, vanilla and salt. Mix about 2 minutes or until well blended. Stir in flour and oats with spoon.

3. Place remaining ¼ cup granulated sugar in small bowl.

4. Measure ¼ cup dough. Shape into ball. Repeat with remaining dough. Roll each ball in granulated sugar. Place 4 inches apart on ungreased cookie sheet. Flatten into 4-inch circles.

5. Bake at 350°F for 8 to 10 minutes. Use back of spoon to flatten center and up to edge of each hot cookie to resemble pizza crust. Cool 5 to 8 minutes on cookie sheet before removing to flat surface.

6. For Pizza Sauce, combine chocolate chips and ¼ cup Butter Flavor Crisco® in large microwave-safe measuring cup or bowl. Microwave at MEDIUM (50% power) for 2 to 3 minutes or until chips are shiny and soft (or melt on rangetop in small saucepan over very low heat, stirring constantly). Stir until smooth. Spoon 2 teaspoons melted chocolate into center of each cookie. Spread to inside edge. Sprinkle desired Pizza Topping over chocolate.

7. For Drizzle, place confectionery coating in heavy resealable sandwich bag. Seal. Microwave at MEDIUM. Knead bag after 1 minute. Repeat until smooth (or melt by placing in bowl of hot water). Cut tiny tip off corner of bag. Squeeze out and drizzle over cookies.

PEANUT BUTTER BEARS

Makes about 3 dozen bears

1 cup SKIPPY® Creamy Peanut Butter
1 cup MAZOLA® Margarine, softened
1 cup firmly packed brown sugar
⅔ cup KARO® Light or Dark Corn Syrup
2 eggs
4 cups all-purpose flour, divided
1 tablespoon baking powder
1 teaspoon ground cinnamon (optional)
¼ teaspoon salt

In large bowl with mixer at medium speed, beat peanut butter, margarine, brown sugar, corn syrup and eggs until smooth. Reduce speed; beat in 2 cups flour, baking powder, cinnamon and salt. With spoon, stir in remaining 2 cups flour. Wrap dough in plastic wrap; refrigerate 2 hours.

Preheat oven to 325°F. Divide dough in half. On floured surface, roll out half the dough to ⅛-inch thickness. Cut with floured bear cookie cutter. Repeat with remaining dough.

Bake on ungreased cookie sheets 10 minutes or until lightly browned. Remove from cookie sheets; cool completely on wire racks. Decorate as desired.

Prep time: 35 minutes, plus chilling
Bake time: 10 minutes, plus cooling

Note: Use scraps of dough to make bear faces. Make one small ball of dough for muzzle. Form 3 smaller balls of dough and press gently into unbaked cookies to create eyes and nose; bake as directed. If desired, use frosting to create paws, ears and bow ties.

Peanut Butter Bears

Peanut Butter & Jelly Cookies

PEANUT BUTTER & JELLY COOKIES

Makes about 4 dozen cookies

1 package DUNCAN HINES® Peanut Butter
    Cookie Mix
¾ cup quick-cooking oats (not instant or
    old-fashioned), uncooked
1 egg
½ cup grape jelly
½ cup confectioners sugar
2 teaspoons water

1. Preheat oven to 375°F.

2. Combine cookie mix, contents of peanut butter
packet from Mix, oats and egg in large bowl. Stir until
thoroughly blended. Divide dough into four equal
portions. Shape each portion into 12-inch-long log
on waxed paper. Place logs on ungreased cookie sheets.
Press back of spoon down center of each log to form
indentation.

3. Bake at 375°F for 9 to 11 minutes or until light
golden brown. Press back of spoon down center of each
log again. Cool 2 minutes on cookie sheets. Remove to
cooling racks. Cool completely. Spoon 2 tablespoons
jelly along indentation of each log.

4. Combine confectioners sugar and water in small
bowl. Stir until smooth. Drizzle over each log. Allow
glaze to set. Cut each log diagonally into 12 slices with
large, sharp knife. Store between layers of waxed paper
in airtight container.

Tip: Also delicious with strawberry preserves instead of
grape jelly.

PEANUT BUTTER AND CHOCOLATE COOKIE SANDWICH COOKIES

Makes about 2 dozen sandwich cookies

½ cup REESE'S® Peanut Butter Chips
½ cup plus 3 tablespoons butter or margarine,
    softened and divided
1¼ cups sugar, divided
¼ cup light corn syrup
1 egg
1 teaspoon vanilla extract
2 cups plus 2 tablespoons all-purpose flour,
    divided
2 teaspoons baking soda
¼ teaspoon salt
½ cup HERSHEY'S® Cocoa
5 tablespoons butter or margarine, melted
    Additional sugar
    About 2 dozen large marshmallows

Preheat oven to 350°F. In small saucepan over very low
heat, melt peanut butter chips and 3 tablespoons softened
butter, stirring constantly until smooth. Remove from
heat; cool slightly. In large mixer bowl, beat remaining
½ cup softened butter and 1 cup sugar until light and
fluffy. Add corn syrup, egg and vanilla; blend thoroughly.
Stir together 2 cups flour, baking soda and salt; add to
sugar mixture, blending well. Remove 1¼ cups batter
and place in small bowl; with wooden spoon stir in
remaining 2 tablespoons flour and peanut butter chip
mixture. Blend cocoa, remaining ¼ cup sugar and
5 tablespoons melted butter into remaining batter.
Refrigerate both batters 5 to 10 minutes or until firm
enough to handle. Roll doughs into 1-inch balls; roll in
additional sugar. Place on ungreased cookie sheet.

Bake 10 to 11 minutes or until set. Cool slightly;
remove from cookie sheet to wire rack. Cool completely.
On paper plate, place 1 marshmallow on flat side of
1 chocolate cookie. Microwave at MEDIUM (50% power)
10 seconds or until marshmallow is softened; place a
peanut butter cookie, flat side down, over marshmallow,
pressing down slightly. Repeat for remaining cookies.
Serve immediately.

GRAHAM PEANUT BUTTER CRUNCHIES

Makes about 6 dozen cookies

1 cup BUTTER FLAVOR CRISCO®
1 cup JIF® Extra Crunchy Peanut Butter
1 cup firmly packed brown sugar
1 cup granulated sugar
2 eggs
1 teaspoon vanilla
2 cups all-purpose flour
2 teaspoons baking soda
½ teaspoon salt
1 cup graham cracker crumbs
⅓ cup milk

1. Preheat oven to 350°F.

2. Combine Butter Flavor Crisco®, Jif® Extra Crunchy Peanut Butter, brown sugar and granulated sugar in large bowl. Beat at medium speed of electric mixer until well blended and creamy. Beat in eggs and vanilla.

3. Combine flour, baking soda and salt. Mix into creamed mixture at low speed until just blended. Stir in crumbs and milk.

4. Form dough into 1-inch balls. Place 2 inches apart on ungreased cookie sheet. Make crisscross pattern on dough with floured fork.

5. Bake at 350°F 10 to 11 minutes or until edges of cookies are lightly browned. Remove immediately to wire rack.

PEANUT BUTTER STARS

Makes 7½ to 8 dozen cookies

1 package DUNCAN HINES® Peanut Butter Cookie Mix
1 egg
2 packages (3½ ounces each) chocolate sprinkles
2 packages (7 ounces each) milk chocolate candy stars

1. Preheat oven to 375°F.

2. Combine cookie mix, contents of peanut butter packet from Mix and egg in large bowl. Stir until thoroughly blended. Shape dough into ¾-inch balls. Roll in chocolate sprinkles. Place 2 inches apart on ungreased cookie sheets.

3. Bake at 375°F for 8 to 9 minutes or until set. Immediately place 1 milk chocolate candy star on top of each hot cookie. Cool 1 minute on cookie sheets. Remove to wire racks. Cool completely. Store in airtight containers.

HAYSTACKS

Makes about 3 dozen cookies

½ cup JIF® Creamy Peanut Butter
¼ cup BUTTER FLAVOR CRISCO®
2 cups butterscotch-flavored chips
6 cups corn flakes
⅔ cup semi-sweet miniature chocolate chips
    Chopped peanuts or chocolate jimmies (optional)

1. Combine Jif® Creamy Peanut Butter, Butter Flavor Crisco® and butterscotch chips in large microwave-safe bowl. Cover with waxed paper. Microwave at MEDIUM (50% power). Stir after 1 minute. Repeat until smooth (or melt on rangetop in small saucepan over very low heat, stirring constantly).

2. Pour corn flakes into large bowl. Pour hot butterscotch mixture over flakes. Stir with spoon until flakes are coated. Stir in chocolate chips.

3. Spoon scant ¼ cupfuls of mixture into mounds on waxed paper-lined cookie sheet. Sprinkle with chopped nuts. Refrigerate until firm.

Peanut Butter Stars

CHOCOLATE CHIP LOLLIPOPS

Makes 2 dozen cookies

1 package DUNCAN HINES® Chocolate Chip
   Cookie Mix
1 egg
2 teaspoons water
   Flat ice cream sticks
   Assorted decors

1. Preheat oven to 375°F.

2. Combine cookie mix, contents of buttery flavor packet
from Mix, egg and water in large bowl. Stir until
thoroughly blended. Shape dough into 24 (1-inch) balls.
Place balls 3 inches apart on ungreased cookie sheets
(see Tip). Push ice cream stick into center of each ball.
Flatten dough ball with hand to form round lollipop.
Decorate by pressing decors onto dough.

3. Bake at 375°F for 8 to 9 minutes or until light golden
brown. Cool 1 minute on cookie sheets. Remove to
wire racks. Cool completely. Store in airtight container.

Tip: For best results, use shiny cookie sheets for baking
cookies. Dark cookie sheets cause cookie bottoms to
become too brown.

Chocolate Chip Lollipops

CAP'N'S COOKIES

Makes about 3 dozen cookies

1 cup firmly packed brown sugar
½ cup (1 stick) margarine or butter, softened
2 eggs
1 teaspoon vanilla
1½ cups all-purpose flour
1 teaspoon baking powder
½ teaspoon salt (optional)
2 cups CAP'N CRUNCH® Cereal, any flavor
1 cup raisins or semi-sweet chocolate pieces

Preheat oven to 375°F. Lightly grease cookie sheet.
Beat sugar and margarine until fluffy. Blend in eggs
and vanilla. Add combined flour, baking powder and
salt; mix well. Stir in cereal and raisins. Drop by
rounded teaspoonfuls onto prepared cookie sheet.

Bake 10 to 12 minutes or until light golden brown.
Cool 2 minutes on cookie sheet; remove to wire rack.
Cool completely. Store tightly covered.

DREAMY CHOCOLATE CHIP
COOKIES

Makes about 3 dozen cookies

1¼ cups firmly packed brown sugar
¾ cup BUTTER FLAVOR CRISCO®
3 eggs, lightly beaten
2 teaspoons vanilla
1 package (4 ounces) German's sweet chocolate,
   melted, cooled
3 cups all-purpose flour
1 teaspoon baking soda
½ teaspoon salt
1 package (11½ ounces) milk chocolate chips
1 package (10 ounces) semi-sweet chocolate chunks
1 cup coarsely chopped macadamia nuts

1. Preheat oven to 375°F.

2. Combine brown sugar, Butter Flavor Crisco®, eggs
and vanilla in large bowl. Beat at low speed of electric
mixer until blended and creamy. Increase speed to high.
Beat 2 minutes. Add melted chocolate. Mix until well
blended.

3. Combine flour, baking soda and salt. Add gradually
to creamed mixture at low speed.

4. Stir in chocolate chips, chocolate chunks and nuts
with spoon. Drop by rounded tablespoonfuls 3 inches
apart onto ungreased cookie sheet.

5. Bake at 375°F for 9 to 11 minutes or until set. Cool
2 minutes on cookie sheet before removing to wire rack.

3. Combine flour, baking powder, baking soda and salt. Add gradually to creamed mixture at low speed. Stir in oats, corn flakes, chocolate chips, nuts and coconut with spoon. Fill ice cream scoop that holds ¼ cup with dough (or use ¼ cup measure). Level with knife. Drop 3 inches apart onto greased cookie sheet.

4. Bake at 350°F for 13 to 15 minutes or until lightly browned around edges but still slightly soft in center. Cool 3 minutes on cookie sheet before removing to wire rack with wide, thin pancake turner.

GRANOLA COOKIES

Makes 4½ to 5 dozen cookies

1 cup sugar
½ cup CRISCO® Oil
⅓ cup honey
¼ cup water
2 eggs
2 cups unsifted all-purpose flour
1¾ cups quick-cooking rolled oats (not instant or old-fashioned), uncooked
1 teaspoon baking soda
1 teaspoon salt
1 teaspoon ground cinnamon
½ cup chopped dried apricots
½ cup raisins
½ cup chopped nuts
½ cup semi-sweet miniature chocolate chips
½ cup flaked coconut

1. Preheat oven to 350°F. Grease cookie sheet.

2. Mix sugar, Crisco® Oil, honey, water and eggs in large mixing bowl. Add flour, oats, baking soda, salt and cinnamon. Mix well. Stir in remaining ingredients. Drop dough by teaspoonfuls about 2 inches apart onto cookie sheet.

3. Bake at 350°F for 8 minutes or until almost no indentation remains when touched lightly. Cool on wire rack.

Granola Bars: Follow recipe above, except spread dough in greased and floured 15 × 10 × 1-inch jelly-roll pan. Bake at 350°F for 15 minutes or until top is light brown. Cool completely in pan on wire rack. Cut into 48 bars.

Brian's Buffalo Cookies

BRIAN'S BUFFALO COOKIES

Makes 2 to 2½ dozen cookies

1 cup BUTTER FLAVOR CRISCO®, melted
1 cup granulated sugar
1 cup firmly packed brown sugar
2 tablespoons milk
1 teaspoon vanilla
2 eggs
2 cups all-purpose flour
1 teaspoon baking powder
1 teaspoon baking soda
½ teaspoon salt
1 cup uncooked rolled oats
1 cup corn flakes, crushed to about ½ cup
1 cup semi-sweet chocolate chips
½ cup chopped pecans
½ cup flake coconut

1. Preheat oven to 350°F. Grease cookie sheet with Butter Flavor Crisco®.

2. Combine Butter Flavor Crisco®, granulated sugar, brown sugar, milk and vanilla in large bowl. Beat at low speed of electric mixer until well blended and creamy. Add eggs. Beat at medium speed until well blended.

Brownie Sandwich Cookies

BROWNIE SANDWICH COOKIES

Makes 25 sandwich cookies

BROWNIE COOKIES
1 package DUNCAN HINES® Chocolate Lovers'
   Double Fudge Brownie Mix
1 egg
3 tablespoons water
   Sugar

FILLING
1 container (16 ounces) DUNCAN HINES®
   Creamy Homestyle Cream Cheese Frosting
   Red food coloring (optional)
½ cup semi-sweet miniature chocolate chips

1. Preheat oven to 375°F. Grease cookie sheets.

2. For Brownie Cookies, combine brownie mix, contents of fudge packet from Mix, egg and water in large bowl. Stir with spoon until well blended, about 50 strokes. Shape dough into 50 (1-inch) balls. Place 2 inches apart on cookie sheets. Grease bottom of drinking glass; dip in sugar. Press gently to flatten 1 ball to ⅜-inch thickness. Repeat with remaining balls.

3. Bake at 375°F for 6 to 7 minutes or until set. Cool 1 minute on cookie sheets. Remove to wire racks. Cool completely.

4. For Filling, tint frosting with red food coloring, if desired. Stir in chocolate chips.

5. To assemble, spread 1 tablespoon filling on bottom of one cookie; top with second cookie, bottom-side down. Press together to make sandwich cookie. Repeat with remaining cookies and filling.

Tip: Keep leftover sandwich cookies fresh by wrapping individually with clear plastic wrap.

CANDY SHOP PIZZA

Makes about 12 servings

1½ cups all-purpose flour
½ teaspoon baking soda
½ teaspoon salt
10 tablespoons (1¼ sticks) butter, softened
½ cup granulated sugar
½ cup firmly packed brown sugar
1 egg
½ teaspoon vanilla extract
2 cups (12-ounce package) NESTLÉ® Toll House®
   Semi-Sweet Chocolate Morsels, divided
½ cup peanut butter
   About 1 cup cut-up fruit, such as bananas and
     strawberries (optional)
   About 1 cup chopped candies, such as
     NESTLÉ® CRUNCH® Bars,
     BUTTERFINGER® Bars,
     ALPINE WHITE® Bars,
     GOOBERS® and RAISINETS®

Preheat oven to 375°F. Grease 12- to 14-inch pizza pan or 15½ × 10½ × 1-inch jelly-roll pan.

In small bowl, combine flour, baking soda and salt; set aside. In large mixer bowl, beat butter, granulated sugar and brown sugar until creamy. Beat in egg and vanilla extract. Gradually beat in flour mixture. Stir in 1 cup Nestlé® Toll House® Semi-Sweet Chocolate Morsels. Spread batter in prepared pan.

Bake 20 to 24 minutes or until lightly browned. Immediately sprinkle remaining 1 cup Nestlé® Toll House® Semi-Sweet Chocolate Morsels over crust; drop peanut butter by spoonfuls onto morsels. Let stand 5 minutes or until soft and shiny. Gently spread chocolate and peanut butter over crust. Top with fruit and candy. Cut into wedges. Serve warm.

KIDS' FAVORITE JUMBO CHIPPERS

Makes about 3 dozen jumbo cookies

2¼ cups all-purpose flour
 1 teaspoon baking soda
 ¾ teaspoon salt
 1 cup butter or margarine, softened
 ¾ cup granulated sugar
 ¾ cup firmly packed brown sugar
 2 large eggs
 1 teaspoon vanilla
 1 package (9 ounces) mini baking semisweet
    chocolate candies
 1 cup peanut butter flavored chips

Preheat oven to 375°F.

Place flour, baking soda and salt in medium bowl; stir to combine.

Beat butter, granulated sugar and brown sugar in large bowl with electric mixer at medium speed until light and fluffy, scraping down side of bowl once. Beat in eggs and vanilla, scraping down side of bowl once. Add flour mixture. Beat at low speed until well blended, scraping down side of bowl once. Stir in candies and chips with wooden spoon. Drop heaping tablespoonfuls of dough 3 inches apart onto ungreased cookie sheets.

Bake 10 to 12 minutes or until edges are golden brown. Let cookies stand on cookie sheets 2 minutes. Remove cookies with spatula to wire racks; cool completely. Store tightly covered at room temperature or freeze up to 3 months.

SURPRISE COOKIES

Makes 1 dozen cookies

2 squares (1 ounce each) semisweet baking
    chocolate, coarsely chopped
1¼ cups all-purpose flour
 ½ teaspoon baking powder
 ¼ teaspoon salt
 ½ cup butter or margarine, softened
 ½ cup sugar
 1 large egg
 1 teaspoon vanilla
    Fillings as desired: maraschino cherries
       (well drained) or candied cherries; chocolate
       mint candies, broken in half; white baking
       bar, cut into chunks; thick milk chocolate
       candy bar, cut into chunks or semisweet
       chocolate chunks; raspberry jam or apricot
       preserves

Preheat oven to 350°F. Grease 12 mini-muffin cups.

Melt chopped chocolate in small, heavy saucepan over low heat, stirring constantly; set aside. Place flour, baking powder and salt in small bowl; stir to combine.

Beat butter and sugar in large bowl with electric mixer at medium speed until light and fluffy, scraping down side of bowl once. Beat in egg and vanilla, scraping down side of bowl once. Gradually beat in chocolate. Gradually add flour mixture. Beat at low speed, scraping down side of bowl once.

Drop level teaspoonfuls of dough into prepared muffin cups. Smooth down dough and form small indentation with back of teaspoon.

Fill as desired with assorted filling ingredients. Top with heaping teaspoonful of dough, smoothing top lightly with back of spoon.

Bake 15 to 17 minutes or until cookies are set. Remove pan to wire rack; cool completely before removing cookies from pan. Store tightly covered at room temperature.

Note: These cookies do not freeze well.

Kids' Favorite Jumbo Chippers

GERMAN SWEET CHOCOLATE BROWNIES

Makes about 16 brownies

1 package (4 ounces) BAKER'S® GERMAN'S®
    Sweet Chocolate
¼ cup (½ stick) margarine or butter
¾ cup sugar
2 eggs
1 teaspoon vanilla
½ cup all-purpose flour
½ cup chopped nuts

Preheat oven to 350°F.

Microwave chocolate and margarine in large microwavable bowl on HIGH (100% power) 2 minutes or until margarine is melted. Stir until chocolate is completely melted.

Stir sugar into melted chocolate mixture. Mix in eggs and vanilla until well blended. Stir in flour and nuts. Spread in greased 8-inch square pan.

Bake for 25 minutes or until wooden toothpick inserted into center comes out with fudgy crumbs. Do not overbake. Cool in pan on wire rack. Cut into squares.

Prep time: 10 minutes
Bake time: 25 minutes

PEANUT BUTTER BROWNIE CUPCAKES

Makes 12 cupcakes

Preheat oven to 350°F.

Prepare German Sweet Chocolate Brownie batter as directed, omitting nuts. In separate bowl, mix ¼ cup peanut butter and 2 tablespoons powdered sugar until smooth. Fill 12 paper-lined 2½-inch muffin cups ½ full with brownie batter. Place a teaspoonful of peanut butter mixture on top of each.

Bake 20 minutes or until wooden toothpick inserted into brownie comes out with fudgy crumbs. Do not overbake. Remove from pan to cool on wire rack.

Prep time: 15 minutes
Bake time: 20 minutes

BROWNIE ICE CREAM CONES

Makes 12 cones

Preheat oven to 350°F.

Prepare German Sweet Chocolate Brownie batter as directed. Fill 12 flat-bottomed ice cream cones half full with batter. Place on cookie sheet.

Bake 25 minutes or until wooden toothpick inserted into brownie comes out with fudgy crumbs. Do not overbake. Cool. To serve, place small scoop of ice cream in each cone. Garnish with candy sprinkles, if desired.

Prep time: 15 minutes
Bake time: 25 minutes

BANANA BERRY BROWNIE PIZZA

Makes 10 to 12 servings

⅓ cup cold water
1 (15-ounce) package brownie mix
¼ cup oil
1 egg
1 (8-ounce) package PHILADELPHIA BRAND®
    Cream Cheese, softened
¼ cup sugar
1 egg
1 teaspoon vanilla
    Strawberry slices
    Banana slices
2 (1-ounce) squares BAKER'S® Semi-Sweet
    Chocolate, melted

- Preheat oven to 350°F.
- Bring water to a boil.
- Mix together brownie mix, water, oil and egg in large bowl until well blended.
- Pour into greased and floured 12-inch pizza pan.
- Bake 25 minutes.
- Beat cream cheese, sugar, egg and vanilla in small mixing bowl at medium speed with electric mixer until well blended. Pour over crust.
- Bake 15 minutes. Cool in pan on wire rack. Top with fruit; drizzle with melted chocolate. Garnish with mint leaves, if desired.

Prep time: 35 minutes
Cook time: 40 minutes

Microwave tip: To melt chocolate, place unwrapped chocolate squares in small microwave-safe bowl. Microwave on HIGH (100% power) 1 to 2 minutes or until almost melted. Stir until smooth.

Top to bottom: Brownie Ice Cream Cones, Peanut Butter Brownie Cupcakes

PUMPKIN CANDY BROWNIES

Makes 26 brownies

1 package DUNCAN HINES® Chocolate Lovers'
    Double Fudge Brownie Mix
2 eggs
⅓ cup water
¼ cup CRISCO® Oil or CRISCO® PURITAN® Oil
1 cup DUNCAN HINES® Creamy Homestyle
    Chocolate Frosting
26 pumpkin candies
½ cup DUNCAN HINES® Creamy Homestyle
    Vanilla Frosting
    Green food coloring

1. Preheat oven to 350°F. Place 26 (2-inch) foil liners in muffin pans or on baking sheets.

2. Combine brownie mix, contents of fudge packet from Mix, eggs, water and Crisco® Oil in large bowl. Stir with spoon until well blended, about 50 strokes. Fill each liner with 2 level measuring tablespoons batter.

3. Bake at 350°F for 15 to 17 minutes or until set. Cool 5 to 10 minutes in pans. Remove to cooling racks.

4. Place Chocolate frosting in small saucepan. Melt on low heat, stirring constantly. Frost top of 1 warm brownie with generous ½ teaspoonful melted frosting. Top with 1 pumpkin candy; push down slightly. Repeat for remaining brownies. Cool completely.

Pumpkin Candy Brownies

320

5. Tint Vanilla frosting with green food coloring. Place in decorating bag fitted with small leaf tip. Pipe 3 leaves around each pumpkin candy. Use small writing tip to pipe vines, if desired.

Tip: For a brighter green frosting, use green paste food color available at cake decorating and specialty shops.

CRUNCH CROWNED BROWNIES

Makes about 2½ dozen brownies

1 package (21 to 23 ounces) fudge brownie mix
1 cup chopped nuts
⅔ cup quick-cooking oats, uncooked
½ cup firmly packed light brown sugar
¼ cup margarine, melted
1 teaspoon ground cinnamon
1½ cups "M&M's®" Plain Chocolate Candies

Preheat oven to 350°F. Prepare brownie mix according to package directions for cake-like brownies; spread batter into greased 13×9-inch baking pan. In large bowl, combine nuts, oats, brown sugar, margarine and cinnamon; mix well. Stir candies into nut mixture; sprinkle over batter.

Bake 40 to 45 minutes or until set. Cool completely in pan on wire rack. Cut into squares.

BROWNIE CANDY CUPS

Makes 2½ dozen brownie cups

1 package DUNCAN HINES® Chocolate Lovers'
    Double Fudge Brownie Mix
2 eggs
⅓ cup water
¼ cup CRISCO® Oil or CRISCO® PURITAN® Oil
30 miniature chocolate-covered peanut butter cup
    candies, wrappers removed

1. Preheat oven to 350°F. Place 30 (2-inch) foil liners in muffin pans or on baking sheets.

2. Combine brownie mix, fudge packet from Mix, eggs, water and oil in large bowl. Stir with spoon until well blended, about 50 strokes. Place 2 level measuring tablespoons batter in each foil liner.

3. Bake at 350°F for 10 minutes. Remove from oven. Push 1 peanut butter cup candy in center of each brownie cup until even with surface of brownie. Bake 5 to 7 minutes longer. Remove to cooling racks. Cool completely.

Tip: Pack these brownies in your child's lunch bag for a special treat.

1. Preheat oven to 350°F. Grease 13×9-inch pan with Butter Flavor Crisco®.

2. For Base, combine ⅔ cup Jif® Creamy Peanut Butter and Butter Flavor Crisco® in large bowl. Beat at medium speed of electric mixer until blended. Add brown sugar and granulated sugar. Beat until well blended. Add eggs and vanilla. Beat until well blended.

3. Combine flour, baking soda and salt. Stir into creamed mixture with spoon. Stir in oats. Press into bottom of greased pan.

4. Bake at 350°F for 20 minutes or until golden brown. Cool to room temperature in pan on wire rack.

5. For Peanut Butter Layer, combine confectioners sugar, milk, 2 tablespoons Jif® Creamy Peanut Butter and 1 tablespoon butter. Mix with spoon until smooth. Spread over base. Refrigerate 30 minutes.

6. For Chocolate Glaze, combine chocolate and 2 tablespoons butter in microwave-safe measuring cup. Microwave at MEDIUM (50% power). Stir after 1 minute. Repeat until smooth (or melt on rangetop in small saucepan over very low heat, stirring constantly). Cool slightly. Spread over peanut butter layer. Cut into bars. Refrigerate about 1 hour or until set. Let stand 15 to 20 minutes at room temperature before serving.

Peanut Butter Bars

PEANUT BUTTER BARS

Makes about 2 dozen bars

BASE
⅔ cup JIF® Creamy Peanut Butter
½ cup BUTTER FLAVOR CRISCO®
¾ cup firmly packed brown sugar
½ cup granulated sugar
2 eggs
1 teaspoon vanilla
1½ cups all-purpose flour
½ teaspoon baking soda
¼ teaspoon salt
1 cup quick-cooking oats (not instant or
    old-fashioned), uncooked

PEANUT BUTTER LAYER
1½ cups confectioners sugar
3 tablespoons milk
2 tablespoons JIF® Creamy Peanut Butter
1 tablespoon butter or margarine, softened

CHOCOLATE GLAZE
2 squares (1 ounce each) unsweetened baking
    chocolate
2 tablespoons butter or margarine

CHOCOLATE PECAN POPCORN BARS

Makes about 30 bars

3 quarts popped corn
2 cups pecan halves or coarsely chopped pecans
2 cups (12 ounces) semisweet chocolate chips
¾ cup sugar
¾ cup KARO® Light or Dark Corn Syrup
2 tablespoons MAZOLA® Margarine

Preheat oven to 300°F. In large roasting pan, combine popped corn and pecans. In medium saucepan, combine chocolate chips, sugar, corn syrup and margarine. Bring to boil over medium-high heat, stirring occasionally; boil 1 minute. Pour over popcorn mixture; toss to coat well.

Bake 30 minutes, stirring twice. Spoon into 13×9-inch baking pan. Press warm mixture firmly and evenly into pan. Cool 5 minutes. Invert onto cutting board. Cut into bars.

Prep time: 15 minutes
Bake time: 30 minutes

Marshmallow Krispie Bars

BAKED S'MORES

Makes 9 squares

1 package DUNCAN HINES® Golden Sugar
  Cookie Mix
1 egg
1 tablespoon water
3 bars (1.55 ounces each) milk chocolate
1 jar (7 ounces) marshmallow creme

1. Preheat oven to 350°F. Grease 8-inch square pan.

2. Combine cookie mix, contents of buttery flavor
packet from Mix, egg and water in large bowl. Stir until
thoroughly blended. Divide cookie dough in half. Press
half the dough evenly into bottom of pan.

3. Break each milk chocolate bar into 12 sections by
following division marks on bars. Arrange chocolate
sections into 4 rows, with 9 sections in each row, over
cookie dough in pan.

4. Place spoonfuls of marshmallow creme on top of
chocolate. Spread to cover chocolate and cookie dough.
Drop remaining cookie dough by teaspoonfuls on top
of marshmallow creme. Spread slightly with back of
spoon.

5. Bake at 350°F for 25 to 30 minutes or until light
golden brown. Cool completely in pan on wire rack.
Cut into squares.

MARSHMALLOW KRISPIE BARS

Makes about 2 dozen bars

1 package DUNCAN HINES® Fudge Brownie
  Mix, Family Size
1 package (10½ ounces) miniature marshmallows
1½ cups semi-sweet chocolate chips
1 cup JIF® Creamy Peanut Butter
1 tablespoon butter or margarine
1½ cups crisp rice cereal

1. Preheat oven to 350°F. Grease bottom of 13×9-
inch pan.

2. Prepare and bake brownies following package
directions for basic recipe. Remove from oven. Sprinkle
marshmallows on hot brownies. Return to oven. Bake
for 3 minutes longer.

3. Place chocolate chips, Jif® Creamy Peanut Butter and
butter in medium saucepan. Cook over low heat, stirring
constantly, until chips are melted. Add rice cereal; mix
well. Spread mixture over marshmallow layer. Refrigerate
until chilled. Cut into bars.

Tip: For a special presentation, cut cookies into
diamond shapes.

MAGIC RAINBOW COOKIE BARS

Makes 2 to 3 dozen bars

½ cup margarine or butter
1½ cups graham cracker crumbs
1 (14-ounce) can EAGLE® Brand Sweetened
  Condensed Milk (NOT evaporated milk)
1 (3½-ounce) can flaked coconut (1⅓ cups)
1 cup chopped nuts
1 cup plain multi-colored candy-coated chocolate
  pieces

Preheat oven to 350°F (325°F for glass dish). In
13×9-inch baking pan, melt margarine in oven. Sprinkle
crumbs over margarine; pour sweetened condensed milk
evenly over crumbs. Top with remaining ingredients;
press down firmly.

Bake 25 to 30 minutes or until lightly browned. Cool.
Chill if desired. Cut into bars. Store loosely covered at
room temperature.

EMILY'S DREAM BARS

Makes about 4½ dozen bars

1 cup JIF® Extra Crunchy Peanut Butter
½ cup BUTTER FLAVOR CRISCO®
½ cup firmly packed brown sugar
½ cup light corn syrup
1 egg
1 teaspoon vanilla
1 cup all-purpose flour
½ teaspoon baking powder
¼ cup milk
2 cups 100% natural oats, honey and raisins cereal
1 package (12 ounces) miniature semi-sweet
    chocolate chips (2 cups), divided
1 cup almond brickle chips
1 cup milk chocolate-covered peanuts
1 package (2 ounces) nut topping (⅓ cup)

1. Preheat oven to 350°F. Grease 13×9-inch pan with Butter Flavor Crisco®.

2. Combine Jif® Peanut Butter, Butter Flavor Crisco®, brown sugar and corn syrup in large bowl. Beat at medium speed of electric mixer until creamy. Add egg and vanilla. Beat well.

3. Combine flour and baking powder. Add alternately with milk to creamed mixture at medium speed until well blended. Stir in cereal, 1 cup chocolate chips, almond brickle chips and chocolate-covered nuts with spoon. Spread into greased pan.

4. Bake at 350°F for 20 to 25 minutes or until golden brown and wooden toothpick inserted in center comes out clean. Sprinkle remaining 1 cup chocolate chips over top immediately after removing from oven. Let stand about 3 minutes or until chips become shiny and soft. Spread over top. Sprinkle with nut topping. Cool completely in pan on wire rack. Cut into bars.

CHOCOLATE CARAMEL PECAN BARS

Makes about 40 bars

2 cups butter, softened, divided
½ cup granulated sugar
1 large egg
2¾ cups all-purpose flour
⅔ cup firmly packed light brown sugar
¼ cup light corn syrup
2½ cups coarsely chopped pecans
1 cup semisweet chocolate chips

Preheat oven to 375°F. Grease 15×10×1-inch jelly-roll pan.

Beat 1 cup butter and granulated sugar in large bowl with electric mixer at medium speed until light and fluffy, scraping down side of bowl once. Beat in egg. Add flour. Beat at low speed, scraping down side of bowl once. Spread dough into prepared pan.

Bake 20 minutes or until light golden brown. While base is baking, prepare topping. Combine remaining 1 cup butter, brown sugar and corn syrup in medium, heavy saucepan. Cook over medium heat until mixture boils, stirring frequently. Boil gently 2 minutes, without stirring. Quickly stir in pecans and spread evenly over base. Return to oven.

Bake 20 minutes or until dark golden brown and bubbly. Immediately sprinkle chocolate chips evenly over hot caramel. Gently press chips into caramel topping with spatula. Loosen caramel from edges of pan with a thin spatula or knife.

Remove pan to wire rack; cool completely. Cut into bars. Store tightly covered at room temperature or freeze up to 3 months.

Chocolate Caramel Pecan Bars

HOLIDAY DESSERTS

PEANUT BUTTER REINDEER

Makes about 2 dozen cookies

COOKIES
1 package DUNCAN HINES® Peanut Butter
    Cookie Mix
1 egg
2 teaspoons all-purpose flour

ASSORTED DECORATIONS
    Miniature semi-sweet chocolate chips
    Vanilla milk chips
    Multi-colored, candy-coated chocolate pieces
    Colored Sprinkles

1. For Cookies, combine cookie mix, peanut butter packet from Mix and egg in large bowl. Stir until thoroughly blended. Form dough into ball. Place flour in jumbo (15 × 13-inch) resealable plastic bag. Place ball of dough in bag. Shake to coat with flour. Place dough in center of bag (do not seal). Roll dough with rolling pin out to edges of bag. Slide bag onto cookie sheet. Chill in refrigerator at least 1 hour.

2. Preheat oven to 375°F.

3. Use scissors to cut bag down center and across ends. Turn plastic back to uncover dough. Dip reindeer cookie cutter in flour. Cut dough with reindeer cookie cutter. Dip cookie cutter in flour after each cut. Transfer cut out cookies using floured pancake turner to ungreased cookie sheets. Reroll dough by folding cut plastic bag back over dough scraps. Decorate as desired making eyes, mouth, nose and tail with assorted decorations.

4. Bake at 375°F for 5 to 7 minutes or until set but not browned. Cool 2 minutes on cookie sheets. Remove to wire racks. Cool completely. Store between layers of waxed paper in airtight container.

SNOW-COVERED ALMOND CRESCENTS

Makes about 4 dozen cookies

1 cup (2 sticks) margarine or butter, softened
¾ cup powdered sugar
½ teaspoon almond extract *or* 2 teaspoons vanilla
    extract
2 cups all-purpose flour
¼ teaspoon salt (optional)
1 cup QUAKER® Oats (quick or old-fashioned,
    uncooked)
½ cup finely chopped almonds
    Additional powdered sugar

Preheat oven to 325°F. Beat margarine, ¾ cup powdered sugar and almond extract until fluffy. Add flour and salt; mix until well blended. Stir in oats and almonds. Shape level measuring tablespoonfuls of dough into crescents. Place on ungreased cookie sheet about 2 inches apart.

Bake 14 to 17 minutes or until bottoms are light golden brown. Remove to wire rack. Sift additional powdered sugar generously over warm cookies. Cool completely. Store tightly covered.

Peanut Butter Reindeer

Left to right: Sparkly Cookie Stars, Black Forest Brownies (page 335)

SPARKLY COOKIE STARS

Makes about 6½ dozen cookies

3½ cups unsifted all-purpose flour
1 tablespoon baking powder
½ teaspoon salt
1 (14-ounce) can EAGLE® Brand Sweetened
    Condensed Milk (NOT evaporated milk)
¾ cup margarine or butter, softened
2 eggs
1 tablespoon vanilla *or* 2 teaspoons almond or
    lemon extract
1 egg white, slightly beaten
    Red and green colored sugars *or* colored sprinkles

Combine flour, baking powder and salt. In large mixer bowl, beat sweetened condensed milk, margarine, eggs and vanilla until well blended. Add dry ingredients; mix well. Chill 2 hours.

Preheat oven to 350°F. On well-floured surface, knead dough to form a smooth ball. Divide into thirds. On well-floured surface, roll out each portion to ⅛-inch thickness. Cut with floured star cookie cutter. Reroll scraps as necessary to use all dough. Place 1 inch apart on greased cookie sheets. Brush with egg white and sprinkle with sugar.

Bake 7 to 9 minutes or until lightly browned around edges (*do not overbake*). Cool. Store loosely covered at room temperature.

Note: If desired, cut small stars from dough and place on top of larger stars. Proceed as above.

FROST-ON-THE-PUMPKIN COOKIES

Makes about 4 dozen cookies

2 cups all-purpose flour
1 teaspoon baking powder
1 teaspoon ground cinnamon
½ teaspoon baking soda
½ teaspoon ground nutmeg
1 cup butter, softened
¾ cup JACK FROST® Granulated Sugar
¾ cup firmly packed JACK FROST® Brown Sugar
1 cup canned pumpkin
1 egg
2 teaspoons vanilla
½ cup raisins
½ cup chopped walnuts
    Cream Cheese Frosting (recipe follows)

Preheat oven to 350°F. In small mixing bowl, combine flour, baking powder, cinnamon, baking soda and nutmeg. Set aside. In large mixer bowl, beat butter for 1 minute. Add granulated sugar and brown sugar; beat until fluffy. Add pumpkin, egg and vanilla; beat well. Add flour mixture to pumpkin mixture; mix until well blended. Stir in raisins and walnuts. Drop by teaspoonfuls 2 inches apart onto greased cookie sheet.

Bake 10 to 12 minutes. Cool on cookie sheet for 2 minutes. Transfer to wire rack; cool completely. Frost with Cream Cheese Frosting. Garnish with chopped nuts, if desired.

Cream Cheese Frosting: In medium mixing bowl, beat 3 ounces softened cream cheese, ¼ cup softened butter and 1 teaspoon vanilla until light and fluffy. Gradually add 2 cups JACK FROST® Powdered Sugar, beating until smooth.

KAHLÚA® KISSES

Makes about 2½ dozen cookies

¾ teaspoon instant coffee powder
⅓ cup water
1 cup plus 2 tablespoons sugar, divided
¼ cup KAHLÚA®
3 egg whites
¼ teaspoon cream of tartar
    Dash salt

Set oven rack in center of oven. Preheat oven to 200°F.

In heavy 2-quart saucepan, dissolve coffee powder in water. Add 1 cup sugar; stir over low heat until sugar dissolves. Do not boil. Stir in Kahlúa®. Brush down sides of pan often with pastry brush dipped in cold water. Bring mixture to a boil over medium heat. *Do not stir.* Boil until candy thermometer registers 240° to 242°F, about 15 minutes, adjusting heat if necessary to prevent boiling over. (Mixture will be very thick.) Remove from heat (temperature will continue to rise).

Immediately beat egg whites with cream of tartar and salt until soft peaks form. Add remaining 2 tablespoons sugar; continue beating until stiff peaks form. Gradually beat hot Kahlúa® mixture into egg white mixture. Continue beating 4 to 5 minutes or until meringue is very thick, firm and cooled to lukewarm.

Line cookie sheet with aluminum foil, shiny side down. Using pastry bag fitted with large (#6) star tip, pipe meringue into kisses about 1½ inches wide at base and 1½ inches high onto cookie sheet.

Bake for 4 hours. Turn oven off. Without opening oven door, let kisses dry in oven 2 more hours or until crisp. Remove from oven; cool completely on cookie sheet. Store in airtight container up to 1 week.

GINGERBREAD MEN

Makes 12 to 14 six-inch tall gingerbread men

1 package DUNCAN HINES® Moist Deluxe Spice Cake Mix
½ cup all-purpose flour
2 eggs
⅓ cup CRISCO® Oil or CRISCO® PURITAN® Oil
⅓ cup dark molasses
2 teaspoons ground ginger
  Raisins, assorted candies, nonpareils or decors

1. Combine cake mix, flour, eggs, oil, molasses and ginger in large bowl. Stir until thoroughly blended (mixture will be soft). Refrigerate 2 hours.

2. Preheat oven to 375°F.

3. Roll dough to ¼-inch thickness on lightly floured surface. Cut with gingerbread man cookie cutter. Place cutout cookies 3 inches apart on ungreased cookie sheets. Decorate as desired using raisins or candies.

4. Bake at 375°F for 8 to 10 minutes or until cookie edges start to brown. Remove immediately to wire racks. Cool completely. Store in airtight container.

Tip: To use as ornaments, press end of drinking straw in top of head section of cookies before baking. String ribbon through holes of cooled cookies. Tie at top.

LINZER TARTS

Makes about 2 dozen cookies

1 cup BLUE BONNET® Spread, softened
1 cup granulated sugar
2 cups all-purpose flour
1 cup PLANTERS® Slivered Almonds, chopped
1 teaspoon grated lemon peel
¼ teaspoon ground cinnamon
⅓ cup raspberry preserves
  Confectioners' sugar

In large bowl with electric mixer at high speed, beat Spread and granulated sugar until light and fluffy. Stir in flour, almonds, lemon peel and cinnamon until blended. Cover; refrigerate 2 hours.

Preheat oven to 325°F. Divide dough in half. On floured surface, roll out one-half of dough to ⅛-inch thickness. Using 2½-inch round cookie cutter, cut circles from dough. Reroll scraps to make additional rounds. Cut out ½-inch circles from centers of half the rounds. Repeat with remaining dough. Place on ungreased cookie sheets.

Bake 12 to 15 minutes or until lightly browned. Remove from cookie sheets; cool on wire racks. Spread preserves on top of whole cookies. Top with cut-out cookies to make sandwiches. Dust with confectioners' sugar.

Gingerbread Men

SPRITZ CHRISTMAS TREES

Makes about 5 dozen cookies

⅓ cup (3½ ounces) almond paste
1 egg
1 package DUNCAN HINES® Golden Sugar
    Cookie Mix
8 drops green food coloring
1 container (16 ounces) DUNCAN HINES®
    Creamy Homestyle Vanilla Frosting
    Cinnamon candies, for garnish

1. Preheat oven to 375°F.

2. Combine almond paste and egg in large bowl. Beat at low speed with electric mixer until blended. Add contents of buttery flavor packet from Mix and green food coloring. Beat until smooth and evenly tinted. Add cookie mix. Beat at low speed until thoroughly blended.

3. Fit cookie press with Christmas tree plate; fill with dough. Force dough through press 2 inches apart onto ungreased cookie sheets.

4. Bake at 375°F for 6 to 7 minutes or until set but not browned. Cool 1 minute on cookie sheets. Remove to wire racks. Cool completely.

5. To decorate, fill resealable plastic bag half full with Vanilla frosting. Do not seal bag. Cut a tiny piece off one corner of bag. Pipe small dot of frosting on tip of

Spritz Christmas Trees

1 cookie tree and top with cinnamon candy. Repeat with remaining cookies. Pipe remaining frosting to form garland on cookie trees. Allow frosting to set before storing between layers of waxed paper in airtight container.

Tip: For fancier trees, pipe frosting on 1 cookie for garland; sprinkle with colored sugars or decors. Repeat with remaining cookies.

CHOCOLATE ALMOND SNOWBALLS

Makes about 2½ dozen cookies

1¾ cups all-purpose flour
⅔ cup NESTLÉ® Cocoa
2 teaspoons baking powder
¼ teaspoon salt
¾ cup granulated sugar
½ cup (1 stick) butter, melted and cooled
2 eggs
1 teaspoon almond extract
    Confectioners' sugar

Preheat oven to 350°F. In small bowl, combine flour, Nestlé® Cocoa, baking powder and salt; set aside.

In large mixer bowl, beat granulated sugar, butter, eggs and almond extract until creamy. Gradually beat in flour mixture. Roll measuring tablespoonfuls of dough into balls. Place 2 inches apart on ungreased cookie sheets.

Bake 6 to 8 minutes. Let stand on cookie sheets 2 minutes. Remove from cookie sheets; cool completely on wire racks. Sprinkle with confectioners' sugar.

SNOWBALLS

Makes about 5 dozen cookies

1 cup butter or margarine, softened
½ cup DOMINO® Confectioners 10-X Sugar
¼ teaspoon salt
1 teaspoon vanilla extract
2¼ cups all-purpose flour
½ cup chopped pecans
    Additional DOMINO® Confectioners 10-X Sugar

In large bowl, beat butter, ½ cup sugar and salt until fluffy. Add vanilla. Gradually stir in flour. Blend nuts into dough. Cover and refrigerate until firm.

Preheat oven to 400°F. Form dough into 1-inch balls. Place 1 inch apart on ungreased cookie sheets.

Bake 8 to 10 minutes or until set, but not brown. Immediately roll in additional sugar. Cool on wire racks. Roll in sugar again. Store in airtight container.

Peppermint Refrigerator Slices

ANISE PILLOWS (PFEFFERNUESSE)

Makes about 5 dozen cookies

1⅔ cups all-purpose flour
1½ teaspoons DAVIS® Baking Powder
½ teaspoon grated lemon peel
¼ teaspoon salt
¼ teaspoon ground cinnamon
¼ teaspoon ground nutmeg
⅛ teaspoon white pepper
⅛ teaspoon ground cloves
⅓ cup BLUE BONNET® Spread, softened
½ cup granulated sugar
1 egg
½ cup milk
½ cup PLANTERS® Walnuts, finely chopped
½ teaspoon anise seed
    Confectioner's sugar

Preheat oven to 350°F. In small bowl, combine flour, baking powder, lemon peel, salt, cinnamon, nutmeg, pepper and cloves; set aside. In large bowl, beat together Spread and granulated sugar until creamy; beat in egg. Add flour mixture alternately with milk, beating well after each addition. Stir in walnuts and anise seed. Drop dough by teaspoonfuls, 2 inches apart, onto lightly greased cookie sheets.

Bake 15 to 17 minutes. Cool slightly on wire racks. Roll in confectioner's sugar while still warm; cool completely.

PEPPERMINT REFRIGERATOR SLICES

Makes about 15 dozen small cookies

3 packages DUNCAN HINES® Golden Sugar
    Cookie Mix, divided
3 eggs, divided
3 to 4 drops red food coloring
¾ teaspoon peppermint extract, divided
3 to 4 drops green food coloring

1. For pink cookie dough, combine contents of 1 buttery flavor packet from Mix, 1 egg, red food coloring and ¼ teaspoon peppermint extract in large bowl. Stir until evenly tinted. Add 1 cookie mix and stir until thoroughly blended. Set aside.

2. For green cookie dough, combine contents of 1 buttery flavor packet from Mix, 1 egg, green food coloring and ¼ teaspoon peppermint extract in large bowl. Stir until evenly tinted. Add 1 cookie mix and stir until thoroughly blended. Set aside.

3. For plain cookie dough, combine remaining cookie mix, contents of buttery flavor packet from Mix, remaining egg and remaining ¼ teaspoon peppermint extract in large bowl. Stir until thoroughly blended.

4. To assemble, divide each batch of cookie dough into four equal portions. Shape each portion into a 12-inch-long roll on waxed paper. Lay 1 pink roll beside 1 green roll; press together slightly. Place 1 plain roll on top. Press rolls together to form 1 tri-colored roll; wrap in waxed paper or plastic wrap. Repeat with remaining rolls to form 3 more tri-colored rolls; wrap separately in waxed paper or plastic wrap. Refrigerate rolls for several hours or overnight.

5. Preheat oven to 375°F.

6. Cut chilled rolls into ¼-inch-thick slices. Place 2 inches apart on ungreased cookie sheets.

7. Bake at 375°F for 7 to 8 minutes or until set but not browned. Cool 1 minute on cookie sheets. Remove to wire racks. Cool completely. Store in airtight containers.

Tip: For a delicious flavor variation, substitute almond extract for peppermint extract.

COOKIE CUTOUTS

Makes about 4½ dozen cookies

1 cup margarine, softened
½ cup granulated sugar
½ cup firmly packed light brown sugar
1 egg
1 teaspoon vanilla extract
3 cups all-purpose flour
1 teaspoon baking soda
    Assorted SUNKIST® Fun Fruits®

In large bowl, with electric mixer, beat margarine with sugars until light and fluffy. Beat in egg and vanilla until smooth. Combine flour with baking soda. Gradually add to margarine mixture, blending well. Cover; refrigerate at least 2 hours.

Preheat oven to 375°F. On lightly floured surface, roll dough ⅛ inch thick; cut into assorted shapes. Place on lightly greased cookie sheets. Decorate with fun fruit snacks.

Bake 8 to 9 minutes or until lightly browned. Cool completely on wire racks. Decorate, if desired, with decorative icing.

Spicy Cookie Cutouts: Increase brown sugar to ¾ cup and add 1½ teaspoons ground cinnamon and 1 teaspoon ground ginger to flour mixture.

Chocolate Cookie Cutouts: Decrease flour to 2¾ cups, increase granulated sugar to 1 cup and add ½ cup unsweetened cocoa powder to flour mixture.

OATS 'N' PUMPKIN PINWHEELS

Makes about 4 dozen cookies

1½ cups sugar, divided
½ cup (1 stick) margarine, softened
2 egg whites
1½ cups all-purpose flour
1 cup QUAKER® Oats (quick or old-fashioned, uncooked)
¼ teaspoon baking soda
1 cup canned pumpkin
½ teaspoon pumpkin pie spice
¼ cup sesame seeds

Beat 1 cup sugar and margarine until fluffy; mix in egg whites. Stir in combined flour, oats and baking soda until well blended. On waxed paper, press into 16 × 12-inch rectangle. Spread combined pumpkin, remaining ½ cup sugar and pumpkin pie spice over dough to within ½ inch from edge. From narrow end, roll up dough, jelly-roll fashion. Sprinkle sesame seeds over outside of roll, pressing gently. Wrap in waxed paper; freeze overnight or until firm.

Preheat oven to 400°F. Spray cookie sheet with nonstick cooking spray. Cut frozen dough into ¼-inch slices; place 1 inch apart on prepared cookie sheet.

Bake 9 to 11 minutes or until golden brown. Remove to wire rack; cool completely.

OATMEAL CRANBERRY-NUT COOKIES

Makes about 4 dozen cookies

¾ cup BUTTER FLAVOR CRISCO®
1 cup firmly packed dark brown sugar
¼ cup dark molasses
1 egg
2 tablespoons milk
1½ teaspoons vanilla
1 cup all-purpose flour
1¼ teaspoons ground cinnamon
½ teaspoon baking soda
½ teaspoon salt
¼ teaspoon ground allspice
1 cup crushed whole-berry cranberry sauce
½ cup sliced almonds, broken
3 cups quick-cooking oats (not instant or old-fashioned), uncooked

1. Preheat oven to 375°F. Grease cookie sheets with Butter Flavor Crisco®.

2. Combine Butter Flavor Crisco® and sugar in large bowl. Beat at medium speed of electric mixer until well blended and creamy. Beat in molasses, egg, milk and vanilla.

3. Combine flour, cinnamon, baking soda, salt and allspice. Mix into creamed mixture at low speed until just blended. Stir in cranberry sauce, nuts and oats with spoon.

4. Drop tablespoonfuls of dough 2 inches apart onto prepared cookie sheets.

5. Bake at 375°F for 12 minutes or until set. Cool 2 minutes on cookie sheets. Remove to wire racks.

Cookie Cutouts

Glazed Sugar Cookies

EUROPEAN KOLACKY

Makes about 3 dozen cookies

1 cup butter or margarine, softened
1 package (8 ounces) cream cheese, softened
1 tablespoon milk
1 tablespoon granulated sugar
1 egg yolk
1½ cups all-purpose flour
½ teaspoon baking powder
1 can SOLO® *or* 1 jar BAKER® Filling (any flavor)
  Confectioners' sugar

Beat butter, cream cheese, milk and granulated sugar in medium bowl with electric mixer until thoroughly blended. Beat in egg yolk. Sift together flour and baking powder; stir into butter mixture to make stiff dough. Cover and refrigerate several hours or overnight.

Preheat oven to 400°F. Roll out dough on lightly floured surface to ¼-inch thickness. Cut dough with floured 2-inch round cookie cutter. Place on ungreased cookie sheets about 1 inch apart. Make depression in centers of dough rounds with thumb or back of spoon. Spoon 1 teaspoon filling into centers of depression.

Bake 10 to 12 minutes or until lightly browned. Remove from cookie sheets and cool completely on wire racks. Sprinkle with confectioners' sugar just before serving.

GLAZED SUGAR COOKIES

Makes 2½ to 3 dozen cookies

COOKIES
1 package DUNCAN HINES® Golden Sugar
  Cookie Mix
1 egg

GLAZE
1 cup sifted confectioners sugar
1 to 2 tablespoons water or milk
½ teaspoon vanilla extract
  Food coloring (optional)
  Red and green sugar crystals or decors

1. Preheat oven to 375°F.

2. For Cookies, combine cookie mix, buttery flavor packet from Mix and egg in large bowl. Stir until thoroughly blended. Roll dough to ⅛-inch thickness on lightly floured surface. Cut dough into desired shapes using floured cookie cutters. Place cookies 2 inches apart on ungreased cookie sheets.

3. Bake at 375°F for 5 to 6 minutes or until edges are light golden brown. Cool 1 minute on cookie sheets. Remove to wire racks. Cool completely.

4. For Glaze, combine confectioners sugar, water and vanilla extract in small bowl. Beat until smooth. Tint glaze with food coloring, if desired. Brush glaze on each cookie with pastry brush. Sprinkle cookies with sugar crystals or decors before glaze sets or decorate as desired. Allow glaze to set before storing between layers of waxed paper in airtight container.

Tip: Use DUNCAN HINES® Creamy Homestyle Vanilla Frosting for a quick glaze. Heat frosting in opened container in microwave oven at HIGH (100% power) for 10 to 15 seconds. Stir well. Spread on cookies and decorate as desired before frosting sets.

BISCOTTI

Makes about 3 dozen cookies

1 (8-ounce) package PHILADELPHIA BRAND®
  Cream Cheese, softened
¾ cup PARKAY® Margarine, softened
¾ cup sugar
1 teaspoon vanilla
½ teaspoon anise extract
4 eggs
3¼ cups all-purpose flour
1 teaspoon CALUMET® Baking Powder
⅛ teaspoon salt
½ cup sliced almonds, toasted

- Preheat oven to 400°F.

- Beat cream cheese, margarine, sugar, vanilla and anise extract in large mixing bowl at medium speed with electric mixer until well blended. Blend in eggs.

- Gradually add combined dry ingredients; mix well. Stir in almonds.

- On well-floured surface with floured hands, shape dough into three 12 × 1½-inch logs. Place logs, 2 inches apart, on greased and floured cookie sheet.

- Bake 15 to 20 minutes or until light golden brown. (Dough will spread and flatten slightly during baking.) Cool slightly.

- Diagonally cut each log into ¾-inch slices. Place on cookie sheet.

- Continue baking 5 to 10 minutes or until light golden brown. Cool on wire rack.

WALNUT CHRISTMAS BALLS

Makes about 1½ dozen sandwich cookies

1 cup California walnuts
⅔ cup powdered sugar, divided
1 cup butter or margarine, softened
1 teaspoon vanilla
1¾ cups all-purpose flour
  Chocolate Filling (recipe follows)

Preheat oven to 350°F. In food processor or blender, process walnuts with 2 tablespoons sugar until finely ground; set aside. In large bowl, beat butter and remaining sugar until creamy. Beat in vanilla. Add flour and ¾ cup ground walnut mixture; mix until blended. Reserve remaining ground walnut mixture. Roll dough into about 3 dozen walnut-sized balls. Place 2 inches apart on ungreased cookie sheets.

Bake 10 to 12 minutes or until just golden around edges. Remove to wire racks to cool completely.

Prepare Chocolate Filling. Place generous teaspoonful of filling on flat side of half the cookies. Top with remaining cookies, flat side down, forming sandwiches. Roll chocolate edges of filling in remaining ground walnut mixture.

Chocolate Filling: Chop 3 squares (1 ounce each) semisweet chocolate into small pieces; place in food processor or blender with ½ teaspoon vanilla. In small saucepan, heat 2 tablespoons *each* butter or margarine and whipping cream over medium heat until hot; pour over chocolate. Process until chocolate is melted, turning machine off and scraping side as needed. With machine running, gradually add 1 cup powdered sugar; process until smooth.

Favorite recipe from **Walnut Marketing Board**

CHERRY PINWHEEL SLICES

Makes about 4 dozen cookies

2 cups all-purpose flour
½ teaspoon salt
1 cup butter or margarine
1 cup dairy sour cream
1 can SOLO® *or* 1 jar BAKER® Cherry, Raspberry or Strawberry Filling, divided
1 cup flaked coconut, divided
1 cup finely chopped pecans, divided
  Confectioner's sugar

Place flour and salt in medium bowl. Cut in butter until mixture resembles coarse crumbs. Add sour cream; stir until blended. Divide dough into 4 pieces. Wrap each piece separately in plastic wrap or waxed paper; refrigerate 2 to 4 hours.

Preheat oven to 350°F. Roll out dough, 1 piece at a time, on lightly floured surface into 12 × 6-inch rectangle. Spread one-fourth of filling over dough and sprinkle with ¼ cup coconut and ¼ cup pecans. Roll up, jelly-roll style, starting from short side. Pinch seam to seal. Place, seam side down, on ungreased cookie sheet. Repeat with remaining dough, filling, coconut and pecans.

Bake 40 to 45 minutes or until rolls are golden brown. Remove from cookie sheets to wire racks. Dust liberally with confectioner's sugar while still warm. Cut into ½-inch slices. Cool completely.

Walnut Christmas Balls

WHITE CHOCOLATE BROWNIES

Makes about 4 dozen small or 2 dozen large brownies

1 package DUNCAN HINES® Chocolate Lovers'
    Milk Chocolate Chunk Brownie Mix
2 eggs
⅓ cup water
⅓ cup CRISCO® Oil or CRISCO® PURITAN® Oil
¾ cup coarsely chopped white chocolate
¼ cup sliced natural almonds

1. Preheat oven to 350°F. Grease bottom of 13×9-inch pan.

2. Combine brownie mix, eggs, water and oil in large bowl. Stir with spoon until well blended, about 50 strokes. Stir in white chocolate. Spread in pan. Sprinkle top with almonds.

3. Bake at 350°F for 25 to 28 minutes or until set. Cool completely in pan on wire rack. Cut into bars.

Tip: For decadent brownies, combine 2 ounces coarsely chopped white chocolate and 2 teaspoons CRISCO® Shortening in small heavy saucepan. Melt over low heat, stirring constantly. Drizzle over brownies. Let stand until set; cut into bars.

White Chocolate Brownies

IRISH COFFEE BROWNIES

Makes 16 brownies

2 cups (11½-ounce package) NESTLÉ® Toll
    House® Milk Chocolate Morsels, divided
½ cup butter
½ cup sugar
2 eggs
1 teaspoon vanilla extract
2 tablespoons Irish whiskey
2 teaspoons NESCAFÉ® Classic Instant Coffee
1 cup all-purpose flour

Preheat oven to 350°F. In small saucepan over low heat, combine 1 cup Nestlé® Toll House® Milk Chocolate Morsels and butter; stir until morsels are melted and mixture is smooth. Cool to room temperature. In large bowl, combine sugar and eggs; beat until thick and lemon-colored. Gradually beat in chocolate mixture and vanilla extract. In cup, combine Irish whiskey and Nescafé® Classic Instant Coffee; stir until dissolved. Add to chocolate mixture. Gradually blend in flour. Pour into foil-lined 8-inch square baking pan.

Bake 25 to 30 minutes or until set. Immediately sprinkle remaining 1 cup Nestlé® Toll House® Milk Chocolate Morsels on top. Let stand until morsels are shiny and soft; spread evenly. Cool completely in pan on wire rack. Cut into 2-inch squares.

BLACK RUSSIAN BROWNIES

Makes about 2½ dozen brownies

4 squares (1 ounce each) unsweetened chocolate
1 cup butter
¾ teaspoon ground black pepper
4 eggs, lightly beaten
1½ cups granulated sugar
1½ teaspoons vanilla
⅓ cup KAHLÚA®
2 tablespoons vodka
1⅓ cups all-purpose flour
½ teaspoon salt
¼ teaspoon baking powder
1 cup chopped walnuts *or* toasted sliced almonds
    Powdered sugar (optional)

Preheat oven to 350°F. Line bottom of 13×9-inch baking pan with waxed paper. Melt chocolate and butter with pepper in small saucepan over low heat, stirring until smooth. Remove from heat; cool.

Combine eggs, granulated sugar and vanilla in large bowl; beat well. Stir in cooled chocolate mixture, Kahlúa® and vodka. Combine flour, salt and baking powder; add to chocolate mixture and stir until blended. Add walnuts. Spread evenly in prepared pan.

Bake just until wooden toothpick inserted into center comes out clean, about 25 minutes. *Do not overbake.* Cool in pan on wire rack. Cut into bars. Sprinkle with powdered sugar, if desired.

CHOCOLATE CHERRY BROWNIES

Makes about 2 dozen brownies

1 jar (16 ounces) maraschino cherries
⅔ cup (1 stick plus 3 tablespoons) margarine
1 package (6 ounces) semi-sweet chocolate pieces (1 cup), divided
1 cup sugar
1 teaspoon vanilla
2 eggs
1¼ cups all-purpose flour
¾ cup QUAKER® Oats (quick or old-fashioned, uncooked)
1 teaspoon baking powder
¼ teaspoon salt (optional)
½ cup chopped nuts (optional)
2 teaspoons vegetable shortening

Preheat oven to 350°F. Lightly grease 13×9-inch baking pan. Drain cherries; reserve 12. Chop remaining cherries.

In large saucepan over low heat, melt margarine and ½ cup chocolate pieces, stirring until smooth. Remove from heat; cool slightly. Add sugar and vanilla. Beat in eggs, one at a time. Add combined flour, oats, baking powder and salt. Stir in chopped cherries and nuts. Spread into prepared pan.

Bake 25 minutes or until brownies pull away from sides of pan. Cool completely in pan on wire rack.

Cut reserved cherries in half; place evenly on top of brownies. In small saucepan over low heat, melt remaining ½ cup chocolate pieces and vegetable shortening, stirring constantly until smooth.* Drizzle over cherries and brownies; cut into squares. Store tightly covered.

*To Microwave: Place chocolate pieces and shortening in small microwaveable bowl. Microwave at HIGH (100% power) 1 to 2 minutes, stirring after 1 minute and then every 30 seconds until smooth.

BLACK FOREST BROWNIES

Makes 2 to 3 dozen brownies

1 (12-ounce) package semi-sweet chocolate chips
¼ cup margarine or butter
2 cups biscuit baking mix
1 (14-ounce) can EAGLE® Brand Sweetened Condensed Milk (NOT evaporated milk)
1 egg, beaten
1 teaspoon almond extract
½ cup chopped candied cherries
½ cup sliced almonds, toasted

Preheat oven to 350°F. In large saucepan, over low heat, melt *1 cup* chips with margarine; remove from heat. Add biscuit mix, sweetened condensed milk, egg and extract; mix until well blended. Stir in remaining chips and cherries. Turn into well-greased 13×9-inch baking pan. Top with almonds.

Bake 20 to 25 minutes or until brownies begin to pull away from sides of pan. Cool. Cut into bars. Store tightly covered at room temperature.

PUMPKIN JINGLE BARS

Makes about 3 dozen bars

¾ cup MIRACLE WHIP® Salad Dressing
1 two-layer spice cake mix
1 (16-ounce) can pumpkin
3 eggs
   Confectioners' sugar
   Vanilla frosting
   Red and green gumdrops, sliced

• Preheat oven to 350°F.

• Mix salad dressing, cake mix, pumpkin and eggs in large bowl at medium speed of electric mixer until well blended. Pour into greased 15½×10½×1-inch jelly-roll pan.

• Bake 18 to 20 minutes or until edges pull away from sides of pan. Cool. Sprinkle with sugar. Cut into bars. Decorate with frosting and gumdrops.

Prep time: 5 minutes
Cook time: 20 minutes

Pumpkin Jingle Bars

CRISPY NUT SHORTBREAD

Makes about 4 dozen cookies

6 tablespoons margarine, softened
⅓ cup sugar
1 egg
1 teaspoon vanilla
½ cup QUAKER® or AUNT JEMIMA® Enriched Corn Meal
½ cup all-purpose flour
½ cup finely toasted, husked, chopped hazelnuts or walnuts
½ cup semi-sweet chocolate pieces
1 tablespoon vegetable shortening Coarsely chopped nuts (optional)

Preheat oven to 300°F. Grease 13×9-inch baking pan.

Beat margarine and sugar until fluffy. Blend in egg and vanilla. Add combined corn meal, flour and ½ cup nuts; mix well. Spread onto bottom of prepared pan.

Bake 40 to 45 minutes or until edges are golden brown. In small saucepan over low heat, melt chocolate pieces and shortening, stirring until smooth.* Spread over shortbread. Sprinkle with coarsely chopped nuts, if desired. Cool completely in pan on wire rack. Cut into squares; cut squares diagonally into triangles, if desired. Store tightly covered.

*To Microwave: Place chocolate pieces and shortening in small microwaveable bowl. Microwave at HIGH (100% power) 1 to 2 minutes, stirring after 1 minute and then every 30 seconds until smooth.

Crispy Nut Shortbread, Peanut Butter Chocolate Bars (page 338)

ALMOND SHORTBREAD

Makes 8 wedges

1 cup all-purpose flour
½ cup sifted powdered sugar
¼ cup cornstarch
½ cup butter
¼ teaspoon vanilla extract
¼ teaspoon almond extract
½ cup BLUE DIAMOND® Sliced Natural
   Almonds, toasted and lightly crushed

Preheat oven to 350°F. In food processor, combine flour, powdered sugar and cornstarch. With on-off pulses, add butter, vanilla, almond extract and almonds until mixture just forms a ball. (To prepare without a food processor, combine flour, powdered sugar and cornstarch in large bowl. With fingertips, work butter into flour mixture until mixture resembles coarse cornmeal. Add vanilla, almond extract and almonds and form dough into ball.)

Press dough into ungreased 8-inch round pie pan; smooth top. Prick top with fork. With knife, score into eight wedges. Decorate edge by indenting with tines of fork. Bake 25 minutes or until firm. Cool in pan on wire rack. Cut into wedges.

PUMPKIN PECAN PIE BARS

Makes 3 to 4 dozen bars

1 cup firmly packed brown sugar
½ cup margarine or butter, softened
1½ cups unsifted all-purpose flour
1 cup rolled oats, uncooked
1 teaspoon baking powder
1 teaspoon salt
1 (16-ounce) can pumpkin (2 cups)
1 (14-ounce) can EAGLE® Brand Sweetened
   Condensed Milk (NOT evaporated milk)
2 eggs, beaten
2 teaspoons pumpkin pie spice
1½ teaspoons vanilla extract
1 cup chopped pecans
   Confectioners' sugar (optional)

Preheat oven to 350°F. In large mixer bowl, beat brown sugar and margarine until fluffy; add flour, oats, baking powder and ½ *teaspoon* salt. Mix until crumbly. Reserve ½ cup crumb mixture. Press remaining crumb mixture on bottom of ungreased 15×10×1-inch jelly-roll pan.

Bake 20 minutes. Meanwhile, in medium bowl, combine pumpkin, sweetened condensed milk, eggs, pumpkin pie spice, vanilla and remaining ½ *teaspoon* salt. Spread over crust. In small bowl, combine reserved crumb mixture with pecans; sprinkle over pumpkin mixture.

Bake 30 to 35 minutes or until set. Cool in pan on wire rack. Sprinkle with confectioners' sugar, if desired. Cut into bars. Store covered in refrigerator.

PUMPKIN CHEESECAKE BARS

Makes 2½ dozen bars

1 cup all-purpose flour
⅓ cup firmly packed light brown sugar
5 tablespoons butter or margarine
½ cup finely chopped pecans
1 package (8 ounces) cream cheese, softened
¾ cup granulated sugar
½ cup LIBBY'S® Solid Pack Pumpkin
2 eggs, lightly beaten
1½ teaspoons ground cinnamon
1 teaspoon ground allspice
1 teaspoon vanilla extract
   Glazed Pecan Halves (recipe follows)

Preheat oven to 350°F. In medium bowl, combine flour and brown sugar. Cut in butter until mixture resembles coarse crumbs. Stir in nuts. Set aside ¾ *cup* mixture for topping. Press *remaining* mixture into bottom of ungreased 8-inch square baking pan.

Bake 15 minutes or until lightly browned. Cool slightly. Meanwhile, in large mixer bowl, combine cream cheese, granulated sugar, pumpkin, eggs, cinnamon, allspice, and vanilla; blend until smooth. Pour over baked crust. Sprinkle with reserved topping.

Bake an additional 35 to 40 minutes, or until slightly firm. Cool in pan on wire rack. Cut into 1×2-inch bars or triangles, if desired. Garnish each piece with a Glazed Pecan Half.

Glazed Pecan Halves: Place greased wire rack over cookie sheet. In small saucepan, bring ¼ cup dark corn syrup to a boil. Boil 1 minute, stirring constantly, until mixture thickens slightly. Remove from heat. Add 32 pecan halves, stirring until well coated. With slotted spoon, remove pecans from syrup. Separate nuts and place on prepared wire rack; cool.

PEANUT BUTTER CHOCOLATE BARS

Makes about 16 bars

½ cup (1 stick) margarine, softened
⅓ cup sugar
½ cup QUAKER® or AUNT JEMIMA® Enriched Corn Meal
½ cup all-purpose flour
½ cup chopped almonds
½ cup peanut butter
¼ cup semi-sweet chocolate pieces
1 teaspoon shortening

Preheat oven to 375°F. Beat margarine and sugar until fluffy. Stir in combined corn meal, flour and almonds. Press onto bottom of ungreased 9-inch square baking pan.

Bake 25 to 30 minutes or until edges are light golden brown. Cool about 10 minutes; spread with peanut butter. In small saucepan over low heat, melt chocolate pieces and shortening, stirring until smooth.* Drizzle over peanut butter. Cool completely in pan on wire rack. Cut into bars. Store tightly covered.

*To Microwave: Place chocolate pieces and shortening in small microwaveable bowl. Microwave at HIGH (100% power) 1 to 1½ minutes, stirring after 1 minute and then every 15 seconds until smooth.

Chocolate Peanut Butter Squares

CHOCOLATE PEANUT BUTTER SQUARES

Makes about 1 dozen squares

1½ cups chocolate-covered graham cracker crumbs (about 17 crackers)
3 tablespoons PARKAY® Margarine, melted
1 (8-ounce) package PHILADELPHIA BRAND® Cream Cheese, softened
1 cup powdered sugar
½ cup chunk-style peanut butter
¼ cup BAKER'S® Semi-Sweet Real Chocolate Chips
1 teaspoon shortening

• Preheat oven to 350°F.

• Stir together crumbs and margarine in small bowl. Press onto bottom of 9-inch square baking pan. Bake 10 minutes. Cool.

• Beat cream cheese, sugar and peanut butter in small mixing bowl at medium speed with electric mixer until well blended. Spread over crust.

• Melt chocolate chips with shortening in small saucepan over low heat, stirring until smooth. Drizzle over cream cheese mixture. Cover; refrigerate 6 hours or overnight. Cut into squares.

Microwave Tip: Microwave chocolate chips and shortening in small microwave-safe bowl on HIGH (100% power) 1 to 2 minutes or until chocolate begins to melt, stirring every minute. Stir until chocolate is melted and mixture is smooth.

CHOCOLATE PECAN PIE SQUARES

Makes about 2 dozen squares

Bar Cookie Crust (recipe follows next page)
1½ cups KARO® Light or Dark Corn Syrup
1 cup (6 ounces) semisweet chocolate chips
1 cup sugar
4 eggs, slightly beaten
1½ teaspoons vanilla
2½ cups coarsely chopped pecans

Preheat oven to 350°F. Prepare Bar Cookie Crust. In large heavy saucepan, combine corn syrup and chocolate chips. Cook and stir over low heat just until chocolate melts. Remove from heat. Beat in sugar, eggs and vanilla until blended. Stir in pecans. Pour over hot Bar Cookie Crust; spread evenly.

Bake 30 minutes or until filling is firm around edges and slightly firm in center. Cool completely in pan on wire rack before cutting into squares.

BAR COOKIE CRUST

MAZOLA® No Stick™ Corn Oil Cooking Spray
3 cups all-purpose flour
1 cup cold MAZOLA® Margarine, cut in pieces
½ cup sugar
¼ teaspoon salt

Spray 15 × 10 × 1-inch jelly-roll pan with cooking spray. In large bowl with mixer at medium speed, beat flour, margarine, sugar and salt until mixture resembles coarse crumbs; press firmly and evenly into bottom of pan.

Bake at 350°F for 20 minutes or until golden brown. Top with desired filling. Finish baking according to individual recipe directions.

GLAZED CRANBERRY MINI-CAKES

Makes 3 dozen mini-cakes

⅓ cup butter or margarine, softened
⅓ cup firmly packed light brown sugar
⅓ cup granulated sugar
1 egg
1¼ teaspoons vanilla extract
1⅓ cups all-purpose flour
¾ teaspoon baking powder
¼ teaspoon baking soda
¼ teaspoon salt
2 tablespoons milk
1¼ cups coarsely chopped fresh cranberries
½ cup coarsely chopped walnuts
1⅔ cups (10-ounce package) HERSHEY'S Vanilla Milk Chips, divided
Vanilla Chip Glaze (recipe follows)
Additional cranberries (optional)

Preheat oven to 350°F. Lightly grease or paper-line 36 small muffin cups (1¾ inches in diameter).

In large mixer bowl, beat butter, brown sugar, granulated sugar, egg and vanilla extract until light and fluffy. Stir together flour, baking powder, baking soda and salt; gradually blend into butter mixture. Add milk; stir until well blended. Stir in 1¼ cups cranberries, walnuts and ⅔ cup vanilla milk chips (reserve remaining chips for Vanilla Chip Glaze). Fill muffin cups about ⅞ full with batter.

Glazed Cranberry Mini-Cakes

Bake 18 to 20 minutes or until wooden toothpick inserted in centers comes out clean. Cool 5 minutes; remove from pans to wire racks. Cool completely. Prepare Vanilla Chip Glaze; dip rounded portion of each muffin into glaze (or spread glaze over tops). Place on waxed paper-covered tray; refrigerate 10 minutes to set glaze. Garnish with additional cranberries, if desired.

Vanilla Chip Glaze: In small microwave-safe bowl, place remaining 1 cup HERSHEY'S Vanilla Milk Chips; sprinkle 2 tablespoons vegetable oil over chips. Microwave at HIGH (100% power) 30 seconds; stir vigorously. If necessary, microwave at HIGH additional 30 seconds or just until chips are melted and mixture is smooth when stirred.

CRANBERRY NUT ROLL

Makes 10 to 12 servings

4 eggs, separated
½ cup granulated sugar, divided
1 cup cranberries, chopped
½ cup walnuts, finely chopped
⅓ cup sifted cake flour
2 tablespoons cornstarch
1 teaspoon ground cinnamon
2 tablespoons (¼ stick) butter, melted
    Confectioners' sugar
2 foil-wrapped bars (4 ounces) NESTLÉ® Premier
    White Baking Bars, broken up
1 cup whipping cream, divided
    White Buttercream (recipe follows)

Preheat oven to 350°F. Grease 15½ × 10½ × 1-inch jelly-roll pan. Line with waxed paper; grease paper. In large mixer bowl, beat egg whites until foamy. Gradually add ¼ cup granulated sugar, beating until stiff peaks form; set aside.

In small mixer bowl, beat egg yolks and remaining ¼ cup granulated sugar until light and fluffy, about 3 minutes. Fold in cranberries, walnuts, flour, cornstarch and cinnamon; gently fold into egg white mixture. Fold in melted butter. Spread in prepared pan.

Bake 20 minutes or until top springs back when lightly pressed. Loosen cake from sides of pan; cool 10 minutes. Sprinkle cloth towel with confectioners' sugar; invert cake onto towel. Peel off waxed paper. Starting at 10-inch side, roll up warm cake with towel inside. Cool cake completely, seam-side down, on wire rack.

Combine over hot (not boiling) water, Nestlé® Premier White Baking Bars and 2 tablespoons cream; stir until baking bars are melted and mixture is smooth. In small mixer bowl, combine melted baking bar mixture and remaining cream; refrigerate until chilled. Beat chilled cream mixture *just* until soft peaks form.

Unroll cooled cake. Spread whipped cream mixture to within ½ inch of edges; roll up cake. Pipe or spread White Buttercream over cake. Refrigerate until ready to serve.

WHITE BUTTERCREAM

3 foil-wrapped bars (6-ounce package) NESTLÉ®
    Premier White Baking Bars, broken up
¼ cup whipping cream
1 cup (2 sticks) cold butter, cut into pieces
1 cup confectioners' sugar

Melt over hot (not boiling) water, Premier White Baking Bars with cream. Stir until bars are melted and mixture is smooth. Transfer to large mixer bowl; cool to room temperature.

Gradually beat in cold butter and confectioners' sugar; continue beating until light and fluffy. Buttercream may be made 1 to 2 days ahead of time and refrigerated; beat until light and fluffy before using.

Makes about 3 cups frosting

PINEAPPLE-CRANBERRY CAKE

Makes about 12 servings

1 can (20 ounces) DOLE® Crushed Pineapple
    in Juice
3 cups all-purpose flour
2 teaspoons baking soda
1 teaspoon ground cinnamon
1 teaspoon ground ginger
½ teaspoon salt
1½ cups sugar
¾ cup mayonnaise
3 eggs
4 cups fresh cranberries, chopped
1 cup DOLE® Raisins
1 cup chopped walnuts
1 tablespoon grated orange peel
    Pineapple Frosting (recipe follows)

Preheat oven to 350°F. Drain pineapple; reserve ½ cup juice. In medium bowl, combine flour, baking soda, spices and salt. In large bowl, beat sugar, mayonnaise, pineapple, eggs and ½ cup reserved juice. Gradually add flour mixture, beating until well mixed. Stir in cranberries, raisins, walnuts and orange peel. Pour batter into greased and floured 13 × 9-inch pan.

Bake 50 to 55 minutes or until wooden toothpick inserted into center comes out clean. Cool completely in pan on wire rack. Frost with Pineapple Frosting. Cover; refrigerate cake to set frosting. Store in refrigerator.

Pineapple Frosting: In medium bowl, beat 1 package (8 ounces) softened cream cheese and ½ cup softened margarine. Beat in 1 cup powdered sugar and 1 teaspoon grated orange peel until light and fluffy. Stir in 1 can (8 ounces) well-drained Dole® Crushed Pineapple.

Cranberry Nut Roll

Classic Christmas Cake

1. Preheat oven to 350°F. Grease and flour two 8½ × 4½-inch loaf pans.

2. For Cake, combine cake mix, pudding mix, eggs, water and Crisco® Oil in large bowl. Beat at medium speed with electric mixer for 2 minutes. Stir in toasted pecans. Pour batter into pans.

3. Bake at 350°F for 55 to 60 minutes or until wooden toothpick inserted in centers comes out clean. Cool in pans 15 minutes. Loosen loaves from pans. Invert onto wire racks. Turn right-side up. Cool completely.

4. For Caramel Glaze, combine butter, brown sugar, granulated sugar and whipping cream in small heavy saucepan. Bring to a boil over medium heat; boil 1 minute. Remove from heat; cool 20 minutes. Add confectioners sugar and vanilla extract; blend with wooden spoon until smooth and thick. Spread evenly over cooled loaves. Garnish with pecan halves and maraschino cherry halves before glaze sets.

CLASSIC CHRISTMAS CAKE

Makes one 10-inch cake

> 1 package (8 ounces) cream cheese, softened
> 1 cup butter or margarine, softened
> 1½ cups granulated sugar
> 1½ teaspoons vanilla
> 1½ teaspoons ground cinnamon
> ¼ teaspoon ground nutmeg
> 4 eggs
> 2¼ cups sifted cake flour
> 1½ teaspoons baking powder
> 1 jar (8 ounces) maraschino cherries, drained and chopped
> 1 cup finely chopped pecans, divided
> 1½ cups powdered sugar
> 2 tablespoons milk
> Pecan halves and red and green candied cherries for garnish

Preheat oven to 325°F. In large bowl, beat cream cheese, butter, granulated sugar, vanilla and spices. Add eggs, 1 at a time, mixing well after each addition. In small bowl, combine flour with baking powder; gradually add 2 cups flour mixture to butter mixture. To remaining flour mixture, add maraschino cherries and ½ cup chopped pecans; fold into batter. Grease 10-inch Bundt® or tube pan; sprinkle remaining ½ cup chopped pecans in bottom. Pour batter into prepared pan.

Bake 1 hour and 15 minutes or until wooden toothpick inserted into center comes out clean. Let cool in pan on wire rack 5 minutes. Loosen edge of cake; remove from pan. Cool completely on wire rack. In small bowl, beat powdered sugar and milk until smooth; spoon over cake. Garnish with pecan halves and candied cherries.

Favorite recipe from **Pecan Marketing Board**

CARAMEL PECAN SPICE CAKES

Makes 2 loaves, 24 slices

CAKE
> 1 package DUNCAN HINES® Moist Deluxe Spice Cake Mix
> 1 package (4-serving size) vanilla instant pudding and pie filling mix
> 4 eggs
> 1 cup water
> ⅓ cup CRISCO® Oil or CRISCO® PURITAN® Oil
> 1½ cups pecan pieces, toasted and finely chopped

CARAMEL GLAZE
> 3 tablespoons butter or margarine
> 3 tablespoons firmly packed brown sugar
> 3 tablespoons granulated sugar
> 3 tablespoons whipping cream
> ½ cup confectioners sugar
> ¼ teaspoon vanilla extract
> Pecan halves, for garnish
> Maraschino cherry halves, for garnish

Autumn Gold Pumpkin Cake

PUMPKIN 'N' SPICE MINI-FLUTED TUBE CAKES

Makes 12 mini-fluted tube cakes

1 package (18.5 ounces) yellow cake mix with
    pudding in mix
1 cup canned LIBBY'S® Pumpkin Pie Mix
⅓ cup vegetable oil
3 eggs
2 teaspoons ground cinnamon
¾ cup sour cream
2 teaspoons firmly packed light brown sugar
    Fresh fruit, cut up, for garnish

Preheat oven to 350°F. Generously grease 6 individual
mini-fluted tube pans with solid shortening. In large
mixer bowl, combine cake mix, pumpkin pie mix, oil,
eggs and cinnamon. Using an electric mixer, beat at low
speed until moistened. Beat 2 minutes at high speed.
Fill prepared pans about half full, using half the batter.
Spread evenly with rubber spatula. Gently tap pans on
counter several times to remove air bubbles.

Bake 20 to 25 minutes, or until wooden toothpick
inserted in centers comes out clean. Cool in pans 4 to
5 minutes. Remove from pans; cool on wire racks. Repeat
process with remaining batter. When cool, place cakes
on serving plates.

Combine sour cream and brown sugar in small bowl,
stirring well. Fill center of each cake with 1 tablespoon
sour cream mixture. Garnish with fresh fruit.

AUTUMN GOLD PUMPKIN CAKE

Makes 12 to 16 servings

CAKE
1 package DUNCAN HINES® Moist Deluxe
    Butter Recipe Golden Cake Mix
3 eggs
1 cup water
1 cup solid-pack pumpkin
1 teaspoon ground cinnamon
¼ teaspoon ground ginger
¼ teaspoon ground nutmeg
1 cup chopped walnuts

FROSTING
1 container (16 ounces) DUNCAN HINES®
    Creamy Homestyle Vanilla Frosting
½ teaspoon ground cinnamon
¼ cup coarsely chopped walnuts, for garnish

1. Preheat oven to 375°F. Grease and flour two 8-inch
round cake pans.

2. For Cake, combine cake mix, eggs, water, pumpkin,
1 teaspoon cinnamon, ginger and nutmeg in large bowl.
Beat at medium speed with electric mixer for 4 minutes.
Stir in 1 cup walnuts. Pour batter into pans.

3. Bake at 375°F for 30 to 35 minutes or until wooden
toothpick inserted in centers comes out clean. Cool
following package directions.

4. For Frosting, combine Vanilla frosting and ½ teaspoon
cinnamon. Stir until blended. Fill and frost cake. Garnish
with ¼ cup walnuts.

Tip: You may also bake this cake in a greased and floured
13×9-inch pan at 375°F. Bake for 28 to 33 minutes or
until wooden toothpick inserted in center comes out
clean.

CHRISTMAS TREE POKE CAKE

Makes 24 servings

2 packages (2-layer size each) white cake mix
1 package (4-serving size) JELL-O® Brand
    Strawberry Flavor Gelatin
1 package (4-serving size) JELL-O® Brand Lime
    Flavor Gelatin
2 cups boiling water, divided
2⅔ cups (7 ounces) BAKER'S® ANGEL FLAKE®
    Coconut, divided
    Green food coloring
½ teaspoon milk or water
5¼ cups (12 ounces) COOL WHIP® Non-Dairy
    Whipped Topping, thawed, divided
    Assorted gumdrops, peppermint candies and
    red string licorice (optional)

Preheat oven to 325°F. Prepare 1 cake mix as directed on package. Pour batter into greased and floured 9-inch square pan.

Bake 50 to 55 minutes or until cake tester inserted in center comes out clean. Cool 10 minutes. Remove from pan; finish cooling on wire rack. Repeat with remaining cake mix.

Christmas Tree Poke Cake

Place cake layers, top sides up, in 2 clean 9-inch square pans. Pierce cakes with large fork at ½-inch intervals.

Completely dissolve each flavor of gelatin in separate bowl, using 1 cup boiling water for each. Carefully pour strawberry flavor gelatin over 1 cake layer and lime flavor gelatin over second cake layer. Chill 3 hours.

Increase oven temperature to 350°F. Spread ⅓ cup coconut in shallow pan. Toast, stirring frequently, 7 to 12 minutes or until lightly browned. Cool. Place remaining coconut in small bowl. Dilute a few drops food coloring with milk; add to coconut in bowl. Toss with fork until evenly tinted.

Dip 1 cake pan in warm water 10 seconds; unmold. Place right side up on large serving plate or cutting board. Cut cake as shown in Diagram 1. Arrange pieces in Christmas tree shape (Diagram 2), using small amount of whipped topping to hold pieces together. Top with about 1½ cups of the whipped topping. Unmold second cake layer; cut into pieces as shown in Diagram 1. Place pieces on first layer, using small amount of whipped topping to hold pieces together. Use remaining whipped topping to frost entire cake.

Sprinkle trunk of tree with toasted coconut. Sprinkle remaining cake with green coconut. Decorate with gumdrops, peppermint candies and licorice, if desired. Chill until ready to serve.

Prep time: 30 minutes
Chill time: 3 hours

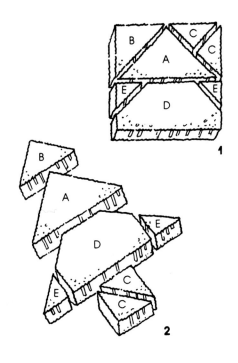

Candy Cane Cake

CANDY CANE CAKE

Makes 12 to 16 servings

1 package DUNCAN HINES® Moist Deluxe Cake Mix (any flavor)

FROSTING
5 cups confectioners sugar
¾ cup CRISCO® Shortening
½ cup water
⅓ cup non-dairy powdered creamer
2 teaspoons vanilla extract
½ teaspoon salt
Red food coloring
Maraschino cherry halves, well drained

1. Preheat oven to 350°F. Grease and flour 13×9-inch pan.

2. Prepare, bake and cool cake following package directions for basic recipe. Remove from pan. Freeze cake for ease in handling.

3. For Frosting, combine confectioners sugar, shortening, water, non-dairy powdered creamer, vanilla extract and salt in large bowl. Beat at medium speed with electric mixer for 3 minutes. Beat at high speed for 5 minutes.

Add more confectioners sugar to thicken or water to thin frosting as needed. Reserve 2 cups frosting. Tint remaining frosting with red food coloring.

4. Cut frozen cake and arrange as shown. Spread white frosting on cake. Mark candy cane stripes in frosting with tip of knife. Place star tip in decorating bag and fill with red frosting. To make stripes, arrange maraschino cherry halves and pipe red frosting following lines as shown in photograph.

Tip: For a quick dessert, serve leftover cake pieces with sugared strawberries and dollops of whipped cream.

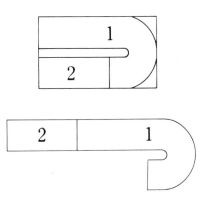

CHOCOLATE AND VANILLA YULE LOG

Makes 10 to 12 servings

4 eggs, separated
½ cup plus ⅓ cup sugar, divided
1 teaspoon vanilla extract
½ cup all-purpose flour
¼ cup HERSHEY'S Cocoa or HERSHEY'S
    European Style Cocoa
½ teaspoon baking powder
¼ teaspoon baking soda
⅛ teaspoon salt
⅓ cup water
    Vanilla Cream Filling (recipe follows)
    Cocoa Glaze (recipe follows)
    Vanilla Leaves (recipe follows)
    Cranberries (optional)

Preheat oven to 375°F. Line 15½ × 10½ × 1-inch jelly-roll pan with foil; generously grease foil.

In large mixer bowl, beat egg whites until soft peaks form; gradually add ½ cup sugar, beating until stiff peaks form. Set aside. In small mixer bowl, beat egg yolks and vanilla extract on high speed about 3 minutes; gradually add remaining ⅓ cup sugar. Continue beating 2 additional minutes until mixture is thick and lemon-colored. Stir together flour, cocoa, baking powder, baking soda and salt; gently fold into egg yolk mixture alternately with water just until mixture is smooth. Gradually fold egg yolk mixture into egg whites; spread batter evenly into prepared pan.

Bake 12 to 15 minutes or until top springs back when touched lightly in center. Immediately loosen cake from edges of pan; invert onto clean, lint-free dish towel sprinkled with powdered sugar. Carefully peel off foil. Immediately roll cake in towel starting from narrow end; place on wire rack. Cool completely. Prepare Vanilla Cream Filling. Unroll cake; remove towel. Spread with Vanilla Cream Filling; reroll cake. Spread Cocoa Glaze over top and sides. Cover; refrigerate until just before serving. Top with Vanilla Leaves and cranberries, if desired.

VANILLA CREAM FILLING

½ teaspoon unflavored gelatin
1 tablespoon cold water
⅔ cup HERSHEY'S Vanilla Milk Chips
¼ cup milk
1 teaspoon vanilla extract
1 cup (½ pint) cold whipping cream

In small cup, sprinkle gelatin over cold water; let stand 1 minute to soften. In medium microwave-safe bowl, combine vanilla chips and milk. Microwave at HIGH (100% power) 30 seconds to 1 minute, stirring vigorously after 30 seconds, until chips are melted and mixture is smooth when stirred. Add gelatin mixture and vanilla extract; stir until gelatin is dissolved. Cool to room temperature. In small mixer bowl, beat whipping cream until stiff; carefully fold into vanilla mixture. Refrigerate 10 minutes or until filling begins to set.

Makes about 2 cups filling

COCOA GLAZE

2 tablespoons butter or margarine
2 tablespoons HERSHEY'S Cocoa or
    HERSHEY'S European Style Cocoa
2 tablespoons water
1 cup powdered sugar
½ teaspoon vanilla extract

In small saucepan over low heat, melt butter; add cocoa and water, stirring until smooth and slightly thickened. Do not boil. Remove from heat; cool slightly. Gradually blend in powdered sugar and vanilla.

Makes about ¾ cup glaze

Vanilla Leaves: Place waxed paper on tray or cookie sheet; set aside. Thoroughly wash and dry several rose, lemon or other non-toxic leaves. In small microwave-safe bowl, place ½ cup HERSHEY'S Vanilla Milk Chips and 1 teaspoon vegetable shortening. Microwave at HIGH (100% power) 45 seconds to 1 minute or until chips are melted and mixture is smooth when stirred. With small soft-bristled pastry brush, brush melted vanilla chip mixture onto backs of leaves, being careful not to drip over edges; place on prepared tray. Refrigerate until very firm. Carefully peel green leaves away from vanilla leaves; refrigerate until ready to use.

Chocolate and Vanilla Yule Log

Brownie Holiday Dessert

BROWNIE HOLIDAY DESSERT

Makes 12 servings

BROWNIES
1 package DUNCAN HINES® Chocolate Lovers'
   Milk Chocolate Chunk Brownies
3 eggs
⅓ cup water
⅓ cup CRISCO® Oil or CRISCO® PURITAN® Oil

FILLING AND FROSTING
1 package (4-serving size) French vanilla instant
   pudding and pie filling mix
¼ cup confectioners sugar
1 cup milk
1 container (8 ounces) frozen whipped topping,
   thawed
1 can (8 ounces) pineapple tidbits, drained and
   divided
¼ cup miniature marshmallows
¼ cup flaked coconut
2 tablespoons chopped maraschino cherries
   Additional marachino cherries, for garnish

1. Preheat oven to 350°F. Grease two 8-inch round
cake pans. Line with waxed paper.

2. For Brownies, combine brownie mix, eggs, water and
oil in large bowl. Stir with spoon until well blended,
about 50 strokes. Pour into pans.

3. Bake at 350°F for 25 to 30 minutes or until set. Cool
in pans on wire racks 15 minutes. Remove from pans.
Peel waxed paper from bottoms. Cool completely.

4. For Filling and Frosting, combine pudding mix,
confectioners sugar and milk in large bowl. Beat at low
speed with electric mixer for 1 minute until well blended.

Fold in whipped topping. Remove 1 cup mixture to
small bowl; stir in ⅓ cup pineapple, marshmallows,
coconut and 2 tablespoons chopped cherries.

5. To assemble, place one brownie layer on serving
plate. Spread with fruit filling. Top with second brownie
layer. Frost top and sides with remaining pudding mixture.
Garnish with remaining pineapple and additional cherries.
Refrigerate until ready to serve.

KAHLÚA® SWEETHEART CAKE

Makes 10 to 12 servings

¾ cup unsweetened cocoa
1 teaspoon instant coffee crystals
1 cup boiling water
½ cup plus 2 tablespoons KAHLÚA®, divided
½ cup butter or margarine, softened
¼ cup shortening
1¾ cups sugar
3 eggs
1 teaspoon vanilla
2 cups sifted all-purpose flour
1½ teaspoons baking soda
¾ teaspoon salt
¼ teaspoon baking powder
   KAHLÚA® Fudge Frosting (recipe follows)

Preheat oven to 350°F. Line bottoms of two 9-inch
round pans with parchment paper; lightly grease sides of
pans. In small heatproof bowl, blend cocoa, coffee and
water. Stir in ½ cup Kahlúa®; cool. In large bowl, beat
butter, shortening, sugar, eggs and vanilla until light and
fluffy. In small bowl, combine flour, baking soda, salt
and baking powder. Add flour mixture to butter mixture
alternately with cocoa mixture, beating well after each
addition. Divide batter evenly between prepared pans.

Bake 25 to 30 minutes or just until wooden toothpick
inserted into centers comes out clean. Do not overbake.
Let cool in pans on wire racks 5 minutes. Loosen edges;
remove from pans. Peel off parchment paper; cool
completely on wire racks. Prepare Kahlúa® Fudge
Frosting. Brush bottom of each layer with 1 tablespoon
of remaining Kahlúa®. Fill and frost layers with Kahlúa®
Fudge Frosting. Decorate as desired. Let stand until
frosting is set.

Kahlúa® Fudge Frosting: In medium saucepan,
combine 1 package (6 ounces) semisweet chocolate
chips, 1 cup butter or margarine and ¼ cup *each*
Kahlúa® and half-and-half. Stir over medium heat until
chocolate melts. Remove from heat; blend in 2½ cups
powdered sugar. Beat until frosting is cool and of
spreading consistency. (Pan may be placed over ice
water to hasten cooling.)

TRIPLE CHOCOLATE FANTASY

Makes 12 to 16 servings

CAKE

1 package DUNCAN HINES® Moist Deluxe
   Devil's Food Cake Mix
3 eggs
1⅓ cups water
½ cup CRISCO® Oil or CRISCO® PURITAN® Oil
½ cup ground walnuts (see Tip)

CHOCOLATE GLAZE

1 package (12 ounces) semi-sweet chocolate chips
¼ cup *plus* 2 tablespoons butter or margarine
¼ cup coarsely chopped walnuts, for garnish

WHITE CHOCOLATE GLAZE

3 ounces white chocolate, coarsely chopped
1 tablespoon CRISCO® Shortening

1. Preheat oven to 350°F. Grease and flour 10-inch Bundt® pan.

2. For Cake, combine cake mix, eggs, water, oil and ground walnuts in large bowl. Beat at medium speed with electric mixer for 2 minutes. Pour into pan.

3. Bake at 350°F for 45 to 55 minutes or until wooden toothpick inserted in center comes out clean. Cool in pan 25 minutes. Invert onto serving plate. Cool completely.

4. For Chocolate Glaze, combine chocolate chips and butter in small heavy saucepan. Heat over low heat until chips are melted. Stir constantly until shiny and smooth. (Glaze will be very thick.) Spread hot glaze over cooled cake. Sprinkle with coarsely chopped walnuts.

5. For White Chocolate Glaze, combine white chocolate and shortening in small heavy saucepan. Heat over low heat until melted, stirring constantly. Drizzle hot glaze over top and sides of cake.

Tip: To grind walnuts, use a food processor fitted with steel blade. Process until fine.

Triple Chocolate Fantasy

CHERRY FRUIT CAKE

Makes 1 cake

¾ cup all-purpose flour
½ teaspoon baking powder
½ teaspoon salt
1 (16-ounce) jar whole maraschino cherries, drained
9 ounces pecan halves
8 ounces diced pitted dates
8 ounces chopped candied pineapple
3 eggs
1½ ounces rum
¼ cup light corn syrup

Preheat oven to 300°F. Combine flour, baking powder and salt in large mixing bowl; mix well. Add cherries, pecans, dates and pineapple. Toss until fruits and nuts are coated with flour mixture. Beat eggs and rum in small bowl until blended. Pour over fruit mixture; mix thoroughly. Grease 9 × 5-inch loaf pan; line with parchment paper and grease again. Turn cake batter into pan, pressing down with spatula to pack tightly.

Bake 1 hour and 45 minutes or until wooden toothpick inserted near center comes out clean. Cool cake in pan 15 minutes. Remove cake from pan; discard paper. Brush warm cake with corn syrup. Cool completely before serving or storing.

Favorite recipe from **National Cherry Foundation**

HOLIDAY FRUIT CAKE

Makes 20 to 24 servings

1 pound diced candied mixed fruits
8 ounces candied cherries, halved
4 ounces candied pineapple, chopped
1½ cups chopped nuts
1 cup raisins
½ cup all-purpose flour
1 package DUNCAN HINES® Moist Deluxe Spice
    Cake Mix
1 package (4-serving size) vanilla instant pudding
    and pie filling mix
3 eggs
½ cup CRISCO® Oil or CRISCO® PURITAN® Oil
¼ cup water
    Light corn syrup, heated

1. Preheat oven to 300°F. Grease 10-inch tube pan.
Line bottom with aluminum foil.

2. Reserve ¼ cup assorted candied fruits and nuts for
garnish, if desired. Combine remaining candied fruits,
nuts and raisins in large bowl. Toss with flour until
evenly coated. Set aside.

3. Combine cake mix, pudding mix, eggs, oil and water
in large bowl. Beat at medium speed with electric mixer
for 3 minutes (batter will be very stiff). Stir in candied
fruit mixture. Spread in pan.

Pumpkin Marble Cheesecake

4. Bake at 300°F for 2 hours or until wooden toothpick
inserted in center comes out clean. Cool completely in
pan on wire rack. Invert onto serving plate. Peel off foil.

5. Brush top of cooled cake with corn syrup and
decorate with reserved candied fruit pieces and nuts, if
desired. To store, wrap in aluminum foil or plastic wrap,
or place in airtight container.

Tip: Store leftover candied fruits in airtight containers
in freezer.

PUMPKIN MARBLE CHEESECAKE

Makes 12 servings

CRUST

2¼ cups gingersnap crumbs
½ cup finely chopped pecans
⅓ cup PARKAY® Margarine, melted

FILLING

3 (8-ounce) packages PHILADELPHIA BRAND®
    Cream Cheese, softened
1 cup sugar, divided
1 teaspoon vanilla
3 eggs
1 cup canned pumpkin
1 teaspoon ground cinnamon
¼ teaspoon ground nutmeg
    Dash ground cloves

• Preheat oven to 325°F.

• For Crust, mix crumbs, pecans and margarine; press
onto bottom and 2 inches up sides of 9-inch springform
pan. Bake 10 minutes.

• For Filling, beat cream cheese, ¾ cup sugar and vanilla
at medium speed with electric mixer until well blended.
Add eggs, 1 at a time, mixing at low speed after each
addition, just until blended. Reserve 1½ cups batter. Add
remaining ¼ cup sugar, pumpkin and spices to remaining
batter; mix well.

• Spoon pumpkin and cream cheese batters alternately
over crust; cut through batters with knife several times
for marble effect.

• Bake 55 to 60 minutes or until center is almost set.
Run knife or metal spatula around rim of pan to loosen
cake; cool before removing rim of pan. Refrigerate 4
hours or overnight.

CHOCOLATE RICOTTA CHEESECAKE WITH GLAZED FRUIT

Makes about 10 servings

Graham Crust (recipe follows)
3 cups ricotta cheese or lowfat cottage cheese
1 cup sugar
4 eggs
1 cup (½ pint) whipping cream
⅓ cup HERSHEY'S Cocoa
¼ cup all-purpose flour
½ teaspoon vanilla extract
⅛ teaspoon salt
Glazed Fruit (recipe follows)
Fresh mint sprig
Sweetened whipped cream

Preheat oven to 350°F. Prepare Graham Crust; set aside. In food processor or blender container, place ricotta cheese, sugar and eggs; process until smooth. Add cream, cocoa, flour, vanilla and salt; process until smooth. Pour batter into prepared crust.

Bake 1 hour and 15 minutes or until set. Remove from oven. Loosen cheesecake from rim of pan; cool to room temperature. Refrigerate several hours or overnight. Remove rim of pan; top with Glazed Fruit or fresh fruit and mint sprig. Pipe border of sweetened whipped cream around edge of cheesecake.

Graham Crust: In small bowl, stir together 1 cup graham cracker crumbs, 2 tablespoons sugar and ¼ cup melted butter or margarine. Press onto bottom and ½ inch up side of 9-inch springform pan. Bake at 350°F for 10 minutes; cool.

Glazed Fruit: Stir 1½ cups sliced peaches, pitted sweet cherries, fresh sliced strawberries or pineapple chunks with ½ cup fruit preserves until fruit is well coated.

TRIPLE CHOCOLATE AND VANILLA CHEESECAKE

Makes one 9-inch cheesecake

1½ cups finely crushed creme-filled chocolate
    sandwich cookies (about 18 cookies)
3 tablespoons margarine or butter, melted
4 (8-ounce) packages cream cheese, softened
1 (14-ounce) can EAGLE® Brand sweetened
    Condensed Milk (NOT evaporated milk)
4 eggs
⅓ cup unsifted all-purpose flour
1 tablespoon vanilla extract
2 (1-ounce) squares semi-sweet chocolate, melted
    Chocolate Glaze (recipe follows)

Chocolate Ricotta Cheesecake with Glazed Fruit

Preheat oven to 350°F. Combine cookie crumbs and margarine; press firmly on bottom of 9-inch springform pan. In large mixer bowl, beat cheese until fluffy. Gradually beat in sweetened condensed milk until smooth. Add eggs, flour and vanilla; mix well. Divide batter in half. Add chocolate to one half of batter; mix well. Pour into prepared pan. Top evenly with vanilla batter.

Bake 50 to 55 minutes or until center springs back when lightly touched. Cool. Top with Chocolate Glaze. Chill. Just before serving, remove sides of springform pan. Refrigerate leftovers.

Chocolate Glaze: In small saucepan, over low heat, melt 2 (1-ounce) squares semi-sweet chocolate with ¼ cup BORDEN® or MEADOW GOLD® Whipping Cream. Cook and stir until thickened and smooth. Remove from heat; cool slightly.   *Makes about ⅓ cup*

Rich Pumpkin Cheesecake

CHOCOLATE CHIP PUMPKIN CHEESECAKE

Makes 10 to 12 servings

1 cup vanilla wafer crumbs (about 30 wafers)
¼ cup HERSHEY'S Cocoa
¼ cup powdered sugar
¼ cup (½ stick) butter or margarine, melted
3 packages (8 ounces each) cream cheese, softened
1 cup granulated sugar
3 tablespoons all-purpose flour
1 teaspoon pumpkin pie spice
1 cup canned pumpkin
4 eggs
1½ cups HERSHEY'S MINI CHIPS® Semi-Sweet Chocolate
Chocolate Leaves (recipe follows)

Preheat oven to 350°F. In medium bowl, stir together crumbs, cocoa and powdered sugar; stir in melted butter. Press mixture onto bottom and ½ inch up side of 9-inch springform pan. Bake 8 minutes; cool slightly. *Increase oven temperature to 400°F.*

In large mixer bowl, beat cream cheese, granulated sugar, flour and pumpkin pie spice until well blended. Add canned pumpkin and eggs; beat until well blended. Stir in small chocolate chips; pour batter into prepared crust.

Bake 10 minutes. *Reduce oven temperature to 250°F;* continue baking 50 minutes or until set. Remove to wire rack. With knife, loosen cheesecake from side of pan. Cool completely; remove side of pan. Refrigerate before serving. Garnish with Chocolate Leaves. Cover; refrigerate leftovers.

Chocolate Leaves: Thoroughly wash and dry several non-toxic leaves (rose or lemon leaves work well). In small, microwave-safe bowl, place ½ cup HERSHEY'S MINI CHIPS® Semi-Sweet Chocolate. Microwave at HIGH (100% power) 30 to 45 seconds or until smooth when stirred. With small soft-bristled pastry brush, brush melted chocolate on backs of leaves. (Avoid getting chocolate on leaf front; removal may be difficult when chocolate hardens.) Place on waxed paper-covered cookie sheet; refrigerate until very firm. Beginning at stem, carefully peel green leaves away from chocolate leaves; refrigerate until ready to use.

RICH PUMPKIN CHEESECAKE

Makes 8 to 12 servings

CRUST
1 package DUNCAN HINES® Moist Deluxe Spice Cake Mix
½ cup butter or margarine, melted

FILLING
3 packages (8 ounces each) cream cheese, softened
1 can (14 ounces) sweetened condensed milk
1 can (16 ounces) solid-pack pumpkin
4 eggs
1 tablespoon pumpkin pie spice

TOPPING
1 package (2½ ounces) sliced almonds
2 cups whipping cream, chilled
¼ cup sugar

1. Preheat oven to 375°F.

2. For Crust, combine cake mix and melted butter in large bowl; mix until crumbly. Press in bottom of ungreased 10-inch springform pan.

3. For Filling, combine cream cheese and sweetened condensed milk in large bowl. Beat with electric mixer at high speed for 2 minutes. Add pumpkin, eggs and pumpkin pie spice. Beat at high speed for 1 minute. Pour over prepared crust in pan.

4. Bake at 375°F for 65 to 70 minutes or until set. Loosen cake from sides of pan with knife or spatula. Cool completely on wire rack. Refrigerate 2 hours. Remove sides of pan.

5. For Topping, preheat oven to 300°F. Toast almonds on baking sheet at 300°F for 4 to 5 minutes, stirring occasionally, or until fragrant and light golden brown. Cool completely. Beat cream in medium bowl until soft peaks form. Gradually add sugar; beat until stiff peaks form. Spread over top of chilled cheesecake. Garnish with toasted almonds. Refrigerate until ready to serve.

Tip: To prepare in a 13 × 9-inch pan, bake at 350°F for 35 minutes or until set.

PRALINE-TOPPED PUMPKIN PIE

Makes one 9-inch pie

1½ cups solid-pack pumpkin
1 cup granulated sugar
2 eggs, slightly beaten
1 teaspoon ground cinnamon
½ teaspoon salt
¼ teaspoon ground ginger
¼ teaspoon ground cloves
¼ teaspoon ground nutmeg
1½ cups *undiluted* CARNATION® Evaporated Milk
1 (9-inch) unbaked pie shell
½ cup chopped pecans
⅓ cup firmly packed brown sugar
3 tablespoons butter or margarine, melted

Preheat oven to 350°F. In large bowl, combine pumpkin, granulated sugar, eggs, cinnamon, salt, ginger, cloves and nutmeg. Gradually add evaporated milk; mix well. Pour into unbaked pie shell.

Bake 30 minutes. Meanwhile, in small bowl, combine pecans, brown sugar and butter. Remove pie from oven; sprinkle pecan mixture over top. Continue baking 20 to 25 minutes or until knife inserted near center comes out clean. Cool completely on wire rack. (Filling will firm up while cooling.)

Traditional Pumpkin Pie

PUMPKIN EGG NOG PIE

Makes one 9-inch pie

1 (9-inch) unbaked pastry shell
1 (16-ounce) can pumpkin (2 cups)
1½ cups BORDEN® or MEADOW GOLD®
    Egg Nog
2 eggs
½ cup sugar
½ teaspoon salt
½ teaspoon ground cinnamon
¼ teaspoon ground cloves
¼ teaspoon ground ginger

Preheat oven to 425°F. In large mixer bowl, combine all ingredients except pastry shell; mix well. Pour into pastry shell.

Bake 15 minutes. *Reduce oven temperature to 350°F;* bake 40 to 45 minutes longer or until knife inserted near edge comes out clean. Cool. Refrigerate leftovers.

TRADITIONAL PUMPKIN PIE

Makes one 9-inch pie

1 (9-inch) unbaked pastry shell
1 (16-ounce) can pumpkin (2 cups)
1 (14-ounce) can EAGLE® Brand Sweetened
    Condensed Milk (NOT evaporated milk)
2 eggs
1 teaspoon ground cinnamon
½ teaspoon salt
½ teaspoon ground ginger
½ teaspoon ground nutmeg
    Quick Sour Cream Topping *or* Streusel Topping
    (recipes follow), optional

Place rack in lowest position in oven; preheat oven to 425°F. In large mixer bowl, combine all ingredients except pastry shell and Toppings; mix well. Pour into pastry shell.

Bake 15 minutes. *Reduce oven temperature to 350°F;* bake 35 to 40 minutes longer or until knife inserted near edge comes out clean. Cool. Garnish as desired. Refrigerate.

Quick Sour Cream Topping: In medium bowl, combine 1½ cups BORDEN® or MEADOW GOLD® Sour Cream, 2 tablespoons sugar and 1 teaspoon vanilla extract. Spread evenly over top of pie after 30 minutes of baking; bake 10 minutes longer. Garnish as desired.

Streusel Topping: In medium bowl, combine ½ cup firmly packed light brown sugar and ½ cup all-purpose flour; cut in ¼ cup cold margarine or butter until crumbly. Stir in ¼ cup chopped nuts. Sprinkle on top of pie after 30 minutes of baking; bake 10 minutes longer.

PUMPKIN CARAMEL TARTS

Makes 14 tarts

1 (15-ounce) package refrigerated pie crusts
12 EAGLE™ Brand Caramels, unwrapped
1 (14-ounce) can EAGLE® Brand Sweetened
 Condensed Milk (NOT evaporated milk)
1 (16-ounce) can pumpkin (2 cups)
2 eggs
3 tablespoons water
1 tablespoon vanilla extract
½ teaspoon ground cinnamon

Preheat oven to 425°F. From each pie crust, cut 7 (4-inch) circles, rolling scraps as necessary. Press into 3-inch tart pans. In medium saucepan, over low heat, melt caramels with sweetened condensed milk, stirring constantly. Remove from heat; stir in remaining ingredients. Pour equal portions into crusts. Place on baking sheets.

Bake 15 minutes. *Reduce oven temperature to 350°F;* bake 20 to 25 minutes longer or until set. Cool. Garnish as desired. Refrigerate leftovers.

Microwave Tip: In 2-quart glass measure with handle, combine caramels and sweetened condensed milk. Cook on 100% power (high) 3 minutes or until caramels melt, stirring after each minute. Proceed as above.

BOURBON PECAN PIE

Makes 6 to 8 servings

 Pastry for single-crust 9-inch pie
¼ cup butter or margarine, softened
½ cup sugar
3 eggs
1½ cups light or dark corn syrup
2 tablespoons bourbon
1 teaspoon vanilla extract
1 cup pecan halves

Place oven rack in lowest position. Preheat oven to 350°F. Roll out pastry and line 9-inch pie pan; flute edge. Beat butter in large bowl of electric mixer on medium speed until creamy. Add sugar; beat until fluffy. Add eggs, 1 at a time, beating well after each addition. Add corn syrup, bourbon and vanilla; beat until well blended. Pour filling into pastry shell. Arrange pecan halves on top.

Bake 50 to 55 minutes or until knife inserted near center comes out clean (filling will be puffy). Cool on wire rack. Serve at room temperature or refrigerate.

Brandied Fruit Pie

BRANDIED FRUIT PIE

Makes 8 servings

1 KEEBLER® READY-CRUST® Graham Cracker
 Pie Crust
2 packages (8 ounces each) mixed pitted dried fruit
¾ cup plus 1 tablespoon water, divided
¼ cup plus 1 tablespoon brandy or cognac, divided
5 thin lemon slices
¾ cup firmly packed brown sugar
1 teaspoon ground cinnamon
¼ teaspoon salt
¼ teaspoon ground nutmeg
¼ teaspoon ground cloves
½ cup graham cracker crumbs
¼ cup butter or margarine, melted
 Prepared hard sauce or whipped cream
 Additional lemon slices for garnish

Preheat oven to 350°F. In medium saucepan, combine dried fruit, ¾ cup water, ¼ cup brandy and 5 lemon slices. Simmer over low heat, stirring occasionally, 10 minutes or until liquid is absorbed. Remove from heat; discard lemon slices. Stir in sugar, cinnamon, salt, nutmeg, cloves, remaining 1 tablespoon water and remaining 1 tablespoon brandy; pour into pie crust. Sprinkle graham cracker crumbs evenly over top of pie. Drizzle melted butter over crumbs.

Bake 30 minutes. Cool on wire rack. Serve warm or at room temperature. If desired, serve with hard sauce or whipped cream; garnish with additional lemon slices.

SOUR CREAM MINCE PIE

Makes one 9-inch pie

1 (9-inch) unbaked pastry shell
1 (9-ounce) package NONE SUCH® Condensed
 Mincemeat, crumbled
1 cup apple juice *or* water
1 tablespoon all-purpose flour
1 medium all-purpose apple, cored, pared and
 chopped
2 cups (1 pint) BORDEN® or MEADOW GOLD®
 Sour Cream
2 eggs
2 tablespoons sugar
1 teaspoon vanilla extract
2 to 3 tablespoons chopped nuts

Place rack in lowest position in oven; preheat oven to
425°F. In small saucepan, combine mincemeat and apple
juice. Bring to a boil; boil rapidly 1 minute. In medium
bowl, stir together flour and apple until apple is coated;
stir in mincemeat mixture. Pour into pastry shell.

Bake 25 minutes. *Reduce oven temperature to 325°F.*
Meanwhile, in small mixer bowl, combine sour cream,
eggs, sugar and vanilla; beat until smooth. Pour evenly
over mincemeat mixture. Sprinkle with nuts.

Bake 20 minutes longer or until set. Cool. Chill
thoroughly. Garnish as desired. Refrigerate leftovers.

TRADITIONAL MINCE PIE

Makes one 9-inch pie

Pastry for 2-crust pie
1 (27-ounce) jar NONE SUCH® Ready-to-Use
 Mincemeat (Regular or Brandy & Rum)
1 egg yolk
2 tablespoons water

Place rack in lowest position in oven; preheat oven to
425°F. Turn mincemeat into pastry-lined 9-inch pie
plate. Cover with top crust; cut slits near center. Seal
and flute. In small bowl, beat together egg yolk and
water. Brush egg mixture over crust.

Bake 30 minutes or until golden. Cool slightly. Garnish
as desired.

Tip: To Use NONE SUCH® Condensed Mincemeat,
combine 2 (9-ounce) packages None Such® Condensed
Mincemeat, crumbled, and 3 cups water in large
saucepan; bring to a boil. Cook and stir 1 minute. Cool.
Turn into pastry-lined 9-inch pie plate. Bake and cool
as directed above.

Left to right: Sour Cream Mince Pie, Traditional Mince Pie

CHOCOLATE PECAN PIE

Makes 8 servings

1 package (4 ounces) BAKER'S® GERMAN'S®
   Sweet Chocolate
2 tablespoons margarine or butter
1 cup corn syrup
⅓ cup sugar
3 eggs
1 teaspoon vanilla
1½ cups pecan halves
1 unbaked 9-inch pie shell
   COOL WHIP® Non-Dairy Whipped Topping,
   thawed (optional)

Preheat oven to 350°F.

Microwave chocolate and margarine in large microwavable bowl on HIGH (100% power) 2 minutes or until margarine is melted. Stir until chocolate is completely melted.

Stir in corn syrup, sugar, eggs and vanilla until well blended. Stir in pecans, reserving 8 halves for garnish, if desired. Pour filling into pie shell.

Bake for 55 minutes or until knife inserted 1 inch from center comes out clean. Cool on wire rack. Refrigerate until set. Garnish pie with whipped topping and pecan halves, if desired.

Prep time: 20 minutes
Bake time: 55 minutes

CRANBERRY CRUMB PIE

Makes one 9-inch pie

1 (9-inch) unbaked pastry shell, pricked
1 (8-ounce) package cream cheese, softened
1 (14-ounce) can EAGLE® Brand Sweetened
   Condensed Milk (NOT evaporated milk)
¼ cup REALEMON® Lemon Juice from
   Concentrate
3 tablespoons firmly packed light brown sugar
2 tablespoons cornstarch
1 (16-ounce) can whole-berry cranberry sauce
¼ cup cold margarine or butter
⅓ cup unsifted all-purpose flour
¾ cup chopped walnuts

Preheat oven to 425°F. Bake pastry shell 8 minutes; remove from oven. *Reduce oven temperature to 375°F.* Meanwhile, in large mixer bowl, beat cheese until fluffy. Gradually beat in sweetened condensed milk until smooth. Stir in ReaLemon® brand. Pour into prepared pastry shell. In small bowl, combine *1 tablespoon* sugar

and cornstarch; mix well. Stir in cranberry sauce. Spoon evenly over cheese mixture. In medium bowl, cut margarine into flour and remaining *2 tablespoons* sugar until crumbly. Stir in nuts. Sprinkle evenly over cranberry mixture.

Bake 45 to 50 minutes or until bubbly and golden. Cool. Serve at room temperature or chilled. Refrigerate leftovers.

APPLE CRANBERRY RASPBERRY PIE

Makes one 9-inch pie

CRUST
   Unbaked 9-inch Classic CRISCO® *Double* Crust
   (page 80)
FILLING
  2 cups chopped, peeled Granny Smith apples
    (about ⅔ pound or 2 medium)
  2 cups whole cranberries, coarsely chopped
  1 package (10 ounces) frozen dry-pack raspberries,
    thawed
1½ cups sugar
  3 tablespoons quick-cooking tapioca
  ½ teaspoon ground cinnamon
  ¼ teaspoon salt
  ¼ teaspoon almond extract

GLAZE
   Half-and-half or milk
   Sugar

1. Preheat oven to 375°F.

2. For Filling, combine apples, cranberries and raspberries in large bowl. Combine 1½ cups sugar, tapioca, cinnamon, salt and almond extract. Add to fruit mixture. Toss well to mix. Spoon into unbaked pie crust. Fold edge under; flute with fingers or fork.

3. Roll top crust between lightly floured sheets of waxed paper. Peel off top sheet. Trim dough to a circle 2½ inches smaller than upside-down pie plate. (An upside-down dessert plate could serve as a guide.) Cut a spiral strip starting from outside, about ¾ inch wide. Flip onto filling. Remove waxed paper. Separate strip gently with knife tip to form opened spiral.

4. For Glaze, brush spiral with half-and-half. Sprinkle with sugar. Cover edge of pie with foil to prevent overbrowning.

5. Bake at 375°F for 25 minutes. Remove foil. Bake for an additional 25 to 35 minutes or until filling in center is bubbly. Cool until barely warm or room temperature before serving.

Creamy Egg Nog Pie

CREAMY EGG NOG PIE

Makes one 9-inch pie

1 (9-inch) baked pastry shell
1 (6-serving size) package vanilla flavor pudding
    mix (*not instant*)
¼ teaspoon ground nutmeg
1½ cups canned BORDEN® Egg Nog
2 tablespoons light rum *or* 1 teaspoon rum
    flavoring (optional)
2 cups (1 pint) BORDEN® or MEADOW GOLD®
    Whipping Cream, whipped
    Additional ground nutmeg

In medium saucepan, combine pudding mix, ¼ *teaspoon* nutmeg and egg nog; mix well. Over medium heat, cook and stir until thickened and bubbly. Remove from heat; stir in rum if desired. Chill thoroughly. Beat until smooth. Fold in whipped cream. Spoon into prepared pastry shell. Garnish with additional nutmeg. Chill 4 hours or until set. Refrigerate leftovers.

To Microwave: In 2-quart glass measure with handle, combine pudding mix, ¼ *teaspoon* nutmeg and egg nog; mix well. Cook on 100% power (high) 6 to 8 minutes or until thickened and bubbly, stirring every 1½ minutes. Proceed as above.

NESSELRODE CREAM PIE

Makes one 9-inch pie

Chocolate Coconut Crust (recipe follows)
1 envelope unflavored gelatin
¼ cup water
1 (14-ounce) can EAGLE® Brand Sweetened
    Condensed Milk (NOT evaporated milk)
¼ cup BORDEN® or MEADOW GOLD®
    Sour Cream
2 tablespoons light rum
½ cup chopped mixed candied fruit
½ cup chopped nuts
¼ cup raisins
2 teaspoons grated orange peel
1 cup (½ pint) BORDEN® or MEADOW GOLD®
    Whipping Cream, whipped

Prepare Chocolate Coconut Crust. In small saucepan, sprinkle gelatin over water; let stand 1 minute to soften. Over low heat, stir until gelatin dissolves. In large bowl, combine sweetened condensed milk, sour cream, gelatin mixture and rum. Chill until mixture mounds slightly when dropped from spoon, about 15 minutes. Fold in candied fruit, nuts, raisins, peel then whipped cream. Pour into prepared crust. Chill 4 hours or until set. Garnish as desired. Refrigerate leftovers.

Chocolate Coconut Crust: In large saucepan, over low heat, melt 2 tablespoons margarine or butter with 1 (1-ounce) square semi-sweet chocolate. Add 1 (7-ounce) package flaked coconut (2⅔ cups); mix well. Press firmly on bottom and up side to rim of buttered 9-inch pie plate. Chill.

KAHLÚA® ICE CREAM PIE

Makes 1 (9-inch) pie

1 (9-ounce) package chocolate wafer cookies
½ cup unsalted butter, melted
10 tablespoons KAHLÚA®, divided
1 teaspoon espresso powder
3 ounces semi-sweet chocolate, chopped
1 tablespoon unsalted butter
1 pint vanilla, coffee or chocolate chip ice cream
1 pint chocolate ice cream
¾ cup whipping cream, whipped
    Chocolate-covered coffee beans, for garnish

Preheat oven to 325°F. Place about half the cookies in food processor, breaking cookies into pieces. Process to make fine crumbs. Repeat with remaining cookies. Add ½ cup melted butter and process with on-off pulses, just to blend. Press crumb mixture evenly onto bottom and up side to rim of 9-inch pie plate. Bake 10 minutes. Cool completely.

In small saucepan, heat 6 tablespoons Kahlúa® and espresso powder over low heat until warm and espresso powder dissolves. Stir in chocolate and 1 tablespoon butter until melted and smooth. Cool completely.

Transfer vanilla ice cream to electric mixer bowl and allow to soften slightly. Add 2 tablespoons Kahlúa® and beat on low speed until blended. Spread over bottom of cooled crust and freeze until firm. Spread cooled chocolate mixture over ice cream mixture. Freeze until firm.

Transfer chocolate ice cream to mixer bowl and allow to soften slightly. Add remaining 2 tablespoons Kahlúa® and beat on low speed until blended. Spread over frozen chocolate mixture. Freeze until firm.

To serve, pipe decorative border of whipped cream on pie around inside edge. Garnish with chocolate-covered coffee beans.

COFFEE TOFFEE PIE

Makes 8 to 10 servings

2 cups chocolate wafer crumbs
¼ cup sugar
6 tablespoons PARKAY® Margarine, melted
1 (8-ounce) package PHILADELPHIA BRAND® Cream Cheese, softened
3 to 4 tablespoons coffee-flavored liqueur
1 (8-ounce) container COOL WHIP® Non-Dairy Whipped Topping, thawed
4 (1.4-ounce) milk chocolate-covered toffee bars, chopped (1 cup), divided

• Preheat oven to 350°F.

• Stir together crumbs, sugar and margarine in medium bowl; press onto bottom and up sides of 9-inch pie plate. Bake 10 minutes. Cool.

• Beat cream cheese and liqueur in large mixing bowl at medium speed with electric mixer until well blended. Fold in whipped topping and ¾ cup candy; pour into crust.

• Sprinkle with remaining ¼ cup candy. Chill until firm.

CHOCOLATE TURTLE PIE

Makes 8 servings

¼ cup caramel or butterscotch flavor dessert topping
1 baked 8- or 9-inch pie shell, cooled
¾ cup pecan halves
1 package (4-serving size) JELL-O® Chocolate Flavor Pudding and Pie Filling*
1¾ cups milk*
1¾ cups (4 ounces) COOL WHIP® Non-Dairy Whipped Topping, thawed

Bring caramel topping to a boil in small saucepan, stirring constantly. Pour into pie shell. Arrange pecans on top; chill.

Combine pudding mix and milk in medium saucepan. Cook and stir over medium heat until mixture comes to a full boil. Cool 5 minutes, stirring twice. Pour into pie shell; place plastic wrap on surface of pudding. Chill 3 hours. Remove plastic wrap. Cover with whipped topping. Drizzle with additional caramel topping and garnish with additional pecans, if desired.

*1 package (4-serving size) instant pudding may be substituted for 1 package (4-serving size) cooked pudding mix. Prepare as directed on package, using 1½ cups *cold* milk.

Prep time: 15 minutes
Chill time: 3 hours

Chocolate Turtle Pie

PINK CHAMPAGNE SORBET

Makes 8 servings

1 package (4-serving size) JELL-O® Brand
    Strawberry Flavor Gelatin
1⅓ cups boiling water
1 bottle (187 mL) pink champagne
¾ cup light corn syrup
2 egg whites, lightly beaten*
    Lime slices (optional)

Completely dissolve gelatin in boiling water. Stir in
champagne and corn syrup. Beat in egg whites with wire
whisk. Pour into 13×9-inch pan. Freeze until firm, about
2 hours.

Spoon half the gelatin mixture into food processor or
blender; cover. Process at high speed until smooth but
not melted, about 30 seconds. Pour into 9×5-inch loaf
pan. Repeat with remaining gelatin mixture; pour over
mixture in pan. Cover; freeze until firm, about 6 hours
or overnight.

Scoop sorbet into dessert or champagne glasses. Garnish
with lime slices, if desired.

*Note: Use only clean eggs with no cracks in shell.

FRUITED CHOCOLATE SORBET

Makes about 8 servings

1 medium-size ripe banana
1½ cups orange juice
½ cup sugar
¼ cup HERSHEY₂S Cocoa
1 cup (½ pint) cold whipping cream

Slice banana into blender container. Add orange juice;
blend until smooth. Add sugar and cocoa; blend until
thoroughly combined. Add whipping cream; blend well.
Pour mixture into 9-inch square pan. Freeze until hard
around edges. Spoon mixture into large mixer bowl or
blender container; blend until smooth. Pour into 1-quart
mold; cover. Freeze 4 to 6 hours or until firm. To serve,
unmold onto chilled plate; cut into slices.

CHOCOLATE-AMARETTO ICE

Makes 4 servings

¾ cup sugar
½ cup HERSHEY₂S Cocoa
2 cups light cream or half-and-half
2 tablespoons amaretto liqueur
    Sliced almonds (optional)

In small saucepan, stir together sugar and cocoa; gradually
stir in light cream. Cook over low heat, stirring constantly,
until sugar dissolves and mixture is smooth and hot; do
not boil. Remove from heat; stir in liqueur. Pour into
8-inch square pan. Cover; freeze until firm, stirring several
times before mixture is completely solid. Scoop into
dessert dishes. Serve immediately. Garnish with sliced
almonds, if desired.

CHOCOLATE FROZEN YOGURT

Makes about 4 servings

¼ cup HERSHEY₂S Cocoa
¼ cup sugar
2 containers (8 ounces each) vanilla yogurt
¼ cup light corn syrup

In medium bowl, stir together cocoa and sugar until
well blended. Add yogurt and corn syrup; stir until well
blended and smooth. Pour mixture into 8-inch square
pan or 9×5-inch loaf pan. Cover; freeze until firm,
several hours or overnight. Spoon into large mixer bowl.
With mixer on low speed, beat until smooth but not
melted. Return to pan or pour into 1-pint freezer
container. Cover; freeze several hours or overnight until
firm. Before serving, allow to stand at room temperature
about 10 minutes.

Clockwise from top left: Eggnog Trifle (page 365),
Sparkling Champagne Dessert (page 365), Pink Champagne Sorbet

DOUBLE ALMOND ICE CREAM

Makes 1 quart

3 cups whipping cream
1 cup milk
¾ cup *plus* 2 tablespoons sugar, divided
4 egg yolks, beaten
1 tablespoon vanilla extract
2 teaspoons almond extract
2 tablespoons butter
1½ cups BLUE DIAMOND® Chopped Natural
   Almonds

Combine cream, milk and ¾ cup sugar in medium saucepan. Cook and stir over medium heat until sugar is dissolved and mixture is hot. Gradually add 1 cup cream mixture to beaten egg yolks, whisking constantly. When mixture is smooth, strain into double boiler. Gradually pour in remaining cream mixture, whisking constantly. Cook over simmering water, stirring frequently, until mixture thickens slightly and coats the back of a spoon, about 8 minutes. *Do not boil*. Stir in extracts. Cool.

Meanwhile, melt butter in small saucepan; stir in remaining 2 tablespoons sugar. Cook and stir over medium heat until sugar begins to bubble (about 30 seconds). Add almonds; cook and stir over medium heat until golden and well coated. Cool. Stir almonds into cream mixture. Pour into ice cream freezer container. Freeze according to manufacturer's instructions.

Double Almond Ice Cream

CHOCOLATE RUM ICE CREAM

Makes about 8 servings

1 cup sugar
2 tablespoons all-purpose flour
1 cup milk
1 egg, slightly beaten
2 bars (2 ounces) HERSHEY'S Unsweetened
   Baking Chocolate, broken into pieces
½ teaspoon rum extract
2 cups (1 pint) chilled light cream

To Microwave: In large microwave-safe bowl, combine sugar and flour; gradually stir in milk. Blend in egg and baking chocolate pieces. Microwave at HIGH (100% power) 2 to 2½ minutes, stirring frequently, just until mixture boils and thickens. Add rum extract; blend with wire whisk until mixture is smooth. Refrigerate until cold. Add light cream to cold chocolate mixture; blend well. Freeze in 2-quart ice cream freezer according to manufacturer's directions.

ESPRESSO PRALINE ICE CREAM

Makes about 1 quart

PRALINE
¾ cup sugar
1 tablespoon *plus* 2 teaspoons water
1½ cups BLUE DIAMOND® Sliced Natural
   Almonds, toasted (see Tip)

ICE CREAM
2 cups whipping cream
2 cups half-and-half
¾ cup sugar
5 egg yolks, beaten
1 tablespoon vanilla extract
1 teaspoon almond extract
2 tablespoons instant espresso powder
2 tablespoons brandy

For Praline, grease cookie sheet. Mix sugar and water together in small heavy saucepan. Over medium-low heat, cook and stir until water evaporates and sugar turns golden brown, about 5 minutes. Working rapidly, add almonds and stir until all almonds are lightly coated. Spread immediately on prepared cookie sheet. Cool. Process in food processor or crush with rolling pin until the size of small peas. Reserve.

For Ice Cream, combine cream, half-and-half and sugar in medium saucepan. Cook and stir over medium heat until sugar is dissolved and mixture is hot. Gradually add 1 cup cream mixture to beaten egg yolks, whisking constantly. When mixture is smooth, strain into double boiler. Gradually pour in remaining cream mixture, whisking constantly. Cook over simmering water, stirring, until mixture thickens slightly and coats the back of a spoon, about 8 minutes. *Do not boil.* Stir in extracts.

Combine espresso powder and brandy in large bowl. Strain cream mixture into brandy mixture, stirring to dissolve espresso. Cool. Stir in praline. Pour into ice cream freezer container. Freeze according to manufacturer's instructions.

Tip: To toast nuts, spread evenly on baking sheet. Bake at 350°F, stirring occasionally, 8 to 10 minutes or until lightly browned; cool.

RICOTTA GELATO

Makes about 6 cups

½ cup golden raisins
¼ cup rum
2 cups milk
⅔ cup sugar
4 egg yolks
1 container (15 ounces) POLLY-O® Ricotta Cheese
    Grated peel of 1 lemon
1 teaspoon vanilla extract

In small bowl, combine raisins and rum. Cover and set aside for several hours or overnight.

In heavy saucepan, combine milk and sugar. Cook over medium-high heat, stirring occasionally, until sugar is dissolved and mixture is hot.

In medium bowl, whisk egg yolks briefly. Gradually whisk half of hot milk mixture into beaten egg yolks. Slowly whisk mixture back into saucepan.

Cook over medium heat, stirring constantly, until custard thickens enough to lightly coat back of spoon, about 8 minutes. *Do not boil.* Immediately pour into large bowl and cool slightly.

In blender or food processor, process ricotta until smooth. Gradually blend in cooled custard, lemon peel and vanilla. Pour into ice cream freezer container.

Freeze according to manufacturer's instructions. About halfway through freezing process, stir in raisins and rum.

Refrigerator-Freezer Method: Pour custard mixture into 13×9-inch pan; cover and freeze until slushy, about 2 hours. Transfer to large bowl; beat until smooth. Return to pan. Cover and freeze until almost solid, about 2 hours. Beat until smooth; stir in raisins and rum. Serve immediately.

Prep time: 20 minutes
Cook time: 10 minutes
Freezing time: 45 minutes

Simple Spumoni

SIMPLE SPUMONI

Makes about 1 quart

2 cups whipping cream
⅔ cup sweetened condensed milk
½ teaspoon rum flavoring
1 can (21 ounces) cherry pie filling
½ cup chopped almonds
½ cup miniature semisweet chocolate chips

Combine cream, sweetened condensed milk and rum flavoring in large bowl; refrigerate 30 minutes. Beat just until soft peaks form. *Do not overbeat.* Fold in remaining ingredients. Pour into 8×8-inch pan; cover. Freeze about 4 hours or until firm. Scoop spumoni into dessert dishes to serve. Garnish as desired.

Favorite recipe from **Cherry Marketing Institute, Inc.**

CREAMY CRANBERRY FRUIT FREEZE

Makes 9 to 12 servings

2 packages (3 ounces each) cream cheese, softened
½ cup KARO® Light Corn Syrup
1 can (16 ounces) whole-berry cranberry sauce
1 can (11 ounces) mandarin orange sections, well drained
1 can (8 ounces) crushed pineapple, well drained
1 container (8 ounces) frozen non-dairy whipped topping, thawed
Fresh fruit and mint leaves (optional)

In large bowl with mixer at medium speed, beat cream cheese until fluffy. Gradually beat in corn syrup until smooth. Reduce speed to low; beat in cranberry sauce until combined. Stir in oranges and pineapple. Gently fold in whipped topping just until combined. Spoon into 8- or 9-inch square pan. Cover and freeze 6 hours or overnight.

Let stand 10 minutes at room temperature before serving. Cut into bars. If desired, garnish with fresh fruit and mint leaves.

Prep time: 15 minutes, plus freezing

Creamy Cranberry Fruit Freeze

FROZEN AMARETTO TORTE

Makes 12 to 15 servings

1 (8½-ounce) package chocolate wafers, finely crushed (2½ cups crumbs)
½ cup slivered almonds, toasted and chopped
⅓ cup margarine or butter, melted
1 (6-ounce) package butterscotch flavored chips (1 cup)
1 (14-ounce) can EAGLE® Brand Sweetened Condensed Milk (NOT evaporated milk)
1 (16-ounce) container BORDEN® or MEADOW GOLD® Sour Cream
⅓ cup amaretto liqueur
1 cup (½ pint) BORDEN® or MEADOW GOLD® Whipping Cream, whipped

Combine crumbs, almonds and margarine. Reserving 1¼ cups crumb mixture, press remainder firmly on bottom of 9-inch springform pan. In small saucepan, over medium heat, melt chips with sweetened condensed milk. In large bowl, combine sour cream and amaretto; stir in butterscotch mixture. Fold in whipped cream. Pour half the cream mixture over prepared crust; top with 1 cup reserved crumb mixture, then remaining cream mixture. Top with remaining ¼ cup crumb mixture; cover. Freeze 6 hours or until firm. Before serving, remove sides of pan. Garnish as desired. Freeze leftovers.

CHOCOLATE TORTONI

Makes 4 servings

1 cup (½ pint) cold whipping cream
½ cup cold HERSHEY'S Syrup
¼ cup almond macaroon crumbs *or* vanilla wafer crumbs
¼ cup plus 2 tablespoons chopped almonds, toasted, divided*
¼ cup chopped maraschino cherries
1½ tablespoons rum *or* ½ teaspoon rum extract
Whole maraschino cherries (optional)

In small mixer bowl, beat whipping cream until stiff; gently fold in syrup. Fold in macaroon crumbs, ¼ cup chopped almonds, chopped maraschino cherries and rum. Divide mixture among 4 dessert dishes; cover and freeze until firm, about 4 hours. Let stand at room temperature several minutes before serving; sprinkle with remaining 2 tablespoons chopped almonds. Garnish with whole maraschino cherries, if desired.

*To toast almonds: Spread almonds on cookie sheet. Bake at 350°F, stirring occasionally, until lightly browned, 8 to 10 minutes. Cool.

CHOCOLATE TAPIOCA

Makes 4 to 6 servings

¾ cup sugar
¼ cup HERSHEY₂S Cocoa
3 tablespoons quick-cooking tapioca
⅛ teaspoon salt
2¾ cups milk
1 egg, slightly beaten
1 teaspoon vanilla extract

Combine sugar, cocoa, tapioca and salt in medium saucepan; blend in milk and egg. Let stand 5 minutes. Cook over medium heat, stirring constantly, until mixture boils. Remove from heat; stir in vanilla. Pour into bowl; press plastic wrap directly onto surface. Cool; refrigerate. Spoon into individual dessert dishes.

CHERRY-CROWNED COCOA PUDDING

Makes 6 servings

1 cup sugar
½ cup HERSHEY₂S Cocoa
⅓ cup all-purpose biscuit baking mix
2 cups milk
1 cup water
1 can (21 ounces) cherry pie filling, chilled

In medium saucepan, combine sugar, cocoa and baking mix. Stir in milk and water. Cook over medium heat, stirring constantly, until mixture comes to a full boil; remove from heat. Pour into dessert dishes. Press plastic wrap directly onto surface. Refrigerate several hours or until set. Garnish with cherry pie filling.

SPARKLING CHAMPAGNE DESSERT

Makes 8 servings

2 packages (4-serving size each) or 1 package
  (8-serving size) JELL-O® Brand Lemon
  Flavor Gelatin
2 cups boiling water
2 cups champagne
3 oranges, sectioned

Dissolve gelatin in boiling water. Let stand about 10 minutes to cool. Add champagne. Chill until slightly thickened.

Measure 1 cup gelatin into small bowl; reserve. Fold orange sections into remaining gelatin. Spoon into champagne glasses or dessert dishes.

Beat reserved gelatin at high speed of electric mixer until fluffy, thick and about doubled in volume. Spoon over gelatin with oranges in glasses. Chill until firm, about 2 hours. Garnish as desired.

Prep time: 15 minutes
Chill time: 2 hours

EGGNOG TRIFLE

Makes 8 to 10 servings

1¼ cups cold milk
1 package (4-serving size) JELL-O® Instant
  Pudding and Pie Filling, French Vanilla
  or Vanilla Flavor
¼ cup rum, divided
⅛ teaspoon ground nutmeg
3½ cups (8 ounces) COOL WHIP® Non-Dairy
  Whipped Topping, thawed, divided
1 prepared pound cake loaf (about 12 ounces)
2 tablespoons strawberry jam, divided
1 can (11 ounces) mandarin orange sections,
  drained, divided
1½ cups strawberries, halved, divided
¼ cup sliced almonds, toasted, divided

Pour milk into medium bowl. Add pudding mix, 2 tablespoons rum and nutmeg. Beat with wire whisk until well blended, 1 to 2 minutes. Let stand 5 minutes or until slightly thickened. Fold in half the whipped topping.

Cut rounded top off pound cake; reserve for snacking or another use. Slice remaining cake horizontally into 4 layers. Sprinkle layers evenly with remaining 2 tablespoons rum. Spread 1 tablespoon jam on surface of 1 cake layer; top with plain cake layer. Cut into 1-inch cubes. Repeat with remaining 1 tablespoon jam and 2 cake layers.

Arrange about half the cake cubes on bottom of 2½-quart straight-sided bowl. Spoon half the pudding mixture into bowl over cake cubes. Top with half the fruit and half the almonds; cover with remaining cake cubes. Spoon remaining pudding mixture over cake cubes. Top with remaining fruit and almonds. Garnish with remaining whipped topping. Chill until ready to serve.

Prep time: 30 minutes

ACKNOWLEDGMENTS

The publishers would like to thank the companies and organizations listed below for the use of their recipes in this book.

American Dairy Industry Association
American Egg Board
Arm & Hammer Division, Church & Dwight Co., Inc.
Best Foods, a Division of CPC International Inc.
Blue Diamond Growers
Borden Kitchens, Borden, Inc.
California Apricot Advisory Board
California Kiwifruit Commission
Carnation, Nestlé Food Company
Celebrate! Kansas Food Recipe Contest
Checkerboard Kitchens, Ralston Purina Company
Cherry Marketing Institute, Inc.
Dole Food Company, Inc.
Domino Sugar Corporation
Essex Agricultural Society
Florida Department of Citrus
Hershey Chocolate U.S.A.
Illinois State Fair
Kahlúa Liqueur
Keebler Company
Kentucky State Fair
Kerr Corporation
Kraft General Foods, Inc.

Leaf, Inc.
Libby's, Nestlé Food Company
Thomas J. Lipton Co.
M&M/Mars
Michigan Apple Committee
Michigan State Fair
Nabisco Foods Group
National Cherry Foundation
National Date Festival
National Peanut Festival
National Sunflower Association
Nebraska State Fair
Nestlé Foods Company
New Mexico State Fair
Oklahoma Peanut Commission
Pecan Marketing Board
Pollio Dairy Products
The Procter & Gamble Company
The Quaker Oats Company
Refined Sugars Incorporated
Roman Meal Company
Sokol and Company
USA Rice Council
Walnut Marketing Board
Western New York Apple Growers Association, Inc.

PHOTO CREDITS

The publishers would like to thank the companies and organizations listed below for the use of their photographs in this book.

Best Foods, a Division of CPC International Inc.
Blue Diamond Growers
Borden Kitchens, Borden, Inc.
Carnation, Nestlé Food Company
Dole Food Company, Inc.
Hershey Chocolate U.S.A.
Keebler Company
Kerr Corporation

Kraft General Foods, Inc.
Leaf, Inc.
Thomas J. Lipton Co.
Nestlé Foods Company
Pecan Marketing Board
The Procter & Gamble Company
The Quaker Oats Company
USA Rice Council
Walnut Marketing Board

INDEX

INDEX

Fruit (*continued*)
Berry Cream Sauce, 261
Berry Good Sundaes, 128
Blackberry Ice Cream Pie, 108
Blackberry-Lemon Ice Cream, 132
Brandied Fruit Pie, 355
Brownie Pizza, 245
Candy Shop Pizza, 316
Cantaloupe Ice, 132
Cherry Fruit Cake, 349
Citrus Cream Cheese Frosting, 20
Creamy Cranberry Fruit Freeze, 364
Eggnog Trifle, 364
Fabulous Fruit Tart, 99
Fresh Berry Ice Cream, 135
Fruit 'n' Spice Parfaits, 147
Fruited Chocolate Sorbet, 360
Fruit Glazed Baked Custards, 167
Fruit in Cream, 260
Fruit Parfaits, 308
Fruit Sparkles, 140
Glazed Fruit, 351
Holiday Fruit Cake, 350
Honeydew Ice, 132
Kiwifruit and Pear Pastry, 170
Mini Fruit Cheese Tarts, 302
Minted Grapefruit Ice, 264
Nesselrode Cream Pie, 358
Pastry Chef Tarts, 252
Pinwheel Cake and Cream, 151
Spring Fling Fruit Tart, 99
Tangerine Sorbet, 131
Trifle Spectacular, 154
Tropical Frozen Mousse, 138
Watermelon Ice, 132
Fruited Chocolate Sorbet, 360
Fruit Flavor Freeze, 131
Fudge Brownie Pie, 301
Fudge Ribbon Cake, 47
Fudgy Chocolate Chip Ice Cream, 306
Fudgy Ice Cream Squares, 127
Fudgy Rocky Road Ice Cream, 306

G

Gelatin
about, 11
Alpine Strawberry Bavarian, 143
Any Berry Pie, 112
Any Season Light and Fruity Pie, 112
Apricot Deluxe Cheesecake, 70
Apricot Glaze, 250
Autumn Harvest Pie, 112
Bavarian Rice Cloud with Bittersweet Chocolate Sauce, 147
Blackberry Ice Cream Pie, 108
Charlotte Russe, 263
Cheesecakes in a Cup, 76
Chilled Raspberry Cheesecake, 291
Chilled Raspberry Soufflé, 155
Chilly Strawberry Soufflés, 154
Choco-Berry Bavarian Cream, 142
Chocolate-Cherry Sundaes, 307

Gelatin (*continued*)
Chocolate Mousse Pie, 118
Christmas Tree Poke Cake, 344
Citrus Snowflake Pie, 112
Cold Apricot Soufflé, 155
Creamy Daiquiri Pie, 112
Elegant Raspberry Chocolate Pie, 117
Frosty Orange Dessert, 141
Frozen Fruity Bars, 307
Frozen Lemon Soufflé, 155
Fruit Flavor Freeze, 131
Fruit Sparkles, 140
Gelatin Banana Splits, 308
Gelatin Poke Layer Cake, 44
Gelatin Sundaes, 308
Heavenly Chocolate Cheesecake, 69
Key Lime Pie, 111
Lemon Cheesecake Cups, 74
Lime Chiffon Squares, 149
Minted Grapefruit Ice, 264
Mocha Chocolate Chip Cheesecake, 71
Nesselrode Cream Pie, 358
No-Bake Peach Cheesecake, 291
Orange Cream Timbales, 262
Orange No-Bake Cheesecake, 70
Orange Terrine with Strawberry Sauce, 145
Peach Melba Dessert, 140
Pink Champagne Sorbet, 360
Raspberry Sorbet, 131
Sparkling Champagne Dessert, 365
Strawberry-Chocolate Bavarian Cream, 263
Strawberry Squares, 148
Tangerine Sorbet, 131
Trifle Cups, 152
Vanilla Cream Filling, 346
Georgia Peach Pie, 89
German Chocolate Cheesecake, 291
German Chocolate Pie, 104
German Sweet Chocolate Brownies, 318
German Sweet Chocolate Cake, 46
German Sweet Chocolate Pie, 119
Gingerbread Men, 327
Gingerbread with Lemon Sauce, 25
Ginger Pear Upside-Down Cake, 26
Gingersnaps, 179
Glazed Cranberry Mini-Cakes, 339
Glazed Fruit, 351
Glazed Sugar Cookies, 332
Glazes
Apricot Glaze, 250
Chocolate Chip Glaze, 54
Chocolate Glaze, 32, 39, 351
Cocoa Glaze, 50, 287, 346
Cream Cheese Glaze, 20
Easy Cocoa Glaze, 245
Easy Cream Cheese Glaze, 32
Lemon Glaze, 68
Mini Chips® Glaze, 192
Quick Cocoa Glaze, 40
Semi-Sweet Chocolate Glaze, 16, 33
Vanilla Chip Glaze, 339
Vanilla Glaze, 40
Golden Bread Pudding, 164
Golden Lemon Sauce, 110
Graham Cracker Crust, 75

Graham Crust, 351
Graham Peanut Butter Crunchies, 313
Granola Bars, 315
Granola Cookies, 315
Grasshopper Dessert, 149
Green Mountain Pie in Chewy Crust, 302
Greeting Card Cookies, 268

H

Halloween Party Cupcakes, 296
Hawaiian Cream Pie, 115
Hawaiian Trifle, 152
Haystacks, 313
Heavenly Chocolate Cheesecake, 69
Heavenly Chocolate Cream Pies, 259
Heavenly Lemon Cream Pies, 259
Heavenly Oat Bars, 220
Heavenly Oatmeal Hearts, 268
Hershey® Bar Cake, 57
Hershey®'s Chocolate Chip Blondies, 241
Holiday Fruit Cake, 350
Honeydew Ice, 132
Hopscotch Cake, 296
Hot Chocolate Soufflé, 265
Hot Fudge Peanut Sundaes, 128
Hot Fudge Sauce, 301
Hot Fudge Sundae Cake, 124

I

Ice Cream (*see also* **Desserts, Frozen; Ices**)
about, 12
Almond Ginger Ice Cream Pie, 115
Alpine Strawberry Bavarian, 143
Banana Cookie Ice Cream, 305
Banana Mocha Ice Cream, 132
Banana Split Bombe, 129
Banana Split Brownie Pie, 301
Banana Split Pie, 303
Berry Good Sundaes, 128
Blackberry Ice Cream Pie, 108
Blackberry-Lemon Ice Cream, 132
Brownie Alaska, 136
Butter Pecan Ice Cream, 135
Butter Rum Sundaes, 128
Charlotte Russe, 263
Cherry Cheesecake Ice Cream, 306
Chocolate-Cherry Sundaes, 307
Chocolate Chip Ice Cream, 133
Chocolate Chip Rugalach, 269
Chocolate Chocolate Chip Ice Cream, 135
Chocolate Coffee Pie, 122
Chocolate Frozen Dessert, 126
Chocolate Frozen Yogurt, 360
Chocolate Mint Baked Alaska, 264
Chocolate Mint Ice Cream, 135
Chocolate Mocha Ice Cream, 135
Chocolate Nut Ice Cream, 135
Chocolate Peanut Butter Ice Cream, 135

METRIC CONVERSION CHART

VOLUME MEASUREMENTS (dry)

1/8 teaspoon = 0.5 mL
1/4 teaspoon = 1 mL
1/2 teaspoon = 2 mL
3/4 teaspoon = 4 mL
1 teaspoon = 5 mL
1 tablespoon = 15 mL
2 tablespoons = 30 mL
1/4 cup = 60 mL
1/3 cup = 75 mL
1/2 cup = 125 mL
2/3 cup = 150 mL
3/4 cup = 175 mL
1 cup = 250 mL
2 cups = 1 pint = 500 mL
3 cups = 750 mL
4 cups = 1 quart = 1 L

VOLUME MEASUREMENTS (fluid)

1 fluid ounce (2 tablespoons) = 30 mL
4 fluid ounces (1/2 cup) = 125 mL
8 fluid ounces (1 cup) = 250 mL
12 fluid ounces (1 1/2 cups) = 375 mL
16 fluid ounces (2 cups) = 500 mL

WEIGHTS (mass)

1/2 ounce = 15 g
1 ounce = 30 g
3 ounces = 90 g
4 ounces = 120 g
8 ounces = 225 g
10 ounces = 285 g
12 ounces = 360 g
16 ounces = 1 pound = 450 g

DIMENSIONS

1/16 inch = 2 mm
1/8 inch = 3 mm
1/4 inch = 6 mm
1/2 inch = 1.5 cm
3/4 inch = 2 cm
1 inch = 2.5 cm

OVEN TEMPERATURES

250°F = 120°C
275°F = 140°C
300°F = 150°C
325°F = 160°C
350°F = 180°C
375°F = 190°C
400°F = 200°C
425°F = 220°C
450°F = 230°C

BAKING PAN SIZES

Utensil	Size in Inches/Quarts	Metric Volume	Size in Centimeters
Baking or Cake Pan (square or rectangular)	8×8×2	2 L	20×20×5
	9×9×2	2.5 L	22×22×5
	12×8×2	3 L	30×20×5
	13×9×2	3.5 L	33×23×5
Loaf Pan	8×4×3	1.5 L	20×10×7
	9×5×3	2 L	23×13×7
Round Layer Cake Pan	8×1½	1.2 L	20×4
	9×1½	1.5 L	23×4
Pie Plate	8×1¼	750 mL	20×3
	9×1¼	1 L	23×3
Baking Dish or Casserole	1 quart	1 L	—
	1½ quart	1.5 L	—
	2 quart	2 L	—